TAKE UP YOUR CROSS

A THEOLOGY OF LITURGICAL ABNEGATION

DAVID W. FAGERBERG

SENSUS FIDELIUM PRESS

Gastonia, North Carolina

ISBN: 978-1-962639-89-7

Cover Illustration by Amit Dey

PREFACE

I can only explain what I am trying to do in this book by providing one bit of personal background.

One cannot tell where prejudices are born, because they are literally pre-judgments: biases in play before judgments are made. I came to realize I had a bias against post-Reformation Catholic spiritual writers. They felt to me overly complex, excessive in mood, and dramatic in form. Their emphasis on suffering, submission, trials, and crosses felt unduly severe. Then I began to read them. Fenelon smuggled himself into my office in a box of books a friend gave me; Libermann walked up to shake my hand in the quotations contained in a study on spirituality; St. Sulpice was a landscape as foreign as the moon, but Olier waved me in. After that it was a matter of friends introducing me to other friends, and the reason for writing this book is to enjoy their company. And to see if the reader would enjoy it, too.

My academic study has not been in mysticism or spirituality, it was in liturgical theology. But I think we have made liturgical theology too small if it cannot include mysticism and spirituality. At one point, I used the Orthodox Christian concept of asceticism to describe the cost of being capacitated to commit liturgy. It resulted in my book, *On Liturgical Asceticism*, and, in a way, I consider this book to be "Volume II," but this time with all Latin authors. Orthodox asceticism had given me a different way of looking at liturgy; now liturgy is giving me a different way of looking at Catholic abnegation. The ascetical scent of liturgy that was taught me by the Orthodox East equips me to find a liturgical aroma in the theologians of abnegation in the Latin West. And that is my thesis in a nutshell: the language of abnegation sounds harsh *unless* it is placed against a more transcendent horizon. That transcendent horizon is the act of liturgizing God.

This book looks at a number of key words in abnegation, but it is not exactly a word study. I'm not interested in counting up the words, or locating words, or comparing who uses which words. I am interested in how the authors use these words to make their point. I want, therefore, very much, to acquaint readers with quotations from primary texts. I do not apologize for the number of quotes because it is much better for the reader to encounter the original writers than to encounter me. My only contribution has been one of selection and organization, like the designer of a collage who glues their words to the page in order to make a picture. I find a passage to cause me to pause and reflect upon what liturgical abnegation is, and it would fulfill a hope if readers came to feel a kinship with some of the authors, and sought them out to read more for themselves.

Biblical passages about the cross have been worn so smooth by familiarity that we hardly hear the words anymore, and are scarcely startled when Paul says that he has been crucified with Christ (Galatians 2:20), that he dies daily (1 Corinthians 15:31), that those who belong to Christ have crucified the flesh (Galatians 5:24), that our old self was crucified with Jesus (Romans 6:6), and that we must die with Christ (Romans 6:8). The overtones of asceticism and abnegation permeate the New Testament's entire description of the Christian life, but we have become insensitive to it. These spiritual writers try to remove the callous and let the words touch us again.

My hypothesis is that abnegation must be connected to liturgy. Hence I call the friends you will meet in the pages ahead *theologians of liturgical abnegation*. The ultimate reason why Christ commands abnegation is because abnegation is constitutive of his program of adoration. It is a matter of justice. Who deserves worship? Liturgical abnegation shapes us into true adorers.

Those are the connections I hope to make ahead. Liturgy can only be done on the terrain of love, and liturgical abnegation is an activity of love. "What is rendered liquid no longer retains its own shape, but takes the form of the vessel in which it is contained. Thus, loving souls do not retain their own wills, but conform them to whatever their beloved wills."[1] Every Christian has his or her own vocation; every vocation will be an exercise of abnegation, in one form or another. All the baptized are ascetics, but not all have a monastic vocation. All the baptized should practice abnegation, but not all will exhibit

---

1. Alphonsus de Liguori, *The True Spouse of Jesus Christ, or, The Nun Sanctified by the Virtue of Her State*, in *The Complete Works of Saint Alphonsus de Liguori, The Ascetical Works, vol. 10* (New York: Benziger Brothers, 1899) 263-64.

it in the same way, so de Sales says everyone is obliged to love the Evangelical Counsels, even if they are not all obliged to practice them. "If a robe of gold does not suit you, will you say that therefore it is worth nothing? Or will you throw a ring into the dirt because it fits not your finger?"[2] I say to the reader that I hope we will both be encouraged by the examples of people we encounter here.

I am grateful to *Sensus Fidelium Press* for showing interest in my effort, and I am enjoying the coincidence that I have it ready by the month of August. I am an adult convert to Catholicism, and when people inquire as to why, I tell them that my birthday is August 15 and Jesus still cannot refuse his Mother anything she asks for.

Solemnity of the Assumption of the Blessed Virgin Mary

August 15, 2024

---

2. Francis de Sales, *Treatise on the Love of God* (Blacksburg, VA: Wilder Publications, 2011) 277-78.

ABOUT THE AUTHOR

David W. Fagerberg is professor emeritus in the department of theology at the
University of Notre Dame, where he taught for twenty years. He holds an M.Div
from Luther Seminary; an M.A. from St. John's University, Collegeville; an S.T.M.
from Yale Divinity School; and the Ph.D. from Yale University. He has explored how
lex orandi is the foundation for *lex credendi* (*Theologia Prima,* 2003), into which he
integrated the Orthodox understanding of asceticism (*On Liturgical Asceticism,* 2013).
He applied liturgical theology to daily life (*Consecrating the World,* 2016) and to
personal spirituality (*Liturgical Mysticism,* 2020). He has treated liturgy's foundation
for dogmatics (*Liturgical Dogmatics,* 2021) and for various theological questions (*The
Liturgical Cosmos,* 2023). His recent work has turned to "theologians of abnegation", i.e.
Catholic spiritual writers 1500-1900 (in *Desiring to Desire God* 2024, and in the present
work).

Contents

LITURGY TRANSFORMING ABNEGATION

Some authors of Catholic spirituality use terms that trouble our modern ears. The authors I have in mind can be found in the bibliography, but here are some of the terms I have in mind: *abnegation, annihilation, indifference, resignation, mortification, abjection, abandonment, self-denial, self-renunciation, self-detachment, nothingness, contempt, hating the world, suffering,* and *bearing crosses*. These words sound harsh when we hear them within a limited horizon, but they might be better understood if we could place them against a more transcendent horizon. That transcendent horizon, I hypothesize, is the act of liturgizing a God whose infinite Justice demands our total worship. Whatever denial we make of self and world is, says Giovanni Bona, because "God will have no Sharers."[1] Two things happen simultaneously, says Saint-Jure: "We must necessarily empty ourselves of self, if we wish to fill ourselves with God."[2]

The thesis of this book is that, on the one hand, liturgy modifies an ordinary understanding of abnegation because liturgy assigns it a completely new motive. On the other hand, abnegation modifies an ordinary understanding of liturgy because abnegation expands liturgy's scope: it is no longer confined to the temple, it becomes constant through daily renunciations that launch us toward God. My hypothesis is that liturgizing God and abnegating self are one and the same motion, as suggested by Grou

---

1. Giovanni Bona, *Manductio ad Coelum: or, a Guide to Eternity* (London: printed for Henry Brome, 1672) 4.

2. Jean Baptiste Saint-Jure, *The Religious: A Treatise on the Vows and Virtues of the Religious State*, vol. 1 (New York: P. O'Shea, 1882) 574.

when he said "Yes, my Divine Saviour! I know that to consecrate my being to Thee and to renounce it are one and the same thing; and that I can live by thy life only in as far as I die to myself."[3] The language of liturgy and the language of abnegation coincide: consecrating is renouncing, oblation is surrender, sacrifice is annihilation, attending God's will is denying self-will, liturgizing is abnegating. A turn toward is also a turn away. Liturgy is embracing, turning toward, and conversion, while abnegation is denial, turning away, and aversion.

So how does liturgy affect abnegation, and vice versa? Granada says that earth will never taste the same once we have tasted heaven. "When the soul has once tasted these spiritual pleasures, none carnal will please her," and therefore "all her endeavors are to disengage herself from the world. She has but one love, and one desire; so that, whatsoever she loves, it is for the sake of one alone, and this one she loves in all things."[4] And Camus explains the reason why: "[what] is this true life, but life everlasting? ... Let them take so full a taste of the Manna of the blessed Eternity [that they] repute all time vain, in respect of Eternity."[5]

Abnegation is a matter of forming but one love, and one desire, and training it upon one God. Abnegation can be put forward as an act of liturgy, since liturgy is an act of love. We see everything by the light of Mount Tabor on the liturgical summit, and Granada says "when our eyes are once cleared up by this heavenly brightness, we discover a new light, which represents things quite different from what they appear to us at first."[6] Those whom I am calling *theologians of liturgical abnegation* describe this illumination, and its affect upon our view of all created things (including ourselves). They describe the consequence of our encounter with God upon our view of the world. They explain abnegation from the summit of liturgy on Mount Calvary, as Louis Tronson does here:

> When we are about to assist at the Celebration of the holy Eucharist
> we should place ourselves in spirit with the Blessed Virgin on Mount

---

3. Jean Grou, *The Interior of Jesus and Mary*, vol. 1 (New York: Benziger Brothers, 1893) 320-21.

4. Louis de Granada, *Sinner's Guide* (Philadelphia: Henry McGrath, 1845) 123-24.

5. Jean Pierre Camus, *A Draught of Eternitie* (London: Scolar Press, 1972) 69.

6. De Granada, *Sinner's Guide,* 95.

Calvary, and there devoutly contemplate the Lamb of God offering upon the Cross the Sacrifice which He mystically renews day by day upon our Altars. Let us reverently endeavour to enter into the feelings which must have possessed the Virgin Mother's sword-pierced soul as she watched the death-pangs of Her Divine Son: so shall our eyes, wholly fixed upon our Dying Lord, refuse to be drawn aside by any outward object; so shall our hearts, filled with the love of God, urge us to cast away all self-love, to crucify in ourselves whatever is displeasing to Him.[7]

We must leave the valley in order to climb the mountain, and only then, from the summit, do we understand why we have left the valley. The piercing sword seems awful, and the death seems terrifying, but Lebrun does not doubt that "it is a sword of love, the sword that has wounded and slain all true lovers of Jesus, that is, all the saints. It wounded them that it might heal them, it killed them to bring them to life."[8] Liturgy fixes our eyes on something new, and whenever we see Jesus as Mary saw him, abnegation follows. That is, we deny anything which attempts to draw our eye off him – beginning with the self, which clamors for attention, and ending with the world, which is ever too happy to flatter the self with the attention it craves.

Adam and Eve were created to be cosmic liturgists, but the Fall was the forfeiture of their liturgical career. Ever since then, we, their children, have used our soul's powers for purposes other than glorifying God. Bona considers it a failure of our most primordial task when we "set up as many Idols as there are Creatures which we love with an inordinate Affection."[9] Men and women now forsake simplicity in adoration, and divide their adoration amongst other objects. Perfection demands simplicity, observes Jean-Joseph Surin, and "perfection consists in this, that the soul, looking simply to God, not only gives the preference to the Creator over all creatures in her esteem, but in truth wishes and desires nothing but Him; has no other care than to be faithful to Him, and passes through

---

7. Louis Tronson, *Examination of Conscience* (Oxford: Rivingtons, 1870) 122.

8. Charles Lebrun, *The Spiritual Teaching of St. John Eudes* (London: Sands & Co., 1934) 107.

9. Bona, *Manductio ad Coelum: or, a Guide to Eternity*, 4.

visible things without delaying till she reaches that Divine Object, and begins to taste the ineffable delights of simple love."[10] Abnegation denies our self-esteem, and withdraws our esteem from the created world, in order that we may give it to the Creator, setting up a tension between the Christian and the world that will last until judgment day. Bossuet sees "how the spirit that influences the world, acts in opposition to the genuine spirit of Christianity. What is the great characteristic of Christianity? Compassion! What is the leading principle among the great? Self-Love!"[11] We may call this a liturgical element of abnegation because, Bona says, "it is the ultimate of all misfortunes to turn away from the sovereign Good through excessive attachments to creatures."[12] Upon entering true and simple liturgy, one's attitude toward all created things, toward all natural desire, and toward all human affection is changed.

When we finally worship the Father in spirit and in truth, then Jesus said nothing will be the same, reports Francis Libermann.

> Then there will be true adorers, persons wholly devoted to my Father, entirely given to adoring my Father, who will forget and lose sight of all created things, renounce all human affection and natural desire, who will constantly practice self-abnegation, so as to become nothing before my Father in order that he alone may reign in them. Nothing will remain in them which tends to their own personal satisfaction or serves their interest or their own glory. Their souls with all their powers will be constantly prostrate before him and tend only towards him, in a spirit of submission and in the sole desire of his glory and reign over them. There you have true adorers, true adorers who will adore my Father in spirit

---

10. Jean-Joseph Surin, *The Foundations of Spiritual Life* (London: James Burns, 1844) 126.

11. Jacques-Bénigne Bossuet, *Select Sermons*, London: Printed for W. Clarke, 1800) 146.

12. Giovanni Bona, *Guidance to Heaven* (Rockford, IL: TAN Books and Publishers, Inc., 1995) 3.

and in truth ... They will prostrate, admit their nothingness before the sovereign Majesty, whom they will see living and reigning in them."[13]

The liturgist of abnegation swoons as de Castaniza does: "O that I were so ravished with Thy love and liking, my only amiable Lord God, that through joy, jubilee, and admiration, I might feel no self at all."[14]

Liturgy provides power to abnegation. It gives the soul a greater fire and a nobler love. In the first stanza of his *Ascent of Mount Carmel*, St. John of the Cross refers to "anxious love inflamed," and explains by saying:

> The soul has passed out and gone forth in the obscure night of sense to the union of the Beloved. For, in order to overcome our desires, and to deny ourselves in all things ... we require another and greater fire of another and nobler love – that of the Bridegroom – so that having all our joy in Him, and deriving from Him all our strength, we may gain such resolution and courage as shall enable us easily to abandon and deny all besides.[15]

Question: why abnegation? Answer: Liturgy. Question: how does our worship become truer, simpler, and more spiritual? Answer: Liturgize with Christ living within you.

The result of liturgy is a new vision of the cosmos, says Jean Grou, and it is a discovery that every Christian must make for himself.

The Christian made this discovery when he turned his thoughts upon his own soul, and reflected on past errors, and acknowledged that he had never found happiness in the

---

13. Francis Libermann, *Jesus Through Jewish Eyes*, vol. 1 (Dublin: Paraclete Press, 1995) 120.

14. Juan De Castaniza, *The Spiritual Conflict and Conquest* (London: Burns and Oates, 1874) 254.

15. John of the Cross, *The Ascent of Mount Carmel,* in *The Complete Works of Saint John of the Cross,* vol. 1 (London: Longman, Green, Longman, Roberts & Green, 1864) 52

enjoyment of this world's goods; when he listened to God in the silence of meditation and prayer. It was then that he really saw the nothingness of earthly things, and understood that they were capable indeed of exciting his passions, but never of satisfying his heart. Then a deep secret touch of grace taught him that man's true happiness lies in God; and that, in order to enjoy and possess it, he must give up, or at least give up his love for, all other joy. From that time forth, all things have seemed insipid, except prayer and communion with God; the world has been crucified to him and he to the world; he has been attracted to God alone; he has sought Him, and found Him within his own soul, which is God's very temple.[16]

This is the experience on the mountain top of liturgy.

Liturgical abnegation is an abnegation stirred up by liturgy; that is, an abnegation stirred up by the desire for God's glory, which is the whole point of liturgy, says Augustine Baker.

> Prayer is an affectuous [sic] actuation of an intellective soul towards God, expressing, or at least implying, an entire dependence on Him as the Author and Fountain of all good, a will and readiness to give Him His due, which is no less than all love, obedience, adoration, glory, and worship, by humbling and annihilating of herself and all creatures in His presence; and lastly, a desire and intention to aspire to a union of spirit with Him.[17]

Abnegation is going forth in full strides of liturgy, indifferent to the distraction of creatures, diffident about our own autonomous powers, detached from our own self-love and self-will. At that point, John of the Cross can see that "the Bridegroom whom thou lovest is 'the treasure hidden in the field' of thy soul, for which the wise merchant gave all that he had, so thou, if thou will find Him, must forget all that is thine, withdraw from all created things, and hide thyself in the secret retreat of the spirit, shutting the door upon

---

16. Jean Grou, *The Spiritual Maxims of Pere Grou* (London: J. T. Hayes, 1874) 95-96.

17. Augustine Baker, *Holy Wisdom, Or Directions for the Prayer of Contemplation* (New York: Burns & Oates, 1911) 341-42.

thyself – that is, denying thy will in all things – and praying to thy Father in secret."[18] Liturgy is discovery of the pearl of great price; liturgical abnegation is denial of all else in order to purchase that field and obtain that pearl.

Suppose with me a man who lives in a garden of extreme beauty and delight. What would it matter to him if his beloved *is not there*? The contents of the garden would not alleviate his sorrow. And what would it matter if his beloved *is there*? It would change the delight the contents of the garden could provide. If the pearl of great price is not in your garden, then leave all to go find it; if the pearl of great price is in your garden, then do not be preoccupied with any of its other worthless pebbles. Knowing that the pearl is within reach changes our attitude toward all else.

God is love; love causes abnegation; abnegation flows willingly from love. Therefore, union with God can be said to cause abnegation, according to John of Avila. "Tell me, has God united Himself to you? The chief sign by which you will know that God is with you is that you will despise everything on earth that is not of God, and your one thought will be to love and please Him, as your only good. And you will know, brother, that the Holy Ghost has come to you if you walk along the path of Jesus Christ, filled with joy and fervor."[19] The joyful path of Jesus Christ is his Incarnate pathway of self-denial for his Father's glory and our salvation. The love can be spoken of as a wound, it is true, but the wound itself is experienced as sweet. Nepveu says this is a paradox that will confound a worldling: "pleasure is found in refusing pleasure for the love of God."[20] The Christian takes pleasure in refusing pleasure, because there is a good higher than the current pleasure. John of the Cross is marveling at the same paradox when he describes these "wounds of love."

> By the wound of love the affections of the will lead most rapidly to the possession of the Beloved, whose touch it felt, and in the same degree also, His absence … They are called the spiritual wounds of love, most sweet to

---

18. John of the Cross, *Spiritual Canticle Between the Soul and Christ* in *The Complete Works*, vol. 2, (London: Longman, Green, Longman, Roberts & Green, 1864)17.

19. John of Avila, *The Holy Ghost* (London: Scepter Limited, 1959) 152.

20. François Nepveu, *The Hidden Life* (London: J. Masters, 1871) 69.

the soul and desirable; and therefore when it is thus wounded the soul would willingly die a thousand deaths, because these wounds make it go forth out of itself, and enter into God.[21]

Liturgical abnegation is linked in an alliance with liturgical latria because to be *drawn toward* is to be *drawn away*. To *go in* is to *go out*. To *ascend* is to *depart*. To liturgize is to abnegate.

But there is more. What we go out of, are drawn away from, what we depart and deny (abnegate) is not only goods of the world, but even ourselves. That is why John of the Cross describes the spiritual running after God as having a twofold meaning. "The first is a going forth out of all created things, hating and despising them; the second, a going forth out of oneself, self-forgetting, for the love of God ... O my Spouse, [the soul] seems to say, by this touch of Thine and wound of love hast Thou drawn me away not only from all created things, but also from myself."[22] We choose whether to love God, or not, and "if we love Him, our heart will not consider itself, nor look to its own pleasure or profit, but to the honour, glory, and pleasure of God; for the more the heart is occupied with self, the less it is occupied with God."[23] The two signs of whether God has really stolen our hearts is whether that heart is anxiously seeking after God (liturgical asceticism), and whether it has no pleasure in anything but Him (liturgical abnegation). The liturgist, continues John of the Cross, demands to know why God does not soon "carry away the heart which Thy love has stolen, to fill it, to heal it, and to satiate it by giving it perfect rest in Thyself?"[24]

Abnegation is a reaction to liturgy present (which is faith: having tasted God, the world becomes vain), or a reaction to liturgy absent (which is hope: the soul is an empty vessel waiting to be filled), or a reaction to liturgy incipient (which is love: the eschatological liturgy is beginning, and we sell all in order to buy the field where that pearl of great price is buried). Jean Croiset says tranquility results from withdrawing into the deep part of the soul – that is why Christians do it!

---

21. John of the Cross, *Spiritual Canticle*, in *The Complete Works*, vol. 2 23.

22. John of the Cross, *Spiritual Canticle*, in *The Complete Works*, vol. 2, 23.

23. John of the Cross, *Spiritual Canticle*, in *The Complete Works*, vol. 2, 49.

24. John of the Cross, *Spiritual Canticle*, in *The Complete Works*, vol. 2, 49.

A man that is not recollected, wanders about without finding rest anywhere. He seeks after all kinds of objects, without feeling satisfied with any. Whereas, if by giving himself to recollection he entered into himself, he would there find God. He would find a satisfaction in God, who by His presence would fill him with so great an abundance of His gifts, that he would no longer go to find elsewhere wherewith to satisfy his desires. This is what may be seen every day, in interior persons. We imagine that the love they have for retirement, and the pain they feel in diffusing themselves outwardly, is an effect of melancholy. But it is not so. They taste Almighty God within themselves; and the ineffable sweetness with which they are filled, makes them feel the divergence and pleasures which are met with in the world so insipid and nauseous, that they have a horror of them.[25]

After feeding upon Christ himself at the altar, there is no pain or melancholy felt when denying the world and self. Hatred of self-will leads to obedience; hatred of self-esteem leads to humility; hatred of self-indulgence leads to renunciation; hatred of pride leads to meekness; hatred of self-love leads us to abandon ourselves and become true servants of God. To describe such servants, De Liguori turns to St. Mary Magdalene of Pazzi.

Whoever, therefore, would make progress in the love of Jesus Christ, must absolutely give a death-blow to the love of self-esteem. But how shall we inflict this blow? Behold how St. Mary Magdalene of Pazzi instructs us: "That which keeps alive the appetite for self-esteem is the occupying [of] a favorable position in the minds of all; consequently the death of self-esteem is to keep one's self hidden, so as not to be known to any one.

---

25. Jean Croiset, *Devotion to the Sacred Heart of Jesus* (London: Burns & Lambert, 1863) 52-53.

And till we learn to die in this manner, we shall never be true servants of God."[26]

This puts an eschatological question to us: what is our last end? Man and woman have gotten their answer to that question wrong since the Garden of Eden. "Naturally we love and seek nothing but ourselves in all things," says Baker, "whatsoever we love and seek. We are our own last end, referring all things, even supernatural – yea, God Himself – to our own interest and commodity."[27] Saint-Jure refers to Thomas in order to remind that sin, in either its mortal or venial form, is a disorderly affection and attachment to the creature in place of the Creator. "The disorder of mortal sin, says St. Thomas, is that it is directly opposed to the end of man; it excites man by the most deplorable of abuses to place in a creature his end and beatitude, which are to be found not in the creature but in the Creator."[28]

God has given all creatures as steps to beatitude, so the sinner commits an offense against God when he employs them in any other way, or for any other reason. The world is a good creation, and we may use the things of this world, but only as a pathway to God. De Liguori imagines how comical it would look otherwise.

> What folly would it not be for a traveler, if when traveling, he were only to think of making himself great in that country through which he only has to pass, without minding the being reduced to live miserably in that country where he will have to spend his whole life? And is he not foolish, who seeks his happiness in this world, where he has to remain but a few days, and who by so doing, runs the risk of being unhappy in the world to come, where he will have to remain for ever?

---

26. Alphonsus de Liguori, *The Practice of the Love of Jesus Christ*, in *The Holy Eucharist*, vol. 6 of *The Ascetical Works* (New York: Benziger Brothers, 1887) 36.

27. Baker, *Holy Wisdom*, 206-207.

28. Jean Baptiste Saint-Jure, *Treatise on the Knowledge and Love of Our Lord Jesus Christ*, vol. 2 (New York: P. O'Shea, 1875) 357-58.

He who possesses anything that is borrowed does not place his affections on it, knowing, as he does, that within a short time he will have to restore it. All the goods of this world are but given to us as a loan.[29]

Therefore, we should refrain from setting our ultimate affections on what will perish. The only method to be followed, says Grou, is "carefully to avoid setting our affection on what must perish, and to use the things of this world, as St. Paul admonishes, as if we used them not."[30] This is the first lesson that Ignatius of Loyola would have us learn in his exercises, announced in three parts. First, "man is created to praise, reverence, and serve God our Lord, and by this means to save his soul"; second, "the other things on the face of the earth are created for man to help him in attaining the end for which he is created"; and third, "hence, man is to make use of them in as far as they help him in the attainment of his end, and he must rid himself of them in as far as they prove a hindrance to him."[31]

Abnegation does not scorn temporal things, but it does scorn us resting in temporal things when we have been made for eternal things. When the soul realizes her liturgical identity, she goes out of herself in self-forgetfulness. Something analogous to this can be experienced even on the natural plane: we can remember times when we became indifferent to an original desire because something more crucial arose. On the supernatural plane, liturgy causes a similar indifference to the world because it presents the most important object of desire we could possibly have, the object which will give us beatitude. We might not know where we are going when our liturgical experience draws us away from the world, but we will discover, as Abraham did, that liturgical abnegation is not mere ignorance, it is holy ignorance (faith). Abnegation does not despise the world; it runs out of the world, and out of self, in order to run after God, into God. A man

---

29. Alphonsus de Liguori, *Preparation for Death* (Philadelphia: J. B. Lippincott & Co, 1869) 27-28.

30. Jean Grou, *Morality, Extracted from the Confessions of Saint Austin*, vol. 1 (London: J. P. Coghlan, 1791) 359.

31. Ignatius of Loyola, *The Spiritual Exercises of St. Ignatius*, trans. Louis Puhl (Westminster, MD: The Newman Press, 1951) 12.

of faith, says Pollien, "can only love by stripping himself, and he only strips himself to love. One must go out of oneself to go to God."[32] When man runs forth from creation to God, creation's purpose is being fulfilled, and the cosmos is happy. The happiness of all creatures is to perform their part in God's design, and natural creatures are happy to sacrifice themselves for our good. Elizabeth of the Trinity confesses that "if I wish my interior city to agree with, to resemble that of the 'immortal King of ages,' and to shine with the great illumination given by God, I must first extinguish every other light, so that the Lamb may be its only Lamp."[33]

Many perishable, created lights dazzle our eyes, but at the liturgical apex we receive a light that annihilates all others. It is the sun that overcomes the pale light of the stars. When the sun rises, the stars are still in the sky but their light is overcome. When the soul finds her way back to God as her first principle, then "all lights that are merely natural or infused are quenched and rendered dark," says Blosius, "for they have always shone below this light, in the same way as all the light of the stars is darkened and falls before the brightness of the blazing sun. For when the uncreated light arises created light vanishes. Therefore the created light of the soul is changed into the light of eternity."[34] Liturgical abnegation is the annihilation and extinguishment of any lamp that blinds us to God and impedes our union with him. As the stars disappear from the sky when the sun fills it, so creatures disappear from our covetousness when God fills out heart. Rigoleuc describes it this way: "The soul, in contemplating God, whom she regards as the one only Being this world contains, the rest being as absolute nothingness in her sight, forgets all else, and divests herself as far as possible of the remembrance of, and affection to, every other creature," and by this act of acquiescence the soul "renders Him the most perfect homage

---

32. François Pollien, ed. Joseph Tissot, *The Interior Life Simplified and Reduced to Fundamental Principle* (London: Burns Oates & Washbourne, Ltd., 1927) 170.

33. Elizabeth of the Trinity, *The Praise of Glory: Reminiscences of Sr. Elizabeth of the Trinity* (London: R. & T. Washbourne, Ltd., 1914) 233-34.

34. Blosius (Louis of Blois), *A Book of Spiritual Instruction, Institutio Spiritualis* (St. Louis: B. Herder, 1800) 107.

that it is possible for a creature to offer."[35] Abnegation produces liturgy; liturgy is the
reason for abnegation.

Annihilation is death, de Ravignan admits – but "what then is it that dies here? That
which is not worthy to live, that which by retiring gives life to [the] soul: pride, frivolity,
vanity, caprice, weakness, vice, and passion."[36] The liturgical soul takes spiritual measure
of the created horizon by placing it against the Uncreated horizon, and then vanities
evaporate, self-will is subdued by obedience, possessions are weighed on the scale of the
temple, honors are evaluated by a different measure, slavery yields to freedom, and success
is no longer appraised by the opinion of the world. The spiritual soul that is formed by
liturgy discovers the logic of abnegation, which will explain the grammar of a spirituality
that otherwise disturbs us. John Evangelist of Bois-le-Duc describes the soul as remaining
"with all her powers naked and converted to God who, at that same instant, infuses into
her His divine light, irradiating the pure soul which, simply for His love, has put herself
into such a state of poverty and detachment from all things."[37]

The soul is made for God, and God alone, and nothing but God, and therefore the
soul cannot rest in the world, or the world in the soul. Since the world was meant to
be only a pathway to God, says Blosius, the soul cannot rest in any of the things of the
world, "seeking in them her own satisfaction, for so perfect is her mortification that in
nothing doth she seek her own convenience or interest, but in all things the good pleasure,
praise and honor of God."[38] Seek none of these things self-interestedly; rather, seek
them liturgically, namely, for the good pleasure, praise, and honor of God. He who loves
God truly is the one "whose taste is for heavenly things, while earthly things are to him

---

35. Jean Rigoleuc, *Walking with God: Or, Dwellers in the Recreation House of the Lord*
(London: Thomas Richardson and Son, 1859), 40, 42.

36. Gustave de Ravignan, *On the Life and Institute of the Jesuits* (Philadelphia: W. J.
Cunningham, 1845) 111.

37. John Evangelist of Boisleduc (Balduke), *The Kingdom of God in the Soul* (London:
Sheed & Ward, 1930) 53.

38. Blosius, *A Book of Spiritual Instruction, Institutio Spiritualis* (St. Louis, MO: B.
Herder, 1800)124.

worthless."[39] The definition of a liturgist is one who has a taste for heavenly things, and although there are many other benefits to abnegation, the primary motive in liturgical abnegation is to please God, according to de Sales. Spiritual lovers, that is, spouses of the heavenly King,

> cleanse, purify, and beautify themselves as well as they can, not in order to be perfect, not to satisfy themselves, not from a desire to make progress in virtue, but out of obedience to the Bridegroom – out of the reverence they have for Him, and the fervent desire which they have to please him. Now, is not that a love pure, simple, and unalloyed, since they do not purify themselves in order to be pure, they do not adorn themselves in order to be beautiful, but only to please their Beloved?[40]

A soul's fervent desire to please God is a liturgical yearning, not a selfish one, and more than a yearning after moral improvement. It is a remarkable thought – perhaps the most lofty anthropology possible – to think that although God does not *need* our praise, he *wants* our praise, and is pleased by our praise. Liturgy arises from the desire to please God. "In Thy praise only I am happy,"[41] exclaims Gertrude More. And Blosius thinks that the ascetical soul

> should accustom herself, by a holy attention of mind, to refer all her actions to the glory of God; as also to unite her deeds as well as her sufferings, by her prayers or her desires, to the sorrows and actions of Our Lord. In this manner, these sufferings, and these actions ... will become infinitely great, illustrious, and pleasing in the sight of God, for they will

---

39. Blosius, *A Book of Spiritual Instruction*, 37.

40. Francis de Sales, *The Spiritual Conferences* (London: Burns & Oates, Ltd., 1909) 228.

41. Gertrude More, *The Writings of Gertrude More* (London: R. & T. Washbourne, Ltd., 1910) 12.

receive ineffable dignity from the merits of Jesus Christ, to which they will be united.[42]

Even our sufferings and sorrows can become liturgies. Daily abnegation can become liturgy. Liturgy can be done upon the cross. Or, actually, as we shall see, liturgy *must* be done upon the cross. The entire apparatus of abnegation operates on a liturgical premise of pleasing God (our sanctification glorifying him) or displeasing God (our sin sorrowing him). Blosius says the reasons why our iniquities displease us is "chiefly because thou knowest that they are displeasing to God, and contrary to His honour and good pleasure."[43] Awareness of sin is an awareness of how much we need God, and our sense of needing God leads us to sell everything and purchase the pearl of great price.

Liturgical abnegation is retracing the steps of the Fall, but this time in reverse. We have been doing creation backwards all this while, and redemption is when we are finally turned forward, as we should have been. John Evangelist of Boisleduc explains.

> We must know that when man lost a happy state and that true life in which God had first placed him, he fell back upon creatures through inordinate affections. First, he fell back upon himself, then upon exterior things, then upon the gifts of God, and last, in a wrong manner, upon God Himself, seeking in God only his (man's) own ease and interest, whereas we ought to seek only God's honour and good pleasure. Now all this life of self love must be thoroughly mortified and utterly destroyed before we can obtain true union with God.[44]

The transition from seeking our own ease and interest to seeking God's honor and good pleasure is a maneuver of liturgical abnegation.

---

42. Blosius, quoted in Georges de Blois, *A Benedictine of the Sixteenth Century* (London: Burns and Oates, 1878) 151.

43. Blosius (Louis of Blois), *Spiritual Works of Louis of Blois*, ed. John Edward Bowden (New York: Benziger Bros., 1903) 110.

44. John the Evangelist, *The Kingdom of God in the Soul*, 51-52.

Asking "Whose liturgy are we doing?" is the same as asking "Who is doing our liturgy?" It is not us, admits Bona. "Sweet heart of my Saviour Jesus Christ, watching over me with careful keeping all the night, I salute Thee with praise and glory for ever. Do Thou to the Father pay for me my debt of praises and thanksgiving."[45] We beg Jesus to pay our debt of liturgy for us; he is the only one who can liturgize adequately, satisfactorily, properly. And he can do so because in the hypostatic union the divine liturgy of the Son unites with the human liturgy of a man. So our liturgizing is cooperation with the Son, through the Holy Spirit, with the service he gives to the Father. He and we co-operate the liturgy: we work it together. In liturgizing God we are content with whatever choice he makes for us, which is another way of describing self-abnegation. Mary Margaret Alacoque exclaims: "Thou art sufficient for me, O my God! Do for me whatever will glorify Thee the most, having no regard either to my interest or satisfaction. It is sufficient for me to know that thou art satisfied."[46] Liturgy is well done when God is satisfied, when it pleases him, and no creature could satisfy the worship God's justice deserves by acting out of his own strength, because the finite cannot satisfy the infinite. Such a liturgy must be made by the Eternal One become flesh.

Our religion is impotent until it becomes liturgy. Therefore, when we liturgize, it must be with Jesus's virtues, just as Bona hopes. "Thou art far above all our praise, O my God. I rejoice that it is so, and that whatsoever mere creatures can do for Thy service is a homage utterly unequal to the worthiness and greatness of Thy Majesty."[47] First, the incarnation causes our liturgy; second, the honor of joining Christ's liturgy causes us to love our own abjection. Alacoque is content in humiliation. "In your visits to the Blessed Sacrament let your prayer be for love of your own abjection in honor of the self-effacement of a God

---

45. Giovanni Bona, *The Easy Way to God* (London: Burns Oates & Washbourne, Ltd., 1876) 207.

46. Mary Margaret Alacoque, *The Autobiography of Saint Margaret Mary* (Charlotte, NC: TAN Books, 2012) 65.

47. Bona, *The Easy Way to God* 129.

hidden away and humiliated for love of us."[48] And Boudon is content with a hidden and interior life of abnegation because then Christians

truly seek the notice, the esteem, and the friendship of God Only, since they have no desire to be seen, esteemed, or loved by any living creature whatsoever; this is why they are transported and exult with joy when they are unknown and unthought of ... Ah! then it is that, thrust aside by men, effaced from their memory, banished from their heart, they cry out with truth that God Only is their all in all. They say it, and God sees it. Then it is that they render Him a glory great beyond all comparison: for, stripping themselves of everything but Him, remembering nothing but Him, they render to His Divinity the highest and the strongest testimony of gratitude and love which they can pay Him, being ready also to sacrifice to Him their life itself. Souls which allow any admixture of the love and esteem of created things are thereby far removed from such pure love and zeal for His glory.[49]

The glory of God is the primary driver in creation, in salvation history, and in the liturgical circulation between heaven and earth, even if we are unaware of it. De la Colombiere wishes we were aware of God's goodness and blessings.

I imagine that as God has His glory as the last end of His actions, He does all these things principally for love of those who think of it and admire His goodness in it; are grateful to Him and sees the occasion to love Him. Others receive the same blessings, but as it were by chance and good luck, almost as, when at a feast a serenade is given to someone, a thousand people enjoy the pleasure because they happen to be in the house with the person for whom it is done ... God ceaselessly refers to us the being,

---

48. Mary Margaret Alacoque, *The Letters of St. Margaret Mary Alacoque* (Charlotte, NC: TAN Books, 2012) Letter 77, Kindle edition.

49. Boudon, *The Hidden Life of Jesus*, 105-06.

the life, the activity of every created thing in the universe. that is His occupation in nature. Ours should be endlessly to receive what He sends us from all parts, and send it back to Him by thanking Him, by praising Him and recognizing in Him the author of all things.[50]

Things are different before and after baptism; dry worship is different from wet liturgy.

The Church celebrates the cult of the New Adam, and he is at work in his baptized children. Christ will apply us to himself, says Saint-Jure.

He will apply us to His virtues, to His humility, His patience, His meekness, His obedience, His intentions, His prayer, His love toward God and man, His conversation, and His contempt of transitory things; giving us grace to know them, to esteem them, to love them, to resolve to practice them in occasions. In applying us, for example, to humility, He infuses the knowledge of the humble thoughts that He entertained, of the abnegations which He practised as man toward the Divinity, and of the love He bore this virtue. Afterward, He will give us strength to practise it in our thoughts, our judgments, our opinions, our affections, our words and our actions.[51]

Christ applies us to himself, heart to heart. He does his liturgy within us, we do our liturgy within him. This is why liturgical theology intertwines with abnegation theology: because when we are incorporated by the Holy Spirit into the abnegations the Son practiced as man toward the Father, then his abnegation will fill us, and we will synergistically liturgize the Father with him. Toward that end, we put aside any doxology

---

50. Claude de la Colombiere, *Faithful Servant* (St. Louis, MO: B. Herder Book Co., 1960) 52-53.

51. Saint-Jure, *The Spiritual Man; or, The Spiritual Life Reduced to its First Principles* (London: Burns and Oates, 1878) 240.

we can generate under our own power. If human worship can give any glory to the Father, it only comes as a result of the person being united to the glory which Christ's own abnegation gives to the Father. Liturgical abnegation is a Christological mystery. Liturgical abnegation is also a pneumatological mystery. Only the Spirit who teaches all truth can convince us of its need, "for, what may he not teach and evince, who evinces the necessity of self-denial, self-forgetfulness, and self-hatred?"[52]

Since the only begotten Son is the one in whom the Father is well pleased, the liturgist wants to be united to Christ, be made a temple for Christ, imitate Christ, take Christ as his model. The Eucharistic liturgy begs God to look with favor on the Church's offering and see neither the sacrifices we accomplish under our own power, nor the victims we devise, but to rather see the pleasing Victim who reconciled mankind to himself. Similarly, de Castaniza imagines liturgical abnegation begging God to look with favor on our self-denial, our resignation, our mortification, and see his Son's activity therein.

> This is the abnegation which Christ our Savior so often inculcated. This is the obedience to which the Son of God invites and directs His faithful followers, both by His words and by His example. This is the desirable cross which his diligent servants are to lay on their shoulders, and so follow the steps of their Savior. This is that love which our Lord so seriously, frequently, and carefully recommended to the whole world, and especially to His disciples, as His particular friends and children, after His last supper.[53]

The more we love the cross, the more Christoform we are. "The more a soul participates of the spirit and interior of the Son of God," says de Berniere-Louvigny, "the more she esteems and loves the cross, and, consequently, does the more glorify God the Father. For, to suffer, is to make a continual sacrifice of our pleasures and interest; uniting

---

52. Louis Bourdaloue, *Sermons, and Moral Discourses, on the Important Duties of Christianity*, vol. 1 (Dublin: Published by James Duffy, 1843) 77.

53. De Castaniza, *The Spiritual Conflict and Conquest*, 7.

ourselves to the design the Son of God had by suffering, viz.: – to repair the glory of his Father."[54]

Liturgical abnegation unites our death with Christ's death, places our prayer in union with his prayer, mingles our trials with his cross. This is made possible by the Holy Spirit, the great uniter in love. And after that, John of Avila thinks we look different to God. "In heaven there is One to Whom you appear all fair, for He looks at you through the apertures of the Wounds He received for you."[55]

Liturgizing involves abnegation because we must take our eyes off ourselves, our self, our selfishness, our self-love, our self-will, our self-esteem, and put them on Christ, whose one desire is to glorify his Father. Then, John of Avila writes, we will "embrace hardships and overcome them by the burning charity God has kindled in us. This love so carries us out of ourselves that it makes us perfectly insensible to dishonor, as wine takes away the reason of a drunkard. Like all strong affection, it makes a man forget himself, and care only for his Beloved, Who in this case, is God Himself, and He is most holy will."[56] We join Jesus in his aspirations: his liturgy subsumes our dispositions. We do not worship on our own, we liturgize in Christ. "Strip thyself of all things," says John de Bovilla so that "He may apparel thee with Himself. Having forgot thyself He will remember thee."[57] Strip yourself, but do not remain unclothed. Become martyrs of love. Love to the point of martyrdom. Abnegation is liturgical ecstasy: a love that so carries us so far out of ourselves that we become insensible to being dishonored, contemned, derided. Liturgical abnegation is forsaking our imperfect happinesses, and finding God to be our full happiness, which diffuses gradually into every corner of our experience. The Christian is not pushed by morality, he is pulled by liturgy.

---

54. Jean De Berniere-Louvigny, *The Interior Christian in Eight Books* (New York: The Catholic Publication Society, 1843) 6.

55. John of Avila, *Letters of Blessed John of Avila* (London: Burns & Oates Ltd., 1904) 96.

56. John of Avila, *Letters of Blessed John of Avila*, 59-60.

57. John de Bovilla, *The Quiet of the Soul* (London: Thomas Richardson and Sons, 1876) 19.

All of these theologians of liturgical abnegation describe any withholding of liturgy as an act of robbery. It robs God of the glory that is his in justice. Grou says, "to God is due the glory of all His works, and that so exclusively that He declares He will never share it with anyone. He requires that in all circumstances it shall return to Him in its entirety; so that in honouring His angels and saints He aims at glorifying Himself. Humility pays this tribute of glory to Him faithfully and joyfully, and would regard the smallest reservation as a criminal act of robbery."[58] Misdirecting worship is not a neutral act, it is robbery. Segneri says, "when is it that thou ascribes to thyself the glory of any good thing that thou mayest have done? It is when thou regardest it with self-complacency, or self-praise, as though thou hadst done it of thyself. This is the greatest robbery of God that thou canst commit: for it is to rob Him of that glory which can only be due to Him."[59] This is not a legal matter, it is a matter of love, so Bossuet traces the offense further upstream from glory to love. "Imprint deeply upon your heart this fundamental truth: that love in its origin is due to God only and that it is an act of sacrilegious robbery to take it from Him and consecrate it to any other than Him."[60] We will not understand abnegation if it is lacking this liturgical motive, and we will not understand liturgy if we do not treat it as an exchange of intimate love.

Creation is put under the reign of God again in the sacrifice of the mass ("thy kingdom come, thy will be done") by a cosmic priesthood that Christ restored to man and woman after they had forfeited it. Christ won it back for them by his merits on the cross so that liturgical responsibility could once again be practiced with justice. This, of course, will be impossible if we are selfish instead of selfless, and therefore de Castaniza imagines the following exchange occurring in the interior heart with the holy guest we receive in the Divine Sacrament. The soul will say

---

58. Grou, *The School of Jesus Christ*, 204.

59. Paul Segneri, *The Manna of the Soul: Meditations for Every Day of the Year*, vol. 2 (New York: Benziger Brothers, 1892), 731-32

60. Jacques-Bénigne Bossuet, *Great French Sermons from Bossuet, Bourdaloue, and Massillon* (London: Sands and Co., 1917) 172.

"What hath moved Thee, O great King of kings, to enter into me, who
am nothing but a miserable, despicable, vile, blind, and naked creature?"
And He will answer thee: – "Love, for thou art My dove, My friend, My
sister, My spouse, and My dearly beloved." Then thou mayest reply: – "O
uncreated Love, O sweetest Dilection, O friendly and faithful Charity!
what wouldst Thou have me do? What demandest Thou? What desirest
Thou?" He saith: – "I ask nothing but love. I would have nothing burn
on the hearth of thy heart but the fire of My love; that it may devour all
foreign love within thee, and destroy all self-will and seeking.[61]

The use of the word "vile" in these quotes will require us to grasp its etymology in order
to replace an original meaning with the one it has come to have. Instead of "disgusting"
or "repulsive," its original meaning was "base, common, worthless (from *vilis*). Camus
makes the contrast intelligible to us when he says that at judgment day a great fan "can
separate the corn from the chaff, and separate precious from vile things."[62]

The fire God kindles in the soul of the liturgist will devour all foreign love within her.
We cannot glorify God, or enjoy peace, without submission to the adorable will of our
Maker. Liturgy is abnegation. If we wish to define true liturgy by its opposite, we may say
that it is not-idolatry. It is the opposite of idolatry in three senses.

First, idolatry directs love to self instead of to God. Idolatry directs itself towards our
glory instead of God's. Self-love is self-worship. Those who have not subdued the love of
self become, Tronson says, "their own idols, and thus they fall into those sins to which
S. Paul alludes as the sad fruits of the love of self. 'In the last days men shall be lovers of
their own selves, covetous, boasters, proud, unthankful, unholy lovers of pleasures more
than lovers of God' (2 Tim. iii. i, 2. 4)."[63] We can deceive ourselves into thinking we
worship God purely, but worship is not pure if we liturgize with a mercenary intention
that mingles other goods with the supreme good. Fenelon traces this to the root: "the

---

61. De Castaniza, *The Spiritual Conflict and Conquest*, 187-88.

62. Camus, *The Draught of Eternitie*, 74-75.

63. Tronson, *Examination of Conscience*, 197-98.

origin of our trouble is, that we love ourselves with a blind passion that amounts to idolatry. If we love anything beyond, it is only for our own sakes."[64]

Second, idolatry is liturgy flowing in the wrong direction. Who receives what? Who is directed to whom? "Do not refer God to yourself," warns Grou, "but refer yourself to God for everything that is of any consequence to you, in time and in eternity, and self-love will be lost in the love of God."[65] This problem is especially noticeable in prayer that has not been purified by abnegation. Prayer is a good action, true, but what we do by ourselves, and for ourselves, is filled with secret pride and self-love. Olier gives an example. "How many persons make use of prayer, to ask for riches, for the gain of a suit, or the attainment of honors, in all which they have frequently no other object, at least ultimately, than to enjoy the pleasures of the world, satisfy their ambition, or take revenge of their enemies. In all this, there is nothing for God or the good of their souls; all this tends, on the contrary, to sin and the satisfaction of self-love."[66]

Liturgy must attend God and be for his glory. The original order must be observed, insists Grou. "Self-love, by which our prayers are as much influenced, to say the least ... reverses the order that has been established by the very nature of things, as well as by divine institution and the example of Jesus Christ."[67] In this backward state, we conceive of prayer as nothing beyond "a request presented to God in order to gain a particular boon from him; it completely ignores the main idea of homage, and the tribute of love and gratitude."[68] If we are truly in love with God, then it should be he who attracts our affection, not the boons we might get from him. Many will protest, and point out their exercises, their devotion, their religious observances, but Baker will not relent. "Let them say what they will, self-love guides their prayers; they pray more to please themselves than

---

64. Fenelon, *Spiritual Progress* (New York: M. W. Dodd, 1853) 30.

65. Grou, *Manual for Interior Souls*, 275.

66. Jean-Jacques Olier, *Catechism of an Interior Life* (Baltimore: Murphy & Co., 1852) 194-95.

67. Grou, *The School of Jesus Christ* (London: Burns Oates & Washbourne, Ltd., 1932) 236.

68. Grou, *The School of Jesus Christ*, 236.

to please God. Their object is to bear witness to themselves that they have prayed; and they think they have a palpable proof of it when they have recited so many forms of prayer that they lose their breath. For the same reason many speak aloud, that the ear may be an additional witness."[69] Abnegation of self and the glorification of God work hand in hand, he adds. "We must destroy self-love in our souls, that so the Divine love may be raised and increased in them."[70] "There is a time appointed for fasting," notes Segneri, "a time for taking the discipline, a time for giving thyself to contemplation; but all times alike belong to the denial of the will. When is it that a horse, and a vicious one, does not require the bit?"[71]

This sort of idolatry has liturgy flowing the wrong direction, as if we have exchanged places with God. It is a sort of infidelity when we want continual assurance that we are doing well, instead of wanting our liturgy to be continual thanksgiving for the goods with which God has blessed us. What shall we do to correct this faulty liturgy? Fenelon says "the safest and shortest course is to renounce, forget and abandon self, and through faithfulness to God to think no more of it. This is the whole of religion – to get out of self and of self-love in order to get into God."[72]

Third, idolatry happens when we give only partial liturgy to God. The fault is not only having the wrong God, it is not having enough God, and not having God alone. Our liturgy must be a full Holocaust, not a partial one, and in Scriptural revelation Grou finds love to be "a purifying fire; destroying, consuming all that clings to corrupt nature and self-love; it is a fire which feeds itself upon sacrifices, which insists upon voluntary victims, and which hates the smallest raid upon the holocaust."[73] Of course, Segneri says we can begin slowly, but be sure to finish. "Would not these poor souls, then, do better to begin gradually and voluntarily to detach themselves from those things from which,

---

69. Grou, *The Characteristics of True Devotion* (New York: Benziger Brothers, 1895) 62.

70. Baker, *Holy Wisdom*, 196.

71. Paul Segneri, *The Manna of the Soul: Meditations for Every Day of the Year,* vol. 1 (New York: Benziger Brothers, 1892) 23.

72. Fenelon, *The Inner Life*, 15-16.

73. Grou, *Meditations Upon the Love of God* (London: T. Baker, 1905) 142.

unless they do it themselves out of love, they will in the end be rent by force?"[74] Our God is a consuming fire who wants the flame of his love to annihilate anything which causes us to divide our selves, a part for him and a part for ourselves. There should be no admixture of self-love in our zeal for God's glory. Our eyes should be fixed wholly, totally, completely upon Jesus, as Tronson notices Mary modeling.

> Let us reverently endeavor to enter into the feelings which must have possessed the Virgin Mother's sword-pierced soul as she watched the death pangs of Her Divine Son: so shall our eyes, wholly fixed upon our Dying Lord, refuse to be drawn aside by any outward object; so shall our hearts, filled with the love of God, urge us to cast away all self-love, to crucify in ourselves whatever is displeasing to Him, and to be willing to sacrifice all for Him Who was slain for us, "that" we should "present" our "bodies a living sacrifice, holy, acceptable unto God" (Rom. xii. i). Then let us, adoring the Holy Spirit from Whom all good thoughts proceed, prepare to assist at the Celebration of the august Mysteries.[75]

Liturgical abnegation is seeing Jesus as Mary saw him on the cross: with eyes refusing to be drawn to any other object, casting away self-love, and crucifying whatever is displeasing to God.

The liturgical heart that has undergone abnegation seeks God alone, desires God alone, loves God alone. Rigoleuc discovers the power to do so from an unexpected place. "What [the soul] on her part does is, to concentrate all her desires in one alone, in order to belong entirely to God, and to die to herself and to creatures. This is the sole desire she reserves to herself, all-absorbing in its strength and intensity, occupying and pervading every faculty; *a desire which is felt rather than produced,* proceeding more from God than from herself."[76] It is astounding to see it in the saints, but Saint-Jure thinks it is just as wonderful if we can see it in partial measure in ourselves.

---

74. Segneri, *The Manna of the Soul*, vol. 1, 278.

75. Tronson, *Examination of Conscience*, 122.

76. Jean Rigoleuc, *Walking with God*, 37-38. Emphasis added.

Behold what self-denial effects in a man! This is why it is called "annihilation," a state of nothingness, because man, by the annihilation and the destruction of self-love, no longer thinks of himself, no longer applies his attention to himself, no longer occupies himself with himself, and no longer acts for himself. His soul and his body, his understanding, his will, his imagination, his passions, his eyes; his ears, his tongue, his senses, his members, and all there is in him, bears him and refers him to God and to his glory.[77]

---

77. Saint-Jure, *The Religious*, vol. 1, 573.

DEFINING ABNEGATION

Jesus, himself, made self-abnegation a condition for being his follower. Mark 8:34, Matthew 16:24, and Luke 9:23 are identical except for Luke's addition of one word: "If any man would come after me, let him deny himself and take up his cross [daily] and follow me." Olier says the reason "why our Lord put abnegation in his gospel as the first step we must take in the Christian life ... [is] because self-centeredness, being filled with the self, blocks Jesus Christ and the fullness of his divine life from entering us. It is the inexhaustible source of every evil and every sin."[1] This point is emphasized in each of the theologians of abnegation, who all take special notice of this verse. Here are some examples.

Grou calls this central to the gospel that Christ proclaims. "In this complete abnegation He admitted no compromise. There is no middle course. He said you must deny yourself, or I shall deny you; you can only belong to Me on that condition."[2] Croiset also places the command of mortification first among Jesus's teachings.

> Mortification is so necessary for the perfect love of Jesus Christ, that it is the first lesson that Jesus Christ Himself gives to those who wish to be His disciples. Without it, we can have no hope of ever being disciples of Jesus Christ. If any man will come after Me, says our loving Savior, let

---

1. Jean-Jacques Olier, *Introduction to the Christian Life and Virtues*, in *Berulle and the French School*, ed. Thompson (New York: Paulist Press, 1989) 262-63.

2. Jean Grou, *The School of Jesus Christ* (London: Burns, Oates & Washbourne, 1932) 81.

him deny himself ... For this reason all the Saints agree in considering that there is no stronger proof of real piety than perfect mortification.[3]

Francis Libermann does not want us to forget that abnegation is Jesus's teaching, not our invention.

> It is not I who preach abnegation, it is our Lord Himself who has set down the conditions under which He will receive us as His followers: "If anyone comes to me and does not hate his father and mother, and wife and children and brothers and sister, yes, and even his own life, he cannot be my disciple." (Luke 14:26-27). No doctrine has ever found more forceful expressions in the Gospels. And to make evasion impossible, the Savior adds: "And he who does not carry is cross and follow me, cannot be my disciple." (Luke 14:27). In other words, it is not sufficient even to renounce all these things; but it is also necessary to carry behind our Lord the pains and adversities which will befall us. Right after this Christ tells us the parable of the man who builds a house, and of the man who goes to war; how they consider their resources, and whether or not they would be able to meet the requirements, so that, should they be deficient, they may abandon their plans. This teaches us, that unless we renounce everything, we do not possess sufficient equipment to follow Christ our Lord to battle. If we are not generous enough to prepare ourselves to renounce everything, we should not follow Him. The words of our Savior allow of no quibbling.[4]

Francis de Sales underscores the traditional doctrine that keeping the commandments is only a beginning, and perfection ultimately involves abnegation.

---

3. Croiset, *Devotion to Sacred Heart*, 77-78.

4. Francis Libermann, *Instructions for Missionaries* (https://dsc.duq.edu/cgi/viewcontent.cgi?article=1021&context=spiritan-rc) 133.

He who keeps the commandments denies himself sufficiently for
salvation; to humble oneself in order to be exalted is quite enough:
but still there remains another obedience, ability and self-abnegation, to
which the examples and instructions of Our Lord invites us. He would
have us learn humility from him ... He would have us renounce ourselves,
after his example, but he has renounced his own will so decisively that he
has submitted to the cross itself.[5]

The reason to renounce our own will is because Jesus has renounced his, and we want
to be like Jesus. If someone denies himself, it is because he wants to act the way Jesus did.
Following Jesus (liturgy) is the cause of mortification. When Bossuet hears Jesus say "I
am in them," he understands it to mean that

they are My living members; they are other Christs; other Selves. They
have in them His spirit, which makes the doctrine of Jesus Christ shine
in their lives; which renders them, like Him, gentle, humble, patient, and
calm in good and evil, whether the world esteems or despises them ... In all
these things, the spirit of Jesus which is in them, as in His living members,
makes them like Him, and prompts them to follow His example ... They
carry the imprint of His cross; and, as Saint Paul says, *always bearing
about in our bodies the mortification of Jesus* (II Cor. 4:10). Thus the
eternal Father sees only Jesus Christ in them.[6]

If one is destined to share the glory of the Son of God in heaven, then it is demanded
that one share Jesus' sufferings on earth. Shall we g rumble over this? de Gergy asks.

---

5. Francis De Sales, *The Catholic Controversy* (London: Burns & Oates, Ltd, 1909)
   193-94.

6. Jacques-Bénigne Bossuet, *Selections From Meditations on the Gospel*, vol. 2,
   (Chicago: Henry Regnery Company, 1962) 186.

"Ought we to resist, put ourselves in trouble, and to complain? Complain that we are destined to share the glory of the Son of God in heaven! No."[7]

Eudes says that when Jesus makes this command he is simply applying to us the conditions under which he, himself, lived.

> Adore our Blessed Lord when He says, "If any man will come after me, let him deny himself" (Luke 9, 23). Adore the thought, the love and the design that He had in your regard when He said these words. Ask His pardon for placing any obstacle in the way of its fulfilment. Give yourself to Him that you may effectuate what He meant by these words, and realize that He Himself first did what He asks of you, having given you the perfect example of self-abnegation. While He was on earth, He never acted according to His own desires, but rather He did the will of His Father. He never sought His own satisfaction nor His own interests, but those of His Father. "For Christ did not please himself" (Rom. 15, 3).[8]

The supreme example of self-denial was given in the incarnate life of the God-man's hypostatic union. It climaxed in the cross, but it began in the incarnation and was maintained throughout his earthly ministry. It was a perfect detachment, made out of love, which we can only approach in tandem with Christ, that is, by following after him in love.

Segneri insists that Jesus' words to deny, take up a cross, and to follow, "were not addressed by Christ to the Apostles only, but to others also. 'He said to all:' that is, to those then living, to those who were to come after, to all Christians without exception,"[9] which is to say, they were addressed to his followers, as Eudes underscores.

---

7. Jean-Joseph Languet de Gergy, *Confidence in the Mercy of God* (London: R. Washbourne, 1876) 231-32.

8. John Eudes, *The Priest: His Dignity and Obligations* (New York: P. J. Kenedy & Sons, 1947) 191.

9. Paul Segneri, *The Manna of the Soul*, vol. 2, 579.

It is no small accomplishment to renounce the world in the manner just described. Yet even this is not enough to give you that perfect detachment which is one of the primary foundations of Christian life. Our Lord cries out to us in a loud voice: "If any man will come after me, let him deny himself and take up his cross, and follow me" (Matt. 16, 24). So, then, if you want to be among the followers of Christ and belong to Him, you have to renounce yourself, that is, your own mind, your own ideas, your own will, desires, inclinations and your self-love, because it is your self-love that leads you to hate and avoid anything that might cause pain or mortification to your spirit or your flesh and makes you love and seek out everything that may give them pleasure and contentment.[10]

The two reasons given for why we are obliged to practice self-abnegation is, first, because everything in us is corrupted and disordered, and, second, because Jesus behaved like a person having no love for himself, but only for his Father in heaven. Jesus was the first to live the Christian life, and then makes many copies of himself. He abnegated himself to ennoble and sanctify our abnegations. "By the use he has made of human nature," and by "all the exercises and functions proper thereto," Quarre says "he sanctified ours, showing that we may imitate him, seeing he became man to be the rule, law and model of our actions, and not only imitate him, but express and represent him to the life, and be so many Christs, as members of the Son of God."[11] Saint-Jure says salvation means that what happened in Jesus must now happen in us.

> The Incarnation and the grace which is a consequence of it, tend only to this, that Jesus Christ the word Incarnate should do by similitude in us, what the Word did in His Humanity; that is, that He should empty us of ourselves, replenish us with His divinity, imprint on us traces of

---

10. John Eudes, *The Life and the Kingdom of Jesus in Christian Souls* (New York: P. J. Kenedy & Sons, 1946) 19.

11. Quarre, *A Spiritual Treasure, Containing our Obligations to God, and the Vertues Necessary to a Perfect Christian* (London: printed by T. R. for Thomas Dring, 1664) 493.

His perfections; that He should unite us to Himself and cause us to live a life divinely human; that He should operate in us without resistance whatever he pleases, make us act in and by His spirit, [and] render us to His Father to be employed in his service now and forever.[12]

John of Avila therefore discovers Jesus to be our exemplar, telling us to do what he has done. We follow the path he took, which was a path of obedience for him, and is a path to holiness for us. "Holiness comes from love, and the greater the love, the greater the saint. The best proof we can give of our love for Christ is to obey His commands and bear the cross for Him ... Contempt for self and abnegation of our will are also signs of this love, for our Lord says: 'If any man will come after me, let him deny himself.'"[13] We need not grope in the dark to discover a pattern for our faith, because Christ has given us his own pattern to follow. Elizabeth of the Trinity notices "the path is traced for us. We have but to deny ourselves, to die to self, to lose sight of self. Is not that the Master's meaning when He says: 'If any man will come after Me, let him deny himself, and take up his cross, and follow me?'"[14] An effect of original sin is the craving to be esteemed, respected, and honored, and mortification primarily targets these, which is why de Bergamo concludes "that if I will not mortify myself with humility – that is to say, crush my self-love and craving for esteem – I shall be excluded as a follower of Jesus Christ."[15]

In what is initially an unexpected turn, we are told that the soul must not only be on the lookout for the operation of self-will in its engagement with the world, but also in her performance of spiritual exercises. John of the Cross thinks people are still succumbing to self-will when they nourish their natural self with spiritual consolations. "They think it enough to deny themselves in the things of this world, without annihilating themselves, and purging away all self-seeking in spiritual things ... They seek only for delights, for sweet

---

12. Saint-Jure, *A Treatise on the Knowledge and Love of Our Lord Jesus Christ*, vol. 2 (New York: P. O'Shea, 1875) 407-08.

13. John of Avila, *Letters of Blessed John of Avila*, 98-99.

14. Elizabeth of the Trinity, *The Praise of Glory*, 244.

15. Gaetano Maria de Bergamo, *Humility of Heart* (Mandeville, LA: Founding Father Films Publishing, 2015) 107.

communications, and satisfactions in God, but this is not self-denial, nor detachment of spirit, but rather spiritual gluttony. They render themselves spiritually enemies of the cross of Christ."[16] The command imposed by Christ applies not only to a portion of our life, but to our entire life, including our religious life.

Grou admits we dislike the command because self-denial is the opposite of self-seeking. The spiritual person under conversion discovers that he is at enmity with his own self-will, and liturgical abnegation is a holy indignation against all selves in that state, even if we would hope to falsely exclude ourselves from that number.

> How is it that we dislike, and indeed have almost a horror of hearing about interior mortification, abnegation, poverty of spirit, or renunciation of every natural inclination, repugnance, desire, or fear? As though all this were not included in the saying of Jesus Christ: *If any man will come after Me let him deny himself!* As though this renunciation, carried to the highest pitch of perfection, were not the characteristic of Jesus Christ's holiness, and ought not to be the characteristic of our own![17]

Self-love is so deadly that Bona observes that "the Lord has not only forbidden it, but even commanded its opposite, hatred, saying (Luke xiv, 26): 'If any man come to me, and hate not his father, and mother, and wife, and children, and brethren, and sisters, yea, and his own life also, it cannot be my disciple.'"[18] The word "hate" sounds harsh to us, because as a noun it means malice and hostility; but as a verb it means to regard with extreme ill-will, or have a passionate aversion to, that is, to treat as an enemy. Our sin is an enemy of our beatitude, and we should treat self-love and self-will as enemies to vanquish.

The liturgical state is the reign of God's will in our hearts, where self-will is expunged by submitting our will to his. Obedience to the true master involves abnegation of self-mastery. Insofar as a devout soul surrenders judgment to God, she no longer directs

---

16. John of the Cross, *The Ascent of Mount Carmel*, in *The Complete Works*, vol. 1, 76.

17. Grou, *The School of Jesus Christ*, 432.

18. Giovanni Bona, *A Treatise of Spiritual Life* (Poplar Bluff, MO: The author, 1893) 261-62.

herself by her own judgment. At that point, Grou adds, we find God's commands sweet, not bitter. "[The Christian] can discern but hidden sweetness in the sentence so terrible to the pusillanimous: 'If any man will come after me, let him deny himself, and take up his cross and follow me.' Earth contains no object which he is not ready to immolate for the name of Jesus; attracted by the owner of his Savior's perfumes, he burns with ardor to follow the blood-stained traces of his sacred footsteps."[19] This abnegation is liturgical because all is done in the name of Jesus, and we find courage in the liturgizing conversion of heart. Unified will is a sign of love, and Christ's possession of our will is a sign of self-love's demise, which is why Castaniza says "the greatest sign of love is to have one and the same will with the beloved, so that the more we have of our own will, so much the less we have of God's will and love."[20]

It will require courage, true; all the theologians of liturgical abnegation admit it; but there is no other way, or Christ would have used it, as de Ravignan points out.

> I say courage, because I know what it costs to embrace this abnegation, this absolute renunciation of self; here is our interior cross, but a cross to which is united every virtue, for in prayer are to be found patience, mortification, zeal, strength, warfare, victory and peace. If it were not so, if there were any better means, our Saviour when consummating His sacrifice upon Calvary, for the expiation of our hardness of heart, in order that we might gain every grace and that the world might be saved, would assuredly have commanded and taught it to us.[21]

Satan has made all this sound bitter to us. Pride has flipped the world upside down, and now we see in mirror images, having confidence in ourselves instead of in God. Where we should not place trust, we do; where we should place trust, we do not. Therefore, the reversal must itself be reversed, and this is done by liturgical abnegation, which puts God

---

19. Grou, *The Interior of Jesus and Mary*, vol. 1, 320.

20. De Castaniza, *The Spiritual Conflict and* Conquest, 428.

21. Gustav de Ravignan, *Conferences on the Spiritual Life* (London: R. Washbourne, 1873) 169-70.

back on his throne. The setback humanity suffered in Eden can only be repaired through faith, and John of Avila says "faith is the beginning of the spiritual life ... This faith is the first reverence by which the soul adores its Creator, thinking of him in all his grandeur, as is fitting."[22] To make the world right side up again, we should have confidence in God and diffidence in ourselves (from *fidere*, to trust + *dis,* away.) This is why Granada says a "condition of true humility is, that it ought to fill you with a greater distrust of yourselves, of your own wit, and of your own strength."[23] The Tempter has hidden half the truth from us, just as he hid half the truth about deification from Adam and Eve. We make two acts simultaneously: by doing the one, we do the other. Deny the false wisdom under which we operate, and accept God's wisdom and grace. As we drop the former, we can pick up the latter; we can only pick up the latter by dropping the former. Thereby, our moral actions become liturgical.

De Sales reminds us that "humility does not only consist in mistrust of ourselves, but also in confidence in God."[24] His friend and brother bishop, Camus, echoes the advice: "Nothing [is] so diligently recommended unto us in holy writ, as the distrust of ourselves (who are but a mere vanity) and to place our whole confidence in God.[25] Put succinctly, have diffidence in yourself and confidence in God. Put more succinctly still, diffide yourself and confide God. This requires an experience of grace, de Alcantara says, because "we do not rest upon our own merits, but upon Almighty God's grace; who is so much the more willing to assist man, by how much the more he is diffident of his own forces, placing a firm hope in the goodness of God, to whom nothing is impossible."[26] Rodriguez says the best means to overcome temptations "is to diffide in ourselves, and to place all our confidence in God," the reason being that it moves God to protect those

---

22. John of Avila, *Audi, Filia* (New York: Paulist Press, 2006) 112.

23. Louis de Granada, *A Memorial of a Christian Life* (New York: The Catholic Publication Society, 1870) 364.

24. De Sales, *The Spiritual Conferences,* 77

25. Jean-Pierre Camus, *A Spiritual Combat* (London: The Scolar Press, 1974) 96-97

26. Peter de Alacantara, *A Golden Treatise of Mental Prayer* (Philadelphia: M. Fithian, 1844) 205.

that hope in him "because they attribute nothing to themselves, and give the glory of all to God. So that as they are regardless of their own honor, and attentive only to that of God, he takes their cause in hand, does his own work, and makes it his own business, is a thing that purely regards his own honor and glory."[27] Too many things we do are done for our self-glory, including some of our pious acts of religion, and liturgical abnegation flips things back to right side up so that the things we do can be purely for God's own honor and glory. Liturgizing God abnegates self-idolization.

The liturgical conquering of idolatry demands abnegation of the idols we serve: self, flesh, world, passions, and vain honor, first among them. De Estella insightfully defines a vain thing as "that which filleth not the place where it is. The things of this world do not fill our soul ... Wouldst not thou take him for a fool, that when he were hungry, would open his mouth and take in the air to satisfy his hunger withal? ... That vessel which is able to contain God himself, can never be full until that God himself do fill it; the cause whereof, is the vanity of these worldly things."[28] This straightening will be accomplished by the ratcheting of the cross. What will be a person's particular crosses? How will he recognize them? From whom will he receive them? How long must he carry them? How broad, how deep are they? These are among the questions asked by theologians of liturgical abnegation, and we will address them in a later chapter. For now, know that the wood of the cross is kindling for the fire that Jesus came to cast upon the earth (Luke 12:49). If Jesus requires crosses of us, he also bestows the power to bear them. Abnegation is not an energy we summon up from ourselves, it relies upon a strengthening by God. Man is only required not to give resistance, which is a trait of patience. Patience is not simply tolerating delay without any irritation, says de Sales; it is the power to surrender to providence.

---

27. Alphonsus Rodriguez, *The Practice of Christian and Religious Perfection*, vol. 2 (London: James Duffy, 1861) 314-15. There are two named Alphonsus Rodriguez, who should not be confused. The *theologian* is referred to as Alfonso (he composed three volumes on Christian and Religious perfection); the *saint* is referred to as Alonso (porter at Majorca for 46 years). In my text, if I am referring to theologian I will use only the last name, if referring to the saint I will add the first name.

28. Diego de Estella, *The Contempt of the World and the Vanities Thereof* (Somers, for John Heigham, 1622) 357, 365.

You must see and speak to God amid the thunders and the whirlwinds; you must see him in the bush, and amid the thorns; and to do this, the truth is that we must take off our shoes, and make a great abnegation of our wills and affections. But the Divine goodness has not called you to the state in which you are, without strengthening you for all this. It is for him to perfect his work. True, it is a little long, because the matter requires it; but [have] patience.[29]

What shall we count amongst the things that we will abnegate? When we say "ourselves," that is only a convenient summary, a shorthand term Eudes says. "If you want to be among the followers of Christ and belong to Him, you have to renounce yourself, that is, your own mind, your own ideas, your own will, desires, inclinations and your self love."[30] When we say "worldly pleasures," that is an exterior description of a deeper and more important interior action. Abnegation might involve acts austerity for some, but even one who cannot practice great external austerity should nevertheless engage in serious interior abnegation.

Mortification rectifies faculties, and things are set in right order when it does, which means that any love we have for creatures can be a means and instrument to increase our soul's love of God. Having affection for creatures is not the problem. Even the affections residing in our sensitive nature is not the problem, since Baker reminds us how different it was for the first and second Adams. "For to Adam in the state of innocency, yea, even to our Lord Himself, many objects were pleasing and delightful to sense: His sight and taste took contentment in pleasurable objects, and there was in nature an aversion from pain, and an earnest desire to prolong natural life; and in all this there was not the least imperfection."[31] But some affections become sinful by migrating from the inferior part

---

29. Francis De Sales, *Letters to Persons in the World* (London: Burns & Oates, Ltd., 1894) 259.

30. Eudes, *The Life and the Kingdom of Jesus in Christian Souls*, 30.

31. Baker, *Holy Wisdom,* 201.

of the soul to the superior part of the soul, there infecting it, and then they need to be denied.

> The affections to creatures, therefore, which we affirm to be sinful, are
> such as are seated in the superior soul or rational will, by which the mind
> and will consider and adhere unto creatures, and knowingly and willingly
> pursue the attaining and enjoying of them, *as if they were the good, not of*
> *sense only (for so they are), but of the person,* which indeed they are not;
> for the only good of an intellectual nature is God, who alone is exalted
> above it; whereas all other creatures are but equal or inferior to it. To the
> superior will, therefore, all things but God must be indifferent as in and
> for themselves, and only to be loved as they are serviceable to the spirit.[32]

Christ's kenosis inspires our abnegation. We have not a glory like his to deny, but we have a will to deny, which we must do if we want to follow his example of having no desire except for his Father.

We should annihilate ourselves when communicating in the Blessed Sacrament, as our Lord annihilated Himself in order to communicate Himself to us in it. De Sales asked this to be explained to his spiritual daughter.

> Tell her to communicate fearlessly, calmly, yet with all humility, in
> order to correspond with the action of that Spouse who in order to
> unite Himself with us annihilated Himself ... Oh! my daughter, those
> who communicate according to the spirit of the Heavenly Bridegroom,
> annihilate themselves and say to our Lord: feed on me, change me,
> annihilate me, convert me into Thyself. There is nothing, I think, in
> the world of which we have more absolute possession, or over which
> we have more entire dominion, than over the food which, for our own
> self-preservation, we annihilate.

---

32. Baker, *Holy Wisdom,* 201, emphasis added.

Well, our Lord has condescended to this excess of love, namely, to give
Himself to us for our food; and as for us, what ought not we to do in
order that He may possess us, that He may feed on us, that He may make
us what He pleases?[33]

To say "annihilate me" is to say "establish Thyself in me." There would be no need to
empty the heart unless something new was going to be put in it; no reason to annihilate
what is there unless something new is about to arrive. Abnegation is renouncing our
first father, Adam, who gave us death, so that we can become children of the New
Adam, who will give us life. If this be so, what ought we not deny, so that Christ can
take possession? What ought we not empty out, that Christ can replace? What ought
we not abnegate, so we can liturgize with him? He has brought the perichoresis of
the Trinity so near to earth that it imprints our liturgical life with the same self-giving
reciprocity. The persons of the Trinity are self-emptying, self-effacing, self-giving, and
if we join them in their liturgical pattern, then we welcome the annihilation of pride,
arrogance, and selfishness in ourselves. The Trinitarian perichoresis is an *eternal* mystery;
the Christological perichoresis is the mystery of the *incarnation*; now we are invited into
a spiritual perichoresis, which is a mystery of *liturgical abnegation*. We are linked to God
the Father by the mystical liturgical chain of Son, Holy Spirit, Church, sacrament, and
our own abnegation.

This is the union the Eucharist brings about. (More on this in the final chapters.) The
union to Christ in the Eucharist is like to that which subsists between him and his Father,
according to Saint-Jure.

As the Father is in the Son and the Son in the Father, so, by analogy,
however, Our Lord is in us and we in Him when we received this august
Sacrament; and by our union with His humanity we are elevated to union
with His Divinity. God the Father is united to His Son in the unity
of essence by the eternal generation; the Son unites Himself to man by
the hypostatic union in the Incarnation, and to all men by the Blessed

---

33. Jean Pierre Camus, *The Spirit of St. Francis de Sales* (London: Burns, Oates &
Washbourne, Ltd., 1925) 396.

Sacrament; by this union with His humanity He unites them to His divinity, and by it He unites them to His Father.[34]

This communion with God also produces perfect charity towards our neighbor. One of love's effects is to make the will of those who love one with the beloved. The spillover from love of God to love of neighbor is affirmed by all these theologians of abnegation, as it is done here by John of Avila.

> The best way to possess true charity and understand what it is, is to consider how the Blessed in heaven practise it ... The love which the saints bear towards God transforms their will, so that it becomes one with His: that is, they can wish, or not wish, only what He does; ... From this overflowing river which gladdens the city of God, comes, as a streamlet, their love for their neighbour. Their one longing and joy is to see the God they love so fervently, possess all glory and honour, and hence they ardently desire that the Blessed, their companions, may be as full of beauty, and felicity, as they are themselves, because God is thus honoured in them.[35]

Liturgical philanthropy – a love rightly ordered toward the neighbor – comes from the constant desire that God be recognized as good, as holy, and as full of excellence as he is. Latria begets benevolence toward the neighbor that increases the glory of God, which is why John of Avila adds loving our neighbor "consists in loving his virtues, and desiring them for him, that God may be glorified in him. Your pleasure should augment in proportion as his sanctity increases and you should regret his sins as offenses against his Creator ... The love for God and man, then, both concur to the one end that God may be praised and worshipped."[36] Charity is the unwavering desire that God possess in himself all the perfections proper to him. Love and justice kiss.

---

34. Jean Baptiste Saint-Jure, *A Treatise on the Knowledge and Love of Our Lord Jesus Christ*, vol. 1 (New York: P. O'Shea, 1870) 606.

36. John of Avila, *Letters of Blessed John of Avila*, 131.

We have experience even in the natural realm of denying ourselves for the sake of love, or for the sake of another's happiness. We see it constantly in one spouse for another, in parents for their children, in friends for their comrades. In the case of liturgical abnegation, this is exercised in the supernatural realm, and with all the more power because abnegation receives energy from devotion to Almighty God. Furthermore, God infuses the soul with grace so she may partake of the perichoretic exchange of love that is his life. Barbanson speaks as though the Trinity is making its force felt.

> God, descending into the soul, not only freely imparts his riches to her, making her partaker of his graces and favors, but also gives himself wholly unto her in his own person. God, who is the glory of angels, before whom the heavens tremble, inclines his affections to the soul as a bridegroom to his bride, taking his delight in her presence. And a participation of the self-same force of love is communicated to the creature, so that, forgetting her meanness, the soul not only beholds this infinite majesty as her God, king and father, for to adore, fear and reverence him; but she dares to approach and unite herself unto him as her equal and friend, nay even as her dear spouse.[37]

Liturgy is participation in the self-same force of love that kenotically extended from the deity to the creature, and it is participation in the self-same force of love that the only begotten Son could return to the Father when he joined mankind. We can join the Son in this because our abnegation is brought about by the self-same force that caused the incarnation. Gay speaks of the Church being an expansion of Christ: "He will expand in reality, beyond and outside Himself, and will fill the universe. In that consists, as you have seen, the mystery of His mystical Body, or of the holy Church. As Christ manifests God, the Church manifests Christ ... The humanity of Christ is the prism of God, the Church ist he prism of Christ."[38] The glory of his Father required the cross, so Jesus

---

37. Constantine Barbanson, *The Secret Paths of Divine Love* (London: Burns Oates and Washbourne Ltd., 1928) 34.

38. Charles Gay, *The Christian Life and Virtues Considered in the Religious State*, vol. 1 (London: Burnes & Oates, 1878) 66.

welcomed it; the glory of the Father will require crosses for us, so we should also welcome whatever instruments God chooses for us individually, concludes Grou. "Provided God be glorified, no matter by what instrument, they are happy, and if permitted to select the means of promoting His glory in their own persons, they would choose such as are most humiliating and most calculated to lead to self-abnegation."[39]

What would it mean to truly believe in the resurrection? It would mean measuring all our present happiness against the certainty of our coming beatitude. The present happiness is real, but it is trivial, comparatively. And the more vivid the faith and hope in the resurrection, the more radical will be the love in Christ's followers, as the martyrs knew. We may never arrive at circumstances where a literal martyrdom will be required, but a willing martyrdom is demanded of us. Overcoming a dissipated heart is the death that a spiritual martyr seeks. Overcoming self-will and self-love may prove hard – certainly harder than the facile religious practices with which we try to placate God – yet de Caussade believes "it is in this destruction of self-love that all true piety and all spiritual progress consist, while for want of real abnegation most devout people have only the appearance of piety."[40] We are willing to do religion, but are we willing to embrace the spirit of abnegation in order to liturgize God? Grou points the way.

> This very necessary renunciation, of which the fruits are so sweet and the reward so great, is the great stumbling-block of the Gospel, and makes mortification of the heart odious to some who are otherwise most devout. Enjoin on them as many pious exercises, as many religious practices, even as many austerities as you will: they will fast, and go without sleep, and spend whole days in the churches; but to do violence to their character, to conquer their sensitiveness, to endure contradiction, to give up their own opinion, in a word to mortify their own mind and their own will is what they will not do, and what seems to them not merely difficult, but impossible.[41]

---

39. Grou, *The Interior of Jesus and Mary*, vol. 1, 233-34.

40. De Caussade, *Abandonment to Divine Providence*, 350.

41. Grou, *The School of Jesus Christ*, 34.

Abnegation is unpleasant and irritating to our corrupted nature, and the sinner finds ingenious ways to cling to the honor and esteem he has crafted for himself in this world, even crafted out of his religious piety. Yet, the only satisfaction for the soul, ultimately, is liturgizing God, since that is what she was created for when she was formed for a body. Surin believes what would please God should also become our pleasure. "This is the fruit of an entire abnegation of self, when, having put all our interests, temporal and spiritual, in the hands of the Lord, we desire only to obtain from Him what it is His will that we should ask. Thus a good man is fully satisfied when God is pleased; His whole pleasure is to see God's will done."[42] Liturgy wants God; abnegation denies whatever is not God, and spurns whatever does not lead to God; liturgical abnegation is the two working simultaneously. Pollien explores their connection.

> I have no other *raison d'etre* than His glory. I only exist to procure this one good for Him. It is for Him, for Him alone that I live, it is for Him that I die, it is for Him that I shall live world without end …

> And every one that calleth upon My name, saith the Lord, I have created Him for my glory, and it is for this that I have formed him and made him.

> This is all man. – God's glory is the whole purpose of my life, it is my all, the whole of me; for if I do not procure it, I have no more *raison d'etre*, I am good for nothing, and am nothing.[43]

Mrs. Murphy is a liturgical theologian because she has become a mystical theologian, exalted above all created things – even above the working of her own natural faculties of memory, intellect, and will. Blosius describes her when he writes, "the contemplation of mystical theology must be accompanied by ardent love, because it is not a purely

---

42. Surin, *The Foundations of Spiritual Life*, 24.

43. Pollien, *The Interior Life*, ed. Tissot, 11.

speculative an intellectual intuition of God, but must affect the will also. It is an experimental perception of God, not merely speculative: practical as well as theoretical; it is a union of will with Him, and not a mere intellectual apprehension."[44] Thus he finds the exalted soul to be "purified in memory from all images, and experiences perfect purity and simplicity! In the intellect it perceives the exceeding bright illuminations of the sun of Justice, and apprehends the divine truth; and in the will experiences a certain heat of calm love, the spiritual contact of the Holy Ghost, as of a living fountain."[45] This is not a matter of intellect alone, as we shall soon see.

How does one *practice* a dogma? Not simply believe a dogma, but practice it? Dogma affirms the infinity, transcendence, superiority, fullness, excellence, goodness, and ascendancy of God Almighty. We believe it, but we must also practice it. In Leen's words: "self-abnegation is but the practical acknowledgement of the fatherhood of God."[46] This remarkably terse description of liturgical abnegation is unpacked by Canfield.

> Having now found by the first point, that nothing is but this Essential Will, and that it is all things: it follows that by the second point we practice the same; i.e. live in this Annihilation of the Creatures, and Contemplation of this All: For, between the Knowledge and the practice of it, there is great difference. And indeed so much, that many have the one, but few practice the other. For many will say that nothing is but God: yet scarce a Man to be found will practice what he says ... Whoso therefore will remove all impediments, and banish whatsoever can step in betwixt God and him; whoso desires everlastingly to abide in the highest Contemplation of all others: And lastly, who so desires to cleave constantly to God ... Then let him follow the practice thereof, losing

44. Blosius, *A Book of Spiritual Instruction*, Preface, x.

45. Blosius, *A Book of Spiritual Instruction*, 97-98.

46. Edward Leen, *The True Vine and Its Branches* (New York: P. J. Kenedy & Sons, 1939) 222.

himself in this Infinite and dwelling therein, beholding it with a fixed eye, and that by the Death and Annihilation of himself.[47]

Everything we will encounter in the pages ahead – abnegation, providence, justice, nothingness, humility, annihilation, crosses, and the Eucharist – will open the eye to deification. This union with God is attained by integrating the acts of virtue (chiefly the three theological ones) with liturgical abnegation. For Saint-Jure,

> it consists ... in honoring and adoring him in the Temple of our souls;
> in performing to him there the Sacrifices of a lively Faith upon the Altar
> of our Understanding; in offering up the Holocausts of perfect Hope,
> an ardent Charity, upon the Altar of our Wills; and in a total subjection
> of our spirits to his, and a union of all our faculties with him; whereby
> we become purified, sanctified, and deified, proportionably as the blessed
> Saints are in heaven, where this perfection is completed.[48]

Liturgical abnegation is performed on the altar of our hearts, where love's sacrificial fire burns a holocaust, annihilating distractive diversions from Almighty God until the day we die. How can God's liturgy be shared with any other god? Jenks thinks we are foolish to even believe we can pull it off?

> 'Tis possible, you'll say, to love the world to a very great degree, and yet
> love God a little better; which if we do, we love him above all things, and
> that's enough to save us. Surely you are not in good earnest. Your whole
> heart is due to him: and can you think you do him Justice, by allowing
> him a little more than half? Your whole heart ought to be a House of
> Prayer: and is it just to make almost one half of it a den of thieves? Your

---

47. Benedict Canfield, *A Bright Starre Leading to & Centering in, Christ our Perfection. The Third part of the Rule of Perfection* (London: Henry Overton, 1646) 80-81.

48. Jean Baptiste Saint-Jure, *The Holy Life of Monsieur de Renty* (London: printed for Benj. Tooke, 1684) 239.

whole Heart ought to be the Temple of God: and dare you offer to defile
it, by making a Partition in it, and erecting Altars to his Mortal Enemies,
the World, the Flesh, and the Devil?[49]

Liturgical abnegation requires grace to harrow our hearts, as Christ harrowed hell.
Canfield knows our hearts resist self-denial and self renunciation. "That which deters
us from an absolute renouncement of ourselves, for the sake of the Will of God, is the
opinion stealing over us that by such renouncement we shall be deprived of what we
desire, and of all that forms our delight."[50] And in order to cooperate synergistically
with grace, the soul must learn a different reality by experience. "When once the
soul has learned the contrary by experience, and has found that by renouncement and
forgetfulness of her own will, and joy for the sake of the Divine Will, her will and joy
are not quenched or brought to nothing, but are, according to His promise, increased
a hundredfold; then she is no longer sad."[51] She can climb the mountain of the Lord
because she desires not worthless things. Her Lord has passed by, she is drawn up Mount
Moriah, and the liturgy she experiences there will inspire her to sacrifice anything.

> She now experiences no reluctance in renouncing self, and in offering to
> God her dear one, her only son Isaac, that is, her joy and her own will,
> because she foresees as a certainty that though he is bound, and laid on
> the altar of the heart in this mountain of prayer, and the sword of justice
> is near falling on his head, and he is about to be burnt by the root of fire
> of renouncement, yet never will he be handed over really to death, but
> he will still live, and, according to his name, will be changed into joy and
> laughter.[52]

---

49. Silvester [sic] Jenks, *Practical Discourses on Morality, part 1* (London: s.n., 1699) 35.

50. Benedict Canfield, *The Holy Will of God: A Short Rule of Perfection* (London: Thomas Richardson and Sons, 1878) 42.

51. Canfield, *The Holy Will of God*, 41-42.

52. Canfield, *The Holy Will of God*, 42.

There is no reluctance in renouncing the world after we have seen the world's Maker, and we can exclaim with Fenelon, in prayer, "I see nothing but thee; all the rest disappears as a shadow before the eyes of him who has once seen thee."[53]

---

53. François Fenelon, *Pious Thoughts Concerning the Knowledge and Love of God* (London: W. and J. Innys, 1720) 19-20.

ABNEGATION AT WORK

I am using the word "abnegation" to sum up all the various terms these authors utilize. This chapter will put forward many definitions, but perhaps Libermann puts it most succinctly when he says "self-abnegation is an efficacious remedy against sin, which is the manifestation of disorder of the soul."[1] In other words, everything here concerns a healing, a therapy, a cure. If that is true, we need not be surprised by the context in which these theologians place abnegation. I will take just one person to make a more detailed illustration. What company does the word keep in Libermann's writings? The spiritual person is advised to perform "an act that contains a movement of humility, abnegation, of oblation of yourself to God";[2] to belong "totally to God in self-abnegation, peace, mildness and humility of heart";[3] to preserve his soul "in a spirit of humility, abnegation and confident abandonment to God";[4] to pursue "a work of patience, abnegation, gentleness";[5] to attain virtues of "humility, obedience, charity, gentleness, simplicity, a life of prayer and abnegation";[6] to maintain a heart in perfect peace ("This peace must be a quiet abnegation of every sort of earthly affection and a total detachment

---

1. Libermann, *Instructions for Missionaries*, 114.

2. Francis Libermann, *Letters to Clergy and Religious*, Spiritan Series 7, vol. 3 (Pittsburgh: Duquesne University Press, 1963) 158.

3. Libermann, *Letters to Clergy and Religious*, Spiritan Series 7, vol. 3, 256.

4. Libermann, *Letters to Clergy and Religious*, Spiritan Series 7, vol. 3, 285.

5. Libermann, *Letters to Clergy and Religious*, Spiritan Series 7, vol. 3, 317.

6. Libermann, *Letters to Clergy and Religious*, Spiritan Series 7, vol. 3, 319.

from everything that is not God");[7] to seek true knowledge and love of God;[8] to engage "zealous ministry, which is a work of abnegation and devotedness";[9] to live with gentleness and humility of heart, which, as "the immediate fruit of a genuine and perfect love, demand perfect interior abnegation and great docility and submission to God;"[10] to perform "acts purely inspired by grace and may love God in God and for God alone";[11] to build a firm foundation on abnegation and "perfect fidelity to grace [so that] we may count upon God living in us to intensify our love for Him in due proportion;"[12] and to overcome superficiality that deprives one of earnestness and calm, accomplished by adhering "lovingly to God, with determination and perseverance, showing earnestness and moderation in every respect. Interior self-abnegation is of great help in aiding us to overcome this obstacle."[13]

Most people would not think to associate abnegation with peace, mildness, humility, confidence in God, patience, gentleness, simplicity, and devotion, perfect love – examples given in the above list – yet that is precisely the environment around abnegation. Abnegation is associated with love because love causes abnegation. God loved us enough to die for us; in return, we love God enough so as even to die (to ourselves) for him. Bruyere writes, "divine love is in very truth a strong and generous wine, sustaining the soul in heights above herself, but that love ever enforces the law of total self-abnegation ... When she lives the true life, God adapts her to Himself, and then everything in her that

---

7. Francis Libermann, *Letters to Clergy and Religious*, Spiritan Series 8, vol. 4 (Pittsburgh: Duquesne University Press, 1964) 38.

8. Libermann, *Letters to Clergy and Religious*, Spiritan Series 8, vol. 4, 401.

9. Francis Libermann, *Letters to Clergy and Religious*, Spiritan Series 9, vol. 5 (Pittsburgh: Duquesne University Press, 1966) 209.

10. Libermann, quoted in Alphonse Gilbert, *You have Laid Your Hand on Me* (Pittsburgh: Duquesne University, 1983) 126.

11. Libermann, *Instructions to Missionaries*, 12.

12. Libermann, *Instructions to Missionaries*, 15.

13. Libermann, *Instructions for Missionaries*, 177.

is unfit for union must irremissibly disappear."[14] Abnegation is about submission and docility to God, yes, but those are acts of love, which are the coin of the realm in liturgy. That abnegation is annihilation merely means purification is sanctification. Abnegation arises out of the liturgical desire to glorify God more fully. The note of liturgy sounded in abnegation is tersely expressed by Faber: "We wish to annihilate our whole being to return Him thanks for it."[15]

Abnegation therefore removes what is not God in order to receive God. Abnegation is cleaning the heart-as-temple to be God's residence. As Jesus once cleansed the temple in Jerusalem, Olier can see him cleansing our souls so they may serve as his temple now.

> The intention of Jesus Christ, as he comes into our hearts to sanctify it and to restore it to its original state of emptiness, is to banish from his temple all that fills it. He cannot tolerate there anything but his Father and his Divine perfections. With the lashes of a whip he drives from it, through persecutions and through crosses, all the buyers and sellers ... That is why Jesus Christ came into the world. He wanted to purify the human heart, empty it of every creature and thus make reparation for the original misfortune and disorder into which we had fallen through the mystery of sin and the goading of the devil.[16]

De Ponte summarizes the choice between two vocations:

> The vocation of the Devil, which, although at first sight it promises delights, honors, riches, liberty, and repose, yet all these are so intermingled with bitterness, that to say the truth, they are most painful ... On the contrary, the vocation of Christ, although it treat of abnegation

---

14. Bruyere, *Spiritual Life and Prayer*, 280.

15. Frederick Faber, *All for Jesus: or, The Easy Ways of Divine Love* (London: Richardson and Son, 1854) 345.

16. Olier, *Introduction to the Christian Life and Virtues*, in *Berulle and the French School*, 249.

and crosses, it is so proportioned by the Divine Providence, so fitted and accommodated to every one's forces, and mingled with such sweetness and celestial graces, that truly it is most sweet, even in this life.[17]

We find it sweet even in this life because Christ promises that "although my yoke be abnegation, yet it is sweet, and although my burthen be the cross, yet is it light to such as are meek and humble like myself."[18]

Abnegation is not required because there is something the matter with matter. God does not desire the death of the material body, he desires the death of sin, in order to liberate the self, so the whole man (body and soul) can be entirely given to God. God's love never lets the heart rest after it has taken possession of it, therefore Alacoque advises us to "surrender ourselves to its ardor, so that we may love Him with our whole being. Everything must be subservient to that, everything bend and yield before this holy love."[19] Abnegation is bending and yielding before holy love, which is another way of calling abnegation the correlative of love and justice. Saint-Jure makes a conclusion from Augustine's example of removing anything from your house that might be displeasing to the eyes of a distinguished visitor, however pleasing it might be in your own eyes, "because you would not wish to offend him whose friendship you should seek. Is it not then very just that we should tear from our hearts all that could displease Jesus Christ, whatever attachment we have to it, since He is the King of Kings, who, to come to us, has wrought such wonders?"[20] By the force of Christ's love, we become insensible to all diversions, even the diversion of created goods that are themselves good, if we did not misuse them.

The tradition has identified three stages in the spiritual growth of a person: purgation, illumination, and union. The language of the first stage is different from the language of the second and third stages. It is rougher and sounds harsher, of course, because the stage

---

17. Louis de Ponte, *Meditations on the Mysteries of Our Holy Faith*, vol. 3 (London: Richardson and Son, 1953) 95.

18. De Ponte, *Meditations on the Mysteries of Our Holy Faith*, vol. 3, 95.

19. Alacoque, *Spiritual Letters,* Letter 24, Kindle edition.

20. Saint-Jure, *A Treatise on the Knowledge and Love of Our Lord Jesus Christ*, vol. 1, 672.

of purgation involves punishing past sins, enduring combats, casting out corrupt habits, and slaying passions. Bona describes the three stages this way.

> In the first stage man learns himself: in the second he searches into God, in the third he aims at being united to, and transformed into God. All the spiritual life may be reduced to these three points, what man is, what God is, and how there may be effected a union between these two by love. When fire works upon green wood, it first expels the cold and moisture, which are obstacles to its operation; then it infuses dryness and heat, as necessary prerequisites to its own entrance; then, lastly, it is united intimately to the wood. So for union of the soul with God, first all impediments must be removed out of the way, then the requisite predispositions must be procured; and, these things being done, union infallibly follows.[21]

The Pentecostal fire of the Holy Spirit works first upon a green wood, and there's usually a lot of smoke. That is what most people associate with abnegation. But when the soul becomes more flammable, the fire can become hotter, and the abnegation more easy, so Bona provides aspirations to use in each of the three stages. Even a brief comparison of a random sampling is enough to remind us that the second and third stages have a different quality than does the first.

The Groans of a Repentant Soul for Beginners

- I am grieved, O my most sweet Lord, that I have sinned; I am grieved exceedingly that I have transgressed Thy law: wash me yet more from my iniquity, and cleanse me from my sin.[22]

- O Ruler of my life, Thou seest that in me is no good thing. There is no health in my soul. Miserable and blind, I can do nothing, and I am nothing, without

---

21. Bona, *The Easy Way to God*, 60.

22. Bona, *The Easy Way to God*, 95.

23. Bona, *The Easy Way to God*, 97.

Thee.[23]

Pius Desires for Those Advancing

- O sweetest Jesus Christ, perfect and re-fashion the powers of my soul by those of Thy own most holy soul. Would that I were made after Thy image in both mind and body.[24]

- Instruct, direct, and help me in all things, that I may speak nothing, think nothing, do nothing, wish nothing, but what is acceptable in Thy sight.[25]

Sighs Of a Loving Soul, for the Perfect

- O Sweetness of my heart, O life of my soul, O essence of my being, and delightful rest of my spirit, drawn me away from all created things that I may repose alone in Thee.[26]

- I will not follow Thee, O Lord, by the way of comforts and delights, but by the way of true and pure love. I do not desire that which cometh forth from Thee, but Thyself. Thee alone do I wish for. I desire only Thee. Out of Thee there is nothing for me.[27]

In my first example in each pair, I selected an aspiration typical for each stage; in the second example in each pair, I sought out a profession of nothingness. Nothingness remains on the mind throughout all three stages, but can we not see that it is experienced differently by the green wood, the dry wood, and the burning wood?

Purgation, illumination, and union are stages on the pathway of love. After all, we only reach God by loving him. Charity is the surest, sweetest, and easiest road to God, says Saint-Jure, because it is the most transformative.

---

24. Bona, *The Easy Way to God*, 108.

25. Bona, *The Easy Way to God*, 111.

26. Bona, *The Easy Way to God*, 120-21.

27. Bona, *The Easy Way to God*, 122.

We have two ways of purifying our soul and acquiring perfection: with
the hammer of mortification; giving blows now to one habit, now to
another, now to pride, now to envy, and so of the rest; by this means we
may, perhaps, accomplish our design, but not so surely or effectually as by
the fire of charity which would burn, in a little while, all the bad habits
of the field of our soul and render it fertile in holy affections and good
works.[28]

Ultimately, those experienced with abnegation will associate it with charity's fire, not
mortification's hammer, even if the latter is required at one's initiation into the spiritual
life. Love is exercised towards God when we rejoice in God's infinite perfections, "which
we taste in Him, as if they were in us ... Here is found true love, which impels the lover to
deprive himself of all things for his beloved."[29] Love produces abnegation.

The provenance of Christian abnegation is the Mystical Body, the Church, where
Christ remains high priest of his people's liturgizing. Everything Christian comes
from Christ, as the name indicates, and everything liturgical must pass through the
hypostatic union before it can be useful to the Church. That includes sacrifice,
priesthood, sacrament, time, temple, icon, and it includes abnegation. Liturgical
abnegation originates from something mystical, not something moralistic. Abnegation
is pneumatological, not psychological. Its home is ecclesial, as de Sales describes. "Such
signal examples and instructions as these, in poverty, chastity, and abnegation of self, –
to whom have they been left? To the Church. But why? Our Lord tells us: *he who can
receive, let him receive* ... Now, there is no mission outside the Church, therefore *he who
can receive let him receive,* is addressed immediately only to the Church, or for those who
are in the Church, since outside the Church it cannot be put in practice."[30] The gifts of

---

28. Saint-Jure, *A Treatise on the Knowledge and Love of Our Lord Jesus Christ,* vol. 1,
243.

29. Saint-Jure, *A Treatise on the Knowledge and Love of Our Lord Jesus Christ,* vol. 1,
262.

30. De Sales, *The Catholic Controversy,* 195.

poverty, chastity, and abnegation of self are given to the Church for her work of glorifying God and sanctifying man.

It is true that natural law, natural religion, and natural philosophy encourage a kind of abnegation; they contain shadows of the truth. But this understanding is different from supernatural, sacramental, liturgical abnegation. Any philosopher who takes an honest look around will acknowledge that persons have reason to be humble, but Nepveu does not think this admission of humility is sufficient for Christian doctrine. "Reason and philosophy go thus far: we need beyond this a penetrating and effective insight into our nothingness, our poverty and impotence" which will lead us into a "self-forgetfulness before God and all his creatures, rejoicing in our hearts that we are nothing of ourselves and that God is everything, and loving our abject poverty and dependence because it makes more apparent the power and greatness and sovereign dominion of God."[31] De Sales deals at length with the difference between Christian and stoical abstention.

> The Stoics, especially good Epictetus, placed all their philosophy in abstaining and sustaining, bearing and forbearing; in abstaining from and forbearing earthly delights, pleasures and honours; in sustaining and bearing wrongs, labours and trials: but Christian doctrine, which is the only true philosophy, has three principles upon which it grounds all its exercises – abnegation *of self*, which is far more than to abstain from pleasures, *carrying the cross*, which is far more than tolerating or sustaining it, *following Our Lord*, not only in renouncing our self and bearing our cross, but also in the practice of all sorts of good works."[32]

The pagans have a kind of virtue, he continues. It is the opposite of vice. But this is insufficient for liturgical abnegation. "These pagan virtues are only virtues when compared with vice, but, when compared with the virtues of a true Christian, they do not merit the name of virtue. Yet because they have something of good in them, they can

---

31. François Nepveu, *The Spirit of Christianity, or the Conformity of the Christian with Christ* (New York: Edward Dunigan & Brother, 1859) 125.

32. De Sales, *A Treatise on the Love of God*, 293.

be compared to worm-eaten apples; for with the colour and a little of the substance of real virtues they have the worm of vanity concealed within them, and so are spoiled."[33]

The difference between a Christian philosopher and a natural philosopher is that the former seeks sanctification through practice of abnegation. De la Colombiere agrees. "To be holy is to be a Christian philosopher; that is to say, it is to be free from error, delivered from all the passions which disturb the tranquility of the soul, to be detached from creatures and from self, and to be so united to God by faith and love that one forgets all that is not God."[34] Stripping ourselves would be no great gain if it did not result in our being clothed in Christ; similarly, denying ourselves would be of no great matter if the result was not total surrender to God. The principles of liturgical abnegation depend less on stoical endurance (abstaining, tolerating, renouncing) and much more on the path to deification (denying self, accepting the cross, following the Lord). Let him who can receive the gifts of abnegation receive them in Christ. We follow behind his liturgy, and are brought to abnegation in the wake of his Paschal Mystery. What is done is conditioned by the reason why it is done, which is why Camus can say that true Christian patience "is neither apathy nor insensibility, nor the adult stupid endurance of the Stoics, but a sweet and reasonable submission to the Will of God, coupled with cheerful obedience to the physician whom He commands us to honor, and a grateful acceptance of the remedies prescribed for us."[35] De Estella observes that "virtue without patience is a widow, and patience is the preserver of all virtue ... An impatient sick man, maketh the physician cruel."[36]

The purpose of liturgy has always been named as twofold: the glorification of God and the sanctification of man. The surprising thing is that the latter is for the sake of the former. God is glorified by sanctifying us; God is glorified when we are saved; God

---

33. Francis de Sales, *The Mystical Flora of St. Francis de Sales* (Dublin: M. H. Gill & Son, 1877) 32.

34. De la Colombiere, quoted in Sr. Mary Philip, *A Jesuit at the English Court: The Life of the Venerable Claude de la Colombiere, S. J.*, (London: Burns Oates & Washbourne, Ltd., 1922) 97.

35. Camus, *The Spirit of St. Francis de Sales*, 427.

36. De Estella, *The Contempt of the World, and the Vanities Thereof*, 277.

is glorified when Satan is defeated. De Ravignan reminds us that this was asserted by the Council of Trent.

> We were created to save and sanctify ourselves and to reach heaven: if we understand this, we shall know, as we are taught by the Council of Trent, "that our salvation gives glory to God." God, Who is Charity, could never have given life to the creature, except to manifest in him the seal of His glory, and to make him a partaker in eternal happiness; to seek and to accomplish the glory of God is alliance with the Divinity Himself, and we ought to bless God for having imposed this obligation upon us![37]

How convenient it is that giving thanks to the Father, always and everywhere, is not only our duty but also our salvation (Eucharistic Prayer II). Abnegation is liturgical because it is meant to form and establish a person in Jesus's liturgical mission to glorify the Father, but, Saint-Jure reminds us, "to glorify God in a manner more excellent, we must empty our hearts of many other things."[38] Deny and overcome anything that impedes and hinders full relationship with the Father through the Only-Begotten Mediator, which Eudes thinks is fundamental.

> Here you have the main foundation, the first principle and the first step in Christian living. It is what is called, in holy Scripture and in the lives of the saints, being lost to self, dying to self and self renunciation. It is one of the chief cares incumbent upon you, one of your principal tasks to practise abnegation, humiliation and mortification, both inward and outward: and this development of self-denial is one of the most effective means to form and establish Jesus in you.[39]

---

37. De Ravignan, *Conferences on the Spiritual Life,* 232-33.

38. Saint-Jure, *A Treatise on the Knowledge and Love of Our Lord Jesus Christ,* vol. 1, 296.

39. John Eudes, *Life and Kingdom of Jesus in Christian Souls* (CreateSpace Independent Publishing Platform, 2013) 80-81.

Abnegation may be thought of as a door through which Christ comes into the soul in order to chastise the disarrayed, constrain the dissipated, and correct the false worship he finds there. We are not united to God without perfect disengagement. Surin thinks of it as a knock on the door. "Question – How is this sweet union of the soul with God formed? Answer – ... The means of obtaining union with God is absolutely to renounce ourselves. How is this? Figure to yourself that God stands at the door of your heart, and that when you open it by entire self-abnegation, immediately He will come in."[40] Leen thinks of it as a channel down which grace flows to the soul. "Losing one's life, selling all that one has, taking up the daily cross and other similar expressions are phrases that but ring the changes in the same theme. They all inculcate self-abnegation. Let but the love of self be removed by constant self-denial, then, just as when, at the raising of the sluice gates, waters pour into the channel prepared for them, so streams of divine grace flow into the soul."[41] Libermann never lets us forget that Jesus lived a life of sacrifice and obedience, humility and love, and he sends forth his followers for the same purpose, and under like conditions. "He commissions us as His Father commissioned Him. 'As the Father has sent me, I also send you.' (John 20:29). We are to Jesus what He was to His Father. In our whole life, in all our works, we ought to seek only His glory. We must reproduce in ourselves His sanctity and mercy, His abnegation and love of suffering, His charity, firmness and gentle forbearance."[42] A Christian must necessarily resemble Jesus if he is to be numbered among the elect, says Grou, because "Jesus Christ was given to us as a model, and it is especially on the hill of Calvary that the Man of Sorrows, the Man stricken of God and humiliated, is held up for our imitation. It is therefore in bearing the cross, in living and dying on the cross, that we ought to resemble Him."[43]

Most of the time we are happy enough to unite ourselves with Christ on our own terms, but this will not do. We must unite with him on his terms. The Master does not imitate the slave, rather the slave should conform to the Master's habits, which, in Jesus's case, Surin notes, was humiliation and the cross.

---

40. Surin, *The Foundations of Spiritual Life*, 149-50.

41. Leen, *The True Vine and Its Branches*, 177.

42. Libermann, *Instructions for Missionaries*, 28.

43. Grou, *The School of Jesus Christ*, 184.

Unite yourself with Him, not only by a feeling of tenderness, but by a generous desire of bearing His Cross. Love must bind you to God, and mortification to Jesus. The love of the Cross is inseparable from self-abnegation, and both are necessary to a perfect and constant union with the Saviour … *The disciple is not above his master.* Matt. x. 24. He has set us the example of entire detachment from all things; we must follow His steps, and teach others to do so.[44]

There are many who wish to seek Jesus, many who say they seek Jesus, even some who do seek Jesus – but on misleading terms. Grou is especially adept at correcting this misunderstanding.

They seek Jesus, and they say they expect to find him – but under what circumstances? In the splendor of his glory; in the sublimity of heavenly lights; in the overflowing abundance of spiritual consolations; in the midst of extraordinary supernatural favors. Great is their mistake, and equally great will be their disappointment. It is not by such signs as these that the Lord Jesus is to be recognized here below. If you desire to find him, seek him in spiritual infancy; seek him in humility of heart; in weakness, in simplicity, and total abnegation.[45]

Seek Jesus in his state of total self-abnegation (kenosis), and be, yourself, in total abnegation in order to seek him (humility). Abnegation is participation in the liturgy Christ gives to the Father in his extreme humility of heart and simplicity.

Christ's sacrifice on the cross is the greatest enactment of his self-denial, but his entire life was an expression of it. Scupoli describes our Divine Shepherd as someone who followed "after His lost sheep for three and thirty years with loud and bitter cries, in a way so painful and so thorny, that He spilt His Heart's Blood and left His life there. The

---

44. Surin, *The Foundations of Spiritual Life*, 243. Emphasis in the original.

45. Grou, *The Interior of Jesus and Mary*, vol. 1, 72.

poor sheep now follows Him through obedience to His commands, or through a desire (though at times faint) to obey Him."[46] Faber describes the sacraments as actions of Christ which continue beyond his historical years. "He instituted them as Man; and thus they are the going on of the Thirty-Three Years upon earth ... The sacraments are then, as we see, in a very special sense the vases of the Precious Blood. They are the means by which the Precious Blood is ordinarily applied to the souls of men."[47] This made Christ's entire life a continual kenosis, and Eudes urges us to "beg Him by the great love with which He annihilated Himself to use ... His great power to annihilate our old selves and to establish Himself within us."[48] His life was a continual accomplishment of the oblation he made of Himself to the Father when he came into the world. Berulle gives the Incarnation this startling explanation: "heaven had many adoring spirits and an adored God, but it did not yet have an adoring God."[49] The Word became incarnate so that in this mystery "he may divinely, substantially, and personally dedicate to God's homage all that is created, just as in the Godhead he dedicates to God his Father all that proceeds and is uncreated."[50] Christ's liturgy is to offer God (himself) to God (the Father); what else does our liturgy do but this same thing: offer God (Christ) to God (the Father)? To do this, we conform to his self-emptying (kenosis).

The Christian is called to trail after his Redeemer, whether in the world or in religious life. Chantal catches a glimpse of the itinerary. "But, O divine Saviour! whither shall we follow Thee? Throughout Thy entire life Thou didst tread the road of perfect poverty, of contempt, humiliation and abjection before creatures, and of incessant labor. Is it in this way that we should follow Thee? Is it in these paths that the Religious obliges herself to follow in Thy footprints? O immense, but precious, abnegation! ... O self, I renounce you,

46. Lorenzo Scupoli, *The Spiritual Combat* (London: James Burns, 1845) 10.

47. Frederick Faber, *The Precious Blood; or, The Price of Our Salvation* (London: Burnes & Oates, Ltd., 1860) 111.

48. Lebrun, *The Spiritual Teaching of St. John Eudes*, 109.

49. Pierre de Berulle, *Discourses on the State and Grandeurs of Jesus* (Washington DC: Catholic University Press, 2023) 46.

50. Berulle, *Discourses on the State and Grandeurs of Jesus*, 153.

as only on this condition can I follow my Jesus."[51] This imitation must penetrate the heart and condition the soul's interior temperament. The whole purpose of our sacramental union with Christ, says Olier, is to produce his dispositions in us. "Q. What do you mean by having the same dispositions that our Lord had? A. It is to have in one's heart and soul the same desires that he had; for example, of being humbled and crucified."[52] It is a grave mistake to think that Jesus suffered the cross, but did not have to, or did not want to. It is an equivalent mistake to think that because Jesus suffered the cross, we do not have to, or should not want to. Liturgical abnegation is the linkage between ourselves and the cross. If abnegation does not make the cross happen in us, then the sacrifice of Christ was nothing more than a past historical fact, while, in truth, the drama on Calvary must play out in our hearts, as Leen describes.

> The mass is the implicit protestation on the part of the Christian of his resolve to tend towards adopting the most characteristic disposition of the soul of Christ. This disposition is one of uncalculating submission to the will of God … It is, or, at least, aims at being a renouncement of making one's own will the ruling principle of one's life, and to substitute for it the holy will of God. This is being a victim … Victimhood and abnegation of self in the interest of God, are one and the same thing. If the creature is to be continually disposed to receive the effectively sanctifying influence of God, he must abide permanently in the disposition of sacrifice. To be sanctified daily demands that one be daily a victim; that is, the practice of self abnegation must be constant.[53]

Victimhood, abnegation of self, sanctification, sacrifice, liturgy – these are all bound together. At the Paschal Triduum we don't just watched Jesus die, we join him mystically, sacramentally, liturgically, *and also* in personal abnegation. Madame Acarie forewarned

---

51. Jane de Chantal, *Meditations for Retreats Taken from the Writings of St. Francis de Sales* (New York: Benziger Brothers, 1900) 88, 90.

52. Olier, *Catechism of an Interior Life*, 23-24.

53. Leen, *The True Vine and Its Branches*, 73-74.

that "we are quite content to look at Our Lord on the Cross and we do not want to carry it ourselves,"[54] and Segneri agrees: "It is true that we do not prize the Cross by merely honoring it as the mass of Christians do, or by preaching and lauding it, but by clasping it to our hearts."[55] Or, in de Sales words, "it is better to bear the cross of our Lord, than only to think on it."[56] This a tree of life only to those who embrace it, lay hold on it (not just to those who honor it or exalt it).

A desire for a cross would sound masochistic *unless* it were understood that the cross accomplished the goals of liturgy in both his case and ours: God is honored and man is redeemed. Jesus desired the cross because it revealed love: his love as Son for the Father, his love as perfect man for the Father, and his Father's love for fallen mankind. Grou summarizes: "Through the cross, Jesus Christ repaired the glory of His Father, appeased His anger, and reconciled Him with the world."[57] And where else, John of Avila wants to know, "did Jesus Christ demonstrate his great love for his Father more clearly than in his suffering for his Father's honor? As he said, 'That the world may know that I love the Father, arise, let us go hence' (John 14:31). But where was he going? Clearly, it was to suffer."[58] Grou therefore concludes that this abnegation is liturgical, not morbid. Faith teaches "that those humiliations were decreed for him in the eternal counsels; that he joyfully accepted and endured them, to glorify his Father, and to expiate our pride, with the many other sins of which it is the source. It teaches us, that in this state, more than in any other condition of his life, Jesus Christ is our model."[59] Amazing audacity: to follow the example of a God-man! Jesus, God made man, is our exemplar.

This is astounding, and is only possible in view of a mystical ecclesiology. He has done first whatever he requires of us, and if we abnegate ourselves it is in imitation of his

---

54. Madame Acarie, "In the footsteps of our Holy Mother, like a daughter following her mother," by Sr Anne-Therese Segura, https://www.madame-acarie.org/en/author/sr-anne-therese/

55. Segneri, *Manna of the Soul*, vol. 2, 619.

56. De Sales, *To the Spiritual Director*, 67.

57. Grou, *Manual for Interior Souls*, 31.

59. Grou, *The Interior of Jesus and Mary*, vol. 2 (Dublin: James Duffy, 1847) 64.

self-denial. Since we can only follow Jesus by the practice of self-denial, says Grou, "it is evident he must have given us the example of that self-denial, for he requires nothing of us which he has not practiced in the highest perfection."[60] Grou adds that we copy Christ more in his interior mind than in his exterior activity, the latter being impossible to us since his ministry and miracles were done as the Son of God, but the former being possible to us because he became a man like us. "By the interior mind of Christ, we mean that which was the principle and rule of His Life ... Jesus is the model of all Christians, and those who would study the interior life, must seek to know what was His mind ... As regards Himself, incarnate Lord as He was, nothing could surpass His humility, His abnegation, His readiness to bear all things."[61]

Eudes reduces the primary reasons for why a human being is obliged to practice self-abnegation to two, one negative and one positive. First, that we should be overcome; second, that we should overcome.

First, everything in you is so disordered and depraved, as a result of the corruption of sin, that there is nothing in you that is not contrary to God, and that does not put some obstacle in the way of His plans, or oppose itself to the love and glory you owe Him. Therefore, if you desire to belong to God, you must necessarily renounce yourself and forget and hate and persecute and destroy and annihilate your own self.

Secondly, Jesus Christ, your head and your model, in whom there is nothing that is not all holy and divine, nevertheless lived in so great detachment from Himself and kept His human spirit, His own will and love of Himself so subordinated that He never did anything according to His own human light or spirit, but all according to His Father's spirit. He behaved like a person having no love for Himself of infinite glory and felicity in this world, and of all human pleasures and satisfactions,

---

60. Grou, *The Interior of Jesus and Mary*, vol. 1, 311-312.

61. Grou, *The Hidden Life of the Soul* (London: Rivingtons, 1871) 101-102.

and sought out and welcomed everything that might cause Him to suffer
in His body or in His soul. Now if you are truly His members, you
ought, therefore, to share His sentiments and dispositions, and make a
firm resolution to live in future in complete detachment, forgetfulness,
and hatred of your own selves.[62]

Jesus not only showed us what God is like, he showed us what man should be like. This
is why he can be called the second Adam – the successful Adam, man as man was meant
to be. Our liturgical abnegation comes from being sacramentally conformed to Christ,
and our denial of self-will is surrender to the will of God, being worked in us through the
gifts of the Holy Spirit. Abnegation is about subordination, says Pollien. "It is putting
God fully in the first place that befits His dignity as my Savior, and putting myself totally
in the second place that befits my humility as His servant. One of my life's acts is perfect,
when it entirely realizes this subordination; and the state of my life is perfect when my
whole existence is thus ordered."[63]

No one is alone in this. We live in a communion of saints, every one of whom bears
the *sphragis* (seal) of the cross inscribed by baptism. True, the saints in the Church
triumphant experience a joy that the saints in the Church militant still await, and we
are anxious to one day receive this happiness for ourselves. But are we as anxious to
participate in their abnegation? asks Grou. "Are we equally anxious to participate in
their virtues, their detachment from created things, their humility, their obedience,
their interior abnegation, their love for the cross, and all the comprehensive perfection
included in attention to the word of God, and fidelity in executing it? This is the only
foundation of real happiness both for the present life and that to come."[64] We should
honor the saints both for their triumph and for their warfare; the second no less than
the first. Each one went to battle because he sincerely believed himself to be the first
of sinners. Abnegation is surrender; abnegation is submission; abnegation is giving up
our judgment; abnegation is abandoning our way of thinking and taking on God's views

---

62. Eudes, *Life & Kingdom of Jesus*, 19-20.

63. Pollien, *The Interior Life*, ed. Tissot, 92.

64. Grou, *The Interior of Jesus and Mary*, vol. 2, 264.

and affections; abnegation is to judge things as God judges them – including ourselves. So "let us honor those sentiments in the saints," recommends Eudes. "Let us bless God for their presence and thank Him for their meritorious application. Let us ask our Lord through the intercession of the saints to let us share their abnegation. Let us ask St. Paul, St. Francis and the other saints to engrave similar sentiments of profound humility in our own hearts."[65] And first among the saints with whom we should seek similitude is Mary. Her abnegation was her liturgy, concludes Eudes. "Offer to God all the glory that she rendered Him by this self-abnegation."[66] How can we resemble the Mother of God? Libermann answers: "by purity of heart, mildness, charity, humility, modesty, heavenly wisdom, self-abnegation."[67]

Abnegation is deification, union with God, participation in the divine perichoresis, a liturgical state. Denial is for the sake of dilation, renunciation is for the sake of expansion, and annihilation is for the sake of purity. Mortification opens the door of the heart wider so that more crosses can fit in, because then, thinks de Sales, more love can fit in. "Keep your heart very wide to receive in it all sorts of crosses and resignations or abnegations, for the love of him who has received so many of them for us."[68] For the love of Christ we accept all sorts of abnegations that will perfect our liturgy.

Human beings are still in a state of becoming, currently unfinished and incomplete, because the ascent from image of God to likeness of God was interrupted. The perfection of our humanity will come with the imitation of Christ, who was the true and complete man. "To acquire this spirit of Christ is one and the same thing as to acquire Christian perfection," says Scaramelli. "These two expressions mean one and the same thing. For Christian perfection, considered either in itself (essential perfection) or as a means (instrumental perfection) consists exclusively in the imitation of our Savior's life and

---

65. John Eudes, *Meditations on Various Subjects* (New York: P. J. Kenedy & Sons, 1947) 142.

66. Eudes, *Meditations on Various Subjects*, 102.

67. Francis Libermann, *Letters to People in the World*, Spiritan Series 6, vol. 2 (Pittsburgh: Duquesne University Press, 1963) 235.

68. De Sales, *Letters to Persons in the World*, 68.

in acquiring His spirit."[69] God desires the resumption of each person's supernatural pilgrimage, a desire unchanged since the first moment he created that person. John of Avila thinks God's persistence will not forsake the initial goal. "Since [God] has placed us in the path of his service, he will not abandon us in the middle of it, for his works are perfect (cf. Deut 32:4), as he himself is."[70]

The excellence and perfection of our humanity turns out to be a liturgical business, because our human perfection and excellence is our participation in the liturgy described in the book of Revelations. All the cosmos glorifies God; man, the rational creature (hybrid of matter and spirit) will join cosmic liturgy to angelic liturgy by being the priestly tongue of mute creation, but only if he will rule creatures, and not be ruled by them. (Enter abnegation.) Man is necessarily detached from God by being attached to self by the concupiscences. Therefore, he must be detached from self in order to be reattached to God, which is holiness, and detached from the world, which is abnegation. Segneri makes this "the true and short rule for acquiring holiness: to act in opposition to all the maxims of the world, to love what it hates, and to hate what it loves."[71] As these writers take pains to point out, all things are at the service of love, even abnegation, which de Sales insists is not an act made out of scorn toward creation. "All these abandonings and renunciations ... must be made not out of contempt, but solely out of abnegation, for the pure love of God."[72] Deification is union with God, who has kenotically opened for us a redemptive gate to his trinitarian self, which Tronson describes as turning on the hinges of abnegation. "Thus may I ever in receiving Thee be filled with the lively faith, deep humility, a burning love, a total abnegation of self, and a fervent longing to be wholly united to Thee in time and in eternity."[73] All things serve love, and abnegation serves

---

69. John Baptist Scaramelli, *Directorium Asceticum; or, Guide to the Spiritual Life*, vol. 1 (New York: Benziger Bros, 1902) 475.

70. John of Avila, *Audi, Filia,* 80.

71. Segneri, *The Manna of the Soul*, vol. 1, 422.

72. De Sales, *The Spiritual Conferences*, 129.

73. Tronson, *Examination of Conscience,* 115.

love by purifying our love. Wanting us for himself, God strips other things away. This mortification is bitter at first, but it does achieve its purpose of causing beatitude.

Numerous things weigh us down and impede our union with God. John Evangelist of Boisleduc calls it a worldly drag on our heavenward flight. The soul of man "is created to live in God as the bird in the air, but is hindered in its heavenward flight by attachments to creatures, be that attachment never so slight."[74] Libermann calls it a blindness that causes us to confuse the real with the counterfeit. "Those who are content with merely observing the commandments are in great danger of falling frequently into sin. They are like men walking above a precipice, upon a slope so steep, that they are constantly drawn downwards and may easily slide into the abyss. They do not see, and they risk mistaking a shadow for a piece of firm ground."[75] De Castaniza therefore says the first task for the faithful is to reverse his descent, and recover the path of ascent. "For as Abnegation and Resignation produceth in the soul a nakedness and clarity, so doth this pure love raise and lift itself up into God; for such is the property of love, and especially of this pure love, which is altogether clear and unmixed."[76] He adds that God, the source of Uncreated truth, beauty, and goodness, shines in the highest supernal glory, and our desire to reach this glory (or even to glimpse it) causes us to renounce created truths, beauties, and benevolences, good though they may be. To find God perfectly requires that "the Abnegation of all creatures and the Resignation of himself be done purely for the love of God. For the soul, being now naked, stripped of all exterior things and freed from all internal adhesion to herself, remains within herself ready to be carried and brought still further; and this happeneth when the pure love of God is adjoined to abnegation and resignation, whereby she is lifted up above herself into God."[77] This interior life of the heart must not be smothered by the exterior life of the world. But do we know how to enter that life? asks Fenelon. "Do they know what it is ever to enter into themselves? Have they ever tried to find the way? ... They are continually out of themselves among the objects of their ambition or amusement ... O my Creator, with my eyes shut to all external

---

74. John the Evangelist, *The Kingdom of God in the Soul*, 65-66.

75. Libermann, *Instructions for Missionaries*, 114.

76. De Castaniza, *The Spiritual Conflict and Conquest*, 338.

77. De Castaniza, *The Spiritual Conflict and Conquest*, 335.

objects, which are but vanity and vexation of spirit, I will find in the most secret recess of my heart and intimate familiarity with thee by Jesus Christ thy Son."[78]

Liturgical abnegation annihilates, relieves, elevates, converts, animates, vivifies. Its motive is not dualistic disdain for matter, its motive is a longing for God. Even if the casual eye of the world sees abnegation as derision of the world, it is not true. Being carried beyond the creature is for the purpose of being carried to the Creator. Faber pictures the elevation. "Earth grows more and more like a speck as our thoughts ascend: our affections detach themselves from it more and more. As life goes on, and life and grace together draw us nearer to God, earth, in spite of all its affectionate memorials, becomes only a pretty planet, and nothing more: but oh! Why is it we let slow time do the work which swift grace would so much better do?"[79] God can use a creature to raise us to himself, but the creature itself hasn't this power. So Faber adds, "all attachment to creatures narrows our capacity for holding God. There are many earthly loves which ennoble us; but they do so by saving us from lower things, not by leading us to higher."[80] When our soul rises to God, she must take the path Christ took, a path of poverty and abnegation, because that if there had been another path, Barbanson supposes Christ would have shown it to us. "By this elevation the soul, now collected within itself, endeavors to raise itself above itself to God, not by imagination or discourse, but by and abnegation of all things in of itself also, in order that it may finally possess God."[81]

The perfection of a person is the one goal worth pursuing, the pearl of great price, the one thing necessary, and de Castaniza thinks this

> perfection consists, not in multiplicity of action, but in simplicity of intention; not in variety of exercises and devotions, but in peace of mind and purity of heart; not in saying or doing much, but in suffering and loving much. Let us sometimes check our importunate spirit, as Jesus

---

78. Fenelon, *Pious Thoughts Concerning the Knowledge and Love of God, 17-18.*

79. Frederick Faber, *The Creator and the Creature, or, the Wonders of Divine Love* (London: Thomas Richardson and Son, 1857) 192.

80. Frederick Faber, *Bethlehem* (London: Thomas Richardson and Son, 1860) 193.

81. Barbanson, *The Secret Paths of Divine Love,* 89.

did Martha: – *Martha, Martha, thou art careful and art troubled about many things. But one thing is necessary,* which is, a real, cordial, and total abnegation of thyself in all things.[82]

The one thing needful is not reserved for a special few, and held back from the ordinary Christian. De Caussade acknowledges that although we all cannot aspire to the distinct favors the extraordinary saint receives, everyone "can attain to the same love, the same abnegation, the same God and His work, and thence it follows naturally, to the highest sanctity."[83] Neither does he think the one thing needful requires success at the beginning, for God looks upon the desire and intention. "Does not God behold these desires, so deep and so hidden, and do they not speak for you to God more powerfully than any words you could utter? Yes, certainly, these desires are acts, and better acts than any others."[84] To want to want God is already a grace God causes in the heart. The one thing needful that Jesus recommended to Martha does not require a special time, or infrequent opportunities.

The one thing necessary can always be found [for the soul] in the present moment. It is no longer a choice between prayer and silence, seclusion and society, reading and writing, meditation and cessation of thought, flight from and seeking after spiritual consolations, abundance and dearth, feebleness and health, life and death, but it is all that each moment presents by the will of God. In this despoilment, abnegation, renunciation of all things created, either in reality or affectively, in order to retain nothing of self, or for self, to be in all things submissive to the will of God and to please Him; making it our sole satisfaction to sustain

---

82. De Castaniza, *The Spiritual Conflict and Conquest*, 442-43.

83. De Caussade, *Abandonment to Divine Providence*, 44.

84. De Caussade, *Abandonment to Divine Providence*, 375.

the present moment as though there were nothing else to hope for in the world.[85]

De Berniere-Louvigny thinks these opportunities can be found in either the city or in the desert. "A soul may be as much separated from creatures in the midst of towns and cities as in the deserts ... When God once makes a soul sensible of his grandeurs ... this soul, thus illuminated, begins to be dead to the world."[86] All baptized Christians are called to abnegation, some are called to religious life.

It is my hope that these authors show us "a mundane abnegation," namely, one that be practiced in the world (*mundanus*) and not merely in the monastery. Let me conclude by reminding us that Christ is the exemplar for all Christians, in whichever world they reside. Gay asks us only to reflect, and we will see clearly that in the hypostatic union of the God-Man "is the finished model of the supernatural state, of the state of grace, of the Christian state, in its substance and in its source."[87] Jesus models the Christian life in two ways, because he was the first to live the Christian life.

First, in his humility. Leen says this takes every individual back to a primordial time, to the battle cry between faithful and fallen angels.

> Humility consists in making God all and oneself nothing in one's life ... It is the practical acceptance of St. Michael's battle cry: *Quis ut Deus*! Who is like unto God! It is the complete obliteration of all the false claims of self, in face of the all pervading sovereignty of God. All that is required on the part of the Christian to make perfect his calling, is to efface himself before God. Hence it is that the whole burden of the Saviour's teaching to men is the practice of self-abnegation. Self-abnegation is something much larger than either suffering or mortification.[88]

---

85. De Caussade, *Abandonment to Divine Providence*, 28-29.

86. De Berniere-Louvigny, *The Interior Christian*, 72.

87. Charles Gay, *The Christian Life and Virtues*, vol. 1, 21.

88. Leen, *Progress Through Mental Prayer*, 10.

Humility checks and inhibits the inclination to gravitate towards self, and "self-abnegation is but humility in act."[89] Humility opens and encourages the inclination to gravitate toward God, because God is all worthy.

Second, in his love. Christ's love is so in conformity with his Father that Saint-Jure says we would hesitate to speak of mortification in his case. "Where there is no contradiction nor resistance, there is no mortification;"[90] "I comprehend not that thing you call Mortification; if one lives in this state of Conformity, for such finding no resistance in His spirit, is not capable of it; whosoever wills whatever God wills, his daily content, let what will happen."[91] As death is trampled down by death, so mortification is trampled down by mortification. Leen agrees, and therefore proposes a difference between abnegation and mortification. Jesus did the former, but not the latter; we sinners can only do the former through the instrumentality of the latter. After quoting the passage about self-denial from Luke 9, Leen says

> What is self-denial? A definition of it presents some difficulty. It is almost as subtle and elusive as its opposite, self-love. It is not to be taken as synonymous with mortification. It is something which strikes much deeper ... To "deny self" is the contrary of "to assert self" or "to put self forward." Self-seeking in all its forms is an evil tendency surviving in men as an effect of original sin ... Instead of glorifying God, [fallen man] has an inveterate inclination to glorify himself.[92]

Self-abnegation and mortification run the risk of being understand as equivalents, but Leen thinks "mortification and self-denial are distinct notions ... Mortifications are not self-denial but a means to it."[93] Consider childlikeness. This is a state in which one does

---

89. Leen, *Progress Through Mental Prayer*, 14.

90. Saint-Jure, *The Holy Life of Monsieur De Renty*, 111.

91. Saint-Jure, *The Holy Life of Monsieur De Renty*, 262.

92. Leen, *True Vine and Its Branches* 178.

93. Leen, *True Vine and Its Branches*, 208-09.

not put oneself forward. Adam was created in such a state, but rejected it; Jesus had such a spirit, and maintained it. Adam's children must *mortify* themselves to attain a childlike spirit, but Jesus maintained his childlike spirit by *self-denial*. Leen therefore says:

> Christ's life, generally speaking, was not characterized by mortification,
> if we are to except the opening forty days of his voluntary fasting,
> and his observance of the penitential prescriptions of the law. It was,
> however, marked by sustained self-denial ... "He did not please Himself,"
> in anything. Self-denial is much broader and more fundamental than
> mortification: it is bound up with the very springs of our activity. It
> aims at purifying that activity at its source. Mortification lops and prunes
> the living plant. Self-abnegation aims at a complete modification of
> the life-giving sap itself. Mortification is medicinal and is, therefore,
> of a rather negative nature. Self-abnegation is spiritually hygienic and
> invigorating and, consequently, highly positive in character.[94]

This alters love, something Leen thinks we intuitively know. "It is scarcely necessary to remark that this love of God is not a sentiment, a feeling, or an emotion. It is of the will, not of sensibility. It consists in a deliberate election, choice and preference of the Supreme and Infinite Good, above all else."[95] Love is moved from feeling to willed choice directed by the intellect. Love is supernaturalized. And where can this be seen? In two, related places.

First, Mary, the New Eve. "We, like Mary, are called to love God. That is why our lives should centre round Jesus. That is why our life should be a life of complete obliteration of self in view of serving Him. Mary had only one thought, only one ambition and that was to promote God's cause and to serve His interests. Our ambition ought to be the same. We should think only of serving His cause, otherwise our religion is not Christianity."[96]

---

94. Leen, *True Vine and Its Branches*, 210-11.

95. Leen, *Progress Through Mental Prayer*, 6.

96. Edward Leen, *Our Blessed Mother* (New York: P. J. Kenedy & Sons, 1946) 43.

Second, in the offspring of this New Eve, the Church, the mystical body brought forth from the side of Jesus on the cross.

> This service is possible to all of us. Jesus Christ is not dead. He lives in the Church. In the Church, His Mystical Body, He lives and suffers and triumphs. An easy mode of self-obliteration is to lose all our self-interest and allow it to be submerged in the interests of the Mystical Body of Christ. We can palpitate in sympathy with Christ, sorrow in His trials, thirst for His glory, make His interests our interests, and thus devote ourselves, as Mary did, entirely to His service. Like Mary, we should live solely for Jesus. The trials and sorrows of His Mystical Body should become our trials and sorrows, the triumphs of that Body our triumphs. Then self-life, self-interest and self-love will disappear, and we shall live only for Jesus.[97]

Living only for Jesus, who lived only for his Father's will and glory, is the liturgical life of abnegation the Holy Spirit intends to work in us, if we will allow.

---

97. Leen, *Our Blessed Mother*, 44.

THE REWARDS OF ABNEGATION

What is life like on the road of abnegation that Christ, our spiritual surveyor, has laid out for each individual person? Although the path is steep, it is comprised of happiness, and leads to even more happiness. "What is happiness?" asks Grou. He answers: "Peace of heart ... Show me any other happiness on earth to be compared with this. There is none. That of innocence is great; that of true, loving penitence is great likewise; that of ordinary Christian holiness is still greater. But that of souls sanctified by God Himself in the interior way of bare faith and self-abnegation is above all."[1] The intensity is even greater when the sensible consolations are withdrawn and the soul is dealing with God alone. The dimmed reason of worldlings is astonished at the thought of the struggle and effort that perfection requires, but de Caussade assures them it is the true path.

> You cannot follow the path of perfection in reality except through losses,
> abnegation, despoilment, death to all things, complete annihilation,
> and unreserved abandonment. We need not be astonished when we
> experience afflictions, when even our reason totters, that poor reason so
> blind in the ways of faith; for it is a strange blindness which leads us to
> aspire after perfection by the way of illumination, of spiritual joy and
> consolation, the infallible result of which would be to revive ever more
> and more our self-love and to enable it to spoil everything.[2]

---

1. Grou, *The Spiritual Maximums*, 233-34.

2. De Caussade, *Abandonment to Divine Providence*, 362.

Pride is so insidious that it might make an appearance as a traveling companion dressed in pious garb, so every precaution must be taken to be on the lookout for a revival of self-love that will spoil everything. Do not let a secret satisfaction of self-will develop, or the terms of passage will be violated. Such persons, Boudon writes, "would have God do their will; hence they readily believe that what is not to their taste is not according to the will of God. They envy the spiritual good of their neighbor, and are troubled when they see themselves outstripped in the ways of grace. In fine, they have no love for the cross and pure mortification, for complete abnegation and annihilation of self."[3] Our judgment must be the first thing we turn over to God, with our will following immediately after, so that we may affix our affections on the Creator instead of upon ourselves or our neighbors, according to Fenelon.

> You have good reason to believe that the self-abnegation which is required in the Gospel, consists in the sacrifice of all our thoughts, and of all the motions of our heart. The self which we must renounce is not a certain I know not what, or a Phantom in the Air; tis our understanding which thinks, tis our will which wills according to its one fashion, by self-love. To reestablish the true order of God we must renounce this corrupt self, by [neither] thinking nor willing but according to the impression of the spirit of grace.[4]

As we have already noted, this spiritual warfare leads from purgation, through illumination, to union, and the throng of travelers is made up of the beginner, the intermediate, and the perfect. The road is steep at first, but Baker assures us that it levels off to a more steady ascent after one becomes accustomed to it. "Now though this most secure practice of love by abnegation and annihilation of all propriety and self-will be at the beginning full of difficulty, because all the comfort of nature lies in

---

3. Henri-Marie Boudon, *Devotion to Nine Choirs of Angels* (London: Burns, Oates, & Co., 1869.) 67.

4. François Fenelon, *An English Nun in Exile Translates the Spiritual Letters of Archbishop Fenelon to Madame Guyon.* http://www.umilta.net/cambray2.html) 185-86. I have made some corrections to punctuation for intelligibility.

self-will, yet by custom it will be less uneasy, and in the end delightful. For most certain it is that Christ's yoke, by constant bearing, becomes easy."[5] Persistence, not speed, is more valuable; patience, not success, is more valuable. The demons immediately tempt us to despair when the sensible consolations are lost, proposing it is due to a lack of progress and compromised verve. Libermann is one of many voices to warn that "in this war which we must wage against the enemies that are within us, we cannot limit ourselves to half-measures. We must fight energetically and generously on every point where the enemy's presence is felt or may be found. In short, the only really powerful remedy we can apply to all our wills is self-abnegation."[6] In other words, the remedy of abnegation is multitherapeutic, to be applied against the pressures exerted by Satan, self, the flesh, and the world. The will be must directed to the climb itself, not to the gifts God supplies to aid the warfare, and not to the rewards at the conclusion, or else one lapses into half-heartedness and lukewarmness – often called tepidity – about which many of our authors warn.

Scaramelli is forthright in saying "God forsakes those souls that cool in their purpose and desire of perfection; for as men loathe the food they have vomited, so Almighty God loathes the lukewarm soul which He has cast out of His divine mouth."[7] Branchereau describes a soul for whom the fervency that begins a retreat does not last. "We had set out with a determination to attend diligently to the things of the soul, but we have grown weary of the struggle, we have become indifferent to our spiritual progress ... Lukewarmness by its very nature has arisen from indifference and neglect; it is a state of drifting."[8] The cause of lukewarmness is easily spotted, Challoner thinks: "Alas! the reason why thou art so lukewarm, or rather downright cold, in thy devotions, is the continual dissipation of thy thoughts at other times, and a habit of indulging vain amusements, which fill thy inward house with such disagreeable company, as keep Christ

---

5. Baker, *Holy Wisdom,* 249

6. Libermann, *Instructions for Missionaries,* 119.

7. Scaramelli, *Directorium Asceticum; or Guide to the Spiritual Life,* vol. 1, 161-62.

8. Louis Branchereau, *Meditations for the Use of Seminarians and Priests, vol. 3, Priestly Life* (New York: Benzinger Brothers, 1912) 159-60.

away from thee, and rob thee of his sweet conversation."[9] But noticing the state is not so easily spotted, de Liguori thinks: "tepidity is a desperate and almost incurable evil. For in order to be able to avoid danger it is necessary to know it. Now the tepid, when they have fallen into that miserable state of darkness, do not even know their danger. Tepidity is like a hectic fever that is scarcely perceived. The tepid man does not see even habitual defects."[10] The way out? Lacordaire's advice: "A man may love God tenderly and fervently in any state of life. But you must will it ... For love springs from sacrifice, and especially from the sacrifice of pride." [11]

Self-love can produce two opposite effects, Croiset thinks: one of excess and one of defect, one too muscular and one too frail. We most easily recognize self-love when it produces pride, but tepidity is an equal, though opposite, problem.

> Though the Son of God has an infinite hatred of sin, He has not a horror of the sinner. He calls him, He seeks him, and has compassion on him. But His Divine Heart cannot endure a tepid soul ... A tepid soul is in a state of blindness, caused by the passions that tyrannize over her; by the continual dissipation in which she lives, and which prevents her from entering into herself; by the multitude of sins that she commits, and by the subtraction of heavenly graces, which her resistance draws upon her ... What makes this state still more perilous, and obliges Jesus Christ to reject a tepid soul, is, that she is in a certain way, beyond hope, for tepidity is scarcely ever cured.[12]

---

9. Richard Challoner, *Considerations Upon Christian Truths and Christian Duties, Digestede into Meditations for Every Day in the Year*, part 1 (Philadelphia: Eugene Cummiskey, 1874) 164.

10. Alphonsus de Ligouri, *Dignity and Duties of the Priest*, in *The Complete Works of Saint Alphonsus de Liguori, The Ascetical Works, vol. 13* (New York: Benziger Brothers, 1889) 93-94.

11. Henri-Domnique Lacordaire, *Letters to Young Men* (London: Art and Book Company, 1902) 209.

12. Croiset, *Devotion to the Sacred Heart of Jesus*, 58.

One should not be dismayed by where one stands in Christ's cortege, since the hierarchy of the pilgrims in its totality praises God, serves God, pleases God, etc. John Evangelist of Boisleduc warns envious persons "not to judge what is altogether unknown to them, and since they believe that hereafter there shall be diversity of degrees in the heavenly glory, they should grant that so also there have always been, and are, different degrees of holiness among the servants of God in the Church Militant."[13] Some spiritual persons will be more explicit in their liturgical abnegation, others more secretive, but it is generally agreed that conducting the internal warfare is harder than bearing external torments. In the words of Fenelon:

> Ten years of bodily austerities are as nothing in comparison with such a cutting off of the jealousies and sensitiveness of a restless personal self-love. Such abnegation would be the greatest of props if it were clearly perceived. But then it would cease to be self-abnegation; it would become the richest and most flattering of possessions. So that this self-abandonment must hide us from ourselves and be itself concealed, and then it will really give us all which it hides from our self-love.[14]

There is every chance that external abnegation can become an occasion of pride if not accompanied by an interior struggle. Abnegation primarily concerns the inward warfare, even if it is abetted by exterior practices. Liturgical abnegation is about love in the soul, not merely discipline of the body, which is why, Libermann says, "abnegation must extend to intellectual objects as well as to those offered by the senses. I mean, to those satisfactions which are created by our mind and our imagination."[15] This means the pathway of liturgical abnegation is universal: it is meant for every Christian, not simply those in religious orders and clergy.

The will is the thing. Look at Mary, advises Blosius.

---

13. John the Evangelist, *The Kingdom of God in the Soul*, 57.

14. François Fenelon, *Letters to Men* (London: Rivingtons, 1877) 105.

15. Libermann, *Instructions for Missionaries*, 135.

Thou must not be pusillanimous, nor imagine thyself to be remote from God, because, perchance, thou canst not practice great austerity of life, or because one dost not feel thyself inwardly impelled and attracted towards it. For it is not in this that true perfection and true holiness consist; they consist in the mortification of self-will and of evil inclinations, and in true humility and charity. We do not read that the Blessed Virgin Mary, Mother of God, led so hard a life as did the holy widow Judith; and yet she was by far more perfect than Judith. All the elect walk not outwardly in the same path; but almost surely follow inwardly the same path, namely, the path of humility, and true charity or holy love.[16]

The will is where the real abnegation occurs; bodily exercises are its trappings. This theme is sounded by Scupoli, which is at least part of the reason why Francis de Sales carried *The Spiritual Combat* around for eighteen years and read it daily. "The mortification and victory over our own appetites, however trifling, is more praiseworthy than the storming of strong cities, the defeat of mighty armies, the working of miracles, or the raising of the dead."[17] This theme is emphasized by Libermann. Priests are cautioned to "avoid performing external actions for the purpose of abasing yourself in the eyes of men. Be satisfied with having this disposition to abasement interiorly."[18] This theme receives focus in Baker, who thinks a daily oblation, which is "the smallest act of love and service to God, performed with a perfect self-abnegation, is more acceptable and precious in His eyes, than the working of a thousand miracles or the conversion of nations, if in these there are mixed interests of nature."[19] It is emphasized by Fenelon, when he replied to this question coming not from a monk in the desert, but from a man in the court of Louis XIV.

---

16. Blosius, *Spiritual Works*, ed. Bowden, 123.

17. Scupoli, *The Spiritual Combat*, Pusey translation 17

18. Libermann, *Letters to Clergy*, Spiritan Series 8, vol. 4, 34.

19. Baker, *Holy Wisdom*, 249.

How can I offer my common daily actions to God; e.g., promenades, service at Court, visits received and paid, dressing, toilet matters, reading, history, etc., the business which comes upon me on behalf of friends and relations, amusements, shopping, and ordering equipages and the like? I want to learn how, by some kind of prayer, to offer all these things to God.

ANSWER. The most unimportant acts cease to be so, and become important, directly that they are done with the intention of conformity to God's Will. Indeed, they are often better and purer than what may seem more religious acts; first, because they are less self-chosen, and more according to the order of God's Providence; secondly, because they are simpler, and less exposed to self-complacency; thirdly, because if performed in moderation, and with a right intention of heart, we may find more means of self-abnegation than in actions where excitement or self have a larger part; and lastly, because these trifling matters are continually recurring, and furnish a constant opportunity for unobtrusively serving God.[20]

He is equally encouraging about the circumstances of the Duchess in Court, for whom he asks God for special help.

I have good reason to believe that, while obliged to be at Court, her heart is a temple through a recollection, self-denial, and devotion to God, consecrated by grace in the Holy Eucharist, fit for the Holy Spirit's indwelling. God grant that His sacred wind may scatter all the dust and rubbish which those who are in the great world cannot fail to gather. God grant that His devouring flames may consume all the straw and foam which will float upon the heart's surface. It is difficult at a period and in a

20. Fenelon, *Letters to Men*, 45-46.

country where everything tends to dissipation to be nowise affected; but it is not impossible to stand fast when strengthened by the Holy Spirit.[21]

The struggle *may* involve exterior austerity, but it *must* involve internal control of eye, ear, and tongue, and, most of all, the will. De Caussade says this is especially relevant to persons in Religion when they are restrained by their superior from exterior mortifications, in case the excessive discipline might make them vain. The Religious can still, nevertheless, perform an abnegation that is interior. "As to what regards exterior mortification, follow in everything the rules of moderation, discretion and obedience, but make up for what they refuse to allow you to do, by interior abnegation in refusing yourself the least little desire, the least little pleasure, and the least thought which is not of God and for God, rejecting all that is useless in order to occupy yourself exclusively with Him."[22] Of course, this must not be used as an excuse to say that abnegation of the will needs no practices of external mortification. To such a dodge de Liguori answers "the fruit of the vineyard does not consist in the surrounding hedge; but still if the hedge be taken away, you will seek in vain for the produce of the vine. Where there is no hedge, says the Holy Ghost, the possession shall be spoiled."[23]

One would be wrong to think that abnegation can only be practiced by the wealthy who have riches to renounce, and the honorable who have esteem to relinquish. Any object, no matter how small, is sufficient to distract the selfish man's attention, and therefore any object, no matter how incidental, can be an occasion for practicing abnegation. So Fenelon says to be on guard at all times. "The moment we perceive that any sovereign object gives us pleasure and joy, let us separate our heart from it: and in order to hinder our heart from taking his rest in this creature, let us present to it immediately it's true object, and its sovereign good, which is God himself."[24] Everyone must practice internal abnegation as a denial of self-will and self-indulgence, because Grou notices that everyone will feel the besiegement.

21. Fenelon, *Letters to Men*, 161-62.

22. De Caussade, *Abandonment to Divine Providence*, 255.

23. De Liguori, *The True Spouse of Jesus Christ*, 123.

24. Fenelon, *Pious Thoughts Concerning the Knowledge and Love of God*, 79.

Can I elevate myself, on supernatural principles, above the influence of transitory things? can I use them without detachment? ... can I resist human respect? can I withstand the maxims, the example, the satire, the ridicule, the opposition of the world without exercising an imminent degree of abnegation? If I mean to secure salvation, does not the practice of that abnegation become indispensable? It is, in fact, closely identified with the eternal interest of every Christian.[25]

No thing is sinful, but anything can be used sinfully, that is to say, used to please ourselves and not liturgize God. That is the definition of pride, which is the thing that abnegation is truly combatting. This egocentric pride created havoc in the Garden of Eden, and Libermann thinks the conflict that began there continues in each heart. "What you ought to do in your combat against the movements of pride is to deaden them, to calm your agitation if it is present and to reject those movements purely and simply, either by thinking of something else, or by performing an act that contains a movement of humility, abnegation, of oblation of yourself to God."[26]

While the natural eye, which is uneducated in the ways of spiritual abnegation, thinks that only persons in religious life renounce property, sex, and liberty (vows of poverty, chastity, and obedience), de Caussade does not want us to think that life in the secular world will exempt us from abnegation!

Suppose that in consequence of this I am obliged to live in the world, what will become of me? These are vain fears put into your mind by the devil to make you lose the peace of your soul. You must abandon yourself entirely to God, and put your whole trust in Him. He is powerful enough to make you stand firm in the world, and good enough to sustain you when it is by the arrangements of His providence that you live in it.

---

25. Grou, *The Interior of Jesus and Mary*, vol. 1, 319.

26. Libermann, *Letters to Clergy*, Spiritan series 7, vol. 3, 158.

You could not do better, therefore, than to practise recollection and abnegation in renouncing your own will in everything, but particularly in your too eager desires, however holy they may be; for this excessive vehemence, and these restless struggles show much imperfection and self-love.[27]

One is not relieved from this combat by being either secular or religious, rich or poor, honored or ignored, because the temptation of pride can plant its seeds anywhere. We can even become proud of the practice of our religion. The problem is personal, not circumstantial, says Barbanson, and the person in Religion is not exempt.

There is neither great nor small, poor nor rich, old nor young, who does not find in his heart a certain inclination to be of some kind of importance in the eyes of the world. Everyone is willing to appear more than he is and to defend his own opinions. There is neither time, place, state, nor person, where this execrable pride doth not seek to sprout up and to produce its pernicious effects. Hence it is not to be wondered at that even in the service of God, in the contempt of the world, in abnegation of self, nay, even in the very exercise of humility, we are not free and secure.[28]

Liturgical abnegation is thus required of every believer who would purify their piety toward the end of offering up a more perfect liturgy. The objective is to liturgize God above all other things, a task that sounds easier when thinking about some trivial possession than when we realize it means preferring God to our own selves.

The full perfection of our beatitude must wait for the time of glory; but during this time of grace, we can begin. Quarre says "*glory* is nothing but *grace consummated, grace glory commenced.*"[29] Even now, liturgizing God is our greatest happiness. Moral

---

27. De Caussade, *Abandonment to Divine Providence*, 165-66.

28. Barbanson, *The Secret Paths of Divine Love*, 20.

29. Quarre, *A Spiritual Treasure*, 491.

acts are good and just, but Christian acts are liturgical and worthy of heaven and God. Quarre continues: "Let us then suppose this to our *perfect Christian,* that to do acts truly *Christian,* and worthy of God, we must *regard* nothing but God, and have no other *intent* then to *please* him … for love, if it be true, makes us quit our own *interests and respects,* to engage us in the *interests* and *respects* of the thing *beloved.*"[30] Remember that liturgy is an act of love: love is the coal in the liturgical engine. If love be true, it makes us negate our own interests for the liturgizing of God-the-beloved.

The twin purposes of liturgy are the glorification of God and the sanctification of man, and Grou says God is unimpressed with anything else.

> Any motive that is not, ultimately at all events, concerned with His glory and our salvation, does not move Him in the least. But how few prayers are pure, with no object but the glory of God! How few souls there are who appeal to His dearest interest, and pray to Him for His sake only! What could He refuse when it was represented to Him that His glory was concerned, and when the prayer had indeed no other intention? So noble an intention implies complete abnegation, absolute death to self, the deepest love and the highest ideals, and is unhappily very rare even among the most fervent Christians. St. Paul bids us perform our most ordinary actions for the glory of God, and surely we ought to consider it far more in our holiest action, which is prayer.[31]

How few prayers are pure! Faber describes the characteristics of a man whose prayer has not been purified: he does not think of God alone, but always of God plus his desires; his submission is not instantaneous; he accepts a cross only if conjointly agreed upon, not if God bestows it without consultation; he would fain talk to God if he cannot persuade God; he expects God to flatter him; his childlike spirit is lost upon questioning the ways of God; and the refinement of his obedience is gone. In summary, absent a profession of nothingness, prayer loses its liturgical purpose of adoration.

---

30. Quarre, *A Spiritual Treasure,* 267-68.

31. Grou, *The School of Jesus Christ,* 275-76.

Men may not *assail* God, even with the impetuosity of their prayer: their business is to adore. Otherwise the gracefulness of submission is gone. The right to more intimate union with God is forfeited. The waters of grace in their soul become shallow, and their spirit of prayer thin, peevish, vexed, and wailing. All this is because in their prayer they have had the habit of being something before God, instead of being nothing. [32]

Our most ordinary actions can become liturgical actions, once abnegation is at the service of the perfection of our prayer. Abnegation originates from an altered vision of reality attained atop the liturgical mountain, where de Caussade says prayer produces its effects. "It is impossible to navigate safely unless guided by the sure and infallible rules of faith which make us turn away from sin, love God and our neighbour, detach us from creatures, and lead us to obedience, self-forgetfulness, complete submission to the will of God, abnegation and mortification. The kind of prayer which produces these effects is, without doubt, the best."[33] Prayer must be continual, and pure from all voluntary defects, says Berniere-Louvigny, "for how can God visit, in such a gracious manner, a soul which is still full of disquietudes and imperfections? How can she hear the voice of God amongst the noise of creatures, if they still live in her with any affection?"[34] The rules of faith, which operate in liturgy and are drilled into the liturgist by repeated practice, detach us from creatures and attach us to Creator by obedience and submission. The best prayer is done out of a state of abnegation, where three rewards can be identified: obedience, liberty, and freedom in death.

The first reward abnegation confers is obedience. De Chantal learned this well from her director. "Our obedience should be established on perfect abnegation of self-will

---

32. Frederick Faber, *The Foot of the Cross or, The Sorrows of Mary* (London: Thomas Richardson and Son, 1858) 174.

33. De Caussade, *Abandonment to Divine Providence*, 226.

34. De Berniere-Louvigny, *The Interior Christian*, 240

and of our own judgment."[35] Obedience means two wills become one, so it is evident that obedience is lacking if one feels a clash of wills. When wills clash, the self-denial is imperfect, and done resentfully or fearfully. Abnegation means a death: it kills an obstinate will. This makes possible a perfect and obedient compliance, which de Caussade says is not a reaction to a threat, but a response to goodness. "This way of uniting yourself to Him by a total self-abnegation is based on the great principle that God, who is Almighty and goodness itself, gives to His children on all occasions and always what He knows will be best for them; and that all perfection consists in a constant adhesion of the heart to His adorable will."[36] Belief that God knows what is best for his children, and gives only what is best for his children, is the underpinning of the doctrine of providence, which deserves closer attention in its own chapter because it is one of the most neglected of Christian doctrines today. Self-abnegation is not simply the negative act, it includes the positive act: we deny self *in order to obey God*. He gives us direction and means and end, and abnegation is our acceptance of them.

The Christian spiritual tradition has identified three states in which a person can stand vis-à-vis God: as a slave, a servant, or a son. The first obeys out of fear of punishment; the second obeys for reward; the third obeys because of love. The first is servile; the second is mercantile; the third is unitive. Both the slave and the servant are self-conscious, i.e., more conscious about their self than they are conscious about God. Their minds are constantly occupied about what they fear to lose, or hope to gain. If one can overcome this self-consciousness, and obey without attention to self, then the theologians of abnegation call it "indifference." Indifference means taking our eyes off ourselves and placing them solely on God. Indifference means being more concerned with the giver than the gift. Indifference means the glory of God is more important than self-esteem.

True worship is found neither in the slave nor the servant. Consider each in turn. First, the slave is such as those who Fenelon finds thinking of God as "something wonderful, far off and unconnected with us. They think of Him as a stern and powerful Being, ever making requisitions upon us, thwarting our inclinations, threatening us with great evils, and against whose terrible judgment it behooves everyone to be on his guard ... In truth,

---

35. De Chantal, *Meditations for Retreats*, 184-85.

36. De Caussade, *Abandonment to Divine Providence*, 375-76.

such a one fears only, but does not love; as the child is in awe of the master who punishes him."[37] Second, the servant is such as those whose mercenary love Fenelon describes as

> that love of God which originates in a sole regard to our own happiness. Those who love God with no other love than this, love him just as the miser his money, and the voluptuous man his pleasures; attaching no value to God, except as a means to an end; and that end is the gratification of themselves. Such love, if it can be called by that name, is unworthy of God. He does not ask it; He will not receive it.[38]

One of the signs of mercantile love is that it ceases when the benefits cease because it is actually a kind of spiritual greediness. Third, the filial love of the son or daughter can be described contrasting it with the others, as Blosius does here.

> The soul which is deeply infected with this fault [of spiritual gluttony] cannot be said to be a modest and faithful handmaid of Christ; for she does not wish to serve God for nought, but loves God's gift rather than God. She is but a hireling slave, not a daughter who is a freewoman. Then, if that sensible sweetness be at all diminished, the soul becomes full of bitterness, full of indignation; she becomes turbulent, impatient; she forsakes the love of piety; and, throwing off the reins of holy fear and modesty, she abandons herself entirely to external consolations. If God in sooth is willing to give her pleasure, she serves God; if not, she departs from Him. But the soul which deserves to be called the faithful handmaid or the chaste spouse of Christ resteth not in God's gift, but in God. Whether or not God poureth into her interior sweetness, she abideth tranquil, she joyfully serves her Spouse, faithfully cleaves to Him,

---

37. François Fenelon, *Spiritual Progress* (New York: M. W. Dodd, 1853) 7.

38. Fenelon, *Maxims of the Saints* (www.ccel.org/ccel/fenelon/maxims/maxims.htm) article 1.

constantly loves Him. She would rather God's will were done than her own.[39]

The pious, but imperfect, person understands that sinners should stop focusing on self because he supposes those still at the first level of slave to be self-centered. What he has not entertained yet is the idea that the same demand must also be made of those at the second level of servants, because, even if pious, their motive for obedience can also include an element of self-regard, self-accomplishment, selfishness. Neither slave nor servant has reached the point of wanting only what God wants for himself. The obedience of liturgical abnegation is neither slavish nor selfish, fearful nor mercantile, because it unifies the will with what God wills, to do what God is doing, namely, giving glory to himself. God is secondarily moved to bestow happiness on us, but he is primarily moved to fulfill his glory. This is Fenelon's final test for the perfection of our liturgy. *"It is true that [God] desires our happiness, but that is neither the chief end of his work, nor an end to be compared with that of his glory.* It is for his glory only that He wills our happiness."[40] The ultimate reason for abnegation is one step higher than one's own salvation; its ultimate reason is God's glory, which is what makes the abnegation liturgical. But how difficult do the exiles of Eden find this, in Fenelon's analysis.

> Men have a great repugnance to this truth and consider it to be a very hard saying, because they are lovers of self from self-interest. They understand, in a general and superficial way, that they must love God more than all his creatures, but they have no conception of loving God more than themselves, and loving themselves only for Him. They can utter these great words without difficulty, because they do not enter into their meaning, but they shudder when it is explained to them, *that God and his glory are to be preferred before ourselves and everything else* to such a degree that we must love his glory more than our own happiness.[41]

---

39. Blosius, *The Manual of the Spiritual Life*, 57-58.

40. Fenelon, *Spiritual Progress*, 13. Emphasis added.

41. Fenelon, *Spiritual Progress*, 13. Emphasis added.

One can utter words about abnegation without difficulty (and even write them!) if one does not personally enter into their meaning.

Only love that has been purified in the fires of abnegation has an obedience that is pure obedience, without any egocentric turn. Liturgical abnegation capacitates a latria suffused with love, and such liturgizing includes the denial of our own will, which is why Grou says "we should ask for such a spirit of obedience as may wholly set aside our own will and judgment, overrule our tastes and opinions, and the light of our own reason, ever remembering that God's ways are not as man's ways, and that if we would win entrance into His Eternal Life; it must be through a total abnegation of self and everything appertaining thereto."[42]

The second reward abnegation confers is liberty. By forsaking perishable things, the soul can turn to eternal things; by embracing eternal things, the soul forsakes perishable things. Perishable things are not renounced because we are disappointed in them being perishable. It is only because they will fall away from under our feet after we have made a ladder of them to heaven. John Evangelist of Boisleduc observes the ascent of the ladder, a common symbol amongst our authors.

> In proportion as man forsakes creatures so he goes to God; as he forsakes himself so does God enter into him, and as he dies to himself so does God live in him. Creatures are at the beginning of the way; God is at the end … Again, mystical writers teach that we must make a scale or ladder of creatures and ourselves by which to ascend to God, and the more a man ascends above creatures the nearer he approaches to God. Moreover, they say that with God and the soul, as in nature, there is never a vacuum. If a vessel be emptied of the liquid it contained, at once it is filled with air.[43]

On the one hand, adds Bona, comfort taken from creatures will exclude the divine, since "*one body driven out of any place, is succeeded by another, that there may not be a vacuum;*" but, on the other hand, "*the soul that expels all created things, and all self-love,*

---

42. Grou, *The Hidden Life of the Soul*, 45-6.

43. John Evangelist of Boisleduc, *Kingdom of God in the Soul*, 46-47.

is forthwith filled with God, in whom it finds all manner of good."[44] God is not excluded from the material cosmos, since he is omnipresent; we can therefore "[make] of creatures a ladder, by which to ascend to God."[45] But, unfortunately, the disordered attraction we have for corruptible creatures has broken that ladder. Its rungs are rotted, and crack under our foot. We have happiness in the world because it contains a glint of God, but the pathway must not satisfy as our homeland. Remain a pilgrim; do not become a squatter. We may use the world, but we must not be ruled by the world. De Estella gives an interesting image about how abnegation protects us: by crippling one foot to halt our pursuit of the world.

> Love is the feet of the soul, and I am carried by love whithersoever I wish to go; and as this body of ours possesses two feet with which it walks, so the soul has two loves and affections which carry it on, *viz.,* Thy Divine and holy love, and the love of worldly things. Afte Jacob had wrestled with the angel ... the angel touched him on one leg and made him lame of one foot.

> O Lord, my soul in learning the excellence of Thy goodness, and in discovering somewhat of Thy Divine perfections, immediately goes halting in respect to the love of the world, and walks straight along the way of Thy holy love.[46]

What is perishable is forsaken for the eternal because we only find gratification in He who is the Eternal Good. This is how charitable abnegation works, according to Baker: love goes beyond creatures themselves to terminate elsewhere. "Charity is only and in the most strict sense a friendship, because therein all our love is terminated in God only: we

---

44. Bona, *The Principles of Christianity,* 85. Emphasis in the original.

45. Bona, The *Easy Way to God,* 200.

46. Diego de Estella, *Meditations on the Love of God* (London: Burns & Oates, Ltd., 1898) 32.

love nothing but Him or for Him; yea, we direct the love, not only of all other creatures, but also of ourselves only to Him."[47] Love nothing but God, and when you love a thing, love it insofar as it is ordered to him, "that is, as a means and instrument to beget and increase His divine love in our souls."[48]

The Israelites had to empty their memories of Egypt in order to be happy in the promised land, and they, like we, had some difficulty doing so. It was not enough to leave Egypt if they were still carrying Egypt in their minds, and Surin says many a spiritual director of monks has had to tell his novice to put down the world he left, and not carry it with him into the monastery. "This joy, this perfect satisfaction, produced by the immediate presence of our Lord, is not a favour common to all the just, nor, perhaps, even to all who have renounced the world ... This gift is only for those who, by complete self-abnegation, and a general renunciation of all that is not God, and that does not tend to God, have perfectly emptied themselves of all creatures."[49] It is an intrepid step of faith: Abraham, the father of faith, began with an act of abnegation. He renounced; he left; he went out. De Sales says Abraham sacrificed the strongest natural inclinations he had when he obeyed the voice telling him to go forth out of his country. "The dear love of country, the sweetness of the society of his kindred, the pleasures of his father's house, did not shake his constancy; he departs boldly and with fervour, and goes whither it shall please God to conduct him. What abnegation, Theotimus, what renunciation! One cannot perfectly love God unless one forsake affections for perishable things."[50] When the liturgist spiritually forsakes known goods for greater goods, all on the word of the Lord, he repeats the withdrawal that his father in faith made centuries ago.

And here enters the liberty of which we speak. The exterior action of leaving the world, such as monks do, can be reenacted interiorly by leaving oneself, says John Evangelist of Boisleduc. "The soul which would come to God must also deny and leave her own self. This S. Gregory plainly affirms, saying: *As much as we leave ourselves we approach to God;* for as long as the soul remains under herself or in herself she cannot be raised to God above

---

47. Baker, *Holy Wisdom,* 246.

48. Baker, *Holy Wisdom,* 200.

49. Surin, *The Foundations of Spiritual Life,* 108.

50. De Sales, *Treatise on the Love of God,* 421.

herself."[51] The soul cannot be raised when she is prone; she cannot breathe when she is smothered; she cannot fly when she is tethered. So the renunciation of anything is really the act of abandoning trust in it, in order to place that trust in God. This is an acceptance of poverty. Pride manipulates creatures with its own hand; humility waits to receive from the hand of the Creator. Pride is an active self-will that takes all things with a worldly mind; humility is an active meekness that takes all things with a spiritual mind. De Sales contrasts the earthly with the spiritual mind by describing the earthly mind as one that "seeks to take its share in all that goes on; and it is so full of self-love that it thinks nothing can prosper without its aid. But the spiritual mind cleaves to God, realizing that whatever is not God, is as nought; and though it takes a charitable and loving share in such matters as come in the way of duty, it willingly abstains from all else, in simple abnegation and humility."[52]

The denial of creatures, as well as self, goes farther and deeper then we expected. At first, God gives encouragement in the form of spiritual consolations, but then we find he also expects us to relinquish these very consolations. It is called the dark night, or dryness, or aridity of the soul. Ultimately, John Evangelist of Boisleduc says we must abnegate not only natural gifts, but also supernatural gifts if the soul is to be set free from self-attachment.

> When once man has withdrawn his affection from all creatures by perfect abnegation and likewise from himself by pure resignation, with his whole affection and adhesion he falls upon the gifts of God. For out of his infinite goodness God presently rewards this abnegation and resignation with interior light, devotion, consolation and strength, to which nature at once turns and rests rightly, just as she formally rested in exterior creatures ...
>
> But although in this life man may well enjoy the interior gifts of God (for to that end they were given him) yet, nevertheless, they greatly hinder him

---

51. John Evangelist, *The Kingdom of God and the Soul*, 69.

when he clings to them or rest in them, and are as great an obstacle to perfect union with God as our attachments to exterior things.[53]

The third reward abnegation confers is freedom in the midst of death, and in the act of dying. Even death can liturgize God, ever since Christ trampled it down by his death, and the divine life he now shares with us protects us from the spiritual death sin imposed. Libermann is more concerned with spiritual death than biological death. "To assure us against a spiritual death, and to help us recover from the ills and infirmities of our soul, to restore the divine life in us in all its perfection, God has taught us the practice of total self-abnegation and of denying to ourselves any pursuit of gratification in creatures."[54] The whole point of dying to ourselves in little things, daily, is to begin an exercise for death as total surrender. Our passions make things of this earth appear different from what they really are, but death will eventually unveil them, predicts de Liguori, showing them as nothing but smoke, dust, and vanity. "At the hour of death, all the glory of everything that is worldly vanishes away, applause, amusements, pomps, and grandeur. Great secret of death! which makes us see that which the lovers of the world do not see. Fortunes which have been envied, the grandest dignities, the proudest triumphs, lose all their splendor when they are reviewed from the bed of death."[55] This deadly revelation of what mortality is truly, can be anticipated in the wisdom abnegation affords.

Such a death must be accepted in completeness, therefore we must train for it by daily mortification. Abnegation crucifies anything that resists, anything that is in rebellion, anything that obstructs the restoration of divine life, anything that diminishes our union with God in the slightest degree. Indeed, says de Caussade, "the practice of complete abnegation consists in having no other care but that of dying entirely to self to make room for God to live and work in us."[56] Natural death is different from supernatural death. In the former, animation ceases, in the latter it increases; the former empties, the latter

---

53. John Evangelist, *Kingdom of God in the Soul*, 79.

54. Libermann, *Instructions for Missionaries*, 113.

55. De Liguori, *Preparation for Death*, 17.

56. De Caussade, *Abandonment to Divine Providence*, 99.

fills; the former enervates, the latter empowers; the individual loses responsiveness in the former, he is roused in the latter. So Barbanson adds:

> The chief exercise of the children of God is to follow the impulses of the Spirit of God in all things, and to be wholly directed by it, not letting themselves be carried away by the affections of flesh and blood. This is that death and burial to which the Apostle so often exhorts us: in fine, this is the Cross and that abnegation of ourselves which the Gospel preaches unto us, to attain unto which we must employ all our endeavors, our prayers, and are holy exercises.[57]

Natural death will come involuntarily, but death can be transformed when it becomes voluntary. With practice, it is transformed into sacrifice, into a liturgy, as Elizabeth of the Trinity says. "If we were to grow more like God every day, with what confidence we should regard the hour in which we must appear before His infinite sanctity! I think you have discovered the secret. It is by self-denial that we reach this divine end; by this we die to self and give place to God."[58]

Liturgizing is an act of love, and love is ecstatic; in liturgical love the soul goes out of herself to dwell in God and, in so doing, leaves the world behind. Absent this, says John of Avila, we do God a great wrong because we love ourselves and not him. But "he who loves Thee with perfect love, dies to self for love of Thee crucified, and is more eager to be disgraced for Thy sake, than to receive all the honours that this world, which is both deceived and a deceiver, can give him."[59] Time was made as a pathway to eternity, and there is no better way to occupy the time we have been given than to prepare for eternity, de Caussade counsels. "The most solid preparation for death is that which we make every day, by a regular life, a spirit of recollection, of annihilation, of abnegation,

---

57. Barbanson, *The Secret Paths of Divine Love*, 30.

58. Elizabeth of the Trinity, *The Praise of Glory*, 276.

59. John of Avila, *Letters*, 76.

patience, charity, and union with our Lord."[60] And, he adds, this death organizes our lives, animates our actions, directs our prayers. "You will never make any prayer that would be better, more useful, or more meritorious; because the prayer of abnegation and suffering being more crucifying is also more purifying for the soul, and makes it die to self more quickly in order to live henceforth in God and for God."[61] This is a repeated refrain among the authors: abnegation is for the purpose of union with God, that is, deification. This is the end abnegation serves, says Saint-Jure,

> This abnegation is so necessary to man, to render himself capable of union with God, that it is absolutely impossible for him ever to arrive at it, if he is not emptied of himself, and annihilated ... In fact, how can you, says Saint Augustine, fill a vase with honey, if you do not first empty it of that with which it is filled? We are all full of ourselves; we must necessarily empty ourselves of self, if we wish to fill ourselves with God: cast out what you have, in order to obtain what you have not ... Therefore, to render a man capable of being changed, and transformed into God, it is necessary that he strip himself of himself, that he die absolutely to his self-love, and to all that feeds self-love in him.[62]

Abnegation and deification are flip sides of one truth: the same liturgical truth. God works unremittingly to get us to leave ourselves so that we can become capable of receiving the plenitude of the divinity, because, in the words of Saint-Jure, "it is impossible to become what one is not, without ceasing to be what one is."[63] We focus on the emptying, but abnegation is really about a filling. The cause-and-effect works in a surprising sequence. The reason that we would empty ourselves is because we have had a taste of God. He stimulates the abnegation. Possessing him leads us to deny all else,

60. De Caussade, *Abandonment to Divine Providence*, 318.

61. De Caussade, *Abandonment to Divine Providence*, 214.

62. Saint-Jure, *The Religious*, vol. 1, 574-75.

63. Saint-Jure, *The Religious*, vol. 1, 608.

according to de la Columbiere. "Once a man has begun to have a relish for God, as he does, there is little room left in the heart for creatures; there is even little left for them in the memory. Everything is taken up, for it is He who fills all."[64]

We are beckoned to drink from an eternal fountain, from which flows the liturgy that the book of Revelation says floods the world. What we really need in order to taste and relish it is not the ceremony itself, but what the cup of liturgy contains, which Blosius describes as "the fountain of water [reference to John 4:14], springing up into life everlasting ... We ought not, therefore, to cease from prayer until we are found worthy to drink of the waters of this fountain. For if we can taste but one little drop of it, we shall no longer thirst for vain things and failing creatures, but for God only, only for the love of God."[65] This changes our taste for the world in two ways. First, as has already been said, a drop of this water makes the world taste insipid. Berniere-Louvigny says the soul, "thus illuminated, begins to be dead to the world ... because the same light that brings her to know and taste God present gives her a disrelish for creatures. Neither is it so much the insufficiency of creatures that causes this disgust as the all-sufficiency of God, and the lively feeling of his divine presence. All this may take place as well among the crowd of men as in deserts."[66] But, second, although the creature cannot satisfy as once it did, the denial of self permits an appreciation of the world in a new way. When we say "denying the world," we really mean denying the selfish advantage we take of the world, according to Saint-Jure.

> In all the assistance and pleasure creatures afford us, as food for the taste, colors for the sight, music for the ears, perfumes for the smell, and in all the other sinless pleasures of the body; also in those of the soul, such as knowledge of truth, the sweet conversation of friends, etc., we will tend directly to God, remembering that He is present in all these creatures, that He causes these delectations, inasmuch as he is our joy our beatitude; that

---

64. De la Colombiere, *Faithful Servant*, 127.

65. Blosius, *A Book of Spiritual Instruction*, 111.

66. De Berniere-Louvigny, *The Interior Christian*, 72.

He sends us through these channels little drops of pleasure which make us sigh after the fountain of all joy, which is Himself.[67]

In conclusion, we assert that love is the basis of abnegation; love is also the basis of liturgy; therefore, we define liturgical abnegation as an act of love that liturgizes God. Picturing love as a companion to abnegation may seem surprising to our initial impressions, but those initial impressions are the very ones I have been trying to correct. The grammar revealed in the examples from this chapter reveals a greater emphasis upon a positive than a negative. Since this has been so aptly described by a more recent writer, Edward Leen, I turn to him for summary.

> It is true that, in the description of the gradual perfecting of the soul, a great deal of stress was laid upon the question of abnegation that conditions this perfection. But there never was an instant in which this abnegation constituted the totality of the soul process. Side by side with the negative movement there went a positive; the relinquishing of oneself was accompanied by the attainment of something infinitely better. There was a passage from nothingness to reality – from darkness to light … The process of self-renouncement is the gradual removal of this curtain of darkness, and as this process proceeds our intuition of the things of God becomes clearer … Hence self-abnegation in its full import is not a merely negative thing; as self in its destruction disappears from our view the vision of Our Divine Lord takes its place.[68]

Our intuition of the things of God become clearer only as the various curtains of self, flesh, world, and the demons are torn in two, like in the temple in Jerusalem upon our Lord's crucifixion. Self-renouncement brings self-knowledge, which is a counterpart to the growth in knowledge of God. Paradoxically enough, we see ourselves truly only when

---

67. Saint-Jure, *Knowledge and Love of God*, vol. 1 (New York: P. O'Shea, 1870) 514-15.

68. Edward Leen, *Progress Through Mental Prayer* (New York: Sheed and Ward, 1935) 122-23.

the self disappears from our view, because we must see ourselves in the light of God. Leen locates what he calls the "focus of infection" in the self, existing "in its varying forms and manifestations. Eliminate this and there ensues necessarily a healthy spiritual life. Hence it is that [Christ] preaches self-abnegation in the first place, He preaches it in the second place: He preaches it all the time. On it all depends."[69] The negative and the positive correspond; aversion and conversion dovetail; closure to self and openness to God harmonize. Self-love paralyzes, but grace re-animates. "If a man practises self-abnegation he does what is required of him. It is always supposed that he does this, urged to it by the desire of possessing God. These two movements of soul must go together. When man fulfils his part, God does the rest. When love of self is banished the desired love of God finds entrance."[70]

It is impossible not to end with de Sales' famous metaphor of the statue standing in liturgical posture, if we want to summarize the mysterious happiness abnegation causes, one unknown to the world.

> If a statue which the sculptor had niched in the gallery of some great
> prince were endowed with understanding, and could reason and talk; and
> if it were asked: O fair statue, tell me now, why art thou in that niche?—It
> would answer,—Because my master placed me there. And if one should
> reply,—But why stayest thou there without doing anything?—Because,
> would it say, my master did not place me here to do anything, but simply
> that I should be here motionless. But if one should urge it further, saying:
> But, poor statue, what art thou the better for remaining there in that sort?
> Well! would it say, I am not here for my own interest and service, but to
> obey and accomplish the will of my master and maker; and this suffices
> me. And if one should yet insist thus: Tell me then, statue, I pray, not
> seeing thy master how dost thou find contentment in contenting him?
> No, verily, would it confess; I see him not, for I have not eyes for seeing,
> as I have not feet for walking; but I am too contented to know that my
> dear master sees me here, and takes pleasure in seeing me here. But if

---

69. Leen, *Progress Through Mental Prayer*, 14.

70. Leen, *The True Vine and Its Branches*, 177.

one should continue the dispute with the statue, and say unto it: But wouldst thou not at least wish to have power to move that thou mightest approach near thy maker, to afford him some better service? Doubtless it would answer, No, and would protest that it desired to do nothing but what its master wished. Is it possible then, would one say at last, that thou desirest nothing but to be an immovable statue there, within that hollow niche? Yes, truly, would that wise statue answer in conclusion; I desire to be nothing but a statue and ever in this niche, so long as my master pleases, contenting myself to be here, and thus, since such is the contentment of him whose I am, and by whom I am what I am.[71]

---

71. De Sales, *Treatise on the Love of God*, 219-220.

PROVIDENCE: A DESIGN FOR OUR PERFECTION

Providence is the execution of God's design for the perfection of a human being as a mystical liturgist living in union with him. De Granada can say that providence is a continuation of creation – no, better, it preserves creation. "Of the blessing of our preservation, observe how thy whole being is protected by Divine Providence; and how thou wouldst not to live without His Almighty Aid; how the whole world was created to serve thee; and how the Holy Angels are entrusted with Thy protection."[1] The God of Israel is not a simple first cause who initiates and then abandons, he adds. "Some mothers are content with giving birth to their child, without afterwards actually nursing or taking charge of it. But with us it is not so; for the same Almighty God takes charge of us altogether, and in such a manner, that He is both the mother who bore us, and the nurse who nourishes us with the food of his divine providence."[2] Behind abnegation is providence; behind providence is God's will; behind God's will is love; resignation is required to believe that this love operates through purgation; this resignation is *from* ourselves *to* God – and this is an act of liturgy, which seeks God alone. Ultimately, Lallemant says providence can be understood within the context of resignation. "To seek

---

1. Louis de Granada, *Considerations on the Mysteries of the Faith* (London: Joseph Masters, 1862) 164.

2. De Granada, *Considerations on the Mysteries of the Faith*, 173.

God is to wish for nothing and to desire nothing but that which He wills, and which He ordains by His providence."[3]

Providence does not primarily concerned a series of incidents of good luck. Attunement to providence is an interior struggle and an interior liturgical accomplishment. The reason we have difficulty understanding the view these authors take of providence is because our view generally restricts itself to exterior issues, while liturgical abnegation gazes fixedly at what God is doing to the soul. Since, Grou says, "the whole spirit of the interior life is summed up in the words 'God Only,'" therefore, "the first step therein is devotion of self to Him – all progress in it is detachment from whatever is not Him, and its end is perfect union with Him."[4] Detachment from what is not God, in order to be united with God, results in what Faber describes as a liberty of spirit. "Liberty and detachment are one, and the same thing. He is free who is detached, and he only. And it is plain that no one can be detached, who is not generous also; for generosity consists in detaching ourselves, always at cost and with pain, from creatures for the sake of the Creator."[5] Generosity consists in abnegation; abnegation can create generosity. In detaching ourselves from creatures for the sake of the Creator, a person can rejoice in a liberty of spirit that allows the discharge of spiritual duties. In the paradox of the Kingdom of God, detachment from creatures finally returns us to creatures – this time not to use them selfishly, but to use them in glorifying God and serving the neighbor.

This resignation to divine will is done through prayer and meditation that produces a peace that does not rely on accidental contingencies. It rather relies upon a confidence in the love that God directs toward us, says Rodriguez.

> This is the confidence, this the tranquility and composure of mind
> we ought to aspire to, by constantly making acts of conformity and
> resignation to the divine will, and by making our way, through prayer and

---

3. Louis Lallemant, *The Spiritual Doctrine of Father Louis Lallemant*, ed. Frederick Faber (London: Burns & Lambert, 1855) 43.

4. Grou, *The Hidden Life of the Soul*, 121.

5. Frederick Faber, *Growth in Holiness; or, The Progress of the Spiritual Life* (Baltimore: John Murphy & Co., 1855) 52.

meditation, to the treasure of the all-fatherly providence of God over us. I
am certain nothing can happen to me without his orders; and that neither
men, nor devils, nor any other creature whatever, can effect anything
contrary to his holy pleasure. Let then his orders be executed upon me. I
must refuse nothing he sends, and I desire nothing but the accomplishing
his holy will.[6]

Such steps must be made in the dark night of faith, a night that tests whether we believe
God knows what we need better than we do. If we have such confidence, observes de
Lombez, then the "soul that is really Christian and really reasonable is never troubled
at the accidents and vicissitudes of this life, because, in them, she recognises the guiding
Hand of a loving Providence, always adorable and always kind, and ordering all things for
our good."[7] Liturgical abnegation asks us to trust God's providence, therefore Scaramelli
can call providence the foundation of abnegation on which our will takes its stand. "This
foundation is a steadfast, firm, and lively conviction, that nothing happens in the vast
system of the universe, that is not in subordination to the will of God ... It is plain that man
cannot render himself conformable to God's will, in all possible circumstances, unless
he be fully persuaded that nothing can happen that is not in some sense willed by the
Almighty."[8] This is quite different from moral stoicism, de Castaniza points out, because
the resignation is not arbitrary, and not an exercise of personal fortitude. This abnegation
is a liturgical act whereby we say: "Lord, I choose Thee and accept of Thy divine pleasure
and providence in all things. I reject whatsoever may possess that place and dominion in
my soul which is due to Thee alone. Dispose of me and mine as shall be most for Thy
honour and glory. Let me be either all Thine, or nothing at all."[9] De Lombez interprets
trust in God's providence as a self-denial that finally resolves into this liturgical shout:
"You are just, O my God! And your decrees are dictated by truth itself, but your mercy

---

6. Alphonsus Rodriguez, *The Practice of Christian and Religious Perfection*, vol. 1
   (London: James Duffy, 1861) 424.

7. Ambrose de Lombez, *A Treatise on the Joy of the Christian Soul* (London: S.
   Anselm's Society, 1894) 6.

9. De Castaniza, *The Spiritual Conflict & Conquest*, 467.

is never separated from your counsels and directs all your ways. Who shall enter into judgment with you?"[10] Trust in providence bears the lineaments of abnegation, because abnegation elides all things that compete with God for our trust.

"Hardly will one annoying person have gone before God sends another to you."[11] This startling and humorous remark by Fenelon seems an appropriate place to begin because it helps to upset our general expectations about providence. A human and natural notion of providence believes it to be an arrangement that will bring good fortune closer to us, but the divine and supernatural design of providence is dedicated to bringing us closer to God. Saint-Jure considers the etymology. "The Latin word, *prudens*, like *providens*, signifies one who sees things at a distance, one who looks forward."[12] While we generally see only as far our self-love can focus, God fixes his eyes upon the end for which we were ultimately made. While we usually do not look beyond the next moment of self-satisfaction, the eyes of the Lord look further down the path to the heavenly abode to which his providence would like to take us. This is one reason why the doctrine of providence is better understood at an older age, in the rear-view mirror, so to speak. Ullathorne writes:

> We see the lower rings of the chains of divine providence, but not those upper rings more golden, that are attached to the throne of God's government ... The action of divine providence is present to our view, but we see the course of that providence more completely in the past than in the present; for it is not of a moment, but is a continuous action, of which one part explains the other. For many things therefore we have to wait the

10. Ambrose de Lombez, *A Treatise on Interior Peace* (New York: Alba House, 1996) 69.

11. François Fenelon, *The Seeking Heart* (Jacksonville, FL: SeedSowers Publishing, 1992) 21.

12. Saint-Jure, *Spiritual Man*, 158.

interpretation of time – that is to say, the future providence will explain the present, to which now in its obscurity we attach our faith.[13]

Our lazy eyes will have to be strengthened by a divine light in order to see what God is doing in order to prepare us for heaven. He can enlist surprising dimensions toward this end: trials, miseries, crosses, as well as consolations, joys, and peace. Such light operating in our eyes is called faith, and if we lack the faith that God is providentially at work even in our chastisements, then fully half – and probably more – of his activity in our lives will be overlooked.

Liturgical abnegation sees providence in an eschatological context, in contrast to our usual understanding of self-denial which is confined to this life. If our idea of moral order were thus restricted, then Grou says

> there might be reason to accuse God of indifference, or of ignorance, or of impotence. But the object of moral order with respect to this present life, is not to reward all that is good, and to punish all that is evil; it is to command the one and to prohibit the other ... As to the effects of these promises, and of these threats, it is reserved for another life, where virtue will be eternally happy, and vice eternally miserable.[14]

We cannot judge the activity of God if we measure his activity merely within the scope of our present life. The next aeon will not cancel or replace this one, it will complete it, and the two ages, separated for any individual by his death, must always be taken as a whole. What goes on then will be a fulfillment of what has now begun; what is going on here must be seen in the light of its fruition there. This requires a God's-eye view. Only God has the natural capacity for such a view; we participate in it by the gift of faith. Providence's energies are intent on making perfect liturgists, and

---

13. William Ullathorne, *The Endowments of Man Considered in their Relations with His Final End* (London: Burns & Oates, 1880) 101.

14. Grou, *Morality, Extracted from the Confessions of Saint Austin*, vol. 1, 324.

providential guidance will be misunderstood so long as it is not grasped in the context of the eschatological liturgical end for which God has created us.

The whole economy of providence is designed to bring about a person's perfection. *Perfectus, perficere,* finishing, completing, accomplishing: providence is the operation performed in our lives to finish and complete and accomplish a Christian soul. Scaramelli says that "to acquire this spirit of Christ is one and the same thing as to acquire Christian perfection. These two expressions mean one and the same thing. For Christian perfection, considered either in itself (essential perfection) or as a means (instrumental perfection) consists exclusively in the imitation of our Savior's life and in acquiring His spirit."[15] Perfection is "union with our Last End,"[16] and the last end intended for every single person is participation in the perichoresis of the holy Trinity, already kenotically extended to invite us to commence our synergistic ascent into deification.[17] Scaramelli adds, a stone attains its perfection when it rests at its center, a flame may be called perfect when it reaches the sphere to which it has always been tending, and "so too is the soul perfect when united with God, Who is the end for which it was created ... Now this, says St. Thomas, is precisely the fruit of the Holy Eucharist, wherein the passion of Christ is commemorated. It perfects our souls by uniting them with the crucified Savior, very God and very Man."[18] This perfection does not merely concern those in Religion, it is effected by the imposition of liturgical abnegation upon every Christian soul, even if in a hidden mode that Boudon says escapes the attention of the world.

> But the world, which has little spirituality about it, regards only what
> is external and showy. O my God, how different are Thy judgments
> from those of men! This high grace, again, is bestowed on certain souls
> destined to serve as victims to divine justice for the sins of others. God,
> in consideration of these souls, bestows the grace of conversion on a large
> number of sinners, draws out of heresy and infidelity many heretics and

---

15. Scaramelli, *Directorium Asceticum; or, Guide to the Spiritual Life,* vol. 1, 475.

16. Scaramelli, *Directorium Asceticum; or, Guide to the Spiritual Life,* vol. 1, 594.

17. My definition of liturgy. *Liturgical Dogmatics* _____

18. Scaramelli, *Directorium Asceticum; or, Guide to the Spiritual Life,* vol. 1, 594.

unbelievers, and sanctifies many souls eminent in the path of virtue: yet all this is hidden from the eyes of men, who are ignorant of the heavy crosses which Divine Providence lays upon them for this end, or, if they know them, understand not the grace nor the purpose for which they are given.[19]

In a word, we may say that what puzzles the world most is when God uses crosses. God can employ crosses for various reasons, as we shall see in a later chapter, and so Grou states:

> The crosses from the hand of Providence ... are inevitable. The wicked are not less exposed to these than the good. But by their resignation, their patience, and submission to the Will of God good Christians sweeten all that is bitter in these inevitable crosses ... Those spiritual crosses which come only from God, to prove and try those who love him, and which, as I have said before, are crosses of pure love, these are the delight of the favoured souls who bear them.[20]

How crosses can be experienced with delight is unknown to anyone who does not see that the cross is an act of pure love, given and received. A cross is a transaction of love, intended in a precise way in every individual life, in every particular moment. God acts mercifully, always. His providence knows the end for which he wants to use crosses. And what is that? De Ravignan answers: "God in His never-failing Providence gives us almost every day some exercise against self-love, against the vanity that is inherent in us. Yes, oh my God! thanks to Thy bounty and to Thy tenderness, there will always be obligations of suffering in this respect."[21] Providential guidance by God aids us in self-abnegation, and empowers the daily and incessant battle against self-love and passions and disorder.

---

19. Boudon, *The Hidden Life of Jesus*, 55.

20. Grou, *Manual for Interior Souls*, 37.

21. De Ravignan, *Conferences on the Spiritual Life*, 130.

Fenelon says no one can find happiness under a cross unless he realizes that God has put it there.

> Happy indeed you are thus to bear a cross laid on you by God's Own
> Hands in the order of His Providence. The penitential work we choose, or
> even accept at the hands of others, does not so stifle self-love as that which
> God assigns us from day to day. In it we find nothing to foster self, and,
> coming as it does directly from His Merciful Providence, it brings with
> it grace sufficient for all our needs. All we have to do is to give ourselves
> up to God day by day ... He will carry us in His Arms as a loving mother
> carries her child.[22]

We are urged not to anticipate crosses. Don't be doubtful. Trust. Providence must keep company with trust, resignation, surrender, renunciation, indifference, and obedience. And patience. Fenelon sees the necessity of patience because it submits to God's planning. "You would perhaps seek some which God would not want to give you, and which would be incompatible with his plans for you. But embrace unhesitatingly all those which his hand offers you every moment. There is a providence for crosses, as for the necessities of life. It is the daily bread which feeds the soul, and which God never fails to distribute to us."[23] Even in suffering, where we should be most passive, we try to be in active control. This is a characteristic of self-will, which exerts itself when we prefer to manage our schedule of activity. Fenelon says we must let God's providence choose what is required of us.

> You will tell me perhaps that you would prefer to be occupied, in a more
> serious and important way. But God does not prefer it for you, since he
> has chosen what you would not choose. You know that his taste is better
> than yours. You would find more satisfaction in the serious things for

---

22. François Fenelon, *Letters to Women* (London: Longmans, Green, and Co., 1900)
   32.

23. François Fenelon, *Christian Perfection* (New York: Harper & Brothers, 1947) 21.

which he has given you the inclination. And it is this satisfaction which he wants to take away from you. It is this inclination which he wants to mortify in you, although it may be a good and healthy one. The virtues themselves need to be purified in their exercise, by the disappointments which Providence makes them undergo, to detach them more completely from all self-will. [24]

Those with intemperate zeal and impatient spirit would have God do their will, according to their timetable, and are therefore tempted to believe that anything not to their taste is not according to the will of God. But Fenelon repeats that trust in providence even requires abstaining from crosses if we are choosing them for self-satisfaction. Do not add to the crosses in your life "either by making vain efforts against Providence from without, or by other no less vain struggles within. You must be motionless beneath the Cross, keep it as long as God gives it, without trying to move it impatiently ... The Cross would cease to be a cross if self-love had the flattering support of believing that it was enduring manfully."[25]

It is easy for vanity to corrupt the good a cross might have done us. The mortification becomes useless if it is directed by our will, instead of our will being united to God's providential choice. A simple faithfulness over mortifications God has chosen is often far more valuable than severe austerities. In other, simple, words, Fenelon says "there is an indispensable Providence for crosses as well as for the necessities of life; they are part of our daily bread; God never will suffer it to fail. It is sometimes a very useful mortification to certain fervent souls, to give up their own plans mortification, and adopt with cheerfulness those which are momentarily revealed in the order of God."[26] The best penance we could sometimes perform might be patiently bearing a cross that comes from God, instead of contriving one for ourselves. And how do we know which is which? De Caussade answers, "all our crosses come certainly from Him when they are the necessary, natural, and inevitable consequences of the state in which divine Providence permits us

---

24. Fenelon, *Christian Perfection*, 9.

25. Fenelon, *Letters to Women*, 83.

26. Fenelon, *Spiritual Progress*, 29.

to be settled. These are the heaviest crosses, but also the most sanctifying because they all come from God. Crosses from our heavenly Father, crosses from divine Providence, how much easier to bear they are than those we fashion for ourselves, and embrace voluntarily."[27] Let God work; he knows what is suitable for each of us.

The confidence we have in God's crosses comes from the twin facts that he loves us and is preparing us for eternity. These guide his providential actions toward us, de Caussade says. "Nothing will console us more at the hour of death than our humble submission to the different arrangements of divine Providence in spite of the subtle imaginations of self-love often hidden under the most spiritual disguise and the most specious pretexts."[28] Imagine our bemusement on judgment day, says de la Colombiere, when we finally understand the reasons why God sent us the crosses that we are now so unwilling to accept.

> So what are we worried about? God is looking after us and yet we are full of anxiety! We trust ourselves to a doctor because we suppose he knows his business. He orders an operation which involves cutting away part of our body and we accept it ... Yet we are unwilling to treat God in the same way! It looks as if we do not trust His wisdom and are afraid He cannot do his job properly ... If we could see all He sees we would unhesitatingly wish all He wishes.[29]

Providence intends to lead us to a state wherein we see all that God sees (faith), wish all that he wishes (hope), and want all that he wants (love). The good news (Gospel) is that we may be even now, already, initiated into this state by the abnegation of our will in preference for God's prudent management in even the smallest duties of our daily life, where de Caussade looks for it.

---

27. De Caussade, *Abandonment to Divine Providence*, 311-12.

28. De Caussade, *Abandonment to Divine Providence*, 177.

29. De la Colombiere, in Saint-Jure, Jean Baptiste & de la Colombiere, Claude, *Trustful Surrender to Divine Providence* (Rockford, IL: TAN Books and Publishers, 1983) 99.

> If they could be persuaded that sanctity is founded on that to which they give no heed as being altogether irrelevant, they would indeed be happy. If, besides, they understood that to attain the utmost height of perfection, the safest and surest way is to accept the crosses sent them by Providence at every moment, that the true philosopher's stone is submission to the will of God which changes into divine gold all their occupations, troubles, and sufferings, what consolation would be theirs![30]

The world is perplexed when God uses suffering providentially, that is, for our purgation and illumination, because the world sees itself as a final end, and not as a place of pilgrimage. In this, it is mistaken. The world is only a place of temporary exile, and in order that we will not "take the place of our exile for that of our country," says Rodriguez, God "permits this life to be full of pain and torment; that the consideration of what we here suffer in it, may make us more ardently sigh after the life to come."[31] We do not run *away* from creation with a sort of anti-cosmic disdain, but we do run *out of* creation, and self, in order to *run after* God so that he may establish his rule in us. This is what Alacoque recognizes in the details of a letter she received.

> On reading your letter I blessed God, my beloved Sister, for giving you tangible proofs of His true love by leading you along the way of self-effacement. Since He has shown you this way, follow it fearlessly. Then I think you will be doing what He requires of you for establishing His reign in your heart. I think He wants to expel from it creatures first and then yourself. That is why you should be glad when you are in any way forgotten or despised. Remember that these things come to you in order that you may banish creatures from your heart, a heart that must no longer go out exterior things, but rather cut off affection for them, in

---

30. De Caussade, *Abandonment to Divine Providence*, 13-14.

31. Rodriguez, *The Practice of Christian and Religious Perfection*, vol. 2, 286.

order to apply itself without reserve to loving God Who dwells within it.[32]

God is great, we are little; he is worshiped, we are liturgists; he commands, and we obey; therefore Boudon rejoices "in all the means with which Divine Providence supplies us for being little thought of in the world, even when we mix in it; as, for instance, low birth, deficiency in natural talents, want of position, or engagement in humble and mean occupations, failure in our undertakings, the little esteem entertained for us, the neglect into which we fall, the exposure of our faults, or the calumnies raised against us."[33]

Providence can be pictured as a spiritual running after God, who does not let us know, at the time, where we are going. De Castaniza therefore considers it our part "to tremble at these imperceivable proceedings of Divine Providence, and to remain always careful and fearful of thine own condition, not intermeddling with that of others, which is concealed from thy knowledge."[34] How tempted we are to judge another person's life, despite the fact that we have no idea at what stage he is on the providential journey God has charted for him, individually. For the disciple of Christ to understand these imperceivable proceedings, faith, hope, and charity must work together, collaboratively and simultaneously. De Castaniza thinks they so operate best in prayer. "If Thou repel me, I will run after Thee. If Thou shut Thy door against me, I will never cease knocking. And if Thou killest me, yet I will trust in Thee [Job 13:15]. I wholly cast myself upon Thy holy will, providence, and protection."[35]

In imitation of the path Christ's own kenosis took, the providential path charted for each Christian will likely lead away from *honor in* the world, to what Leen calls *abandonment by* the world.

---

32. Alacoque, *Spiritual Letters,* letter 69, Kindle edition.

33. Boudon, *The Hidden Life of Jesus,* 124.

34. De Castaniza, *The Spiritual Conflict & Conquest,* 134.

35. De Castaniza, *The Spiritual Conflict & Conquest,* 257-58.

> Little by little the soul grows in that basic humility so characteristic of
> Christ; complete dependence on and loving subjection to God become
> as it were the leaven which spreading by imperceptible degrees pervades
> its every action; it is marked by a self-abnegation which aims at purging
> from it everything that is not God, so that "conformed to the image of
> His Son" it may live its life in full accord with the designs of Providence
> in its regard.[36]

Providence moves us toward our end little by little, slowly, indiscernibly, almost unnoticeably. Such is the way of the interior life: it seems invisible while we watch it, and only evident after a while. John Evangelist of Boisleduc is among many who compare progress in the interior life "to the growing of a tree which grows in size and strength imperceptibly; and the tree which takes the longer time to grow remains green for a longer time than the tree which grows more quickly."[37] Look at the tree ten years later and you will see that it has grown, but you cannot detect that hour by hour. And providence often doesn't work in a linear fashion, first taking care of A, then B, then moving on to C. Providence works more like a painter on a canvas, and sometimes God is working on one corner, other times on another. One virtue is strengthened, and another vice combatted; the ground for one glory is being laid, while another vainglory is being stripped. The tempo of providence is one of the more difficult things for finite creatures to understand, because we are eager (even anxious) to chart our progress along the two-dimensional dotted line we are walking, while God sees the whole three-dimensional map from a higher vantage point. He is more patient than we are.

Providence is mysterious to the eyes of a worldling because people suffer, which shouldn't happen if God exists to do their will. But suffering is no longer mysterious to the eyes of a believer because we exist to do God's will, something that providence is working out. Alacoque says the stripes administered by providence are by a friend because

> He wants to bring you to the end He has in mind for you which is, if
> I'm not mistaken, to establish in your heart the reign of His pure love, so

---

36. Leen, *Progress Through Mental Prayer*, 15.

37. John Evangelist of Boisleduc, *The Kingdom of God in the Soul*, 121-22.

that you may reign, I fondly hope, forever in heaven. This can be attained only by traveling the humble, selfless, lonely way. You should consider immeasurably precious all the opportunities He offers you. These are but the blows of a friend, blows inflicted by a Heart truly in love with yours, of which He is extremely jealous. That is why He is eager to destroy everything earthly and purely natural in you. And He will, if only you will let Him, follow His lights, and cooperate to carry out His adorable will.[38]

Because the same charity runs through both creation and redemption, de Sales thinks we can "diversify the name of providence, and say that there is one providence natural, another supernatural, and that the latter again is general, or special, or particular."[39] Before concentrating on the *redemptive providence* that works for our deification in the next chapter, let us conclude this chapter with some remarks about *natural providence* that preserves order in the natural creation.

De Granada presents an image: "in the same manner in which the movements of a clock depend upon the pendulum, so does the whole mechanism of the world depend solely upon Divine Providence; so that if that failed, all the rest would immediately come to nought."[40] In fact, Eudes says belief in providence comes in the wake of belief in *creation ex nihilo*. "Faith, which tells us there is but one God who created all things, also obliges us to believe that this great God orders and governs all things without exception, either by absolute or by permissive will; and that there is nothing accomplished in the world that does not come under the ordering of His divine guidance, or pass through the hands of His absolute will, or His permission, which are like the two arms of His Providence, by which He controls all things."[41] Still, we must not separate the two providences, cautions de Sales. Natural providence is teleologically tied to supernatural providence because salvation gives creation its trajectory, as fruit gives the vine its purpose.

---

38. Alacoque, *Spiritual Letters,* letter 80, Kindle edition.

39. De Sales, *Treatise on the Love of God,* 81.

40. De Granada, *Considerations on the Mysteries of the Faith,* 174.

41. Eudes, *The Life and the Kingdom of Jesus in Christian Souls,* 60.

The principal reason of planting the vine is the fruit, and therefore the fruit is the first thing desired and aimed at, though the leaves and the buds are first produced. So our great Saviour was the first in the divine intention ... and in view of this desired fruit the vine of the universe was planted, and the succession of many generations established, which as leaves or blossoms proceed from it as forerunners and fit preparatives for the production of that grape which the sacred spouse so much praises in the Canticles, and the juice of which rejoices God and men.[42]

This is liturgical cosmology: the end of a watch is to tell time, the end of a pen is to write, the end of a human being is to be a liturgist, the end of nature is super nature, the end of cosmos is consecration. "If the divine providence has been so careful in providing what regards nature only," marvels de Granada, "how much more solicitous will it be in furnishing us with such things as regard grace, which are infinitely more excellent, but, at the same time, far above the reach and power of man!"[43]

Of course, there is one thing not caused by God, and that is sin. "St. Francis [de Sales] looked over secondary causes, and in all events considered the hand of God as ordering and governing all things. 'Nothing can happen to us,' he said, 'except sin, that is not ordered by God, whether prosperous or adverse, for God is the fountain of good.'"[44] Often we find it difficult to distinguish sin and misfortune, and Rodriguez worries over how the devil will use this ambiguity to his advantage. "It is a truth so firmly supported by the authority of Holy Scripture, that all misfortunes and sufferings come from the hands of God, that it would not be necessary to stop any longer to prove it, if the devil, by his vain subtilties, did not endeavour to obscure it, and render it doubtful."[45] The devil would have us believe chastisements come not from God, but only proceed from natural causes,

---

42. De Sales, *Treatise on the Love of God*, 85-86.

43. De Granada, *The Sinner's Guide*, 112.

44. Camus, *Beauties of de Sales*, 57.

45. Rodriguez, *The Practice of Christian and Religious Perfection*, vol. 1, 390.

or from irrational creatures, or from the malice of other persons. But Eudes reminds us that faith has the clearer sight, and "gives a most certain knowledge that Divine Providence directs and guides all things that happen in the universe, with great holiness and wisdom, in fact, in the best way possible. His disposal of all things deserves to be infinitely adored and loved by all creatures that are subject to His order, whether in justice or in mercy, in heaven, on earth or in hell."[46]

Providence serves the twin goals of liturgy: the glorification of God and the sanctification of man. Concerning the latter, de Granada says our last perfection and happiness is given when "from this fatherly providence, as from a fountain, flow all the favors God bestows on those who serve him. For it belongs to this providence to supply them with all necessaries for the obtaining of their end, which is their last perfection and happiness, by assisting them in all their wants, and infusing into their souls such virtues and habits as are requisite for this end."[47] Concerning the former, de Granada says providence lays up riches by which we can participate in glorifying God. "He offers us inestimable riches for this life as well as for the next. Of all which the chiefest is, the fatherly love and providence wherewith he assists those he looks on as his children, and this is infinitely beyond whatever affection the most tender father in the world can show; for never was there any one yet who laid up such riches for his children as God does, which is no less than the participation of his eternal glory."[48]

I have been at pains to point out that upon accepting a theology of abnegation, we will no longer think of providence as good luck, blessed fortune, or personal success. If we can shake this off this secular expectation, then providence will no longer awaken mercantile speculation about personal profit. The primary ordering of providence in our lives, says de Sales, is Christ's cross.

> Our Lord loves with a most tender love those who are so happy as to
> abandon themselves wholly to His fatherly care, letting themselves be
> governed by His divine Providence without any idle speculations as to

---

46. Eudes, *The Life and the Kingdom of Jesus in Christian Souls*, 9.

47. De Granada, *The Sinner's Guide*, 108.

48. De Granada, *The Sinner's Guide*, 97.

whether the workings of this Providence will be useful to them to their profit, or painful to their loss, and this because they are well assured that nothing can be sent, nothing permitted by this paternal and most loving Heart, which will not be a source of good and profit to them. All that is required is that they should place all their confidence in Him, and say from their heart, 'Into Thy hands I commend my spirit', my soul, my body, and all that I have, to do with them as it shall please Thee.[49]

And, he concludes, "it is our duty to adore this amiable Providence, by casting ourselves into its arms."[50]

---

49. De Sales, quoted by Camus in *The Spirit of St. Francis de Sales*, 279.

50. De Sales, quote by Jean-Joseph Huguet in *Consoling Thoughts of de Sales* (Dublin: M. H. Gill & Son, 1877), 114.

PROVIDENCE: A MATTER FOR THE WILL

Having concluded the last chapter with a brief look at natural providence, let us turn our attention in this chapter to redemptive providence. It must be approached in a particular way, since providence presents a challenge to both believers and theologians, alike. I am not thinking here of some intellectual puzzle presented to our reason, I am thinking of the existential challenge providence presents to the heart. Leen describes it as a challenge of resentment. "*The moment that we feel resentment at anything painful that happens to us through the activity of MEN OR THINGS, at that moment we are resentful against God's Providence.*"[1]

Adoring God's secret plans of providence is a matter for the will, not the understanding. Faith soars up to God in liturgy, it does not plod along the surface of rationality where curiosity wants to know what will happen because it fears what will happen. Bona warns,

> curiosity, by which we often enquire what shall become of us hereafter, is the part of a man who loves himself, and is afraid of suffering. Our most gracious God looking back through the glass of his divine Providence, knows what is most convenient for every one; and sweetly and powerfully

---

1. Edward Leen, *Likeness of Christ* (New York: Sheed and Ward, 1936) 184. Italics and capitalization in original.

> disposing all things, *takes a special care of man, when he sees him take no thought of himself, but cast all his care upon him.*[2]

God sees the whole history of the soul through his looking glass of providence, and Rigoleuc knows this is sufficient. When the soul has reflected on the triad of God's attributes – wisdom, goodness, and omnipotence – she then "remains in silence before Him, who is all-sufficient in supplying her necessities, and who alone can do it efficaciously. This one thought fully satisfies. It suffices to her that God sees her … She places all her interests in the hands of God, throws the burden of her cares upon Divine Providence, *letting God will for her.*"[3] The memory and contemplation of the love of Jesus enkindles the heart, animates every hope, and "we leave to Him the care of obtaining for us what we seek of His Eternal Father, and we entirely and sweetly repose in Him," in short, passing "from confidence to resignation, and we protest to God that we neither will or desire aught but that which it is His good pleasure to bestow."[4] That is trust in providence.

While cataphatic theology employs words to say the limited things we can comprehend about God, apophatic theology confesses mysteries of God that we cannot comprehend, and the hardest apophatic challenge is not an epistemological one (e.g., can we believe the proofs of God's existence?), the hardest apophatic challenge is an ascetical one: will we obey God's providence even though it is beyond our short-sighted reason? When the soul has dismissed all comprehensible things from the mind, then she is left with God the incomprehensible; similarly, when the soul has dismissed all created things from desire, then she is left with God the All. The infinity of God reveals our nothingness, Fenelon says, but that nothingness makes us rejoice in God's infinity.

> O how sweet is this voice. It makes all my entrails to leap for joy. Speak, O my spouse, and let none other venture to speak but thou alone. Be silent, O my Soul, speak thou, O Love. I say that then, *we know all, without*

---

2. Bona, *The Principles of Christianity*, 150.

3. Rigoleuc, *Walking with God*, 37.

4. Rigoleuc, *Walking with God*, 39.

knowing any thing. 'Tis not that we have the Presumption to think, that we possess all Truth in our selves. No, no: quite the contrary; we are sensible that we see nothing, that we can do nothing, that we are nothing. We feel this, and we are ravished at it.[5]

There is an undercurrent connection between abnegation, providence, and apophaticism, articulated repeatedly by Alonso Rodriguez:

- Contemplatives call this ignorance a cloud. Raised up and carried on the ray of divine ignorance the soul's surmounts this, not in order to understand, but so that it may know that God is sweet. In this way it knows by taste what it does not comprehend by intelligence. The less it understands God, the more ignorant it is of him, the sweeter the soul finds him.[6]

- Almost whenever he wants and in whatever situation he may be, this person is always alone with his God, without any effort, or any process of reasoning, for he already has him who is usually sought in the process of reasoning, namely God.[6]

- The little light and knowledge of God gained by reasoning is that of a penny candle. But when God, by himself and without the process of reasoning, gives the soul this divine light, there is a greater difference between it and the light of reasoning than there is between the entire light of the sun and the light of one candle.[6]

---

5. Fenelon, *Pious Thoughts Concerning the Knowledge and Love of God,* 74-75.

6. Alonso Rodriguez, *Saint Alphonsus Rodriguez: Autobiography* (London: Geoffrey Chapman, 1964) 40.

6. Alonso Rodriguez, *Saint Alphonsus Rodriguez: Autobiography,* 106.

6. Alonso Rodriguez, *Saint Alphonsus Rodriguez: Autobiography,* 116.

- If he descends to the world, as far as his soul and body are concerned, he is plunged into the abyss of all that he owes to God, and he says to them, "Lord, where is the love with which I love you? How is it that I do not to die for your love? ... There is scarcely room for reasoning here, rather in an intellectual vision the light shows the soul all the benefits God has given the soul and body, and they surpass understanding.[6]

There is scarcely room for reasoning about providence when resignation to it is a matter of aligning our will with God's will, our thought with God's thoughts, our affections with God's affections. The reason our self-love finds this a struggle is because his thoughts are not as our thoughts. "Does God judge as we do for the welfare of our souls, in His wisdom, in His prudence, in the workings of His Providence?"[10] asks de Ravignan. God's judgment about the welfare of our soul operates on a different logic than the one we use to judge what happens to us. One can only judge a means against its end, and if we do not know the end for which God is preparing us, then we will misjudge his means. But this is an attempt to make ourselves a deity higher than the true God, Eudes observes. It is another idolatry. "There is another and a last extremity of sin, the deepest abyss of iniquity, which consists in making oneself the god of God. The sinner would wish God to prefer his interests, will, pleasure and honor to the interest, will, pleasure and honor of His divine majesty. He would wish that his human will might rule the Providence of God and that God should be guided by the sinner's whims and fancies."[11] Trust in God's providence puts all this to the liturgical test of latria.

Liturgical abnegation is not a matter of forecasting the future according to plans we have made, since that could warp into infidelity. To avoid this, and prevent discouragement in times of mortification, we must have confidence in God's wisdom (faith), in God's goodness (hope), and in God's providence (love). Faith, hope and love can look at higher mysteries than reason, optimism, and natural affection can understand. Then, de Ravignan asks, "if you were to experience a reverse of fortunes, if you were to find yourself suddenly in an inferior position, ought you to be discouraged, ought

---

6. Alonso Rodriguez, *Saint Alphonsus Rodriguez: Autobiography*, 144.

10. De Ravignan, *Conferences on the Spiritual Life*, 83.

11. Eudes, *Meditation on Various Subjects*, 121.

you to let yourself be cast down? I do not pretend to bid you rejoice, but I tell you that then you should raise your eyes to heaven, and lift your thoughts higher and higher, till they rest upon the Divine Providence."[12] These higher thoughts rest upon a foundation that stands beyond nature, beyond the temporal, beyond self-will, beyond plans we have designed for our personal happinesses. The higher thoughts rest upon a providential application of grace, even if that involves a personal share in Adam's judgment, Job's strikes, and Christ's cross. De Castaniza says the first question we must ask is "What is God's will?"

> First, then, let us seek God purely in all – see Him present in all; take as from Him all; return back unto Him all. Let us be indifferent in all; praise God in all; be quiet and content in all – in sickness and health, in light and darkness, in peace and trouble, in life and death; to be expelled out of Paradise with Adam; to lie full of sores and sorrows with Job on a dunghill; to be forsaken by all with Christ on the cross; to be poor, naked, nothing, being ever ready to say cordially, cheerfully, and with an humble and habitual indifference: – 'Yes, O Father, yes, I will; it pleaseth Thee, it shall please me; well, good, best of all; so be it, my good Lord, for time and eternity, in this and in all things.' A soul thus resigned can never be troubled with any cross or calamity, for she eyes God's will, and embraces His providence in all occurrences; nothing troubleth her, but only that His divine pleasure is not perfectly performed in herself and in all creatures.[13]

And here is one of the most mysterious paradoxes: if we will whatever God allows to happen, then nothing can happen that does not please us. Scupoli describes an invariable rule: "keep thy wishes so far removed from every other object, that they may aim simply and solely at their true and only end, i.e., the Will of God," and in that case the will is not only tranquil, but contented, because "as nothing can happen without the Supreme Will, thou, by willing the same, wilt come, at all times, to will at once and to have, all

---

12. De Ravignan, *Conferences on the Spiritual Life,* 84-85.

13. De Castaniza, *The Spiritual Conflict & Conquest,* 371-72.

that happens and all that thou desirest."[14] Desire what God gives, and you will always get what you desire. Desire even the crosses God gives, and you will never be discontented. Nothing will displease you, says Croiset.

> Since we will whatever God allows to happen, nothing can happen that does not please us ... All our application and all our delight should be to do what God wills, when He wills it, in the manner He wills it. Without this, there can be no virtue; all is illusion and self-love. This perfect conformity to the will of God, and perfect submission to the appointments of Divine Providence, which lead us to wish for nothing but what God wills that we should do ... are not only the shortest and most secure path, but properly speaking, the only one, by which to acquire perfect purity of heart, a great love of Jesus Christ, and at the same time, great merit.[15]

This involves a conversion of will, which Leen defines as "the faculty by which we move towards and cleave to what is presented to us as being good, that is, as satisfying a want in us."[16] Can it be purified? Yes, he answers. That "consists in the gradual elimination from its tendencies of all that is not God or does not lead directly to Him. Thus it attains its perfection in an unquestioning submission to the action of Divine Providence, and in embracing wholeheartedly the dispensations of that Providence in the minutest details of life."[17] Saint-Jure defines the will by noting its role within the three human faculties of understanding, will, and affection. The first is presented as a torch, the second is blind, and the third must be instructed. "Such is the order established by nature, that [since the will is] a blind power, it is the function of the understanding to lead it, bearing before it the torch which directs its affections according to the nature of the knowledge it gives,

---

14. Scupoli, *The Spiritual Combat*, 109.

15. Croiset, *Devotion to the Sacred Heart of Jesus*, 169-70.

16. Leen, *Progress Through Mental Prayer*, 206.

17. Leen, *Progress Through Mental Prayer*, 206.

and a thing is loved or hated according as the understanding represents it as being worthy of love or hatred."[18]

It is a maxim shared by all the theologians of liturgical abnegation that absolutely *all* things God gives, or even allows, come from the same providential hand. He is the primary cause. They acknowledge that secondary causes are also involved, but such causes are instrumental to, not obstructive of, the primary cause. Some speak of secondary causes as *chance*, but even this word is only invoked when providence takes on its hidden quality. Rodriguez proposes a helpful example. If a master sent his servant on some business, and afterward sent another to the same place on a different errand, and did so with the intention that the two servants should meet one another on the way, then

> their meeting, in regard to themselves, would be purely by chance; but in regard to their master, it would be a premeditated design. It is the very same with things which seem to happen here below by chance. In respect of men, who see these accidents happen contrary to their inclination, and without ever having so much as thought of them, it is an effect of chance; but, in regard of God, it is a necessary consequence, and an execution of the eternal order of his providence, who would have it thus for secret and hidden ends, which are known to none but himself.[19]

Yet take caution, he adds, for using the word "chance" could become misleading. "There is nothing, in respect of God, that happens by chance. He has regulated all things, and appointed everything from all eternity."[20] Even things proceeding from secondary causes do not happen without the command and will of God. This is less a debate about physical and contingent causes as it is about finding the reason and purpose behind all things, something that human beings have always sought, but often in the wrong source, says Blosius.

---

18. Saint-Jure, *Knowledge and Love of Jesus*, vol. 1, 51-52.

19. Rodriguez, *The Practice of Christian and Religious Perfection*, vol. 1, 389.

20. Rodriguez, *The Practice of Christian and Religious Perfection*, vol. 1, 388.

Wait everywhere on the Providence of God: in every event that occurs,
lean steadfastly on Him, believing that nothing can happen without
a cause, nor without a cause proceeding from the reasonable order of
things. Attribute what happens neither to fortune nor to the stars. Detest
the superstitious and impious fables of astrologers, who put the life,
the manners, the actions and designs of man under subjection to the
stars, and attempt by them to pry into and predict future events, beyond
the natural properties of the elements, and of corruptible things. This
temerity partakes of the remains of idolatry, and is most baneful to the
Christian religion.[21]

The theologians are basing themselves on Jesus's own words when they believe that
"without this divine permission not a hair can fall from our heads, or a leaf in Autumn
from all the innumerable trees of the forests. This is of faith. Could Jesus Christ have more
clearly expressed than by these words, that there is no event, great or small, in the world
which has not been expressly arranged by the sovereign providence of God?[22] Those are
de Caussade's words, but we find others repeating it, because they return repeatedly to
these words of our Lord. Rodriguez says,

He has taken an account of every hair of your head, and not one of them
shall fall to the ground without his order. But why do I speak of men,
since his providence extends itself over all other creatures? "Are not two
sparrows," says Jesus Christ, "sold for a farthing? and not one of them
falls to the ground without the permission of your heavenly Father."
(Matt. x. 29.) No; there is not a leaf that moves upon a tree but by his
will.[23]

Blosius says,

---

21. Blosius, *Spiritual Works of Louis of Blois*, 29.

22. De Caussade, *Abandonment to Divine Providence*, 269.

23. Rodriguez, *The Practice of Christian and Religious Perfection*, vol. 1, 388.

In all things attend wisely to the divine dispensation, without which not even one leaf falls from the tree. God, who created all things, governs also and rules all things, from the highest angelic spirit to the vilest worm of the earth. If thou dost undoubtingly believe this, thou wilt be able more easily to keep thy mind even and undisturbed amid the various circumstances of the present life.[24]

Ravignan says,

Remember that the Saviour never tries you, but that He may bless you; remember that from the heights of heaven His unsleeping Providence and divine mercy are ever watching over you, and not one hair falls from your head unseen.[25]

And de Sales says,

Not only does His providence watch over the most important things of our salvation, but even over the most trifling events of our life. A hair of our head does not fall without His providence, and He knows even the number of them. Without His permission, neither men nor demons dare touch one of them ...

O religious souls! our true to-morrow is Divine Providence. Behold the lilies of the fields, they neither sow nor do they spin, and the sweet

---

24. Blosius, *Spiritual Works of Louis of Blois*, 117.

25. De Ravignan, *Conferences on the Spiritual Life*, 148.

providence of our heavenly Father clothes them better than Solomon was clothed in all his glory.[26]

Nothing is too small or vile to be guided by God's providence, so remain undisturbed. In the smallest of affairs He is directing us to the end most salutary to us, and exercises control over both the visible and invisible worlds to do so.

God's providence cares for the cosmos and for mankind in general, but this fatherhood has a special affection for each individual person, and invites a personal response from each of its recipients. Action creates reaction; energy creates synergy; agape creates charity; fatherhood creates filiality. "What motives should we not find of loving God, and giving up ourselves without reserve to him, if we only considered as we ought, his paternal providence and the tender affection he has for us?" asks Rodriguez. "Hence arises that filial confidence which the true servants of God have in him."[27] Providence extends to all creatures, but de Granada thinks the Almighty is particularly attentive to those he has chosen for himself "because they, being his children, and receiving as his gift, an affection truly filial for him, he, on his part, loves them with a truly fatherly love, and his love is the measure of the care he takes for them."[28] This filiality also finds tender expression in in maternal images for providence, which are abundant. Take this example from de Lombez.

> That providence carries you as a mother carries her unborn babe. How great is the repose you enjoy! How sweet the rest you find in its bosom! You are on all sides sheltered, as with an impenetrable buckler, from the arrows which fly by night and by day. Either it repels them, or if it permits them to reach you, it assures you they come not from the hand of a

---

26. De Chantal, *Meditations for Retreats*, 160 and 162-63.

27. Rodriguez, *The Practice of Christian and Religious Perfection*, vol. 1, 422.

28. De Granada, *The Sinner's Guide*, 97.

pitiless enemy, but from that paternal goodness which never gives a useless wound, and can heal as quickly as it can afflict.[29]

The mother gives freedom by providing direction, thinks Fenelon. "There is no freer heart than that which God leads by this simple path. You will find yourself going on like a little child whose mother leads it by the hand, while it never questions whither they are going."[30]

Overwhelmed by this love, we should throw ourselves (abnegation) into God's providence with devoted recklessness. Abnegation is abandonment *of something* in order to abandon ourselves *to someone*. "Abandon yourselves to the Providence of God" commands de Ravignan, because "it is He Who by work, rule, obedience and duty, leads you by the hand. Blessed children, you have God for a father, learn to conceive your own happiness!"[31] Happiness abounds; there are riches in store; blessings are forthcoming. Here is a short list by de Granada.

> And what fruits can be more precious than those we have here given an account of? What more delicious fruit than the fatherly care and providence which God has over those that serve him? What more pleasant than his divine grace, than the light of wisdom, the consolation of the Holy Ghost, the joy of a good conscience, the help of a secure confidence in him, the true liberty of the soul, the inward peace of the heart, the being heard by him in our prayers, the being consoled by him in our tribulations, the having of our temporal necessities supplied, and, in fine, the comfort of a sweet and quiet death at last?[32]

---

29. De Lombez, *A Treatise on Interior Peace*, 80.

30. Fenelon, *Letters to Women*, 251.

31. De Ravignan, *Conferences on the Spiritual Life*, 185.

32. De Granada, *The Sinner's Guide*, 200.

God knows what he is doing, because God knows what he wants. Therefore de Chantal is content to deliver "over all those rough winds to the Providence of God; let them bluster as it pleases Him; tempest and calm are all the same to me."[33] Three enemies attempt to draw us away from such trust: the devil, the world, and the flesh. They tempt us to abandon our liturgical duty of piety, but de Castaniza knows "perfect obedience breaks through this snare, and a total resignation to God's good will and pleasure is the secure refuge against this deceit. How can a soul be disquieted to receive or refuse, act or omit, that which she truly conceives to proceed both in substance and circumstance from the divine providence and permission?"[34]

We are repeatedly warned by the theologians of liturgical abnegation not to confuse means with end. The end of abnegation is not suffering; suffering is only the means to the end of perfection. Any suffering we undergo comes from the friction between our disordered self and God's righteousness, but Baker believes our Father in heaven is repairing the discord as rapidly as we will let him. "The highest perfection is not to desire to be always suffering, but to be content to suffer all that by God's providence shall befall us ... Therefore, let souls never be solicitous, nor set themselves to devise or procure mortifications, as if they thought God had forgotten them."[35] The theologians can picture providence as the proportionment of abnegation to our several needs. First, Baker sees providence proportioning abnegation to prayer. "According to the ordinary established course of Divine Providence, perfection in prayer is accompanied with a proportionate perfection in mortification."[36] Second, Surin sees providence proportioning abnegation to the intensity of purity of heart that God desires to create in an individual soul. "In fact, nothing more raises the mind, and prepares it better for Divine illumination, than perfect purity of heart, with a complete renunciation of all

---

33. Jane de Chantal & Francis de Sales. *I. The Mystical Explanation of the Canticle of Canticles by St. Francis de Sales; II. The Depositions of St. Jane Frances de Chantal in the Cause of the Canonisation of St. Francis de Sales* in *Library of St. Francis de Sales* (London: Burns & Oates, 1908) 164.

34. De Castaniza, *The Spiritual Conflict & Conquest*, 227.

35. Baker, *Holy Wisdom*, 485.

36. Baker, *Holy Wisdom*, 206.

created things, and an absolute resignation of self into the hands of Providence."[37] Third, Lallemant sees providence proportioning abnegation to a liturgy of adoration.

> Adore with all humility and from the bottom of our heart, this will of God and disposition of His providence, and submit ourselves thereto with perfect resignation; considering that what on the part of men is an effect of their hatred or envy in order to our humiliation, on the part of God is a means which His goodness employs to exalt us to a higher degree of glory, if we are but faithful to Him. We see this in the example of Joseph, and in that of Jesus Christ Himself. Let us learn, then, to serve our Lord with an entire abandonment of ourselves.[38]

In each of these, providence proportions abnegation with the merits of Christ, which de Sales knows is the ultimate foundation of our confidence in God. "It must be grounded on the infinite goodness of God, and on the merits of the Death and Passion of our Lord Jesus Christ with this condition on our part that we should preserve and recognise in ourselves an entire and firm resolution to belong wholly to God, and to abandon ourselves in all things and without any reserve to His Providence."[39]

Resignation to God's providence depends upon purity of heart, which is an ongoing commission. Purity of heart, we are told, is to will one thing, and the pure of heart are blessed because they will see God. Abnegation works a brilliance into the pure heart by removing, one by one, all the contrary objects that Lallemant can see distracting our will from God. "Purity of heart consists in having nothing therein which is, in however small a degree, opposed to God and the operation of His grace. All the creatures there are in the world, the whole order of nature as well as of grace, and all the leadings of Providence, have been so disposed as to remove from our souls whatever is contrary to God."[40] Without

---

37. Surin, *Foundations of the Spiritual Life*, 50.

38. Lallemant, *The Spiritual Doctrine of Father Louis Lallemant*, ed. Faber 73.

39. De Sales, quoted by Camus, *The Spirit of St. Francis de Sales*, 40.

40. Lallemant, *The Spiritual Doctrine of Father Louis Lallemant*, ed. Faber, 96.

a desire for such purity, providence could easily cause anxiety and fear, something de Lombez wants to avoid.

> Your first and greatest fear is that God has withdrawn Himself from you because of your faults, and loves you no longer because He looks on you with the eye of severity. But let me ask you, is it only to punish our sins that God acts in this rigorous manner toward us? Is it not sometimes and very often to perfect our virtue? This apparent coldness – is it not rather a means of His providence to root out our self-love and confirm us in patience and humility, to purify our charity? To render us more perfect and the practice of good works, and make us more conformable to Jesus Christ, our Lord and Savior, the model of predestination, to enable us to merit a richer crown in heaven and draw upon ourselves more abundant graces on earth."[41]

So purity of heart weighs what happens on a new scale. It places events in a new balance. De Sales, and others, call it the scale you find in the temple, not in the world. "This purity of heart consists in setting on all things their true value, and in weighing them in the balance of the sanctuary, which balance is only another name for the will of God."[42] This balance of the sanctuary is a liturgical scale, unknown to the world, which is why providential actions are mysterious to the world. "Purity of heart consists in valuing all things according to the weights of the sanctuary, which are nothing else than the will of God; do not love, then, anything too ardently, not even virtue, which we sometimes lose, by wishing for it beyond the bounds of moderation."[43] What is providence for? To complete the will of God. What is God's will? to love us. What is God's will for us? to bring us into his love.

---

41. De Lombez, *A Treatise on Interior Peace,* 71.

42. De Sales, quoted by Camus, *The Spirit of St. Francis de Sales,* 298.

43. Jean-Joseph Huguet, *The Consoling Thoughts of St. Francis de Sales* (Dublin: M. H. Gill & Son, 1877) 80.

God leads us, guides us, steers us to that love by putting us in his yoke. Or, rather, Camus says, "hearken to him who promises us to lighten our burden, by putting himself into the yoke with us.[44] Such a savior we have! He yokes himself to us, to go through our life with us. A yoke is made for two, Francisco de Osuna reminds us, and "the one with the highest collar does most work and draws the heavier weight. Christ first undertook his part and is figured by Saul who had higher shoulders than the rest of the people and consequently, in his extreme humility and meekness, did more work."[45] The yoke is sweet because the Lord carries the chief part. Moral imitation tries to yoke man to Jesus; in liturgical abnegation, Jesus yokes himself to you. "The yoke of Christ," says Ullathorne, "is the discipline of humility in self-abnegation…. We are no longer under the yoke of Satan, no longer under the yoke of the world, no longer under the yoke of pride; we bear the yoke of Christ, whose yoke is sweet and his burden light."[46] The yoke is a matter of freedom, so long as we are united willingly, so de la Colombiere asks why the faithful soul would seep. And he hears God answer:

> What reason do you have to afflict yourself, my Beloved, since I love you and I am happy with you? It is myself who has given you the blow of which you complain, and since you have offended me in nothing, you well can think that it is not in my anger that I strike you … Consider that the evils that you endure serve not a little to increase the glory that I prepare for you … Do you think that this happened without my permission or that I permitted it unintentionally? And, loving you as I do, can I have an intention that be not for your benefit?[47]

---

44. Camus, *A Spiritual Combat*, 99

45. Francisco de Osuna, *Third Spiritual Alphabet* (New York: Benziger Brothers, 1931) 360.

46. Ullathorne, *The Groundwork of the Christian Virtues* (London: Burns & Oates, Ltd., 1890) 201.

47. De la Colombiere, *Sermons,* vol. 1, *Christian Conduct,* 66-67.

All things – benefactions as well as trials – are tools in the hands of God who is shaping us up for beatitude. The Scriptural image of God as potter, and ourselves as clay, is presented quite often. Here is Rodriguez: "For by this resignation a man places himself in the hands of God, as a piece of clay in the hands of the potter, that is, that divine Providence may dispose of him at pleasure; not desiring anything for the future in order to himself, nor to live for himself, neither to eat, sleep, or work for himself, but to do all things for God alone, and for his service and glory."[48] Here is Libermann:

> You should remain in the Lord's presence like clay before the potter. The workman does what he pleases with it: he beats it, presses it, and beats it again to make it supple. The clay offers no resistance; it leaves the potter perfect liberty to do with it what he wishes. The potter fashions a vase and it often happens that when it is half-finished he breaks it up and reduces it to a shapeless mass. He then starts anew to make of it the particular vase he wants. The more the clay has been battered and crushed, the easier it is for the potter to achieve his purpose...[49]

"Allow God full liberty to handle you,"[50] Libermann concludes, because we are his possession, his property, and he does with us what he wills. "Does the earthen vessel say to the Potter, 'Why do you make me thus?' Does it not allow him to fashion it according to his wishes?"[51]

And why? Because it pleases God. (We have now reached the liturgical foundation of providence.) De Chantal records that Francis de Sales wrote to her one day saying that it is

---

48. Rodriguez, *The Practice of Christian and Religious Perfection*, vol. 1, 394.

49. Libermann, Vol. 5, 116.

50. Libermann, Vol. 5, 116.

51. Libermann, Vol. 2, 78.

a great satisfaction to my soul, which is truly dedicated to God, to walk along with my eyes shut, just as and where Divine Providence leads me from time to time; for His reasons and judgments are impenetrable, yet always sweet and pleasant to those who trust in Him. What do we will, except what God wills? Let us leave Him to guide our soul, which is His vessel; He will bring it safe to port. Oh ! how happy are those souls which only live in this Divine Will![52]

This requires spiritual powers. I will name two here, and others elsewhere. The first spiritual power is *patience*. The glory is eternal, so the fruits that providence is growing in our souls may have to wait for eternity. What appears to have been thwarted now may be part of a greater picture which will only succeed later, in God's own time. De Caussade acknowledges that God may defer the accomplishment of our most holy desires, but his designs will never be ruined. "His providence can be hidden, but infallible means [to] cause things to succeed in spite of every obstacle, even when success seems absolutely impossible. God often allows His work to be thwarted in order to make the exercise of His power more striking, and to show us that He is absolute master of all."[53] God has promised to grant what we need – but not immediately! And Scaramelli is sure the delay will work in both our favors, his and ours.

> For although God has promised to grant us the favours we seek at His hands, provided they help us to attain to our last end, eternal life, He has not promised to grant them immediately, nor even soon. To some, He grants what is asked at the outset; but others are kept praying and waiting for weeks and months, nay, for years together. Some obtain whatever they ask for without any delay; others only insensibly and by slow degrees. All this happens through the hidden and unsearchable counsels of the providence of God, which we cannot pretend to fathom. Suffice it for us

---

52. De Chantal, *The Depositions of St. Jane Frances de Chantal*, 187-88.

53. De Caussade, *Abandonment to Divine Providence*, 163-64.

to know, that in this diversity of conduct God has no other end but our greater advantage, and His own greater glory.[54]

So do not be impatient, counsels Libermann. "It happens on numerous occasions that at any price we want our Lord to act according to our little lights, according to our will," and we are never satisfied because "if we were judges of the events we would decide quite differently. In everything that concerns ourselves we keep wanting to change God's plans to conform them to our petty little ideas and shadowy prudence."[55] This is a weakness of faith expressed in the form of a weariness of patience. God will use the trials we suffer now in order to bring us home, but we must not upset the divine economy he has designed for each one of us. His infinity does not mean he cares only for large things; his infinity means that he can care for each individual thing. Let God choose the path, Libermann continues, and then be patient. "We should give our attention to God alone Whose divine Providence will arrange everything according to His wishes. Let us always follow the good desires for His glory which He inspires, and then wait peacefully until He accomplishes His design."[56]

The second spiritual power is the strength to bear trials with *indifference*. We have already seen the usefulness of this word to describe the overthrow of mercantile service to God. Here it is useful in understanding that God determines the path of providence, God sets providence in motion, and we should not criticize providence. One cannot hold a doctrine of holy indifference if one does not hold the doctrine of providence, and I suppose we find the former difficult because we do not believe the latter. The indifference about which the theologians of abnegation speak depends upon a massive, tectonic shift from the terminal world to eternal God (which is called conversion), and results in a profound peace that is unavailable by any other means. It sounds like we are abjuring the world, but it is not for gnostic reasons; it is only, says Boudon, because a temporal good cannot feed an appetite for the eternal.

---

54. Scaramelli, *Directorium Asceticum; Or, Guide to the Spiritual Life*, vol. 1, 393.

55. Francis Libermann, *Jesus Through Jewish Eyes*, vol. 3 (Dublin: Paraclete Press, 2005) 117-18.

56. Libermann, *Letters to Religious Sisters and Aspirants*, Spiritan Studies 5, vol. 1, 62.

Fear nothing and hope nothing from any living creature. In these few
words is comprehended a peace which is beyond all thought. To this we
may add, Believe only in God, hope only in God, love but God only;
never believe the world, or its arguments, or its maxims; never hope for
anything from the world, from its honours, its pleasures, or its goods;
never love the world, and behold you are settled in a profound peace. No
longer make account of any created things; never look at them save in their
nothingness; never desire any share in the esteem or in the heart of any
one; banish the good from your heart as well as others; make no exception;
be ready to suffer at the hands of all creatures without reserve, of your
nearest friends as well as of your enemies; never believe that any injury
can be done to you, but live in a state of entire abandonment to Divine
Providence, prepared to enter upon ways the most distressing, be they
exterior or interior; make no reservation with respect to any particular
cross; entertain no longer any desires; lose them all in the good pleasure
of God; let God alone suffice you, and behold you already enjoy the peace
of Paradise![57]

Though we suffer a disturbance in the inferior part of the soul, we may have peace in
the superior part of the soul, which sometimes remains hidden even from us.

The addition of this second spiritual power of indifference to the first power of
patience, yields tranquility. What is the state of the soul? – that's what we want to know.
Peace, answers Tronson. "She only desires that which God willeth: she loves what He
loveth: that alone which is displeasing to Him is hateful to her. So entirely is her heart
in conformity with God's holy Will, that she longs far more ardently that It should be
accomplished than that any desire of her own should be fulfilled. Thus does she dwell
always in perfect peace, abandoning herself wholly to God, and submitting joyfully to
whatever His Providence might appoint."[58] The peace that comes from the world is

---

57. Henri-Marie Boudon, *Devotion to the Nine Choirs of Holy Angels* (London: Burns,
     Oates, & Co., 1869) 133-34.

58. Tronson, *Examination of Conscience Upon Special Subjects*, 17-18.

of a different kind than this peace. The former comes from imposing one's will on surrounding conditions, the latter comes from obedience to God. The former is rigid and inflexible, the latter brings supple sweetness, which Libermann describes this way:

"Souls that come under that divine action of grace have sweetness and peace while still remaining strong and constant .... Holy Scripture describes the action of merciful Providence as 'reaching from end to end (i.e. from the beginning of its action to its fulfilment) with might, and disposing all things with sweetness.' Jesus' divine action, vigorous yet sweet, will, some day, take place in the soul of His beloved spouse."[59]

Access to this peace does not depend upon our biological death, and does not wait for us to leave the world for the desert. It depends on our baptismal death, and waits for us to leave worldliness for righteousness. St. Paul told us to be obedient in whatever state God's providence places us (1 Cor. 7:20), which de Sales interprets to mean that "one of the felicities of this life is to be pleased with the condition in which Providence has placed us: he who desires another, is never at peace. We should duly estimate the blessings which fall to our lot; but great care must be taken not to idolize them."[60]

Such peace is a characteristic of paradise, which is a place ablaze with the glory of God, and to such a place does liturgical abnegation direct us. The providential activities of God are designed to bring him glory, and we will never understand spiritual annihilation, resignation, purgation, or hidden sainthood if we cannot turn our attention to the liturgy he deserves. The soul is being prepared for Paradise, even here, says Surin, even now, "because she sees that all things are done as Providence ordains, and is infinitely better pleased than in doing her own will. She regards only the glory of God, seeks only to please Him, reposes sweetly on Him with a pure and disinterested love, possesses and embraces Him lovingly in her inmost heart, and in order to be more closely united with Him, detaches herself from all that might separate her from Him."[61] Resignation to the purifying and sanctifying stages of providence pleases God, and pleasing God is what we seek to do in liturgy. "Let's have no other thought in mind," begs Libermann, "except

---

59. Libermann, *Letters to Religious Sisters and Aspirants,* Spiritan Studies 5, vol. 1, 7.

60. De Sales, quoted in Camus, *Beauties of de Sales,* 215.

61. Surin, *Foundations of the Spiritual Life,* 18.

that of walking in the way traced for us by God's providence and endeavoring to foster His glory and save souls."[62]

We do not abandon ourselves to God's care for some utility we will derive, or for the mercantile motive of blessings we will derive. The primary motive of abandoning ourselves to providence is to liturgize God by giving him glory, by pleasing him, by honoring him with our surrender of faith, hope, and love. Then we can exclaim, with de Sales, "Oh my God! what consolation I feel in the certainty that we shall be one day eternally united in the will to serve and praise God! May His Divine Providence lead us by whatever way seems best to Him."[63] If we don't want to do this now, what makes us think we will want to do it in heaven? Our confidence (hope) comes from knowing (faith) that God wills our good (charity). These three theological virtues are celebrated repeatedly. "It is always for our good, if we on our part make use of it" (Eudes);[64] "he will turn all, even our frailties and failings, to our spiritual good" (de Castaniza);[65] "he lets nothing pass but what contributes, in a special manner, to our greater good and profit" (Rodriguez);[66] and "this providence is so powerful, that it not only delivers us from evil and leads us to good, but what is more, very often, by a wonderful effect, draws even good out of evil, which sometimes God permits the just themselves to fall in" (de Granada).[67]

This is the lesson of the cross imprinted upon the cosmos. Providence sweeps up into its eternal movement both material creature, other human beings, and our very soul. Our beatitude is the purpose of creation, says de Lombez, so both natural providence and redemptive providence will work hand in hand. "If God has created other men to enjoy His benefits with us, it is that we may have fellow-workers and fellow-helpers, all sharing in the good gifts of His Providence. He has made us for each other; and He has made us

---

62. Libermann, *Letters to Clergy and Religious*, Spiritan Series 9, vol. 5, 245.

63. De Sales, quoted by de Chantal, *The Depositions of St. Jane Frances de Chantal*, 88.

64. Eudes, *The Priest*, 57.

65. De Castaniza, *The Spiritual Conflict & Conquest*, 423.

66. Rodriguez, *The Practice of Christian and Religious Perfection*, vol. 1, 420.

67. De Granada, *The Sinner's Guide*, 99.

all for Himself. When He first created all these good things, were we not, each one of us, separately and individually, present to His all-seeing Eye?"[68]

---

68. De Lombez, *A Treatise on the Joy of the Christian Soul*, 51.

JUSTICE AND HOPE

The topic of justice could be approached in a variety ways: I could define it, locate it in the virtues, identify it in God's nature, see how Jesus's cross satisfied it, or consider the judgment of heaven and hell. But here I want to confine myself to one essential question: is it just of God to command abnegation? Is it upright, virtuous, and good of God to do so? What does the justice of God intend to do?

The Father's desire is for us to participate in the glory his Incarnate Son offers up, and bestows gifts of the Holy Spirit to make this possible for us. In short, God desires to include us in the perichoresis of love that flows within him: that is our liturgical life. But we are weighed down by the weight of worldliness, that chains us to honor, wealth, pride, pleasure, and in order to ascend with the Dove (Holy Spirit), we must be cut free from what oppresses. The annihilation of the old Adam is part of liturgizing in God – that is the connection I am trying to make between liturgy and abnegation.

John of Avila distinguishes two meanings of the word "world," and it is almost as if there are actually two worlds. "The word here does not refer here to the world created by God, which is good, created by the one who is the supreme Good. It is used for those who have no other feeling and no other love than for what is visible. Saint John calls this the 'pride of life, the concupiscence of the flesh, and the concupiscence of the eyes' (1 John 2:16-17)."[1] Cutting us free from that latter world is what the justice of God intends to accomplish. Liturgical abnegation is an operation put in motion by the justice of God. Both the motivation and extent of self-denial are conditional upon what God's justice seeks to attain, which is why Rodriguez correctly connects justice to holiness: "We give

---

1. John of Avila, *Audi, Filia*, 275.

the name of justice to righteousness and holiness of life, and we call those just, who are holy and virtuous."[2]

The classic definition of justice is "giving someone his due" – even the pagan philosophers realized this – and de Granada sketches its trifold application. "As it is the property of justice to give every one his due, whether it be God, our neighbor our ourself, so there are three sorts of virtues that compose it; some are particularly for the performance of the duty man owes to God, some, again, for that he owes his neighbor, and others for that he owes to himself."[3] Summarizing these in reverse order we find that justice in our case is to make our state of life orderly according to the law of *ordo amoris*; the justice in our neighbor's case is to give him the mercy and charity God has commanded him to have; and the justice in God's case is "that virtue which the divines call religion, whose object is the worship of God."[4] Religion is the act of justice we owe God. These three arenas of justice are interrelated, and we shall keep them together in our mind. Grou can therefore answer his own question about what God is up to with abnegation. "What does God ask of us, when He commands us to annihilate ourselves and to renounce ourselves? He asks of us to do ourselves justice, to put ourselves in our proper place and to acknowledge ourselves for what we really are."[5] Humility is putting ourselves into our exactly proper place, but since self-love continually deceives us on this point, Fenelon says we must let God's justice appraise us, instead of evaluating ourselves. "Instead of sitting in judgment on God, let Him judge you, and confess that you greatly need His ruling."[6]

When God bestows his gifts he does not relinquish his original claim to them. The earth, the heavens, and all therein remain his possession, so we may describe liturgical sacrifice as a sort of restoration – returning what we have stolen – and liturgical abnegation is founded upon this act of justice. When we deny the claims we have hitherto made upon creatures, deny our self-will, deny the belief that we are the ground of our own

2. Rodriguez, *The Practice of Christian and Religious Perfection*, vol. 1, 8.

3. De Granada, *The Sinner's Guide*, 329.

4. De Granada, *The Sinner's Guide*, 353.

5. Grou, *Manual for Interior Souls,* 187.

being, then justice is served, because justice is giving everything what it is due, and God is due all. This is why Bona places religion in

> the first place among the moral virtues; for it is devoted to those things which are directly and immediately appointed for the divine honor, and it is a sort of justice of the creature towards God, by which that same creature pays due worship to its Creator and Lord, But the excellence of the divine Majesty urges us to offer supreme honor to God, since he alone is good and powerful; he, "the King of kings and Lord of lords: and we, his people, and the sheep of his pasture," have been created to worship and love him; he, our end, our beatitude and supreme good."[7]

Just as a finite creature cannot compensate for sin against an infinite God, in the same way the finite creature cannot accomplish just worship to an infinite God. That is why Christ placed his liturgy in the hands of his Church to use. For our liturgy to be just, it must be united to the worship of the God-man.

What is just when it comes to God? In his book on humility, de Bergamo zeroes in on obedience. "Justice consists in our recognizing that God as our Creator has a right to command us, and that we as His creatures are bound to obey Him."[8] We are blessed if we hunger and thirst after justice because de Ravignan understands Jesus to be talking about the "hunger which establishes the kingdom of God in ourselves and others."[9] Grou summarizes by uniting justice, holiness, happiness, and abnegation. "By justice [Jesus] means holiness and the whole series of virtues that compose it. For only holiness can bring us near to God, who is holy in His essence and cannot be united to anything that is not so. To be happy, then, it is necessary that the Christian should desire to be holy, and make every effort to become so. The more he is devoured by that hunger and thirst the more he

---

7. Bona, *A Treatise of Spiritual Life*, 376.

8. De Bergamo, *Humility of Heart*, 42.

9. Gustave de Ravignan, *Ravignan's Last Retreat* (London: Burns and Oates, 1859) 96.

will one day be satisfied."[10] Justice is integrally bound to holiness: it serves holiness, seeks holiness, brings about holiness, and is ultimately for our beatitude.

The one thing God cannot unite himself to is sin, so if we join ourselves to God's justice, we must "take part with God against ourselves,"[11] says Olier. That is the hard part of abnegation, Eudes also recognizes: "Let me share in the zeal of Thy divine justice and in Thy hatred for sin, so that I may hate my sins as Thou dost hate them."[12] God's judgment on the sinner is God's censure of sin, and the sinner approves of this even in his own case, begging that justice will destroy whatever alienates him from God. Alonso Rodriguez finds a parallel increase of love (for God) and hate (for having offending God).

> The more this love of God increases in the soul, so its hate and abhorrence of self grow in proportion, as the soul becomes angry with itself or having offended a God of such tremendous Majesty, whom it has now come to love and know so well, and from whom it has received so many favors, to which it has responded by so many sins. It is angry and at odds with itself, and desires to avenge his ingratitude ... From this genuine contempt and abhorrence of self comes contempt for all the things of the world, its enjoyments and pleasures and amusements, for the soul is then entirely set upon pleasing its God and this is all its enjoyment and happiness, cost what it may.[13]

We actually desire to be put under justice, surprisingly enough. De Condren pictures the souls under the altar described in the book of Revelation, where they expect "from Him the last effect of divine adoption, the redemption and resurrection of their bodies. In this consists the justice they demand from God; crying with loud voice, that is, sighing with an ardent desire after the perfect reign of Jesus Christ and asking by zeal for the

---

10. Grou, *The School of Jesus Christ*, 104.

11. Olier, *Catechism of an Interior Life*, 108.

12. Eudes, *The Life and the Kingdom of Jesus in Christian Souls*, 121.

13. Alonso Rodriguez, *Saint Alphonsus Rodriguez: Autobiography*, 125.

justice of God, which is the cry of the soul, that sin may be entirely destroyed, and the reign of the prince of darkness be for ever at an end."[14] The unrepentant sinner flees God's justice; the converted sinner is drawn to God's justice, and zealously desires God's justice to reign. The righteous hunger and thirst for the fulfillment of divine law, even if it chastises now, because, de Estella points out, the great power of love can so subdue the flesh as to make it subject to the Spirit, and unite with the soul in rejoicing before God. "Holy love anticipates the joys of the resurrection, when the spirit shall have entire dominion over the flesh, by subordination, even here, the body to the soul."[15] Love accomplishes abnegation; abnegation is an anticipation of the joy of the resurrection.

Blosius outlines the steps a true penitent should take considering by eavesdropping on what God says about the penitent soul. (1) It is amazed to find that My mercy is so great ... that I receive him into My friendship just as if he had never been guilty at all; and (2) he finds his past falls affords him fresh occasions for love. Then

> (3) The same considerations fill him with a greater degree of self-hatred and displeasure, he is wroth with himself and detests himself for having despised Me, his loving God, who although I could justly have condemned and destroyed him have on the contrary spared and consoled him ...

> (4) The effect of these feelings is that the more clearly he sees My mercy towards him, the greater indignation does he feel against himself, as if he desired to avenge on himself the contempt he has manifested to Me.

> (5) From this it comes to pass that not content with seeking pardon for his sins and a return to My favour, he also desires to suffer, to be humiliated and punished for his past wicked opposition to Me. Wherefore, the more

---

14. Charles de Condren, *Eternal Sacrifice* (London: Thomas Baker, 1906) 152-53.

15. De Estella, *Meditations on the Love of God*, 10.

he finds himself comforted by Me, the more he abhors and detests his own unworthiness, [and] grieves for the enormity of his sins.[16]

To repeat, the same considerations of God's astonishing goodness also brings the penitent to hate having hated God, to detest himself for having despised God, to be wroth with himself, to feel an indignation against himself, to stir a desire to avenge his contempt, suffer, be humiliated, and grieve for his sins. Self-denial is a regret for having denied God. Put as a challenge, Blosius asks if we can love God's justice as much as we love his mercy. "When a soul has risen to this degree of zeal against itself and loveth My justice as much as My mercy, then its sins are all consumed as a little drop of water in a blazing furnace."[17]

God's just law is the destruction of sin, and a holy indignation is stirred up when Grou recognizes the convert hating himself for having been God's enemy.

> The first sentiment that every truly converted sinner experiences with
> regard to himself, is a hatred of himself. This hatred principally arises
> from his love for God. He considers himself as having been God's enemy;
> under this aspect he cannot but hate himself, because he loves God ...
> From hence follow the motions of a holy indignation against himself ...
> He enters into the interests of God against himself, he revenges them
> on himself; he arraigns himself with zeal, and declares against himself an
> implacable war.[18]

A holy anger is inspired in a person, but for this good: to make the person an ally in God's fight against sin! This is why the saints can sound so hard on themselves: the more they love God, the more they hate the sin they find concealed in the recesses of their soul. Love of God plus holy anger at sin co-operate a surrender to justice – they together

---

16. Blosius, *Comfort for the Fainthearted* (Westminster: Art and Book Company, 1908) 147.

17. Blosius, *Comfort for the Fainthearted*, 147.

18. Grou, *Morality Augustine*, vol. 2, 227-29.

accomplish a surrender willingly made, with all the disciplines included. We should deny what God denies, says Charles Gay.

> That which God denies in us is that blind and perverse power which strives to ruin His designs, to contradict His instructions, to disregard His rights, to calumniate His perfections, to violate His precepts, to repel His gifts, to struggle against His love, and to drive away from us His Holy Spirit. What in us God detest and denies is, then, positively what deceives, perverts, and depraves us; what kills, what destroys us, both in this world and in the next.[19]

Who should not deny such things when found in oneself? Who would not willingly place oneself under justice's opposition to such things? It is an act of hope to align oneself with God. The sacraments aid in this. Olier sees it in the very first sacrament: "it is then an effect of the justice of God, that, in Baptism, the love of contempt, sufferings and poverty, is imprinted in the heart of man,"[20] and de Condren sees it in the sacrament of Holy Communion, which we approach in order that Jesus "may destroy whatever in us is contrary to God the Father – the old Adam and his sorrowful heritage, the reign of sin and Satan, and the cruel tyranny of self-love; and so coming we must ask of the Divine Humanity to put forth the Right Hand of His Justice, to crucify the old man in us and to confirm the Kingdom of the Adorable Trinity."[21]

We can also learn something about justice by considering its opposite, namely, injustice.

Justice is humility that liturgizes God, so Eudes understands pride as "that injustice which robs God of His glory to attribute it to self."[22] Lallemant agrees. "The desire

---

19. Gay, *The Christian Life and Virtues*, vol. 1, 306-07.

20. Olier, *Catechism of an Interior Life*, 51.

21. De Condren, quoted in H.L. Sidney Lear *The Revival of Priestly Life in the Seventeenth Century in France* (London: Rivingtons, 1873) 121.

22. Eudes, *Meditation on Various Subjects*, 214.

we have to be esteemed, praised, and honoured, is nothing but injustice."[23] As perfect justice himself, God is moved to hate the pride of both Satan and sinner, and so moves to overcome pride with its opposite, namely, humility. Grou finds the whole system of humility a reason for hope.

> Is it not evident that the entire system of Christian morality bears on humility, inculcates humility, inspires humility? To embrace interior abjection, to submit to exterior humiliation, to dread only what exalts us in our own opinion and that of others, to have no desire but for contempt, to entertain a holy ambition for it, to believe that we can never meet it in proportion to our deserts, this is the foundation, the progress, and the consummation of Christian perfection. Thus alone is God really glorified by his creatures.[24]

God is only liturgized when his creatures are humble, embrace abjection, and deny themselves. This the fallen angels would not do: the angelic fall was a breach of liturgy. As an idol is the opposite of God, so anti-liturgy is the opposite of liturgy. The disruption echoed from the spiritual to the material realm, and when Adam and Eve sought their own divinity, their fall was a breach of peace. The citizens of Eden could not say what de Caussade believes every person in peace can say: "I feel pleasure in finding myself rebuffed, when it pleases him thus to mortify and humble me in his presence; so that his divine contentment is always mine, because everywhere and in all things I wish only for his good pleasure."[25] Nothing discontents a humility that is not upset even with contradictions to its own will. This humility was lost in the Fall. Pride is anti-liturgy because a person resists God in favor of himself, and anti-liturgy is a condition of injustice, thinks Grou.

---

23. Lallemant, *The Spiritual Doctrine of Father Louis Lallemant, ed. Faber*, 288.

24. Grou, *The Interior of Jesus and Mary*, vol. 1,145-46.

25. Jean-Pierre de Caussade, *On Prayer: Spiritual Instructions on the Various States of Prayer According to the Doctrine of Bossuet, Bishop of Meaux* (New York: Benziger Brothers, 1931) 240.

When we can well understand this fact, it is easy to understand also
how unjust is the human. This injustice consists in man having a
great consideration for himself, esteeming himself, loving himself, and
thinking himself worthy of esteem and love; in his constituting himself
the centre of everything, and referring everything to himself; in making
the love he has for himself and his own interests the secret motive of all
his thoughts, words, and actions. He looks at everything from his own
point of view; he seeks himself in everything; it seems to him as if the
whole universe, and all creatures, and even God Himself, only existed on
his account.[26]

Justice is giving what is due, and if we constitute ourselves as the center of everything,
we give neither God nor ourselves what each is justly due. When a proud person sets
himself up as his own judge, then his attentions, affections, motives, relationships, and
intentions all blindly revolve around himself, as Libermann points out. "When the
passions are strong and strongly influence a judgment, then not only is balance of justice
upset but the judge becomes blind about the object of his judgment."[27]

Our injustice offends God in three ways. First, we want to lead ourselves, when the
Almighty himself should be our governor. Libermann thinks our blindness would be
comical if it were not so hazardous to our soul's health.

How unjust we are, dear Father, and how wanting in good sense! A blind
man entrusts himself to a small dog which leads him wherever the animal
wishes to go, and the man follows without knowing where he is going.
But we, wretched men, more blind than those born blind, although we
have such a clear-sighted and tender-hearted leader, do not permit Him to

---

26. Grou, *Manual for Interior Souls,* 180-81.

27. Francis Libermann, *Jesus Through Jewish Eyes*, vol. 2 (Dublin: Paraclete Press, 1999)
162.

guide us. This is, to my thinking, the greatest blindness imaginable. What
an injustice toward our most sweet and most lovable Lord Jesus![28]

Second, although God has renounced his right of punishment, yet, sighs Lallemant,
we will not renounce ourselves in the slightest.

> Strange injustice of the human heart! God has forgiven us venial sins
> innumerable ... and yet we cannot forget a disobliging word which has
> been said to us, or a slight affront which has been offered us; we continue
> to preserve the remembrance of it, and wait only for an opportunity to
> testify our displeasure. This comes of the foolish esteem and false love
> which we entertain for ourselves. We think more of our own interests
> than those of God; pride blinds us.[29]

And third, we spurn our freedom, as well as its price, only to return to what Crasset
calls pernicious masters.

> Do you know the price that was paid for you? Do you know what you
> owe? You owe your life to the Son of God, who has given his for you. What
> injustice, then, to give it to the world, the flesh, and the devil, which are
> your most deadly enemies. Did the enemy of souls die for you? Did the
> prince of this world and concupiscence shed their blood for you? Have
> they ever done you good? Can they ever do you good? Can they love
> you? Have they a heaven to offer you? My brethren, you belong, not to
> yourselves, but to Him who, in dying for you, paid an infinite price for
> your salvation.[30]

---

28. Libermann, *Letters to Clergy and Religious*, Spiritan Series 8, vol. 4, 113.

29. Lallemant, *The Spiritual Doctrine of Father Louis Lallemant, ed. Faber*, 106.

30. John Crasset, *Christian Considerations; or Devout Meditations for Every Day in the
    Year* (New York: P. O'Shea, 1864) 259.

When the theologians of liturgical abnegation speak about our "nothingness" it is to avoid these offenses. Our existence is a free gift, our forgiveness is a free gift, our virtues are freely given, and yet we posture ourselves as though we had something to offer to God in negotiation. The concept of nothingness will deserve its own chapters, but Grou can summarize it for us here by saying it means humility and full dependence upon God. "What rights can a thing have that is nothing? ... If his very existence is a free gift, certainly everything else he has is much more so. It is then a formal injustice on our part to refuse to be treated, or to refuse to treat ourselves, as if we were really nothing."[31] If we come from nothing, and if we live entirely from God's grace, such that both our existence and salvation comes from beyond our own power, then we can be said to be doing nothing. Justice is giving someone his due, and God is due our love, so Gay makes this the basis of the Christian life. "The love with which God loves us is the rule and the model of that with which we ought to love Him ... What then must we do to imitate in its activity, the love of God for us? Make many acts of love; do many acts for love; do all your acts through love."[32]

Humility will also receive its own chapters, but we can summarize what our authors will say by naming the three steps of perfection in humility: accept humiliation, be not offended if despised, and take pleasure when we are contemned by others. It is not enough for us to know that we possess no virtue without God; we must also be pleased that others know it. Croiset catches out this failure by noticing how we are led up to it.

> How come so many Professors of Piety to be so very sensible in the imaginary points of Honour? The tone of a voice, a disobliging word disturbs them. Let them make as much use as they please of the words Modest, and humble, true humility is inseparable from Patience and sweetness. Many think that they are truly humble because they have a mean opinion of themselves, but they deceive themselves if they are not willing that others should have the same thoughts of them. It is not

---

31. Grou, *Manual for Interior Souls,* 188.

32. Charles Gay, *The Christian Life and Virtues Considered in the Religious State*, vol. 3 (London: Burnes & Oates, 1879) 4 and 29.

sufficient to know that we have no true virtue or merit, we must be willing to have others believe it too.[33]

That satisfaction is the final accomplishment of humility. In the final stage of humility, we do not merely accept whatever comes, we want whatever comes – it is the final stage of surrender to justice, Croiset says. "Any one who is convinced that he is very miserable, is not offended if he is despised: he sees that it is only just. A humble man, whatever bad treatment he may receive, thinks that justice is done him. Men do not esteem me; they are right, they agree in this with God, and with the Angels. Whoever has deserved hell, thinks that contempt is his due."[34]

A common misunderstanding of humility thinks it involves making a low estimate of oneself, and taking a lower place than deserved in the hierarchy. This is not true, says Grou. "Humility [is] a virtue which does not consist, as it is generally reckoned, in placing ourselves beneath what we are, but in doing ourselves the exactest and the strictest justice."[35] In other words, humility does not degrade: it knows the grade precisely. Humility understands a thing's position on the scale of God's justice. Once a nun described humility to Madame Acarie "as the self attribution of all sorts of defects," but she replied, "Sister, humility is not to be found in all that; it consists in complete recognition of one's own nothingness in all things. There is in me much that prevents God's action in my soul. A leather bag is best filled by being laid flat on the ground. I fail exceedingly in not humbling myself before God."[36] That is why Lallemant calls the knowledge of God the root of humility. "For it is impossible to know and feel our baseness, except in relation to some grandeur with which we may compare it. In vain do we think of the little that is in us: we shall never again feel humbled about it if we do not

33. Jean Croiset, *A Spiritual Retreat for One Day in Every Month* (London: Printed by Thomas Hales, 1704) 260.

34. Croiset, *Devotion to the Sacred Heart of Jesus*, 82-83.

35. Grou, *Morality Augustine*, vol. 1, 242.

36. Madame Acarie, in *Barbe Acarie, Wife and Mystic. A biography by Lancelot Sheppard* (London: Burns Oates, 1953) 147-48.

compare it with God's infinite perfections."[37] Grou adds that this conclusion can only come out of the twin knowledge of God and ourselves.

> If we know ourselves, we do ourselves justice; we think of ourselves exactly as we are; we see ourselves as God sees us. And what does He see? Sin and nothingness; and no more. We have no other possessions of our own; everything else comes from God, and must be attributed to Him. If we know ourselves thus, what must be our humility, and our contempt and hatred of self?

> I am absolutely nothing. Throughout eternity I was not, and there was no reason why I should exist, nor why I should be what I am. My existence is the simple effect of God's Will; He bestowed it on me as it pleased Him. He preserves it; if His mighty Hand were not upholding me every moment, I should fall back into nothingness.[38]

A power or vitality will be required in order to restore us to justice before God, but a power cannot be exercised without the guidance of the intellect, so Grou finds the starting point for our recovery to be a true view of reality. "Where is the man who studies his self-love seriously, perceives its injustice, and is willing to admit that it opposes, not religion alone, but also reason? ... Hardly anyone is willing to face self-knowledge; and the obstacle is self-love, which shrinks from the sight of its own deformity."[39] Such knowledge would give us hope; justice produces hope, and hope embraces justice.

God's commands are reasonable, and reason could recognize his justice if it were not warped into self-justification by self-love. Having been created in a disposition of tending towards God alone, this should be easy and natural. It belongs to the order of things.

---

37. Louis Lallemant, *The Spiritual Doctrine*, ed. by Patricia M. Ranum (Boston: Institute of Jesuit Sources, Boston College, 2016) 289.

38. Grou, *The Spiritual Maxims*, 6.

39. Grou, *The School of Jesus Christ*, 75.

But Grou diagnoses how the sinner violates this order. "The malice of the sinner consists in knowing the justice of this order, and in voluntarily transgressing it; he inverts the established law of God, and for an inferior advantage which his passions propose to him, he makes no account of his sovereign good: and this is at once the excess of blindness and of injustice."[40] God alone determines the order of justice that leads to happiness, and we are not in a position to negotiate those terms. The terms of happiness have been fixed by God Incarnate, whom Grou says is the only proper judge.

> The person who offers a prize has a right to fix the terms on which he will award it. Eternal happiness is the prize that Jesus Christ offers us, and the condition on which He promises it to us is that we should be just. But our justice must conform to His meaning of the word; it must be a justice of which He alone is the judge, and which therefore must be conceived and determined in accordance, not with human, but with divine ideas.[41]

We live now in a state of injustice, no longer in the original justice gifted to Adam and Eve, and de Ravignan knows that our perfection consists "in obtaining a victory over ourselves – in surmounting our passions and appetites and reestablishing ourselves as much as it is possible in a happy state of original justice."[42]   Doing so requires prayer, though he reminds us that prayer is only a means and not the end. The end is submission of the will. "Though iron is hard, yet fire softens it and renders it fit for any use we please. Prayer works the same effect upon our heart, which being naturally hard, has a repugnance to mortification and contempt, and feels it very difficult to submit to the will of another."[43] This difficulty, this repugnance, this loss of the instinctive turn toward God, means that divine love has become difficult to us, and de Ravignan admits it is what gives abnegation its bad name.

---

40. Grou, *Morality Augustine*, vol. 1, 226-27.

41. Grou, *The School of Jesus Christ*, 123.

42. De Ravignan, *The Practice of Christian and Religious Perfection*, vol. 1, 269.

43. De Ravignan, *The Practice of Christian and Religious Perfection*, vol. 1, 269.

We are not inclined for it, it is hard to us to love God. And when, in the purity of His spirit, in His holiness, He wishes us to love Him for His own sake, we prefer this earth and carnal things which flatter and please our senses to Him; we pursue an ideal which is but of this world. The love of God is not the end to which we instinctively turn, and if grace sometimes leads us back towards it, sometimes in our days of retreat, recollection, and a prayer, it does not last; and yet, in God alone is to be found rest and ' happiness![44]

Yet longing for justice gives us hope.

Loving God for his own sake is the state of "indifference" to which Fenelon so often refers, and it enables a person to continue loving God even when the sensible pleasure of grace is wanting. The strength of indifference enables a person to continue loving God in his superior soul even when the inferior soul has lost its consolations. There is a love of perfection that is superior to all agreeable sensation, and which can continue to motivate docility to God. The saints suffered, Fenelon acknowledges, yet "these divine Lovers continued steadfast in their submission to the supreme will; not because it was delightful, but because it was just."[45] Why obey? Why submit? Why deny self, flesh, and world? Because it is just to do so. We may be confident that God intends our happiness, but we also assured that happiness stands on the shoulders of justice, which is only observed when we love God for his supreme perfection alone, independent of our own desire for happiness or fear of punishment. Therefore Crasset says the first duty of justice is to submit our minds to God, "for as a man has received every faculty he possesses from God, he ought to offer Him principally the homage of his mind and will, which are above all the rest."[46] It is right and just for God's will to be ours, and for our will to correspond

---

44. De Ravignan, *Conferences on the Spiritual Life*, 212.

45. Fenelon, quoted in Andrew Ramsay, *The Life of François Fenelon, Archbishop and Duke of Cambray*. (London: printed for Paul Vaillant, 1723) 181-82.

46. Crasset, *Christian Consideration*, 127.

to his in all things; then Crasset can exclaim: "Oh, what happiness, not to have any other rule of judgment than the judgment of God, no rule of the will but the will of God!"[47]

It is true that justice will involve chastisement. The adversities and trials we undergo will be both purgative and punitive, and John of the Cross says the latter will bring about the former. But since this is all an exercise of divine justice, "be not made sad by the adverse events of this life, for you know not the good they bring with them, ordained in the justice of God, for the everlasting joy of the elect."[48] The just soul – the one that has a rightly-aligned will – shall attain happiness, and that same soul should not grumble in the desert when the ascetical struggle against the passions includes punishment of sins. She will not grumble if her eyes have been opened, Fenelon concludes.

> The condemned creature will only see justice in his condemnation. Thou wilt show him clearly that thou hast done all that thou shouldest for the cultivation of thy vine ... Now man does not see this point, because he does not know his own heart. He realizes neither the graces offered to him, nor his own real feelings, nor his inner resistance. In thy judgement thou wilt unfold it all to his own eyes. He will see himself. He will be horrified by the sight.[49]

There is a risk of despair when the sinner sees what he has done against himself, but there is hope in justice upon sight of what God is doing on the sinner's behalf.

The punishment of sin is a mark of God's justice. We admit this happily and readily in the abstract, but we hesitate when it comes to applying it to our personal case. We should not, says Grou. The just soul should accept chastisements simply because they are a satisfaction of God's justice, and the soul delights when God is satisfied. "She [the soul] does not consider what happens to her as a trial, but rather as a just chastisement, too slight in comparison with what her sins deserve. Acquiescing with all that God makes her suffer,

---

47. Crasset, *Christian Considerations*, 416.

48. John of the Cross, *Spiritual Maxims*, in *The Complete Works of Saint John of the Cross*, vol. 2, 358.

49. Fenelon, *Christian Perfection*, 127.

she finds her peace, her strength, and her happiness in humility; she is delighted that God should be satisfied, and that at the expense of all that she has He should receive what is due to His Divine justice."[50] Punishment of sin is a mark of God's justice – even when it is a punishment of *our* sins. Perhaps especially if it is a punishment of our sins, Grou adds. "If He makes us experience some of the effects of His justice, we should humbly submit ourselves to Him, saying with the prophet, 'I will bear the weight of the anger of the Lord, because I have sinned against Him.' It is quite right that, as I am a sinner, I should satisfy the Divine justice; I ought not to wish to dispute the right of God to punish me."[51]

So here is a deep mystery. When fallen creation is rectified, then God is glorified, which means our very punishment can become part of the liturgy being rendered to God. We liturgize God by accepting his justice, even in its punitive form, says Eudes. "In homage to His divine justice, I submit with my whole heart to the sentence of death Thou didst pass upon me even at the beginning of the world, recognizing that I have deserved it not only by original sin, but each time I have committed sin."[52] Liturgical abnegation is submitting to God's justice, submission is reverence, reverence is adoration, and adoration is liturgical homage, so Eudes counsels his readers to "humble yourself in face of all your faults and infidelities as a whole, and adore God's justice, offering yourself to Him to suffer all the pains ordained by His holy will, in homage to His justice, and considering yourself most unworthy that this divine justice should be exercised upon you."[53] But the lesson of Job is difficult for us.

This mystery is profound, and when inadequate language tries to express it, it can sound harsh to anyone who does not penetrate into the mystery far enough. But it is not as harsh as we may suppose when we place it in the context of justice, Grou points out. "We are not always willing to accept the doctrine of our own nothingness, or of the necessity of a death unto self; and yet it is a true doctrine, and not really harsh as we may suppose. When God requires such humiliation of self, He only exacts that which is

50. Grou, *Manual for Interior Souls*, 312.

51. Grou, *Manual for Interior Souls*, 211.

52. Eudes, *The Life and the Kingdom of Jesus in Christian Souls*, 312.

53. Eudes, *The Life and the Kingdom of Jesus in Christian Souls*, 86.

His due, He would only have us realise our true position."[54] We readily confess our sins
at the beginning of each mass, but rarely connect this to its consequence. De Sales asks
"who is there that has not sinned and consequently has not deserved punishment? Has
anyone offended you? Well, think how often you have offended God! Surely, therefore,
it is meet that creatures, the instruments of His justice, should punish you."[55] Eudes
notes that the punishment is not pointless; it serves expiation. "In homage to Thy divine
justice, I now willingly accept all the sufferings and penances it shall please Thee to inflict
upon me, whether in this world or in the next, in expiation of my faults, to satisfy for the
dishonor I have given Thee today."[56] But de Granada admits this is sometimes hard to
understand until a person recognizes his state of heart, and this must sometimes be done
retrospectively.

> My desires gave law to my life. I blindly obeyed my concupiscences, and
> I made as little account of thee as if I had never known thee. I was that
> fool who said in his heart there is no God, (Psalm xiii. 1.) because I lived
> a long time in such a manner as if I believed that there was none. I never
> did anything for love of thee; I never dreaded thy justice; I never refrained
> from evil for fear of thy laws; I never gave thee the thanks I ought for thy
> benefits; and knowing that thou art everywhere, I never abstained from
> sin in thy presence. I granted my eyes whatsoever they desired, and never
> used the least resistance to my heart to restrain it from any pleasure.[57]

Though difficult for our clouded eyes, de Sales requires the sinner to recognize that
"justice is no less the child of [God's] infinite goodness than his compassion."[58] God's

54. Grou, *The Hidden Life of the Soul*, 181.

55. De Sales, quoted in Camus, *The Spirit of St. Francis de Sales*, 172.

56. Eudes, *The Life and the Kingdom of Jesus in Christian Souls*, 122.

57. De Granada, *A Memorial of a Christian Life*, 275.

58. John Camus, *The Beauties of St. Francis de Sales* (London: Longman, Rees, Orme, Brown, and Green, 1829) 52.

goodness produces both justice and compassion, and if we love his goodness, we should love both the offspring. Both, I say. We may not, therefore, suppose some conflict between the goodness and justice of God; or between the wisdom and mercy of God; or between the justice and mercy of God. John of Avila seems to suggest God uses both his right and left hands on us: "in his infinite wisdom he sees [our] infirmity and, by his mercy and justice together, cures and heals them."[59] He adds that all God's attributes stream forth from his simplicity. "The Lord God is just and merciful. When he looks upon our faults in his justice, they provoke him to wrath, and the more sins we have, the greater is the punishment to which we provoke him. But when he looks upon our sins in mercy, they do not move him to wrath but to compassion, and he does not regard them as an offense against him but as an evil for us."[60] The sinner and saint (often the same person) willingly embrace the suffering, even if their inferior nature is reluctant, because it will honor God. "In spite of the reluctance of my own mind," confesses Eudes, "I desire to embrace this affliction to the full extent of my will in homage to Thy divine justice, in submission to Thy holy will, in honor of Thy extreme sufferings on earth, in satisfaction for my sins, to accomplish Thy designs for me, and as something which comes from Thy beloved hand and from Thy Heart overflowing with love for me."[61]

Understanding the justice of God requires a true view of the world, a true view of God, and a true view of ourselves in our fallen state. It was the first sin, says de Granada, "that made God draw the sword."[62] If a person is born in original sin, and if he has further stained himself with actual sins, and has accumulated innumerable debts against divine justice, then "whatever trial he may suffer from God, whatever ill-treatment he may have to bear from his neighbour, has he any right to complain?" asks Grou. "Can he accuse God of severity, or men of injustice?"[63] Adding personal sins to our solidarity with Adam

---

59. John of Avila, *Audi, Filia*, 66.

60. John of Avila, *Audi, Filia*, 85.

61. Eudes, *The Life and the Kingdom of Jesus in Christian Souls*, 162.

62. De Granada, *The Sinner's Guide*, 229.

63. Grou, *Manual for Interior Souls*, 190.

has compounded our guilt, and where there is guilt, we can expect to find God's justice, says de Granada, because this is reality.

> Turn your eyes which way you please, and you shall scarce see any thing but sins, like men in the midst of the sea, who have no other object but sky and water. And can you see all these sins without seeing justice too? Can you be in the middle of the ocean, and see no water? And if all this world is nothing but an ocean of sins, it must needs be an ocean of justice. There is no need of going down into hell to see how the divine justice manifests itself there, we may see it plainly enough in this world.[64]

Grou surveys three types of persons who suffer God's just punishment, and asks for which one is it terrible? Only one, he suggests.

> Is it for those *children of God who love Him* and serve Him as a Father, who are determined to refuse Him nothing and to displease Him in nothing? No. If these children love God, God loves them still more; He sees that their faults are not faults of malice, but of imperfection and human weakness; at the first look of love and sorrow that they turn to Him He will forgive them; and even if He has to punish them He will punish them in this world, in the way that is most advantageous for their salvation.

> *Is it for the sinners who return to God* sincerely that His justice is terrible ? No. They experience the effects of His great mercy; and often they are treated with so much tenderness and love that even the just are jealous of them; we have only to think of Mary Magdalen and of the Prodigal Son.

---

64. De Granada, *The Sinner's Guide*, 233, 234.

The Divine justice is only terrible for *those who will not have recourse to His mercy*, either through presumption or through despair.[65]

Wrath is love destroying that which would destroy love. Justice is love destroying that which would destroy man, and denigrate the neighbor, and dishonor God. Justice repairs these dislocations, like easing a bone back into its socket. We long for the day of justice, instead of fearing it. Abnegation is the doorway to the land of the living, and liturgy is doing the world the way the world was meant to be done (as my teacher, Aidan Kavanagh, used to say), wherein a man daily receives humility, his neighbor receives charity, and God receives worship.

---

65. Grou, *Manual for Interior Souls*, 272-73, emphases added. Nearly the same wording is also used in *Hidden Life of the Soul*, 131-32,

JUSTICE AND MERCY

The paradoxical relationship of justice with mercy is a mystery to our finite minds because we think there are two purposes when we see two operations, as if God sometimes feels merciful toward us, but is other times stirred to justice. But this is not true. He is *always and only* working toward our holiness, for his glory (the twin purposes of liturgy), and does so with both his justice and mercy. Justice wants our perfection, and God's mercy works for our perfection. Love seeks happiness in the objects it loves, but God alone gives us our felicity, and Massillon calls the search for happiness in a creature an "injustice of that love."[1] So when mercy brings us to love our Creator, mercy is restoring justice. Mercy serves justice, it does not negate it, cancel it, sidestep it, or bypass it.

We make a mistake by pitting mercy against justice, and to give an example, it is like the mistake of pitting meekness against anger. Nepveu defines meekness as "a virtue which has for its object to repress or to govern anger: it represses anger when that passion is excited without reason or contrary to reason."[2] So meekness is not an alternative to anger, it is the governance of anger. One does not choose between being meek or being angry, one should be both, and simultaneously. One can use anger insofar as it is "a movement excited in the soul to repel an evil which threatens or offends us."[3] And one must use meekness because it is where we find rules for anger's proper government. Nepveu identifies three possibilities of anger according to the evil it must repel. Anger is called *indignation* if

---

1. John-Baptist Massillon *Sermons by John-Baptist Massillon, Bishop of Clermont* (London: Printed for Thomas Tegg, 1839) 233.

2. Francis Nepveu, *The Spirit of Christianity, or the Conformity of the Christian with Jesus Christ* (New York: Edward Dunigan & Brother, 1859) 206.

3. Nepveu, *The Spirit of Christianity*, 207.

an evil has offended what reason knows is our good. Anger is called *zeal* if the evil has offended God by attacking his truth or justice. Anger is called *resentment* or *desire of vengeance* if an evil has wounded our own self-love and so stirred animosity. The first is just; the second is holy; the third is disorderly and unjust. Meekness governs the first by not letting it degenerate into bitterness or spite; it moderates the second by not letting it be carried into indiscretion; it stifles the third entirely, because resentment and desire of revenge is irregular.

Now, God would never be angry in the irregular sense of having a desire for revenge. He is not angry out of an excited passion, or without reason, or contrary to reason. But he can be angry in the first two ways: indignant over what the devil is doing, and zealous for restoring truth and happiness. And I am suggesting that as meekness and anger co-ooperate, so mercy and justice co-operate. Wrath can be called love destroying that which would destroy love, and mercy and justice cooperate in wrath. Justice and mercy are not opposed to each other, they rather join hands to lead us to an indissoluble union with God in heaven. Both are acts of the same God – as if he is ambidextrous. He will accomplish his end by both his left and right hands.

Both justice and mercy are tools in service of his holiness, as Libermann makes abundantly clear.

> God is infinitely and essentially holy. This holiness of God in his dealing with his creatures appears in two ways: through his mercy and through his justice. When it shows itself through his mercy, it transmits itself to creatures; when through his justice, it rejects them.

> Nevertheless God created us in a design of mercy and in order to communicate himself to us in his holiness, thus his mercy is never taken back. It always far surpasses justice in his dealings with us.[4]

How does God choose whether to use mercy or justice on us?

---

4. Libermann, *Jesus Through Jewish Eyes*, vol. 3, 209.

God's justice only acts when forced to, that is to say, when the creature refuses mercy. First, it acts when forced to for this reason, that God necessarily has dealings with his creature; these dealings have only one purpose: to draw the creature towards himself or to repel it. Now if the creature in his free will refuses God's merciful action of drawing it to himself, then God has to repel his creation. This is his justice. Both actions give him glory, because both are manifestations of his holiness. Therefore we necessarily procure the glory of our Creator God. If we are not willing to bring it about for our happiness by accepting divine mercy, we will bring it about for our unhappiness by becoming the object of his holy and infinite justice.[5]

Both mercy and justice give God glory (his ultimate purpose) because both are manifestations of his holiness. Souls will not enter into God until they have gone completely out of themselves: deification twins with abnegation. Mercy's goal is for us to enter into God. But how can that be done? By being taken out of oneself, which is accomplished by the trial of inexorable justice. An anonymous writer puts these words in God's mouth: "The hour of Justice always announces the hour of mercy close at hand; the heaviness in my arm as Dispenser of Justice always signals the pressing need to pour out my Heart as Savior. The function of my justice is to 'clear the way' for mercy. Justice is its herald."[6] We often think of mercy and justice as antipodes, like weights on different trays of the scale. If we start from that perspective, then God seems to change – at one point feeling justice toward us, and at another feeling mercy toward us. But Fenelon recognizes that this cannot be.

He forms no new will respecting us; it is not He that changes, but we. When we are righteous and good, we are conformable to his will and agreeable to Him; when we depart from well doing and cease to be good, we cease to be conformable to Him and to please Him. This is the immutable standard which the changeable creature is continually

---

5. Libermann, *Jesus Through Jewish Eyes*, vol. 3, 209.

6. Anonymous, *The Redeemer's Call to Consecrated Souls*, 168.

approaching and leaving. His justice against the wicked and his love towards the righteous are the same thing; it is the same quality that unites Him to everything that is good, and is incompatible with everything that is evil. Mercy is the goodness of God, beholding our wickedness and striving to make us good; perceived by us in time, it has its source in the eternal love of God for his creature.[7]

Mercy beholds our wickedness, pities us, and thus justice begins its operations against sin and wickedness. Justice beholds our weakness, pities us, and thus mercy begins its operation of redemption. Do not pit the two poles of the paradox against each other. Justice and mercy are not antithetical, they are antinomical. So Eudes says that God "deserves no less praise for the effects of His justice than for those of His mercy, since all His divine attributes are equally holy and worthy of adoration. Many are the reasons to bless and glorify Jesus, who so commands your adoration and love![8]" De Granada admits the effects of each are different, but insists that both justice and mercy stream from the one heart of the one God.

> the purity of God's essence allows of no difference or distinction. So that his being is his essence, his essence is his power, his power is his will, his will is his understanding, his understanding is his being, his being is his wisdom, his wisdom is his justice, his justice is his mercy. And though the effects of the one are contrary to those of the other, because the duty of mercy is to pardon, and that of justice to punish; they are, notwithstanding, so perfectly one and the same thing in him, that his mercy is his justice, and his justice is his mercy.[9]

---

7. Fenelon, *Spiritual Progress*, 5.

8. Eudes, *The Life and the Kingdom of Jesus in Christian Souls*, 214.

9. De Granada, *The Sinner's Guide*, 12.

Justice wants what mercy wants, and mercy wants what justice wants, and God uses both pardon and punishment to bring about his designs, as de Castaniza recognizes. Even our chastisements include mercy.

> In this fatherly chastisement there is both Mercy and Justice. *Justice*, because we have often shut the doors of our hearts against God, giving a deaf ear to His calls, and therefore it is just that we should now call and knocked at the gate of His mercy, and not be heard. *Mercy*, because our sufferings are small in comparison to our deserts. If this be most true, why lament we are misfortune? Is there any proportion between time and eternity, betwixt this desolation and the never-ending lamentations of the damned in hell?

> Let us, then, receive and kiss His paternal rod with filial reverence.[10]

Justice demands that the debt owed to God must be paid in order to gain admittance to heaven; the debt is paid by making sacrifice; the sacrifice God will not refuse is his own Son's sacrifice; a humble and contrite heart attains that merit; mercy creates such a heart; mercy fulfills justice; thus they do not contradict each other. De Condren summarizes:

> He who gains admittance into the temple of the heavenly sacrifice must have paid all that he owes to the divine justice; he must have purified himself from the smallest stains, which the holiest contract on earth. Hence the Council of Trent does not only say that the whole life of a sinner should be a continual penance, but the whole life of a Christian; in order to will, preserve, and increase the innocence and purity demanded by the sacrifice and communion of the holy and adorable Eucharist.[11]

---

10. De Castaniza, *The Spiritual Conflict*, 476.

11. De Condren, *Eternal Sacrifice*, 201.

In fact, we may measure God's justice by his mercy: the amount he gives of one is the amount he will give of the other, in de Granada's view.

> Since God is equal in all his attributes, because all that is in him is God, it follows, that his justice is no less in itself than his mercy is; and as, by the thickness of one arm, we may judge how big the other is, so may we know how great the arm of God's justice, by that of his mercy, since they are both equal ...

> If, then, he punishes with so much rigor, with what sweet delights must he fill the souls of those that love him? If his arm is so heavy, when he holds it out to chastise, how light must it be when stretched out to caress. For he is more wonderful in his works of mercy than in those of justice.[12]

Some of Crasset's passages reflect on justice and mercy, involving God and ourselves. If we are frightened of God's justice, it is because we are unaware of the greatness of His mercy.

> O God, my Father
> I have not known You till now.
> I was frightened at Your justice.
> I knew not the greatness of Your mercy.
> However enormous my crimes,
> They are not greater than Your goodness.
> I will never distrust Your love.
> When I see the abyss of my misery,
> I will invoke the abyss of Your mercy

---

12. De Granada, *The Sinner's Guide*, 81 and 120.

Since fulness flows into emptiness,
And abundance seeks for indigence.[13]

The attributes of justice and mercy are not really in conflict, they only appear in conflict because man oscillates between the despair and presumption.

Why fly from God who seeks you?
Waits for you, opens His arms,
Loves you so tenderly?
Despair is worse than presumption.
Presumption combats the justice of God.
Despair combats His mercy.
It is more natural for God,
To pardon than to punish.[14]

God desires mercy, but our sin requires justice, so the path to peace is to learn how to properly use mercy.

God is for you a rule of mercy.
You are for Him a rule of justice.
Unless you use mercy as He does,
He will take vengeance as you do.
If you love; He will love you.
If you hate; He will hate you.
If you excuse; He will excuse you.
If you condemn; He will condemn you.
If you pardon; He will pardon you.
If you punish; He will punish you.[15]

---

14. Crasset, *Meditations for Every Day in the Year, Pentecost to Advent*, 70.

15. Crasset, *Meditations for Every Day in the Year, Pentecost to Advent*, 349.

If the objective is beatitude, then justice must mortify whatever would poison our happiness. And although shocking to common opinion, Grou says this makes justice sweet! It works for our happiness, not against it. "O Jesus, how sweet would this penance be to me, if I did but practice it. How merciful is Thy Justice! in order to satisfy it, to expiate my sins, it does but sentence me to mortify the passions which poison the happiness of my life, to renounce a world whose seduction can only make me unhappy, and to live with Thee only, and for Thee only, Who art alone the Source of all consolation."[16] To what does justice condemn us? Simply the mortification of the passions which make us unhappy. Justice is a compensation borne by Jesus for humanity's offense against the majesty of God; mercy inscribes his compensation into our hearts and his penance onto our body; the mercy-act takes us up into *his* justice-act so it can meritoriously affect us. Libermann sees both sides at work.

> Man is a sinner, and should feel all the weight of divine justice before
> beholding the kingdom of God, His love and His life established in
> himself. Jesus should enjoy, love and live in our souls; and it is we that
> should suffer, since all evil resides in us, and all good in Him alone. But
> by His inconceivable mercy, He takes all the weight of justice and all our
> sorrows upon Himself, and He seems to deliver His life, His reign, and
> His love unto us and place them at our discretion.[17]

Liturgical abnegation is the linkage between ourselves and the cross. This is different from a simple historical linkage, or a formal linkage, or the linkage of personal piety and imagination. It is a liturgical, mystical, sacramental linkage between us and the cross. If abnegation does not follow upon liturgy, then the sacrifice of Calvary is nothing but a past historical fact. The formula of Christianity is not so much "Christ was crucified for us," as "Christ crucified in us." We join his submission to God by death to self. For him, this is self-denial; for us, it is mortification and self-denial. Liturgical abnegation is discerned in our attitude toward the cross, because, Grou says, the crucified Christ is our model. "Let

---

16. Jean Grou, *The Practical Science of the Cross in the Use of the Sacraments of Penance and the Eucharist* (London: Joseph Masters, 1871) 54.

17. Libermann, *Letters to Clergy and Religious*, Spiritan Series 8, vol. 4, 210.

me become, by the cross which it shall please Thee to give me, the victim of Thy adorable Justice, as Thy Son, my Saviour, and my Exemplar did become."[18] Jesus's cross is our hope – which is why liturgical abnegation willingly accepts crosses. How does God satisfy his own justice? asks Grou. "You are bound to satisfy divine justice: allow it to achieve its own satisfaction by means of crosses. This form of retribution, carried out in this world, is full of mercy."[19] Therefore, what Jesus demands is that "we should take our cross from the hand of God, place it upon our own shoulders, and bear it with a willing heart and entire submission to His will."[20] Because sinners do not like abnegation, Tronson says they usually pit *false mercy* against justice. "Have we not, on the other hand, presumed too much upon His Mercy, persuading ourselves that His Goodness being infinite, we have no cause to fear His Justice; and have we not, consequently, allowed ourselves as it were to stagnate in our sins, putting off our repentance, neglecting our duties, and thus hindering the great work of our salvation?"[21]

The rectification of the disaster in Eden has been going on during the whole of salvation history, and it is a good example to make our point. Saint-Jure agrees with the Church fathers that Adam was "banished from the terrestrial paradise, not only through the justice of God punishing him for his sin, but also through His mercy, that he might not eat of the fruit of life, which would prevent is dying, and thereby leave him in this state of imperfection and misery."[22] Adam and Eve were not exiled because God punished them in a fit of pique; they were exiled because his justice would not let them steep in their sins. And yet, the finish line is more sublime than we expected. On the cross, Jesus fulfilled what justice demanded: the majesty of God was honored. But this did not satisfy the love of Jesus: therefore he went on to fulfill the designs of mercy. The glory of the Father was accomplished, but the Trinity's love desired more. The cross does not take us back

---

18. Grou, *The Practical Science of the Cross*, 56.

19. Grou, *The School of Jesus Christ*, 183.

20. Grou, *The School of Jesus Christ*, 181.

21. Tronson, *Examination of Conscience*, 9.

22. Jean Baptiste Saint-Jure, *A Treatise on the Knowledge and Love of our Lord Jesus Christ*, vol. 3 (New York: P. O'Shea, 1875) 357.

to Eden, it takes us forward to heaven. Grou marvels over the design of the Incarnation where God selected one man from among the sons of Adam, destined to be the Mediator of reconciliation. "That chosen Being was designed to satisfy the justice and to disarm the anger of God, by bearing in his own person all the punishment due to sin; and, by his obedience and self-immolation, he was to restore to God a degree of glory far transcending that of which sin had deprived him, as well as to exalt man to a state of being preferable to that whence he had fallen."[23] De Ravignan says that after we beg God "to put us beneath the press of His justice, in order that all our impurities may pass away," only one thing alone remains: "the purity acquired for us in the blood of Jesus Christ."[24] On the one hand, mercy cannot be had without justice. Do not ask God to stop being God by asking him not to be just in his condemnation of sin. On the other hand, mercy always accompanies justice. Upon being united with Christ in his mystical body, he gives us his heart, the heart that the Son has for his Father, a heart with fear and reverence, a heart with zeal for his Father's honor.

Strange to say, pride would rather work its own redemption through justice, than receiving redemption through mercy. De la Colombiere thinks this needs correction in our confused minds: "I would rather owe my grace to God's mercy than my own efforts, because that would be more glorious to God and make Him much more lovable to me."[25] If the heart of the Begotten Son infuses his filial status with created sons, then de Granada thinks we can give God the heart his justice demands. It is a heart of liturgical abnegation.

> Consider, then, with yourself what kind of a heart it is that a son has for his father, what love he bears him, with what fear and reverence, with what obedience he serves him, with what zeal for his honor, and with how much disinterestedness; with what confidence he runs to him in all his necessities, with what humility he receives his corrections, how submissively he bears his reprimands, and how willingly he embraces all

23. Grou, *The Interior of Jesus and Mary*, vol. 1, 18.

24. De Ravignan, *Ravignan's Last Retreat*, 31.

25. De la Colombiere, *Faithful Servant*, 15.

that comes from him. Do but give God such a heart as this is, and you will perfectly discharge the part of justice."[26]

Pride is the enemy of both justice and mercy, because it rankles under the former and is insulted by the latter. "Jesus, knowing that creatures are prone to put themselves forward in all things," marvels Boudon, showed us by his own example that, "in order to satisfy the justice of His Father, offended by so monstrous a perversion, hides himself in an infinitely astonishing manner, and endures annihilations at which we stand aghast."[27] We are aghast at the thought, even though Jesus says that those who suffer for justice's sake are blessed (de Sales's translation of the eighth beatitude[28]).

Why annihilation? Because we are disciples of the one who did not count equality with God a thing to be grasped. Boudon asks us to "contemplate awhile this Divine Infant, and you will see that He hides in an ineffable manner all the splendours of His eternal generation; yea, He hides them so effectually that the great Apostle declares, by the inspiration of the Holy Ghost, that He annihilated Himself."[29] By his incarnation-annihilation Christ shows man how man is supposed to live his humility-annihilation, and continues to do so with his Eucharist-annihilation. In Crasset's words:

> Jesus annihilates Himself on the altar.
> He gives up the being He had.
> He hides divinity and humanity,
> Under the lowly appearance of bread.
> He is there more humbled,
> Than at the crib, the cross, or the tomb.
> He is despised by idolators, heretics,

---

26. De Granada, *The Sinner's Guide*, 353.

27. Boudon, *The Hidden Life of Jesus*, 61.

28. De Sales, quoted in Camus, *The Spirit of St. Francis de Sales*, 202.

29. Boudon, *The Hidden Life of Jesus*, 12.

And by wicked Catholics.

He there receives the greatest insults.

He visits the sick in wretched hovels.

He enters the heart of a Judas.

My God and my Saviour!

You are truly a hidden God.[30]

Jesus annihilates himself – why? To sanctify our acts of abnegation. Because the being we have by grace is elevated, and all our actions must be elevated and done in Jesus. Jesus annihilates himself first, for the glory of the Father (he takes nothing to himself but gives all to the Father), and second, for our salvation (to mercifully appease the justice that confronts the self-exaltation of creatures). We have again stumbled across the twin purposes of liturgy: glorification of God and sanctification of man. We join Jesus in his kenosis. Our life is hidden in Christ; our righteousness is hidden, too, in abnegation. That is de Sales' hope. "Should God have given me one particle of justice, enabling me thereby to do some little good, it would be my wish that in the Day of Judgment, when all secrets are revealed, God alone should know my righteousness, and that my sinful actions should be proclaimed to all creatures."[31]

Jesus died in order to repair the offense done to the majesty of God, and to satisfy the justice of his Father. Eudes asks: Are we going to say he was wrong in doing so? Or that we are wrong in following him to Calvary?

In honor of Thy exceeding great love and most profound humility with which Thou didst hear and accept the sentence of death, spoken by Pilate, the Roman Governor, but willed by Thy Eternal Father, in honor of and in homage to His divine justice, I submit with my whole heart to the sentence of death Thou didst pass upon me even at the beginning of the world, recognizing that I have deserved it not only by original sin, but each time I have committed sin.[32]

---

31. De Sales, quoted in Camus, *The Spirit of St. Francis de Sales*, 202-203.

32. Eudes, *Meditation on Various Subjects*, 170.

Upon seeing how low Christ stooped in annihilating kenosis for his creatures, Grou says we should be inspired to liturgical abnegation, which is an act of justice. "When shall we understand that the humiliations thou didst embrace in obedience we should embrace in justice; that, as beings formed of clay and still more as sinners, humiliation is our lawful inheritance ... This is the foundation, the progress, and the consummation of Christian perfection. Thus alone is God really glorified by his creatures."[33] Injustice – failed conformity to the justice at play between the Son and the Father – is stolen liturgy says Crasset.

Ungrateful that I am!
I dishonour instead of glorifying Him.
Far from giving glory to Him,
I take honour to myself for His gifts.
I take His graces, and steal His glory.
O my God, what injustice![34]

The idea of stealing God's glory is used repeatedly by these theologians of liturgical abnegation, and can clarify the connection of liturgy, justice, and abnegation. God is the sovereign Lord, the beginning, the end, and the center of all things. Therefore, "we cannot refuse Him our homage," says Grou, "without falling into the sin of rebellion, neither can we share it with any other object without the greatest injustice."[35] Latreutic theft is the greatest injustice. It is fraud, Grou continues. "Thus I owe whatever I am or have to God – my intellect, my memory, my will – all are of Him; and if I use them as my own, if they move me to vanity or self-conceit, I defraud Him of His right."[36] Justice demands liturgy; liturgizing God is justice-in-motion; want of liturgical posture is unjust. Back to Crasset:

---

33. Grou, *The Interior of Jesus and Mary*, vol. 1, 145-46.

34. Crasset, *Meditations for Every Day in the Year, Pentecost to Advent*, 206.

35. Grou, *Manual for Interior Souls*, 278.

36. Grou, *The Hidden Life of the Soul*, 79.

Are we not creatures of God?

Ought we not to give Him daily homage?

Thank Him for His benefits?

Appease His justice?

Offer Him this most pleasing victim?

Why are we so seldom at the sacrifice?

And with such coldness and apathy?

Because we do not believe in God.

Because we know Him not.

Nor our dependence on Him.

Nor our extreme want of His help.

Nor our duty of satisfying His justice.[37]

The sinner's sin is to forsake the Creator for love of the creature, while the saint's righteousness is to annihilate self-love in order to become an agent of liturgy. For de Granada, "he who dishonored God should humble himself ... It is thus a soul renders herself the throne of God, and becomes the palace in which the Divine Wisdom is pleased to make its abode."[38] Justice means giving someone what he is due; all glory is due God.

What could possibly lead someone to withhold from God what is his just due? We know the answer, but let Grou describe it.

> We will now look more closely into the various devices used by self-love
> for the corruption of true piety. Its chief aim is to appropriate the work of
> grace, and rob God of the glory of good actions, or claim a share in such
> glory; thus robbing us of all merit, for that is based wholly on humility.
> So S. Philip Neri said to the Lord: "Beware of me, as of a great robber."
> Self-love is jealous of the property of God, and endeavours to rob Him of
> it. This property is the glory which belongs to God alone, and which He
> cannot give to another. He allows us to make use of His blessings, but all
> glory must be rendered back to Him. This is exactly what self-love desires

---

37. Crasset, *Meditations for Every Day in the Year, Pentecost to Advent,* 26-27.

38. De Granada, *A Memorial of a Christian Life,* 117.

to appropriate, prompting us to glory in ourselves, against the express precept of the Apostle "He that glorieth, let him glory in the Lord."[39]

Self-love produces false piety. True piety, to the contrary, is a virtue that Saint-Jure says "has reference to justice; by it we give to God *latria*, the supreme honor which is His due;" and true piety will also show its virtue in "our duties toward our parents, our country, and all that belong to us."[40] All the virtues are all grounded in this latria (we are describing liturgical morality!) because, in de Granada's words, "moral virtues are nothing before God, as considered in themselves," and because "all that God values is the spirit of love sent down from heaven, and whatsoever springs from this root."[41] Virtues are expressions of justice, and, like the prophets, we thirst for a justice that will establish our lives in virtue. And our societies, too. Such justice is greater than the secular realm can accomplish because it is concerned with God's glory. Fenelon explains how worship is the canon for social order.

> Let justice be done, and let justice be done to God. Did we make
> ourselves? Do we exist for God or for ourselves? Has he made us for
> ourselves or for himself? To whom do we belong? Has God made us for
> our own beatitude or for his glory? If it is for his glory, then we must
> conform to the essential order of our creation. We must wish his glory
> more than our beatitude, so that we refer our whole beatitude to his own
> glory.[42]

Eudes laments that we are unfaithful servants who do not even liturgize our God. "We who are full of evil and void of all good cannot humble ourselves! We even strive

---

39. Grou, *The Spiritual Maxims*, 172.

40. Saint-Jure, *The Spiritual Man,* 153.

41. De Granada, *The Sinner's Guide*, 357.

42. Fenelon, *Christian Perfection*, 139.

to rob God of what belongs to Him, and to attribute it to ourselves!"[43] Our sin (which is injustice) is to serve ourselves instead of serving God, to praise ourselves instead of praising God, to keep our latria from joining that of the heavenly hosts. Incredible though it may sound, Grou says this sin wounds God: "Sin is the greatest of all evils, since it is the evil which hurts God."[44] The moral context speaks about sin violating the law, but the liturgical context speaks about sin hurting God. Rodriguez agrees: "when, therefore, it happens, that we seek to attract to ourselves the esteem and praise of men, we pervert that order which God established, and we do him an injury."[45] An amazing thought – that we can do God injury – and it comes from failing what he, in justice, commands from us, namely, our liturgy. The order is upset, perverted, debased, and God is injured when his justice is offended.

To grasp this, we must keep love on the table when talking about justice, liturgy, and abnegation. It is uncomfortable, says Grou, because although we love truth when it applauds us, we do not when it "exposes us to vain glory [sic], to pride, and to the temptation of robbing God of the praise which is due to him for the good that is in us."[46] This attitude requires a severe shift from the state of original sin that we have inherited, and it requires constant attention, because, Crasset says, Satan is at our side every day, and all day.

> The beginning in everything is very important. The first-fruits of our thoughts, of our affections, of our works, are tributes due to God. The manner in which we spend our day depends very much upon the beginning; this is why the Evil One makes every effort to destroy the tree at the root and to rob God of this first homage due only to Him. Therefore

---

43. Eudes, *Meditation on Various Subjects*, 112.

44. Grou, *The Practical Science of the Cross*, 25.

45. Rodriguez, *The Practice of Christian and Religious Perfection*, vol. 1, 111.

46. Grou, *Morality Augustine,* vol. 2, 357-58.

when you get up in the morning your first thought, your first word, your first action, should be given to God. Do you do this?[47]

Grou proposes that we define this robbery as an usurpation. "If we claim any right of disposing of ourselves as it shall please us best, we are usurpers; we rob God of a possession which belongs to Him."[48] Usurping is the injustice of taking credit which is due another. We unjustly usurp glory from God and give it to ourselves, first, and creatures, second. Liturgical abnegation is required to restore order, and give glory to the rightful recipient. So says John Evangelist of Boisleduc: "the coming into God's kingdom in the soul must be preceded by spiritual death. By this death man dies to all that which he unjustly usurped when he was forced to leave the kingdom of God, wherein he was first created and constituted."[49] So says John of the Cross: "One thought of man is of more value than the whole world; God alone is, for that reason, the worthy object of it, and to Him alone is it due; every thought of man, therefore, which is not given to God, is a robbery."[50] So says de Caussade: walking in justice means the interior disposition of nothingness because "outside this stage there is nothing but falsehood and injustice towards God. Injustice because we deprive Him of the glory that belongs to Him; falsehood because we flatter ourselves in appropriating what can never belong to us."[51]

Why let liturgy into the conversation? Because, Lallemant says, this theft is blasphemy. "We take God's share to ourselves; we desire to have the glory as well as the profit of our possessions. This injustice is a kind of blasphemy; for nothing is due to nature, considered

47. Francis de Sales & Jean Crasset, *The Secret of Sanctity According to St. Francis De Sales and Father Crasset*, (New York: Benziger Brothers, 1892) 24.

48. Jean Grou, *Self-Consecration, or the Gift of one's Self to God* (New York: E. & J. B. Young & Co., 1887) 24.

49. John Evangelist, *The Kingdom of God in the Soul*, 49.

50. John of the Cross, *Spiritual Maxims*, in *The Complete Works of St. John of the Cross*, vol. 2, 369.

51. De Caussade, *Abandonment to Divine Providence*, 116.

in itself."[52] We must let liturgy enter the conversation because this disobedience is idolatry, which Rodriguez finds built into even the Old Testament.

> Hence you may infer why Samuel, in his speech to Saul, compares the sin of disobedience to idolatry. "To resist God's orders", says he, "is like the sin of witchcraft, and not to submit, is like the crime of idolatry" (Kings, xv. 23). St. Gregory and St. Bernard infer from these words that disobedience is a very enormous crime, since holy writ compares it to idolatry and magic. The reason they give to prove the comparison is drawn from the nature of idolatry and witchcraft, which rob God of the worship due to him in the same manner as disrespect and disobedience to a superior deprive him of the honour and deference due to the person who represents him. Besides, as by idolatry we adore an idol of wood or stone, instead of the true God to whom that adoration alone is due, so by the spirit of disobedience we stray from the true rule, which is God, and follow a deceitful one, which is that of our own judgment and of the maxims of the world.[53]

To be sure, God does give us blessings and goods to use. But Grou points out how things go wrong when "self-love is jealous of the property of God, and endeavours to rob Him of it. This property is the glory which belongs to God alone, and which He cannot give to another. He allows us to make use of His blessings, but all glory must be rendered back to Him. This is exactly what self-love desires to appropriate, prompting us to glory in ourselves."[54] Abnegating the world is a steppingstone, an instrument for dealing a death blow to self-love, because the real battle is love of God versus self-love. Rodriguez despairs over what we do when we endeavor to get others to praise us. "What is this but to rob God of his creatures' hearts, and in a manner, to drive him out of his own house? Can

---

52. Lallemant, *The Spiritual Doctrine of Father Louis Lallemant*, ed. Faber, 57.

53. Alphonsus Rodriguez, *The Practice of Christian and Religious Perfection*, vol. 3 (London: James Duffy, 1861) 286.

54. Grou, *The Spiritual Maxims*, 172.

one commit a greater evil than this? Or imagine anything worse, than in such a manner to rob God of his glory? For though by your words you exhort men to regard none but him, yet you wish in the bottom of your heart that they would turn their eyes from him, and fix them upon yourself."[55] Self-esteem, self-justification, self-glorification, and vainglory are more than matters of ethics, morality, or virtue, because at bottom they are matters of latreutic fidelity. The reason why we attribute nothing to ourselves (in other words, profess our nothingness), is a liturgical one: we seek not our own glory, but God's alone.

Latreutic theft diverts minds and affections from God, derailing the praise and admiration he is owed, and we are so practiced in this sin of self-love, that de Bergamo notices we can commit robbery against God even while we are doing our morality and religion.

> Do you sometimes do good from motives of human respect, in order to be seen – esteemed? "Take heed," Christ says to you, "that you do not your justice before men, to be seen by them" [Matthew 6:1)]. You are merely robbing God of glory, when from the gifts He has given you, you reserve some of the glory for yourself. Examine your intentions; are they purely directed to the glorification of God?[56]

This is a manifestation of pride, of course, which Grou describes as nothing but trespassing the first commandment. "The injustice and wickedness of pride consists in recognising greatness in something other than God; in regarding any perfection there may be in us as belonging to us and existing for ourselves; in desiring to be praised for our qualities and actions, good though they may be, with praise that ends in ourselves; and in appropriating any glory whatever to the exclusion of God, or even sharing it with Him."[57] This is robbing God of a possession that is essentially his own, of which he is especially jealous, and which shall not be given to another (Is. 42:8). Why would anyone not give himself to God? Because he loves himself more than he loves God, admits Grou. "All tells me that I ought to love God for Himself, above all things and in all things, and

---

55. Rodriguez, *The Practice of Christian and Religious Perfection*, vol. 1, 111.

56. De Bergamo, *Humility of Heart*, 158-59.

that no duty is as just as this, as it is itself the source of all justice; for nothing is just if this commandment is not so."[58]

If I were responsible for engendering love, if love were my creation and possession, then I could choose whether to direct it to God or to myself. If the love were mine, the choice would be mine. I would not offend God by saving some love for self because I could generate some more tomorrow, and maybe even have a little bit leftover for him. But if love comes from God, then not *returning* it to God is theft. God does not claim something of ours; he claims his own. That is why holding anything back is an act of injustice. None of the saints retained any of God's love for themselves – they gave it back, and they gave it to their neighbor. We are touching on what Scripture means by calling God a jealous God, says Grou. It is a prerogative of God, according to Scripture.

> The love of God does not admit, either, any division of our hearts. God is supremely jealous; He wants the whole of it, because He deserves it; He wants it wholly to Himself, because he is the only One Who merits it, and because He made it only for Himself. If I transfer the least affection from it towards the creature, I take it from God; I take from Him a right that belongs to Him, and that He can yield to no one … This commandment of loving God with all our hearts absolutely forbids self-love, which makes us love ourselves, without any relation to God, and love all else in relation to ourselves.[59]

We are familiar enough with Jesus's command to love the Lord our God with all our heart, soul, and mind, but we neglect the consequential fact that this requires the annihilation of self-love, because self-love is caught in the act of diverting to our own heart, soul, and mind a small portion of the love that God is due. But we have no just claim to this, says Grou. "We do not deserve to be loved and served for our own sakes; it is an injustice, it is a theft from God, when we desire to be loved in this way. But God does deserve it, and He alone has the right to claim such a love as this; He would have a

---

58. Jean Grou, *Meditations upon the Love of God* (London: T. Baker, 1905) 46-47.

59. Grou, *Meditations on the Love of God,* 39.

right to it for many reasons even if, through His infinite goodness, He had not promised to reward our love and service."[60]

Rodriguez titles one of his chapters "In what the Malignity of Vainglory Consists." Malignity is defined as hatred, intense ill will, something that gives birth to enmity, so he is saying vainglory is not our personal innocent and accidental business, it is hatred of God.

> The malignity of this vice consists in this; that those who are infected with it endeavour to rob God of the glory that belongs to him alone, according to the words of St. Paul; "To God alone be glory and honour" (1 Tim. i. 17); of which he is so jealous that he himself says, in the prophet Isaiah, "I will not give my glory to another." (Isa. xlii. 8; Aug. c. 16. Solil.) Wherefore St. Austin [Augustine], speaking on this subject: Lord, says he, whoever would be praised for your gifts, and seek not your glory, but his own, in the good he does, is a robber; and is like the devil himself, who attempts to rob you of your glory. In all the works of God there are two things, utility and glory; as to the utility he leaves that entirely to men; but he reserves all the glory of them to himself alone.[61]

The vainglorious man is a thief like the devil himself. The devil was the first anti-liturgist, after which true piety was corrupted, divine governance was denied, human independence was declared, grace was declined and replaced by human merit, and glory was curved back upon the creature. (I make reference to Augustine's definition of sin as *incurvatus in se*). The vainglorious man will not give glory to God because he is sitting upon his accumulated pile of glory as his own personal throne. Pride makes a man a thief, appropriating to himself that which is God's. It is a greater sin to rob God of what belongs to him, than to rob any person of whatever belongs to that person, because he is God almighty. Whatever virtues a person has are gifts from God – even his very existence, reminds John of Avila. "You must be most loyal to our Lord Jesus Christ by giving Him the glory for any virtues you possess. This is the matter, above all others, on which He is

---

60. Grou, *Manual for Interior Souls*, 230.

61. Rodriguez, *The Practice of Christian and Religious Perfection*, vol. 1, 110.

susceptible to injustice, and He leaves those who defraud Him of these His claims without honour or graces."[62]

Liturgizing the Almighty in due and proper measure burns self-love out of our hearts and produces abnegation to the point of humility, and humility simply means an exercise of truthful justice upon ourselves. Ullathorne says "Humility is the immolation of self-love to justice."[63]

> When, by the grace of God, we come to His light that reveals all things, and when we exercise that truthful justice upon ourselves that we call humility, and give to all what in justice is their due, to God what is due to God, to every creature what is due to that creature, and to ourself what is due to us; we shall find ourselves stripped of much that our self-love and our vanity have appropriated, and reduced to our native poverty, which God alone can enrich with His truth and good, whenever He finds us sufficiently humble and sincere to ascribe His gifts to Him and not to ourselves."[64]

This dimension of justice, therefore, leads us first to nothingness, in the next two chapters, and then to humility, in the two chapters after that. Justice, humility and nothingness are interrelated, exclaims de Bergamo. "To be humble[,] let us listen to the revelation of the Holy Ghost which is infallible. 'Behold you are nothing, and your work is of that which hath no being.' But who is really convinced of his own nothingness?"[65]

---

62. John of Avila, *Letters*, 98.

63. Ullathorne, *The Groundwork of the Christian Virtues*, 232.

64. Ullathorne, *The Endowments of Man*, 145.

65. De Bergamo, *Humility of Heart*, 8.

NOTHINGNESS AS A
ONTOLOGICAL FACT

Perhaps the most difficult word to grasp in the lexicon of abnegation is the insistence on nothingness, so I will devote two chapters to the idea. This one will see nothingness as a fact of creation: the status of a creature before the Creator. The next one will see the embrace of nothingness as a liturgical act.

Any study of being (ontology) would see that creatures are dependent on a creator. "What is the creature but the emptiness which the Creator fills?"[1] asks Faber. How can the former distract us from the latter, adds de Ponte, when "in the presence of the divine being they are like a drop of water which cannot quench my thirst, or satisfy the least part of my desires."[2] God says: *Yahweh* (I am). Man replies: *I am not* (I am nothing). As a category, nothingness is understood in contrast with God, not in contrast with anything else. It is a theological category, not a social, moral, personal, psychological, or philosophical category. Admitting nothingness is not self-contempt, or shame, or disgrace, it is admitting my being comes from God. "Whence do I draw my origin?" asks Huby. "Who is the author of my existence? – An inquiry which I cannot neglect to make, without renouncing my religion and my reason ... The weakness, the frailty, and the mutability of my being, are evident proofs of its having had a beginning, and of its

---

1. Frederick Faber, *The Foot of the Cross: Or, the Sorrows of Mary* (London: Thomas Richardson and Son, 1858) 179.

2. Louis de Ponte, *Meditations on the Mysteries of Our Holy Faith*, vol. 6 (London: Richardson and Son, 1854) 27.

approaching dissolution. It will soon finish ... Before I existed I was nothing: and, what is nothing, can do nothing."[3]

Nothingness is fact of our finite existence, and admitting it is the contrary of an independence that is an expression of pride. Nothingness means that God alone has life in himself, and of my own accord I revert to nihility; nothingness recognizes God as a necessary being, and acknowledges the absolute and continual dependence of contingent beings on him. Scupoli revels in God's revelation of his name. From *I Am that I Am* he can perceive "how vain is that man who loves creatures, and attaches himself to them ... That man is vain, I say, because he loves vanities. He is vain, because he thinks to satisfy himself with things which have no being in themselves."[4] Love Being, use beings.

Nothingness figures in the middle of the divine economy, because from the moment you began to live Boutauld says "you have been obliged by the very Laws of your Being, to endeavor after the Knowledge of three grand Truths: the *first*, that there is a God, who made you; the *second*, that there is a State of Nothingness, out of which you [were] produced, and a State of Death, to which you are going; the *third* that there is a Saviour *Jesus Christ* who has redeemed you, and who will raise you up at the last Day."[5] He further finds three voices that are ready to teach these lessons: the Voice of Nature, the Voice of Death, and the Voice of Grace and the Gospel. If only we would listen.

The knowledge comes out of a two-sided prayer, such as this very short one, composed by Grou: "Lord, make me to know Thee, and to know myself. The prayer is short, but its meaning is infinite. Knowledge of God elevates the soul; knowledge of self, humbles it. The former lifts it to the abyss of Divine perfections; the latter sinks it to its own abyss of nothingness and sin."[6] Mere moralizing – true and reasonable as it is – does not go deep enough. It does not go as deeply into the heart as liturgizing does. We are not moralizing

---

3. Vincent Huby, *The Spiritual Retreat of the Reverend Father Vincent Huby, of the Society of Jesus* (Philadelphia: Printed for Mathew Carey, 1795) 2

4. Scupoli, 179.

5. Michel Boutauld, *The Counsels of Wisdom. Or A Collection of Such Maxims of Solomon as are Most Necessary for the Prudent Conduct of Life* (Oxford: Printed at the Theater, 1736) 289-90.

6. Grou, *The Spiritual Maxims*, 1.

when we say that we are nothing; we are confessing and petitioning and praising. "Jesus, and Jesus all alone! The rest is nothingness, misery, and abomination" (Libermann).[7]

Confession of nothingness is not a melancholic expression, it is recognition of a ontological fact, which means it concerns the nature of being. How did you come to have existence? Segneri provides a provocative example of how to think about this.

> If thou hast an existence, it is only because God gave it thee, and preserves thee in it. And if this is so, thou hast no existence of thyself. Wouldst thou say that the reflection in a mirror has any existence? Certainly not: and why? Because it is entirely dependent on thee. Just so art thou with regard to God, Whose image thou bearest ... "Man was made to the image of God." If He does but turn His face away from thee for a moment, thou returnest at once to thy original nothingness.[8]

De Ponte also explores the theme. While it is the "*essence* of God to be *He that is*, this cannot be said of any other whatever besides Himself," and all other things which receive their being from God "are capable of not being, and are of themselves as things vain and destitute of being ... and shall come to perish, if God do not always give them being, and preserve them in it."[9] Or, in Saint-Jure's language: "When God bade Moses to order Pharao [sic], on His part, to let the Israelites leave his dominions, He said to him: *I am who am*; in like manner each of us may say to himself: I am who am not."[10] So Ullathorne concludes, "the word *being* in its absolute sense belongs to God alone: the word existence properly belongs to the creation. God *is*, the creation *exists* from Him."[11] And Ullathorne

---

7. Libermann, *Letters to Clergy*, Spiritan Series 8, vol. 4, 200.

8. Segneri, *The Manna of the Soul*, vol. 2, 168-69.

9. Louis de Ponte, *Meditations on the Mysteries of Our Holy Faith*, vol. 6 (London: Richardson and Son, 1854) 24.

10. Saint-Jure, *A Treatise on the Knowledge and Love of Our Lord Jesus Christ*, vol. 2, 538.

11. Ullathorne, *The Endowments of Man*, 81.

thinks man can find plenty of evidence of his nothingness "when considered in himself, and as he would be were God to leave him to himself, unenlightened, ungraced, unhelped even in the order of providence, vacant of all but himself, stained, too, and disordered with sin, that we say that man is nothing before God."[12]

All non-divine creatures are capable of not being – and de Ponte knows that includes the human creature. "My 'flesh' is 'a flower,' and soon 'withers like grass;' my life is a breath of wind, and as 'a vapour' that soon passes,"[13] so all persons must face the fact that "I was created out of nothing, and that of myself I am 'nothing;' that I merit nothing, and that presently I shall be turned into nothing if God do not continually preserve me; neither should I be able to do anything if God did not continually aid me."[14] As we will see later, the fruit that sprouts from this root of nothingness is humility, which is crucial for the spiritual life. So de Ponte adds:

> This truth well pondered, will lead to the principal foundation of the spiritual life, for upon it is grounded that *profound humility* which we ought to feel in the presence of God, and which is felt by the angels, the blessed spirits, the Virgin our Lady, and even by the soul of Christ our Lord. I have, therefore, great reason to study to attain the same humility, but considering that as God alone is *He that is*, even so I am *he that is not*.[15]

Admitting our nothingness is also a key ingredient for our liturgical confrontation with the holy and transcendent God. Faber protests that "all our duties to God, and to ourselves no less, are founded on the fact that we are creatures. All religion is based on the sense that we are creatures," and "there is nothing in the whole range of asceticism

---

12. Ullathorne, *The Groundwork of Christian Virtues,* 101.

13. Louis de Ponte, *Meditations on the Mysteries of Our Holy Faith*, vol. 1 (London: Richardson and Son, 1852) 104-05.

14. De Ponte, *Meditations*, vol. 1, 106

15. De Ponte, *Meditations*, vol. 6, 24.

which does not turn out at last to be, a natural and logical result of our position in the world as the creatures of a Creator."[16] Alacoque recalls God addressing her vanity with a look of severity when they were alone together: "What hast thou to boast of, O dust and ashes, since of thyself thou art but nothingness and misery!"[17] Confessing nothingness is confessing that God is God, and we are not, so she concludes "he is pleased only with souls that are reduced to nothingness, souls that are all in Him and find everything in Him, since they are nothing in themselves."[18] All that is not eternal is nothing: this is not a judgment on the value of temporal goods, it is a sober acknowledgement that temporal things are temporary.

Related to this is the Latin term *annihilare*, which means "reducing to nothing, bringing low, humbling." It leads Saint-Jure to summarize the Incarnation this way: "as the essence of the Name of God is *to be*, the name of creature is *not to be*, because the creature is nothing of itself. Hence, St. Paul had great reason to say that Jesus Christ, in becoming a creature, *annihilated Himself*."[19] The Eternal Word assumed a human nature that can be humbled, brought low, annihilated, and place all its confidence in God. Canfield therefore say sthe kenosis of Jesus revealed what the human soul can, and should, be.

> The soul is elevated by the very same things which bring her low. Her very nothingness, which shows before her eyes what she is in herself, clearly reveals also how she is all in God, and how by abandoning the finite she may be united to the Infinite. From this she knows full well that, as she is of herself nothing, so she cannot by herself subsist, but only by Him Who Is, that is, God. And if it is by Him she subsists, by Him equally is

---

16. Frederick Faber, *The Creator and the Creature, or, The Wonders of Divine* Love (London: Thomas Richardson and Son, 1858) 25 and 21.

17. Alacoque, *Autobiography*, ch 62, Kindle edition.

18. Alacoque, *Letters*, letter 106, Kindle edition.

19. Saint-Jure, *A Treatise on the Knowledge and Love of Our Lord Jesus Christ*, vol. 1, 282.

she kept in being, and therefore He is in her and she in Him, in whom is the true exultation of the mind.[20]

In short, he adds, confessing nothingness confesses that the creature is no more than a mere dependence on God, and he gives a brilliant illustration of what dependence means.

'Tis such as cannot well be expressed in words: yet by a similitude we may come to some notion thereof. So then is the Creature to God, as the beam to the sun, or heat to the fire. For, as the beam and heat do so absolutely owe themselves to their productive causes, as that without their perpetual sustentation and communicating, they cannot subsist: even, in like manner, so omnimodous is the creature depending on God, that without his continual preservation they cannot endure ... The sun is no sooner hid, but the beams cease to be; so, if God hides himself, and withdraw his hand from the Creatures, they've suddenly returned to their Nothing.[21]

Upon encounter with God, Canfield concludes, the soul submits to the theological certainty "that He is the only Being to be found: that all the rest is nothing: for though the rest of things have a certain borrowed essence, yet she sees that they are to be esteemed as nothing when there is question of the Divine Essence."[22]

Philosophy, the handmaiden to the Queen of Sciences (theology), lends us the useful word "contingency." God is necessary; creation is not. God is essential Being; creatures are contingent beings. We cannot imagine God not being; we could imagine any creature not being. God is All; our contingent existence does not add to God. In Crasset's words, "it was not necessary that I should come into he world; but, since I am here, it is necessary that I should be all to God, and live only for God."[23] De Berniere-Louvigny recognizes that "whatever the glorious angels or saints in heaven, or his servants on earth, can do for

---

20. Canfield, *The Holy Will of God*, 59.

22. Canfield, *The Holy Will of God: A Short Rule of Perfection*, 53.

23. Crasset, *Christian Considerations*, 488.

God adds nothing to him."[24] One is not surprised at this in the human case, since every person is part of the *creatio ex nihilo*, as Blosius observes.

> If he considers himself to be something, he is still a very long way off from God. Let him always, therefore, think and acknowledge that of himself he is nothing, and can do nothing. For every creature, since it was made from nothing, of its own nature is nothing; but man, furthermore, by sin has reduced himself to nothing. Moreover, as he is created, compared to the Creator, he is nothing. Therefore, the servant of God, considering the abyss of his own nothingness, and plunging himself into it, must dwell in the deepest valley of humility.[25]

Since nothingness is a corollary of dependence upon God, the more totally one feels one's dependence on God, the more complete is one's profession of nothingness. Saint-Jure says, "another means proper to make us practise humility is, to approach God in thought, to consider ourselves in His presence, to measure our being with His, to compare ourselves with Him, for thus shall we clearly see our nothingness in His being, and our littleness in His grandeur."[26] Our being comes from God, and apart from him is nothingness; in the same way, whatever goodness and virtue we have comes from God, and apart from him we claim nothing. "Our being is linked to you, O my God, through your grandeur and its poverty, that is, by its need to be sustained by you so as not to fall into the nothingness from which your powerful hand has drawn it. Our being is also linked through your goodness and its powerlessness, since it is unable to accomplish any work of salvation if it is not joined to you through grace."[27] The state of nothingness is

---

24. De Berniere-Louvigny, *The Interior Christian*, 47.

25. Blosius, *A Book of Spiritual Instruction*, 17-18.

26. Saint-Jure, *A Treatise on the Knowledge and Love of Our Lord Jesus Christ*, vol. 2, 589.

27. Berulle, *Discourse on the State and Grandeurs of Jesus*, in *Berulle and the French School*, 121.

the opposite of the state of God, and that is just a recognition of pure fact. Pollien says we may define a creature as not-Creator. "By creatures, I mean universally all that is not God, all created things ... The word "creatures" has, then, an absolutely universal sense, and denotes all that is not God, all that is between God and me, all that is, and all the takes place in happens around me, in me, for me or against me."[28]

The fact of nothingness is not found only at the beginning, or only at the end, it is found in every moment. Do not say "God created," say "God is creating." Our existence depends on God being a constant creator, says Olier. "We are so totally and truly nothingness that if God does not communicate existence to us at all times, then there is nothing in us. Only nothingness remains. This is our core and our true reality."[29] We can speak of the Creator sustaining us, with Eudes ("if God were to withdraw His Almighty Hand which sustains me, and were to cease for a single moment to preserve me, I would at that very instant return to the nothingness from which He drew me"[30]); or preserving us, with Blosius ("if He by His power preserved not the things which He hath made, all would presently go back into nothingness; for of themselves they are nothing, and are altogether dependent upon God, by whom they were made"[31]); or preventing a relapse, with Eudes again ("at every successive moment, He has prevented it from falling back into the nothingness from which He drew it and He continually preserves it, which preservation is a perpetual creation"[32]); or being more involved in his work than an artisan is in his, with Froget:

> God, then, is not present to the world like the artisan or the artist; [the
> artisan] is external to his work, and does not often touch it in a direct
> way, but rather through his instruments, or is present to his work when

---

28. Pollien, *The Interior Life*, ed. Tissot, 23.

29. Olier, *Introduction to the Christian Life and Virtues*, in *Berulle and the French School*, 237.

30. Eudes, *Meditation on Various Subjects*, 47.

31. Blosius, *The Manual of the Spiritual Life*, 65.

32. Eudes, *Meditation on Various Subjects*, 53.

he produces it, but later on withdraws from it without endangering its existence. [But] God is so intimately united to the works of His hands that if, after calling a created thing into being, He should withdraw from it and cease to sustain it, it would immediately fall into the nothingness out of which it was made.[33]

Nothingness is not only a past ontological fact, but it is also a present possibility, because existence depends upon God as a ray of light depends upon the sun. We cannot preserve our being independently of God, any more than Saint-Jure says a ray of light can be "produced or preserved independently of the sun: if separated for a moment from its source, it immediately flickers and dies out."[34] We have nothing in ourselves, by ourselves, to keep ourselves afloat in being, says Grou. "We live always suspended, as it were, in this state of nothingness, and unless we were drawn out of it by an almighty Hand should sink into it with all our weight."[35] God would not even have to exercise a direct power to annihilate the soul of man, thinks Fenelon, "He would only have to withdraw that which has continued his being, every moment from his birth, to replunge him into the nothingness from whence he originally drew him, as a man would merely open his hand to let a stone fall that he had held in the air."[36] Eudes says, provocatively, that "by counting every moment that has elapsed since you came into the world, you may know how many times you would have been annihilated if God had not performed as great a miracle to preserve you as He did to create you."[37]

Created nothingness is an acknowledgment of the contingency of creation. God has necessary existence, but contingent beings do not, and the admission of nothingness is

---

33. Barthelemy Froget, *Indwelling of the Holy Spirit* (New York: Paulist Press, 1921) 4.

34. Saint-Jure, *The Spiritual Man*, 33.

35. Grou, *The School of Jesus Christ,* 197.

36. François Fenelon, in *Letters and Reflections of François de Fenelon*, ed Kepler (New York: The World Publishing Company, 1955) 108.

37. Eudes, *Meditation on Various Subjects*, 104.

a confession of that ontological fact. Fenelon also finds it to be the cause of unceasing gratitude in the cosmic liturgy.

> It did not follow necessarily that because we were yesterday, we should exist to-day; we might cease to be, we might relapse into the nothingness from whence we came, if the same all-powerful hand who called us from it did not still sustain us. We are nothing in ourselves; we are only what God has made us to be, and that only while it pleases him. He has only to withdraw the hand which supports us in order to replunge us into the abyss of our nothingness, as a stone which one holds in the air falls from its own weight, as soon as the hand is unclosed which supported it. Thus do we hold existence only as the continual gift of God.[38]

The stone would fall from its own weight: *depend* literally means "to hang from," and it describes us perfectly, Libermann points out. "The little being we have, we hold from God ... Our little existence is in a complete dependence of a foreign hand and in no way in ours."[39] But God depends on nothing else: it is as if he hangs from nothing. He is his own foundation. The Absolute God has the property of necessity, but there is nothing necessary about our existence. We could just as well have not existed. God's being demands our reverence because it is so different from ours, concludes de la Colombiere.

> God is a being that has nothing of nonbeing, who can lose nothing, gain nothing, who enfolds in Himself all being, who is the source of all being, who cannot depend on any other in any sense at all, neither for His being more for His better being; if I have been penetrated with profound reverence for this incomprehensible greatness, I do not think that I have

---

38. François Fenelon, in *Selections from the Writings of Fenelon,* ed. Hassard (New York: P. O'Shea, 1864) 97.

39. Libermann, *Of Humility,* 8.

ever understood so well the nothingness of all things as when considered against this idea.[40]

The embrace of nothingness should facilitate a purification of the particles of pride that flow in our veins as traces of original sin, because de la Colombiere points out that "anyone who thinks of what he is, what he has been, and what he can do of himself will find it difficult to be proud. To shatter pride it is enough to remember that the first sign of real virtue is to consider self as nothing at all."[41] Nothingness means desiring nothing but God, allowing nothing but God, letting nothing separate us from God, begging God to possess us entirely, in Alacoque's terms. "I cannot understand how a heart that seeks its God and wants to love Him can relish any pleasure outside of Him. There must be no more this thing called *self*. I can see no other happiness in this life than to remain always hidden away in one's own nothingness, suffering and loving in silence, embracing our crosses and praising and thanking Him Who sends them."[42] Why abnegation? Because Jesus should be the only Spouse of our souls. Abnegation struggles to overcome adultery (otherwise called infidelity); nothingness is spiritual monogamy. "We must give all in order to possess all. Divine love admits of no alloy."[43]

Nothingness is a corollary of grace. When liturgical abnegation says "we have no good of ourselves," it is the same as saying "of ourselves, we have no being; of ourselves, we do not merit grace." Nothingness means I have done nothing by myself, for myself, and am nothing of myself. The key is in the words *of myself*, thinks Bona, because "I by the grace of God am rich," but in God's unchangeable truth "*I clearly see that of myself I have nothing, I am nothing, and can do nothing.*"[44] We are rich by God's grace, but of myself, without that grace, we have nothing. Nothingness involves willing ourselves to God absolutely,

---

40. De la Colombiere, *Faithful Servant*, 72.

41. Claude de la Colombiere, *The Spiritual Direction of Saint Claude de la Colombiere* (San Francisco: Ignatius Press, 1998) 77.

42. Alacoque, *Spiritual Letters,* letter 15, Kindle edition.

43. Alacoque, *Spiritual Letters,* letter 7, Kindle edition.

44. Bona, *The Principles of Christianity,* 113. Emphasis in original.

and holding nothing back. Abnegation puts the "absolutely" in belonging to God. If God alone is the one whom we wish to please, then we should turn away from – abnegate – pleasing everyone else.

The order of nature and the order of grace reflect each other. De Bergamo says if God were to withdraw his omnipotent preserving hand in the order of nature, "I should at once show what I am capable of when left to myself, by returning immediately into my nothingness. And, in the order of grace, the nothingness into which I relapse when left to myself is sin."[45] What is true of our natural being is true of our supernatural being; what holds in our natural faculties also holds in the operations of grace. Alphonsus Rodriguez writes,

> We have already shewn, that we hold our natural being and faculties from God; because of ourselves we were nothing, and therefore incapable either of the operations of our senses, or of those of our memory, will, or understanding; it being God alone that has made us capable of them, by giving us our being; and consequently it is to him we ought to ascribe both the being we have, and the natural faculties which accompany it. The same may be said of our supernatural being, and of the operations of grace; and with so much the more reason, as grace is infinitely above nature; for we hold not from ourselves supernatural being, but from God; which is a being of grace, that he has freely added to our natural being.[46]

Therefore, nothingness concerns both being and doing: if I am only because God, I should do only what glorifies God, according to de la Colombiere.

> After I recognized and confessed that before God I am nothing, and that by myself I have done nothing, I understood how just it is that God alone be glorified, and I thought that a man who happens to be praised for some virtue and some good action should be as ashamed as would be a man of

---

45. De Bergamo, *Humility of Heart*, 14.

46. Rodriguez, *The Practice of Christian and Religious Perfection*, vol. 2, 248.

honor who was taken for another and praised for something he had not
done ... On the day of judgment God will bring forth this man, let all the
world see all that he has received and all that he has of himself, and then
ask him while reproaching his vanity: "What have you that you have not
received, and if you have received why do you glory?" [I Cor 4:16].[47]

He who is truly humble is never astonished at his nothingness; he knows it comes from
being not-God. Why is that so difficult for us to admit? The confession of nothingness
acknowledges *both* man's finitude and fallenness. It is applicable to both the doctrine
of creation and redemption. Two things lift a person to God, according to Libermann:
"the feeling of his own nothingness and the deep wounds made in him by sin, a feeling
animated by true holiness."[48] The liturgical state is animated by God's omnipotence
(which produces a sense of nothingness), and by God's holiness (which produces a sense
of sin).

Eudes suggests there are two experiences of nothingness: one from out of innocent
finitude, the other from out of guilty fallenness. "By the first creation, God drew us
from utter nothingness; by the second, He drew us from the nothingness of sin which
is a much deeper abyss. The former void is not opposed to the power of God; but the
latter infinitely resists Him by its infinite malice."[49] Here is the Christian ontological
view: we are creatures, coming from nothingness and owing existence to God. Here is the
Christian soteriological view: we are creatures, coming from sin and owing salvation to
God. "Convinced of their nothingness," says de Caussade, "and that everything deriving
from themselves is damaging, they surrender themselves to God so as to have nothing
but him, and from him and through him. And so God becomes the source of life for
these souls."[50] Even our slow process of sanctification must be kept under this rule, lest
we mistake our spiritual life as personal accomplishment. De Sales says spirituality is not

---

47. De la Colombiere, *Faithful Servant,* 39.

48. Libermann, *On The Episcopate,* 7.

49. Eudes, *Meditation on Various Subjects,* 79.

50. Jean Pierre De Caussade, *The Sacrament of the Present* Moment (San Francisco:
    HarperSanFrancisco Reissue edition, 2009) 16-17.

done for our gain, but for liturgical surrender to God. "It would be no great matter to accept our nothingness ... if the result of this were not the total surrender of ourselves to God."[51]

The therapy for both finitude and fallenness is the embrace of nothingness that is called annihilation. If we would bind together God's gift of creation and God's gift of sanctification, then we must also, on the reverse side, bind together our created nothingness and our sinful nothingness. The latter is added to the former, the criminal to the natural, as Boudon explains.

> Nothingness belongs to us, because it is from nothingness that we are drawn, and it is into nothingness that we would fall again, if the all-good God ceased for a moment to preserve us: but to this natural nothingness we add the criminal nothingness of sin; so, here is nothingness upon nothingness. We are nothing by our natural origin, and we are nothing by sin. This is not all, we are even less than nothing because the one who sins is the slave of sin: being, then, nothing in so many ways, we also put ourselves below nothing.[52]

De Berniere-Louvigny says "it is my duty, who am a mere nothing by the condition of my being, and who have become less than nothing by the enormity of my sins."[53]

This feature makes nothingness distasteful to the proud man. For a finite creature to admit finitude is a simple fact, but a proud creature finds it revolting to count himself as nothing. Fenelon guides his spiritual directees through this. "If you would fully comprehend the meaning of self-abandonment, recall the interior difficulty which you felt, and which you very naturally testified when I directed you always to count as *nothing* this self which is so dear to us. *To abandon one's self* is to count one's self as nought; and he who has perceived the difficulty of doing it, has already learned what that renunciation

---

51. De Sales, *The Spiritual Conferences*, 17-18.

52. Henri-Marie Boudon, *The Holy Slavery of the Admirable Mother of God* (CreateSpace Independent Publishing Platform, 2013) 150.

53. De Berniere-Louvigny, *The Interior Christian*, 178.

is, which so revolts our nature."[54] As we shall see, overcoming this distaste will require humility, which Saint-Jure says is

> so taken up in the greatness of God, that it becomes lost in reverence of him, and self-abasement and annihilation. This is the grace of Christians in their Pilgrimage, who divested and spoiled of all, esteem themselves but a Nothing, and very puff of being, which have nothing but what it received from God, hath not instinct or inclination, but for God: It's a brave humility to see nothing in oneself but Nothingness.[55]

Annihilation is a verb that brings us to the noun of nothingness. Embracing nothingness means annihilating self (self-will, self-love, vainglory, etc.). Self-abasement is a miracle, admits Segneri, but what a miracle! It was figuratively predicted by the Old Testament. "Of your own free choice, you wish to engage in God's service, in preference to that of this vain, transient world, to mortify and subdue yourselves, and to realize thereby, in your own persons, that miracle of self-abasement, figuratively predicted, when even the lions would one day openly forsake their predatory life, and like so many oxen learn to abhor bloodshed and be content to eat straw."[56]

Although nothingness is the opposite of God, nevertheless they are in a relationship. Saint-Jure says it "always points towards God, like a needle touched with a Loadestone."[57] The opposite of nothingness is Greatness, meaning a God so great that he is incomprehensible. Augustine said it most succinctly when he wrote, *si comprehendi, non est Deus*: If you can comprehend it, it's not God. God's Being and our nothingness brings us to admit we cannot finally, fully know God. In apophatic theology we come to know what we do not know. "O my God, I elevate myself as much as I am able, to find thee,"

---

54. Fenelon, *Spiritual Progress*, 30.

55. Saint-Jure, *The Holy Life of Monsieur de Renty*, 55.

56. Paul Segneri, *Quaresimale: Lenten Sermons*, vol. 2 (New York: Christian Press Association, 1874) 307.

57. Saint-Jure, *The Holy Life of Monsieur de Renty*, 55.

writes a confused de Berniere-Louvigny, "and I discover that thy being depends not upon imagination, or sense, or reason; but that thou art, above all, incomprehensible."[58] But then he comes to rejoice in this very ignorance.

> O eternal Being! thou never had beginning, nor ever shall have end! O
> infinite Being! thou art nothing of what we see or know here below;
> thou art an infinity to whom nothing is wanting; to whom nothing
> can be added; from whom nothing can be taken away. Thy perfections
> are infinite. O immense Being; thou fillest all things without extension,
> without quantity, without parts or composition; it is thou alone in whom
> is the eternal source of life and being. When I search for thee, if I go out of
> myself what do I find by privation and nothing? O my God, what damage,
> what annihilation, is it when we fall into sin or imperfection? for this is
> to go out of our being, to plunge ourselves into the abyss of nothingness.
> *Ad nihilum redactus sum;* "I am brought to nothing." Psalms 72:22.[59]

Yet we can love what we cannot comprehend. The mystics speak of this in paradoxical terms: "bright darkness," or "ignorant knowing," or "tasting the incomprehensible." The soul is carried on what Alonso Rodriguez calls a ray of divine ignorance, "so that it may know that God is sweet. In this way it knows by taste what it does not comprehend by intelligence. The less it understands God, the more ignorant it is of him, the sweeter the soul finds him."[60] Acknowledging nothingness means not reducing God to rational categories, or confining him to attributes we contrive. Malaval points this out when we so much as say the Sovereign Name. "[This] could not be done save by this universal concept of the Being of Beings; an idea which in a short time is no longer an idea but a taste; no

---

58. de Berniere-Louvigny, *The Interior Christian*, 98.

59. De Berniere-Louvigny, *The Interior Christian*, 98-99.

60. Alonso Rodriguez, *St. Alphonsus Rodriguez: Autobiography,* 40.

longer a thought but an experience; no longer a significant expression but a satisfying sentiment, a vivifying light, a knowledge wholly effective, and wholly affective."[61]

As a philosophical admission we can use Grou's formulation: "Throughout eternity I was not, and there was no reason why I should exist, nor why I should be what I am. My existence is the simple effect of God's Will."[62] But this acknowledgement becomes even clearer as a liturgical admission, for which we can use Saint-Jure's formulation.

> I believe most firmly, O my God, that Thou art essentially a necessary
> Being, sovereign and independent: and I believe with equal firmness that
> I am essentially a mere nothing, a miserable being, entirely dependent on
> Thee: that Thou hast drawn me out of nothing, in the obscurity of which
> I had dwelt for eternity, to call me to life by giving me the being I have, and
> which Thou dost preserve to me: that I am in such absolute and continual
> dependence on Thee, that if Thou shouldst cease for a moment to sustain
> me, I should immediately fall back into my original nothingness, and so
> remain for all eternity. I believe that of my self I am nothing as to soul or
> body, as to the goods of nature, grace and glory: and that whatever I have
> or am is Thy gift, the result of Thy bounty.[63]

Have we forgotten the dimension of sin when considering abnegation and nothingness? asks Tronson. "Do we remember that having offended God, sin has reduced us to less than nothing, because it adds to our nothingness the guilt of treason against the Divine Majesty?"[64] He thinks we can therefore call neither our being nor our virtues our own, just as Scripture says. "Are we fully persuaded that we can call nothing our own; that

---

61. François Malaval, *A Simple Method of Raising the Soul to Contemplation* (London: J. M. Dent and Sons, Ltd., 1931) 125.

62. Grou, *The Spiritual Maxims*, 6.

63. Saint-Jure, *A Treatise on the Knowledge and Love of Our Lord Jesus Christ*, vol. 2, 491-92.

64. Tronson, *Examination of Conscience Upon Special Subjects*, 51.

we are nothing: and that we can do nothing of ourselves; no, not even conceive a single good thought? 'Not that we are sufficient of ourselves to think anything as of ourselves; but our sufficiency is of God' (2 Cor. 3. 5)."[65] Libermann thinks the rescue of humanity from this state will require a power humanity lacks in itself. "We must remember that we have fallen into such extremes of corruption and evil by our sin that by themselves our souls are unable to tend Godwards; our mind cannot conceive divine things or what could save us and our will is unable to love him. Then God has to raise us from our extreme nothingness and incapacity in order that we may have life."[66] When Olier asks "What then is our own in us?" he answers "Our nothingness and sins; this is all we can boast of."[67] In the meantime, "man, of himself, being nothingness and sin ... ought to have no other desire for himself than to be treated as he deserves, that is to say, to suffer contempt, persecution, poverty, etc."[68]

Calumny, maltreatment, and want are precisely what the saints embrace, and embrace all the more strongly as they are being sanctified by a power not their own. Rodriguez says the cause why saints are so humble, and have so low an opinion of themselves is because "as they increase in sanctity, they increase in humility, and in a contempt of themselves. The more God enlightens them, and communicates himself to them, the more they perceive that they have of their own only nothingness and sin."[69] Saint-Jure finds a twinned revelation by the divine lights, which not only teach the soul "the greatness, the goodness and the other ineffable perfections of the Divinity," but at the very same time exhibit to the soul "her inherent nothingness and her continual need of God."[70] The former is taught by the latter: by embracing nothingness we learn the ineffable perfections of God. The book of grace has the perfections of the Divinity written on one page, and the inherent nothingness of the soul on the other.

---

65. Tronson, *Examination of Conscience Upon Special Subjects*, 51.

66. Libermann, *Jesus Through Jewish Eyes*, vol. 2, 74.

67. Olier, *Catechism of an Interior Life*, 86.

68. Olier, *Catechism of an Interior Life*, 51-52.

69. Rodriguez, *The Practice of Christian and Religious Perfection*, vol. 2, 163.

70. Saint-Jure, *The Spiritual Man*, 217.

Libermann identifies "only two principles: God, who is truth, and sin, which is lie, nothingness, the negation of truth and the exact opposite of God."[71] God and not-God, truth and lie, righteousness and sin, glory and vainglory, being and nothingness. Unfortunately, pride regularly chooses sin, falsehood, and nullity, so God must take us away from self and world in order to bring us toward himself. Human beings are creatures made to be raised higher. This is the incredibly optimistic anthropology of Christian doctrine. Unfortunately, de la Colombiere says, we cannot be raised if we commit ourselves to the not-God.

> The thought of the greatness of God and of the nothingness of all created things has made me understand the foolishness of those who make themselves dependent upon other people and the happiness of those who depend only upon God. There is only one way of raising ourselves above our own nothingness, and that is to cling to God: "He who is joined to the Lord is one spirit" (I Cor 6:17). By doing this we rise above the things of earth and become in some measure like unto God.[72]

So in order to elevate us, God must humble us; in order to show us the sublime, he must show us our nothingness; in order to give us true knowledge of himself and ourselves, he must break through the false revelations in which we incarcerate ourselves. Saint-Jure thinks "pride is inseparable from false revelations, because, in proportion as God elevates a soul to sublime favors, He humbles her by communicating His light more abundantly, to enable her clearly to see her sins, defects and nothingness."[73] Those false revelations tell us lies about the world, and lies about ourselves, from which we must be disabused, which will involve embracing nothingness, according to Libermann. "All here is vanity and nothingness. *God alone* must be our entire happiness. Blessed are we if, in the end,

---

71. Libermann, *Jesus Through Jewish Eyes*, vol. 2, 204.

72. De la Colombiere, *The Spiritual Direction of Saint Claude de la Colombiere*, 84.

73. Saint-Jure, *The Spiritual Man*, 100.

we are totally His. Let us not put our confidence in man. *God alone!*[74] Fenelon thinks a new vision is offered to the world, which it can find either disheartening or inspiring. That choice is the choice of conversion.

> Show as much as you please of the vanity and nothingness of the creature by the faults of creatures. Call to notice the brevity and uncertainty of life, the fickleness of fortune, the faithlessness of friends, the illusion of great places, the bitterness which is inevitable there, the disappointment of the most beautiful hopes, the emptiness of all the good things we possess, the reality of all the evils we suffer: all this moralizing, true and reasonable as it is, only skims the heart. It does not sink in. The inner man is not changed at all. He sighs to see himself a slave to vanity, and does not get out of his slavery. But if the ray of the divine light shines within, he sees the abyss of good which is God, the abyss of nothingness and evil which is the corrupted creature. He despises himself. He hates himself. He leaves himself. He flees himself. He fears himself. He renounces himself. He gives himself up to God. He loses himself in him. Happy loss![75]

The sight of God everywhere strips our false estimates of everything else. The world is frail, fragile, finite – why ever should it command our allegiance? Fenelon images dialogue with the world. We should repudiate it: "With what boldness do you hope to impose on us, vain and fantastic form which passes and disappears? You are only a dream, and you want us to believe in you!"[76] When we become aware that of its charade behind masks, we should say to it: "The moment you offer yourself to us with a smiling face, you cause us a thousand pains. The same moment you are going to disappear, and you dare promise to

---

74. Libermann, *Letters to People in the World*, Spiritan Series 6, vol. 2, 146.

75. Fenelon, *Christian Perfection*, 146.

76. Fenelon, *Christian Perfection*, 72.

make us happy? Happy only is he who sees his nothingness in the light of Jesus Christ!"[77] The correct use of the world depends upon seeing it in light of judgment day.

The first name for sin is self-complacency: being pleased with oneself, instead of with God. The second name for sin is being complacent with the world: finding one's pleasure in what is not-God. Bourdaloue says God has commanded love of us, but it must take a certain form. God does not command a love of tenderness and feeling (not always in our power), or a forced love (not honorable for God), or a fervor (which may be beyond our discernment), "but he requires, under pain of everlasting reprobation, that I love him as God, in preference to all that is not God."[78] Abnegation aids love – is, in fact, a form of love – because it is obedience, and as such does battle with self-love, self-will, self-complacency.

Liturgical abnegation is the source and cause of our realization that the contingent world is not permanent, and neither are we, which makes abnegation of all the grandeurs of the world easier, notices Fenelon.

> For it is in seeing God that we see the nothingness of the world, which will vanish in a little while like smoke. All the grandeurs, and their paraphernalia, will flee away like a dream. All height will be brought low, all power will be crushed, every superb head will be bowed beneath the weight of the eternal majesty of God. In the day when he will judge men, he will obliterate with one look all that shines in the present night, as the sun, in rising, puts out the stars. We shall see only God everywhere, so great will he be. We shall seek in vain, we shall find only him, so shall he fill all things. "Where have they gone," we shall say, "those things which have charmed our hearts? What is left of them? Where were they?" Alas, not even the marks of the place where they have been remain.[79]

---

77. Fenelon, *Christian Perfection*, 72.

78. Louis Bourdaloue, *Sermons, and Moral Discourses, on the Important Duties of Christianity*, vol. 2 (Dublin: Published by James Duffy, 1843) 98.

79. Fenelon, *Christian Perfection*, 71.

NOTHINGNESS AS LITURGICAL AFFECTION

Our nothingness is an ontological fact – can we understand it as a liturgical opportunity? Malaval finds a way to put it in a verb form: "recognizing its impotence to do anything for God, *it naughts itself* in His presence."[1] Guillore makes numerous connections between true worship and nothingness. "God is All, man nothing; the soul must bow before Him in a deep penetrating sense of its own nothingness, while a true offering of self to suffer all His Will is a necessary element of real worship" (66). "The more you are stripped of self and self-conceit ... the more capable you will become of true adoration" (70). "Strange to say the very greatness of our distance from God, and the self-abasement with which our knowledge of it fills us, promotes this union" (70). "The only way to pray profitably is in the spirit of earnest adoration, self-abnegation, silence and resignation" (80). And "among the various ways in which man may bow in adoring homage before his Creator, there is none more complete and effectual than a voluntary abasement" (275).[2] Latria comes from the depths of my nothingness.

How can the Being of God and the Nothingness of man possibly coexist? It seems quite impossible, and yet Boutauld has encouraging words to say.

> Infinity elevates him above you, and an Infinite Goodness ... lessens him
> so far, as to be equal with you ... He alone is your Master and equal;
> and therefore it is of him, you may say with Truth, *my beloved to me,*

---

1. Malaval, *A Simple Method of Raising the Soul to Contemplation* 33. Emphasis added.

2. François Guillore, *Self-Renunciation*, (London: Rivingtons, 1871).

and I to him, notwithstanding he is God, and I am nothing; yet by an ineffable Mystery, he is fit for me, and I for him. His Wisdom has taken my measure upon him, and rendered my littleness capable after some manner of containing his Immensity."[3]

The key to this linkage between the supreme and the inferior, the great and the little, the elevated and the near, is obedience. "I have nothing," admits Bossuet. "I am nothing; and so, it is only a question of abasement, or rather, only of keeping my nothingness obedient to You."[4]

Malaval first God to sanctify his own name, and then asks him to "sanctify our nothingness to the end that our thoughts may be reduced to silence, to adoration, to love," and we are actually led to "glorify Thee that Thou art *He who is* and that Thy creature are nothing in themselves. I rejoice that nothing can equal Thee, that nothing can express Thee, that nothing can praise Thee, but Thyself."[5] This is liturgical employment of nothingness, indeed. Crasset marvels that nothingness is the cause of opportunity. "Oh sacred nothingness, wherein the soul loses its being to be transformed into God!"[6]

To be, is to come from God; not to be, is to return to Him. Until a soul finds its nothingness, it cannot find God. He is hidden under the veil of creatures, and it is only when men have penetrated and looked beyond that material veil that they will see Him, to so speak, in plain view.

---

3. Michel Boutauld, *A Method of Conversing with God* (Liege: printed by H. Dessain & Sisters, 1789) 105-06.

4. Bossuet, *Selections from Meditations on the Gospel*, vol. 2, 19.

5. Malaval, *A Simple Method of Raising the Soul to Contemplation*, 126-27

6. Crasset, *Christian Considerations*, 270.

> To know all, it is necessary to know nothing; to taste all, to taste nothing; to have all, to have nothing. To become all, it is necessary to be nothing.[7]

Nothingness does not appear as a threat in liturgical abnegation because it is a cause for gratitude. The nothingness as revealed by liturgical abnegation is different from all other teachings about nothingness in two ways. First, Libermann says it is not a lesson that can be learned from the world, it is a lesson that must be learned from the holiness of God. "This is what constitutes the humility of the intellect: the clear and intimate knowledge of our nothingness, baseness and sin, and the existence, greatness and holiness of God. This is also what these words mean: *the knowledge of what one is in oneself and in relation to God*."[8] Second, Baker says it is not a lesson that can be learned from speculative knowledge, it is an admission that must come from affective knowledge.

> You must note that there is a great difference between the *knowledge* of our nothing and the *feeling* of our nothing. By a little consideration, according to the light of natural reason or of faith, we may know our own nothing, and realise that our being is wholly dependent on the only true being of God. But this knowledge, although it be good and may help us to attain the feeling, is not the feeling. And many men have that knowledge, while very few have that feeling.[9]

If the last chapter tried to provide some knowledge, this chapter will invite a feeling which arises from an encounter with the Transcendent One.

The liturgical question is: in what do we glory? to whom do we pay homage? what do we fear and reverence? As a friend of mine said, "If you do not fear God, what *do* you fear?" Liturgical abnegation answers that everything beyond nothingness already belongs to God, so he is the one who should be receiving its glory. Pride glories in the world, but Bona

---

7. Crasset, *Christian Considerations*, 441.

8. Libermann, *Of Humility*, 2.

9. Baker, *The Cloud of Unknowing, With a Commentary on the Cloud by Father Augustine Baker*, 342

thinks this false glory – vainglory – should be "overcome by the love of righteousness. *We ought to glory in nothing.* What is ours, is nothing. Of ourselves we can do nothing; for it is God that works in us both to will and to do."[10] Nothingness therefore aids our worship, and de Bergamo describes worshipers actually rejoicing in the fact that God is Almighty, and we are not.

> If we wish to discern what belongs to God and that which is our own,
> it is sufficient for us to reflect that by rendering to God all that is His,
> nothing is left to ourselves but nothingness. So that we can truly say with
> the prophet: "I am brought to nothing." (Ps 72:22) This is a true saying,
> that all that is within us that is more than nothingness belongs to God,
> and He can take away what is His when He chooses without doing us
> any wrong. Therefore in what can we pride ourselves, since God can take
> anything away from us the moment that we begin to glory in it?[11]

All that is within us that is more than nothingness belongs to God: that would be everything! If everything we possess (starting with being itself) is a gift from God, therefore we cannot glory in anything as if it is our own. This is a liturgical confession of nothingness; this is a liturgical consequence of nothingness. Things seem to have an existence, but compared with God, they are nothing, since they only possess substance on loan from God. Accepting nothingness (i.e. annihilation) is itself a liturgical act because it is returning all things to God in order that God may be glorified. For Eudes, men are "nothing but dust, corruption and nothingness. We are nothing and can do nothing of ourselves. Every creature has come forth from nothingness, therefore it is nothing, has nothing, and can do nothing of itself, without the sustaining power of its Creator,"[12] and for John of Avila, this applies not only to any being we have, but also to any righteousness we have. "If God's hand were withdrawn from you, you would return in that instant to the

---

10. Bona, *The Principles of Christianity,* 134.

11. De Bergamo, *Humility of Heart,* 103.

12. Eudes, *The Life and the Kingdom of Jesus in Christian Souls,* 40.

abyss of nothingness in which you were before. Likewise, if God were to stop protecting you, you would return to the sins from which he drew you, and to others greater."[13]

By God's gift we have being and virtue; by our own capacity we are nothingness and sin, so where would we be if God took back creation and grace? John of Avila wants to know.

> He who is taught by divine truth attributes nought to himself save his sins and his own nothingness. If all that God gave us at our creation, and which by His power He daily sustains, were withdrawn from us, there would remain only nothingness and we should return to the nothingness from which we were formed. And if God took from us the grace which He bestows on us for the sake of Jesus Christ, what would the most holy amongst us be, but what Peter was when he denied our Lord, or Paul when he persecuted his Redeemer? We know but too well what we were before God touched our souls, and taking from us our old hearts gave us new ones in their stead.[14]

So liturgical abnegation combats pride by recognizing God's sustenance of creation. God is worthy of liturgy because he created the heavens and earth; he is equally worthy of liturgy because he is sustaining that same heavens and earth, and if he did not, they would return instantly to nothingness. Scaramelli suggests we should see the first chapter of Genesis outside our window every morning: "he repeats the gift at every instant, and preserves us by the working of a power which yields in nothing to that by which He created us."[15] But making this acknowledgement depends upon a battle between pride and humility, vainglory and meekness, thinks de Bergamo. "No one can fall who lies on

---

13. John of Avila, *Audi, Filia*, 197.

14. John of Avila, *Letters*, 153.

15. John Baptist Scaramelli, *Directorium Asceticum; or, Guide to the Spiritual Life*, vol. 3 (New York: Benziger Bros, 1902) 598.

the ground; and no one can sin so long as he is humble. My God! My God! let me remain
in my nothingness, for it is the surest state for me."[16]

Pride blurs our vision, but recognizing nothingness is clear-sightedness. God's optical
correction can be startling, but it is necessary. God will permit our disappointment in
order to wake us up, suggest de Castaniza. "This pride – whence this deceit proceeds
– so hoodwinks the eyes of our soul that we see it not at all, and are therefore justly
permitted to fall and fail of our expectation, that we may thereby truly come to the
knowledge of our own nothingness, and learn to ground all our good designs upon the
Divine goodness, grace, and power, and not at all on our own strength or endeavours."[17]
Scripture recognizes a deceptiveness of pride[18] and de Bergamo wants to know where
it comes from. "In reality a lie dwells essentially in that pride which makes us esteem
ourselves above what we are. Whoever regards himself as more than mere nothingness is
filled with pride, and is a liar."[19] Recognition of nothingness is necessary in the search for
truth about God, ourselves, the world, and our neighbor. It is necessary because Tronson
says we are so easily we are so easily fooled. "Do we not quickly lose this consciousness
of our nothingness when we are flattered and applauded by the world; and do we not
suffer ourselves to be dazzled and intoxicated by praise, instead of humbling ourselves?"[20]
The point is not to make us feel bad about ourselves. The point is obedience, submission,
service, and oblation – all liturgical verities. To reference de Bergamo again:

> But when this person says of himself: "I have riches, I have health, and I
> have knowledge," etc., what is meant by this "I"? Nothingness; and yet
> this "I", this nothingness, that derives all it possesses from God, dares to
> disregard this same God by disobeying His sovereign commandments,

---

16. De Bergamo, *Humility of Heart*, 34.

17. De Castaniza, *The Spiritual Conflict and Conquest*, 93.

18. "If any man think himself to be something whereas he is nothing, He deceives
   himself" (Gal 6:3).

19. De Bergamo, *Humility of Heart*, 10.

20. Tronson, *Examination of Conscience*, 53-54.

saying to Him, if not in words most certainly in deeds, which is far worse, "I will not serve"; no, I will not obey. Oh, pride, pride! But, O my soul, "Why doth thy spirit swell against God?" (Tobias 15:13)[21]

If one thinks the riches and honors one receives from the world are adequate, why worship God? If one worships God, then the riches and honors one receives from the world are nothing.

We know from the book of Genesis that although the fall consisted in disobedience, it came from pride, and de Bergamo calls this pride the greatest of all sins, because proud persons "rebel against God, setting themselves in opposition to God, nor do they mind displeasing God in order to please themselves, leaving the All to attach themselves to their own nothingness."[22] Pride tries to pry the creature apart from the Creator, whereas the creature, in fact, is nothing in its independence. So why seek it? Libermann brings us back to the liturgical verity of glory.

> Pride has an invincible tendency to seek glory, glory inherent in the creature as such. There follows from this another invincible tendency, to seek glory in the good opinions of others, a glory which is basically a lie, since the creature to which it relates has only its own nothingness and consequently is devoid of true glory. It is formally a lie, for it only exists in the form of an idea held by others of the one whom they esteem. The latter draws nothing authentic from this good repute to really enhance itself.[23]

The creature's full glory is to be found only in glorifying the Creator, and all other glory is empty, whether given or received. Nothingness is concerned with giving latria to the right object, in the right way, for the right reason, in the right measure. In other words, Libermann says it is concerned with justice in worship. "When people glorify themselves

---

21. De Bergamo, *Humility of Heart*, 118.

22. De Bergamo, *Humility of Heart*, 187.

23. Libermann, *Jesus Through Jewish Eyes*, vol. 3, 219-20.

before others on whatever good quality it may be, it is not God they glorify nor is God glorifying them; it is nothingness glorifying nothingness through another nothingness, and consequently the glory is nothing: 'it is nothing'."[24] The sinner loses the point of view that he is a creature, which does not exist for his own sake, but exists for God's pleasure.

Fenelon says the sinner knows this at one level, and dares not deny it, "but it escapes him, and he wants always unconsciously to come back to bargaining with God to seek his own interest."[25] Bargaining with God has been going on even before the fall in the garden; the fallen angels tried it, too. All sin is the failure to recognize that God is God, and we are not. So the battle cry against the rebelling angels, that first rang in the heavens, was the faithful angel crying out "who is like God?" (Mikha'el). Libermann finds it laughable when he sees us misdirect our worship to other creatures (other contingent beings). "This little being is so little that it could be called nothing, even during the time of its existence. And how to boast of nothingness before other nothingness? Men believe us: that's enough to satisfy us! ... Nothingness has esteem for another nothingness! Will we be less stupid and miserable for this?[26]

Being restored to such a state is an operation of grace, of course. We must surrender ourselves entirely to the guidance of grace, which follows a different course than nature, one mapped by Grou's careful tracing.

> First of all it fills the Christian with a consciousness of his nothingness, his incapacity to obtain any supernatural gift, his need of being absolutely dependent on God and perpetually appealing to Him, and of mistrusting himself entirely. It teaches him to keep his sins in mind, in order to maintain a salutary feeling of shame and repress every impulse of pride at its birth: and not to flatter himself that they are easily forgiven, but to expiate them by penance, of which the humiliation – the portion of the sinner – forms the principal part.[27]

---

24. Libermann, *Jesus Through Jewish Eyes*, vol. 2, 214.

25. Fenelon, *Christian Perfection*, 138.

26. Libermann, *Of Humility*, 8.

27. Grou, *The School of Jesus Christ*, 220.

When we see by the light of grace, we see into the least of our imperfections, which is the reason, again, why the more sanctified the saint, the more he professes his nothingness. "The more sensible he is of the goodness and mercy of God, the more acquainted he is with his own misery," says Rodriguez. "If we set any value upon ourselves, the reason is, because we have little knowledge of God, and are not illuminated with light from heaven: the rays of the sun of justice have not yet penetrated into our soul."[28] That *we* are nothing means *God* is everything. That *we* are nothing means everything we have comes from *God*, and this includes being, goods of nature, redemption, deification – everything. Saint-Jure says "the mind of St. Catherine of Genoa was so filled with this knowledge, that she would not even name herself, regarding herself as pure nothingness, and as not having anything but what God had given her."[29] Liturgical obeisance produces an abnegation that climaxes in claiming our nothingness. Because we recognize God's omnipotence, we confess our nothingness; because we recognize our weakness, we confess God's sovereignty; because we recognize our helplessness, we confess God's supremacy.

But it is crucial to remember that nothingness does not disconnect us from God. It cannot, because our being is linked to him in two ways. First, poverty is linked to his grandeur, and second, powerlessness is linked to his goodness. De Bergamo thinks nothingness actually connects us to God as a form of liturgizing the Creator-Savior in a reception of grace.

> The soul is truly humble when it recognizes that its true position in the order of nature or of grace is entirely dependent on the power, providence and mercy of God; so that finding in itself nothing but what is of God, it appropriates to itself only its own nothingness, and abiding in his nothingness. It places itself on the level of all other creatures without raising itself in any way above them. It annihilates itself before God, not so as to remain in an otiose inactivity, but seeking rather to glorify

28. Rodriguez, *The Practice of Christian and Religious Perfection*, vol. 2, 253.

29. Saint-Jure, *A Treatise on the Knowledge and Love of Our Lord Jesus Christ*, 539.

Him continually, conforming with exact obedience to His laws and with perfect submission to His will.[30]

When the soul recognizes her nothingness with a vivid, immediate, and affective knowledge, then Eudes thinks the knowledge gained will know that "when He gives you some helpful thought of pious inspiration or some other grace, your pride and self-love may not claim it as your own, ascribe to your own effort, vigilance and cooperation but rather refer it to Him."[31]

Who does this sound like? Who do we know who refrained from claiming as his own the gifts he received from God, his Father? Surprising as it sounds, Jesus is our model. His annihilation (kenosis) is the model for our nothingness (abnegation). The faithful one follows Christ's path from kenosis to glorification that occurred in the mystery of the Incarnation. Startling as the thought is, admits Lallemant, "it may be said that the Divinity in some wise annihilated itself in this mystery of the incarnation, by uniting itself personally to a nature drawn from nothingness."[32] Christ's kenosis was a self-emptying, a sort of annihilation, and in this Christians should imitate him. Alacoque found that through our own abjection, we can honor Christ's abjection. "Love, then, of our own abjection in the love of Our Lord Jesus Christ is sufficient for us, in order to honor the mysteries of His holy Passion and death. These He wishes us to honor. And we must observe a holy silence, as He did, in all humiliations and sufferings."[33] How to be a true disciple (follower)? Eudes wonders.

> If I wish to come after Thee I must not only renounce all things, but
> my own self as well. To this end, I give myself to the power of thy divine
> love by which Thou didst reduce Thyself to nothingness, and in union
> with that same love I profess to renounce entirely and forever everything

---

30. De Bergamo, *Humility of Heart*, 40-41.

31. Eudes, *The Life and the Kingdom of Jesus in Christian Souls*, 86-87.

32. Lallemant, *The Spiritual Doctrine of Father Louis Lallemant*, ed. Faber, 236.

33. Alacoque, *Spiritual Letters*, letter 101, Kindle edition.

belonging to myself and to the old Adam; to annihilate at Thy Feet, as far as possible, my mind, my self-love, my own will, my life and my being.[34]

We are perhaps surprised at associating nothingness with Jesus, but why would that be? We are not surprised at associating humility, meekness, lowliness with him. The reason Jesus was humble in such a superlative degree was twofold: the knowledge of God he had in his divine nature, and the knowledge of man he had in his human nature. Grou discovers that "Jesus Christ was humble in a degree only possible to a soul that possessed the most perfect knowledge of God's infinite Being, and also of the creature's nothingness. Not only had He the knowledge of these two extremes – infinite being and nothingness – but He was also most vividly and profoundly conscious of them, since they were united in His own Person."[35] The Son liturgizes the Father in his subordination and submission, and Baker sees the Holy Spirit wanting to unite us to his liturgy.

By virtue of this indispensable subordination, or comparing of God with His creatures, the most perfect, most holy, and most sublime of all God's creatures do most profoundly humble themselves in His presence. The glorified saints do prostrate themselves before Him, casting their crowns at His feet: the Seraphim cover their faces, and our blessed Lord as Man, having a most perfect knowledge, perception, and feeling of the nothingness of creatures, and the absolute totality of God, did more than all saints and angels most profoundly humble Himself before the Divine Majesty of His Father, remaining continually plunged in the abyss of His own nothing. Moreover, in virtue hereof, He submitted Himself to all creatures, yea, forasmuch as concerned suffering, even to the devil himself. As a creature, He saw nothing in Himself but the nothing of a creature, and in all other creatures He saw nothing but God.[36]

---

34. Eudes, *The Life and the Kingdom of Jesus in Christian Souls*, 145.

35. Grou, *The School of Jesus Christ*, 194.

36. Baker, Holy Wisdom, 313.

Regrettably, we do not embrace our nothingness, even when we have seen Christ
model humility for us. "Even after His infinite example of humility," Eudes regrets,
"nothingness still wants to be exalted, and then, indeed, He finds this more than
unendurable."[37] The Lord therefore imposes crosses upon us – pieces of his own cross,
really – and Surin warns us "not [to] be surprised to find that God loves to see His servants
in a condition in which their own nothingness is forced upon them."[38] Libermann admits
the cross must be imposed because we do not take it up voluntarily. "He imposes upon
you His most lovable and admirable Cross, for the purpose of effecting in your person
this disposition of nothingness. He destroys, crushes and annihilates the flesh with its
powers, and He alone will remain the Master."[39] If Christ is master, then we rejoice in
the very things the world despises. Rejoice in weakness, says Libermann: "Rejoice at the
sight of your weakness, abjection, uselessness and nothingness. Remain thus absorbed
in our Lord who is in you and become, as it were, annihilated in order that He alone
may exist in you."[40] Rejoice in tribulation, Libermann adds: "Jesus alone is great and
glorious! To Him be all glory and to us, poor creatures, be all shame! Remain in your
nothingness before Him, and consider yourself most blessed when, for love of Him and
for His glory, you are weighed down by tribulation."[41] And rejoice in annihilation,
concludes de Lombez: "Say to Him ... *You delight, dear Lord, to work upon nothing; behold
me, and if I am yet something in my own eyes, hasten my annihilation that You may begin
your work.*[42]

Rejoice in nothingness. Although the unbeliever finds this difficult, the liturgical soul
finds it a happy state because it glorifies God. Our humility is his glory, explains Saint-Jure.
"I esteem myself happy in being nothingness that Thou mayest be all, in being darkness

---

37. Eudes, *The Life and the Kingdom of Jesus in Christian Souls*, 43.

38. Surin, *The Foundations of Spiritual Life*, 13.

39. Libermann, *Letters to Clergy and Religious*, Spiritan Series 8, vol. 4, 248.

40. Libermann, *Letters to Clergy and Religious*, Spiritan Series 9, vol. 5, 71.

41. Francis Libermann, *Letters to Religious Sisters and Aspirants*, Spiritan Series 5, vol.
    1 (Pittsburgh: Duquesne University Press, 1962) 102.

42. De Lombez, *Interior Peace*, 110-11.

that Thou mayest be light, weakness that Thou mayest be strength, poverty that Thou mayest be riches, misery that Thou mayest be beatitude, an abyss of imperfections that Thou mayest be the sovereign perfection ... I beg of Thee ... that Thou wouldst unite Thy being to my nothingness, and work great things in me, for Thy own sake."[43] This is perfection, insofar as "perfection consists in seeking to please God, and only God, in all things."[44] De la Colombiere expresses this same sentiment repeatedly on the same page: "It is He alone whom I wish to please ... It is a great happiness to belong altogether to God, seeing that His greatness is infinite ... I have understood this from the comparison of a king who chose one of his subjects to be solely his, and who would not allow him to give any service to anyone other than to his own person, as he wished his friendship entire."[45]

We rejoice in poverty and nothingness because it permits sacrifice (a liturgical reason for rejoicing). Remain in poverty and nothingness, says Libermann, so you can "offer Him your body and soul constantly to be sacrificed to His glory, whenever and wherever He chooses. Be prepared before Him as is a victim lying on the altar before the sacrificing priest."[46] Indeed, the nothingness has nothing else but a liturgical purpose: sacrifice.

O chosen vessels ! If you are faithful, Jesus will use you for the salvation of many. But He will sacrifice you. He will teach you how you must suffer for His glory. Be faithful, therefore, and follow every impulse which Jesus wishes to give to your souls. Live by Him and in Him, keeping in mind your poverty, nothingness and incapacity. Don't say: "I am going to save many souls." It is Jesus who will decide that. He is the Lord who can at will foster His glory by means of the poorest instrument as well as by the richest. His Father made out of nothing this whole beautiful universe and the creatures of heaven. If nothingness has been the starting point for

---

43. Saint-Jure, *Knowledge and Love of Christ*, vol. 1, 263.

44. De la Colombiere, *Faithful Servant*, 56.

45. De la Colombiere, *Faithful Servant*, 56.

46. Libermann, *Letters to Religious Sisters and Aspirants*, Spiritan Series 5, vol. 1, 20.

such a magnificence, a poor man can also serve as His instrument for the diffusion of His grace.[47]

We are powerless to scale heaven, but there is something we can do. We can "resign ourselves entirely to God by a total self-renunciation," de Caussade says, and "lose self in the abyss of our own nothingness to find it no more save in God."[48] This is the one thing needful that Jesus referred to in his gospel, because "the more completely a soul annihilates itself the more precious does it become in the sight of God. To lose yourself in your own nothingness is a sure way of finding God."[49] If the divine hand accomplishes the will of His Father, Libermann is sure it will be in our poor nothingness,[50] because there a soul is kept "in complete forgetfulness of self, and of everything that relates to self. Be like a machine in the hands of your Master, doing all things by the sole movement of Jesus."[51] Nothingness does not belittle self, it forgets self. Alacoque was shown that forgetting self is not belittlement, it is a release to serve. "Once He said to me with a voice full of authority: 'I am going to make you so poor, so despicable, so abject in your own eyes, I am going to destroy your self-esteem so completely that upon your nothingness I shall be able to establish Myself'."[52]

The choice of Incarnation is an enigma to us. Why would the Word humble himself so low? What could possibly be his motive? What should possibly be our response? Alacoque hazards a guess.

Ah, my beloved Sister, if only you realized the honor and partiality the King of Heaven is showing you in so lowering Himself as to come down

---

47. Libermann, *Letters to Clergy and Religious*, Spiritan Series 9, vol. 5, 303.

48. De Caussade, *Abandonment to Divine Providence*, 99.

49. De Caussade, *Abandonment to Divine Providence*, 99.

50. Libermann, *Letters to Clergy and Religious*, Spiritan Series 8, vol. 4, 308.

51. Libermann, *Letters to Clergy and Religious*, Spiritan Series 8, vol. 4, 225.

52. Alacoque, *Spiritual Letters*, letter 70, Kindle edition.

into your heart! ... He wishes to mean everything to you, wishes you to take these humiliations as a sign that He is waiting for you in the depths of your heart. You must leave everything and go and keep Him company in the way that pleases Him, whether that be by rendering homage to His omnipotence by your powerlessness and thus letting Him act in you and for you, or by new humiliations He will make you find within yourself. These are like so many stairs by which you can go down into the depths of your own nothingness, they are to find your pleasure with Him. For this Sovereign of our souls takes pleasure only in souls empty of self ... To belong entirely to Him one must no longer retain anything of self.[53]

Strange though it sounds to the ears of the world, our powerlessness renders liturgical homage to God's omnipotence. God desires a liturgy emerging like a butterfly from the chrysalis of poverty, dependence, submission, and nothingness. Meanwhile, the world has other plans – plans that Libermann thinks God must ultimately confound. It is reminiscent of the Tower of Babel.

When God has designs of grace and mercy in regard to good souls who love Him, even though they may love Him with an impetuous love, He thwarts their beautiful schemes. They hurry, rush forward and are out of breath: they want to reach the goal before they have started. God arrests their progress by placing all kinds of obstacles in their path. They fall, rise, and start to run once more, and are out of breath. He closes one exit after another and finally they are brought to a full stop. They then collapse, full of sadness, agitation and discouragement. But bit by bit they come to realize their weakness and their nothingness. They humble themselves before God, and realizing their extreme need of help, turn to God to find support. Peace gradually returns to their souls.[54]

---

53. Alacoque, *Spiritual Letters,* letter 80, Kindle edition.

54. Libermann, *Letters to Religious Sisters and Aspirants,* Spiritan Series 5, vol. 1, 130.

Libermann knows the cross and nothingness are no less a stumbling block and foolishness to modern man than they were to the Jews and Gentiles, nevertheless, they are still God's good pleasure, and if we wish the Christ to live in us "we should abandon ourselves, and keep ourselves in our nothingness before Him and in Him .... He knows how He lives in us, and His Father knows also: why, then should we want to interfere?"[55] Christ went the way of the cross, and so must we. His state is intended to be our state. He accepted kenotic annihilation, we should accept the abnegation God wills for us in his mysterious providence. Rejoice, Libermann says, at the fact that Jesus keeps us in our state of nothingness.

> Do not feel sad about it, but, on the contrary, rejoice in it with all your soul. For, if our Master wishes to keep us thus in poverty, weakness and nothingness, and takes delight in it, is it not proper that we who are such wretched servants, should rejoice when we see that our sovereign and well-beloved Lord does with us according to His wishes and at our expense?

> Suppose even that we could make use of admirable graces and gifts such as we behold in saints, we should not be able to succeed. This shows us how weak we are, how utterly incapable of accomplishing anything that is worthwhile. We are not even capable of using the things Our Lord puts at our disposal and in our hands. He Himself has to launch, propel, conduct us at every step and in every one of our actions.[56]

Acknowledging the liturgical origin and liturgical purpose of nothingness is startling, Saint-Jure admits. "God's glory is the end of our creation and preservation: save for it we would still be in nothingness, therefore we ought to refer to it all that we are,

---

55. Libermann, *Letters to Clergy and Religious*, Spiritan Series 8, vol. 4, 220.

56. Libermann, *Letters to Clergy and Religious*, Spiritan Series 8, vol. 4, 351.

since we exist only for it."[57] Startling or not, Tronson says this is the very reason why Jesus displayed cruciform nothingness. "Let us adore our Lord Jesus Christ, Who, although, as God, He is co-equal with His Father, yet, as Man, shows us by His own Example how we should prostrate ourselves before the Divine Majesty, acknowledging our nothingness in His Presence."[58] The cross is a school of liturgy, says Crasset, where prayer "gives us a knowledge of ourselves, which teaches us wise lessons of humility, makes us realize and appreciate our nothingness, and reveals to us the greatness and sanctity of God, before Whom our imaginary virtues have no existence, beauty, form, or measure."[59] Christ's kenosis teaches us how to glorify the Divine Majesty, and embracing our nothingness ensures that adoration is given to God alone. Madeline Saint-Joseph knows that "adoration is what God looked for from the beginning in his creatures, in the angels in heaven and in men on earth, because adoration is a duty and a respect that the lesser owes to the greater, the subject owes to the sovereign Lord. Through it the creature experiences its nothingness in order to offer homage to its Creator."[60]

Grou finds this to be the state and status of the angels in heaven in their liturgical vocation, and if it is not ours, as well, we should distrust the worship we are presenting. "If you be devoid of this feeling; if you do not approach God with a profound consciousness of your own nothingness; if while the pure and holy beings in Heaven cover their faces with their wings in His presence – you, a sinner, be not possessed by religious awe, you should mistrust your prayer."[61]

Neither our spirituality, nor our liturgy, nor our abnegation should become self-serving, when it is God whom those should be serving. Boudon knows that Jesus knows this tendency in us.

---

57. Saint-Jure, *Union with Our Lord Jesus Christ in His Principal Mysteries*, 76-77.

58. Tronson, *Examination of Conscience*, 51.

59. De Sales & Crasset, *The Secret of Sanctity*, 156.

60. Madeleine de Saint-Joseph, *The Spiritual Letters of Madeleine de Saint-Joseph*, in *Berulle and the French School*, 200.

61. Grou, *The School of Jesus Christ*, 246.

Jesus, knowing that creatures are prone to put themselves forward in all things — some of purpose and design and with manifest knowledge of what they do, others through a subtle and almost imperceptible self-seeking: some in temporal things, others, who have renounced mere material aims, in spiritual things, and even such are most divine – and knowing, on the other hand, the infinite greatness of His Eternal Father, who ought to be the supreme object of regard in everything, and that in strict justice He alone ought to be magnified in all, it being the part of creatures to remain in their own nothingness – Jesus, I say, in order to satisfy the justice of His Father, offended by so monstrous a perversion, hides Himself in an infinitely astonishing manner, and endures annihilations at which we stand aghast.[62]

John of Avila uses the illustration of being dependent on God for both being and holiness the way the light in a room is dependent on the lamp. "Consider that you are so dependent on God's power that, if it were to fail you, you would, in that moment, also fail. It is just as the light in a room would fail if the lamp lighting it were taken out, or as light is taken away from the earth by the absence of the sun. With profound reverence, then, adore this Lord as the principle of your being."[63] The light failing absent the lamp applies both to being (we would cease to be) and to the good action done by grace (all our virtue is God's work).

What is the result of this contemplation upon nothingness? Where have we wound up? We can explain the conclusion in numerous ways. We may say with Eudes that we give ourselves to God for his honor and homage.

O Most Lovable Jesus, I fall at Thy feet in the utmost depths of my nothingness ... I offer Thee all the honor that has been given Thee during this night in heaven and on earth.

---

62. Boudon, *The Hidden Life of Jesus*, 61.

63. John of Avila, *Audi, Filia*, 191.

O my Saviour, I offer and consecrate myself entirely and forever to Thee and through Thee to Thy Eternal Father. I offer Thee my body, my soul, my mind, my heart, my life, all the parts of my body, all the powers of my soul, every breath I draw, every throb of my heart and veins, every step I take, every look, every use I make of my senses and in general everything that has been, is and shall be in me. It is my desire that all these things may be consecrated to Thy glory and become so may acts of praise, adoration and love of Thee. Then may it please Thee, O my God, in Thy great power and mercy, to make this be so, in order that everything in me may render to Thee continual honor and homage.[64]

Or we may say with him that we give adoration to the Incarnate One.

Let us adore this precious Heart, offering It all the adoration ever accorded to It in heaven and on earth. O my Saviour, may the whole universe unite in adoration of Thy divine Heart! I willingly consent to be reduced to nothingness now and forever, by means of Thy grace, so that the Sacred Heart of Jesus may be incessantly adored by the whole universe.[65]

Or we may say with Libermann that we give love to God before all other things.

Instead of cherishing and desiring that which raises them in the eyes of men, they will esteem, love and seek only their knowledge of their nothingness, of their weakness, of their uselessness, of their profound wretchedness. Instead of being complacent about that which exalts them, they will try to establish themselves in the humility of heart, loving lowly things and being pleased to suffer the contempt of others. Love for God that is most pure, detachment from themselves, and perfect obedience will be the foundation of that so holy and humble life. True zeal for the salvation of souls, a spirit of mental prayer, perfect observance of the rules

---

64. Eudes, *The Life and the Kingdom of Jesus in Christian Souls,* 112.

65. John Eudes, *Sacred Heart of Jesus* (New York: P. J. Kenedy & Sons, 1946) 91.

will result from those dispositions. But if they are inspired by pride, they will become useless or even harmful instruments for the glory of God while, on the contrary, they would become true apostles if they practiced those virtues perfectly.[66]

(Liturgy is, after all, a love-activity, a fact that should never be forgotten).

Prayer is profitable when it humbles the soul, says Grou, and that means prayer which "impresses her deeply with the conviction of her Maker's sovereign perfection, and her own absolute nothingness; which mortifies her pride, wounds her self-love, and annihilates her natural feelings and inclinations; in a word, which experimentally proves to her the folly of relying on her own efforts, and deprives her of all resources in self."[67] Tough prayer. Difficult liturgy.

Libermann says Jesus's statement to the Samaritan woman means we can no longer bring our homage to God while still harboring evil dispositions in our hearts, so he interprets Jesus' response to her as:

A time will come when the face of all things will be changed. Then there will be true adorers, persons wholly devoted to my Father, entirely given to adoring my Father, who will forget and lose sight of all created things, renounce all human affection and natural desire, who will continually practice self-abnegation, so as to become nothing before my Father in order that he alone may reign in them. Nothing will remain in them which tends to their own personal satisfaction or serves their interest or their own glory ... They will prostrate, admit their nothingness before the sovereign Majesty, whom they will see living and reigning in them."[68]

Adoration requires putting ourselves in the holy presence of God, in a way that is lively and sensitive. When we give all glory, laud, and honor to God, then we will be spared what

---

66. Libermann, *The Rule,* 181-82.

67. Grou, *The Interior of Jesus and Mary,* vol. 1, 63.

68. Libermann, *Jesus Through Jewish Eyes,* vol. 1, 120-21.

Libermann feels is an unseemly sight of manipulating esteem for ourselves. "Let men judge, examine, praise or blame your conduct; let them love, esteem, hate, despise you, or be indifferent toward you. Your soul, in all circumstances, should remain in lowliness before God, praising, adoring, blessing Him, and trying to be sacrificed to Him in all things and in all circumstances."[69]

The duties owed to our creator are adoration, love, and sacrifice: this is what we practice in the virtue of religion, and it can be more perfectly practiced from the valley of nothingness than from the hilltop of self-esteem. Libermann understands it is why Jesus had to teach it to us from Golgotha. "Since by our sin we had abandoned the service of God, then the Word, to repair his original work, came on earth, mingled among us and became united to our nature. And to all who would unite themselves to him through genuine faith he gave a share in the divine sonship."[70] Liturgical abnegation is a matter of retraining our homage so we can redirect it to the right object, and Surin says that at the moment when saints find esteem to be nothing in their eyes, and find themselves ashamed at being devoid of virtue, "they lift up their eyes to Heaven, they admire the greatness of God, they contemplate Him in His glory; and, dazzled with the splendour of Its rays, they hide themselves in their own nothingness, and would descend, if it were possible, to the very centre of the world, to humble themselves more profoundly before His Supreme Majesty."[71] Retraining esteem means forsaking self-esteem, and this means annihilation of self.

The act of accepting nothingness is the heart's act of conceding to God. Nothingness means God is all. Nothingness means nothing else but God – God alone. De la Colombiere drives the point home with repetition (emphases added): "perfection consists in seeking to please God, *and only God*, in all things"; "it is *He alone* whom I wish to please"; "it is a great happiness to *belong altogether* to God"; "he wished his *friendship*

---

69. Libermann, *Letters to Clergy and Religious*, Spiritan Series 9, vol. 5, 177.

70. Libermann, *Jesus Through Jewish Eyes*, vol. 1, 15.

71. Surin, *The Foundations of Spiritual Life*, 232.

entire";[72] "*you alone* are worthy of being loved, served, and praised";[73] "I do not know where to go *to serve anyone but Thee* who art my God";[74] "Dear God, *alone* good, *alone* lovable, must I sacrifice [my friends] to You, since You wish me to be *Yours entirely?*";[75] "when we find something *very perfect in any order*, we cannot bear with all the rest";[76] and if you feel a disturbance in your soul, cast yourself at the feet of Jesus and say, "What, my Jesus, I still desire something apart from You! *You alone* do not suffice for me, and I do not love *You alone*, and it isn't *enough* for me to be loved by You?"[77]

Why love God exclusively? Can't we divide our heart? No! exclaims Jean Vianney. "As if we could divide our heart into two parts! No, my friend: you either belong wholly to God or wholly to the world."[78] Must our love for God push all other loves off the page? Yes! exclaims Guillore. "His jealous Love knows no limit, He is not content to let us have the smallest reserve from him, nor will He endure that we divide our hearts which are His only."[79] Can we only return the sort of love we receive? Yes! exclaims de Liguori. "In order to increase our confidence, God emptied himself, became nothing (Phil 2:7)" and went farther still to hide himself under bread and wine "in order to be our companion forever and to be united with us with the greatest intimacy ... In short, God loves you as

---

72. De la Colombiere, *Faithful Servant*, 56.

73. De la Colombiere, *Faithful Servant*, 65.

74. De la Colombiere, *Faithful Servant*, 66.

75. De la Colombiere, *Faithful Servant*, 74-75.

76. De la Colombiere, *Faithful Servant*, 76.

77. De la Colombiere, *Faithful Servant*, 112.

78. John Vianney, *Sermons for the Sundays and Feasts of the Year* (Long Prairie, MN: The Neumann Press, 1995), 13-14

79. Guillore, *Self-Renunciation*, 105.

much as if he had no other object of love except you alone. And so you should love none other than God."[80]

This knowledge is of the heart, and not of the mind alone, requiring nothingness to be known by liturgical embrace, not by theory. It is known affectively, not speculatively. It is unfortunate that we think of affection as "suffering emotions" over which we have no control, when these theologians rathe think of affection as an act of the will. The will can make acts of resolution; it also makes acts of affection. So Baker finds that "the feeling of our own nothing will never be attained by study or meditation alone, but by the raising and purifying of our souls by prayer."[81] Liturgical worship of God is to *our* benefit, not his, and nothingness scrubs clean the altars of our heart to prepare for it. Worship of God is to the advantage of man, not of God, for who, asks Scaramelli, "would ever dream that it was a benefit to the fountain that we should drink of its waters, or to the light that we should gaze upon it?"[82]

How do we start? By casting a twin glance at God's supreme perfection and our own nothingness, as the past two chapters have said. Where do end? In humility, the place where justice has conducted us, as the next two chapters will say. Ullathorne knows that "the more a soul is made conscious of her nothingness apart from God, the more need she feels for that fundamental justice which we call humility, which subjects her to God, and opens her spirit to the grace and inspiration of His Holy Spirit."[83] Place your own nothingness within the envelope of God's magnificence.

80. Alphonsus de Liguori, 274 *A Way of Conversing Continually With God as With a Friend* in *Alphonsus de Liguori: Selected Writings* (New York: Paulist Press, 1999) 274.

81. Baker, Holy Wisdom, 318.

82. Scaramelli, *Directorium Asceticum; or, Guide to the Spiritual Life*, vol. 3, 199-200.

83. Ullathorne, *The Endowments of Man*, 164.

HUMILITY OF MIND

Due to the abundance of material on this virtue, I am going to divide my treatment of humility into several chapters – and I am still omitting much. I will limit myself to humility directly, even though it is frequently presented as one of a pair of virtues (humility and meekness, humility and patience, humility and charity, humility and obedience), and even though it is opposite to many vices (pride, vanity, vainglory), and even though it is but one element in a spiritual complex (keeping company with poverty of spirit, mortification of the flesh, contempt of this world, simplicity, chastity, mercy, discretion, zeal, devotion, love of the cross). And I will limit myself to definitions of humility, even though the theologians of abnegation also treat methods and means of becoming humble, and the special humility of religious orders, and the contrast between interior and exterior humility, and give the Blessed Virgin her own, individual treatment on this reality. Throughout it all, de Bergamo would have us remember that we cannot know humility by theory alone. "Consider for a little while in what esteem you hold humility. Do you love it? Do you desire it? What do you do to acquire it?"[1] Though all we can do here is think together, it is hoped that an increased light of understanding can feed an increased flame of will.

The world of abnegation feels like living in an upside down world, because our sense of direction was upset by original sin. Boudon sees "nothingness wishes to be, while the Great All annihilates Himself."[2] After Adam and Eve's disorienting tumble, the sinner is mixed up and thinks that pride leads upward, and humility downward. In our topsy-turvy orientation we think the stairway of pride leads to exaltation, and the stairway of humility

---

1. De Bergamo, *Humility of Heart*, 110.

2. Boudon, *The Hidden Life of Jesus*, 69-70.

leads to abasement. But this is not so. Lucifer discovered that by pride he was cast down; the Son of Man creates a cross-ladder for humility to ascend. Humility aims high, Segneri finds. "Commend thyself to Him, confess thy weakness to him at every step, and then aim as high as thou wilt, even, as Lucifer did, to be like God, and still thou wilt not be proud like him, but, on the contrary, truly humble.[3] And Jenks observes, "The humility of saints and he humility of sinners is the same in substance, though they differ in perfection. We wonder not to see a man stand steady upon even ground. But when we see the same man and as firm upon a lofty pinnacle, we gaze and wonder at him."[4]

Humility elevates to greater rank; pride reduces to lower rank. No wonder abnegation is confusing when it upends our ordinary definition of humility. Bossuet calls the paradox in which one grows richer by being stripped. An astonishing antinomy. "You are not ignorant of the truth that it is the chief characteristic of humility that it impoverishes itself and strips itself of all its own advantages, yet at the same time, by some marvellous contradiction, the more it despoils itself the richer it grows, securing to itself everything that it casts away."[5] Bona admiringly claims that it is not a matter of lowering, but raising. "This virtue, though it may seem by its very name to denote something mean and small, is nevertheless the virtue of the great, since it is the virtue of the perfect, and it does not lower the mind to base things, but raises it to those that are more noble; for while it attributes nothing to itself, it is wholly turned to God, believing it can do all things in him, by whom it is strengthened. Therefore, it is brave and magnanimous."[6] De Sales distinguishes between true humility, as Christ teaches, and false humility, as the world assumes. "There are some who amuse themselves with a false and foppish humility, which hinders them from considering in themselves, the good gifts which God has bestowed on

---

3. Segneri, *Manna of the Soul*, vol. 2, 362.

4. Sylvester Jenks, *A Contrite and Humble Heart, with Motives and Considerations to Prepare It* (Dublin: P. Wogan, 1799) 159

5. Bossuet, *Great French Sermons from Bossuet, Bourdaloue, and Massillon*, 201.

6. Bona, *A Treatise of Spiritual Life*, 428-29.

them; such men are much in the wrong; the goods which God has put in us, require to be acknowledged, esteemed, and highly honored."[7]

The worldly understanding of humility might have this mistaken character of timorousness, falling down, shrinking small, but Segneri jibes that this would mean "the idle, the timid, the pusillanimous, the slothful, would be the humblest men in the world."[8] This is not so; humility means thinking we can do nothing *of ourselves.* Heavenly humility is different, which is why Alonso Rodriguez says we must seek it from the correct source. "This humility which makes a man feel how lowly he is, is not itself a lowly thing, nor a fruit which grows in the earth. It is a thing of heaven and God gives it to whoever possesses it here on earth and there in heaven. For this reason it must be asked for from God."[9] Saint-Jure simply defines humility "to be a just knowledge of the truth, which makes a man to take himself for what he is, and nothing more."[10]

We are led to this chapter on humility by the chapters that have gone before: the chapters on justice convicted us of stealing from God when we act self-reliantly in either the order of nature or of grace, and the chapters on nothingness recognizes what we are outside of God. Building off those two truths, humility has a double task: first, knowing our abject state, and second, to love being known for what we are. And what are we? Olier wants to know. "We can never tolerate what Jesus Christ wishes to accomplish in us through his spirit of humility, that is, to love being known for what we are: nothingness and sin. We are nothing more than this in ourselves and of ourselves. All else comes from God, and we are stealing from him everything that we wish to attribute to ourselves

---

7. Francis De Sales, The *Spiritual Director of Devout and Religious Souls* (Dublin: Printed by James Mehain, 1777) 97.

8. Segneri, *Manna of the Soul*, vol. 2, 520

9. Alonso Rodriguez, *St. Alphonsus Rodriguez: Autobiography*, 215.

10. Saint-Jure, *A Treatise on the Knowledge and Love of Our Lord Jesus Christ*, vol. 2, 536.

besides nothingness and sin."[11] We neither know nor love our existence without a supernatural touch.

This is why abnegation in general, and humility specifically, must be placed against the transcendent, supernatural horizon. For Bruyere, "there can be no true prayer without humility, which is the purity of the mind, just as chastity is that of the body."[12] For de Sales, mere knowledge of misery and poverty "is moral and human humility. What then is Christian humility. It is the *love* of this poverty and abjection, contemplating these in our Lord."[13] For Saint-Jure, it is one thing to know what poverty is, it is another thing to love it; and another thing, still, to love it because of a supernatural touch. "As the mariner's compass does not turn to the pole till it is touched with the loadstone, so our will does not of itself incline to humility, to contempt, to opprobrium; it must first be touched with the humility of Jesus Christ, who, communicating His virtue, makes us perform cheerfully what we had previously held in horror."[14] Liturgical humility is humility caused by God, not self-depreciation, which means it must come from contact with the humility of Christ. There is a sacramental cast to it. The abnegation, the nothingness, the humility that our fallen nature holds in horror, is transformed upon the liturgical transaction with the Trinity, as it was for Our Lady. as de Sales witnesses.

> In Latin abjection means humility, and humility means abjection, so that when Our Lady says in the Magnificat that all generations shall call her blessed, because God hath regarded the low estate of His handmaiden, she means that He has accepted her abjection and lowliness in order to fill her with graces and favors. Nevertheless, there is a difference between humility and abjection; for abjection is the poverty, vileness, and littleness which exist in us without our taking heed to them; but humility implies a real knowledge and voluntary recognition of that abjection. And the

---

11. Olier, *Introduction to the Christian Life and Virtues*, in *Berulle and the French School*, 237-38.

12. Bruyere, *Spiritual Life and Prayer*, 154.

13. De Sales, *Letters to Persons in the World*, 141.

14. Saint-Jure, *Spiritual Man*, 241.

highest point of humility consists in not merely acknowledging one's abjection, but in taking pleasure therein, not from any want of breadth or courage, but to give the more glory to God's Divine Majesty, and to esteem one's neighbor more highly than one's self.[15]

This terse explanation by de Sales gives us crib notes to our entire thesis about liturgical abnegation, here applied specifically to humility. In the orders of both nature and grace we are constantly dependent upon God; from this vantage point we have real knowledge of our state of poverty, vileness, and littleness; and we happily acknowledge and accept our state *because* it gives more glory to God. Saint-Jure thinks our Lord speaks of this kind of poverty in the first beatitude, for indeed, "there is no people in the world more poor in spirit, than the truly humble, because they account themselves to be nothing, to have nothing, to be able to do nothing, and to be worth nothing ... and to have need of every thing, not assuming any praise to themselves for any thing whatsoever."[16] Such self-knowledge does not come from a false and weak humility, it comes only from a true and courageous humility that finds pleasure in liturgizing God by confessing his Majesty. The objective here is not simply to know our humble state, but to believe it. And that requires grace, Saint-Jure says with everyone else. "What is more easy than to say, 'I am a vile, miserable sinner'? But to say this in the heart, and to *believe* it firmly, is not quite so easy, because for this our own efforts are not enough without a particular grace."[17] Liturgical humility requires a particular grace that comes from God, and only

---

15. Francis de Sales, *Introduction to the Devout Life* (New York: Vintage Spiritual Classics, 2002) 102. In another location he repeats himself. "My child, in Latin, abjection is called humility and humility abjection, so that when our Lady says: *Because he hath had regard to the humility of his handmaid* she means, because he hath had regard to my abjection and vileness. Still there is some difference between humility and abjection, in that humility is the acknowledgment of one's abjection. Now the highest point of humility is not only to know one's abjection, but to love it." Francis de Sales, *Letters to Persons in the World*, 286-87.

16. Saint-Jure, *The Holy Life of Monsieur de Renty*, 53.

17. Saint-Jure, *Spiritual Man*, 101.

then, Libermann says, is genuine humility "based upon complete disregard of self, and upon perfect union with God, who alone can give it to us."[18]

No wonder we are confused. Grou shakes his head in incredulity. "The world's horror of humility leads it to misrepresent it, and form notions of it that are altogether untrue."[19] The world regards humility as a useless virtue, whereas it is the noblest of all; as pusillanimous, whereas it is capable of the noblest enterprises; as worthy of contempt, whereas it actually attracts paeans of praise. The following passages gathered from across many authors seem reminiscent to me of the rejoicing of the O antiphons.

- O holy humility! Thou art the key of perfection, the gate of paradise, and the seat of divine grace, and there is no other reason why we make no progress and why our way seems so long and tedious, but that we do not learn wholly to leave ourselves (Barbanson).[20]

- O holy self-knowledge! O sacred humility! thou art the key of all perfection, the door of all solid virtue, piety, and devotion (de Castaniza).[21]

- O amiable humility, how necessary art thou for me, how pleasing to God and man! With what comfort and quiet dost thou enrich thy possessor! O heaven upon earth! What do I not get by humility! What do I lose by pride and presumption! (de Castaniza)[22]

- O, humility! who understands thy value? who prefers thee before all treasures? who endeavours to reap from every occurrence of life the precious fruit of self-abjection? Such a soul is great in the sight of God (Grou).[23]

---

18. Libermann, *Letters to Clergy and Religious*, Spiritan Series 9, vol. 5, 68.

19. Grou, *The School of Jesus Christ*, 208.

20. Barbanson, *The Secret Paths of Divine Love*, 22.

21. De Castaniza, *The Spiritual Conflict and Conquest*, 265.

22. De Castaniza, *The Spiritual Conflict and Conquest*, 416.

23. Grou, *The Interior of Jesus and Mary*, vol. 2, 160.

- O incomparable humility! I know thee not, and unless the strong, clear light of heaven reveals thee to my view, I never shall know thee (Grou).[24]

- O humility! first virtue and first duty of the Christian, who shall fear to exceed in thee, seeing the extremes to which Christ carried thee even before his birth? (Grou)[25]

- O mystery of humility! What St. John considers a degradation to the Son of God the Son of God considers a duty which justice requires him to fulfil (Grou).[26]

- Oh, how precious are those humiliations by which we acquire. and learn to exercise, humility! ... Oh, how precious humility must be when God recompenses it with eternal glory! (de Bergamo)[27]

- Oh, humility! Virtue of Jesus Christ, with what confusion dost Thou cover our pride and vanity! (Saint-Jure)[28]

The theologians of liturgical abnegation exclaim the mysteries of humility with wonder and affection.

Humility is abjection that is recognized voluntarily, according to de Sales, which includes an affection for it – even a pleasure in it – and this is a great challenge for us. The saints must know something that we do not. That is why Rodriguez admits that they say things that "seem to us mere exaggerations; as for example, that they were the greatest sinners in the world, and several such like expressions. For so far are we from saying or thinking such things of ourselves, that we cannot so much as comprehend how others could say so; the reason is, because we are not endowed with so profound humility as

---

24. Grou, *The Interior of Jesus and Mary*, vol. 2, 168.

25. Grou, *The Interior of Jesus and Mary*, vol. 1, 62.

26. Grou, *The Interior of Jesus and Mary*, vol. 1, 144-45.

27. De Bergamo, *Humility of Heart*, 77 and 81.

28. Saint-Jure, *A Treatise on the Knowledge and Love of Jesus Christ*, vol. 2, 628.

they were, and so know not the excellence and secrets thereof."[29] We are ignorant about humility, and Grou thinks the reason why is easy to see. "Let us face the fact: we esteem and love humility in others, but have not the greatness of soul nor the courage to practice it ourselves."[30] The repair of our ignorance will not come from additional study (from reading this book, or from writing this book). De Ravignan rather counsels that the repair of our ignorance can only happen only by asking for "the grace of light in order that we may be humiliated, and covered with confusion; it is an act of humility already to feel that we stand in need of it."[31] We love humility, but not humiliation. We are willing to pray "Oh God, give me humility;" we are not willing to pray "Oh God, humiliate me this day." Crasset bemoans, "Are you afraid of the opinions of men? You are then base and haughty. You are vain and ambitious .... Oh, Jesus my Saviour, how can I esteem humility and despise the humiliations which attend it? How can I acquire this essential virtue unless I improve every occasion that offers to humiliate myself?"[32]

On the one hand, humility seems easy because we have so much to be humble about; on the other hand, de Sales knows that acquiring humility is a life-long labor.

> To-day we love humility, and exclaim, therefore: "Ah! what a lovable
> virtue is humility! It is surely the most admirable and the most necessary
> of all!" And so that day we are bent upon trying with all our strength to
> acquire it. But on the morrow we shall be disgusted with it; or, at least,
> not prize or esteem it as we did yesterday. We shall say that it is certainly a
> very great virtue, but not the most lovable of all: and then it is really quite
> piteous to think of all the trouble that must be taken to acquire it, with
> such small results, or even none at all. See how changeable and inconstant
> we are![33]

---

29. Rodriguez, *The Practice of Christian and Religious Perfection*, vol. 2, 247.

30. Grou, *The School of Jesus Christ*, 209.

31. De Ravignan, *Ravignan's Last Retreat*, 35.

32. Crasset, *Christian Considerations*, 36.

The reason we should love humility is because it is a truth-telling posture, or what Bona calls an affection "by which a man wishes to be deemed as such by others as he knows himself before God."[34] If we do not want to deceive the world about ourselves, then "a truly humble man wishes himself to be judged and reckoned by others, such as he knows himself to be by the verdict of truth and in the eyes of God."[35] Humility is the daughter of truth, and the supreme truth is God, therefore Alonso Rodriguez confesses our Lord as a friend of humility. "The reason is that God is supreme truth, and humility consists in the souls walking in truth in the presence of God ... The soul has to walk in truth before God and man, knowing itself as it is, not desiring to be held for anything except for what it is."[36]

Though our mind is changeable and inconstant, our nature is not, and stands in unchanging and constant need of humility. Humility would be natural if we saw ourselves in a true fashion, but no one does. De Bergamo says no one can relax – but do not worry! Opportunities will present themselves constantly.

> Nothing is more natural to us than humility, because we are drawn towards it by our own misery; and nothing is easier, since it is enough for us to open our eyes and to know ourselves; this is not a virtue we need go far to seek, as we can always find it within ourselves, and we have an infinity of good reasons in ourselves for doing so. Nevertheless we must labour as long as life lasts to acquire humility, nor must we ever imagine that we have acquired it.[37]

Perhaps the main reason that something so natural is so hard, something so near is so far away, and something so easy is so difficult, is because the estimate of humility the world has given us is so different from the estimate offered by the Church. Grou says Jesus

---

34. Bona, *A Treatise of Spiritual Life*, 427.

35. Bona, *A Treatise of Spiritual Life*, 436.

36. Alonso Rodriguez, *St. Alphonsus Rodriguez: Autobiography*, 131-32.

37. De Bergamo, *Humility of Heart*, 21.

unfolded to the world's view a "heavenly kingdom, totally different in its elements from the kingdoms of the earth; of a kingdom whose long-scaled portals could be opened only by the cross, and whose low and narrow entrance could give admittance only to humility and detachment."[38] Neither cross nor humility are especially welcome in the kingdoms of the earth, because these kingdoms place such a premium on self that they give no esteem to humility. "What is the result?" asks de Bergamo. "One does not esteem a virtue which one does not love, and one has but little desire to acquire a virtue which one neither esteems nor loves; and if this be the case, woe is me!"[39]

Humility might be honored by the world insofar as it can advance one's status, enhance one's reputation, or stroke one's ego, but the world retreats from it when it is in service to redemption from sin, because sin is an uncomfortable topic. John of Avila says that humility is not "a fruit which springs from this earth, but grows in heaven. God bestows it on those who search deeply in the mire of their own souls, and diligently turn over in their minds the remembrance of their sins and frailties."[40] Humility is a preparation for, as well as a response to, this grace from heaven, so John adds that any absence of humility means that no place has been prepared for the arrival of this grace. "Nothing so offends its Creator as a self-satisfied heart, because it contains no empty vessel into which He can pour the riches of His mercy. It will remain in its natural poverty, for it can offer no place into which the waters of grace may flow, to make it live happily with God, and bring forth much fruit, like a well-watered garden."[41]

The human race has found humility difficult ever since the Garden of Eden, when mankind abandoned submission in favor of autonomy. De Ravignan identifies humility with the former. "If there is anything that may be called humility, it is certainly this perfect submission, which renders our will conformable to the will of God, and removes everything that is opposed to Him."[42] Humility is a component of abnegation because

---

38. Grou, *The Interior of Jesus and Mary*, vol. 1, 170.

39. De Bergamo, *Humility of Heart*, 31.

40. John of Avila, *Letters*, 148-49.

41. John of Avila, *Letters*, 152.

42. De Ravignan, *Ravignan's Last Retreat*, 109-10.

abnegation is the denial of everything that is opposed to God, and this denial is made in willing submission to him. Grou knows that Adam and Eve had natural reasons to be humble before God. "God's supreme dominion over our thoughts, words, and actions; his right to exercise that dominion without prejudice to our liberty; our absolute obligation to obey his will and cooperate with his grace, all concur to prove that humility is the natural appendage of humanity."[43] But sinners don't do nature naturally any more, and humility must become our schoolmaster. Since recognition is the first step to recovery, de Sales says "the principal fruit of humility is to show us the need we have of correction."[44]

Whence humility? asks Saint-Jure. "Humility, what is thy father's name? And the answer given with a smile, in a sweet, pleasing voice, was: Why desire to learn the name of my father? He has none. When you shall be in the possession of God, then you shall understand it; as the sea is the mother of fountains, so is humility the mother of discretion, and of all virtues."[45] A sign of this mother's prudence working in us is when we cease giving resistance to God. Resistance comes from pride, as the serpent knew, and it leads to disobedience. If pride renders a person haughty and sets him against God, Saint-Jure says that "humility, which is its opposite, renders man pliable to all the movements of God; the humble man will never make the least opposition to the dispensations of providence, either in his acts or by his words, or even in his thoughts: thus God can use him without fear of opposition, now in one office, now in another."[46]

Grou observes a kind of contest between man and God, but he surprises us with who he thinks will win. "There is a sort of contest between God and the soul, and none can say where victory lies, for as the soul becomes ever more humble God grows ever more loving; and so the rivalry goes on. It is a contest very pleasing to God, who loves to be conquered by the humility of His creature."[47] The spiritual tournament is a contest for the increase

---

43. Grou, *The Interior of Jesus and Mary*, vol. 1, 266.

44. Francis de Sales, *Maxims and Counsels* (Dublin: M. H. Gill & Son, 1884) 142.

45. Saint-Jure, *Knowledge and Love of our Lord Jesus Christ*, vol. 2, 623.

46. Saint-Jure, *A Treatise on the Knowledge and Love of Jesus Christ*, vol. 2, 195–96.

47. Grou, *The School of Jesus Christ*, 207.

of God's love by the decrease of our conceit, the increase of his glory by the abnegation of our self-esteem. Then we can join Grou in prayer, saying "if I long to make myself more pleasing in Thy sight there is no other path for me to tread but the way of humility. Humility will cover my faults; humility will supplement my imperfect virtues; humility will serve me in the place of merit and win me everlasting light from Thee. Amen."[48] The world considers humility some sort of concession or defeat – and so it is to the ego – but the faithful ones schooled by Christ's humility know that humility is not discouraging. "Humility should never be an occasion for discouragement," urges Libermann. "When you compare yourselves with others, you imagine that you are not accomplishing anything worthwhile and that you are useless. It is good that you remain very humble in God's presence and consider yourselves useless servants, but you ought to avoid grieving over your lowliness."[49] The reputation humility has in the world suggests that the soul is beaten down by any recognition of sins, weakness, fault, and lowliness. To the contrary, when the believer recognizes his sinful, weak, faulty, and lonely condition, Libermann believes it should be with a confident soul, full of gratitude for God's boundless goodness. "Be full of confidence: He loves you and wants to take you to Himself – to place you in the assembly of His angels and saints that you may sing, praise, bless, and adore for all eternity His infinite mercy toward you."[50]

God's final desire is to position each person in heaven's liturgical assemblage, but we must remember that we cannot finish then what we do not start now. "Humility on earth is the seed of exaltation in heaven,"[51] warns Olier. Humility now is the seed of glory then, and the degree of humility attained now will determine the degree of glory bestowed then. Crasset writes, "glory is the portion of the other life, humility of this ... Your elevation will be in proportion to your former humility; your glory in heaven will be proportioned to

---

48. Grou, *The School of Jesus Christ*, 202.

49. Libermann, *Letters to Clergy and Religious*, Spiritan Series 9, vol. 5, 43.

50. Libermann, *Letters to Clergy and Religious*, Spiritan Series 7, vol. 3, 251.

51. Olier, *Introduction to the Christian Life and Virtues*, in *Berulle and the French School*, 241.

your lowliness on earth."[52] Humility will be perfect in heaven because it will be perfected by charity, and as love abides, so de Bergamo thinks humility will abide, too. "O my soul, it is through humility that we shall reach paradise. And what shall we do in paradise? There the practice of all other virtues ceases and only charity and humility remain."[53] Without humility now, we shall not please God either here or in heaven, Eudes warns. "Humility is the measure of perfection and holiness of souls on earth and of their glory in eternity, for the Son of God said when He was here on earth: "Whosoever therefore shall humble himself as this little child, he is the greater in the kingdom of heaven" (Matt. 18, 4)."[54] Humility brings tranquility, because its happy effect is a freedom from worldliness while the soul passes through the world. The soul walks through the world untouched by worldliness. Grou thinks that if we take the first beatitude about the poor in spirit to mean the humble, then "we cannot doubt that the humble are happier than the proud ... Pride is in itself, in fact, the most unquiet of all the vices, and humility is the most tranquil of the virtues."[55]

Not only does this humility make peace between ourselves and God, it also makes peace between ourselves and our neighbors. Grou thinks the latter is easier to understand in many ways, because we experience it. "It is nothing but pride that leads us to quarrel with our neighbours, by making us hard to please, fastidious, sensitive, arrogantly determined to secure our rights and inclined to think we owe nothing to others. Humility, on the other hand, is gentle, considerate, kind, unpretentious, unassuming, tolerant of the faults of others and always anxious to save them from suffering."[56] Vainglorious competition for esteem and reward turns everyone around us into our rival and adversary, but humility allows us to see both our imperfections and their perfections in an entirely different light, a light described by de Sales.

---

52. De Sales & Crasset, *The Secret of Sanctity*, 261, 262.

53. De Bergamo, *Humility of Heart*, 136.

54. Eudes, *The Priest*, 256.

55. Grou, *The School of Jesus Christ*, 95 and 211.

56. Grou, *The School of Jesus Christ*, 207.

Humility enables us to view our imperfections undisturbed, remembering those of others. For why should we be more perfect than others? In like manner, it enables us to view the imperfections of others without trouble, remembering our own. For why should we think it strange that others have imperfections, when we have them ourselves? Humility makes our heart meek towards the perfect and the imperfect, towards the former through reverence, towards the latter through compassion. Humility helps us to receive sufferings meekly, knowing that we deserve them, and favours reverently, knowing that we do not deserve them.[57]

Humility neuters quarreling. Knowing our nothingness is the most certain path to humility and charitable compassion for our neighbor.

Humility draws man and God together. If we made a sum of all Christian philosophy, Blosius says it would be this: "to strive to follow Jesus our leader, by cultivating true humility ... The more humble a man is, the nearer he is to God, and the more advanced in evangelical perfection."[58] Humility is the way to knowledge of God because it acknowledges that God's ways are not our ways, and that we are unable to measure his mysteries. Recognizing this inability is the surest means to know God, and, Fenelon says, "it is, in fact, upon the basis of *humility*, that faith, and the whole fabric of religion, principally repose. The first law of Christianity is the strict injunction to submit our reason to word of God, and our wills to his command."[59] De Bergamo thinks we can equally say humility goes hand in hand with holiness, because it is a means to sanctity. "The soul is holy in measure as it is humble, because in the same measure that it has holiness it has grace, and in the same measure that it has grace it has humility, because grace is only given to the humble."[60] Humility is part and parcel with our liturgical adoration

---

57. De Sales, in Huguet, *The Consoling Thoughts of St. Francis de Sales*, 124.

58. Blosius, *The Manual of the Spiritual Life*, 17.

59. François Fenelon, *On the Use of the Bible* (London: Booker, New Bond Street, 1837) 68.

60. De Bergamo, *Humility of Heart*, 131.

of God because abjection recognizes the creature's nothingness, which is a counterpoise to the Creator's resplendence, which Baker says is humility's acknowledgement of the sublimity of God. "Humility may be defined to be a virtue by which we, acknowledging the infinite greatness and majesty of God, His incomprehensible perfections, and the absolute power that He hath over us and all creatures (which are as nothing before Him), do wholly subject ourselves, both souls and bodies, with all their powers and faculties, and all things that pertain to either, to His holy will in all things, and for His sake to all creatures, according to His will."[61]

I have been gathering a bouquet of definitions that indicate the wonder and affection with which our theologians held humility, but it is important to acknowledge that they have no less affection and wonder for more blunt definitions. We saw de Sales say that there is one summit higher than acknowledging one's abjection, and that is to take pleasure therein. Therefore, our theologians of liturgical abnegation do not shrink from giving definitions that sound harsher to our ears. For example, de Granada: "true humility causes a man to regard himself as one of the vilest and most abject creatures in the world, unworthy of the bread he eats, of the earth he tramples under his feet, and of the air he breathes."[62] And "it is pure divine truth itself that forces such a confession from the perfectest soul; insomuch as that he that does not know, yea, and endeavours not experimentally to feel himself to be, the most vile and wretched of all creatures, does in vain challenge the title of being humble or true."[63] For example, Baker says humility must become a matter of the will, "for to make Humility a virtue it is the will that must even compel the understanding to say, 'I will believe myself to be inferior to all, according as I find just cause by these considerations,' and the same will will upon occasion force practices suitable to such a belief."[64] For example, Lallemant says at this stage one no longer measures against others, but against God himself, and then we will "know and feel

---

61. Baker, *Holy Wisdom*, 310.

62. De Granada, *Memorial*, 362.

63. Baker, *Holy Wisdom*, 312.

64. Baker, *Holy Wisdom*, 316.

our own vileness ... It is in vain that we think of the little that is in us; we shall never be any the more humble, unless we compare it with the infinite perfections of God."[65]

Humility is born from self-knowledge, painful though that may be. Grou thinks "hardly anyone is willing to face self-knowledge; and the obstacle is self-love, which shrinks from the sight of its own deformity. And yet, where there is no self-knowledge there is no humility."[66] We are not describing a human humility that comes from natural knowledge of self, we are attempting to describe a self-knowledge illumined by a supernatural light that penetrates deeper than our natural knowledge. So Grou says, "humility should be the fruit of the first supernatural light vouchsafed to us, and then humility will be the source of all the lights which follow."[67] And de Granada says "Because the knowledge of man's self is the chief foundation of humility, so that of pride is man's ignorance of himself."[68] Humility is the opposite of pride; pride keeps the mind in ignorance; so the knowledge that is the opposite of ignorance can only be won at the cost of defeating pride. And this means going to war with self-love.

Knowledge puts things into context. A sort of self-knowledge can be created by placing ourselves in the context of the world, another sort by comparing ourselves to our neighbor, but both of these types of self-knowledge are corruptible by self-love. The self-knowledge which comes from supernatural light will place us in a liturgical context, i.e., before God. And this, says Libermann, is what constitutes the highest "humility of the intellect: the clear and intimate knowledge of our nothingness, baseness and sin, and the existence, greatness and holiness of God. This is also what these words mean: the knowledge of what one is in oneself and in relation to God."[69] It is theological knowledge (of our nothingness); knowledge dawning from liturgical theology (of God's holiness). Barbanson warns that we are not prepared for how far humility will force us to go.

---

65. Lallemant, *The Spiritual Doctrine of Father Louis Lallemant, ed. Faber*, 432.

66. Grou, *The School of Jesus Christ*, 75.

67. Grou, *The Interior of Jesus and Mary*, vol. 1, 340.

68. De Granada, *The Sinner's Guide*, 286.

69. Libermann, *On Humility*, 1.

Humility is a certain self-knowledge which causes a man to annihilate himself, both interiorly in the presence of God and exteriorly before men. It is a virtue which makes us joyfully and voluntarily to embrace all injuries, contempt, corrections and humiliations, with as much content as worldlings accept of honor and riches. It is a total destruction of self-love, of desire of honor, vain praise, or the favor and affection of men … It is to walk before God in truth, recognizing that we are poor and destitute of all good.[70]

We can never separate knowledge of self from knowledge of God. Alonso Rodriguez is referring to himself in the third person in his Autobiography when he writes:

Without any process of the reason, God plunged him into great knowledge of himself. In this knowledge of God he was inflamed and on fire with his love, and with this knowledge and love of God there came to him another great knowledge, namely of himself. For with such knowledge of God the soul comes to know itself in all truth, since it is easy to see black when it is placed next to white … When such a bad soul comes before so good a God, the soul does not base its opinion of itself on anything other than what it really is."[71]

Knowledge of self increases as love of God increases; love of God increases as knowledge of self increases; so Alonso adds, "the extent of its knowledge of itself is the measure of its growth in the contempt and loathing and hate and abhorrence of itself.[72]" One only sees oneself in truth when one is extracted from one's self and hidden in God, Alonso concludes.

---

70. Barbanson, *The Secret Paths of Divine Love*, 23.

71. Alonso Rodriguez, *St. Alphonsus Rodriguez: Autobiography*, 64.

72. Alonso Rodriguez, *St. Alphonsus Rodriguez: Autobiography*, 120.

This happens when without any process of reasoning, God alone places the soul within himself, so that it may see itself as it is with the real knowledge of itself. There it sees so many and such great evils in itself that for loathing it would rather not see itself ... Hence no matter how many evil things [others] may say about the soul it never gets angry, because it sees that they speak the truth, and it is glad that they know it and tell it about its evils so that it may correct them.[73]

Abnegation makes theory existential, once again. The intellectual self-knowledge that we are sinners becomes affective self-condemnation. The affection that properly belongs to humility, says de Granada, "is a hearty contempt of self; from whence is derived a true knowledge of ourselves and of our sins."[74] We must therefore move from a humility of mind, in this chapter, to a humility of heart, in the next.

---

73. Alonso Rodriguez, *St. Alphonsus Rodriguez: Autobiography*, 124.

74. De Granada, *Considerations on Mysteries of the Faith*, 24.

HUMILITY OF HEART

There are two kinds of humility, humility of mind and humility of heart. We looked at the former in the last chapter, but Eudes warns us that "humility of the mind would be useless without humility of the heart; it would be what St. John calls a 'diabolical humility,' for the demons full well know their own nothingness and worthlessness. True humility ... is humility of the heart ... which consists in loving our baseness and abjection."[1] The devils well know their own worthlessness, but only Christians love their own abjection. The stepping stones from humility of mind to heart are as follows: first, knowledge of self recognizes our nothingness. Second, we reflect on whether there is "any thing beyond nothing? Yes doubtless, there is something" Rodriguez answers. "There is sin which you have added thereunto. And what an abyss is that? It is much greater than the abyss of nothing, because sin is worse than nothing."[2] Third, this leads us to distrust ourselves, distrust our own strength, as Grou says. "This experimental knowledge of himself, joined to the lights he receives from above, inspires him with humility ... The more he advances the deeper becomes this conviction, and the more deeply is humility rooted in his heart. Hence springs his contempt of himself, his salutary distrust of his own strength."[3] And fourth, Grou adds, distrust in ourselves can become trust in God, if touched by grace. "The more humble a man is, the stronger his confidence in God will be, and confidence grounded on humility will never be presumptuous."[4]

---

1. Lebrun, *The Spiritual Teaching of St. John Eudes*, 183.

2. Rodriguez, *The Practice of Christian and Religious Perfection*, vol. 2, 155.

3. Grou, *The Characteristics of True Devotion*, 111-12.

4. Grou, *The Hidden Life of the Soul*, 131.

Self-knowledge means knowing ourselves as we really are, and we really are in a state of original sin to which we add our actual sins. Although the world thinks of humility as having a *low* estimate of oneself, theology thinks of humility as having a *true* estimate of oneself. The reason for the confusion is that humility leads to a recognition of our poverty. Ullathorne summarizes: "As humility is the just thought of what we are, and the right action of our will towards God from the knowledge of what He is to us, we come to see our poverty in the light of his excellence. And then, descending from our conceits and renouncing our fictitious independence, we honestly endeavour to be the subjects of God."[5] When humility speaks of a "vile sinner" it is only acknowledging that original sin has had its way with us. The saints adopt a God's-eye view of themselves, says Rodriguez, and see both what they are without God, and what they are with God's grace.

> The knowledge of our own weakness, which is the root of humility, was so fixed in [the saints'] hearts, that they easily distinguished, what they were in themselves, from what they were by grace; wherefore considering, that if God left them but one moment, they might have grown the greatest sinners, they always looked upon themselves as such; and upon the gifts of God, as borrowed favours, which, instead of making them less humble, did, on the contrary, inspire them with a more profound sense thereof.[6]

Temptations are a time of contest, and before it begins we are either cowardly or presumptuous; "only in the very time of the struggle we learn to judge ourselves rightly,"[7] Grou says. A good preparation will combine knowledge of one's indigence with a firm hope that God, will supply all that we lack in his goodness. This paradoxical combination of a confession of sin with confident hope allows the humble person to see himself as he appears in the sight of God, which is what Scaramelli thinks is exactly the self-knowledge desired.

---

5. Ullathorne, *The Groundwork of the Christian Virtues*, 401.

6. Rodriguez, *The Practice of Christian and Religious Perfection*, vol. 2, 256.

7. Grou, *The Spiritual Maxims of Pere Grou*, 160.

It suffices that we know ourselves as we really are, and appear in the sight of God, in order to level with the earth the vain and groundless opinion we have formed of ourselves, and to attain that lowly, mean and vile appreciation of self wherein humility of the mind wholly consists. For if this self-knowledge be illumined with a ray from on high so as to show us our true selves, without flattery, we shall discover within ourselves an abyss of nothingness, an ocean of evil and misery, which will force us to exchange the high idea we had formed, for another far less favourable, far less flattering, and immeasurably more lowly. This humble-mindedness being pre-supposed, it gives birth, by a sort of natural consequence, to the affection of humility in the will; that is, to a certain disesteem and contempt for self, and for whatever belongs to self.[8]

One of the additional benefits of self-knowledge will be the ability to discern true humility from false humility, something Saint-Jure says is crucial. Alas, it is all too true "that a man may speak ill of himself through pride, upon design to skim off to himself by this false humility, a little glory, and to get some reputation of an humble person."[9] Fenelon agrees. Our sinful vertigo still affects us, and "when we think we are humbling ourselves we are exalting ourselves; when we think we are annihilating ourselves we are seeking our own life."[10] There are numerous signs of false humility, and they are easy to detect if one knows what to look for. Here are six quick examples. First, "if, when stung by slander or ill nature, we wax proud and swell with anger, it is a proof that our gentleness and humility are unreal, and mere artificial show"[11] (de Sales). Second, "humility which loves the light is usually nothing better than vanity in disguise"[12] (Grou). Third, "many

---

8. Scaramelli, *Directorium Asceticum; or, Guide to the Spiritual Life,*, vol. 3, 588-89.

9. Saint-Jure, *The Holy Life of Monsieur de Renty*, 70.

10. Fenelon, *Christian Perfection*, 207.

11. De Sales, *Introduction to the Devout Life*, 109.

12. Grou, *The Interior of Jesus and Mary*, vol. 1, 206.

who pray for humility would be extremely sorry if God were to grant it to them"[13] (Grou). Fourth, "if they were really humble, they would not, when reprimanded, show so much resentment as they do, nor take such great care to excuse and defend themselves, nor would they show so much trouble and uneasiness"[14] (Alphonsus Rodriguez). Fifth, very often "pride is irritated by a view of its defects, and this sentiment is mistaken for humility"[15] (Fenelon). And sixth, "the humility that can yet talk, has need of careful watching; self-love derives comfort from its outward words"[16] (Fenelon).

Fenelon thinks one of the most frequent features of false humility is that it is accompanied by talkativeness. "Talkative humility is always suspicious; talk is a certain relief to self-conceit."[17] "The humility that can yet talk, has need of careful watching; self-love derives comfort from its outward words."[18] De Sales also thinks this kind of talkativeness is frequently a sign of self-conceit: "words of humility coming merely from the lips, and not from the heart, lead surely to vanity."[19] Even words *about* humility can be a sign: false humility might mean being too talkative, or it might mean talking about humility too much, as Libermann explains in a lengthy passage in one of his spiritual letters.

> If you have a real desire to practice this virtue, don't be satisfied with talking about humility from morning until night ... Everyone considers it laudable to speak constantly about humility, but hardly anyone possesses that virtue. It is scarcely possible to open one's mouth about any spiritual

---

13. Grou, *The School of Jesus Christ*, 216.

14. Rodriguez, *The Practice of Christian and Religious Perfection*, vol. 2, 173-74.

15. Fenelon, *Spiritual Progress*, 39.

16. Fenelon, *Spiritual Progress*, 102.

17. Fenelon, *Letters to Women*, 142.

18. Fenelon, *Spiritual Progress*, 102.

19. Camus, *The Spirit of St. Francis de Sales*, 150.

topic whatsoever without somebody saying immediately, "But there is no virtue like humility."

The right means to acquire humility is not to have the word constantly on your lips. I have often noticed that this word rarely has any genuine meaning when used by the greater number of seminarians. It is for this reason that I rarely named it in our spiritual talks, because the term has been so often misused that scarcely anyone understands its true meaning.

Many who claim to understand it desire to acquire it by natural activity, by strenuous efforts, by troublesome and anxious endeavors. Strange humility! You should take care that your virtues are not merely topics of speech, products of the imagination, natural efforts and anxious endeavors of your mind, which becomes troubled and painfully scrutinizes itself in order to find out whether you are humble and to what extent you possess that virtue.[20]

These signs of false humility are essentially simple forms of hypocrisy, because "true humility does not affect to be humble,"[21] says de Sales, but the trouble is deeper than that, and therefore all the parts of a person must be engaged in humility. "Our minds prepare for God a mortified flesh free from the rebellion of the senses, prayer free from distraction, a loving heart free from all bitterness, a humility free from all taint of vanity."[22]

Hypocrisy around other people is an annoying fault, but hypocrisy with God is a damning lie. False humility before God is a cloaking device by which we attempt to hide a persistent pride. "We look upon ourselves," observes Rodriguez, "as if the execution and

---

20. Libermann, *Letters to Clergy and Religious*, Spiritan Series 9, vol. 5, 66-67.

21. De Sales, *Introduction to the Devout Life*, 99.

22. De Sales, *Maxims and Counsels*, 94.

success of these things were to depend on our own strength, instead of turning our eyes upon God."[23] That is why Grou warns that true devotion would be equally on guard against "a false humility, which is never satisfied with its progress and finds fault with all its actions, and against a false confidence, which applauds itself for whatever it does and easily presumes on its advancement."[24] An operation of secret self-love works in two directions: outwardly and inwardly. It dishonestly praises humility in others by flattery, or praises humility in self by vanity. There could be sort of refined pride still lurking at the bottom of the person who claims humility, which can sometimes be detected in the fact that he does nothing more than profess with his lips that he is a miserable creature. Rodriguez says that if humility "consisted in that, nothing in the world would be easier; we should all be humble, for we all speak in that manner,"[25] but, alas, when such persons speak ill of themselves "they speak not in the spirit of truth, and according to the sentiments of the heart, as Job did ... They would fain be thought humble, but in reality they are not."[26]

This is why the distinction between interior humility and exterior humility is considered so important. The external acts of this virtue are nothing by themselves, and very often come from pride. This virtue lies only in the interior. It is the interior that gives humility merit and beauty, and one must look beneath exterior signs at the interior conviction to judge humility truly. Libermann says genuine humility consists neither "in external activity, in anxiously seizing upon everything that is outwardly humiliating," nor in "lowly and humble attitudes or actions in the presence of others."[27] Such attitudes and actions may be, and often are, the result of genuine humility. But to know for sure, one must look inside to find "an awareness and interior conviction which prompts us to acknowledge, with perfect peace, meekness and love before God, that we are but poverty wretchedness, and incapacity and that we are detestable on account of our many sins."[28]

---

23. Rodriguez, *The Practice of Christian and Religious Perfection*, vol. 2, 166.

24. Grou, *The Characteristics of True Devotion*, 135-36.

25. Rodriguez, *The Practice of Christian and Religious Perfection*, vol. 2, 151.

26. Rodriguez, *The Practice of Christian and Religious Perfection*, vol. 2, 173-74.

27. Libermann, *Letters to Clergy and Religious*, Spiritan Series 9, vol. 5, 67.

28. Libermann, *Letters to Clergy and Religious*, Spiritan Series 9, vol. 5, 67.

In the words of de Sales, those truly humble of heart do not wish to appear humble, they wish to *be* humble. "Humility is so delicate a virtue that it is afraid of its own shadow, and cannot hear its own name uttered without running the risk of extinction."[29]

Why would someone indulge in false humility? Because it is so satisfying! And because it hoodwinks others. But there is an easy test to apply, says Rodriguez: examine the moment of humiliation. "There are persons who outwardly seem to have the spirit of meekness and humility, so long as nothing thwarts them, and all things happen as they wish; but upon the least cross accident that occurs, this peace vanishes, and they presently take fire, and discover what they are."[30] Persons may act in a self-humiliating way in order to convince themselves that they are humble, or they may do so in order to make others believe that they are, but Libermann thinks such persons scarcely notice their real motives. He gives some amusingly familiar examples.

> Sometimes the whole thing remains on the level of the imagination. In reality those people would be very much pained if others actually despised them or ill-treated them.

> And they would be particularly resentful if others despised them for other reasons than those that have their approval. To give an example, if, in order to parade his humility, a person performed an action that would indicate a low degree of intelligence, he would be very annoyed if someone actually concluded from it that he is wanting in intelligence. To give a second example, a person might feel very sad if he were looked upon as possessing only ordinary holiness or even false notions of sanctity.

---

29. Camus, *The Spirit of St. Francis de Sales*, 150.

30. Rodriguez, *The Practice of Christian and Religious Perfection*, vol. 1, 70.

This goes to show that all such seeming humility does not have true humility as its foundation.[31]

Therefore, prepare yourself, de Sales warns. "Do not pretend to wish to be last and least, unless you really and sincerely mean it."[32]

False humility is a chameleon that can take many disguises. It can look like a fear of God, though it is actually false fear and saps one's confidence in God. It can look like deference to another person, though it is actually a felt superiority. "These acts of humility are sometimes sincere and sometimes not," admits Libermann, "but, fundamentally, such persons always think well of themselves in their own conduct. They have a certain self-satisfaction and self-complacency because they feel they have privileges that others do not possess ... The soul is puffed up as it were by that feeling of superiority, in a vague and indefinite fashion."[33] Sin is sneaky. The proud person can "request to have their faults pointed out in order to make others say they have done well,"[34] which Rodriguez thinks is "humility with a hook."

> We sometimes make use of a hook to pull things to us which you cannot otherwise reach ... A preacher, for example, will come out of the pulpit fully persuaded that he has done marvelously well, and then will ask some of his friends to tell him, in charity, wherein he failed. To what end is all this dissembling? For you do not believe you have failed in anything, nor is it your intention to be found fault with, but to be praised, and to have others of the same opinion with yourself, it is that which you seek, and that which tickles your vanity.[35]

---

31. Libermann, *Letters to Clergy and Religious*, Spiritan Series 9, vol. 5, 68.

32. De Sales, *Introduction to the Devout Life*, 99.

33. Libermann, *Letters to Clergy and Religious*, Spiritan Series 7, vol. 3, 93.

34. Rodriguez, *The Practice of Christian and Religious Perfection*, vol. 2, 175.

35. Rodriguez, *The Practice of Christian and Religious Perfection*, vol. 2, 175.

It would be much safer if we are not the ones to call ourselves humble, only letting other people do so, because Grou says this virtue is safer if hidden from our own eyes. "To call oneself humble would be a folly so outrageous that I doubt if there be any person capable of committing it; to think oneself humble would be the effect of a particularly subtle and deliberate kind of pride."[36]

The main dangers of false humility are theological, by which I mean they are dangerous to our friendship with God. Secret pride is as hard an obstacle as overt pride, and God will reject all of our rationalizations. De Bergamo concludes "it will be useless then to excuse ourselves by saying that we fell into such and such a sin from want of grace. 'Grace was there,' the Lord will answer; 'but you ought to have asked for it with humility and not forfeited it by your pride.' Pride is an obstacle harder than steel which hinders the beneficent infusion of grace into the soul."[37] Madame Acarie's maxims identifies several signs of true humility: "One has to be very humble in order to give exact account of one's faults and to accuse oneself of them properly;" and "We must rejoice when we see that our faults are known, and that we are embarrassed and reproved as a result."[38] Other authors give marks of true humility, and I will name three. The first in Fenelon: "true humility lies in seeing one's own unworthiness, and giving one's self up to God, never doubting that He can work out the greatest results for and in us."[39] The second in de Sales: "That humility which is prejudicial to charity is undoubtedly a false humility."[40] And the third in Scaramelli:.

> [These people] eventually lose heart and say to themselves, and at times
> to others also, that God does not hear them, that the Saints will not listen
> to them; and as they fear lest by such sentiments they may be disparaging

---

36. Grou, *The School of Jesus Christ*, 203.

37. De Bergamo, *Humility of Heart*, 49.

38. Madame Acarie, quoted in Jean-Philippe Houdrey, "Madame Acarie, or an Abyss of Humility," https://www.madame-acarie.org/en/author/jean-philippe-houdrey/

39. Fenelon, *Letters to Women*, 38.

40. De Sales, in Huguet, *The Consoling Thoughts of St. Francis De Sales*, 102.

God's goodness, they add, that they mean not by such language to charge the goodness of God with being unwilling to do them favours, but they will have it that their sins and their wickedness render them unworthy to be heard. And the worst of it is, that they believe such vile faint-heartedness to be true humility. The Director must open the eyes of these blind persons, and show them that this depression of spirit is not humility, but its poisonous counterfeit, which the devil puts into their minds in order to disgust them with prayer, or at all events to render their prayers ineffectual with God.[41]

True humility sounds diffident, but is, in fact, confident. It produces courage, not faint-heartedness.

False humility settles for less than God intends for us, which Jesus said was to be perfect as our heavenly Father is perfect. To refuse this graced perfection is neither humility nor modesty, it is cowardice, says Scaramelli. Each says to himself, "perfection is not for me. I recommend myself to God, but I do not deserve to be heard on account of my sins."

Whence they fall into a certain torpor of spirit, and care not, or neglect, to do good. All this is mistaken by them for humility, as it is based on a knowledge of their own weakness, and on this account they do not resist the temptation; but it is, in very deed, pusillanimity, littleness of soul, a faint-heartedness founded on a subtle pride. Do you know why these persons are disquieted after their sin? It is because they had conceived the vain notion that they were very strong, He who is really humble will not be surprised or disturbed after having fallen into sin.[42]

Such a person is certainly not seeing himself in truth, in a trustworthy light, or with veritable self-knowledge. Feigned humility is actually lost confidence, which translates into forsaken effort and dying verve.

---

41. Scaramelli, *Directorium Asceticum; or, Guide to the Spiritual Life,* vol. 1, 413.

42. Scaramelli, *Directorium Asceticum; or, Guide to the Spiritual Life,,* vol. 3, 666-67.

If we do not look at ourselves, or the world, or God in a trustworthy light, then certainly we will not see humility in a true light. De Osuna gives a list of erroneous views: many think humility is pusillanimity, a mean-spirited disposition, inclined to petty interests, weak health, commonplace speech and manners and clothes, faint-heartedness, timidity, wanting in ability, and concealing what we have. Such a list overlooks the power of humility as a true incorruptibility of the soul. It thinks humility shrinks, when actually it enlarges. "The heart of the sinner is called a broken vessel that cannot contain divine things, but the heart of the just does not leak; it is joined and mended with humility ... This vase of the heart, repaired by humility and restored so as to hold its own small measure of contents must be so formed that, without breaking, it can enlarge automatically to receive divine grace."[43]

We could summarize all this by identifying humility's two locations. First, humility is located in truth. "One of the reasons why God loves humility, is, because he loves the truth above all things. Now humility is truth itself; whereas, pride is a mere deceit and a lie, for you are not in effect what you think you are, nor what you would have others think you to be,"[44] according to Rodriguez, leaving Saint-Jure to "define it to be a just knowledge of the truth, which makes a man take himself for what he is, and nothing more."[45] Quarre also insists that humility is simply truth, and

> to be humble, is to walk in the spirit of truth. I say, humility is truth,
> because true humility conists in this, that God by his infinite bounty, by
> his operations of love and grace infuses into the soul, a light which makes
> it see the truth in all things, more or less, at it pleases God. This light,
> which brings with it knowledge, abaseth and annihilateth the soul in her
> self, and causes that in all things she annihilate herself, because this truth
> teacheth her what God is ,and what the creature is.[46]

---

43. De Osuna, *The Third Spiritual Alphabet*, 391.

44. Rodriguez, *The Practice of Christian and Religious Perfection*, vol. 2, 152.

45. Saint-Jure, *A Treatise on the Knowledge and Love of Jesus Christ*, 536.

46. Quarre, *A Spiritual Treasure*, 193.

Second, humility is located in justice. For Grou, humility is "a virtue which does not consist, as it is generally reckoned, in placing ourselves beneath what we are, but in doing ourselves the exactest and the strictest justice."[47] God, who knows all truth and is all justice, knows exactly where a person should be. Humility is not taking a place lower than we deserve, it is taking exactly the place we deserve. Contrary to the popular opinion that thinks humility means sinking lower and lower, it actually means accepting the place where God places us. This is truthful justice, which is why Segneri says humility comes with the Holy Ghost's gift of *understanding*. "Thou wilt find that as humility is the foundation of all other virtues, so it is built upon the knowledge of ourselves."[48] Therefore, "no virtue is more suitable to man's nature, than humility: a body formed out of dust, and a soul out of nothing."[49] Fenelon says humility is accepting God's providential placement, and "if humility is real, it will make us pay continual homage to God through our lowliness, abiding in our proper."[50] And de Bergamo says humility means being in the place where we justly and truthfully belong, "recognizing that God as our Creator has a right to command us, and that we as His creatures are bound to obey Him."[51]

All of these theologians of abnegation make comments that are provocative for their brevity and imagery. Fenelon is among the best: "people who think they are lowering themselves have a good deal of conceit."[52] But he is not the only one. Nicolas of the Cross says Christ's heart wounded by the humble soul, because "there is not a hair of her head, dart of her eye, least motion of her heart or limb, which caused him not a wound, because they all import acts of obedience, humility, and love towards him; and therefore it was a pleasing wound, since it was to be to them matter of all their

---

47. Grou, *Morality, Extracted from the Confessions of Saint Austin*, vol. 1, 242.

48. Paul Segneri, *The Knowledge of Ourselves; With Practical Thoughts of Humility Divided into Meditations for Every Day in the Week* (York: C. Croshaw, 1834) 5.

49. Paul Segneri, *The Knowledge of Ourselves*, 2.

50. Fenelon, *Letters to Men*, 273.

51. De Bergamo, *Humility of Heart*, 42.

52. Fenelon, *Christian Perfection*, 206.

spiritual benedictions."[53] Eymard writes to a directee, "Work hard at humility: it's
the queen, but a genuine humility, that is, draw humility from yourself, let it feed on
your weaknesses, cover it over with your faults; be patient and peaceful toward your
poor weak human nature. However, let your humility be simple like a child's, without
self-consciousness and without frustration."[54] Huby recommends the full treatment.
"But why this excess of humiliations and sufferings? ... The excess of our pride demanded
an excess of humiliations; our passion for riches could only be healed by the most
necessitous poverty; our thirst for pleasure by the weight of the crosses ... The hardness of
our hearts, which still resist in spite of his example, ,justifies only too well the wisdom of
the choice of Jesus and his conduct."[55] Jenks acknowledges that "whoever is a saint, the
greater saint he is, the easier it is for him to be humble. Sinners, indeed, have much more
material for humility to work upon."[56] And Swetchine sits back to watch the seed grow.
"Christianity, even before it is accepted, is, as it were, outlined in truly noble souls. It is
deposited there in germ; and the little seed grows up in the shadow of humility to be an
impenetrable asylum from every storm."[57]

False humility is a clandestine pride, which will accept abasement only because of an
expectation for final elevation. If a person remains where God wants him, not trying to
go lower or higher, then he will not become puffed up with the pride of humility, which is
a truly deadly state. Fenelon will even surprise us by saying humility can accept greatness,
if that is the will of God.

---

53. Nicholas Cross (Nicolas of the Holy Cross), *The Cynosura, or a Saving Star that Leads to Eternity* (London: printed by I. Redmayne for Thomas Rooks, 1679) 255.

54. Peter Eymard, *Life and Letters of Saint Peter Julian Eymard,* vol. 1 (Curia Generalizia, Congregation of the Blessed Sacrament, 2010) 193.

55. Vincent Huby, *Spiritual Works of Pere Vincent Huby, S.J.* (London: Burns Oates & Washbourne Ltd., 1930) 125.

56. Jenks, *A Contrite and Humble Heart,* 161.

57. Anne-Sophie Swetchine, *Life and Letters of Madame* Swetchine (New York: The Catholic Publication House, 1869) 137.

Many men deceive themselves herein; seeking to be humble by an effort of will, and failing in perfect resignation and self-renunciation, they sin against Divine Love ... But the really humble man does not do anything of the sort: he lets himself be carried hither and thither; he is satisfied that God should do as He will with him, as the wind with a straw; and there is more real humility in accepting even greatness in such a spirit, than in thwarting God's plans beneath a pretext of lowliness. He who chooses abasement rather than elevation is not necessarily humble, though he may wish to be; but he who lets himself go, – up or down, – heedless whether he be praised or blamed, unmindful of what is said of him, is really humble, whatever men may think, if it be because he waits solely on God's Pleasure.[58]

Only truth and justice will produce true humility; otherwise, it will be a sham, thinks Alacoque. "The best humiliations are those we do not recognize as such. For humility has this peculiarity: it disappears as soon as one notices it in oneself."[59]

This is not an escape clause. We may not conclude that we need not be so hard upon ourselves as we initially thought. What does true knowledge and true justice show us? Our natural place. And Grou wants to know what is the natural place for "a soul that has come from nothingness and possesses only a borrowed existence, a soul that depends entirely upon grace for the attainment of its final destiny, a soul that has sinned and is always liable to sin? Evidently the place assigned to it by humility."[60] Humility comes from a combination of four factors: self-knowledge, justice, nothingness, and sin. If we see ourselves exactly as we are, then Grou says we can discern our ontological contingency and hierarchical dependence.

If we know ourselves, we do ourselves justice; we think of ourselves exactly as we are; we see ourselves as God sees us. And what does He see? Sin

---

58. Fenelon, *Letters to Men*, 276.

59. Alacoque, *Spiritual Letters,* letter 80, Kindle edition.

60. Grou, *The School of Jesus Christ*, 210.

and nothingness; and no more. We have no other possessions of our own: everything else comes from God, and must be attributed to Him. If we know ourselves thus, what must be our humility, and our contempt and hatred of self? I am absolutely nothing. Throughout eternity I was not, and there was no reason why I should exist, nor why I should be what I am. My existence is the simple effect of God's Will: He bestowed it on me as it pleased Him. He preserves it.[61]

There is one final step to take in order to reach perfection, as we have said throughout. For our humility to be perfect we must go beyond merely acknowledging what we are, and actually taking pleasure in appearing to others as we are. De Bergamo says it can only be accomplished by grace. "What good qualities have we of our own for which we can praise ourselves? All the good that is in us comes from God, and to Him alone we must give praise and honour."[62] It is not easy, admits Olier.

Humility is that virtue which gives us this pleasure and this satisfaction of appearing as we are, of being seen as people who are nothing and who are accursed sinners in everyone's eyes. For in ourselves we are nothing but that. For if there are graces in us or any gifts, these do not come from us, but from God. If we wish to be appreciated and esteemed for that, then we unjustly steal what does not belong to us, and we claim for ourselves what belongs to God alone.[63]

Outside the universe of liturgical abnegation it is difficult to understand experiencing pleasurable satisfaction in being what we are, namely, contingent beings (with no claim on existence), and admitting what we are, namely, sinners (with no claim on righteousness). But within the universe of liturgical abnegation, obeisance smiles because Grou calls it a

---

61. Grou, *The Spiritual Maxims*, 6.

62. De Bergamo, *Humility of Heart*, 68.

63. Olier, *Introduction to the Christian Life and Virtues,* in *Berulle and the French School,* 238.

"special characteristic of humility to keep guard over the rights of God, and preserve them against the usurpations of the creature."[64]

Humility places us on God's side instead of on our own, desiring that his will be fulfilled, instead of our own; desiring that his glory be full, instead of siphoning some off for ourselves. The main business of the virtue of humility is to start by cutting off the branches of pride, and ultimately putting an axe to the root. Liturgical abnegation emerges from the confrontation of God's glory with creation's finitude and man's sin, but God's glory is always mingled with a mercy and that modulates our abjection. It transforms pusillanimous fear into liturgical fear, which is the fear of God that angels, patriarchs, and saints know beatifically. Liturgical humility is confident while it admits sin, yet not despairing, which is a relief to de Bergamo. "To fix our thoughts solely on our own wretchedness might cause us to fall into self-distrust and despair, and in the same way to fix our thoughts solely on the contemplation of the divine goodness might cause us to be presumptuous and rash. True humility lies between the two."[65]

We have been looking at definitions of humility in this chapter, gathering them from various authors. I will conclude by pointing to two particularly dense summary definitions. Here they are from Ullathorne's book on humility.[66] "Humility consists in our subjection to God in all things" (84). "Humility is an obedient reflection of the truth of what we are, as we see ourselves in God's truth, and the just conformity of ourselves to the Divine Justice" (163). "In its essence humility is that absence of egotism and exclusiveness from which spring generosity and devotedness to what is beyond us" (166). "Humility is the vacancy made in the soul by the removal of our unsound and unsupporting self-love, and of the unsubstantial inflation of pride" (218). "We may, therefore, give a final definition of humility as the grateful acknowledgment to God of all we are and have, and as the sacrifice and surrender of our whole being to God, that He may reform it to perfection by His goodness" (106). Here is a second compressed summary from Fenelon.

---

64. Grou, *The School of Jesus Christ*, 203.

65. De Bergamo, *Humility of Heart*, 90.

66. Ullathorne, *The Groundwork of the Christian Virtues*, page numbers in text above.

He who imagines himself to be something is not truly humble; neither is he who seeks anything for himself. But he who so entirely forgets himself that his thoughts do not recur to self or self-seeking; who is lowly within, never offended at anything, though not affecting outward tokens of patience; who speaks of himself as he would of another; who does not pretend to ignore himself while really bursting with self-consciousness; who gives himself up for love's sake, without considering whether to do so looks like pride or humility; who is content to be thought deficient in humility – in short, he who is full of love, such an one is truly humble. He who does not seek his own interest, but solely God's interest in time and eternity, he is humble. The purer his love, the more perfect his humility. Do not test humility by external appearances, by this or the other action, but solely by love.[67]

---

67. Fenelon, *Letters to Men*, 237.

HUMILITY: FLEEING SATAN

To recap: humility is banded together with justice, faith, charity, and purity – all things which must be known experimentally, i.e. by giving it a trial. Ullathorne says "it was to destroy this supremacy of self-sufficiency that Christ brought these four virtues to mankind, that by *humility* the soul might know herself and all that God is to her, by *faith* she might be the humble subject of His truth and authority, by *charity* she might have her life in God, and by *purity* she might be holy in body and spirit. To have these virtues is to know them; not to have them is to be completely ignorant of them, because they are not theories of the mind but experiences of the soul."[1] It would seem, then, that we will only know what humility is by using humility. So let me put the question this way: what good is humility? For what can it be used? If we attain it, how should we employ it? And the answer is two-sided: to flee Satan and to adhere to Christ. This chapter concerns the former, the next chapter concerns the latter.

Satan hates humility. It offends him. De Sales pictures it as hurting Satan's ears. "The swallow with its sharp cry and keen glance has the power of frightening away birds of prey, and for that reason the dove prefers it to all other birds, and lives surely beside it; even so humility drives Satan away, and cherishes the gifts and graces of the Holy Spirit within us."[2] It is the reason, says Blosius, why all the saints have esteemed the grace of humility above all other virtues. "Remember that our Lord Jesus Christ, and the blessed angelic spirits, and all the citizens of heaven are humble and detest pride; that, on the contrary, the wicked demons are proud and pursue humility with hatred."[3] Satan finds

---

1. Ullathorne, *The Groundwork of the Christian Virtues*, 79. Emphases added.

2. De Sales, *Introduction to the Devout Life*, 96.

3. Blosius, *Spiritual Works of Louis of Blois*, 120.

humility offensive. His mind has been perverted in such a way that he finds submission oppressive, beatitude cheerless, and love painful. He experiences the good aroma of Christ in Christians like a stench that repels him. Humility disarms temptation – so use it! says de Bergamo. "Humility causes the evil one to flee because he cannot face the humble on account of his great pride, and it causes every temptation to vanish suddenly because there can be no temptation without a touch of pride."[4]

In the face of humility, what is Satan's stratagem? He seeks to create a *counterfeit humility*, which, according to Scaramelli, is a deception that induces us to give up possession of grace and surrender our right of friendship with God.

> There are, then, two sorts of humility; one is the gift of the bountiful hands of God, the other comes from the crafty hands of the devil. The humility which is God's gift brings with it, indeed, a knowledge of our sins and miseries, but has this property, that while it lowers the soul in its own estimation, it raises it to hope, and finally leaves it in great calm, and reposing within the arms of the Divine Goodness. The humility, however, which is counterfeit and from the devil, brings with it, in like manner, a knowledge of our own sins and weakness; but it has this most injurious quality, that while it bends low the soul, it takes away hope, or at least diminishes it, and leaves us full of cowardice, diffidence and discouragement. The humility which is God's gift, is holy. That which comes from the devil, is wicked. The former disposes us for pardon; the latter prevents forgiveness.[5]

God-given humility brings knowledge of sin, but raises the soul to hope; Satan-inspired humility brings knowledge of sin, but leaves discouragement. Teresa of Avila says we can

---

4. De Bergamo, *Humility of Heart*, 46.

5. Scaramelli, *Directorium Asceticum; or, Guide to the Spiritual Life*, vol. 1, 497.

detect the difference between the two because "the humility the devil leaves behind is false, unquiet, and without sweetness."[6]

Satan cannot create, but he can corrupt. His animus toward humility means he must present himself as an imposter, and cannot attack it head on, but Teresa of Avila knows he has ways of weakening it. "Great are the wiles of the devil; for he will turn hell upside down a thousand times, in order to make us imagine we possess a virtue which in reality we do not. And with reason (does the devil act in this way); for thus he effects much mischief, because these counterfeit virtues are always attended with some vain-glory, coming from such a source."[7] All the spiritual writers have marveled at the irony that we can be made proud of our humility. The remedy can be turned into another variation of the original disease! De Bergamo wonders how this comes about so easily, and understands that "the strongest subterfuge which the devil can employ in order to make us fall into temptation is to flatter our humility."[8] Satan beguiles us with words we find pleasing, with undue and insincere praise – in short, flatters us, which stirs up vainglory.

Realizing that Satan can only swindle and cheat should convince us of his weakness, and stir up more courage to oppose him. A temptation is not greater in strength than a will supported by grace, therefore, says Scaramelli, if Satan cannot strip persons of God's grace, "he strives to rob them at least of the humility which they have been taught in their struggles, and which is the main end that God has in view in permitting them. He endeavours either to make them vain of their triumphs, or, if wearied by their continual conflicts, to draw them into want of trust, into discouragement, disquiet, trouble, and complaints; all of which are contrary to holy humility."[9] His hatred is not stronger than love, his seeds of doubt are not stronger than faith, so he turns his efforts to distorting theology: he presents a bogus picture of God. Teresa of Avila thinks it looks like this:

---

6. Teresa of Avila, *Life of Saint Teresa, Written by Herself* (New York: P. J. Kenedy & Sons, 1870) 227.

7. Teresa of Avila, *Interior Castle*, 83.

8. De Bergamo, *Humility of Heart*, 47.

9. John Baptist Scaramelli, *Directorium Asceticum; or, Guide to the Spiritual Life*, vol. 2 (New York: Benziger Bros, 1902) 486.

In that other humility which the devil suggests, there is no light for anything that is good, but it seems to the soul as if God were ready to put every one to fire and the sword. He represents the divine justice to her, and though she has faith in God's mercy, because the devil has no power to destroy that, yet, she believes in such a manner, that her faith gives her no comfort; but rather when she considers God's great mercy, the tempter makes this serve for her greater torment, because she thinks she ought to have served God so much the more.

This is a stratagem of the devil, and one of the most painful, the most subtle, and disguised that I have ever known.[10]

Perhaps the saddest consequence of these seeds of distrust is their effect on prayer. A soul outside prayer is like a fish outside water, so Boudon says "the devil ... leaves no stone unturned to divert souls from it; and sometimes he tries to surprise them under fine pretexts of humility, persuading them that they are unworthy to converse with God."[11] Loss of prayer is loss of the lifeline that keeps us connected to God, by which we can petition grace for protection.

Like opposite trays on a scale, the lessening of humility is the increase of pride, which is precisely the state this fallen angel chose for himself. Flattered humility becomes vainglorious, and, being puffed up with vainglory, Blosius sees the soul's self-reliance leading to a downfall. "God has decreed from all eternity to open heaven to sinners by works of humility and love, and He wills that measure and discretion be observed in all things. But the devil in his envy often persuades an imperfect man to fast beyond his strength, or to take up exercises that he cannot bear, or to aim at what is too high for him."[12] We have already learned that humility means abiding exactly where God has placed us, not higher and not lower; now we also learn that humility means performing

---

10. Teresa of Avila, *Life of Saint Teresa, Written by Herself*, 269-70.

11. Boudon, *The Holy Slavery of the Admirable Mother of God*, 234.

12. Blosius, *Spiritual Works of Louis of Blois*, 218.

exactly the mortifications God requires of us, no more and no less. The devil will tempt us to greater ambition so we can boast of our accomplishments, and from that height Bovilla says we will despise others.

> That he may shift thee from thy humility, [the devil] will seek that thou
> lay something to thine own industry and endeavour, above that of others;
> whereby thou mayest come to despise somebody or other in thy own
> thoughts, as less disposed than thou to receive God's gifts. This is the
> door of vanity and self-conceit. Be advised, then, and speedily pull thyself
> down, lest thou fall into the pride of the Pharisee. For if the proud fiend
> enter thy soul, he will soon, to thy great loss and damage, plant in it every
> kind of vice.[13]

With another of his vivid illustrations, de Sales says humility is a guard of the virtues, because "he who would lay up virtues without humility is like one who carries a precious dust in his hand exposed to the wind."[14]

Boudon advises comfort and security in an abased state. "Be comforted, ye poor and simple men and women, in your littleness, so only that it be accompanied with humility, for this it is on which God sets a value: and of this the devils will never be able to perform the slightest act."[15] The Lord will preserve and protect all who are endowed with sincere humility if they piously seek and invoke him, but Blosius warns against those "who are proud, and who conceal within themselves any duplicity and dissimulation, miserably mislead themselves, and fall of their own accord into the nets of the devil."[16] If Adam and Eve could be seduced in their innocence, so can their children be in their humility. This is why humility is foundational for Fenelon. "All the saints are convinced that sincere humility is the foundation of all virtues. This is because humility is the daughter of pure

---

13. Bovilla, *The Quiet of the Soul*, 33-34.

14. De Sales, *Maxims and Counsels of St. Francis de Sales*, 160.

15. Boudon, *The Hidden Life of Jesus*, 17.

16. Blosius, *Spiritual Works of Louis of Blois*, 191.

charity, and humility is nothing else but truth. There are only two truths in the world, that God is all, and the creature nothing. In order that humility be true, we need to give continual homage to God in our lowliness, and to stay in our place, which is to love being nothing."[17] Humility is truth; humility is born of charity; out of this truth and love comes continual homage to God; this liturgizing gives us constant joy. Lose humility, lose liturgy, lose beatitude.

In his goodness, God has gifted us with many ways of practicing humility, though we are not so happy about it! De Bergamo wonders at "how many occasions we have of humbling ourselves secretly, in all places, at all times, at every turn – towards God, our fellow-men, and even towards ourselves!"[18] The reason God has given us so many opportunities for practicing humility is because it is so essential to our Christian life. A theoretical knowledge of abnegation might be found in the library, but the practical knowledge of it comes from daily humiliation. More on that in a moment, but let us first notice some four dimensions of humility that we could consider as guides to its practice.

The world tells us to look upon status in society ("high birth") as something meritorious, but Grou wonders "what is it in God's sight? Nothing. What is it according to the standard of the Gospel? An obstacle to humility."[19] The mindfulness of our nothingness that weighs upon us from introspection, the memory of death, prayer, and obedience should crush the feelings of self-love. Eudes says humility is pitted against vanity. "Should we not, indeed, employ every means at our disposal to banish vanity from our lives and preserve within our hearts a Christ-like humility?"[20] Since pride is the opposite of humility, the two cannot coexist any more than darkness and light can coexist at the same time. Abasement expunges pride, and de Bergamo thinks it should expunge it even from our consciousness. "He who thinks himself humble is no longer so. In the same way that to recognize that we are proud is the beginning of humility, so to flatter ourselves that we are humble is the beginning of pride, and the more humble we think ourselves the

---

17. Fenelon, *Christian Perfection*, 205.

18. De Bergamo, *Humility of Heart*, 127.

19. Grou, *The Spiritual Maxims of Pere Grou*, 132.

20. Eudes, *The Priest*, 111.

greater is our pride."[21] Because everything that pride touches can be stained, including efforts at humility, this expunction requires supernatural force. No grains of sand can be left in the ointment because, says de Bergamo, "humility is like purity: however little it may be contaminated it becomes impure. Purity is corrupted not only by an impure act, but also by an immodest word or thought. And humility is also so fragile that it is easily tainted by the love of praise, by a word or thought of self-esteem, by vainglory or self-love."[22]

Humility needs protection by abasement in order to be preserved, and the supernatural energy of God must work both upon our will and upon our understanding. First, humility is sister to truth: humility is seeing ourselves truly, which, to Olier, means seeing ourselves as does God. "This is the true touchstone to recognize authentic humility: that in interior dryness, aridity, abandonment and rejection by God, the soul takes God's side and approves of his prosecution of itself; that it humiliates itself and annihilates itself in prayer, condemning itself and saying that it deserves no other treatment. We should admit that he is right to reject our works and our very selves."[23] Second, humility is sister to justice: perfected humility is desiring God's righteousness to take effect. Again, for de la Colombiere, this moves the soul to the other side of the table. "Place yourself on his side and be glad to see him chastising you in proportion to your sins. Try to please him by perfect acceptance of the severest measures of his justice, and this by willingly accepting all that happens, all that is humiliating to body and soul ... Let your compunction be mingled with a certain pleasure at the sight of yourself: poor, miserable, humbled, deprived of all merit in virtue."[24] When the saints accuse themselves of being the worst sinners, they mean it.

This fragile gift of humility, so easily tainted, should keep itself free from boasting, which is helped by embracing our annihilation. The soul that is truly humbled and annihilated leaves herself in God's hands, and when we recognize that all goods we possess

---

21. De Bergamo, *Humility of Heart*, 20.

22. De Bergamo, *Humility of Heart*, 31.

23. Olier, *Introduction to the Christian Life and Virtues*, in *Berulle and the French School*, 240.

24. De la Colombiere, *The Spiritual Direction of Saint Claude de la Colombiere*, 50-51.

are given by God freely, liberally, and undeservedly, then Grou says we will no longer brag of them as our own.

> If we were really humble with the humility which is fitting for us, we should make no account, either in ourselves or in others, of good birth, or of intellect, or of beauty, or of riches, or of any other natural gifts; we should never make of any of these things an occasion for thinking more highly of ourselves or for despising others who do not possess them. For all these advantages do not really belong to us, to us who are only nothingness: God has given them to us out of pure liberality, and His intention never was that we should be vain of them.[25]

The gifts are from God; also from God is our very ability to deny that we have earned the gifts. So what is our part in acquiring humility? Reception, not accomplishment. The tower of virtue rests upon a foundation of humility, and that foundation must itself be laid by God. According to Boudon, self-abnegation is his work, not our own. The virtue of humility "must be accompanied with an entire distrust of ourselves. If we put any confidence in our own strength, in our experience, our discretion, our resolutions, we are lost; sooner or later we shall infallibly perish: and we must be greatly on our guard against a secret self-reliance, which is sometimes imperceptible to ourselves."[26] Doctrine reminds us that merit is a mystery whereby a sinner who cannot act autonomously is given the power to receive. So take hope! urges Crasset. "Do not heed these discouraging thoughts. God is leading you through this hard and stony desert to the promised land flowing with milk and honey. He is establishing you in humility in order to fit you to receive the great favors He intends to bestow upon you. He is despoiling you in order to enrich you, and to make you merit what He yearns to give you. Your whole duty consists in fidelity."[27] Our duty of fidelity means cooperation, practice, effort, voluntariness.

---

25. Grou, *Manual for Interior Souls*, 209-10.

26. Boudon, *Devotion to the Nine Choirs of Holy Angels*, 81.

27. De Sales & Crasset, *The Secret of Sanctity*, 208.

Though we cannot accomplish humility out of our own strength, we are obliged to do more than stir up a casual wish for it. De Ravignan explains more precisely. "It is not difficult to desire it, but to practise, to accept, to go in quest of humiliation is another thing. Humility itself is sweet, very sweet; but it is a fruit, a product, and we must labour and work for a long time, and pray above all things before gathering it."[28] These humiliations are the hard thing – but fortunately for us, we are given much opportunity for practice. The person who humiliates me may have no thought of my salvation, but he is nevertheless a medium for it, thinks de Bergamo. "I ought to be most grateful to any one who helps to keep me in humility by subjecting me to humiliations of word and deed, because he is co-operating with the divine mercy to fulfil the work of my eternal salvation. And although he has no thought of my salvation when he offends me, he is nevertheless an instrument thereof, and all the evil comes from me if I do not make a good use of it."[29]

The deep soteriological paradox of salvation is applied to the virtue of humility: like salvation itself, it consists of grace and works, gift and labor, being free and costly. Surin observes a kind of excuse often used, when we announce we are far from perfect, and since we cannot be perfect without special grace, there is nothing we can do. We are off the hook.

> People say this; but they do not see, that if the Saints received great assistance from Heaven, as they assuredly did, it was always their principal care to co-operate with it; that they laboured much, did themselves much violence, that they spent ten or twenty years in conquering themselves and mortifying their passions; in a word, that the perfection that they acquired cost them much, and that it is with extreme labour that they arrived at it.[30]

---

28. De Ravignan, *Ravignan's Last Retreat*, 106.

29. De Bergamo, *Humility of Heart*, 85.

30. Surin, *Foundations of the Spiritual Life*, 28.

On the one hand, "The Lord Himself it is that buildeth this house of peace. Without Him thou dost toil thyself in vain. But the foundation thereof is humility"[31] (Bovilla). On the other hand "We must work with very great care to acquire this virtue. It is so necessary and so valued by God because it makes us worthy to have his Spirit dwelling within us"[32] (Madeleine de Saint-Joseph). Humility is like a gate in the sheepfold through which the graces can be herded for distribution, which is what makes it so important. Humility is the virtue that makes other virtues virtuous, which is why Blosius says "humility alone will preserve the good that is in thee uncorrupted,"[33] and de Bergamo agrees that, "though destitute of some of the other virtues, we may yet be saved, but never without humility."[34] In Crasset's words,

> Either humble thyself,
> Or God will humble thee ...
> Virtues without humility cannot save you;
> Vices with humility will not damn you;
> For humility vanishes all vices,
> And puts charity in their place.[35]

If it was lacking, whatever we did would be displeasing in the sight of God precisely a position Satan would have us occupy. Humility makes salvation possible because it keeps a pressure on sin that drives us to the cross to be united with Jesus.

In fact, de Bergamo goes so far as to say the humble person is not the person with no sin, he is rather the person who knows how to use his sins profitably. Turnabout is fair play: if the devil will use humility to make us proud, God will use sins to make us convert.

---

31. Bovilla, *Quiet of the Soul*, 11.

32. Madeleine de Saint-Joseph, *The Spiritual Letters of Madeleine de Saint-Joseph*, in *Berulle and the French School*, 196.

33. Blosius, *Spiritual Works of Louis of Blois*, 68.

34. De Bergamo, *Humility of Heart*, 1.

35. Crasset, *Meditations for Every Day in the Year, Pentecost to Advent*, 187.

"How many great sinners have become great saints without having done anything more than keep their sins constantly before their eyes end humble themselves in shame and confusion before God and their fellowmen! ... We shall never be able to make the excuse that we could not become saints because we committed grave sin, when those, very sins might have been the means of sanctifying us by urging us to a deeper humility."[36] We acquire the spirit of humility the way we acquire all other virtues: by repetition. This is why Christians have turned away from the world, as de Sales knows. "Humility makes us annihilate ourselves in all things which are not necessary for our advancement in grace, such, for instance, as a gift of expression, gracefulness of manners, great talent for business matters, a capable mind, eloquence, and so on, for in all these outward matters we ought to desire that others should do better than we do."[37] If God's providence has placed one in a position of responsibility in the world, then one must remain in it, but one should not hold dear anything that does not contribute to one's advancement in grace. Real humility would not take account of any natural advantages, according to Grou, because "they are not our own work, and God does not give such gifts to nourish pride and vanity. Of themselves they are not profitable to our salvation; – it may be that through misuse we have turned them into occasions of sin, and far from glorying in them, perhaps they ought to deepen our humility. Real humility would hold itself unworthy of the praise of men, and would refer all such to God."[38]

What, then, are the goods of humility? We can name two, and they both irritate Satan. Its primary good, according to Olier, is to please God. "It must be presupposed in every work of piety. Without it, we will never make any progress. Pride, which is the opposite of this virtue, is the vice that displeases God the most."[39] Its secondary good, according to de Lombez, is an acquisition of interior peace, which humility can do

---

36. De Bergamo, *Humility of Heart*, 57.

37. De Sales, *The Spiritual Conferences 73*.

38. Grou, *The Hidden Life of the Soul*, 196.

39. Olier, *Introduction to the Christian Life and Virtues*, in *Berulle and the French School*, 232.

because it modifies the passions, insensibly weakens them, and finally destroys them as far as they can and ought to be destroyed. It is a short means of attacking them almost all at once...

A soul truly humble is always tranquil. What can trouble it? The praises it receives rather surprises than inflates it; reproach and blame rejoices it instead of dejecting it, and it is glad to find others have the same opinion it has of itself. Calumny, though grievous, such as giving scandal to truth and justice, does not disconcert it. Prosperity does not exalted; adversity neither weakens nor discourages.[40]

The man of vanity is always on a restless quest for additional honors and acclamations from the world, but the man of humility finds peace even in dry times. Teresa of Avila knew something about stretches of aridity. "Believe me, that wherever this virtue is really found, though our Lord may give no delights at all, yet He will bestow a certain peace and conformity, which will satisfy you more than pleasures and favours do others."[41] Thus it becomes clear that when the tradition of abnegation speaks about humility, diffidence, and loathing. Camus says de Sales identified exactly what is being despised.

We ought not under pretence of humility to slight and despise the graces which God has given us. To do so would be to throw ourselves over the precipice of ingratitude in order to avoid perishing in the pitfall of vanity, "Nothing," said [de Sales], "can so humble us before the mercy of God, as the multitude of his benefits; nothing can so abase us before the throne of His justice, as the countless number of our misdeeds. We need never fear that the good things God has given us will feed our pride, as long as

---

40. De Lombez, *A Treatise on Interior Peace*, 57.

41. Teresa of Avila, *Interior Castle*, 31.

we remember that whatever there may be *in* us that is good, it is not *of* us."[42]

Satan hates humility because he hates the truth; fallen man hates humility for the same reason; Jesus loved humility because he loved the truth; and if we loved Jesus, then we would love humility, as well. But such humility must make its dwelling in the heart, and not on the tongue. "To learn one's own nothing, and not to be willing to be treated as we deserve, is, in [Alonso Rodriguez's] language, merely to know the road, yet never to undertake the journey."[43] It is one thing to approve of humility, and another to love it, desire it, embrace it as Christ embraced his. "Humility is in reality a confession of the greatness of God, who after His voluntary self annihilation was exalted and glorified,"[44] observes de Bergamo. Read the Gospels. The motive of Christ's humility was love, which is the motive for all humility – love for God's glory and man's sanctification (the two-headed liturgical motive). Both Christ's kenosis in the flesh and his sacramental presence in the Eucharist inspire charity. De Castaniza finds Christ making moves that are exactly the opposite of Satan's moves. "O strange humility of my Saviour! Not only to descend unto, but into, a wicked worm; not only to eat with a sinner, but to be eaten by a sinner."[45] We hesitate at calling human beings worms, but the theologians of liturgical abnegation secure their footing on Scripture. De la Colombiere notes that the Son of God is insulted when the crowd prefer Barabbas to him, and "this is what is strange: we complain of the advantages given to others, but Jesus Christ has no complaint to make. He even placed himself lower than they have placed Him by this unjust comparison. At the same time He said in His heart to His Father: 'I am a worm and no man' (Ps 21:7)."[46] De la Colombiere is using the Vulgate numbering, and we would recognize this as verse six

---

42. Camus, *The Spirit of St. Francis de Sales*, 167-68.

43. Francis Goldie, *The Life of St. Alonso Rodriguez* (London: Burns and Oates, 1889) 299.

44. De Bergamo, *Humility of Heart*, 4.

45. De Castaniza, *The Spiritual Conflict and Conquest*, 415.

46. De la Colombiere, *Faithful Servant*, 46.

of Psalm 22, which begins "My God, my God, why have you forsaken me?" This Psalm, which Jesus referenced on the cross, represents his position during the entire trial which preceded it: "I am a worm, and no man; scorned by men, and despised by the people." De Castaniza thinks this is a sign of the ineffable humility of the heart of Christ,[47] and the impact of hearing Christ apply the verse to himself should lead us to say "O strange pride in me, to see the Lord of heaven and earth so humbled in His Incarnation, Passion, Communion, and yet to see a beggar so proud, a sinner so lofty-minded, and dust and ashes, have such difficulty to stoop!"[48]

Satan wished for a place higher than the one he was assigned, and to attain it, he diverted creation's glory from God to himself. He broke the hierarchy, and created anarchy. But humility can teach man the role of cosmic priesthood by mingling together nothingness and liturgical glorification of God. The homage and glory that our liturgical humility gives to God is homage and glory presented in mystical union with Christ. Our natural religion is graced to become supernatural liturgy, and in the process we receive self-knowledge of our nothingness. Blessed Elizabeth of the Trinity is said to have learned quickly the "self-knowledge which is both the foundation and the summit of humility. God made use of temptation to show her the abyss of her own nothingness, and to insure that glory would be ascribed to Him alone for the graces which He intended to bestow upon her soul."[49] Liturgy and nothingness are connected in what de Bergamo describes as a binocular vision. "Humility has two eyes: with one we recognize our own misery so as not to attribute to ourselves anything but our nothingness; with the other we recognize our duty to work and to attribute everything to God, referring all things to Him: 'Not unto us, O Lord, not unto us, but to Thy name give glory'."[50] Abnegation of self, i.e.,

---

47. "In the following Lent, 1678, [De la Colombiere] captivated his audience by the way in which he spoke of the ineffable humility of the Heart of Christ. "*Ego autem sum vermis et non homo, opprobrium hominum et abjectio plebis* – I am a worm and no man, the reproach of man and the outcast of the people." Sr. Mary Philip, *A Jesuit at the English Court*, 134.

48. De Castaniza, *The Spiritual Conflict and Conquest*, 415.

49. Elizabeth of the Trinity, *The Praise of Glory*, 81.

50. De Bergamo, *Humility of Heart*, 41.

denial of self-reliance, opens up the soul to a dependency upon God that is our true place before him (justice and truth unite). Then abnegation permeates adoration. "Humility can nowhere more appear," says de Castaniza, "than when a soul is so annihilated as to trust neither little nor much to herself. O rich nothing! What spiritual mines, what masses of treasure doth a soul find that hath thus happily lost herself in her loving Lord. Adoration, sacrifice, devotion, and all sorts of Religion are here effectually practiced."[51]

This affects the soul's relationship to both Creator and creation. It places us in justice before God, which is a humble place, and it determines our proper use of all things, which we do with humility. Satan rebelled against his subordination, but the believer performs all his actions in subordination to the divine Spirit, and therefore we will be able to use everything according to its proper and true end. Barbanson says we are wrong to reason that "I will first abstract myself, then recollect myself, and then raise myself to God." Rather, say

> I will endeavor with humility to lift my heart to God, to kindle my affection towards him and replenish it with the desire of his love. Thus shall I be able to neglect all things within and without, and to recall my mind from all vanity, extravagant or exterior affection, human respect, and such like. Nor is such abstraction to be thought of as a bitter thing, but as sweet, because it has undergone for the love of God.[52]

The tradition of abnegation recognizes three degrees of humility. A number of authors treat of this, relying as far back as Benedict and his Rule, but I will use only three for summary, and notice that they all have a liturgical element. First, Nepveu says humility is a thorough knowledge of ourselves, which shuts out self-esteem and the love of men's praise, and it has several degrees. "The first consists not only in acknowledging on our knees before God that we are nothing ... but also in feeling content that it should be so ... The second degree of humility consists in submitting patiently to contempt ... [And]

---

51. De Castaniza, *The Spiritual Conflict and Conquest*, 391.

52. Barbanson, *The Secret Paths of Divine Love*, 133.

the highest degree of humility reaches the point of even loving contempt."[53] Anything
that causes humility is a blessing, and real blessings ought always be desired. "Is it not a
blessing when [humility is] viewed by the light of faith, since it enables us to sacrifice to
Christ that which is dearest to us – our honor; since it renders us the objects of God's
good pleasure and love, Who cannot but be pleased with so costly a sacrifice; since it is a
method of becoming like unto God Who was despised and emptied of His glory?"[54]

Second, Rodriguez says the first degree of humility is to have a humble opinion of
oneself, the second consists in being glad that we are despised, and the third "consists
in not being exalted with the gifts we have received from God, and in not ascribing the
glory of them to ourselves, but wholly to him as the author and dispenser of all good."[55]
The saints practiced humility without glorying in the gifts heaped upon themselves, and
instead made these gifts a cause for liturgizing. "Applause and honours raised in them
no vain thoughts; because they knew how to distinguish, what did, and what did not
belong to them; so that looking upon the favours which were heaped upon them, and the
honours and respects which were paid them, as things received from God, they gave him
all the glory."[56] A person who attains this third degree of humility is not inflated in ego,
and can therefore give God all thanks in a glorious act of liturgy.

> We have shewn that a man attains the third degree of humility, when,
> having received great gifts from God, and seeing himself honoured and
> esteemed, he is neither puffed up, nor does he attribute any thing to
> himself; but ascribes all to the fountain of all things, which is God; giving
> him the glory of every thing, and retaining as deep a sense of humility and
> lowliness, as if he did nothing, and were not endowed with any virtue at
> all.[57]

---

53. Nepveu, 146-47.

54. Nepveu, *The Hidden Life,* 147.

55. Rodriguez, *The Practice of Christian and Religious Perfection,* vol. 2, 239.

56. Rodriguez, *The Practice of Christian and Religious Perfection,* vol. 2, 244.

57. Rodriguez, *The Practice of Christian and Religious Perfection,* vol. 2, 245.

And third, Grou wraps it up. Rendering God glory requires us to acknowledge our nothingness, not because God is pleased to see us grovel – this is the lie Satan told – but because we mustn't steal the glory for ourselves.

> To God is due the glory of all His works, and that so exclusively that He declares He will never share it with anyone. He requires that in all circumstances it shall return to Him in its entirety …

> If the glory for which human pride is so greedy belongs only to God, what is due to the creature? There is nothing that he can ascribe to himself, nothing that he has any right to claim in the way of praise and applause, either in the natural or the supernatural order, whether in self-congratulation or being congratulated by others. No honour of any kind is due to him, either for his fine qualities of mind or heart, or for his achievements and acts of benevolence, or for his virtues, or for the special gifts and graces he has received from God. Humility regards it as a duty to recognise this. It cannot endure that the smallest particle of these things should be appropriated by the creature; it rejects with horror all the feelings of vanity, self-complacency and appropriation, however slight, that arise in the soul in this connection. As for the praises of men, humility refuses to hear them or discuss them, but simply returns them to God without leaving a fragment to the creature.[58]

These are lessons hard to learn, but the truth is taught by during aridity and spiritual consolation, both in trials and successes. Praise is directed only to God – never to ourselves; abnegation stops up our ears against both the praise from other men and the flattery of the demons. Rodriguez believes the reason why God sometimes refuses to give us the graces we ask for is so that "we should know by experience, how little ability we have of ourselves to do any thing that is good; suffering us to remain a long time in this state, to teach us humility, and not at all to confide in, or attribute any thing to ourselves,

---

58. Grou, *The School of Jesus Christ*, 204.

but to render the glory of all to God alone."[59] The dark night of the soul is a time of liturgical preparation, a sort of apprenticeship in the cross for the perfection of our liturgy. Through all this time, God's jealousy is not petulant. "God's first aim in man's sanctification is His own glory," insists Grou, and "He would have us acknowledge that we can do nothing of ourselves ... God is jealous of His glory."[60] Liturgy consists of the twin blades of glorifying God and sanctifying man, and God has not forgotten the latter even while he corrects our errors in doing the former.

If the word "annihilation" is offensive to our too delicate ears, what about the word "submission"? Either word is equally offensive to Satan, so Scaramelli can coordinate them by saying "humility of heart towards God consists not only in the deepest reverence in His sight, but in an entire submission of soul to Him as to the source of all our good, rendering to Him all the honour, praise, and glory of our every excellence ; without keeping back any share of it for ourselves."[61] Liturgy is submission to God; liturgizing God requires submissiveness. In saying so, we are talking about annihilation, which Saint-Jure describes as such a profound humility that one is "as it were, annihilated in His presence, remembering only that He looks on them, and abasing themselves before His august Majesty."[62] This submission is, of course, interior, and not merely an exterior performance, but this is no reason to excuse us from exterior liturgy. Interior humility is the perfecting of corporate, ritual, sacramental liturgy. Saint-Jure believes we could "approach God in thought, to consider ourselves in His presence, to measure our being with His, to compare ourselves with Him, for thus shall we clearly see our nothingness in His being, and our littleness in His grandeur."[63] If the word annihilation is too hard, and the word submission is too hard, surely it would not be too hard for anyone to admit that God is great. Except for Satan.

---

59. Rodriguez, *The Practice of Christian and Religious Perfection*, vol. 2, 316.

60. Grou, *The Spiritual Maxims of Pere Grou*, 214.

61. Scaramelli, *Directorium Asceticum; or, Guide to the Spiritual Life*, vol. 3, 620.

62. Saint-Jure, *The Spiritual Man*, 141.

63. Saint-Jure, *A Treatise on the Knowledge and Love of Jesus Christ*, vol. 2, 589.

Humility: Adhering to Christ

I asked, what good is humility? The last chapter described its first good of fleeing Satan; I turn now to its second good, which is to adhere to Christ.

We could say that humility attaches us to Christ, and therefore our theologians of abnegation place humility within the context of a liturgical act. They turn to Christ in prayer because, Crasset says, prayer "is a respectful homage which we render to the divine grandeur and majesty by the submission of all our powers."[1] Prayer unifies the mind with truth, unifies the heart with goodness, and makes a liturgical act of submission. Eudes composes one such prayer.

> I give myself to Thee, my Lord Jesus, that I may enter into Thy spirit of humility. I wish to spend all the days of my life with Thee, in this holy virtue. I call down upon myself the power of Thy spirit of humility in order to annihilate my pride and bind me close to Thee in humility. I offer up to Thee all the opportunities for humility that shall present themselves in my life. Deign, I beseech Thee, to bless them. I renounce myself and all things which may prevent me from sharing in the grace of Thy humility.[2]

---

1. De Sales & Crasset, *The Secret of Sanctity*, 153.

2. Eudes, *The Life and the Kingdom of Jesus in Christian Souls*, 50.

Hostius can say it more briefly: "I renounce myself, because I am thine."[3]

Prayer is necessary because Christian humility is different from social modesty or moral unpretentiousness: it is the humility of Christ infused. It is a divine product, accomplished by a divine operation. Boutauld says it is God who works in saints "the Miracles of becoming Nothing by their Humility, and at the same time, of elevating them to an Equality with the Holy Angels, by the Means of a *new and Virgin* Heart."[4] And Blosius reminds us that Christian humility consists of embracing the cross. "Give me grace to take hold of the cross of self-denial with ardent devotion, and to imitate, with the most fervent charity, the example of Thy virtues, and to follow Thee in all humility even unto death."[5] We will find such humility beyond our capacity, which is why de Castaniza counsels a prayer filled with necessary introspection.

> How much, O my God, do I wish to leave all, and lose myself to find
> Thee, to humble myself to please Thee, and to hate myself to love Thee.
> But these hard and high matters I dare scarcely promise. How, then, and
> when shall I practise them? Yet without Thee, O sacred humility, there is
> no solid centre to rest in, no true sweetness to take delight in; therefore,
> O my God, I come to Thy school to learn this necessary lesson; teach me,
> touch me, wound me, and win me unto Thee.[6]

Christ's humility carved the path to salvation when he embraced our condition of contingency, sin, and nothingness for himself. Grou says the purpose of Jesus's incarnation was for him to join us in our state, and "we cannot examine one single fact in the life of Jesus Christ without observing that humility was the groundwork of his whole

---

3. James Merlo Horstius, *The Paradise of the Christian Soul, Delightful for Its Choicest Pleasures of Piety of Every Kind* (London: Burns & Lambert, 1850) 637.

4. Boutauld, *The Counsels of Wisdom*, 256.

5. Blosius, *Oratory of the Faithful Soul* (London: Richardson and Son, 1848) 51.

6. De Castaniza, *The Spiritual Conflict and Conquest*, 346.

existence."[7] First, his kenosis was an act of self-abasement whereby the Only Begotten and Uncreated Son joins humanity in its order of contingent existence. Second, he takes upon himself the consequences of original sin, even though he is without sin himself. Third, he gave a continual glorification of his Eternal Father by his thought and will out of the nothingness due a creature. Joining our condition was the very purpose and unfolding of his humility, as Lallemant summarizes.

> The grounds of His humility are, first, the continual sight of the
> annihilation of the Word; secondly, the clear knowledge of what He is
> as man – that the human nature He has taken, and which in its union
> with the Person of the Word is rendered impeccable and infinitely holy,
> is in itself subject to sin, miseries of all kinds, and damnation; thirdly, the
> infinite rectitude of His will, which, with the knowledge that nothing
> is due to the creature but lowliness, abjection, poverty, labor, and pain,
> makes Him desire nothing else; and this it is He chose for his portion on
> earth.[8]

Christ's kenosis was an act of self-abasement whereby the Only Begotten and Uncreated Son joins humanity in its order of contingent existence. Berulle says "we see that the eternal Father does not treat this man as God. We see that he leaves him in infancy, in the common life, in the suffering life, as though God were not residing and living in this man,"[9] leaving me to define abnegation as being in the deity of the Father without being in the glory of the Father – not until he asks for it, to be received after the Resurrection. Berulle speaks of two lives bound together, and in the state of the Son of God's life we find the instructions for putting our life together: joining bliss-merit, joy-suffering, greatness-humility.

---

7. Grou, *The Interior of Jesus and Mary, vol. 1,* 176.

8. Lallemant, *The Spiritual Doctrine of Father Louis Lallemant, ed. Faber,* 372.

9. Berulle, *Discourses on the State and Grandeurs of Jesus,* 233.

O state that experiences the Son of God's striving over himself and his own life! A constant and ongoing striving for thirty-four years, without a single moment of interruption! A striving over the state not of nature or of grace but of glory ... A state, striving, and miracle of the Son of God over himself ... A striving that instructs and urges us to make a salutary striving over the state of our defective, wretched, and imperfect life, so that we might honor the one who for our salvation undertakes a striving.[10]

Our humility should manifest itself in our lives the way his humility manifested itself in his. What else does the disciple imitate? (*De Imitatione Christi.*) Otherwise, asks Barbanson, "how shall we be able to appear before that great mirror and pattern of all humility, our Redeemer Jesus Christ, in the manger, on the cross, and in the other miseries of his life, if we will not conform ourselves to the example which is there showed us?"[11] His humility was expressed in a cruciform shape, which is the shape his followers must also take. He deifies our humility by making it Christoform. De Ravignan interprets the beatitude "Blessed are they who suffer persecution" to mean "detachment from all earthly things, then, the desire of receiving insults, – yea, nothing more than this to imitate and to follow Him, and to fight Satan. The desire of receiving insults is nothing but true humility which consists itself in the love of God, joined to the knowledge of ourselves."[12]

Why did Jesus choose humility? Why does he love it? (And why do we hate it so much?) De Bergamo gives the question a liturgical answer. "He chose the way of humility as the most suitable one for rendering unto God, by His own humility, that honour of which the pride of man has deprived Him."[13] Teresa of Avila confirms this liturgical homage as the way of truth.

---

10. Berulle, *Discourses on the State and Grandeurs of Jesus*, 72.

11. Barbanson, *The Secret Paths of Divine Love*, 20.

12. De Ravignan, *Ravignan's Last Retreat*, 101.

13. De Bergamo, *Humility of Heart*, 132.

I was once considering the reason why our Lord loved humility so much, when, without much consideration, I suddenly remembered, that God was essentially the Supreme Truth, and humility is walking in the truth; for it is a very great truth, that of ourselves we have no good, but misery and nothingness; and he who does not understand this, walks in falsehood; but he who understands it the best, is the most pleasing to the Supreme Truth, because he walks in it.[14]

The economy of salvation, which led to and flows from the incarnation, has all been designed to correct the flawed state of sin and restore the glory of the Father. To accomplish this, de Sales says Christ must heal our present condition. "Our first parents, and almost all others who have sinned, were led to do so by pride. For this reason our Lord, as the wise and loving Physician of our souls, goes to the root of the evil, and instead of pride He comes to plant, first of all, the very beautiful and useful plant of holy humility, a virtue that is all the more necessary because the contrary vice is so general amongst men."[15] Above the temporal and trivial contests that distract us, a crucial conflict is going on between sin and holiness, disobedience and obedience, pride and humility. The first Adam, having stumbled in the first confrontation, is now replaced by a stronger, second Adam, who will defeat the tempter by a victorious humility. (Jesus in the wilderness is like a do-over of Adam in the garden.) De Ravignan therefore thinks we should see the whole human race – ourselves included – in the actions of this true Adam.

What did Jesus, your example? What did He choose? Poverty and humiliation. It was to expiate your pride, your self-love, and to teach you a great lesson. What did He constantly preach? what has He taught? Always humility, that is to say the love of God, even unto sacrifice and contempt of oneself. Alas! this sentiment of self-contempt ought not to be so difficult a one. We have sufficient material within us make us to despise ourselves, and if our lives were laid open to the eyes of men, if we were known for exactly what we are, or what we have been, ah, what a

---

14. Teresa of Avila, *Interior Castle*, 164.

15. De Sales, *The Mystical Flora of St. Francis De Sales*, 38-9.

small amount of respect would our imposing exterior receive! When one
sees so much that is lamentable within oneself, we must at least humiliate
ourselves before God, if we cannot do so before men![16]

Christ's humility was his love of God. Our lack of humility is our disregard for God.
  We have been saying that we should imitate Christ, and that is true. His humility exists
to call ours forward, his cross exists to imprint itself on our lives, and his grace exists
to animate us toward this end. But there is another sense in which the theologians of
liturgical abnegation admit we cannot imitate Jesus, because his humility is unique and
incomparable with ours. His is a kenotic abnegation of glory performed out of grace; ours
is an abnegation of self, demanded by justice. His is the humility of a God made man;
ours is the humility of a sinner. As Grou puts it, "never was there humility like to that of
Jesus Christ, voluntary, deep, practical; taking upon Him man's nature, bearing all that
is most despised of men: – we cannot be humble in like manner; nothing to begin with,
we cannot go lower; – sinners, meriting God's sentence, how can we humble ourselves
below our natural condition?"[17] De Bergamo therefore considers the humility of the
God-man to be different from the humility of a mere man. "Humility is a virtue that
belongs essentially to Christ, not only as man, but more especially as God, because with
God to be good, holy and merciful is not virtue but nature, and humility is only a virtue.
God cannot exalt Himself above what He is, in His most high Being, nor can He increase
His vast and infinite greatness; but He can humiliate Himself as in fact He did humiliate
and lower Himself."[18] The hypostatic union makes possible this new humility, Grou says,
unseen among the children of men. "Jesus Christ was humble in a degree only possible to
a soul united in substance to Divinity, and dependent upon it in every free action, whether
natural or supernatural."[19] When we humble ourselves, we enter our natural state; when
Christ humbled himself, he entered our state.

---

16. De Ravignan, *Conferences on the Spiritual Life*, 130-31.

17. Grou, *The Hidden Life of the Soul*, 195.

18. De Bergamo, *Humility of Heart*, 4.

19. Grou, *The School of Jesus Christ*, 195.

Christ's majesty as God makes his humility different from the humility we are capable of performing in our human nature, which is why Saint-Jure thinks Christ's humility exhilarates us more than does the humility of any human saint. "In His Divinity He humbled Himself to such an excess that His humility will excite the admiration of the Blessed for all eternity, and it may be said that He alone could really humble Himself, since He alone is great by essence. When a mere man humbles himself, he only enters his natural state; however great his abasement, he can never descend to the nothingness from which he was drawn."[20] He goes on to describe this as the humility by which Jesus liturgizes his Father in heaven with submission and adoration. "The soul of Our Lord was, in the first moments of its creation, and will be for all eternity, the most humble of all creatures, rendering to God the most perfect submission, the most profound respect, the most excellent adorations, the greatest homages, the most ardent thanksgiving, the most faithful in referring to Him the glory of its perfections and its works."[21]

We might be able to compare a long line with a short line, but we certainly cannot compare an infinite line with a finite line. The distance Christ traveled in his kenosis is infinitely longer than the distance any one of us will travel in our abjection. "In the first place," Grou explains, "Christ possessed perfect comprehension of the infinite distance between the majesty of the self-existing God and the lowliness of the creature drawn from nothing, and as he united these two extremes in his own person he was at all times penetrated with the strongest possible conviction of God's greatness and his own abjection."[22] His hypostatic union made him more conscious of the sort of humility he would exercise, a humility "only possible to a soul that possessed the most perfect knowledge of God's infinite Being, and also of the creature's nothingness. Not only had He the knowledge of these two extremes — infinite being and nothingness — but He was also most vividly and profoundly conscious of them, since they were united in His own Person."[23] Owing to the hypostatic union, Christ perceived God's greatness and man's lowliness, God's sovereign power and man's lowly dependence, the glory that was his by

---

20. Saint-Jure, *A Treatise on the Knowledge and Love of Jesus Christ*, vol. 2, 625.

21. Saint-Jure, *A Treatise on the Knowledge and Love of Jesus Christ*, vol. 2, 626.

22. Grou, *The Interior of Jesus and Mary*, vol. 1, 261.

23. Grou, *The School of Jesus Christ*, 194.

justice and the nullity that is man's by right. The result? A liturgy unique to him – yet not confined to him! Amazingly, he mystically shares his liturgy with us by incorporating the Mystical Body into the liturgy of the Head. "We can see that His whole created being was continually prostrated in reverence and adoration before the Supreme Being. The united worship of angels and men is nothing in comparison with His."[24]

Jesus's humility differed from ours both in its nature and extent, says John of Avila, because his was perfect, and ours is not. His humility outweighed the collection of all other humilities combined. "Just as in his personal being he did not depend on himself but on the person of the Word, which exceeds all souls and heavenly spirits, so he exceeds them in this holy humility. His soul is farther from giving glory to itself or depending on itself than all of the others together."[25] This is why Christian humility, in contradistinction to all other forms and sources of humility, must look to Christ alone, and not to other inspirations. If we may put it so, it gives us a humility over our humility! Grou drives the point home: Christ's humility was voluntary, ours is compulsory.

> We cannot be humble in the same manner that Jesus Christ was humble. If humility consists in abasing ourselves lower than we are, it is Jesus Christ alone Who could be truly humble ... He alone was truly humble, because He united Himself to a nature infinitely inferior to His own ... He was humble of heart, because His humility was a humility of choice ... It is therefore impossible for us to be humble in the same way that Jesus Christ was. As we are nothing from the very beginning, how can we make ourselves any less, or place ourselves below what we are by nature? Sinners by our own free will, deserving of the curse of God and of the punishments of hell, worthy only of contempt and horror, and thus infinitely below nothing, to what a state could we be further reduced which might pass for a state of humility? When we place ourselves on the level of nothing, we are only doing ourselves simple justice, even if we had never been guilty of any sin. And when we consent to be treated by God and all creatures as a sinner deserves to be treated, still we only do

---

24. Grou, *The School of Jesus Christ,* 194.

25. John of Avila, *Audi, Filia,* 189.

ourselves simple justice, even if we had only committed one mortal sin. how then shall we humble ourselves, how shall we lower ourselves?[26]

And yet, and yet, Jesus nonetheless wishes to teach his humility to us, to convey his humility to us, to infuse us with his humility. What is impossible in the natural state of affairs is made possible by grace that perfects. What Christ does as God-Man, he wants to teach human beings, and "what man can dare to reject a doctrine that is taught by a God, that is practiced by God, even to the highest degree of perfection?"[27] wonders Grou. Barbanson says Christ came to teach this doctrine, and teach it by example. "The first lesson in the school of our Lord Jesus Christ is the virtue of humility, the contempt of ourselves, pronounced by his sacred lips in these words, so clear, so serious, so important: Unless ye become like unto little ones, ye shall not enter into the kingdom of heaven. Whence we may gather that without humility it is impossible to please God, and that there is no other way of gaining heaven."[28] This was the strategy of incarnation, and the resultant curriculum that Grou calls the school of Jesus. "The lesson that Jesus Christ desired most of all to imprint upon our hearts was that of humility. There is not a page of His Gospel that does not teach it; and the quality that shines out most clearly in His life, and particularly in His birth and death, is humility."[29] He sets himself before us as example – not a philosophy, not a moral clause, not a human hero, but himself. Therefore, "the greatest motive we have to oblige us to be humble," says de Bergamo, "is the example of our Lord Jesus Christ, who came down from heaven to teach us the humility of which we stood in such need to cure our pride, the cause of all our ills, and the greatest impediment to our eternal salvation."[30]

---

26. Grou, *Manual for Interior Souls*, 207-08.

27. Jean Grou, *Morality, Extracted from the Confessions of Saint Austin*, vol. 2 (London: J. P. Coghlan, 1791) 117.

28. Barbanson, *The Secret Paths of Divine Love*, 19.

29. Grou, *The School of Jesus Christ*, 193-94.

30. De Bergamo, *Humility of Heart*, 131.

This lesson is more than didactic. This lesson occurs outside the classroom. It cannot be learned by speculative knowledge alone, as many worldly-wise Christians incorrectly suppose. Grou thinks such Christians imagine themselves to be knowledgeable in religion from having studied it, "yet, if they have not viewed it under the aspect of humility, directing their principal attention to this grand point; if they have not commenced the sacred study by the humiliation of mind and heart, although they may argue profoundly on theological questions, they are ignorant of the first elements of that Divine science which forms humble saints, not subtle disputants."[31] The knowledge of humility such Christians possess is merely speculative, and the real investigation of its true depths requires an examination of the heart of Jesus, not just his external actions. "It is in the interior dispositions of Jesus, far more than in the external display of his abjection, that we should seek illustrations of this great virtue,"[32] and if such Christians turn out to be utter strangers to this truth, it is because the truth is concealed from them. It is concealed "because they bring to the perusal of the Gospel, and even to the very feet of Jesus Christ, minds inflated with pride and self-sufficiency, because they have never thoroughly humbled their souls at prayer."[33]

In order to discover true, interior humility of heart, we must pass through a series of concentric, intensifying circles, wherein the lesson becomes more and more demanding and potent. First, according to Rodriguez, the lesson is more than verbal lecture, it is given by actual activity. "To comprehend well the excellence of this virtue, and the need we have thereof, we are to consider, that the Son of God descended from heaven to teach it us; not only by his words, but more especially by his actions; and that his whole life was nothing else than a long example and living model of humility."[34] Second, according to Fenelon, the lesson is by more than actions alone, it involves filling those actions with charity. "Let us not make it depend on one action or another, but on pure charity. Pure charity divests man of himself. It reclothes him with Jesus Christ. That is in what true humility consists,

---

31. Grou, *The Interior of Jesus and Mary,* vol. 1, 338.

32. Grou, *The Interior of Jesus and Mary,* vol. 1, 336.

33. Grou, *The Interior of Jesus and Mary,* vol. 1, 336-37.

34. Rodriguez, *The Practice of Christian and Religious Perfection,* vol. 2, 133.

which makes us live no longer for ourselves, but lets Jesus Christ live in us."[35] Third, and finally, according to de Castaniza the lesson is more than putting our own charity in motion, it comes from mystical union with Christ. "Draw humility out of your frailty, saying: – 'What am I proud of now? Where are my strong resolutions? Why do I judge others? Who is so feeble, fickle, frail as I am? O Lord, this is the worm that is so proud!' Then cast all into Christ's sacred wounds, and leaving all there, go on with as much quiet and confidence as if you had not sinned."[36] Christian humility feeds upon the grace that flows from the sacred wounds of the God who emptied himself of a throne of glory in order to be enthroned upon a cross, and it is to the cross Canfield says we must go for our final lesson. "There seems therefore a lack of humility in that soul, which, despising the Passion of the Lord, would be carried to His Godhead only."[37] Only then will one's sufferings be properly used, and transformed from carnal affliction into spiritual trial. De Sales invites us to

> say humbly with the good thief: *We receive in our sufferings that which we have deserved by our sins*. It is thus we shall, by our humility, render our thief's cross, the cross of a true Christian. Let us, then, like the good thief, unite our sinner's cross with the cross of Him who has saved us; and, by this loving and devout union of our sufferings with the sufferings and cross of Jesus Christ, we shall enter, like so many good thieves, into His friendship and company in paradise.[38]

Behold the crucified Christ as an icon beholds its prototype, and unite all your crosses to his.

The sort of humility we are talking about here is interior, Fenelon claims, not merely exterior. "Only Jesus Christ can give that true humility of heart which comes from him ...

---

35. Fenelon, *Christian Perfection*, 206.

36. De Castaniza, *The Spiritual Conflict and Conquest*, 489.

37. Canfield, *The Holy Will of God: A Short Rule of Perfection*, 64-65.

38. Huguet, *The Consoling Thoughts of St. Francis de Sales*, 197.

It does not consist, as one imagines, in performing exterior acts of humility, although that is good, but in keeping one's place."[39] Keeping one's place is the definition of justice, as we noted earlier, and external humility is important, but Libermann insists that interior humility be its source. "Be humble in your interior more than in your exterior, in your thoughts more than in your words, in your desires more than in your actions, in your sentiments more than in your bearing and manners."[40] On its own, external humility "might lead to vanity and to the conducting of yourself in such a way as to lead others to think that you are humble."[41] De Bergamo adds a harder lesson. It is easy to think that an experience of humiliation means one has attained humility, when, in fact, perfect humility means interiorly embracing the humiliation. Though we might keenly feel the insult or calumniation, "it is not the humiliation nor the suffering alone which makes the soul humble, but the interior act by which this same humiliation is accepted and received through motives of Christian humility and especially of a desire to resemble Jesus Christ, who, though entitled to all the honours the world could offer Him, bore humiliation and scorn for the glory of His eternal Father."[42]

Learn from Christ. Learn how to be humble. Learn what humility is. His humility comes forth from liturgizing, charity, submission, obedience. His humility comes from spurning the honors the world could offer, not simply missing out on them (which could be caused by a lot of other reasons). Christian humility is mystical in nature. Christ teaches us humility by infusing his own humility into us. De Granada links this to Christ's identity as mediator, who will give the key to reconciliation with God. "The humility of Christ was sufficient to overcome the heart of God, to procure his favor, and to cause him to become gentle and mild towards us, and shall it not suffice to overcome thy heart, and to make it humble and meek?"[43]

---

39. Fenelon, *Christian Perfection*, 205.

40. Libermann, *Letters to Clergy and Religious,* Spiritan Series 8, vol. 4, 156.

41. Libermann, *Letters to Religious Sisters and Aspirants,* Spiritan Series 5, vol. 1, 35.

42. De Bergamo, *Humility of Heart,* 22-23.

43. Louis de Granada, *Granada's Meditations Containing Fourteen Devout Exercises, for the Seaven Daies of the Week* (London: For Joseph Browne, 1623) 510.

Is there evidence as to whether someone has learned the lesson of humility? Yes, in fact. There are proofs. One is "to be horrified by any spirit of notoriety or vanity, to love contempt and obscurity, to choose always, in all things, whatever is more cheapening and humiliating, and to be ready to be humbled even to the point to which Jesus Christ was humbled in His Incarnation, His life, His passion and His death"[44] (Eudes). Another is an embrace of nothingness. "True humility desires to be nothing, neither in its own eyes nor in anyone's mind. It is careful to not stand out in anything. It creates a great desire to be hidden and to love being unknown, passing for nothingness ...We should destroy our own being in order to be clothed with Jesus Christ, so that we are noticed only under him and in him"[45] (Olier). Another is to receive all occasions of humiliation as coming from the hand of God, which is accomplished when prayer and mortification are combined simultaneously, and the suffering is placed *between* God and the soul. "Hence I have to forget the instrument with which he sends me the suffering, be it man or devil, but looking at this Lord I say to him, 'My Lord and my love! I shall love you more and more for the great favour you do me in giving me something whereby I may in some way suffer for your love', and receive it from the Lord himself and not from any creature"[46] (Alonso Rodriguez). Another is to receive all the occasions of humbling ourselves as coming from the hand of God, "mounting, as it were, by three steps, of which the first is to bear crosses with patience; the second, to accept them promptly and readily; and the third, to embrace them with joy; because we must not stop till we are come to be glad to suffer affronts and contempt, the better to resemble Jesus Christ, who, for love of us, vouchsafed to become 'the reproach of man, and the outcast of the people' (Psalm 21:7)"[47] (Rodriguez). One last proof is for the soul to care not for speaking well of herself, but rather wishing God to divide the fruits, "so nothing sticks to her fingers. All the good that she has is directed

---

44. Eudes, *The Life and the Kingdom of Jesus in Christian Souls* 46.

45. Olier, *Introduction to the Christian Life and Virtues*, in *Berulle and the French School*, 240.

46. Alonso Rodriguez, *St. Alphonsus Rodriguez: Autobiography*, 133.

47. Rodriguez, *The Practice of Christian and Religious Perfection*, vol. 1, 359.

and referred to God; and if she should say anything of herself, it is for His glory, for she knows that she has nothing of her own"[48] (Teresa of Avila).

These are proofs of progress in humility, that is, signs that one is going down the Christian path of the cross instead of down a path of simple social mores of modesty. Christian humility is the love of littleness, the love of baseness, and the love of degradation. It places what Olier calls the abasements of Jesus within our own soul.

> This type of humility has its source in God himself, who, although incapable by nature of being abased, due to his infinite perfections, nevertheless has in himself an inclination toward little things. For in himself he loves what is lowly ...

> The immense power of the Godhead first filled the soul of Jesus Christ with its inclinations and placed in him an infinite tendency toward baseness, which is continually at work in him, but is never fulfilled or satisfied. All the scorn, abasement and degradation that exists is like nothing to his soul before this immense thirst that engulfs him.

> This is what constitutes the humility of God and that of Jesus Christ, in which we should commune and which he pours forth in the heart of Christians, to whom he gives the same tendency and the same inclination toward lowly things. This is true Christian humility.[49]

Certain people are called to make special imitation of Jesus. De Bergamo mentions examples of anchorites who imitate his desert solitude, apostles who imitate his teaching,

---

48. Teresa of Avila, *Life of Saint Teresa Written by Herself*, 189-90.

49. Olier, *Introduction to the Christian Life and Virtues*, in *Berulle and the French School*, in 235.

saints who perform similar miracles, and martyrs who imitate his agony.[50] These Christic reproductions require a special vocation which comes from divine law, and special permission which comes from ecclesiastical law, but general humility, he says, is given as an example for *all* to imitate. "He has not called every one to be doctors, preachers or priests, nor has He bestowed on all the gift of restoring sight to the blind, healing the sick, raising the dead or casting out devils, but to all He has said: 'Learn of Me to be humble of heart,' and to all He has given the power to learn humility of Him. Innumerable things are worthy of imitation in the Incarnate Son of God, but He only asks us to imitate his humility."[51]

Let me pause here to give special attention to Jesus command *"learn of me."* When Jesus says this he is not offering an opportunity, he is issuing a command. This is not an advertisement, it is a mandate. "Have not we a strict obligation to imitate him?" Saint-Jure asks. "If we do not, are we not worthy of severe punishments? God humbled himself and put himself beneath all to give us an example, and we still wish to raise ourselves up?"[52] Humility was a virtue so dear to the Son of God, "and was so conspicuous both in his person and whole life," says de Granada, "that, designing to give us a perfect model for ours, he comprehends all in these words; 'Learn of me, for I am meek and humble of heart' (Matt. xi. 22.)."[53] Is there a method to learning humility? That is a wrong way of putting the question. It makes it sound as though there is some procedure of techniques to learn, when in fact, learning humility requires drawing nearer and nearer to Jesus. Grou, our proctor in the school of Jesus, thinks that "when all is said, I know no method equal to that which Jesus Christ expressed in the words: *Learn of Me.* You have *My lessons* in the Gospel: study them, and put them in practice. You have *My example*, for My whole life was a mirror of humility: make Me your pattern. You have *My interior grace*, which will persuade and help you to profit by My lessons and My example."[54] Any soul that

---

50. De Bergamo, *Humility of Heart*, 134.

51. De Bergamo, *Humility of Heart*, 2-3.

52. Saint-Jure, *Union with our Lord Jesus Christ in his Principal Mysteries*, 193.

53. De Granada, *A Memorial of a Christian Life*, 362.

54. Grou, *The School of Jesus Christ*, 216.

aspires to humility must carefully study Jesus' humility. "Follow Him from His Crib to His Cross, and as you mark His actions one by one, say to yourselves: This is what He was; this is what my Master, my Pattern, my Saviour, my Judge was willing to be."[55]

Why did Jesus wish to teach is humility? For the sake of our salvation, according to John of Avila. "The Son of God came down from heaven and taught us by His life and words the way to heaven, and that way is humility."[56] Jesus is jealous of our salvation, so for the glory of his Father, he eagerly teaches whatever humility his students are willing to learn. As we have seen above, the humility of the God-Man is different from ours, giving evidence that there are two sorts of humility. One is in the understanding, whereby a sinner considers his misery and believes he deserves to be contemned; another is in the will, which makes someone desire to be despised and disesteemed by all the world. Rodriguez thinks Jesus only had the latter, but we must have both.

> Jesus Christ could not have humility of the first description, which is that of the understanding because, says [St. Bernard], "he knew himself, and thinking it no robbery to be equal to God," (Phil. 2. 6), he could not despise himself, nor believe himself worthy of contempt. But he had the second sort of humility, which is that of the will and heart; "when he made himself of no reputation, taking upon him the form of a servant," (Phil 2: 7), and when for the love he bore to men he was pleased to humble himself, and appear contemptible in their eyes, and therefore be says to us, "Learn of me, who am meek and humble of heart." – (Matt 11:29.) But as for us, we ought to have humility of both kinds; for the first without the second is false and deceitful, there being nothing more unjust than to desire to pass for what we are not.[57]

There is nothing more unjust than to desire to pass for what we are not: to pass for righteous when we are sinners, to pass for something in the eyes of the world when we

---

55. Grou, *The School of Jesus Christ*, 219.

56. John of Avila, *Letters*, 121.

57. Rodriguez, *The Practice of Christian and Religious Perfection*, vol. 2, 181.

are nothing except by virtues bestowed by God, to pass as self-made when we are actually children of grace.

Our lives are made up of many hidden dimensions, and abnegation takes a different form in each of them, from mortification of the senses to warring with the passions. As master Pedagogue, Jesus makes our entire lifetime a class for humility. We learn by practical experience. De Bergamo does not think we should be attending this school for theory alone.

> He is our Master, and we are His disciples; but what profit do we
> derive from His teachings, which are practical and not theoretical? How
> shameful it would be for any one, after studying for many years in a school
> of art or science, under the teaching of excellent masters, if he were still to
> remain absolutely ignorant! My shame is great indeed, because I have lived
> so many years in the school of Jesus Christ, and yet I have learnt nothing
> of that holy humility which He sought so earnestly to teach me.[58]

Why would Jesus give the command "learn of me" if he didn't want us to follow it? Why would he demonstrate it if he didn't want us to practice it? As the Father sent him, so he sends his disciples. Saint-Jure can almost hear him say "My Father sent Me to convert and save men by humility, by the suffering of the Cross; I send you for the same design, and I give you the same means to execute it."[59] What the Father sent him to do, he sends others to do. Assimilating this requires more than listening, his disciples must watch; and it requires more than watching, his disciples must imitate; and it requires more than imitating autonomously, his disciples must be graced, because refusing grace is forsaking discipleship, Grou says. "If we sincerely desire to imitate him, and humbly implore from himself the grace to do so, our prayer will be granted. If, on the contrary, we refuse to follow him by this path we cannot hope to be one day recognized as his disciples."[60]

---

58. De Bergamo, *Humility of Heart*, 5-6.

59. Saint-Jure, *A Treatise on the Knowledge and Love of Jesus Christ*, vol. 2, 202.

60. Grou, *The Interior of Jesus and Mary*, vol. 1, 70.

Grace makes Christian humility a liturgical mystery instead of a moral accomplishment. Christian humility is Christoform and cruciform and deiform. "The motives and impressions which produced the humility of Jesus Christ may and ought to lead to the same result in every Christian," says Grou, although "according to the individual capacity of each. God is the great All: we have nothing in the order either of nature or grace except what we derive from him."[61] Forget not that Jesus joined us in this exact humility, as Guillore notices.

> In truth, God Alone has any independent Being; all creation is but a handful of clay moulded by His Hands. It was before this Infinite Being of God that Jesus humbled Himself in His Sacred Humanity: inasmuch as He took upon Him the form of man, He partook of the weakness and nothingness of created beings, Holy and pure as He was in His Incarnation; as man His life had a beginning, and like other men, there was a time when He was not.[62]

Jesus himself made the connection between humility and liturgy at the end of his life, when he established the Eucharist and founded the priesthood. Humility was so important a lesson that he did not rest content with everything he had taught so far, he made a final exhibition of it on the last night of his life. "Learn of me" bled into "a new commandment I give to you." The humility that he had sought to inspire in his disciples now received an irresistible presentation. Rodriguez pictures humility as his last will and testament.

> And doubtless humility must be a virtue of great importance and difficult to practice, since Jesus Christ is not content with so many examples which he had already given us, nor with so many others which he was about to give; but that knowing well our infirmity, and the malignity of the humour of pride, which is predominant in us, he does so many things to

---

61. Grou, *The Interior of Jesus and Mary,* vol. 1, 263.

62. Guillore, *Self-Renunciation,* 277.

cure it; and that in fine, to make a stronger impression of humility on our hearts, he yet recommends it to us, as it were, by a declaration of his last will.[63]

Grou says this final, strongest impression had to be made because "he knew how strongly our pride would revolt against this command, and therefore he would require nothing of us, which he had not first practised."[64]

Basil, bishop of Caesarea, once imposed a trial of humility upon one of his priests. He commanded the priest to bring water, which the priest did with ready cheerfulness. Then Basil commanded the priest to wash the feet of his bishop, which the priest also did readily and cheerfully. But finally Basil commanded the priest to let his bishop wash his feet. Baker reports what happened.

> The humble and virtuously simple man, without any excuses or contestations, quietly and calmly, as it became one perfect in obedience, suffers his feet to be washed by him, who was then the most eminent and most reverend prelate in the Eastern Church. Upon this proof, St. Basil was satisfied that he had found an attendant fit for the employments to which he destined him, and, with many thanks to the neighbour bishop, took the priest with him for his inseparable companion.[65]

There is more humility in letting your own feet be washed than in washing another's; there is more humility in letting your own sins be forgiven than in forgiving another's; there is more humility in suffering than in acting. This is why humility is connected with lowliness, powerlessness, abnegation, and annihilation. On his last night on earth, Jesus

---

63. Rodriguez, *The Practice of Christian and Religious Perfection*, vol. 2, 190.

64. Grou, *The Interior of Jesus and Mary*, vol. 2, 12.

65. Baker, *Holy Wisdom*, 329-30. Comments on Christ's foot washing are also made by Grou, *The Interior of Jesus and Mary*, vol. 2, 12; Alphonsus Rodriguez, *The Practice of Christian and Religious Perfection*, vol. 2, 190; and Saint-Jure, *The Religious*, vol. 1, 406.

desired his disciples to have the humility to let him wash their feet. He washed their feet before he gave them his flesh to eat. What he has done to them, they should do to others: Grou says that was the point of the example.

> How powerful an inducement to the practice of humility! Can a true disciple of Christ require a stronger, or could a more irresistible be presented? As our Lord and Master, Jesus Christ, was authorized to impose commands at his own option, while that two fold title assuredly dispensed him from giving to the world so astonishing an example of annihilation. But he knew how strongly our pride would revolt against this command, and therefore he would require nothing of us, which he had not first practised.[66]

If humility is to be more than an intellectual lesson, then we must ask how we can excite our will. If we are commanded to seek more than exterior humility, how does it become interior? Libermann directs us to Jesus, of course. "To powerfully excite our will to embrace this own abjection and all the other movements that belong to humility, we must constantly consider the mysteries of the humiliations of Our Lord."[67] With that, we have transitioned to the relationship of liturgy to humility.

In the liturgical sequence of a life, the first step is lifting one's heart to God with humility, then kindling affection towards him, and then finding it possible to recall the mind from vanity, prestige, and the seductions of temporal goods. Liturgical abnegation is not a bitter thing, it is sweet because it is undergone for the love of God. The glory of God is the supreme motive for our worship – even more than our own salvation – and when we worship with Christ's latria, passing through us, and returning to the Father through him, then our liturgizing gives a glory to God that is impossible to craft by human nature alone. Christ stands beside us, and we liturgize thorough him, with him, and in him, as the Mass puts it. He liturgizes within us – but only, Eudes says, if we make room for his liturgy by annihilating our self-love.

---

66. Grou, *The Interior of Jesus and Mary*, vol. 2, 12.

67. Libermann, *Of Humility*, 6.

Of yourself, you cannot entertain a single holy thought, nor perform a single act that is pleasing to Him. Therefore you must annihilate yourself at His feet, offering yourself so our Lord Jesus Christ, that He may establish Himself in you, that it may be He Himself who prays within you, since He alone is worthy to appear before God's face to glorify and love Him, and to obtain from Him the answer to all petitions.[68]

Humility is required in order to converse rightly with God. As courtiers "pay their court well to their Prince," Surin writes, so do true liturgists approach him in a reverential manner, and "one who disregards the inspirations of Heaven, or speaks unworthily of the presence of God, lacks this humility. We must in all times and in all places show profound reverence for the Divine Majesty. And this is not a weariness to souls which are wholly devoted to the Lord; for He is in such manner their King, that He is also their Spouse."[69]

While we liturgize God, we retain a sense of our nothingness; our sense of nothingness convinces us that whatever virtues we have are bestowed by God. Having emptied ourselves of self, liturgy can come from the Trinity, down Christ, in the Holy Spirit, through us, and reascend to the Father. Professing our nothingness does not mean we do not act our part, or that we have no share in the work we do. Our free will does certainly operate jointly with God, and we put ourselves forward in action. But the merit is not ours. This is the antinomy of grace and works again: having done all that depends on ourselves, we diffide in ourselves and confide only in God. We have done as nothing, so Libermann can describe adoration as "the most perfect humility and the destruction of pride. Adoration, then, includes all the virtues of religion and all our duties towards God."[70]

One of the crucial components of liturgy – both ritual liturgy and lived liturgy – is prayer, and humility quietly goes about the perfection of prayer. De Sales says "the first condition necessary for praying well is that we must, in our humility, be little in our

---

68. Eudes, *The Life and the Kingdom of Jesus in Christian Souls*, 31.

69. Surin, *Foundations of the Spiritual Life*, 46-47.

70. Libermann, *Jesus Through Jewish Eyes*, vol. 1, 123.

own eyes ... And as this humility raises the soul nearer to God, it makes the angels say: 'Who is she that goeth up out of the desert?'"[71] The Angels and the church triumphant both rejoice to see holy prayer in the ranks of the church militant as it resists crippling misunderstandings of prayer. (Grou warns: "nothing more infallibly leads to pride and illusion or more surely renders the soul the sport of imagination and self-love than the habit of such prayer as is ill understood and worse practised."[72]) Prayer, like all liturgizing, is done for the glory of God, not out of self-conceit, vainglory, or complacency. Rodriguez detects a mutuality at play, because "as humility is a means to gain the gift of prayer, so prayer is a means to obtain and conserve humility." [73] Therefore if we rise from any prayer "with a sort of satisfaction ... imagining that we have already made great progress in spirituality, and are become very intelligent therein; we must, I say, when we find ourselves thus disposed, always suspect our prayer was not as it should have been."[74] Prayer is our perfection, and humility perfects prayer, because humble prayer seeks nothing but God's glory, and Crasset confesses "there is nothing which honors Him so much as humble patience and patient humility; if it is our own merit, there can be no merit without humility and patience; if it is our perfection, humility must its foundation, and patience its crowning glory."[75]

Why would humility appear in prayer? Because it is nothingness before the All, the little before the Great, the annihilated before the Life-giver, the sinner before the Holy One. The person praying is filled with a humility that seems to result from the pressure of these two tectonic plates rubbing together. Grou writes:

> He who prays is God's creature: it is God to whom he prays. The thought of the relation between them should in itself be enough to fill the created being with the deepest humility; and how much greater will his humility

---

71. De Sales, *Mystical Flora*, 52-53.

72. Grou, *The Interior of Jesus and Mary, vol. 1,* 153-54.

73. Rodriguez, *The Practice of Christian and Religious Perfection*, vol. 1, 295-96.

74. Rodriguez, *The Practice of Christian and Religious Perfection*, vol. 1, 295-96.

75. De Sales & Crasset, *The Secret of Sanctity*, 206.

be when he remembers that he is a sinner, and God is infinitely holy; that
he is guilty, and God is not only offended by his guilt but is also his judge!
He can only approach God, then, in a spirit of reverent awe.[76]

We have already said above that humility has two eyes. Now Scaramelli realizes what
they are each looking at.

> He that prays must have one eye fixed on himself and on his own miseries,
> that the sight may humble him and fill him with confusion, by bringing
> home to him his unworthiness to receive any favour; the other eye must
> rest upon God's mercy, His liberality and His promises, so as to make the
> heart expand with a lively hope of receiving every good and perfect gift.
> Humility and confidence are the two wings on which prayer soars aloft
> to God; the two arms which force His hands to shed every blessing.[77]

Admitting unworthiness releases the power of prayer. Humility bends the archer's
bow, so to speak, allowing prayer "to penetrate the clouds" (Eccl. 35:21). Rodriguez
concludes that prayer "is of no effect without humility, and with humility it pierces the
heavens."[78] The recitation of the Divine Office in concurrence millions of angels and
saints, with the Queen of Angels and Saints, is an action thoroughly holy and divine. How
does a faithful priest feel in that company? wonders Eudes.

> Consider, then, the greatness and sanctity of this act and realize that of
> yourself you do not possess the least qualification to recite it worthily,
> but rather that your whole nature hinders you. Realize that you are
> completely unworthy to stand before the face of God and enter into the
> presence of such exalted Majesty. Annihilate yourself, therefore, at the
> feet of your Heavenly Father. Offer yourself to Jesus, and implore Him to

---

76. Grou, *The School of Jesus Christ*, 245-46.

77. Scaramelli, *Guide to the Spiritual Life; or, Guide to the Spiritual Life,* vol. 1, 391.

78. Rodriguez, *The Practice of Christian and Religious Perfection*, vol. 2, 141.

annihilate you and to establish Himself in you, so that He Himself may perform this function on your behalf, that He Himself may glorify His Father and Himself in you, since He alone is worthy to do so.[79]

Humility serves the sacraments (another component of liturgy), as well as prayer, and Grou thinks a faithful priest surely knows this. "If, at the beginning of Mass, we said simply and earnestly: 'Lord, cause me to assist at Thy holy Sacrifice in a manner worthy of Thee: I cannot do so of myself:' we should feel the effects of our faith and humility: Christ would act upon our souls, and keep them in a reverent and loving silence."[80] And such humility is demanded not only for the priest giving sacraments, but also for the laity receiving them. De Sales advises the lay person to make three preparations for any sacrament. The first preparation is purity of intention; the second preparation is attention; and "the third preparation is humility, which is a virtue most necessary to enable us to receive abundantly the graces which flow through the channels of the Sacraments. And this because waters, generally speaking, flow much more swiftly and with greater force when the channels are situated in sloping and low-lying places."[81]

Liturgy is sanctity; no sanctity is secure without humility; humility is preserved by holy fear; abnegation causes a fear that is holy. Humility rejoices in abnegation because its new righteousness causes it to desire that justice should be done. The Christian learns this from the liturgy of his Lord Jesus.

---

79. Eudes, *The Life and the Kingdom of Jesus in Christian Souls*, 175.

80. Grou, *The Spiritual Maxims of Pere Grou*, 60.

81. de Sales, *The Spiritual Conferences*, 349-50.

THE PROBLEM OF SELF

De Berniere-Louvigny outlines the terms: "God ... will admit no rival."[1] De Ponte outlines the choice: "all religion is founded upon the mortification of self-will, which if it lives religion dies, and if religion is to live self-will must die."[2] Liturgical abnegation consists of turning self-love to love of God, and submitting self-will to the will of God, which is a struggle that Huby says dates back to the beginning. "The world owes its ruin to self-will, by the disobedience of the first Adam; the world owes its salvation to the obedience of the second Adam."[3] But do not think this is a merely a historical problem. De Osuna says the heart of man can be called earthly paradise. "Its name is paradise because wherever God is and gives Himself to be enjoyed, is paradise," and God can be said "to have planted this paradise, which is the heart, 'from the beginning,'"[4] (i.e. at the beginning of our conversion, at baptism). Then, just as the earthly paradise grew a tree of knowledge of good and evil, so that tree exists in our heart. "The forbidden tree is self-will [and] of this we must not eat because we are not to follow our will."[5] Self-will can be basically called a self-chosen path, summarizes Guilloré, "and it is a principle in all theology that he who forsakes God's manifest Will, in order to do that which God has

---

1. De Berniere-Louvigny, *The Interior Christian*, 88.

2. De Ponte, *Meditations*, vol. 1, 299.

3. Huby, *Spiritual Works of Pere Vincent Huby*, 114.

4. De Osuna, *The Third Spiritual Alphabet*, 67.

5. De Osuna, *The Third Spiritual Alphabet*, 67.

not made manifest, is guilty of self-will; we cannot serve two masters, or obey God's Will and our own ... It is the poison of all spiritual life."[6]

The addition of the prefix "self-" to almost any word indicates a problem. We shall see momentarily that there is an appropriate sense of self, a proper love of self, a reasonable interest in self, but we are here talking about what happens when this is soiled by sin. For de Castaniza, "pride, presumption, vanity, self-esteem, self-complacency, self-praise, self-seeking, self-delight, with all the rest of like nature, are but several nooses of the same net, and sprouts out of the same main root – self-love."[7] I have watched for even more threads of this net, and compiled this list of terms that have appeared across the texts: *self-love, self-will, self-esteem, self-complacency, self-regard, self-centeredness, self-display, self-sufficiency, self-exaltation, self-reliance, self-interest, self-satisfaction, self-pleasing, self-perfection, self-seeking, self-glorification, self-confidence, self-congratulation, self-judgment, self-advertisement, self-appetite, self-indulgence, self-conceit, self-flattery, self-government.* The appearance of "self-" indicates a prideful egocentricity that derives from original sin and corrupts each of the terms. Camus connects the problem of self to a secret presumption that interferes with the affairs of God. "This self-love being always accompanied with some secret presumption, is consequently always blind. And indeed what greater blindness can befall us than to think that, of ourselves, we are able to do anything in things that are above us, and which pass the bounds of nature?[8]

It is impossible to dedicate a chapter to each of the above terms, so I have confined myself to the first two, which are the two major disasters: self-will and self-love. The error of the former is directing a *will* intended for God toward self, the error of the latter is the corruption a suitable *love* of self into defective self-love. They are connected in a way aptly described by Scupoli: "self-love sways thy will, and is its moving spring."[9] Or by Ullathorne: "Self-will is the product of self-love, and the cause of all pride, sinfulness, folly, and vanity. Take away self-will and you take away all evil. Why, then, did God give

---

6. François Guilloré, *Self-Renunciation* (London: Rivingtons, 1871) 145-46.

7. De Castaniza, *Spiritual Conflict and Conquest*, 224.

8. Jean-Pierre Camus, *A Spiritual Combat* , 93-94.

9. Scupoli, *The Spiritual Combat,* 187.

us this will? He gave us our free-will, but not our self-will; this *self* is the addition we have made to it, and was first inspired by the devil."[10]

The two problems are connected because they both fundamentally have to do with a preoccupation with self. Olier lists "the effects of self-centeredness" by making a list of 31 entries describing the characteristics of self-centeredness in one column, opposite the characteristics of abnegation in the other. The following long quotation is an only slightly abbreviated list from the former column. Notice him get down to specifics! The self-centered person, he says

> dwells in himself ... Is full of himself ... Places his trust in himself and relies on himself ... Is always preoccupied with himself ... Thinks highly of himself ... Wishes to make an impression and show off ... Loves praise and seeks it ... Speaks about himself ... Has difficulty tolerating any praise given to his neighbor ... Never speaks of another's perfections, or if he does, he diminishes them ... Cannot tolerate being contradicted and gives in to no one ... Is obsessed with his own opinion and judgment ... Acts on his own and with his own power, without paying any attention to his weakness ... Acts independently and always follows his own will ... Desires and draws everything to himself and wills good only for himself ... Acts in all things for himself ... Values his own pleasure and satisfaction in everything and seeks it everywhere ... Is attached to everything ... Stands out in everything ... Gets along with no one ... Withdraws from everyone, and is happy to remain by himself and with those who esteem and approve him ... Draws the world to himself and becomes more possessive, detaching others from everyone else out of love for himself ... Wants to fill the heart and mind of every creature with himself ... Is willing to be developed in consolation, abundance and praise, but he abandons all in desolation, dryness and scorn ... Always wants to be in charge and speaks to his brothers arrogantly and generally in a loud voice ... Wants the very best for himself and clothes, food, lodging ... Wants to pass for the author of everything and wishes that the glory be given only to him ... Wants to appear involved in everything ... Is always agitated, troubled, and anxious,

---

10. Ullathorne, *The Groundwork of Christian Virtues*, 376-77

always frustrated and hindered, always timid, frivolous and unstable ... Is
generally sad, closed, lost in reverie and withdrawn ... Becomes upset by
the most insignificant statement ... Gets angry at everything and suspect
that everything is done and said in relation to him ... Becomes exceedingly
joyful in his self-love and pride succeed ...[11]

The handling of self is so important because it concerns the good as a final appetite.
Will and love are complexly connected as they direct us to our good, whom de Sales knows
is God. "To will is nothing more than to love what is good, and love is the willing or
desiring what is good."[12] Sin is closely connected to both self-will and self-love. There
is almost a perichoresis between the three. First we read de Granada saying that "all sins
originally proceed from self-love, for they are all committed through a desire of some
particular good this self-love makes us covet."[13] Next we read Saint-Jure saying that
without self-will "there is, and can be no sin; that it is the cause of all the sins we commit.
Hence, after all the definitions given to sin, by theologians, to explain its nature, it must
be said, that it is the effect of self-will."[14] This is why abnegation must be exercised on
each. Abnegation is denial, but it is not denying will or love, it is denying the independent
rule we exercise over them. Abnegation of self-love is required to make God's love our
only desire, and abnegation of self-will is required to make God's will our only intention,
according to Fenelon.

All sensitiveness springs from self-love; we only suffer because we have
so much will. If we wished for nothing save God's Will, we should be
perpetually satisfied, and everything else would be as unpalatable as black

---

11. Olier, *Introduction to the Christian Life and Virtues*, in *Berulle and the French
    School*, 263-66. (In the column opposite this list he describes the characteristics of
    the Christian who practices abnegation.)

12. Camus, *The Spirit of St. Francis de Sales*, 54.

13. De Granada, *The Sinner's Guide*, 282.

14. Saint-Jure, *The Religious*, vol. 1, 577.

bread offered to a man who had just made a luxurious meal. If we were contented with what is God's Will at the actual moment, we should not stretch our inquisitive longings into the future. God will do His Will; He will not do ours, but He will do perfectly right.[15]

On the one hand, says Libermann, self-will corrupts self-love. "Self-love is blind; it always wants enjoyments ... It never takes the will of God into account. Let us scoff at this silly love, pay no attention to it."[16] On the other hand, Saint-Jure says self-love corrupts self-will. "Self-love, the special venom of nature, resides peculiarly in the will, and, rushing in all directions from this source, it spoils everything; because nature does not wish to die to self, and, openly or secretly, seeks her own contentment in every possible way."[17] Scripture unapologetically affirms that God's love is jealous, and Grou thinks "the jealousy of God is too much interested in the matter to leave His work unfinished."

If this soul does not withdraw herself from the kingdom of God, she may be quite sure that God will not desist until He has finished His work in her according to His designs. Now this work of God consists in purifying her entirely from self-love, in not leaving a single fibre of it in her, and in utterly destroying the human *I*, in such a manner that the soul can lose nothing and desire nothing. Then God finds no more self-love, no more self-interest in that soul, and His jealousy is satisfied.[18]

Abnegation appears loathsome when understood as an *unnatural* resistance to *natural* things. But, in fact, to the contrary, abnegation is *supernatural* resistance to *unnatural* things. De Sales is particularly good on this point, basically saying nature is good, but we don't do nature naturally any more.

---

15. Fenelon, *Letters to Men*, 162.

16. Libermann, *Letters to Clergy & Religious,* Spiritan Series 7, vol. 3, 7-8.

18. Grou, *Manual for Interior Souls*, 326.

The love of ourselves is deeply rooted in our nature ... By the love of
self I mean a natural, just, and legitimate love, so legitimate indeed as
to be commanded by the law of God which bids us love our neighbors
as ourselves ... Nevertheless, this love of ourselves, however just and
reasonable it may be, turns only too easily, and too imperceptibly, into
a self-love ... We often think we love someone, or something in God, and
for God, when it is really only in ourselves, and for ourselves, that we do
so. We think sometimes that we have only an eye to the interests of God,
which is His glory, when it is really our own glory which we are seeking
in our work.[19]

God gifted an intellectual capacity to a creature of clay that positioned it above all
other creatures. That capacity directs a volitional faculty (will) that should seek the end
determined by the intellect; that capacity also grants a special type of consciousness that
makes possible a love of self unknown to the animals. Had everything gone as planned,
these human beings would have maintained a right relationship under God, beside other
persons, and over creatures. But the devil's deceit produced depravity in what Baker
identifies as both nature and act.

Hence will appear how inexpressibly depraved both our nature and all
our actions, outward and inward, must be, since whereas we were created
only to love and enjoy God, yet we love and seek nothing but ourselves.
Our sensitive affections are carried to nothing but what is pleasing to
sensuality; and our spiritual affections to nothing but propriety, liberty,
and independence, self-esteem, self-judgment, and self-will, and to those
things only that do nourish such depraved affections. By this means we
are quite diverted from our last end and felicity.[20]

---

19. Camus, *The Spirit of St. Francis de Sales*, 277-278.

20. Baker, *Holy Wisdom*, 244.

The devil's ultimate goal, summarizes Grou, was "to usurp the place of God in the heart and to induce us to transfer from our Creator to himself our adoration and allegiance."[21] In the fallen state, a volitional faculty that should be directed to regulated goods is turned back upon itself, as self-will; and a love for self that should be governed by God is turned back upon itself, as self-love. This state of affairs demands a duty of fervently cooperating with divine grace, which is the only way, Baker says, we can be led back "to the same perfection for which we were first created, and which was practiced by Adam in innocence; to wit, an utter extinguishing of self-love and all affection to creatures, except in order to God, and as they may be instrumental to beget and increase divine love in us."[22]

Return to Eden, but get it right this time in imitation of the New Adam. No one should disdain any creatures, and neither should anyone disdain himself; nevertheless, all creation must be put at the service of glorifying God and increasing divine love. Self-will and self-love disrupts liturgizing God, which is why they must both be annihilated. This is merely the language of St. Paul – or have you forgotten? Grou asks. "My chief enemy, the enemy through whom all other foes, the world and the devil, reach me, is myself, the 'old man,' the 'old Adam' of which St. Paul speaks."[23] This old man must be devastated, with alacrity, because the old Adam's self-love and self-will has grown "faster than my mental growth, and has been strengthened by my passions, by my natural want of perception, the weakness of my will, the abuse I have made of my freedom, my bad habits and sins."[24] This terrible foe is impossible to overcome by our own efforts, without Christ, because our very efforts seem to give the old Adam new strength. This is a conundrum, Grou admits.

> Self-love finds food in every thing it contemplates, and admires itself in
> every attempt I make to conquer a fault or acquire a virtue; it drinks up
> the praise bestowed upon me, it takes pride even in what I need to be acts

21. Grou, *The Interior of Jesus and Mary*, vol. 1, 161-62.

22. Baker, *Holy Wisdom*, 33.

23. Grou, *The Hidden Life of the Soul*, 179.

24. Grou, *The Hidden Life of the Soul*, 179.

of self-humiliation. It forcibly appropriates what is God's work only, and would fain take His glory for itself. There is no hope save in Him; and He must fight for me. My self-love is His enemy too. He must subdue, crush, destroy it in me, or I can never get the victory. Blessed and All-powerful Lord, I give myself up to Thee, deal with me as Thou wilt.[25]

The catastrophe of original sin has injected pride into our reactions, our instincts, and our efforts, redirecting love and volition from God to self. "What has ungrateful man done?" Eudes shakes his head. "He has become separated from God and devoted his interests to self. Instead of employing his love for God, he has devoted it to himself and developed self-love ... Instead of referring to God all the blessings of nature and grace, man appropriates them to himself by complacency and self-esteem, as if they came from himself, who is only nothingness."[26] We thus see, again, how important the recognition of nothingness is: because it is recognition of divine blessing.

Unfortunately, nature is now always prone to self-seeking, and shall continue to be so inclined during our exile. This makes for a constant spiritual combat, as Scupoli famously titles his book. When experiencing anxiety over tribulation, "examine and discover whereto these events are adverse, whether to the soul, or to self-love and self-will."[27] There is a test to perform. After reflection upon the state of the soul (does it love or desire, is it glad or sorrowful?). Scupoli directs us to next consider the object that stirred the soul. Is it desired in accordance with the laws of God?

> And so of joy or sorrow, [ask] whether they be produced by such things as God would have us to be glad or sorry for; or whether all springs from the world, and from attachment to creatures, in that it lingers, busying itself with them, not of necessity, or as far as the occasion calls for, and as

---

25. Grou, *The Hidden Life of the Soul*, 179-80.

26. Eudes, *Meditations on Various Subjects*, 120.

27. Scupoli, *The Spiritual Combat*, 71-72.

God willeth. If this be so, it is plain that self-love sways thy will, and is its moving spring.[28]

Does the will lament if it is crossed? If so, it is self-will. Do you even do your good works, prayers, and fasting for your own satisfaction? If so, it is self-will. Are your operations done more to please yourself than God? If so, it is self-will. Scupoli directs us to a dialogue with God over the Eucharistic table (our final chapter) where we can ask what the Highest King of Heaven has brought. He will answer *Love*. And now what does he want from us?

> "Nothing," will He answer thee, "but love." "I would have no other fire to burn upon the altar of thy heart, and in thy sacrifices, and in all thy works, but the fire of My Love, which consuming all other love, and all self-will, will be a most sweet savour unto Me.

> "This I have required of thee, and still require, because I desire to be wholly thine, and thou wholly Mine, and this will never be, till, making that entire resignation of thyself which so delights Me, thou be detached from all love of self, from self-opinion, self-will and self-esteem ... I ask thy whole self, that I may become wholly thine.[29]

The sinner squanders the love of God, i.e., fails to take advantage of divine love. The failure is liturgical: he diverts the stream of affection he should be returning to God toward himself, or toward worldly honors. Original sin has had cardial effects upon all the descendants of Adam and Eve, and Grou does not find the heart they have now to be in the shape it was when given them by God.

---

28. Scupoli, *The Spiritual Combat,* 187.

29. Scupoli, *The Spiritual Combat,* 142-43.

By "the heart" we must understand that hidden depth of evil, perversity
and self-love, which is in us all, and which affects even our best actions
more or less; for who that knows himself ever so little but is conscious how
self-love tarnishes and hinders almost all he does? This is a consequence
of original sin, which diverted what would have been our natural leaning
to God, and turned the stream of our affections upon self. Deal honestly
with yourself, and you will see that in fact we measure everything by the
standard of self, by our own interests and opinions; whereas rightly. we
ought to refer all to God, His Spirit and Will.[30]

On the one hand, self-love has spoiled self-will by moving the target of the good from
God to self. On the other hand, self-will has spoiled self-love by producing a love exclusive
of God. That's the original sin, says Grou: namely, reversing "the order of God's creation:
He gave man a heart which tended to love Him above all else, but sin has taught us
self-love, and that self-love does not seek what alone would bring happiness, but rather
draws us down to earthly things, which blind us to those which are heavenly."[31] Sin
is a coronary thrombosis, and abnegation is surgery on the spiritual heart to remove
the blockage. Empty the heart, says de Sales, "in order to receive God's Grace in our
hearts, they must be as empty vessels – not filled with self-esteem."[32] The defense against
pride ruling the heart is to turn will and love from self to God, which involves admitting
nothingness. (All our chapters are connected.) Saint-Jure exclaims, almost in despair, "is

---

30. Grou, *The Hidden Life of the Soul*, 164. Grou expresses the same in *Manual for
   Interior Souls*: "By these words, "the human heart," we mean that depth of malignity,
   of perversity, and of self-love, which is in every one of us, and the venom of which
   extends over all our actions, even the best of them: for there is scarcely any action we
   do that is not spoilt by self-love and deprived of all its goodness. This perverse and
   corrupt element in our nature is a consequence of Original Sin, which has led astray
   the primitive uprightness of our hearts, and has concentrated upon our own selves
   that affection which ought to be given to God alone." (160-61)

31. Grou, *The Hidden Life of the Soul*, 209.

32. De Sales, *Introduction to the Devout Life*, 95-96.

it possible that being what I am, that having committed so many sins, pride and self-love can enter my heart? Is it possible that being nothing, possessing nothing but what I hold of the pure liberality of God, I can esteem myself? On what do I ground my self-esteem? Certainly it cannot be on that, the glory of which belongs to God."[33] The heart will glorify God as it embraces its nothingness, and the heart will become stronger as self-will and self-love are weakened.

The fall consisted in disobedience, but it was caused by pride, and pride went on to distort both volition and affection into self-will and self-love. From the root of self-love comes the three branches of which St. John speaks, namely, lust of the flesh, lust of the eyes, and the pride of life (1 Jn 2:16). More plainly put, these branches are the love of pleasures, the love of riches, and the love of honor, and from them de Granada says the seven vices arise. "From the love of pleasures arise three capital vices, luxury, gluttony and sloth. From the love of honor comes pride, and covetousness from the love of riches. And as for the other two, anger and envy, they serve every one of these unlawful loves. For anger is caused by meeting with any obstruction in the obtaining of what we desire; and when another gets that which self-love desired for itself, then envy is excited."[34] Physicists speak of a gravitational field so strong that it can bend light; the self is like a gravitational field so powerful that it can bend the light of the Kingdom. Will is knocked off its duty of obedience to God, and love is knocked off its trajectory toward the Creator, and both land their attention, instead, upon inferior temporal creatures.

When combined, lust of the flesh, lust of the eyes, and the pride of life sap a soul of energy and unnerve her, causing her it to lose firmness of purpose. This is often called "tepidity" by our authors, and it concerns them plenty. Here are some examples. First, from de Castaniza. "The true cause of which tepidity is, that our affections being fastened to earthly things, we prize them in our wills, though we slight them in our understandings ... we do not seriously seek to be separated from them."[35] Second, this is especially treated by those writing about the Sacred Heart, since tepidness is cooled ardor, and devotion to the Sacred Heart is a rekindling of ardor. Jesus says to Mary Margaret

33. Saint-Jure, *A Treatise on the Knowledge and Love of Our Lord Jesus Christ*, vol. 2, 590-91.

34. De Granada, *The Sinner's Guide*, 282.

35. De Castaniza, *Spiritual Conflict and Conquest*, 200.

Alacoque, "know that I cannot endure the least want of straightforwardness, and I shall make thee understand that, if the excess of My love has led Me to constitute Myself thy Master, in order to teach and fashion thee after My manner and according to My designs, nevertheless I cannot bear tepid and cowardly souls."[36]   Third, when de la Colombiere is asked by a sister for spiritual advice on the subject, he wonders whether he will have to send a book instead of a letter.

> I would rather have a great sinner to convert than a religious who has fallen into tepidity. It is an evil almost without remedy. Few surmount it; age which cures other faults only augments this ... This evil of tepidity is only too common. Religious houses are full of people who keep the rule: rise, go to Mass, meditation, confession and Communion, because it is the custom, because the bell rings and others go; they do all this and more without any interior devotion ... So after one, two, or three years, it is seen that the negligent are still negligent, the slack still slack, the bad-temperate have not become gentle, nor the proud humble, the lazy are still lacking in fervor and the selfish in detachment, and so of the rest. Such communities, which ought to be furnaces where all can enkindle their love of God and purify their souls more and more, remain always in this terrible lukewarmness.[37]

And fourth, Croiset finds tepidity where self-love has sucked us back into ourselves with no struggle. "As soon as a soul gives herself up to tepidity, she no longer thinks of anything but herself. She continually seeks after what can give her pleasure. She has a delicacy that sometimes surpasses that of the most sensual persons: a love of self, which not being weakened by foreign objects, is the stronger from being shut up in herself alone, and is entirely applied in forming for herself and easy and tranquil life."[38]

---

36. Alacoque, *Autobiography*, ch 51, Kindle edition.

37. De la Colombiere, *Spiritual Direction*, 130-132.

38. Croiset, *Devotion to the Sacred Heart of Jesus*, 60.

Already, Saint-Jure admits, self-will has caused so much evil to accrue to us that it deserves a special attention. "Do all that is possible to destroy, to annihilate it, and to conform it to that of God; that it may be therein absorbed, and that of two wills, there may be made but one."[39] Why is it called annihilation? Because man's mind is changed upon the destruction of self-will and self-love. Saint-Jure says such a person "no longer thinks of himself, no longer applies his attention to himself, no longer occupies himself with himself, and no longer acts for himself," with the result that "Self-denial ought to destroy and annihilate this *my, to my*, and *for my*; it ought to exterminate this *mine* and *thine.*"[40] This makes perfect sense in any friendship or natural love relationship: the father who loves his child, the woman who falls in love with her fiancé, no longer apply their attention to themselves, occupy themselves with themselves, no longer act for themselves. So it should be with our relationship to God.

The gravitational force of self also affects the other natural forces our authors have named – esteem, complacency, regard, sufficiency, reliance, interest, satisfaction, confidence, etc. – rendering them now unnatural, and also in need of annihilation, but I will stop here. Let me turn specifically to self-will and self-love in the next two chapters.

---

39. Saint-Jure, *The Religious*, vol. 1, 581.

SELF-WILL

How should the self-will be treated? Seriously! insists Eudes. "We should treat self-will as a beast of prey, a ravening wolf, a ferocious lioness, the source of hell, for without it there would be no hell. It is the mother of all the abominations of the earth. Self-will is a venomous serpent, a detestable homicide that kills body and soul at the same time, an execrable deicide that kills God insofar as it is able."[1] Could one have made a different use of free will than to offend God? Of course! It could have been used to cooperate with grace. Such cooperation would not be Pelagianism, since we would not be reaching heaven by our own initiative; but withholding such cooperation now is as astounding as Grou found it to be to Augustine. "Where then, does he exclaim, was my free-will during so many years? What a strange abuse! What! I only made use of it to offend God! What a wonderful depravity."[2] ("Wonderful" means an object of astonishment.)

In Grou's own words, we should be stupefied at the impertinence of using the gift of free will to mutiny against the one who gave us the gift.

> It is the same with all sinners. When they return to God, their
> astonishment is extreme that they should have had the insolence to
> disobey him, and openly to rebel against him ... The first effect of their
> conversion, is to pull down this pride, to remind them of what they are,
> and of what God is in himself, and what he is with regard to them ...
> They understand what the evil is of self-will; that it is what corrupts the
> intelligent creature, and renders it capable of every excess; that it provokes

---

1. Eudes, *Meditations on Various Subjects*, 217.

2. Grou, *Morality Extracted from the Confessions of Saint Austin*, vol. 2, 200.

the wrath of God, animates his vindictive justice, that it has formed hell; that it is the only source of all crimes ... This inspires them with a holy hatred against themselves.[3]

We are left astonished and disturbed when we commit some fault, but de Sales wants to know why we should find it surprising. "We wish *what* He wishes, but not *as* He wishes it. We do not submit ourselves wholly and as we should do to His will."[4] Self-love insinuates itself into our motives, thereby spoiling both what we will, and how we will it. So, he continues, "Why are we so astonished, disturbed, impatient when we commit some fault? Doubtless because we thought that we were good, stedfast, firm; and finding that it is quite otherwise, we are vexed and put out; whereas, if we realised what we are, so far from marveling because we fall, we should rather marvel how we ever stand upright!"[5] It is a first step to will what God wishes, but the final step is to also will *as* he wishes, which is particularly difficult when it comes to trials and sufferings. The sinner will talk glibly enough about God residing in him until it upsets the plans self-will has devised. Libermann says that Jesus' life will be truly in you, only "if you have no desires, no will of your own, but make His love your only desire and His Will your will. Replace self-love with the love of Jesus."[6] It would seem, says Baker, that the choice between heaven and hell can be made already, now. "In a word, the difference between heaven and hell is, that hell is full of nothing but self-love and propriety; whereas there is not the least degree of either in heaven, nor anything but the fulfilling of God's will and seeking of His glory."[7]

Self-love causes self-esteem, which blinds us to the faulty activity of our self-will. "All sins, whether of the mind or the flesh, originate in our insane self-esteem and inordinate

---

3. Grou, *Morality Extracted from the Confessions of Saint Austin*, vol. 2, 200-01.

4. Camus, *Spirit of St. Francis de Sales*, 251.

5. De Sales, *Spiritual Letters*, 12.

6. Libermann, *Letters to Religious Sisters and Aspirants,* Spiritan Series 5, vol. 1, 35.

7. Baker, *Holy Wisdom*, 249.

self-love,"[8] says Grou, and the vanity known as self-esteem is an even more dangerous snare in the spiritual life because some secret self-esteem is probably inspiring our good works. Fenelon observes that "corrupt nature is nourished very subtly on the graces most contrary to human nature. Self-love feeds itself not only on austerity and humiliations, not only on fervent prayer and self-renunciation, but still more on the purest abandon and the most extreme sacrifices."[9] Vainglory is desiring honor from other human beings, but pride is snatching credit from God upon believing that we have willfully saved ourselves. When self-will is at the helm of the spiritual voyage a person will become proud from treating his spiritual successes as self-accomplished. even of his humility. We are therefore recommended to speak neither in praise nor blame of ourselves, because de Sales finds both springing from the same root of vanity.

> [Boasting is] so ridiculous a weakness that it is hissed down by even the vulgar crowd. Its one fitting place is in the mouth of a swaggering comedian. In like manner words of contempt spoken of ourselves by ourselves, unless they are absolutely heartfelt and come from a mind thoroughly convinced of the fact of its own misery, are truly the very acme of pride, and a flower of the most subtle vanity; for it rarely happens that he who utters them either believes them himself or really wishes others to believe them: on the contrary, the speaker is mostly only anxious rather to be considered humble, and consequently virtuous, and seeks that his self-blame should redound to his honour. Self-dispraise in general is no more than a tricky kind of boasting.[10]

We saw earlier that humility should be defined as accepting exactly the place where one should be, according to justice and truth. Here we see a parallel realization: submissively accepting from God either blame or praise, instead of organizing them ourselves. Most of our theologians call this "naked faith," which Grou says glorifies God the most "because

---

8. Grou, *The School of Jesus Christ*, 414.

9. Fenelon, *Christian Perfection*, 171.

10. De Sales, in Camus, *The Spirit of St. Francis de Sales*, 155-56.

He is hereby served in a manner worthy of Himself, which yields no pleasure to self-love, and wherein we in no wise seek ourselves, but practise self-forgetfulness and self-sacrifice, and give ourselves over to bear all such rigour as it shall please a merciful justice to exercise upon us."[11] Giving oneself over to whatever rigor mercy plus justice chooses to exercise upon us is challenging for self-will, but God is best liturgized when we give up our own judgment. How is a heart mortified? De Chantal answers: "by renouncing self-will, self-judgment, the passions and inclinations, submitting in all things, condescending cheerfully to the will of others."[12] So Grou calculates that "in proportion as self-love is weakened, and we give up our own judgment and bend our own will to the will of God, which is His own glory and His own good pleasure, so will our difficulties be overcome, our conflicts will cease, our troubles will vanish, and peace and calm will be established in our hearts."[13]

The will has an attraction to what gives it delight. Of course it has! Will was made to seek the good, so Blosius points out how important self-examination is in order to discern what delights it. "The only thing which disturbs thy soul, defiles it, and keeps it from the embrace of the heavenly Spouse, is the preposterous love with which thou seekest thyself, reflectest on thyself, and delightest not in God, but in thyself. From this perverse self-love arise all vicious passions and affections, all confusion and irregularity, and indeed all evil within thee."[14] How strange that the proximity and rule of God, for which we were made, should cause any discomfort, yet precisely such is a consequence of self-will. Crasset says it even spoils prayer. "There is a feeling of disquiet in the depth of my heart which fills my meditation with bitterness. Whence is this? The cause is not difficult to find; you do not come to meditation alone, self-will accompanies you ... What wonder that you are troubled! Banish this self-will, and your trouble will cease; purify your intention before entering upon meditation; do not seek your own satisfaction, but that of God."[15]

---

11. Grou, *The Spiritual Maxims*, 149.

12. De Chantal, *Meditations for Retreats*, 196.

13. Grou, *Manual for Interior Souls*, 303.

14. Blosius, *Spiritual Works*, 25.

15. De Sales & Crasset, *Secret of Sanctity*, 188.

Self-will is an enemy of salvation, because Eudes knows self-will is agitated by misreading God's rule in our life as interference.

> Let us regard our own will as the sworn enemy of our salvation, and even
> of our happiness in this life. There is nothing on earth nor in hell we
> should fear more than self-will for it is the source of all the miseries and
> evils of earth and hell. It is a dragon which will strangle us if we do not
> crush it. Fear it more than all the demons for they are chained dogs that
> can bite only those who come within their reach, but self-will is a serpent
> which we bear in our very selves.[16]

De Sales diagnoses self-will as making us willing enough to do things of our own election, but not if it was chosen for us by another, or by obedience. But, on the contrary, "if we had the perfection of the love of God, we should prefer to do what was commanded because it comes more from God, and less from us."[17] The might of God and the nothingness of man would together yield latria. Alas, we instead resist the imposition of the commandments, like a horse resists the bit and bridle (Psalm 32:9). Libermann thinks this weakness of will

> is still rooted in the extreme tenderness we have for ourselves: the love of
> enjoyment. From this is born a laziness of will that causes us great evils. It
> is a love of rest that holds the will in great weakness, produces neglect and
> discouragement, and exposes us to all sorts of temptations, while robbing
> us of the strength we need to fight them.

---

16. Eudes, *Meditations on Various Subjects*, 218-19.

17. De Sales, *Letters to Persons in the World*, 345.

We can easily see that this laziness has its source only in self-love. These souls so lazy, so careless and indifferent to divine things, will be very active and very animated when it comes to giving pleasure to oneself.[18]

De Caussade notices that weakness, laziness, and carelessness make it difficult to maintain the mortification originally willed.

Nature, though mortified by its previous renunciation, awakes again, retrieves its old domination and soon self-love glides with its self-interest, subtlety, and almost without our knowledge into our hearts, substituting itself for the good motives by which our actions had been undertaken and begun. The result of which in numberless cases is what, as S. Paul said, we begin with the spirit and finish with the flesh.[19]

The highest point of obedience, and its accompanying joy, is reached when the satisfaction of self-love is abnegated in order to serve another's will. De Sales writes, "to govern ourselves and to act by our own will or our own choice, always gives much satisfaction to our self-love; but to allow ourselves to be employed in things which others will and we do not – that is, which we do not choose – in this lies the highest point of abnegation."[20] The first battle of grace is for conversion, the last battle of grace is forsaking of self. (There is much resistance between that alpha and omega.) Most of the authors who have written spiritual letters have communicated something like de Caussade writes in one of his.

It seems to me that no one has ever offered so much resistance as you. This proceeds from a very strongly rooted self-love, from a secret great presumption and confidence in yourself that, possibly, you may never have found out; for, mark well, that directly you are spoken to about

---

18. Libermann, *Instructions on the Spiritual Life*, 14-15.

19. De Caussade, *On Prayer*, 195.

20. De Sales, *The Spiritual Conferences*, 65.

this total abandonment to God you feel a certain interior commotion as though all were lost, and is if you had been told to throw yourself, with your eyes shut, into an abyss. It seems a trifle, yet it is very much the contrary, for the greatest assurance of salvation in this life can only be obtained in this total abandonment, and this consists, as Fenelon says, in becoming thoroughly tired of, and driven to despair oneself, and made to hope only in God.[21]

Liturgical abnegation is at the summit because its motive is more profound than mere altruism. De Sales thinks it is true that a lower scale can be used to measure the goods attained by overcoming self-will, however, the inspirations that come from God are different in kind, and a higher scale must be used to measure the good attained by embracing the death of self-will because "our one aim must be to make the love of God reign supreme over self-love."[22] Liturgical abnegation is not simply done for our tranquility (although that is one benefit); it is done out of faith in our sanctification, hope for our deification, and love for God – it is to be measured by those three theological virtues. It is more a matter of transformation than improvement, says Saint-Jure. "Therefore, to render a man capable of being changed, and transformed into God, it is necessary that he strip himself of himself, that he die absolutely to his self-love, and to all that feeds self-love in him."[23] It is a matter of replacing one will with another, says Crasset. "A man who has no self-will does the will of God, for God's will takes the place of his own."[24] It is a matter of dying to new life, says de Chantal. "Ah! self-will, it is time for you to die, since I no longer desire to live but in the will of my God."[25] Saint-Jure summarizes by saying that if a soul is lost upon separating itself from the will of God, it shall be restored upon adhering to the will of God.

---

21. De Caussade, *Abandonment to Divine Providence*, 190-91.

22. De Sales, *The Spiritual Conferences*, 278.

23. Saint-Jure, *The Religious*, vol. 1, 575.

24. De Sales & Crasset, *Secret of Sanctity*, 261.

25. De Chantal, *Meditations for Retreats*, 168.

Man became lost for having separated himself from the will of God, and for following his own. Now, as maladies are cured by their contraries, it is necessary that man recover and save himself by renouncing his will and embracing that of God. Herein consists the regulating of man's will, and following upon it, his salvation, his holiness, his perfection, his deification, and his transformation in God.[26]

Worldliness supposes that the world could satisfy the soul, whereas the proper element for the soul is divine life. Baker describes a soul that fails this

like a whale that has been stranded in a brook: the great creature has not space enough to swim or plunge in its waters. Hence it ever desires the ocean, which, for its depth and wideness, is capable of containing it and millions of others. Here these huge creatures find no bottom, but can swim in all fullness, and enjoy security from danger; for here they are in their element and, as it were, in their own kingdom.[27]

Poor souls! The liturgies in which they swim are too shallow, and they are left like minnows flailing on the floor of the boat. Abnegation serves deification by denying everything that is too small for the soul, everything that would separate us from the ever-loving and ever-living God. De Bernicre-Louvigny can put it in the form of liturgical impetration:

O my God, separate me by thy holy grace from everything which hinders this divine transformation. Grant that I may cease to be what I am according to nature, and that I may become what thou art by the power of grace. When shall I be wholly united and transformed into thee? When

---

26. Saint-Jure, *The Religious*, vol. 1, 577.

27. Augustine Baker, *The Inner Life of Dame Gertrude More* (London: R. & T. Washbourne, Ltd.) 165.

shall I entirely forget myself, and act only in thee, and that thou in me, and continue thus absorbed in thee all the days of my life?[28]

Saint-Jure thinks this transformation is delicate because the self-will still standing in the way operates covertly, and still with permission of the sinner. "The sick are insensible to their wounds, they even like them; often they prefer sickness to health. The greater part of the maladies of the body are visible and palpable, and can therefore be easily healed; but those of the soul are hidden, the corporal eye sees them not; to destroy them invisible enemies must be combated."[29]

Yet, even though the various manifestations of self-will are difficult to see, they have been recorded and plotted on the sinner's diagnostic chart. Obviously, the self-will has been deluded about its strength and capacities. It is almost as if someone has been lying to it, and it is obvious who. It is time to bring Satan into the descriptive picture. Saint-Jure calls the devil "the father of lies and the king of the proud," and he "always inspires self-esteem and pride, and produces in the soul a certain audacity and self-confidence which clearly evince his presence."[30] He tempts us to place too much trust in our own mind, memory, and judgment, and finds a ready mark for his con. John of Avila describes the trap the devil lays:

> He exalts us with vanity and lies, and afterward knocks us down in a truly miserable fall. He puffs us up with thoughts that incline us to high self-esteem in something, and thus makes us fall into pride. He knows through experience that this evil was enough to change him from an angel into a demon. So he works with all his might to make us like him in pride so that we may be like him in his torments.[31]

---

28. De Berniere-Louvigny, *The Interior Christian*, 192.

29. Saint-Jure, *A Treatise on the Knowledge and Love of Our Lord Jesus Christ*, vol. 2, 211.

30. Saint-Jure, *The Spiritual Man*, 101.

31. John of Avila, *Audi, Filia*, 75.

This constant rising and falling, exalting and knocking over, is designed to discourage, then dissuade, then destroy the soul, and a soul that is touchy with self-will and self-love is easily stirred. After that, Libermann says, we join the devil as co-agent of our discouragement.

> All discouragement proceeds from the devil, from self-love, or from both. The devil looks for nothing better than to discourage us. As soon as he has succeeded, he feels confident that he will gain the mastery over our soul in a very short time. On the other hand, our self-love which is very foolish, and very much hurt when it sees how truly miserable we are, is not slow in succumbing to sadness and discouragement.[32]

Where is the devil's house? Whence does he rule? If John of Avila we reflects carefully, he finds "that it is the evil self-will of the wicked. There the devil sits like a king on his throne, and from there he gives orders to everyone."[33]

Taken seriously and soberly, this means not only that we are in his house, it also means that he is in ours. The devil is an antichrist, and insofar as we are sinners, "we carry about, within ourselves, a devil, a Lucifer, and an antichrist, which is our own will, pride and self love; and they, indeed, are worse than all the demons, than Lucifer and antichrist, for all the malice of the demons, Lucifer and antichrist is derived from self-will, pride, and self-love."[34]

On the one hand, we are victims, and on the other hand, we give permission. It is an antinomy wherein both are true. He stirs up self-will and self-love, and we, in turn, give him power as they operate in us. According to Grou, self-love is the one source of all illusions in the spiritual life.

> By its means the devil exercises sleights, leads souls astray, drags them sometimes to hell by the very road that seems to lead to heaven. We

---

32. Libermann, *Letters to Clergy & Religious,* Spiritan Series 8, vol. 4, 178.

33. John of Avila, *Audi, Filia,* 285.

34. Eudes, *The Life and the Kingdom of Jesus in Christian Souls,* 42.

long eagerly for spiritual delights; the devil gives false pleasures, which
feed vanity and sensuousness; we wish ardently for extraordinary favours:
the devil transforms himself into an angel of light, and counterfeits the
Divine operations. ... Then we fancy ourselves the recipients of peculiar
light, and grow wilful, obstinate, and deaf to good advice; we shake off
the yoke of authority, and, under the deceitful guise of sanctity, conceal
the pride of Lucifer.[35]

Our willfulness is the coin of the devil's realm, and he cares not about external
austerities "provided you nourish your self-will"[36] (de Sales). He does his utmost to
discover what designs God has for a particular soul, that is, the designs that God is
using to bring a particular soul to sanctity, and then attempts to corrupt them. Even
the institutions of grace, says Boudon. God's salvific economy intends to lead toward
perfection, but the devils urge us to pursue it with a natural eagerness that proceeds only
from self-love;[37] God wishes us to go to confession, but the devils make us approach this
sacrament not so much from the love of God and movement of his grace, but self-love;[38]
God requires us to go to communion, but the devils induce souls to approach it who
have not the necessary dispositions, and are sometimes prompted by a secret movement
of self-love they do not perceive.[39] All together this can be called a spirit of pride, a
spirit of the world, a spirit of untruth and vanity and boasting and malice. "In a word,"
summarizes Libermann, "it is the spirit of the devil, who is the ruler of this world ... This
spirit inspires the worldings with the desire for display, for self-esteem, for self-love, a spirit
that attributes everything to self, instead of directing all things to the love of God alone.

---

35. Grou, *The Spiritual Maxims*, 177-78.

36. De Sales, *Spiritual Letters*, 206.

37. Boudon, *Devotion to the Nine Choirs of Holy Angels*, 63.

38. Boudon, *Devotion to the Nine Choirs of Holy Angels*, 65.

39. Boudon, *Devotion to the Nine Choirs of Holy Angels*, 65.

It makes them seek their own interest, and not the interest of *God alone*, as Our Lord did and taught."[40]

As one might expect, the deceiver produces a delusional piety. A counterfeit devotion is produced from the combination of the deceitfulness of the devil, the wiliness of the world, and the spirit of self-regard. Grou describes such persons as "narrowminded, pharisaically precise in their devotions, full of self-esteem, touchy, self-conceited, obstinate, unyielding or affected in outward manner, – altogether deficient in truthfulness, simplicity, and reality. They secretly esteem themselves more highly than other men, and they may even despise and condemn the true piety of others, which they are unable to perceive."[41] Hardly a pure liturgy to give to God! This ersatz piety comes from a mind Fenelon describes as "buoyed up with thoughts and projects of self-pleasing, and a will divided between duty to God and inclination to all that fosters self-will."[42] And since the repair requires an abnegation of self-will, which opens the soul to prayer and sincere contrition, Fenelon counsels to "pray about everything; you cannot pray too much. If you decide or act without prayer, your self-will is sure to disturb you much, to involve you in many annoyances, to cause you harassing doubts and misgivings, so that you will waste your strength for nothing."[43] Nature will be fooled without the grace of supernature, because at bottom, says de Castaniza, it will be deceived about its own motivation.

> For Nature doth so secretly seek herself in our enterprises, that those very things which thou thinkest please or displease thee only for the love of God, are principally willed or refused for thy self-interest.

> Wherefore, at the beginning of any action whatsoever, free thyself to the utmost of thy power of all intentions which have the least mixture of this

---

40. Libermann, *Letters to People in the World*, Spiritan Series 6, vol. 2, 40.

41. Grou, *The Hidden Life of the Soul*, 14-15.

42. Fenelon, *Letters to Men*, 227.

43. Fenelon, *Letters to Men*, 87.

self-interest; nor do thou venture to act or omit anything till thou feelest and findest thyself inwardly moved to begin and go on with it purely for the will and pleasure of God only.[44]

Failing to align our volition with God's will decays the willingness we think we feel. Imperfect souls receive advice by which they could improve their discretion, but Baker observes that "if they practice them with any willingness, it is to be feared that the true ground is because thereby they do covertly comply with nature some other way, nourishing self-esteem, contempt of others not so courageous, nor affording so great edification, &c."[45]

True piety, exercised in submission to God, is at peace, Fenelon writes to one of his directees. "From the moment you give up all self-will, and seek absolutely nothing but what He wills, you will be free from all your restless anxiety and forecasting; there will be nothing to conceal, nothing to bring about. Short of that you will be uneasy, changeable, easily put out, dissatisfied with yourself and with others, full of reserve and mistrust."[46] In order to attain this shalom a guard must be stationed at both the door of love and the door of will to determine what comes into the heart and what goes out of the heart. That guard keeps order between the primary and secondary goods, so we do not mistake God as accidental to us, or anything of the world as our final good. Once this order is restored, Lacordaire can chart the change that happens to self-will. "A man is a slave when he serves against his will; serve by your own inclination, and slavery would be destroyed. You have been told that the greatest misfortune and the greatest humiliation is servitude; and I say to you, make an act of love of servitude; [and then] that which was ignominy will become a glory, that which was slavery will become devotedness."[47]

Then Blosius says we can have a totally different relationship with the world.

---

44. De Castaniza, *Spiritual Conflict and Conquest*, 25.

45. Baker, *Holy Wisdom*, 222.

46. Fenelon, *Letters to Men*, 305.

47. Jean-Baptiste Henri Lacordaire, *Conferences of the Rev. Pere Lacordaire, Delivered in the Cathedral of Notre Dame, in Paris* (New York: P. O'Shea Publisher, 1870) 405.

Make use of creatures here for the honour of God; but beware of clinging to them with faulty affection. Keep thyself free and pure within, as far as thou art able. Do thou refer entirely to the Creator, and to thy heavenly home, whatever beauty, elegance, sweetness, fragrance, melody or perfection, thou perceivest in created things; for all the fairness, sweetness, and perfection of creatures flows from God. Thou mayest indeed receive some solace in God from these created things; but them shouldst not cling to them, nor perversely seek in them thy self-will or thy own delight.[48]

The will that is peculiar to self, and identical neither with the will of God nor even of other persons, is a disfigurement of the soul, and Eudes thinks such a soul is best approached by prayer. Here are two prayers he suggests. "At the beginning of your actions, lift your heart to him in this way: 'O Jesus, with all my strength, I renounce myself, my own mind, my own will and my self-love. I give myself completely to you, your holy spirit and your divine love. Free me from myself and guide me in this action according to your holy will.'"[49] And "O Most Powerful and Most Good Jesus, do Thou employ Thine own power and infinite goodness to annihilate me and establish Thyself in me, to destroy in me my self-love, my own will, my own mind, my pride, and all my passions, sentiments and inclinations, in order to establish Thy holy love and make it reign in me, together with Thy divine spirit, Thy most deep humility and all Thy blessed virtues.[50]

Spiritual diagnostics must analyze the comorbidities. Fenelon writes to one, "not merely self-will, but a refined spirit of pride overpowers you, and makes you reject God's Gift, because it does not come in a fashion pleasing to your fastidiousness."[51] And he writes to another, "you see what God requires of you: can you refuse? You see that your

---

48. Blosius, *Spiritual Works*, 128-29.

49. Eudes, *The Life and Kingdom of Jesus in Christian Souls*, 309.

50. Eudes, *Life and the Kingdom of Jesus in Christian Souls*, 81.

51. Fenelon, *Letters to Women*, 109.

resistance is but a refinement of self-love: dare you oppose such refinements, such subtle self-seeking to His Mercy?"[52] In all cases, abnegation is necessary, forcing self-will to abandon its desires, because emptying permits filling, uprooting permits planting, denial permits accepting. Liturgical abnegation is an exchange of wills, thinks de Caussade, and when "one finds oneself reduced to nothing ... this love is then absolutely pure because self-love has nothing to lean upon, and, consequently, nothing to become attached to, or to corrupt."[53]

The will we are adopting (God's) is the opposite of the will we should be abandoning (ours), because his will is governed by a charity that seeks not its own, and our will seeks little else than our own fortune. Our rescue will not come through reason; it will only come through charity. Fenelon bluntly says, "*the will can only change through love.*"[54] In other words (theological words), we are speaking about grace-in-action. Turn the rescue operation entirely over to God. Fenelon advises a person to leave God to work his will – and "what is His Will for you? That you should have none; that you should leave all the Him and His Holy Spirit ... Do not hinder Him by any effort of self-will, by straining to shape things your way."[55]

We turn all we touch into an opportunity for exerting self-will, like King Midas turned all he touched into gold, with disastrous effect. We are bothered by those providences God sends for our correction, including other people, so we become anxious to reverse roles with our neighbor. Fenelon writes, "our own imperfection makes us hasty to rebuke the imperfect; and it is a very subtle and all-permeating self-love which cannot forgive the self-love of others. The stronger it is, the more critical the censor will be; there is nothing so irritating to a proud, self-willed mind, as the self-will of a neighbour; and another man's passions seem intolerably ridiculous and unbearable to one who is given up to his own."[56] Self-will prefers a future it can determine over the providence it cannot control. Indeed,

---

52. Fenelon, *Letters to Women*, 108.

53. De Caussade, *Abandonment to Divine Providence*, 224.

54. Fenelon, *Letters to Men*, 194; emphasis added.

55. Fenelon, *Letters to Men*, 153.

56. Fenelon, *Letters to Women*, 221-22.

Grou notices, "if there are few who attempt this entire gift of themselves to God, there are still fewer who persevere and really accomplish it. Even after once offering the sacrifice, it is not long before they take back and govern themselves more or less as self-will and self-love prompt them. It costs nature too much to rest continually under God's Guiding Hand."[57] So if anyone complains about what is hard and humiliating, or about aridity in prayer, or about a darkness that prevents him from seeing any good in suffering, Boudon may reply

> you thus betray your self-love, although it disguises itself under fair
> pretexts; for if the love of God were strong within, could you desire aught
> else but what He wills? ... In this state, then, we must abide, since such
> is the order of God's Providence. But self-love is not satisfied with this
> dispensation; it wishes to see, it wishes to know, it wishes to have lights
> which God is not pleased to give it.[58]

The sinner lacks resignation to God, surrender, and relinquishment to God, because it costs annihilation of self. And John Evangelist of Boisleduc thinks the want of resignation that proceeds from self-will and self-love is "the cause of all man's worries and anxieties and holds him out of God ... When he is denied what he wants he becomes melancholy and disturbed, which is a sure sign of self-love."[59]

We do have an exemplar and engenderer of submission to God: it is Jesus, who models abnegation and initiates its activity in us. He has a sweet familiarity with us, even in our sinful state, so he can break open the barricades that self-will has built around itself. He can take the soul out of her self. Canfield rejoices:

> By this the soul is stricken with wonder much greater still: that the King
> of Kings and Lord of lords should enter into familiar communication
> with a slave, who borrows all she has from Himself; nay, that He should

---

57. Grou, *Self-Consecration,* 18.

58. Boudon, *The Hidden Life of Jesus,* 169.

59. John Evangelist, *The Kingdom of God in the Soul,* 70-71.

converse and associate with one that is sinful and His enemy ... [that] he should so behave Himself towards her as if she were so precious to Him that He could not do without her. This not only melts her into wonder, but the vehemency of her amazement ravishes her out of herself ... [She says] after His example I desire to renounce self-will.[60]

Sanctification involves a death to self, that Guillore calls casting forth the body of sin. "Where self-will is eradicated, a long stage has been won in the way of holiness."[61] But no one can accomplish this renunciation of on self his own, because, Fenelon says, no one can "make a division between me and self."[62] The renunciation of self-will consists of making opposing acts: to oppose what mere nature feels when it settles for less than eternal life, and to oppose to the smugness that fallen nature feels when it prefers to be its own master. The method of self-renunciation is laborious and challenging, admits Canfield, because it is

brought about by making contrary acts, that is, by renouncing the pleasure felt, and by drawing the mind off another way; by closing all the entrances of the spiritual powers against the like pleasure, and by darting in opposition all their force into God. Thus the soul offers herself to God as a vessel by which He may accomplish the work she does for His honor only, and for His will, without respect to any advantage the creature may get thereby. It comes to pass, by this means, that the soul, which would otherwise be seeking her delights rather from the sensual and pleasing nature of the thing done than from God's Will, does now, on the contrary,

---

60. Canfield, *The Holy Will of God*, 55-56.

61. François Guilloré, *Self-Renunciation* (London: Rivingtons, 1871), 98.

62. Fenelon, *Pious Thoughts Concerning the Knowledge and Love of God* (London: W. and J. Innys, 1720) 22.

after a spiritual act made in this wise, place all our delight in the only Will of God.[63]

The telos of abnegation is to act *only* according to the will of God; to do *all* things from God's will; to have *no other* motive than the will of God. Arriving at this state means slowly eradicating (annihilating) other motives until there is only one remaining.

Jesus teaches and empowers us to do so. The soul desires abnegation because of him. Though Jesus was without sin, and did not engage a struggle against the passions as we do, he nevertheless shared the abnegation commanded of other men because he was fully human. Eudes writes:

> Our Lord Jesus Christ is our leader and exemplar. There was nothing in him that was not completely holy and divine. Nevertheless, he was so detached from himself and so abnegated in his human spirit, his own will and self-love that he never did anything according to his own insight or human spirit, but according to the guidance of his Father's spirit. He behaved toward himself as someone who had no love, but rather an extreme hatred toward himself. He deprived himself, in this world, of infinite glory and happiness.[64]

To be a member of Christ requires a believer to share in these exact sentiments of abnegation, and beg for a firm resolution to live in detachment from his own self. "To this end," Eudes counsels, "make sure that you adore Jesus often in this detachment from himself and give yourself to him, begging him to detach you entirely from yourself, your own mind, your own will, and your self-love so that He may unite you perfectly to Himself, and govern you in all things according to his mind, his love and his pure will."[65]

---

63. Canfield, *Holy Will of God*, 25.

64. Eudes, *The Life and Kingdom of Jesus in Christian Souls*, in *Berulle and the French School*, 309.

65. Eudes, *The Life and Kingdom of Jesus in Christian Souls*, in *Berulle and the French School*, 309.

Our Lord Jesus makes possible the necessary renunciation of self-will by providing us with the graces necessary for it. Surin presents this as a truth of which we must be convinced:

> Our Lord makes us find in him immense treasures of supernatural gifts
> for those who, through a generous and fervent practice of abnegation,
> renounce themselves and everything they possess, and who have the
> courage and the faithfulness to mortify all their passions, their natural
> impetuosity, and all the plans suggested by self-love. By keeping to that
> road, they reach the kingdom of God, which is hidden in us and which
> we do not find unless we dig around in our interior in order to find our
> defects, our vanities, our curiosities, our self-wills.[66]

This is a side of Christology often overlooked, but revealed by liturgical abnegation. Though he is God-man, and we are only human, we wait in hope for a deification that will make us as devout as he was, and the way to that deification is through the gates of abnegation.

Liturgy must be done with such devotion. In almost syllogistic form, Grou says "surrender of liberty is the same thing as devotion to God; because devotion is only an engagement to forsake self-will, and follow the will of God."[67] That is to say, liturgy must be done out of abnegation, and abnegation perfects liturgy. Abnegation is obedience, which is denying self-will, which is necessary if we are to liturgize God instead of lauding ourselves, which is something both self-will and self-love desire. "Perfect forgetfulness of self ... casts us upon God, as a babe rests upon its mother's breast," says Grou. "It is not by great deeds, long prayers, or even by heavy crosses that we may best give glory to God; self-will may taint all these, but total self-renunciation does in truth give Him all the glory."[68] In short, if there is to be genuine forgetfulness of self, we must stop speaking of self. If we do not stop speaking, the sweetness of the cross will be blown away under the

---

66. Jean-Joseph Surin, *Into the Dark Night and Back: The Mystical Writings of Jean-Joseph Surin* (Leiden: Brill, 2019) 468.

67. Grou, *The Spiritual Maxims*, 15.

68. Grou, *The Hidden Life of the Soul*, 66-67.

breath of our own speech, says Alacoque. "I see I am satisfying my self-love in speaking of the cross which is like precious perfume: it loses its sweet scent before God and is dissipated by too much talking. It is my portion always to suffer in silence."[69]

We cannot attain to total self-renunciation by our own power alone, because God alone can extinguish the flames of self-love and self-will. This he does when he destroys the old Adam and raises up mystical life in the heart, at which time we can exclaim with St. Paul "I live, yet not I, but Christ lives in me" (Galatians 2:20). Then the reversal caused by original sin is itself reversed, and from exile we are put back on the path to our last end and felicity. We do not even have to reach a complete and final happiness in order to please God: he is pleased if we but begin our liturgy with what Fenelon calls a first step of abnegation. "Can we glorify God better than by freeing ourselves from all self-will, so that he can act according to his good pleasure? It is then that he is truly our God, that his kingdom does come within us, when independently of all outer aid and all inner consolation, we only see, within and without, the hand of God who does all, and whom we ceaselessly adore."[70] Whatever is done or omitted, let it be done or omitted for the glory of God.

Liturgy requires purity of intention in the will, and purity of intention means willing without self-love. Then de Granada sees the pure intention as something comparable to what is done in heaven. "As the whole exercise of the heavenly choirs is the performing of God's will with a most pure intention only to please him, so should the inhabitant of the earth, as long as he lives here, imitate this custom of heaven as far as possibly he can."[71] The false motives that lead to insincere worship done with merely external form are almost too numerous to count. How many ways are there to liturgize for reasons other than love of God? Let de Castaniza count some.

> Who is not generally more diligent in the performance of his duty for the fear of hell and hope of heaven than for the sole and substantial love of his Creator? Who hath not rather some small clause and secret condition of

---

69. Alacoque, *Spiritual Letters*, letter 132, Kindle edition.

70. Fenelon, *Christian Perfection*, 79.

71. De Granada, *The Sinner's Guide*, 358.

self-interest in his actions than the only fulfilling of God's holy will, and
the following of His divine inspirations? Whom shall we find, though
they be never so great pretenders to perfection, so totally disentangled
from the net of self-love, that they neither hover after human respects
and praises nor look upon rewards or punishments, nor overvalue their
own ways and exercises, nor solace themselves with the sweets of sensible
devotion, nor pride themselves upon their high-towering contemplations
and raptures into God's immediate perfections; nor, finally, dress up
devotion after the pattern of their own passions, and so fall in love with
their own conceptions, and make to themselves in Bethel golden calves,
instead of the cherubim in Jerusalem? Whose will is so truly divested of
all self as to remain untouched, unmoved, undisquieted, resolute, and
resigned in all temporal chances and changes, and in all spiritual dryness,
desolation, dereliction, and affliction whatsoever?[72]

The man of self-will holds self-esteem more precious than wealth, sensual gratification, or even life itself, a point proven by the fact that he is willing to risk those three for the sake of reputation. De Bergamo therefore believes that when we offer "our self-esteem with humility to God we offer that which we deem most precious. This is truly offering 'sacrifice to God, and a good savour' (Ecclesiastes 45:20)."[73] The platitude of "offering oneself" sounds easy, but this whole chapter on self-will reveals how difficult it really is. Grace and discipline is required to offer our self-esteem, self-renown, self-display, self-sufficiency, self-confidence, self-judgment, and self-conceit. From purity of heart (which is to will one thing) comes purity of worship. Without conquering (annihilating) self-will, liturgy will be nothing more than ceremony.

However, a serene piety arises with liturgical abnegation. A serenity arrives upon making our will one with God's will. After that a person "always does *his own will*," de Ponte marvels, "because he has placed his will in the will of God, and of His divine Spirit; in doing, therefore, the will of God, he does his own will, because his own will is no other than the will of God. For which reason St. Bonaventure says, that those who

---

72. De Castaniza, *The Spiritual Conflict and Conquest*, 222.

73. De Bergamo, *Humility of Heart,* 120.

are conformed to the divine will are Gods, omnipotent to do what they will."[74] Self-will wants to rule its little kingdom, and does not realize the size of the Kingdom it is being offered, if only it takes up the will of the true King.

---

74. De Ponte, *Meditation on the Mysteries of Our Holy Faith*, vol. 5 (London: Richardson and Son, 1854) 230.

SELF-LOVE

"As he himself loves us exceedingly, [God] desires in return all our love," de Liguori says, and that means *all* our love because God is "jealous of any one else sharing the affections of our hearts, of which he desires to be the sole possessor."[1] There is this thing called "self" – do you seek it or renounce it? do you please it or deny it? Do you struggle with it or surrender to it? To Bona, "all improvement of the soul is vain and imperfect, unless it be enhanced by renouncement of self-love."[2] The previous chapter asked whether volition (will) is exercised by self instead of surrender to God's will; the present chapter will ask whether our desire (love) is for self or for God. "Divine love enters the soul in proportion as self-love disappears"[3] (Ullathorne), and "this transfer of love from self to God is the whole sum of Christian perfection"[4] (Bruyere).

Of course, there is a right way and a wrong way to do self-love. Jenks calls it *vicious* (a vice) "when we love what we ought not to love; or, when we love it more or less than we ought," and calls it *foolish* "when we love what does not deserve our love; or, when we love it more or less than it deserves."[5] So there can be a proper, rightly ordered self-love. To the person who doesn't believe he can love himself, Jenks answers: "Pray, is it not a

---

1. de Liguori, *The Practice of the Love of Jesus Christ*, 372-73.

2. Bona, *A Treatise of Spiritual Life*, 258.

3. Bruyere, *Spiritual Life and Prayer*, 337.

4. Ullathorne, *The Endowments of Man*, 127.

5. Sylvester Jenks, *An Essay Upon the Art of Love, Containing an Exact Anatomy of Love and all the Other Passions which Attend it* (London: s.n., 1702) 10.

very good thing to be what God has made us? Our Personal Being – is it not made to the Image of God Himself? ... Is this not good for us? Is it not desirable by us? ... He, who made us, planted Self-love in the Center of our Nature."[6] Yet as with every fallen state of nature, we don't do nature naturally any more, so de Liguori makes a firm distinction between "two sorts of self-love – the one good, the other pernicious. The former is that which makes us seek eternal life – the end of our creation; the latter inclines us to pursue earthly goods, and to prefer them to our ever-lasting welfare and to the holy will of God ... Christian perfection, then, consists in self-abnegation."[7] Most others make the same distinction, but I will only mention five.

First, Saint-Jure uses plain terms: a *good and bad* kind. "It must first be known that there are two self-loves: the one good; the other bad."[8] We know the good kind exists because Jesus himself acknowledges it: "Our Lord Himself teaches us this clearly, when He commands us to love our neighbor as ourselves. It is evident that He supposes we love ourselves, and with a good and reasonable love, since He gives it to us as the rule and the measure of that which we ought to bear towards our neighbor."[9] Such love is good if it is conformable to reason and obedient to the commandments of God. In another place Saint-Jure uses the categories of *virtue and vice* to distinguish the two types of love of self. "Man can love himself with a good and laudable love, which consists in loving himself for eternity, which is, to love God ... [But] there is a love of self which is vicious, having its source in sin; this is commonly called self-love. From it, as from a poisoned principal, flow all our evils and all the sins we commit, because every sin is the act of taking some forbidden pleasure which self-love makes us seek."[10]

---

6. Jenks, *An Essay Upon the Art of Love*, 26-27.

7. Alphonsus Liguori, *The True Spouse of Jesus Christ, The First Sixteen Chapters*, The Ascetical Works, vol. 10 (New York: Benziger Brothers, 1888) 129.

8. Saint-Jure, *The Religious*, vol. 1, 564.

9. Saint-Jure, *The Religious*, vol. 1, 564.

10. Saint-Jure, *A Treatise on the Knowledge and Love of Our Lord Jesus Christ*, vol. 3, 151.

Second, Fenelon uses the terms *innocent and selfish*. God created us to have an innocent and natural love of self, and there is no reason not to designate it with the name self-love. Unfortunately, it has become unregulated in us. "The simple desire of our own happiness, kept in due subordination, is innocent. This desire is natural to us; and is properly denominated the principle of self-love. When the principle of self-love passes its appropriate limit, it becomes selfishness. Self-love is innocent; selfishness is wrong. Selfishness was the sin of the first angel, 'who rested in himself,' as St. Augustine expresses it, instead of referring himself to God."[11] In his pastoral letter about indifference, Fenelon contrasts an innocent desire for salvation with a selfish interest that signifies a mercenary affection for God.[12]

Third, Scaramelli uses the terms *regulated and inordinate*. There is a well-regulated affection whereby we love ourselves and our neighbor, but by self-love he means "that inordinate love which makes us seek our own convenience, our own satisfaction, our own honour and interest, without any regard for God and right season. This kind of self-love is the sworn foe of charity, which it banishes from our hearts."[13]

Fourth, Grou uses the terms *well-directed* and *dishonest*. "It is well-directed love that makes me desire my happiness, and that seeks it in God, as in the source of all perfection and of all felicity ... The sin of self-love consists in viewing nothing honestly, neither happiness nor even God Himself, except in relation to self. It consists in appropriating all to itself, inasmuch as its one end is its own welfare, and it only looks upon the possession of God, and of His love, as a means to this end."[14]

And fifth, Surin contrasts true things with misrepresented things. A *proper and improper* understanding of anything will yield two different viewpoints. In order to make good use of anything in this life we must consider its ordered use, and "all things have two faces, and may be viewed from two different sides; 1st, as they are in themselves, and in the sight of God; 2nd, according to the common opinions of men, and the misrepresentations of self-love. It is then true wisdom to regard them only with relation to God's judgment,

---

11. Fenelon, *Maxims*, article 16.

12. Fenelon, *Pastoral Letter on the Love of God*, 12.

13. Scaramelli, *Guide to the Spiritual Life*, vol. 4, 165-66.

14. Grou, *Meditations Upon the Love of God*, 16.

and to the end for which they were created."[15] In another place, he contrasts a sight that sees under the light of grace with a corrupted sight afflicted by the vices. "If one lacks the courage to root out little defects, and particularly to root out everything having to do with self-love, one leads a dragging life and one remains in one's imperfections; and that is done voluntarily."[16]

These theologians have no problem with a good, innocent, regulated, well-directed, and proper self-love. Their problem is with a bad, selfish, inordinate, dishonest and improper self-love. And perhaps the easiest way to define the latter is to follow Grou when he says this false love of self presents itself as a contender for the love of God. "Nothing better marks the character of self-love, or should make it more hateful to us, than this title: Rival of the love of God ... We can bestow our whole love on but one only of two objects: God or self. To set God above all things, and refer all to Him, is to be actuated by charity ... To refer all things to self, is to be filled with self-love."[17] The self desperately wants to make a faux peace that will compromise between the two loves, but Grou says this can never be because "these two loves are entirely contrary to one another; not only rivals but enemies, disputing the possession of the same heart. No compact can exist between them. They hate, attack, and persecute each other to the death."[18] Things which are opposite cannot be combined, as John of St Samson reminds us. "Two contraries cannot exist together, such as living and dying, living according to self-love and dying (*to it*). Self-love must die and be completely destroyed if the love of God is to rule the soul as its own kingdom."[19] Opposites operate in opposite ways, for opposite purposes, with opposite results, so a choice must be made. Either "we turn all evil into good by bearing it patiently for the love

---

15. Surin, *Foundations of the Spiritual Life*, 57-58.

16. Surin, *Into the Dark Night and Back: The Mystical Writings of Jean-Joseph Surin*, 496.

17. Grou, *The Spiritual Maxims of Pere Grou*, 169.

18. Grou, *The Spiritual Maxims of Pere Grou*, 169.

19. John of St. Samson, *Prayer, Aspiration and* Contemplation (New York: Alba House, 1975) 138-39.

of God," Fenelon says, or "we turn all good into evil when we cleave to it in self-love."[20] Therefore, avoid the illusion of parceling love out, giving God a part or a share. Such apportionment will never be equitable because God is God, and deserving of all love.

God is not so touchy or narcissistic that he cannot endure living without our attention; this is not what Scripture means by the jealousy of God ("He is a holy God; he is a jealous God" (Joshua 24:19)). God's jealousy is rather aroused when Israel fails in her identity as a worship partner: "they moved him to jealousy with their graven images" (Psalm 78:58). We upset the rank of primary and secondary goods whenever we withhold liturgy to God by placing our esteem on something that is not our final end. Even spiritual piety can be corrupted, Grou says, if we liturgize for our own sakes.

> Now, what is self-love? It is that love of ourselves which begins and ends with ourselves, and which has not God for its final end. This self-love intrudes even into spiritual things, when we love virtue, and the gifts of God, and the holiness of God, and God Himself, only for our own sakes, or for the enjoyment we find in these things, or for the advantage we derive from them, in one word, when we set up our own selves as the center and object of our affections.[21]

Love of God is pure only when it is unmixed with love of self; self-love is the great enemy of pure love, and these two cannot exist together. For Grou, "this commandment of loving God with all our hearts absolutely forbids self-love, which makes us love ourselves, without any relation to God, and love all else in relation to ourselves."[22] It is permissible to love ourselves properly, but not permissible if it becomes an act of idolatry whereby we credit ourselves instead of God's grace. The foundation of religion is the admission and avowal of our inability to save ourselves, while self-love, to the contrary, "urges us none the less powerfully to take pride in our feeble efforts, to give ourselves

---

20. Fenelon, *Letters to Men*, 105.

21. Grou, *Manual for Interior Souls*, 328.

22. Grou, *Meditations on the Love of God*, 39.

credit for our virtues."[23] Any virtue we possess is derived from God, and it is self-love's pride to think otherwise. Self-love is an obstacle to God's glory, and must be annihilated for God to receive true liturgy.

One characteristic we should acknowledge in our definition of self-love is its hidden quality ("Our self-love endeavors studiously to hide our intentions from ourselves"[24]) and the theologians of liturgical abnegation are embarrassed by its ingeniousness. Here is Grou's understanding.

> I shall not enter upon the discussion of the species reasonings with which self-love skillfully conceals itself ... One would blush to give ear to it. It assumes the fairest colorings, and the most seductive guise. Its motive is always zeal for God's glory; its aim is the perfection of one's own soul of the spiritual welfare of others. Its true purpose lies hidden in the depths of the heart; it professes other objects which are good and holy, adroitly intermingles them with its views, and deceived by means of the admixture.[25]

This is paradoxical, or at least ironic, since the self-love that shows itself everywhere else tries, in this case, to hide itself from the person it afflicts. It does not like to be observed. Here is how Baker understands it to operate surreptitiously even in people who seem to have a natural kind of devotion.

> Yet even these, whatsoever they appear outwardly in show, are full of self-love, which is the principle of all their actions. If they love quietness, it is because nature takes a contentment in it; and their self-love is more abstruse and more deeply seated in the root of the spirit itself; and therefore ofttimes is hard to be cured because not so easily discovered. Neither indeed is there any hope of remedy, till by prayer they get a light

---

23. Grou, *The School of Jesus Christ*, 129.

24. Grou, *The Spiritual Maxims of Pere Grou*, 65.

25. Grou, *The Spiritual Maxims of Pere Grou*, 178-79.

to discover the said secret self-love, and grace by mortification to subdue it.[26]

It is difficult to cure what is hidden, because the patient might not believe he stands in need of a cure. Excuses abound.

On the one hand, self-love is responsible for hiding itself. Saint-Jure says it is stealthy so that it can get its own way: "self-love can use a thousand artifices to get what it desires, and it is not always easy to know *precisely* what is necessary."[27] The world tempts us from without, but Fenelon says we carry self-love within. "We are sharp, oversensitive, difficult, hard to get along with. It is self-interest which causes all this, but the self-interest screens itself with a hundred fine reasons."[28] Self-love hides itself for the same reason Adam and Eve hid themselves after eating the forbidden fruit, namely, Fenelon says, because

> self-love cannot abide to see itself, the sight would overwhelm it with shame and vexation; and if it catches an accidental glimpse, it seeks some false light which may soften and condone what is so hideous. And thus we always keep up some illusions so long as we retain any self-love. To see ourselves perfectly, self-love must be rooted up, and the love of God reign solely in us, and then the same light which shows our faults would remove them.[29]

On the other hand, we are responsible for hiding self-love from ourselves. Surin observes that for want of examining our intentions we sometimes "feel a repugnance to certain things prescribed to us by obedience, without knowing, or to speak more correctly, choosing to know the cause, so much concealment and disguise do we use with ourselves.

---

26. Baker, *Holy Wisdom*, 207.

27. Saint-Jure, *The Spiritual Man*, 77.

28. Fenelon, *Christian Perfection*, 60.

29. Fenelon, *Letters to Men*, 113.

We find reasons to excuse ourselves, which are nothing but pretences; the true cause is self-love."[30]

It should be further observed that in addition to hiding itself, self-love hides other things. A mirage appears in the desert because the wavy lines refracted by the heat distorts the vision. Self-love creates mirages in our minds when it radiates in a way that refracts our vision of reality. Scaramelli says that when the soul is called upon to give judgment about its own affairs, this "self-love ... inclines it to choose what is advantageous and agreeable rather than to right conduct."[31] Fenelon knows that self-love hides true motivations, frequently persuading us "that we are acting for conscience' sake, when it is itself the mainspring of our determination."[32] Unwilling to admit our status in nothingness, Boudon says we accept "a vicious self-love, hidden even from ourselves, [and] are always desiring to be successful in whatever we undertake!"[33] Thanks be to God, we shall soon see that he has his own ways of dealing with this self-flattering mirage.

The more subtle and imperceptible the self-love, the greater the number of consequences it spawns and the greater the number of vices it conceals, until, says de Caussade, "from this poisonous root grows an infinite number of imperfections of which you are scarcely conscious; useless self-examinations, still more useless self-complacency, idle fears, fruitless desires, frivolous little hopes, suspicions unfavorable to your neighbor, little jokes at her expense, and airs full of self-love."[34] The opaque lens of self-love limits what Surin considers a truthful perception of God, neighbor, reality, and self, because "one who thinks only of himself, who loves himself alone, is always in darkness, and cannot, in this state, perceive the truth, because he sees all things in the false colors with which self-love depicts them to his imagination, as when we look through a blackened glass, all that we see appears dark."[35] And if a man thinks he has succeeded in attaining

---

30. Surin, *Foundations of the Spiritual Life*, 95-96.

31. Scaramelli, *Guide to the Spiritual Life*, vol. 3, 52.

32. Fenelon, *Letters to Men*, 27.

33. Boudon, *The Hidden Life of Jesus*, 53.

34. De Caussade, *Abandonment to Divine Providence*, 264.

35. Surin, *Foundations of the Spiritual Life*, 77-78.

pure love, he should doubt himself with salutary distrust. De Castaniza believes a person should have a healthy distrust of himself, believing himself "to be yet possessed with self-love, though covertly; or at least deem that his love of God is not so pure as is here required; and therefore, he must diligently search his interior."[36] Boudon says even a fall from grace in one battle can often serve the ultimate victory in the war. "We must be greatly on our guard against a secret self-reliance, which is sometimes imperceptible to ourselves; it appears to us that when we have gone through certain devotional exercises the victory is gained, and then our Lord permits us to fall grievously."[37]

Curiously, this is all the more true as spirituality increases. Like the risk of being proud of our humility, there is a risk of piety increasing our self-love. This is one of the many mysteries of iniquity. Grou has noticed it. "The proud soul will ... feed on the heroic sentiments which inspire her with an equal share of esteem for self and contempt for others."[38] Surin fears that our best devotion, our most upright intention, our strongest efforts to lift ourselves up to God will become mingled with a little self-love, resulting in an internal weight and suffering. When we find ourselves weary, tired, and dissatisfied "this was caused, and is almost invariably caused, by a secret self-seeking. We think we have the best intention possible; we could swear that in the undertaking we have in hand, we regard God Alone; and yet we are sad, and feel a certain distaste which troubles our peace of mind. This is to be attributed only to this unregulated self-love."[39]

The serpent of self-love was once visible coiled upon the tree of knowledge, but he is now invisible to us, coiled upon the branches of the new tree of paradise God has planted in hearts by baptism. We need Christ as a new St. George. De Caussade says, "oh, God! how subtle is this wretched self-love! It turns and twists like a serpent, and is only too successful in preserving its life in the midst of the most fearful deaths ... Have a horror of this accursed self-love, but learn that, in spite of all your efforts it will not die completely

---

36. De Castaniza, *Spiritual Conflict and Conquest*, 338.

37. Boudon, *Devotion to 9 Choirs*, 81.

38. Grou, *The Interior of Jesus and Mary*, vol. 1, 69.

39. Surin, *Foundations of the Spiritual Life*, 78.

and radically until the last moment of your life."[40] Our own efforts at spirituality will not slay this dragon, he adds. In fact, we must embrace nothingness as the condition for even discovering it. You must "believe that you do nothing for God, and that the little you try to do is spoilt by an admixture of self-love, is nothing but the truth ... However, this truth is so shrouded in darkness for us, so completely hidden in the folds of our self-love, that we cannot be too grateful to God when He is pleased to allow us to grasp it."[41] But take heart. Summon fortitude, Saint-Jure commands. Even if this serpent's death will come only in the next world, our duty in the meantime is obvious.

> It will only be in the next world, where God will accomplish the promise he made by Isaias: "Behold, here I have created new heavens and a new earth." There He will give to man a true soul, a celestial and divine subsistence, and a body, originally formed out of the earth, elevated to the highest purity; but all that we can or ought to do, is to cultivate this earth, to cut and root up the weeds, without expecting to be able to destroy its natural disposition to sin, and to absolutely *kill* self-love. It is in this medium degree, we must understand all that has been said here regarding the annihilation and abnegation of ourselves.[42]

If self-love frets over its upcoming death, use meditation on death to spiritual advantage! De Bergamo says "our self-love is wounded at the thought that we must soon die, and when we least expect it, and that with death everything comes to an end for us in this world; but at the same time this reflection weakens and humbles our self-love."[43]

If we like, we could change the metaphor from dragon-slaying to garden-pruning, to discover that abnegation is an act done not only once, but repeatedly. De Sales likes to point this out, and here are a number of passages.

---

40. De Caussade, *Abandonment to Divine Providence*, 183.

41. De Caussade, *Abandonment to Divine Providence*, 238.

42. Saint-Jure, *The Religious*, vol. 1, 568.

43. De Bergamo, *Humility of Heart*, 70.

To renounce ourselves is simply to purify ourselves from everything that
is done through the instinct of self-love, which, so long as we are in
this mortal life, will not fail to produce off-shoots, which should be
immediately cut away, just as we do with the vine.

And as it is not sufficient to trim the vine once a year, but it must be cut at
one time and at another stripped of its leaves, so that the vine-dresser must
have the pruning-hook continually ready to cut off the useless shoots; in
the same way we must deal with our imperfections.[44]

How long will self-love require the pruning hook? It "can be mortified in us, but still it
never dies; indeed, from time to time and on different occasions, it produces shoots in us,
which show that though cut off it is not rooted out."[45] The weed control must continue
our whole life long. "We must make two equally firm resolutions: one, to be ready to see
weeds growing in our garden; the other, to have the courage to see them pulled up, and
to pull them up ourselves, for our self-love, which produces these miseries, will never die
while we live."[46] God might allow some respite, for short times, but "we must be in no
way surprised to find self-love in us, for it never leaves us. It sleeps sometimes, like a fox,
then all of a sudden leaps on the chickens; wherefore we must constantly keep watch on
it, and patiently and very quietly defend ourselves from it. But if sometimes it wounds us,
we are healed by on saying what it has made us say and disavowing what it has made us
do."[47]

---

44. De Sales, *Mystical Flora*, 18.

45. De Sales, *Letters to Persons in the World*, 345.

46. De Sales, *The Spiritual Conferences*, 162.

47. De Sales, *Letters to Persons in the World*, 346-47.

To cure a disease, a doctor needs a chart of its symptoms. In order to combat self-love, spiritual theologians need the signs of its presence. Here is a collection of tersely worded signs of self-love.

- Libermann: "One of the most dangerous fruits of self-love is confidence in oneself and presumption."[48]

- Fenelon: "What is more delicious to a delicate self-love, than to hear itself applauded for not being self-love?[48]

- Grou: "Self-love intensely dreads obscurity, it is tenacious of being seen, known, and esteemed."[48]

- De Sales: "Discouragement is a mark of excessive love of self and of zeal unaccompanied by knowledge."[48]

- De Bergamo: "My great agitation is an evident proof which ought to convince me that my self-love is great and dominant and powerful within me, and is the tyrant which torments and gives me no peace."[48]

- De Sales: "Complain as little as possible of your wrongs ... self-love always magnifies our injuries."[48]

- And, de Caussade: "The signs of a self-seeking nature are the confusion, haste, and anxiety of a self-love that is perpetually eager, anxious, and impetuous."[48]

---

48. Libermann, *Letters to Clergy & Religious,* Spiritan Series 7, Vol. 3, 294.

48. Fenelon, *Spiritual Progress,* 31.

48. Grou, *The Spiritual Maxims of Pere Grou,* 180.

48. Camus, *The Spirit of St. Francis de Sales,* 443.

48. De Bergamo, *Humility of Heart,* 44.

48. De Sales, *Introduction to the Devout Life,* 93-94.

48. De Caussade, *Abandonment to Divine Providence,* 152.

If such symptoms appear in your spiritual life, there is good reason to think it suffers the sickness of self-love.

There are lengthier, more analytical observations of how self-love manifests itself because it has, after all, been a point of examination since the beginning of Christian theology. Saint-Jure traces it back to St. Paul.

> "Men," says St. Paul, "are enamored of themselves." And what is the
> consequence of this? "They are," he continues, "full of concupiscence,
> of self-esteem, ambition and pride; they are blasphemers, disobedient
> to their parents, ungrateful, wicked, unfriendly, quarrelsome, and are
> calumniators; there is no sensual pleasure after which they do not run;
> they are destitute of sweetness and patience; they are rude and savage
> natures, traitors, full of vanity; they love their satisfaction much more
> than God; hypocrites! they seek after the reputation of virtue, without
> wishing to practice virtue, and under the fine exterior of apparent piety,
> they are really impious."[55]

Gay calls the triple concupiscence "the daughter, and at the same time the mother, of sin."[56]

Self-love stands at the end of some chains and at the beginning of others. Go upstream from anger or impatience and discover self-love at the headwaters: Boudon says self-interest sets everything in motion, "which causes division between nearest relatives, and is the source of all disputes and all law-suits, of sadness, and weariness, and disquietude, of wars between States, of eagerness in all transactions, of disturbance in all consciences, in fine, of all the miseries we see in this wretched life."[57] Go downstream and discover self-love has poisoned everything it touches. Libermann asks for self-examination. "Examine what in you causes that impatience; you will find that it is self-love. Examine the sort of movement of self-love you have. It may be a certain

---

55. Saint-Jure, *The Religious*, vol. 1, 567.

56. Gay, *The Christian Life and Virtues*, vol. 1, 302.

57. Boudon, *Devotion to Nine Choirs of Angels*, 191.

sensitiveness and self-pity; your imagination is aroused; you become unyielding and stern and your mind indulges in reasonings."[58] But most effects of self-love share an anxiety and restlessness that Bona describes thus:

> He who nurtures this venom within his vitals is displeasing to himself, and driven from his normal state of mind by deceptive tricks, as it were, roams about inconstant, and repeatedly changing business, pursuits and pleasures, never finds rest; through senselessness he understands not salutary admonitions, pines away with continual cares, odious to all, intolerable to himself; with sacrilegious perversity he diverts right intention from God to himself, and though deceived by a miserable error he may seem to himself to do things for God, still, in reality he regards only himself, seeks only himself, and in a manner disputes with God himself for the supremacy of end.[59]

Besides signs as obvious as the ones I have listed above, there are other signs of self-love not so easily detected, because they are slighter faults, and often escape the eye of even spiritual persons, Scaramelli says.

> As, for instance, to eat, drink, take rest and recreation; to devote ourselves to occupations suitable to our condition, not out of the virtuous motive of their fitness, and still less from the hallowed purpose of doing God's will, but only to gratify ourselves by feeling complacency in our own actions; to listen with pleasure to our own praises; to be put out when anything unfavourable is said of us; to resent offences; to chafe under admonition; to be slow to forgive, at least heartily; to indulge personal attachments, not indeed such as imply any dangerous affection, but loving with too much partiality and fondness; to omit good works out of human respect; to give way to over-refinement in dress, lodgings,

---

58. Libermann, *Letters to People in the World,* Spiritan Series 6, Vol. 2, 220.

59. Bona, *A Treatise of Spiritual Life*, 259.

furniture, and in a thousand other ways; so that there is no action, not only indifferent, but even holy, which is not tainted in some measure by self-love, owing to some wrong attachment of the heart.[60]

These are all often named together under the category of *worldliness*. By "worldly things" Eudes means "everything the world values, loves and seeks so ardently, that is, the honors and praises of others, vain pleasures and satisfactions, wealth and temporal comforts, friendships and affections based on flesh and blood and on self-love and self-interest."[61]

Worldliness offers false goods, and from the theologians I will name three. First among the false goods the world offers is pleasure and self comfort. It is a pincer movement of temptation: the world without, and tenderness toward self within. When worldliness and self-love unite, the former gives the latter much to feed upon. According to Baker, "when we seek pleasure and riches, &c. to ourselves, the love that we bear unto them is indeed self-love, because it is only for our own sakes that we love them, to give satisfaction to our natural desires."[62] According to de Granada, the slightest burst upon the sensible faculties can make the wicked man turn from God to the world for happiness. "For self-love, the cause of all these desires, having got so much power over them, and they placing all their happiness in earthly riches and pleasures, it is impossible they should not, with greediness, hunger and thirst after those things on which they imagine all their happiness depends."[63] According to Saint-Jure, this all enervates the strength of a person, sapping virtue of its power until a "man seeks to gratify his inclinations in eating and drinking, apparel, the arrangement of his chamber and in everything; he is very tender of himself, he fears hunger, thirst, heat, cold; he complains of the least inconvenience. This vice inclines

---

60. Scaramelli, *Guide to the Spiritual Life*, vol. 4, 170-71.

61. Eudes, *The Life and Kingdom of Jesus in Christian Souls*, in *Berulle and the French School*, 304.

62. Baker, *Holy Wisdom*, 245.

63. De Granada, *The Sinner's Guide*, 161.

the body and soul to what is contrary to chastity, because it excites them to seek their pleasure."[64] Quarre observes that "self-love draws us to the Creature, and involves us in a multiplicity"[65] and Brother Lawrence agrees that love of self exists when we surround ourselves with things of sense, which is why we turn from things created, namely, to find our joy, for a single moment, in the Creator. "What offering is there more acceptable to God than thus throughout the day to quit the things of outward sense, and to withdraw to worship Him within the secret places of the soul? Besides by doing so we destroy the love of self, which can subsist only among the things of sense."[66]

Second among the false goods the world offers self-love is flattery and vain honor. Self-love is unbridled because pride makes us regard everything in relation to ourselves. Self-love loves to be praised! Everyone notices this; let us let Surin describe it.

> A man who has to speak in public, or who loves to be applauded, is always in danger of drawing down vexation on himself; for if he does not succeed, or another succeeds better than he, it causes him much sorrow ... It is certain then that they who seek themselves find themselves at length, but to their own harm; and nothing torments them more than their own vanity. How unhappy are the ambitious, the avaricious, the voluptuous! They have always some wound in the soul, some bitterness in the heart; for if they succeed once, they fail a hundred times.[67]

This is a common weakness, and produces a desire to speak much, which Baker calls "much and willing speaking." It is "the effect of tepidity, self-love, and pride. For

---

64. Saint-Jure, *A Treatise on the Knowledge and Love of Our Lord Jesus Christ*, vol. 2, 383.

65. Quarre, *A Spiritual Treasure*, 320

66. Brother Lawrence, *The Spiritual Maxims of Brother Lawrence* (Philadelphia: The Griffith and Rowland Press, 1907) 16.

67. Surin, *Foundations of the Spiritual Life*, 117-18.

commonly it flows from an opinion that we can speak well, and consequently out of a desire of gaining estimation from others, by showing our wits and abilities."[68]

The proper term for this is flattery, not in the innocent sense of paying compliments but in the original sense of dishonest cajolement. It is empty praise. Flattery increases our vanity because self-love is fed by praise. Libermann knows that "men contribute to our vanity by praising us, revealing their high opinion of us and expressing their affection. This is very harmful, for it prompts us to esteem ourselves and make us acquire habits of self-love."[69] The vanity within runs parallel to a vanity without. De Caussade knows that "a subtle self-love feeds on these vanities of the spirit, in the way that worldly pride is satisfied with the beauties of the body."[70] Yet self-love finds it pleasant. Fenelon asks, "what is there sweeter and more flattering to a sensitive and delicate self-love than seeing itself praised as though it were not self-love? ... This moderation and this self-detachment, which would be the death of our nature if it were a real and effective sentiment, becomes, on the contrary, a more subtle and imperceptible food for a pride."[71] Such flattery disguises poison as nutritious, and we secretly hope the flattery is true. De Bergamo wonders, "when you hear yourself praised, what precautions do you take? Self-love is quick to mingle some grain of its own incense with that which it receives from others. I mean by this that through the corruption of our nature we are very ready to approve these praises as if they were truly and justly due to us, and to flatter ourselves with vainglory."[72] Grou knows that a secretly aided self-love lets its guard down against the praises of others. "It spurs us on ardently to desire them, to seek for them, and to court them with a foolish vanity, and to receive them with as much confidence, as if they came from the mouth of truth itself."[73]

---

68. Baker, *Holy Wisdom*, 231.

69. Libermann, *Letters to People in the World,* Spiritan Series 6, Vol. 2, 213.

70. De Caussade, *Abandonment to Divine Providence*, 184.

71. Fenelon, *Christian Perfection*, 179.

72. De Bergamo, *Humility of Heart*, 180.

73. Grou, *Morality Extracted from the Confessions of Saint Austin*, vol. 2, 442.

Even those in religious life must take special caution over this, lest even their life under religious vows be lived in a merely natural way. Lallemant sees these religious displaying nothing of the gifts of the Holy Spirit, but rather living a life wholly natural. "When they are blamed or disobliged, they shew their resentment at it; they exhibit exhibit so much eagerness for the praises, the esteem, and the applauses of the world; they take so much pleasure in them, and are so fond of their own comfort, and seek it so carefully, as well as everything that flatters self-love."[74]

Third among the false goods the world offers self-love is what Rodriguez calls "an infinity of excuses; it ... teaches us how to lessen our own faults."[75] As a result, flattery breaks out from its interior incubation and causes an antagonistic jealousy toward our neighbor. Grou's careful observation of human nature sees evidence that self-love is offended whenever it feels the neighbor is superior to oneself.

> Every good quality possessed by our neighbour offends our self-love,
> unless we think we see something better in our selves; and this same
> self-love is flattered by our neighbour's defects, as though we were the
> more admirable because he was less so. We can forgive him any description
> of merit as long as we think it inferior to our own, and the public shares
> our opinion; but if we cannot hide his superiority to ourselves, and his
> reputation equals or excels our own we are filled with jealousy.[76]

Grou concludes that strife between persons is therefore a result of self-love. Its cause "is our essentially exclusive self-love, which claims everything for ourselves, gives only in order to receive more in return, and regards our neighbour as an enemy who disputes our rights and seizes for himself the things that we think are only ours. In the depths of our heart we have no regard for anyone but ourselves, and we base this regard on contempt

---

74. Lallemant, *The Spiritual Doctrine of Father Louis Lallemant, ed. Faber*, 148.

75. Rodriguez, *The Practice of Christian and Religious Perfection*, vol. 1, 207.

76. Grou, *The School of Jesus Christ*, 397.

for others."[77] An inverse relationship is established whereby we can only rise as he falls. We laud ourselves by looking with contempt on another, and, to Grou, that means the termination of charity.

> As long as there remains in us any vestige of self-love, we can never love our brothers, as Jesus Christ has commanded us to love them. Self-love concentrates us on ourselves, and makes us exclusive; it makes us look upon our neighbor as a stranger ... More than this, this same self-love is the cause of a thousand sins against charity. It makes us touchy, ready to take offense, ill-tempered, suspicious, severe, exacting as to what we think are our rights, easily offended: it keeps alive in our hearts a certain malignity, a secret joy at the little mortifications which happened to our neighbor ... It nourishes our readiness to criticize, the unjust partiality of our words and actions, are disliked to certain persons, our ill-feelings, or bitterness against them, and a thousand other imperfections most prejudicial to charity.[78]

Since increased self-regard is our objective, we necessarily adopt an attitude of criticism of our neighbor. "We imagine that it is a good thing to make others realize how wrong they were and how far they went out of bounds,"[79] Libermann says, but we are only flattering our own self-love under the pretense of correcting another. Self-love points out the failure of another in order to highlight one's own success. That, says Grou, is why self-love is ever occupied in comparisons:

> exulting in superiority, or vexed and annoyed if forced to yield to others. It blames all conduct but its own; its own way of prayer must be the best; or else it envies souls which it supposes to be more advanced and more favoured of God. It notes the faults of others, criticises actions, judges and

---

77. Grou, *The School of Jesus Christ*, 32.

78. Grou, *Manual for Interior Souls*, 143-44.

79. Libermann, *Letters to Clergy & Religious,* Spiritan Series 7, Vol. 3, 223.

condemns motives, and ever whispers to itself; "I would not have acted thus; I would not have spoken thus."[80]

Criticism is easier and more comfortable because it directs our gaze outwardly, and not inwardly. "When it is a question of discovering self-love in others we show great sagacity; but we shut our eyes to our own," and Grou finds hardly anyone who "is willing to face self-knowledge; and the obstacle is self-love, which shrinks from the sight of its own deformity."[81]

Our natural needs and wants, good in themselves and in their originally created state, can be preyed upon by self-love, and misdirected. Nature seeks its own interest – that is the law written in it for its survival – but mutual love requires overcoming exclusive self-regard. That is why self-love sulks. "It is pained," says Libermann, "grows angry and discouraged, as soon as anything happens that is not perfectly suited to its taste or wishes, or when men think or act differently from what is expected of them. Self-love always condemns others; it is distrustful, easily suspects evil, and never judges itself."[82] We can only go beyond our nature, out of ourselves, if we combat what Surin calls the "too merely natural love which enters every where, and disguises itself by a thousand artifices."[83] Boudon sees the idolatrous coloring of self-love: "the self-love of the creature is so preposterous and so extravagant that it even goes the length of wishing to be preferred before God Himself."[84]

As ruinous as the relationship with our neighbor can become, even more serious is the ruin of our relationship with God caused by the infection of self-love. Sin threw Adam's whole nature into disorder, and Grou spends a good deal of time analyzing this. It has affected each faculty: "it obscured his intelligence, inclined his will towards evil ... subjected him to the senses ... lit within him the fires of desire ... inspired in him the

---

80. Grou, *The Spiritual Maxims of Pere Grou*, 175.

81. Grou, *The School of Jesus Christ*, 75.

82. Libermann, *Letters to Clergy & Religious*, Spiritan Series 8, Vol. 4, 172.

83. Surin, *Foundations of the Spiritual Life*, 181-82.

84. Boudon, *The Hidden Life of Jesus*, 19.

detestable quality of pride, which causes every form of submission and dependence to be hateful to him."[85] Unbridled self-love made Adam "regard everything in relation to himself, concentrate all his thoughts on self, and love nothing except for his own sake; thus turning himself into a sort of god, and assuming divine rights while completely disregarding the supreme love that he owes to God."[86] In pride man reconstructs himself as his own deity. How strange! Fallen man developed a repugnance for the most delightful of all duties, namely, liturgizing God. The degradation must be deep, supposes Grou, "when we find it a matter of so much difficulty to love God with our whole heart!"[87] And why? Because self-love "persuades us that our interests are safe only so long as we have them in our own hands. We cannot make up our minds to trust them to God, to look on Him as our Father, and to believe in His love."[88] Now the most just, most sacred, most attractive and delightful of all duties – liturgizing God – creates an antagonistic opposition arising from the fact that our inordinate love for ourselves is directly opposed to the love we owe to God. How foolish! "As if we could possibly have any true interests different from His, and as if, supposing that were possible, we ought not to sacrifice our own to His!"[89]

The devil obviously has his hand in this situation. He allies himself with the world, our nature, and our self-love, increasing the force of them all. Crasset looks both inside and outside: "within us we have self-love, which always seeks sensible pleasure; without us, the Evil One, who tempts us; the world, which attracts us; objects which flatter us; occasions which encompass us."[90] Our passions and temptations arise from this matrix, and the whole network must be resisted, counsels Grou. " "It is the devil, it is our self-love,

---

85. Grou, *The School of Jesus Christ*, 24.

86. Grou, *The School of Jesus Christ*, 24.

87. Grou, *The Interior of Jesus and Mary*, vol. 1, 284.

88. Grou, *The Spiritual Maxims of Pere Grou*, 109.

89. Grou, *The School of Jesus Christ*, 30.

90. De Sales & Crasset, *Secret of Sanctity*, 125.

it is our nature, always so eager for consolation, that suggests these thoughts to us,"[91] nevertheless, the devil has no power except what we cede to him. Camus writes a book of encouragement for the person troubled by temptation, titled *A Spiritual Combat*. He compares Satan to a mastiff "which barks only at strangers, never at those of the same family,"[92] so it is a good sign if he yaps at you when you pass by. "All the temptations which do not please, cannot hurt,"[93] because Christ so weakened the devil "that he can gain no advantage against us but by our own disloyalty and dastardliness: all the feelings which he can raise up in us, not being able to form any sin at all without our consent.."[94] This leads Camus to an unlikely comparison. "Like as a Maide can never be married while she saith, No, because it is the consent that ties the knot of marriage; so temptation can never cast a soul into sin, and by sin, marry her to death and hell, till free-will yield itself up to so loose a disloyalty as to forsake the Creator for the Creature, and the living fountain for a dry Cistern."[95]

We have seen that self-love produces envy, and envy is the premier mark of the devil's pride. It caused his conflict with God, and will cause the same conflict within us if we allow it to grow. So Eudes advises, "banish every shadow of self-love, pride, ambition or vanity. Have no other thought than to please God and to save souls. Satan was damned because he envied God's glory and sought to become like unto Him."[96] *Martyria* means "witness," one faces a choice between being a divine witness of the love of God, or a diabolical witness to the devil's tyranny. Choose carefully which you love the more, says Eudes. "If you live under the tyranny of sin, you will be a martyr to your self-love and your passions, and

---

91. Grou, *Manual for Interior Souls*, 267.

92. Camus, *A Spiritual Combat*, 127.

93. Camus, *A Spiritual Combat*, 18

94. Camus, *A Spiritual Combat* 41

95. Camus, *A Spiritual Combat*, 211

96. Eudes, *The Priest*, 77.

consequently a martyr of the devil. But if you desire to be a martyr of Jesus Christ, you must strive to live in the spirit of martyrdom."[97]

The devil has twin objectives in stirring up self-love. On the one hand, he wants to keep a soul from even beginning its ascent to God. A tool in his arsenal for this is a fear that paralyzes. Such fear must be driven away, de Caussade almost shouts. "Salutary fear causes neither disturbance, uneasiness, nor discouragement. [But] if fear produce contrary effects you must drive it away, and not allow it to take possession of you, as in this case it comes either from the devil, or your own self-love."[98] On the other hand, the devil wishes to nullify whatever spiritual progress the soul has made, or the virtues that have been developed. Crafty as he is, the devil can turn even our progress to his advantage, says Baker. "The devil can be content, yea will suggest the exercise of the greatest virtues to hearts which he knows will intend only the satisfaction of natural pride, or the interests of self-love, in them."[99] Then our deceitful enemy, as de Castaniza calls him, "tempts us also by those very virtues which we have acquired, and casts them, as it were stumbling-blocks, in our way, to occasion our ruin. To this end he strives to make us please and delight ourselves in them, that being puffed-up in our self-conceits, we may fall afterwards into the dangerous precipice of pride."[100] Having made himself into an antagonist of God, the devil becomes our antagonist as well. Grou wants us to remember that the devil "is our enemy as well as God's. He desires our ruin; but still more to prevent us from glorifying God by our devotion."[101]

The devil is a deceiver, so it goes without saying that he tricks us into efforts that lead not to true devotion, but to a counterfeit piety. This opponent of God also opposes the liturgy of God, which seeks the sanctification of man and the glorification of God. Self-love seeks to please itself, not God, and can evern be busy with self while in the midst of prayer and the most beautiful reflections. Boudon sorrows: "Oh, how much self-love

---

97. Eudes, *The Life and the Kingdom of Jesus in Christian Souls*, 96.

98. De Caussade, *Abandonment to Divine Providence*, 155.

99. Baker, *Holy Wisdom*, 17.

100. De Castaniza, *Spiritual Conflict and Conquest*, 120-21.

101. Grou, *Self Consecration*, 85-86.

is mingled with the most pious conversations, associations for good works, spiritual friendships and intimacies! Oh, how much gratification does nature find in all these!"[102] There are specific dangers to pious souls, and they warrant their own chapter.

102. Boudon, *The Hidden Life of Jesus*, 172.

THREE DANGERS OF SELF TO PIOUS SOULS

Before we begin, let me call to mind an observation these theologians repeatedly make, namely, that it is easier to talk about the self than overcoming the self.

- We must not reason with [self-love], for it feeds and grows fat on arguments.[1] (Alacoque)

- Self-love easily flatters itself that it has attained the attitudes which it has admired in books.[2] (Fenelon)

- This is something we shall always find among the learned – even those well-versed in sacred science – when they are affected by some passion, and do not seek diligently to overcome their self-love. This self-love is often shocked when required to do things which ought to help towards their salvation or sanctification.[3] (Libermann)

- Try to discuss little, but to do a great deal. If one does not take care, one's whole life slips away in theorising, and we want a second career for practice. There is always a risk lest we fancy ourselves to have advanced in proportion

---

1. Alacoque, *Spiritual Letters,* letter 90, Kindle edition.

2. Fenelon, *Letters to Men*, 94.

3. Libermann, *Jesus Through Jewish Eyes*, vol. 2, 120.

4. Fenelon, *Letters to Men*, 35.

to our theories about perfection; whereas all such grand ideas, so far from really promoting self-mortification, do but tends to foster the old Adam in us through self-confidence.[4] (Fenelon)

- What do you expect? That He should work miracles to convince you? No miracle would conquer this irresolution of a self-love which fears to be sacrificed. What do you want? Never-ending arguments, while all the time you know in your conscience what God's claims are? Arguments will never heal the wound in your heart.[5] (Fenelon)

It seems wise to bear these words in mind as I begin writing this chapter, and you begin reading it.

I will divide the following material into three parts. First, the false effort that self produces; second, the false piety that self produces; and third, contrast this to true piety.

First, false effort produces false piety. We identify false effort from true effort by discerning the alternative between constructing our own piety or accepting the three theological virtues. In other words, we face a choice between faith in God and autonomy of self, between hope in God and self-reliance, and between love of God and love of self. This choice was the test failed in the garden, and it is the same test we face in purifying our devotion. "In truth," de Lombez admits, there is "a great fund of self-love hidden under this veil of devotion. We are quite troubled at having so little fervor, because we had the presumption to believe we could attain it by our own strength."[6] Shall we live by grace? Why would anyone avoid grace? Because it threatens our control. About such a prospect Boudon thinks "we ought to have a horror ... lest self-love should mingle anything of its own with works composed even in compliance with a movement of grace."[7] That is why

---

4. Fenelon, *Letters to Men*, 35.

5. Fenelon, *Letters to Men*, 13.

6. De Lombez, *A Treatise on Interior Peace*, 105.

7. Boudon, *The Hidden Life of Jesus*, 15.

de Castinza thinks a beginner will "make choice of such exercises as are most pleasing to themselves, rather than most profitable unto their souls."[8]

Self seeks control, so overcoming self requires abandoning control, otherwise called patience. Relax in the hand of God, Libermann says, and do not "be over-eager or strain after piety. Such straining is usually the result of self-love or vanity or springs from the natural satisfaction we get from piety. Accept from God whatever He gives you and do not fail to profit by it."[9] Eagerness betrays self-control, self-direction, and self-determined ends, so Boudon says, "too much eagerness to attain perfection is a hurtful temptation, for we often desire it from self-love. Our pride makes us wish to see ourselves speedily perfect, and leads us to be astonished when we fall, which is all that of ourselves we can do."[10] The soul should seek God, not seek herself, even if in God.

In short, self-love is only overcome by self-abnegation, and a test of purity of love is the acceptance of mortification. Because self-love easily masquerades, a person might talk a great deal about abnegation, but want no part of annihilation and nothingness, as John of St Samson describes.

> Some souls in this group are by nature inclined to seek themselves when they experience a sensible desire for God, to speak to him and love him. In this they are only seeking their own interests, and not, as they think, God's interests. With the strength and facility that this inclination gives them, they are able to talk to God all day long. But it is without fruit, because they do not leave their senses and natural desires. Thus they satisfy only themselves, not God. They abound in affective conversations which are accompanied by certain natural delights. But when it is a question of really dying to themselves, as for example, when they are hurt by others either intentionally or unintentionally, they want no part of it ... Everything they do is only a product of their self-love.[11]

---

8. De Castaniza, *Spiritual Conflict and Conquest*, 34.

9. Libermann, *Letters to Religious Sisters and Aspirants,* Spiritan Series 5, vol. 1, 36.

10. Boudon, *Devotion to Nine Angels*, 86.

11. John of St. Samson, *Prayer, Aspiration and Contemplation*, 46.

Self can take on the colors of holiness like a spiritual chameleon, but taking personal advantage of God's blessings to feed our self-love is Pharisaism, according to Leen. "It would be an error to think that Pharisaism was merely a passing phase or an accidental product of the Jewish religion. It is of all times, for it springs from a permanent tendency of fallen human nature. In pious persons who are proud and self-seeking, there is always an instinct to strike a compromise between the demands of God and of self."[12] Malaval admits that "it is not always from humility that we refuse the favors of Heaven; it is sometimes from pride, not wishing to give up our own way. It is also very often from cowardice and pusillanimity."[13]

Alas, there is nothing that cannot be corrupted by pride – even humility, says de Bergamo, which is its polar opposite. "Humility is also so fragile that it is easily tainted by the love of praise, by a word or thought of self-esteem, by vainglory or self-love."[14] Even mortification, says Fenelon, which should starve it: "the hardest of all penances is humiliation of the inner mind; it implies a ceasing to bear and believe in self; it implies a meek submission to God's minister; it is that poverty of spirit which, according to Jesus Christ, makes a man blessed. Without it one can turn even mortification into food for self-love."[15] Even grace, says Fenelon, which should purify it: "self-love is fed, not merely by humiliations and austerities, by fervent prayer and mortification, but even by the fullest self-renunciation and utter sacrifice."[16] This is a very deceptive road, indeed.

One reaction is to be too hard on ourselves, another reaction is to be too easy on ourselves. The former is scrupulosity, the latter is softness. "Scrupulous persons imagine their love for God is great, while yet they have many hesitations in His service which seemed more the product of self-love," observes de Lombez. "So much delicacy in their way of thinking, and measured exactness of manner, are very striking characteristics of

---

12. Leen, *True Vine and its Branches,* 194.

13. Malaval, *A Simple Method of Raising the Soul to Contemplation,* 167.

14. De Bergamo, *Humility of Heart,* 31.

15. Fenelon, *Letters to Men,* 232.

16. Fenelon, *Letters to Women,* 269.

vanity and often proceed from no other source."[17] Jenks says a productive scrupulosity does exist, whereby the experience of weakness humbles the person, but he warns to be beware of a sinful scrupulosity. The latter is a fruit of self-love, and he lists the fears such persons have: that confessions are never exact, that they do not love God above all things, that they never do sufficient penance for their sins, that they are not in a state of grace, or in the number of God's elect.[18] "The true and proper cause of our being proud and wilful in our scruples, are the esteem of our judgment, and the love of our liberty."[19] Overcoming this requires careful self-examination, because de Bergamo knows "self-love is cunning, and knows how to work secretly ... Examine yourself, and you will probably find that the true reason of your scruples lies in your self-love, that is, in your pride."[20] Dalgairns puts it forcefully: scrupulous persons are those "who dispense themselves from fighting against their most real sins by occupying themselves with imaginary ones."[21]

The latter reaction is softness, which denies God's justice. Self-love prefers a sort of holiness that is quiet, comfortable, and easy-going, acquired quickly and cheaply, as if to be had merely for the wishing. Grou calls this an empty phantom of holiness, that is, "wishing to be holy without taking any steps to become so. Therefore it is soft, indolent, lazy, full of unfruitful desires, impatient, repelled by the slightest difficulties, weary and exhausted as soon as the first step has been taken. No mention must be made of steep ascents; self-love requires a road either level or of easy acclivity."[22] If few results are seen of the workings of grace, Bossuet says the explanation is that "we weaken the effect of the grace by our own softness and self-indulgence. There is a species of repentance so feeble

---

17. De Lombez, *A Treatise on Interior Peace*, 9.

18. Sylvester Jenks, *The Blind Obedience of a Humble Penitent: The Best Cure for Scruples* (London: Burns Oates and Washbourne, 1926) 90 ff.

19. Jenks, *The Blind Obedience of a Humble Penitent*, 4.

20. De Bergamo, *Humility of Heart*, 151 and 159.

21. John Dalgairns, *The Holy Communion, its Philosophy, Theology, and Practice* (New York: the Catholic Publication House, 1868) 291.

22. Grou, *The Spiritual Maxims of Pere Grou*, 174.

and so languid that it throws no energy into any of its purposes of amendment ... Such is the condition of our nature that well-doing must of necessity cost us something."[23]

On the one hand, Fenelon notices that self-love wants to hide because "self-love cannot endure to see itself; it would die of shame and vexation! If by chance it gets a glimpse, it at once places itself in some artificial light, so as to soften the full hideousness and find some comfort."[24] On the other hand, Boudon says the servant of God, De Renty, noticed that self-love wants to be seen, because he was convinced

> that the greater proportion of our evils proceeds from our taking pleasure in seeing and being seen; ... that what sullies the purity of acts of piety is that self-love desires to have them known and observed; that we always exhibit ourselves in the best light, and hide our defects and the reverse of the picture; that our whole exterior is so studied, that our interior is often more occupied therewith than with God; and that there are few persons who do not care about the vain regard of creatures either in a passive or in an active way. This is not the case in the hidden life; they who really lead this life say God Only, and say it truly.[25]

It is a melancholic sight that when persons of piety are noticed by the world, they perform many good works, but when the esteem of the world is wanting, pious persons lose all desire to work. It is a melancholic sight to watch persons of piety perform many good works when they are noticed by the world, but losing all power of working when the esteem of others is wanting. "Oh, how pitiable to be always wishing to see and be seen!"[26]

Lallemant laments a virtue practiced without the prior purification of our interior, because "we shall mix therewith a thousand effects of self-love; we shall be always seeking

---

23. Bossuet, "On Penance," in *Great French Sermons from Bossuet, Bourdaloue, and Massillon* (London: Sands and Co., 1917) 146.

24. Fenelon, *Letters to Women*, 220.

25. Boudon, *The Hidden Life of Jesus*, 105.

26. Boudon, *The Hidden Life of Jesus*, 140.

ourselves in the holiest practices."[27] John of the Cross calls them travelers on a false road, who have confused primary and secondary purposes, and so "labour more for their own ends than for the glory of God."[28] "One thing is clear," Grou is sure: "true love and self-love cannot dwell together – which ever is strongest will uproot the other. Self-love has its root in our own interests, it keeps them ever in view. God is not its aim and end; even in spiritual things it seeks Him for its own gratification, its own advantage."[29]

We have seen this characterized as a *mercenary stage* of love: Fenelon repeatedly describes it as a "love of God which originates in a sole regard to our own happiness."[30] It is activity for our gain, instead of activity for the glory of God. Camus summarizes the mercenary habit of mind as one which shows up "when we stop short voluntarily, deliberately, and maliciously at our own self-interest, neglecting and putting on one side the interests of God, and when we look forward only to the honours, satisfactions, and delights given to the faithful, and exclude, as it were, the tribute of glory and homage which they render for them to God."[31] Keeping love pure requires a struggle, not a conversation, because Saint-Jure says we can even engage in self-love while we discuss how to overcome it! "There are some who have spoken very subtilely [sic] concerning self-love, and who have made many researches into its failings, and for the remedies that must be brought to bear upon them. But since this love seeks itself in everything ... the remedy for this love ought to be to renounce all its researches and to change it into the love of God."[32] Fenelon notices the peculiar fact that self-love can grow fatter with practices of abnegation, if we are not careful. "We feed our self-love with good works and austerity. We

---

27. Lallemant, *The Spiritual Doctrine of Father Louis Lallemant, ed. Faber*, 329.

28. John of the Cross, *The Ascent of Mount Carmel*, in *The Complete Works of Saint John of the Cross*, vol. 1, 313.

29. Grou, *The Hidden Life of the Soul*, 90.

30. Fenelon, *Fenelon's Maxims of the Saints*, 1. This is the topic of much of Fenelon's pastoral letter explaining his concept of indifference. *The Archbishop of Cambray's Pastoral Letter concerning the Love of God* (London: Robert Nelson, 1715).

31. Camus, *The Spirit of St. Francis de Sales*, 25.

32. Saint-Jure, *The Religious*, vol. 1, 569-70.

go over our mortifications with ourselves secretly, our victories over our own tastes, our righteous deeds, our patience, humility and detachment. We think we are seeking spiritual consolation in all these things, and we are seeking in them a helpful witness to our own righteousness."[33] It is a false project, indeed. Self-love operates on both the natural and supernatural levels, as Boudon summarizes.

> We wish to seem of importance by our wealth and possessions, our station and office, our resources and connections, our friends, and the interest we possess with influential persons. Our manner of proceeding is the same in supernatural things; we wish to appear mighty in works and in words, in the great results they produce, in the large number of persons of consequence who highly esteem our teaching or our direction, and in the striking actions we perform in public; the amount of our alms, our severe austerities, the sublime knowledge we possess of the spiritual life, and extraordinary graces.[34]

Second, false piety is produced by the sort of false efforts we have been describing. We boast of our spiritual prowess, and the result is an ersatz piety. Grou shows it up in this series of depictions:

> A soul tainted with this poison, desires holiness as an embellishing ornament and distinguishing perfection. It desires to be pure, but only in order to contemplate its own purity; it fears sin, less as an offence against God than as a spot on the brilliancy of its own beauty. It is more astonished than abashed by its faults, scarcely conceiving how it was possible for it to fall; its repentance savours more of vexation than of regret; and what it believes to be an act of contrition and love of God, is merely an act of inordinate self-love.[35]

---

33. Fenelon, *Christian Perfection*, 48.

34. Boudon, *The Hidden Life of Jesus*, 34.

35. Grou, *The Spiritual Maxims of Pere Grou*, 173.

The goal should be true sanctity, and de Sales says true sanctity consists in the love of God, "not in foolishnesses of imaginations, of ravishments, which feed self-love, but starve obedience and humility: to wish to play the extatic is an abuse."[36] Such people may appear to be ablaze with a zeal, but Olier thinks it is "a zeal generated by a spirit of pride and self-love, which relishes great things and wants to be involved in brilliant and extraordinary works."[37] Grou contrasts a gross self-love with a spiritual self-love, and believes the latter to be more dangerous because it "glides artfully into pious practices ... [and] is proud, avaricious, envious, voluptuous, greedy, vindictive, and slothful."[38] Under pretense of this higher spirituality, we feed our pride and self-love.[39] This is a problematic temptation for Christians in all states of life, and Baker explicitly includes those in religious profession. "Such may call themselves monks and contemplatives, being yet able to show no signs of such a profession but the habit, and a certain outward, formal, solemn, and severe comportment, under which may be hidden a secret most profound self-love and pride."[40] False piety consists of being pleased by anything other than God, which, remarkably, includes being pleased by our own righteousness. In the words of Fenelon, ever watchful for this:

> We take a great pleasure in seeing ourselves righteous, and feeling
> ourselves strong, in admiring ourselves in our goodness, as a vain woman
> is pleased to consider her beauty in a mirror. Our devotion to this
> contemplation of our virtues tarnishes them, feeds our self-love, and
> stops us from detaching us from ourselves. Thence it comes that so
> many souls, otherwise righteous and full of good desires, only revolve
> around themselves, without ever advancing toward God. Under pretext

---

36. De Sales, *Letters to Persons in the World*, 399.

37. Olier, *Introduction to the Christian Life and Virtues*, in *Berulle and the French School*, 270.

38. Grou, *The Characteristics of True Devotion*, 101.

39. Barbanson, *The Secret Paths of Divine Love*, 52.

40. Baker, *Holy Wisdom*, 166.

of wanting to keep this witness within, they are always complacently occupied with themselves.[41]

Can we detect this sham piety? Not easily, says de Sales. "Beware that you be not deceived by self-love, for sometimes it counterfeits the Love of God so cleverly that you may mistake one for the other."[42] Yet there are signs.

(i) Examine your self complacency (de Castaniza). "We fall into self-complacency and secret pride; and though we cannot digest a hard word, much less blows, yet we devote ourselves to high contemplations."[43]

(ii) Examine your relationship with your neighbor (Fenelon). "Nothing so feeds self-conceit as this sort of internal testimony that one is quite free from self-love, and always generously devoted to one's neighbours. But all this devotion which seems to be for others is really to yourself. Your self-love reaches the point of perpetual self-congratulation that you are free from it."[44]

(iii) Examine what motivates your generosity (Fenelon). "Eagerness to help others often springs only from human generosity and a refinement of self-love."[45]

---

41. Fenelon, *Christian Perfection*, 49.

42. De Sales, *Introduction to the Devout Life*, 123.

43. De Castaniza, *Spiritual Conflict and Conquest*, 91.

44. Fenelon, *Letters to Women*, 118.

45. Fenelon, *Letters to Men*, 261.

(iv) Examine your attitude toward your own sins (de Bergamo). The proud man dwells on the little good he does, and "puts behind him the multitude of his sins, so that he need not be ashamed and humble himself; and he reflects often upon certain of his minute exercises of Christian piety, so as to indulge his self-complacency."[46]

(v) Finally, examine what things can disturb your heart (Fenelon). We may not go straight toward worldliness "with bent head, but we let ourselves be drawn into it as though by accident. We still cling to self in all these things, and a sure sign that we cling to it, is that if anyone disturbs these natural supports, we are desolate … we feel within ourselves a sharp pang, which shows how much self is still alive and sensitive … It is only times of loss which show us the true depths of our hearts."[47]

Third, let us examine what true piety actually looks like. Can we detect it from false piety? Yes, says Libermann, because true piety is peaceful while false piety is agitated. "The state of true perfection is always one of peace. Troubles come usually, nay always, from a source that is not God. This source is usually either self-love, excessive self-indulgence, or lastly a too great eagerness to possess graces, perfection, or the gifts of God which we particularly esteem."[48] Yes, says de Sales, because "self-love is a restless, anxious, overeager love, and so the work done on its behalf is troubled, vexatious. and unsatisfactory; whereas the Love of God is calm, peaceful, and tranquil. and so the work done for its Sake, even in worldly things, is gentle, trustful, and quiet."[49] He thinks true and false piety have different agents and objects.

---

46. De Bergamo, *Humility of Heart*, 177.

47. Fenelon, *Christian Perfection*, 189-90.

48. Libermann, *Letters to Religious Sisters and Aspirants,* Spiritan Series 5, Vol. 1, 6.

49. De Sales, *Introduction to the Devout Life*, 123.

If anyone strives to be delivered from his troubles out of love of God, he will strive patiently, gently, humbly. and calmly, looking for deliverance rather to God's Goodness and Providence than to his own industry or efforts; but if self-love is the prevailing object he will grow hot and eager in seeking relief, as though all depended more upon himself' than upon God. I do nor say that the person thinks so, but he acts eagerly as though he did think it.[50]

Yes, says Grou, because true piety is hopeful and false piety despairs. "Sorrow comes from God: despondency arises from self-love. We will humble ourselves, patiently, quietly, placidly. We will despair of ourselves; but we will expect everything from God."[51] Discouragement will not get anyone anywhere, because it is only "the despair of a vexed self-love."[52]

Finally, true and false piety can be contrasted by how one reacts to faults. On the one hand, we can use Fenelon's description of true piety. "The light of God makes us feel even our least faults, but it does not discourage us. We go forward with him, but if we stumble we hasten to resume our way, and we think only of advancing. O, how happy is this simplicity! But how few, people have the courage never to look behind them! Like Lot's wife, they draw the curse of God on themselves by these restless returns of a jealous and fastidious self-love."[53] On the other hand, we can use de Sales' description of false piety. "All this anger and irritation against one's self fosters pride, and springs entirely from self-love, which is disturbed and fretted by its own imperfection. What we want is a quiet, steady, firm displeasure at our own faults."[54]

---

50. De Sales, *Introduction to the Devout Life*, 190.

51. Grou, *The Spiritual Maxims of Pere Grou*, 218.

52. François Fenelon, *Spiritual Letters of François De Salignac De La Mothe-Fenelon [to Countess Gramont]* (Cornwall-on Hudson, NY: Idlewild Press, 1945) 22.

53. Fenelon, *Christian Perfection*, 52.

54. De Sales, *Introduction to the Devout Life*, 111-12.

What is God's providential plan? To raise us to happiness because it serves his glory. God secondarily desires happiness for us, but he is primarily desirous for his glory. Two goods can be understood in this sequence: God's work is for his glory; our sanctification glorifies him; our sanctification is our happiness; God can give us this happiness; eternal life is eternal happiness. If we do not accept these terms, we will not accept the beatific vision.

Grou returns to this point repeatedly. "Heaven is closed against self-love; all motives of self-interest are banished from it."[55] "As long as there remains in the soul any admixture of self-love it cannot be raised to the beatific vision."[56] "Heaven would be no longer Heaven if self-love could find entrance there."[57] "Self-love, which is the fruit of original sin, can have no place in Heaven, and that the sole love which can exist there is the pure love of God."[58] God must do this work, and only him. So what is man's part? "He can give himself up simply to God; he can leave God to work the destruction of that self-love, he can second the dealings of God's loving jealousy, he can lie still under the Hand which strips and chastens him in seeming severity."[59] The exact problem we face is how self-love can annihilate itself when it loves itself. Self-love will not give up its throne of self-governance until God unseats it. "So soon as a Christian really gives himself to God and to His service, divine love takes possession of his heart, sets up its throne within it, and forthwith proceeds to drive out self-love."[60] Self-love mingles itself even with religion, and adulterates it, so neither our abnegation nor our happiness can be left to our hands alone. "Self-love, when chased from one spot, returns in another and assumes new forms. I do not think it is possible without special grace to banish it entirely from the soul, unless God Himself takes the work in hand, and uses the crucible of trials to separate all foreign

---

55. Grou, *Meditations Upon the Love of God*, 131.

56. Grou, *The School of Jesus Christ*, 111.

57. Grou, *The Hidden Life of the Soul*, 89.

58. Grou, *Manual for Interior Souls*, 326.

59. Grou, *The Hidden Life of the Soul*, 89.

60. Grou, *The Spiritual Maxims of Pere Grou*, 170.

alloy from our love of Him."[61] Only upon the inverse relationship of deescalated self-love and escalating divine love does the soul realize the force that self-love has been exercising over it. "We seldom realise the force of self-love until God's dealings are tearing it out of our hearts."[62] More on this in the next chapter, concerning crosses.

We find, then, the key to annihilation language. We cannot be our own physician. Self-love is too touchy. Fenelon says sickly self-love "cannot be touched without screaming; the mere tip of a finger seems to scarify it,"[63] and Grou says wounded self-love "is irritable and intolerant of the slightest touch."[64] Obviously, then, "self-annihilation" does not mean an operation done under our own power. It means precisely the opposite: annihilating the self's power. Annihilation of self is simply another way of saying grace alone. Do not try to do it yourself, let God do it; do not try to do it to yourself, let God do it to you. This, says Olier, "is why our Lord put abnegation in his gospel as the first step we must take in the Christian life! ... Because self-centeredness, being filled with the self, blocks Jesus Christ in the fullness of his divine life from entering us."[65]

The first step in the Christian life is not *us* taking a step, but rather letting *God* take his. Let God direct, let him act, let him enter – our responsibility is to be home, waiting. How easily the old Augustine-Pelagian problem is solved. De Osuna says a man would be greatly to blame if

> when some high dignitaries were about to visit him, [he] left his home
> at the time they were expected. It would appear insulting, and the
> guests might seek some other dwelling, leaving their indifferent host
> to himself....Every devout soul [should] be spiritually solicitous while
> awaiting to welcome within itself God, who is to be its guest.

---

61. Grou, *The School of Jesus Christ*, 63.

62. Grou, *The Hidden Life of the Soul*, 4.

63. Fenelon, *Letters to Women*, 72.

64. Grou, *The Hidden Life of the Soul*, 178.

65. Olier, *Introduction to the Christian Life and Virtues, in Berulle and the French School*, 262-63.

We are certain and know by the mouth of the Son of God himself that he and the Father and the Holy Spirit will come to dwell with one who loves them and will make their abode with him in no other place but in his soul, which is the dwelling-place of God; but the man himself must be there to receive him.[66]

The Trinity will come to take up its abode in our hearts, but we must be home when he comes. Spread out all the sails of your heart, then, says Surin, "in order to catch the winds of the Holy Spirit, abandoning your power to divine love. If you act through that love, you will find a marvelous strength for everything, in order to collect all the Holy Spirit's gusts."[67] The startling consequence – hard to grasp – is that not only should the *irreligious* man stop his self-direction, even the *religious* man should stop directing himself because, as de Granada knows, "self-love is naturally very subtle and always seeking itself, even in exercises of the utmost piety and devotion. This it was gave a holy man frequent occasion to say, 'Do you know where God is? He is where you are not.' Giving us hereby to understand, that the less advantage and self-interest there was to be expected, the action was so much the more pure and divine, because a man then proposes nothing to himself but the search of God."[68]

What God does for our salvation, he does through Jesus who assumed human nature in order to save it. The God-man knows the strategy of the hidden serpent because he suffered the consequences of sin, even if he did not personally sin. Boudon's meditations on Jesus persuades him that the Word Incarnate now knows that "creatures are prone to put themselves forward in all things" (some overtly, others with a more subtle self-seeking); he also knows "the infinite greatness of His Eternal Father, who ought to be the supreme object of regard in everything;" he therefore satisfies the justice of His Father

---

66. Francisco de Osuna, *The Third Spiritual Alphabet* (New York: Benziger Brothers, 1931), 147.

67. Surin, *Into the Dark Night and Back: The Mystical Writings of Jean-Joseph Surin*, 490.

68. De Granada, *Sinner's Guide*, 362.

and "hides Himself in an infinitely astonishing manner, and endures annihilation that which we stand aghast."[69] Jesus pits his humility against our pride. He pits his wanting to glorify the Father against our wanting to glorify ourselves. In short, Eudes sees Jesus contrasting his life against the life of the world. "The spirit of Jesus is a spirit of modesty, of self-distrust, of mortification and abnegation, of constancy and of firmness. But the spirit of the world is, by contrast, a spirit of pride, presumption, disordered self-love, fickleness and inconstancy."[70] How is self-love overcome in humiliation and subjection and mortification? Surin answers that

> it is done by casting one's eyes on Jesus Christ, who was given to us as a model and whom all predestined persons ought to resemble. We see that he, the Son of God, the chief and the king of all men, who guides us by divine wisdom and by zeal for the glory of his Father and for our salvation, chose a type of life where he fought unto death against self-love, living in abjection, in poverty, in suffering. He took on human lowliness, scorn, rejection, contradictions, in order to give us courage, and he acquired for us a treasure and a fund of grace by dying for us.[71]

True discipleship is the student following his teacher to learn self-abnegation. Christ is our pedagogue of abnegation. "Oh! How far we are from the life of Jesus Christ!" de Ravignan moans. "In the days of our youth, when we feed upon the desire of pleasing, upon all which flatters our self-love and vanity, how far are we from the despised, rejected Savior!"[72] Fenelon thinks the reluctance of our self-will and our wisdom to follow the movements of Christ shows clearly "that we are only held back from them by sensitiveness and by the pull of self-interest. The more we fear to do these things, the more we need

---

69. Boudon, *The Hidden Life of Jesus*, 61.

70. Eudes, *The Life and the Kingdom of Jesus in Christian Souls*, 16.

71. Surin, *Into the Dark Night and Back: The Mystical Writings of Jean-Joseph Surin*, 497.

72. De Ravignan, *Conferences on the Spiritual Life*, 130.

them, because the fear only comes from fastidiousness, stiffness, and attachment either to our own tastes or to our own views."[73]

All the external good works, virtues, and mortifications will fail to bring a man to perfection if he lacks the right intention in performing them. Many are the people who deceive themselves by thinking they would gladly suffer a grand martyrdom, or mimic the heroic saints in the desert, but are unwilling to undergo the small mortifications that will work their conversion, slowly, daily. This is a point made repeatedly by our theologians. For example, de la Colombiere: "there is no one to whom, each day, there do not happen a hundred minor things contrary to one's desires and to one's inclinations," so he counsels that instead of waiting for an opportunity of heroic proportions, be on guard "to offer to God all these little annoyances and to accept them as being ordained by Providence."[74] For example, Grou: "little things do not expose us to the same danger; it is easier in them to reserve humility; in them there is nothing for self-love to fix upon is a matter for glorification ... Therefore, the faithful practice of little things is incomparably safer for us ... And if the death of self-love is more gradual, it is none the less sure."[75] For example, Fenelon: "be stedfast in thwarting your vanity and the sensitiveness of self-love directly that God points them out to you ... I pray that God may make you gentle, lonely, and childlike, as our manger-born Lord Jesus. Do not seek to be clever, or dogmatic, or keen to the faults of others, or sensitive and touchy, or to be thought better in appearance than you are in reality."[76]

If we are made over in the image of Christ, then in him, through him, and with him we may participate in his supreme activity of serving and glorifying the Father. We may become his apprentice liturgists. Fenelon wants to know what it means to glorify God on earth, and he finds Jesus explaining it "clearly in the words, 'I have finished the work which Thou gavest Me to do.' So that to glorify God we must know and perform that

---

73. Fenelon, *Christian Perfection*, 164.

74. De la Colombiere, *Sermons vol. 1: Christian Conduct*, 134.

75. Grou, *Manual for Interior Souls*, 118-19.

76. Fenelon, *Letters to Men*, 44.

which He gives us to do."[77] However, to the contrary, "all the work which I undertake from vanity, from a desire to get on in the world, from temper, fancy, taste, self-will, or human respect, is not that which God has given me to do, and consequently none of this can glorify Him."[78] Self-love likes to present its piety for boasting, but if we are in Christ, then de Sales says our sanctity is hidden from our own eyes, and "God alone sees it, and delights Himself in her simplicity, by which she ravishes His heart and unites herself to Him. She makes short work of all the suggestions of her self-love – that self-love which takes such supreme delight in attempting the great and splendid things which will make us esteemed far above others."[79] From this place of secret sanctity liturgy ascends on the wings of abnegation.

"How should I become good when I pray so badly?"[80] A good question that Grou puts to liturgical theology! Liturgizing God affects morality in a way that few understand or practice. Liturgical morality consists of forgetting oneself – not for stoical reasons, or social altruism, or even personal happiness – but in order to look to God's glory and consider one's own personal interests subordinate to his. Grou bemoans that "the greater number, even in the holiest conditions in life, serve God from self-interest, and not for the glory of their Creator; their only object is to secure salvation, and if they form any occasional aspirations after sanctity, it is to appropriate this perfection, and to feed their self-love on the gratifying vision of their virtue and regularity."[81] We cannot become good unless we refer ourselves unreservedly to God, the Supreme Good, and occupy ourselves with the promotion of his honor, and the accomplishment of his will. Liturgy looks upon the human being as a creature devoted to God's glory, and liturgical abnegation as the denial of anything that stands in that way. So Baker concludes "it is by Mortification that self-love and all other our natural deordinations, which hinder a

---

77. Fenelon, *Letters to Women*, 4.

78. Fenelon, *Letters to Women*, 4.

79. De Sales, *The Spiritual Conferences*, 248.

80. Grou, *The School of Jesus Christ*, 250.

81. Grou, *The Interior of Jesus and Mary*, vol. 1, 37.

divine union, are removed; and it is by Prayer that we directly tend to a divine union."[82]
Liturgical devotion serves this mortification, because the motive of devotion is to attack
self-love at its foundation – "pursue it to its entire extinction," says Grou, "substituting in
its place the love of God, the love of our neighbor, and the well-regulated love of self. Thus
devotion re-establishes in man his primitive rectitude, restores order in his affections,
forbids every sentiment that proceeds not from God and which tends not to God."[83]
Such liturgy must be done with purity of intention, which Barbanson says only happens
when our corrupt nature "with all its worldliness and self-love begins to die, only to rise
adorned with grace and interior light, so that henceforth it may converse in the house of
God."[84] Liturgizing God correctly means we can do the world correctly.

The world is good, but all good is valued as nothing when compared to Divine
goodness. This means we may use the world placed at our disposal, so long as we use it
and enjoy God, not vice-versa. Bona explains.

> The love of God therefore is then esteemed perfect, when all good things
> are loved for him, by whom and for whom they are good ... All good
> compared to the Divine goodness is valued as nothing. But we must
> chiefly be aware that we be not involved by the frequent use of sensible
> things, that the vigor and energy of the will in the love of God be not by
> little and little dissolved; *because the affections to eternal things are slow,
> but to sensible things quick, though those are more valuable* ... As a full vessel
> cannot receive what it has not, unless it first pour out what it has; so the
> evil love of the world ought by us to be excluded, that we may be fitted
> with the good love of God. Love not the world, says the apostle whom
> Jesus loved, nor the things that are in the world, I John 2:15. By which
> words we are prohibited so to love those things which God hath made,
> that we forget the Creator. Those things indeed are beautiful, but how

---

82. Baker, *Holy Wisdom*, 196.

83. Grou, *The Characteristics of True Devotion*, 153.

84. Barbanson, *The Secret Paths of Divine Love*, 110.

much more excellent is he that made them? God hath given us those things that we may use them for him, but must enjoy himself.[85]

The conversation we have with God in his house enables us to come to our true selves, and so at last do the world correctly, i.e. with purity of intention, which, Grou says, is when

> God alone is its object; it is mingled with no self-interest ... What must we do to acquire this precious purity of intention? We must continually watch our motives, in order to cast aside not only the palpably bad, but the imperfect. But we only discern our imperfections as we advance, and as our spiritual lights increase. God increases our lights progressively, according to the use we make of them.[86]

God increases our liturgical lights, so abnegation can watch our motives.

Because true liturgy is liturgy done in the heart, with purity of intention, Grou is certain that true worship is more than devotional routines. "It is not what we do that glorifies Him, but the disposition of our hearts while we are doing it. We find a difficulty in understanding this because we cannot agree to put ourselves entirely on one side, and because our wretched self-love will glide in everywhere, and will corrupt and poison everything."[87] Watch out for ruinous self-love intruding even into the work of liturgy. "If God's service meant no more than a certain devotional routine, readily fitting in with an easy comfortable life, and with the indulgence of self-love and self-esteem, we should find more saints in the world ... But while abrogating those externals, Jesus Christ has laid upon us an internal rule which is incomparably harder to keep."[88]

---

85. Bona, *The Principles of Christianity,* 165-66.

86. Grou, *The Spiritual Maxims of Pere Grou,* 67.

87. Grou, *Manual for Interior Souls,* 229.

88. Grou, *The Hidden Life of the Soul,* 26-27.

Liturgical abnegation is the connecting rod between exterior liturgy and interior liturgization. It is the connecting rod between worship and the virtues. The virtues themselves need to be purified by detaching them from self-will, and this is accomplished by providence making a person undergo disappointments so that the virtues don't serve his ego, but rather serve simplicity of piety. Fenelon is all for simplicity.

> O, how simple and serene piety can be! How likeable, discreet and
> sure in all its proceedings! One lives much as other people do, without
> affectation, without any show of austerity, in an easy and sociable way,
> but continually bound by all one's duties, but with an unrelenting
> renunciation of all which does not moment by moment enter into God's
> plans, in short with a pure vision of God to which one sacrifices the
> irregular impulses of human nature. This is the worship in spirit and in
> truth which Jesus Christ and his Father seek. All the rest is only a religion
> of ceremony, and the shadow rather than the truth of Christianity.[89]

Liturgy takes our eyes off ourselves and focuses them on God (to the discomfort of self-will). "All sensitiveness springs from self-love; we only suffer because we have so much will."[90] Liturgy done with purity of love is a liturgy done with love for God himself alone, which stirs abnegation and brings it to life.

---

89. Fenelon, *Christian Perfection*, 9.

90. Fenelon, *Letters to Men*, 262.

On the Use of Crosses

With the problem of self causing an infectious corruption of our love, will, esteem, interest, judgment, appetite, and conceit (to pick a few from the list in a previous chapter), what are we to do with the self? The answer is an uncomfortable one: crucify it. Self-will and self-love will hate crosses, but, their acceptance is necessary because, as Alacoque says, "the cross is the throne of the true lovers of Jesus Christ."[1] Segneri says the Paschal Mystery plays out in our hearts as abnegation

> There is nothing which is so great an obstacle in every one to this cheerful bearing of the cross as self-love,. For just as Christ here made it a necessary preliminary disposition for the perfect following of Him even to Calvary, that a man should accustom himself to the daily carrying of his own cross, so, too, did he make complete self-abnegation a necessary condition for that daily carrying of his own cross. This is the meaning of the words, "If any man will come after Me, let him deny himself:" not only must this abnegation concern his possessions, *sua*, but *se*, himself.[2]

In this chapter, I am more interested in understanding how God employs crosses than I am in defining them, but if one wants a condensed definition, I can offer the reader this one from Grou.

---

1. Alacoque, *Spiritual Letters,* letter 16, Kindle edition.

2. Segnerei, *The Manna of the Soul*, vol. 2, 582.

As a rule when we speak of a cross we mean certain dispensations of Providence, either natural or supernatural, which thwart us, humiliate us, give us pain or sorrow, and try us in a variety of ways. Such crosses may be caused by nature, like bodily afflictions, infirmities, and illnesses; or by our condition in life, like poverty, toil, and dependence; or by some state that we have adopted, such as marriage; or by man's injustice, or by fortuitous accidents, or the malice of evil spirits. Or they may come to us directly from the hand of God. They attack our health, our possessions, our peace of mind, our reputation, our person or the persons of those we love; they mortify our feelings, our pride, our self-love; they exact a variety of sacrifices from us, some outward and some inward. Crosses in this acceptation of the word, which is the commonest, are the usual lot of humanity and there is no one who can completely avoid them. Everyone has his own; for some they are larger and more numerous; for others they are smaller and fewer. But no man is altogether exempt from them.[3]

Grou is capable of stating the situation still more succinctly: "crosses are the tests to which God puts our love, the sacrifices He expects it to make."[4]

But I repeat that I am more interested in knowing the purpose and effect of crosses than in defining the idea, so, as usual, I must begin with a reminder that reading alone will not be sufficient. This one comes from de Caussade.

The doctrine concerning pure love can only be taught by the action of God, and not by any effort of the mind. God teaches the soul by pains and obstacles, not by ideas.

This science is a practical knowledge by which God is enjoyed as the only good. In order to master this science it is necessary to be detached from all personal possessions, to gain this detachment, to be really deprived of them. Therefore it is only by constant crosses, and by a long succession of all kinds of mortifications, trials, and deprivations, that pure love becomes

---

3. Grou, *The School of Jesus Christ*, 180.

4. Grou, *The School of Jesus Christ*, 184.

established in the soul. This must continue until all things created become as though they did not exist, and God becomes all in all.[5]

A paradox presents itself at the outset. One can be sincere in wanting God to defeat self-love and self-will, and at the same time resist his crosses – such is the divided heart Fenelon observes us to suffer. "The same hidden root of obstinate self-love which makes us need crosses makes us repulse them and hinder their work. And so it is to begin again perpetually; we suffer, yet do not allow the work that suffering has to do to be achieved. I pray our Lord that none of us may fall into that torpid state in which our crosses do us no good."[6] God must reapply crosses when we impede their work, which we do out of trepidation. If we neutralize the efficacy of the crosses, or backtrack from the little progress they make in our lives, then God must go at it again. Being "generally desirous of bargaining with God," Fenelon says

> we would like at least to impose the limits and see the end of our sufferings. That same obstinate and hidden hold of life, which renders the cross necessary, causes us to reject it in part, and by a secret resistance, which impairs its virtue. We have thus to go over the same ground again and again; we suffer greatly, but to very little purpose. The Lord deliver us from falling into that state of soul in which crosses are of no benefit to us![7]

The self feels itself in a precarious position when it is forced to depend upon grace instead of its own will. It feels like a man not trusting the rope which supports him as he ascends the mountain. The first requirement of accepting crosses is to be convinced that love is behind them, and we should accept our suffering as a dependence upon God. The starting point for the believer is to "accept the dependence in which God places you," says Fenelon.

---

5. De Caussade, *Abandonment to Divine Providence*, 50.

6. Fenelon, *Letters to Men*, 99.

7. Fenelon, *Spiritual Progress*, 87.

It is good for you, and will tend to conquer your self-esteem and to make you lowly – you whose tendency is to lead others. I feel for all your crosses. I seem to be closely united to all who suffer in our Lord. Suffering is only sent to lead us on. When God purposes to accomplish a great work in a short time, He sends many crosses, and His blows fall heavily; but oh, how full of love they are, even when they seem to crush us pitilessly. The cross is a holy relic to be kept close, and love without the cross would be a frenzy, and become an illusion.[8]

Crosses help with abnegation, if we are docile to them. "Crosses, as it were, take us out of ourselves more and more, they empty us of ourselves and fill us with God," Libermann says, making us humble and small in our own eyes, making us "live in entire dependence on Jesus, our only love, and realizing that dependence, we are aware of our poverty, weakness, and wretchedness. Blessed are we when, thus destitute of everything, we realize our nothingness and weakness."[9] So take heart! Take the leap of faith – you have nothing to lose. Vianney understands our great fear of crosses, but "whatever we do, the cross holds us tight – we cannot escape from it. What, then, have we to lose? Why not love our crosses and make use of them to take us to Heaven?"[10] "Do you dread trials?" Grou asks. But "they are indispensably necessary for your admission to heaven."[11]

Notice at the outset that the theologians of liturgical abnegation speak of crosses in the plural. Our salvation (healing) cannot be done with one stroke; it requires repeated therapeutic applications of the cross. Virtues require repetition. Crosses must be used repeatedly, persistently, and stubbornly by God if they are to work their effect. One cannot be said to be obedient by obeying one time, or to have patience by enduring

---

8. Fenelon, *Letters to Men*, 101.

9. Libermann, *Letters to Religious Sisters and Aspirants*, Spiritan Series 5, vol. 1, 9.

10. John Vianney, *The Little Catechism of the Curé of Ars* (Rockford, IL: TAN books, 1951) ch 18.

11. Grou, *The Spiritual Maxims of Pere Grou*, 151.

only one inconvenience. Likewise, the uprooting of self-love requires numerous occasions of dependence, of suffering, of abnegation, and the process can be compared to a child growing into an adult. A child does not rise as an adult after one night, says Fenelon, and a person does not shed self-will after one cross.

> The operation of grace in turning us thus from self cannot – save through
> a miracle of that same grace – be other than painful, and God does not
> perform continual miracles in the order of grace any more than in the
> order of nature. It would be as great a miracle in the first sense were we to
> see one full of himself die suddenly to self-consciousness and self-interest,
> as to see a child go to bed a mere child, and rise up the next morning a man
> of thirty!"[12]

God is willing to be patient; we are not. Impatience is our problem. The irritation we feel about crosses is expressed as an irritation with God, or with ourselves, or with both. The healing is slow and steady, therefore de Caussade thinks it "necessary to bear the little crosses we encounter every day, for by them God will enable us to destroy our self-love."[13] The order of divine will is designed to save us, sanctify us, bring us into union with God, but "this order of the divine will ... is continually present under the veil of crosses, and of the most ordinary actions."[14] God is present, but under a veil; God is at work, but in the darkness; and it requires patience to become convinced that love is operating.

The hiddenness of God behind suffering makes the crosses a challenge to faith, hope, and love simultaneously. We prefer to deal with God where he seems more evident to us, and appears more merciful (according to our definition), and we do not like this strange terrain. All the authors admit that no one feels a natural inclination for this state of life. De la Colombiere says "it seems that we never have too much inclination for the cross,"[15]

---

12. Fenelon, *Letters to Men*, 298.

13. De Caussade, *Abandonment to Divine Providence*, 168 .

14. De Caussade, *Abandonment to Divine Providence*, 83.

15. De la Colombiere, *Faithful Servant, 279.*

but if we are to find God, we must look in the place where he has hidden himself. De Caussade admits that God and his grace are given in a hidden and strange manner, and that is why "the soul feels too weak to bear the weight of its crosses, and disgusted with its obligations. Its attractions are only for quite ordinary exercises."[16] But God is the master, and if he lays more crosses upon a person than the person asked for, he does so "in order that they may love Him more," confesses Grou, and "at the same time He communicates to them an unseen strength."[17] As Jesus's cross was the way to his resurrection, so our crosses are the way to our sanctification. Grou says we may ask him: "Why must we bear so many internal and external trials? Can we acquire holiness at no less price?" He will answer his own question. "No; the Gospel affirms that holiness is only to be attained by suffering, or at least by the will to suffer. Holiness consists in readiness to embrace all the crosses that it may please God to send us."[18]

We lack this readiness. We prefer to focus our attention on getting rid of our crosses, rather than on making good use of them. This was a constant complaint by Alacoque.

- The afflictions our Lord sends "are the surest marks of His love. I beg His divine goodness to give her the grace to make as good use of them as she can buy submission and conformity to His good pleasure and most holy will."[19]

- "If it be not the will of the Lord to deliver her from suffering, He will at least grant her perfect conformity to His most holy will. I think He is making use of this means to purify and sanctify her. But she must put it to good use."[20]

- "Exhort him to patience in his illness, since it is not God's will to free him from it just now. He must try to make good use of it."[21]

---

16. De Caussade, *Abandonment to Divine Providence*, 68.

17. Grou, *The Spiritual Maxims of Pere Grou*, 151.

18. Grou, *The Spiritual Maxims of Pere Grou*, 151.

19. Alacoque, *Letters*, letter 77, Kindle edition.

20. Alacoque, *Letters*, letter 84, Kindle edition.

21. Alacoque, *Letters*, letter 99, Kindle edition.

- It is not necessary to seek humiliations, slights, and the low esteem of self with which Christ nourishes his faithful friends, it is only necessary "to make good use of those He sends us."[22]

- "I urge her to make good use of her illness so that God may sanctify her through it."[23]

- "Let us not give way to discouragement, dear friend, but take in good part and in a spirit of submission the little mortifications His sweet Providence allows to come to us and try to make good use of them."[24]

We admire the conclusion of every saint's story, but are less fond of what went before. We are attracted to the heroic virtues at the end, but are less taken with the daily means to it. But there is no shortcut, and one must learn to make good use of crosses, because Fenelon says "that which strikes at your supersensitiveness and your scornful fastidiousness goes right to the mark. God knows well how to choose what we need, and all the blows which he gives us are in mercy."[25] Our daily life is the realm of the crosses, the place where God does his transforming work. Libermann is certain that God pours our blessings on our labors, but "the crosses and contradictions He mingles with them are as salt for our food; they preserve our soul in a spirit of humility, abnegation and confident abandonment to God. In the eyes of God and His Saints, those crosses give a special savor to your works."[26] Being a Christian means following Jesus to abnegation, who descended from heaven in order to share our suffering, and live among our crosses to give us encouragement. Meditate on the Gospel, says Scaramelli, and you will see Jesus doing exactly that.

---

22. Alacoque, *Letters*, letter 106, Kindle edition.

23. Alacoque, *Letters*, letter 114, Kindle edition.

24. Alacoque, *Letters*, letter 123, Kindle edition.

25. Fenelon, *Spiritual Letters of François De Salignac De La Mothe-Fenelon*, 68.

26. Libermann, *Letters to Clergy & Religious*, Spiritan Series 7, vol. 3, 284-85.

[Our blessed Savior] saw that the miserable earth on which we dwell is, so to speak, covered, sown broadcast with crosses. He knew that it was not possible to live in this vale of tears and in this painful exile, without trials and afflictions, grief and bitterness. What, then, did our good Captain do to encourage us to endurance? He took upon His own divine shoulders, the heaviest, the most weighty Cross, the Cross most full of pain; and, turning to us His soldiers, enrolled under His banner, He addresses us in the terms which Abimelech used to his men: "Do what you see Me do. Behold Me, laden with the Cross, groaning under its crushing weight, languishing and dying upon it He who would boast of being My follower, let him take up his Cross, follow Me, tread in My footsteps, and become like unto Me."[27]

Jesus was without sin, yet accepted its wages (death), in solidarity with us, in order to accompany us in what Alacoque calls our exile. "Although the cross is my lot just as a great sinner, still it is the cross which makes bearable the length of my exile, in which there can be no pleasure for me but to love God and suffer for this love. What, alas, would I do if the cross were taken from me, since it is that which makes me hope in His mercy! That is my whole treasure in the adorable Heart of Jesus Christ."[28] Therefore, our love must not only *respond* to his, it must *correspond* to his. We do out of love for him what he did out of love for us, which was to be annihilated for the beloved. Eudes articulates the equation: "cultivate the spirit, the love and desire which annihilated Christ, that you, too, may be annihilated for Him."[29]

A cruciform thread runs from Christ, through his Church, connecting him to each individual Christian soul. First, there is the historical Christ, in whom we see the Mystery-made-flesh vanquish death and Satan for the life of the world; second, the Head communicates with his Mystical Body in the sacramental crosses where he invades our lives through all seven sacraments in order to set us free; third, we see the Mystery as

---

27. Scaramelli, *Guide to the Spiritual Life*, vol. 3, 413-14.

28. Alacoque, *Spiritual Letters*, letter 8, Kindle edition.

29. Eudes, The Priest, 193.

a spiritual cross in our heart, liturgically animating us to bear crosses for love of him. In Christ, Leen sees humanity expressing its submission to God. "The Passion was a gesture of obedience and submission on the part of Christ as Head of the redeemed race contained potentially in him."[30] The Church stresses this Christ's obedience as the predominant characteristic of the Passion, and then liturgical abnegation reproduces that obedience in us. On Good Friday we don't watch Jesus die, we join Jesus (liturgically) by dying ourselves, ourselves submitting to God. "Without crucifixion, our souls will always remain blinded to God ... [And] if we do not see God, we are not saved. Therefore the whole of Christianity is not expressed in the formula: 'Christ crucified for us.' True Christians rejoice also that Christ is crucified *in* us."[31] Saint-Jure compares our cross to the sword of sorrow that pierced the heart of Mary, and if we are to come at last to the glory that awaits us with Jesus and Mary in heaven, we must take it up daily. "All the saints have always loved afflictions and gloried in them. We have the greatest veneration for Our Lord's cross, we even render it the worship of latria; we should then revere our own crosses, which are, as it were, off-shoots of His, and which He has sanctified."[32]

What do crosses accomplish? To that question a variety of answers is given: crosses give peace, they give life, they convert everything to love, they are a path to deification, they are a place of union with God, and more. They get us moving! And how Libermann sees we need to. "Oh! how difficult it is to go out of ourselves, to divest ourselves of self, to be unreservedly detached and abandoned! This we should never be able to attain, if God did not aid us with His almighty power. But, desiring to take pity on us, He overwhelms us with crosses and, whether we wish it or not, we must leave self, forget and lose ourselves, and thus belong to Him alone."[33] So from the very outset, Barbanson insists we firmly assert that the crosses are in service to love and salvation, as is every weapon Christ wields to slay sin. "Everything, whether it be crosses, dereliction, bitterness, trouble, or

---

30. Edward Leen, *Why the Cross* (New York: Sheed and Ward, 1938) 357-58.

31. Leen, *Our Blessed Mother, 64.*

32. Saint-Jure, *A Treatise on the Knowledge and Love of Our Lord Jesus Christ,* vol. 3, p 220.

33. Libermann, *Letters to Clergy and Religious,* Spiritan Series 8, vol. 4, 327

tribulation, is converted into love, and tends ever to the soul's greater perfection."[34] A cross of painful thorns is made soft when burned by love, according to Vianney's arresting image. "Crosses, transformed by the flames of love, are like a bundle of thorns thrown into the fire, and reduced by the fire to ashes. The thorns are hard, but the ashes are soft."[35] Because crosses are beautiful and infallible marks of salvation, Boudon calls them objects of sweet expectation, and "a house all full of crosses is a place of blessing."[36] Looking upon the blessing, the soul is compelled to exclaim:

> Ah, how sweet it is, but how useful and advantageous it is, how glorious it is to live and die overwhelmed by crosses! We are, [the Canticle] also says, the living stones of which the City of Paradise must be built, in which all the elect will have a divine dwelling. If we, who are these mystical stones are, so to speak, cut and trimmed by a large number of torments, it is an obvious sign that our celestial house must be ample and magnificent: because the greater and higher the building must be, the more work the laborers do to polish the stones. Those which are not trimmed and cut are not employed, but are thrown outside; the same goes for the reprobate who are left to their desires, and abandoned to the joys and honors of the world. Oh how precious is, therefore, the grace of crosses, and how necessary it is to preserve it attentively! how we ought to take care to handle all the moments of suffering which are given to us: and how we should be convinced, that to lose one moment of them is to suffer a loss which cannot be understood![37]

Strange language to our ears, indeed. Why is suffering precious? Why is humiliation desirable? Why are afflictions embraced? The answer is out of this world, that is,

---

34. Barbanson, *The Secret Paths of Divine Love*, 235.

35. Vianney, *The Little Catechism of the Curé of Ars*, ch. 18.

36. Boudon, *The Holy Slavery of the Admirable Mother of God*, 171.

37. Boudon, *The Holy Slavery of the Admirable Mother of God*, 191-92.

must come from beyond this world. Crosses can only be understood eschatologically. Bourdaloue says we are deceived because we "form our judgment of things according to the time in which we now are, and which passes away; but ... the judgment of God is formed relatively to eternity, in which we shall hereafter be, and which will never pass away."[38] Divine Providence is just, but Leen says original sin has caused a reduction of horizon in us, and blinded our eyes. This is what the contact with faith overcomes. "The Christian's trials are lifted above the terrestrial plane. They are wholly transmuted by being thus mingled with what Christ underwent on Calvary. Christ's passion is now ours and ours becomes His."[39] Jesus descended from the homeland to which he intends to bring us, and Boudon says that state is "more enviable than we are prone to think! How great will be their confidence at the hour of death who have had no share in the esteem and friendship of creatures! With what joy will they depart from the world to which they never belonged!"[40]

A higher horizon is required to understand crosses, which is generally true for all liturgical abnegation. Grou admits man is certainly born for happiness, "but its enjoyment is reserved for the next life; this life is the season for trial and for acquiring merit. God only prepares crosses for His friends on earth."[41] Crosses are designed to increase our attachment to God, while decreasing our attachment to this passing world. Therefore, Libermann counsels,

> be humbly submissive to the divine will which crucifies you; love the hand of God that leads you with such severity. Have courage, this present life is nothing. The sorrows we suffer here pass quickly; this life is only a painful dream which will be followed by a joyful awakening. The more you suffer,

---

38. Bourdaloue, *Sermons, and Moral Discourses*, vol. 1, 234.

39. Leen, *The True Vine and Its Branches*, 76.

40. Boudon, *The Hidden Life of Jesus*, 59.

41. Grou, *The Spiritual Maxims of Pere Grou*, 146.

the more detached you will become from yourselves and the world. This, at least, should be your aim.[42]

This the worldling will never understand. Abnegation will forever puzzle him, and Languet knows accepting the cross will feel like foolishness and a stumbling block.

> Let the people of the world be saddened, O my good God, with Your chastisements; let them desire to turn them aside; let them seek in creatures, and in worldly amusement, their frivolous consolations; let them address to You their prayers to obtain deliverance from these salutary trials. For myself, I have but one prayer to offer You, and but one only desire – I wish to carry the amiable Cross of my Savior, to carry it with Him, to be attached to it with Him, to die on it with Him. This Cross, in which I desire to glory, and in nothing else, shall take the place of every other joy; and when all the consolations of the earth shall have abandoned me, it will be itself my great consolation.[43]

A man should "kiss the hand that afflicts him"[44] (Alacoque) because crosses bring about an increase of love. It is true that *self-love* is being crucified, but that is only for the purpose of exchanging it for superior love. This enlarges the definition of abnegation that this book has been trying to present.

- Abnegation is unification (de Caussade). "It is most difficult indeed to love God and happiness without any admixture of self, or of vain self-complacency, but in the time of crosses, and of interior spiritual privatizations, all that is needful in order to be certain of the purity of our love, is to endure them patiently, and to abandon ourselves sincerely."[45]

---

42. Libermann, *Letters to Religious Sisters and Aspirants*, Spiritan Series 5, vol. 1, 28.

43. Languet, *Confidence in the Mercy of God, 232-33*.

44. Alacoque, *Letters*, letter 199, Kindle edition.

45. De Caussade, *Abandonment to Divine Providence*, 243.

- (ii) Annihilation is conformity to Christ (Grou). "Those who would follow His steps must share His humiliations, interior and exterior – a sharp Cross which pierces the very secrets of the soul; in comparison of which all the rest are light, which has no limit save in the total annihilation of self-love and self-seeking."[46]

- (iii) Crucifixion is purification (de Caussade). "The crushing weight that you feel in your heart is one of the most salutary operations of that crucifying love which does in your heart what fire does to green wood. Before the flame can make its way the wood crackles, smokes, and gives out all the damp with which it is saturated; but when it is perfectly dry it burns quietly, diffusing all round it a brilliant light. This will be the case with you after your heart is been purified by many crosses."[47]

- (iv) Crosses are given to little ones, not to the wise of this world (Bona). "Verily, Thou art a hidden God, dwelling in unapproachable light. Yet to those who have the crucified Jesus imprinted on their hearts and bodies thou dost lovingly communicate the plentifulness of Thy light ... Souls such as these dost Thou deeply penetrate in living power ... Thou piercest to the very marrow of these souls. They feel Thy spiritual touch."[48]

- (v) And this reveals the deepest mystery (Grou). ""He teaches to the humble and to the little ones the mysteries He has hidden from the wise and prudent. It is here that He reveals to them the wisdom of the Cross."[49]

Some of our authors compare crosses to a ladder, since Grou notices that "God has promised, not that [we] shall be free from crosses, rather they form the ladder by which the soul mounts upwards."[50] And Barbanson expects God to remain with his servants on

---

46. Grou, *The Hidden Life of the Soul*, 119.

47. De Caussade, *Abandonment to Divine Providence*, 347-48.

48. Bona, The *Easy Way To God*, 22.

49. Grou, *The Practical Science of the Cross*, 61.

50. Grou, *The Hidden Life of the Soul*, 143.

each step, "hence the soul is not sad at the cross of poverty and privation, but ever cheerful and light-hearted; for love changes everything which happens to us into a ladder which ascends on to God."[51] Grou notices that the more annihilated the soul is, the more she loves God. "Hence all the crosses and trials and deprivations of all kinds, and everything that tears us from ourselves, are the only steps by which we can ascend to the true love of God."[52] Jesus pursues us in order to bring us to where he is, and where is he, asks Surin but on the cross, glorifying his Father.

> And since the cross, rejected by mortals,
> Serves to favor the painful climb,
> He uses it as a ladder ...
> And, keeping his Lover attached to its wood,
> Never permits him to be torn from it.[53]

Other authors change the metaphor, and instead of a ladder they compare the cross to a bridge. Christ is love pursuing his lover's good, and the bridge he constructs to reach us feels more solid to the foot than the bridges we construct for ourselves. Vianney describes crosses planted on the road to heaven as "a fine bridge of stone over a river, by which to pass it," but Christians who spurn suffering "pass this river by a frail bridge, a bridge of wire, always ready to give way under their feet."[54] There is no path to deification except the route that Jesus took. If Jesus "established the glory of His Father only by poverty, contempt and pain, by persecutions and crosses" then obviously, Boudon thinks, we must not "aspire to take other ways."[55]

---

51. Barbanson, *The Secret Paths of Divine Love*, 244.

52. Grou, *Manual for Interior Souls*, 348.

53. Surin, *Into the Dark Night and Back: The Mystical Writings of Jean-Joseph Surin*, 411.

54. Vianney, *The Little Catechism of the Curé of Ars*, ch 18.

55. Boudon, *The Holy Slavery of the Admirable Mother of God*, 228.

The life where we are and where soon we shall not be any more, which passes so fast, and which hardly allows the leisure look at it, is given over to sufferings. It is necessary, then, to be crucified in it with Jesus, Whose spirit is the soul of our souls, Who alone gives us life, preserves it for us, and without Whom there is only death; and as He was the man of sorrows, we ceaselessly have to be inviolably attached to the cross. The spirit of Jesus is the spirit of crosses, but the spirit of Jesus is a spirit which gives us life: if, then, we want to live, it is necessary to live on the cross.[56]

In bearing crosses we resemble Jesus – that alone is enough to make crosses dear to Christians. In fact, crosses are greeted in prayer, like this one that Baker offers. "My God, I know that to fly Thy cross is to fly Thee that diedst on it; welcome, therefore, be (these) Thy crosses and trials."[57] Or this one one that de Chantal offers.

O Jesus, my Spouse! in kissing and embracing Thy own Cross, Thou didst embrace all our little crosses, thus to render them more amiable. O little crosses, little trials, little repugnances, humiliations, trifling though you may be, my Jesus has seen, has kissed, has sanctified you ... At every step we meet with crosses. If my flesh trembles at the sight of them, my heart loves them. Yes, I love you, little and great crosses, interior and exterior, corporal and spiritual, though I am unworthy of the honor of your shadow.[58]

God has a plan for redemption that is unique to each soul, designed and crafted for each soul, but while "there are a great many ways which lead to heaven," says Libermann,

---

56. Boudon, *The Holy Slavery of the Admirable Mother of God*, 172.

57. Baker, *Holy Wisdom*, 646.

58. De Chantal, *Meditations for Retreats*, 139.

"there is none that is not strewn and bristling with crosses ... Jesus and Mary have been constantly on the cross; should we be spared?"[59]

Christians honor crosses because they worship a crucified Lord, whom they seek to resemble. They also honor crosses because by them they have an intimacy with his Mother.. Boudon writes, "as all rivers pass into the sea, we also find in the holy heart of our glorious Mistress all sorts of crosses. As the bottom of the sea cannot be found, it is also not possible to know the greatness of her pains."[60] Eve was close to the tree of death in paradise, so she picked some fruit from it, and ate it. "Mary being very close to the Cross where hung the fruit of life, picked it, participating ... in an incomparable manner in the Passion of her Son; but this Mother of the living, in order to make us live, gives us to eat of the fruit of the Cross: it is necessary to taste it, and it is necessary to eat it."[61] She is first of the human race to follow the path to heaven blazed by the God-man, because she preferred his bitter cross to any sweet contentments the world had to offer. Grou describes her as supremely patient.

> Mary preferred the most severe sacrifices to the sweetest enjoyments ... She never allowed herself to desire that her exile should be abridged, and the moment of re-union with her Son in the kingdom of glory accelerated. Do we thus love the cross, especially overwhelming interior crosses? Do we not lose patience if they are protracted? Do we not sigh for their termination? Do we not pant for consolation? How few sacrifice themselves generously, absolutely, and irrevocably! To make a perfect offering of self, and never to revoke the oblation, is an event of rare occurrence in the spiritual life.[62]

---

59. Libermann, *Letters to Clergy and Religious,* Spiritan Series 8, vol. 4, 116.

60. Boudon, *The Holy Slavery of the Admirable Mother of God,* 169.

61. Boudon, *The Holy Slavery of the Admirable Mother of God,* 171.

62. Grou, *The Interior Life of Jesus and Mary,* vol. 2, 267-68.

There are various ways to describe contact with Jesus in the crosses we receive. Eudes speaks of embracing them: "with all my heart I love and embrace all the crosses, bodily or spiritual, it may please Thee to send me in my whole life, uniting them to Thine, and begging Thee to grant me a share of that great love with which Thou didst bear them."[63] Fenelon speaks of an intoxication. "What should we do without crosses! We should be given up to ourselves, and be intoxicated with self-love. Tis needful that we have crosses."[64] And Saint-Jure speaks of adoration. "We have the greatest veneration for Our Lord's cross, we even render it the worship of latria; we should therefore revere our own crosses, which are, as it were, off-shoots of His, and which He has sanctified."[65]

We join Christ at his cross, he joins us on ours. The bridegroom has a secret exchange with his spouse, Grou says. "Our Divine Saviour, in accepting [sufferings & trials] for His spouses, lays upon them His cross, the very same cross which He bore for them."[66] Do you desire to be his spouse? Libermann asks. If so,

> you have only one right, namely, to remain at the foot of the Cross, to embrace that Cross of your Beloved, to cling to His divine wounds, to rest in His arms, to abandon yourself to Him in your anguish, and feed on His divine love. What, my poor friend, is more desirable than this? You desire to be the spouse of Jesus Crucified; would you then want to avoid the blows that are aimed at Him, and ought to not accept to be struck and torn to pieces? You desire to rest on the divine Heart of Jesus, you want to be the spouse of His Heart, and would you refuse the bitterness with which His Heart was filled?[67]

---

63. Eudes, *The Life and the Kingdom of Jesus in Christian Souls*, 239.

64. Fenelon, *An English Nun in Exile Translates the Spiritual Letters of Archbishop Fenelon to Madame Guyon*, 182.

65. Jean Baptiste Saint-Jure, *Knowledge and Love of Jesus*, vol. 3 (New York: P. O'Shea, 1875) 220.

66. Grou, *Manual for Interior Souls*, 34.

67. Libermann, *Letters to Religious Sisters and Aspirants*, Spiritan Series 5, vol. 1, 144.

De Berniere-Louvigny realizes that if a soul ceases to love the cross, she is no longer conformed to the soul of Jesus, which means she no longer glorifies the Father. However,

> when she feels in herself a love for the cross, she highly glorifies the eternal Father who takes great delight that she resembles his well-beloved Son.

> When a soul is enlightened with these irradiations she sees that her glory is to be despised; because her glory is to procure the glory of God which she does most effectually by humiliations. She finds her delights to be in suffering; because her delight is to honor the eternal Father. A faithful soul will never part with an esteem and love of the cross as to the interior, because her desire is to please God.[68]

If your soul resembles Jesus, then Libermann says he will be "pleased to present you before His Father in a state of crucifixion similar to His own. Man of sorrows and of crosses, how blessed you are to have so excellent and continual a part in the divine Cross of Jesus."[69] The crosses we bear are but fragments of his.

We are naïve to think we can bear the name of Christian without bearing crosses. Jesus gives us not only his name, but his mark, and Scaramelli hears him say "whoever has not on his shoulders the mark of the Cross shall never be acknowledged by Me for one of Mine."[70] If the Master accepts the cross, the servant must as well, because the servant is living under the Master's law. Grou realizes "you cannot think that God will establish a new order of things on purpose for you, and exempt you from a general law from which even His own Son was not exempt."[71] The Christ whom we follow is the crucified one, and this is not over and done with. Just because we were not physically at Calvary does

---

68. De Berniere-Louvigny, *The Interior Christian*, 48.

69. Libermann, *Letters to clergy and Religious*, Spiritan Series 8, vol. 4, 322.

70. Scaramelli, *Guide to the Spiritual Life*, vol. 3, 412-13.

71. Grou, *The School of Jesus Christ*, 182.

not mean we cannot have an abundant participation in the cross of Jesus. Indeed, asks de Ravignan, "what time, what place, what state, was ever exempt from sufferings? ... Is not the earth one immense Calvary?"[72] We seek abnegation only because it is a state of voluntary, obedient death in imitation of the God-man's voluntary, obedient death. De Castaniza sees that "the Son of God chose the way of thorns and crosses by which He would enter into his glory, and this for thy love; and that thou shouldst imitate Him who left thee this exact pattern of perfect patience."[73] And this applies equally to the purgative, illuminative, or unitive stage. One never outgrows the cross, says Teresa of Avila. "Whether in the beginning, the middle, or the end, all bear their crosses even though these crosses be different. For all who follow Christ, if they don't want to get lost, must walk along this path that He trod."[74]

As we have seen, our admission of nothingness is simply a profession that God is All. This is the source of joy for de Castaniza. "Good Jesus, how truly happy and holy should I be if I could clearly behold my own *Nothing* in Thy *All*; if I could embrace crosses as crowns."[75] Despite the huge ontological difference between ourselves and God Almighty, we have one thing in common with the second Person of the Trinity! When the Incarnate Word preaches the cross to you, Grou says, it is while "He is laden with His own, which combines and surpasses all the crosses of mankind put together. It is in your name and as your representative that He bears it; it is on account of His love for you."[76] Jesus explained to his disciples that to suffer is the greatest happiness of Christianity: they will be blessed when they are hated, when their reputation is torn apart, when they are spoken ill of and persecuted – in short, when they become what Boudon calls living crosses. "Blessed, then, are those who suffer, more blessed those who suffer more; but very happy those who are

---

72. De Ravignan, *The Jesuits*, 50.

73. De Castaniza, *The Spiritual Conflict and Conquest*, 44.

74. Teresa of Avila, *The Book of Her Life*, in *Saint Teresa of Avila, Collected Works, vol. 1: The Book of Her life, Spiritual Testimonies, Soliloquies* (Washington, D.C.: ICS Publications, 1987) 112.

75. De Castaniza, *The Spiritual Conflict and Conquest*, 350.

76. Grou, *The School of Jesus Christ*, 183.

crucified from everywhere, who cannot either set foot, or rest their head, or lean on their hands, or support their bodies except on the cross, who are living crosses, who have no part in the body or in the spirit that is not crucified."[77]

For this reason, Vianney preaches that Christians have the opposite reaction to crosses than worldlings have. "Worldly people are miserable when they have crosses, and good Christians are miserable when they have none. The Christian lives in the midst of crosses, as the fish lives in the sea."[78] This life is one immense Calvary, but it is leading to resurrection if we stay faithfully upon the path our Lord marked out. A trail through the woods will be posted with signs; this trail to heaven is posted with crosses. Following Jesus to heaven requires uniting "our little crosses to his great one"[79] (de Sales), "our little crosses … to the heavy cross of our Lord and Savior"[80] (Grou). We are bold to admit that the cross of Christ saves, and we like to preach this good news, however we are much more hesitant about the subsequent fact that his cross must be established in us. When Jesus gave his disciples their mission to convert the world, he told them they were being sent as his Father had sent him, "as if He would say: 'My Father sent Me to convert and save men by humility, by the suffering of the Cross; I send you for the same design, and I give you the same means to execute it.'"[81]

---

77. Boudon, *The Holy Slavery of the Admirable Mother of God*, 175.

78. Vianney, *The Little Catechism of the Curé of Ars*, ch 18.

79. De Sales, *Letters to Persons in the World*, 420.

80. Grou, *Manual for Interior Souls*, 350.

81. Saint-Jure, *A Treatise on the Knowledge and Love of Christ*, vol. 2, 202.

CROSSES ARE TOTALLY CHANGED

Thanks be to God, de Sales says that when we accept the cross of Christ, then our own crosses are totally changed. "Plant in your heart Jesus Christ crucified, and all the crosses of this world will seem roses to you. Those who are pricked with thorns of the crown of our Lord who is our head, scarcely feel of the thorns."[1] The more crosses sent by our divine Spouse, "the more progress you will make in His holy love," reminds Libermann, and it does not matter whether the crosses be exterior or interior, it only matters that, "reserving your soul in peace and humility before God, you bear them with love as did our Divine Model."[2] This is not a matter of deceiving oneself by covering crosses with faux roses to ward off our initial fear and resistance, it is a matter of finding where the real joy lies, according to Alacoque. "What really ought to give you the greatest joy is to feel the pricks of the thorns hidden beneath the roses. Then it will please the Lord to make you like unto Himself. Then He will make you see that He is not less lovable in the bitterness of Calvary than in the sweetness of Thabor."[3]

A cross is bitter to the world, but made sweet to the disciple of Christ because of love for the Savior who is on it, and whose life the disciple imitates. Jesus testified that he came into this world, not to do his own will, but the will of his Father, and Bona says "to this our will ought to be inclined, that laying aside all property, it may embrace the cross of Christ, *to nature bitter, but to the spirit most sweet.* For this our Christian profession requires of us,

---

1. De Sales, *Letters to Persons in the World*, 368-69.

2. Libermann, *Letters to Religious Sisters and Aspirants*, Spiritan Series 5, vol. 1, 8.

3. Alacoque, *Letters*, letter 3, Kindle edition.

that we say by Christ's example in every work and event, *Not my will, but the will of God be done.*[4] To explain this sweetness, Vianney invokes the imagery of the cross as a wine press. "If you put fine grapes into the wine press, there will come out a delicious juice: our soul, in the winepress of the Cross gives out a juice that nourishes and strengthens it … Thorns give out a perfume, and the Cross breeds forth sweetness. But we must squeeze the thorns in our hands, and press the Cross to our heart, that they may give out the juice they contain."[5]

In short, the view of crosses is totally changed when crosses become matters of love. Many still see the cross as foolishness and a stumbling-block, but de Estella wonders what would they think when their view of the cross changed radically.

> What will Thy brethren, Thy sons and Thy friends … think when Thy love is more unfolded? This is what makes them beside themselves, remaining enraptured … Hence arises their self-suppression; and the kindling of their affections; hence the desire of martyrdom; hence their contentment with tribulations; hence their delighting in what the whole world fears, their embracing what the world abhors. The soul which is betrothed unto Thee, O Redeemer of the world, and which voluntarily unites itself to Thee in the bridal chamber of the cross, holds nothing to be more glorious than to bear within itself the offence of the Crucified … O cross! Open a place for me and receive my body within thee, and deliver me to my Lord! Enlarge thyself, O crown, that I may be able to place my head within thee.[6]

We beg Christ not to remove the crown of thorns from his head, but to enlarge the crown so members of the Mystical Body can be placed within their Head.

Yes, crosses are destructive: they destroy self-love. Then we may be imprinted with love for Jesus, and imprinted with Jesus's love. De Caussade says this is the reason to bear them.

---

4. Bona, *The Principles of Christianity*, 106.

5. Vianney, *The Little Catechism of the Curé of Ars*, ch 18.

6. De Estella, *Meditations on the Love of God*, 94-95.

"It is necessary to bear the little crosses we encounter every day, for by them God will enable us to destroy our self-love,[7] and Grou adds that as self-love decreases, a different sort of love will increase: "The love of crosses is one of the first feelings that God implants in their hearts, and that love is always on the increase."[8]

> Since crosses are the great scourges by which self-love is destroyed, and the best means of establishing in the soul the reign of Divine Love, my duty is to value them, to cherish them, to desire them, if God inspires me to do so; to await them at least with quietness, to receive them with submission, to bear them with patience and self-abandonment, and to make it my happiness here below to glorify God by this great feature of resemblance to Jesus Christ.[9]

Can this be done painlessly? No. Self-love will resist self-surrender, and that causes the suffering we associate with crosses. The mystery of iniquity not only injures the soul, it resists its rehab. "How strange," observes Grou, "that man's pride and inconceivable self-love should make him rebel against his inevitable subjection to crosses, when it was nothing but his own sin that brought him to his present state! He was the cause of the disease, and yet rejects the remedy."[10] Self-love finds the antidote bitter, the cure painful, the remedy objectionable, but "be brave!" exclaims Alacoque. "Medicines the most conducive to health are often the most bitter to the taste. In a word, God, wishing to possess our heart completely, will not let it taste anything but bitterness in creatures and all things here below, so that, in drawing all its affections away from them, it may remain quite buried in Him and united with Him by the love of its own abjection."[11] The comfort comes in due time, in due order, and in the meantime Fenelon is sure that

---

7. De Caussade, *Abandonment to Divine Providence*, 268.

8. Grou, *The Spiritual Maxims of Pere Grou*, 150.

9. Grou, *Meditations Upon the Love of God*, 174.

10. Grou, *The School of Jesus Christ*, 183.

11. Alacoque, *Spiritual Letters*, letter 98, Kindle edition.

"He does not give poisoned comfort, which only fosters the venom of self-love, as men do; He does not comfort until He has deprived our proud, self-seeking nature of every resource."[12] God's love went as far as the cross in order to reach us; the question is whether our love for God will go as far as bearing a cross in order to surrender to that love? Fenelon counsels, "Seek only self-denial and the Cross. Love, and live by love alone. Let Love do whatsoever He will to root out self-love."[13]

Why must it be done this way? Why must God use crosses? Why can't he simply leave our own recovery up to us? The answer is simple enough, Grou says: self cannot kill self.

> Crosses are the great means which God employs to destroy self-love in us and to increase and purify His love within us. Whilst we, on our side, labour for these two ends by the means which He has placed at our disposal.

> The crosses finish the work; without them it would be imperfect.

> The reason of this is clear.

> Self cannot kill itself; the blow must be struck from elsewhere, and self must rest passive in receiving it.[14]

What self would choose death without God's aid? The blow must come from elsewhere, that is, our life must be sown with spiritual crosses not of our own choosing.

---

12. Fenelon, *Letters to Women*, 46.

13. Fenelon, *Letters to Women*, 178.

14. Grou, *Meditations upon the Love of God*, 170.

The aid God gives increases love, which is necessary because mere obedience to moral duty will not get us out of our fix.

Self-love is pride, and "what are crosses but remedies for the pride they humiliate and the self-love they mortify?" Grou asks. "Accept them, and you are cured."[15] Pride reigns over a false ontology wherein God is not God, God is not love, and God is not life. That is why self-love in the land of pride must be expelled, according to Fenelon, because "self-love is unreal life; The love of God is our only true life: so soon as the last expels the first all is safe. There is no life save in this blessed death."[16] Crosses work for the perfection of love by overcoming the imperfect, incomplete, misdirected, ersatz versions of love by which we normally live. Crosses filled with love replace illusion. Surely you recognize, says Grou, that "self-interested, calculating love, is not the 'perfect love' which alone is worthy of God. That love knows neither limit or measure, human prudence cannot restrain it, it reaches out to 'the foolishness of the cross.' That was the love wherewith Jesus loved us."[17] God must send many crosses to accomplish so great a work, which makes Fenelon exclaim "Oh, how full of love they are, even when they seem to crush us pitilessly. The cross is a holy relic to be kept close, and love without the cross would be a frenzy, and become illusion ... Suffering is a merciful purgatory in this world; but who bears it like the souls God is purifying in the next?"[18]

Reality is repaired, and peace is restored, at the cost of a cross. What we are talking about is simply a contest for love. Who will win our love, Libermann wants to know: God or ourselves? "Don't love yourself too much! The more you love yourself with excessive tenderness, the less you draw Christ's love to yourself. Love Jesus, who is the love and joy of our hearts in the life of our souls. This, dear girl, is what your pains and crosses must help you to accomplish in your soul."[19] John of Avila can hear the soul saying to God: "Therefore on Thy cross I seek Thee: there do I find Thee, and finding Thee, Thou dost

---

15. Grou, *The School of Jesus Christ*, 183.

16. Fenelon, *Letters to Women*, 204.

17. Grou, *The Hidden Life of the Soul*, 6-7.

18. Fenelon, *Letters to Men*, 101.

19. Libermann, *Letters to People in the World*, Spiritan Series 6, vol. 2, 201.

heal me and deliver me from myself, – me, who only obstruct Thy love for me which is my salvation. Now, delivered from my self-love, which is Thine enemy, I give Thee my love."[20] The soul is in love; the soul finds itself in love; and in love, the soul surrenders. "Lay upon me whatever external problems and crosses are needful to keep me under Thy yoke."[21]

Now that the soul has a taste for purity, she welcomes purification. Now that the soul has a taste for humility, she welcomes humiliations. Now that the soul has a taste for life, she welcomes death.

Libermann especially explores this theme, and uses numerous metaphors by which to get us to think differently about crosses. He takes a familiar image from Jeremiah and Isaiah.

> Please, dear friend, do not seek to hasten things that concern God. You should remain in the Lord's presence like clay before the potter. The workman does what he pleases with it: he beats it, presses it, and beats it again to make it supple. The clay offers no resistance; it leaves the potter perfect liberty to do with it what he wishes. The potter fashions a vase and it often happens that when it is half-finished he breaks it up and reduces it to a shapeless mass. He then starts anew to make of it the particular vase he wants. The more the clay has been battered and crushed, the easier it is for the potter to achieve his purpose.[22]

He speaks of the cross as a plough that harrows hard soil.

> Crosses in the beginning are hard and painful. They tear up, plough deeply, "penetrating to the very division of the soul." But they are necessary in order to do away with our self-love and wicked affection for

---

20. John of Avila, *Letters*, 74-75.

21. Fenelon, *Letters to Men*, 59.

22. Libermann, *Letters to Clergy and Religious*, Spiritan Series 9, vol. 5, 116.

earthly things, that are like briars and thorns growing in, and covering the soil of our wretched soul.

Those crosses have still another result: they soften the hardness of our heart and make it receptive for the seed which the Divine Master desires to cast in our soul.[23]

He adds the image of a blacksmith forging iron.

Remain, dear friend, before your Divine Master like an anvil before the blacksmith, or rather like a red hot iron which he holds in his tongs. He strikes it over and over again and the iron assumes every shape he wishes it to take. You are still like crude, unwrought iron, rough, hard, and unyielding. Our Lord has to break you and render you supple by means of contradictions and crosses.[24]

And he speaks of a spade uprooting false will.

Our will is something that is most intimate in us; submitting and abandoning it entirely to our Lord in order that He may vivify and rule it is most difficult and the acme of divine love. To produce this effect most perfectly, our divine Master ordinarily, and even almost always, digs down to the utmost depths of our soul. He uproots everything that belongs to our own love in our own life in order to substitute for them His own divine life and love.[25]

But the main purpose to which Libermann puts his metaphors is to assert that crosses sanctify. This softening, yielding, nourishing, sweetening, and uprooting serves the process of sanctification. "Nothing is more sanctifying than crosses ... This is the only

---

23. Libermann, *Letters to Clergy and Religious,* Spiritan Series 8, vol. 4, 340.

24. Libermann, *Letters to Clergy and Religious,* Spiritan Series 7, vol. 3, 100.

25. Libermann, *Letters to Clergy and Religious,* Spiritan Series 9, vol. 5, 182.

sacrifice that satisfies a soul that is devoted to God."[26] Persons without crosses may enjoy a peaceful life, one without contradiction, but they do not learn to love God in a pure manner because persons "who have no crosses and meet with no contradictions, do not sanctify themselves."[27] "You cannot be sanctified without crosses. And the heavier these crosses are, and the more contrary they are to your desires and tastes, the truer will be your sanctification."[28] This is the reason why God sends a life of crosses and pains: "they are for your sanctification; they must help you to detach yourself from the world and from all that it contains."[29] This only happens under one condition, however, which is that crosses must be well borne. It is possible that if our crosses be not well carried, they will be injurious instead of sanctifying. "Our Lord's cross and sufferings are able to sanctify ours and render them salutary ... [Therefore we should] take great pains to unite ourselves to our Lord afflicted, suffering and dying, and to beg him to bless, to purify, to sanctify and deify our afflictions and sufferings."[30] Our suffering must be connected to Christ's, our crosses must be connected to Christ's. We do not suffer masochistically, we do not suffer moralistically, we suffer liturgically.

Crucial to this new view of crosses is to let God choose them for us in his wisdom, because if they do notcome from God's hand, then they will not be sanctifying. Receive them, do not choose them for yourself – this is affirmed repeatedly by the theologians of abnegation. Fenelon says, "do not make to yourself more crosses than those which God's Own Hand lays upon you."[31] Blosius says, "the crosses and afflictions which God lays upon a man are much more safely borne, than those which a man takes upon himself by his own will."[32] And Bona adds,

---

26. Libermann, *Letters to People in the World*, Spiritan Series 6, vol. 2, 245.

27. Libermann, *Letters to Clergy and Religious*, Spiritan Series 9, vol. 5, 94-95.

28. Libermann, *Letters to Clergy and Religious*, Spiritan Series 8, vol. 4, 309.

29. Libermann, *Letters to People in the World*, Spiritan Series 6, vol. 2, 200.

30. Saint-Jure, *Union with our Lord Jesus Christ in his Principal Mysteries*, 183-84.

31. Fenelon, *Letters to Men*, 131.

32. Blosius, *Spiritual Works*, 137.

The short and ready way to Bliss, is that which our Blessed Saviour hath shewed us, saying, 'Let him that will come after me, take up his Cross and follow me.' His Cross, he says, not that which was to be another man's burden; the Cross which God lays upon him, and has fitted for him, and given him strength to bear: not that which he foolishly shall take up, and soon after poorly sink under ... Now this is every man's Cross, to discharge well the duties of his place and of his several relations, to bear patiently those afflictions which he daily meets in his way, and constantly, by doing better and better that which belongs this province, to endeavour after the highest perfection attainable therein.[33]

The patient does not choose his own way to health, the physician does. The sinner does not choose his own way to bliss, the Divine Physician does.

We have a tendency (out of defensive self-love) to choose the wrong kind of crosses for ourselves. Sometimes we fashion crosses for ourselves by an uneasy anticipation of the future, which Fenelon can readily understand. "We tempt [God] by our false wisdom, by wishing to foresee his plan ... The crosses of the present moment always bring with them their grace, and consequently their amelioration. We see in them the hand of God which is making itself felt. But the crosses of uneasy anticipation are seen outside of God's plan. We see them without the grace to endure them."[34] Sometimes we fashion crosses that feed our own self-esteem, or attract false praise from those to whom we show them off, which de Sales can readily understand. "We do not love crosses, unless they are in gold, with pearls and enamel,"[35] but if the crosses have been placed on our shoulders by Jesus, then we should often "kiss [them] in spirit" without looking "whether they are of a precious

33. Giovanni Bona, *Precepts and Practical Rules for a Truly Christian Life* (London: Printed by M. Clark, 1678) 34.

34. Fenelon, *Spiritual Letters of François De Salignac De La Mothe-Fenelon*, 77.

35. De Sales, *Letters to Persons in the World*, 25.

or fragrant wood; they are truer crosses, when they are of vile, abject, worthless wood."[36] We should kiss the cross because it leads us to God, not because we are proud of it, and Alacoque concludes that in that case, "it matters little of what wood it is made. It should be enough for us that it comes from the Sacred Heart of Our Lord."[37]

All our authors are astute observers of human nature – what it is attracted to, and what it avoids. Croiset gives a description of our natural desire for self-control:

> We propose to ourselves certain plans of life which we intend to carry out at certain times; and, as if our conversion and sanctification were secure, we take no further trouble about correcting our imperfections. Though we are convinced that mortification is absolutely necessary if we would be holy, we refuse the crosses that present themselves under the pretext that they are too small. We sigh after greater crosses, only because we see them at a greater distance. We satisfy ourselves in the meantime with these idle imaginations.[38]

When we are vain about the crosses we carry, then we become talkative, whereas Alacoque says a true cross "is a precious treasure which cannot be preserved unless it be buried in humble silence."[39] Remember that the point of crosses is not to attract flattery, but to produce obedience, resignation, and subservience. In short, Bovilla says, a cross is a changing of will.

> Seeing that thy soul is the temple of God, in which He doth lodge, do thou keep it void of all other things for Him alone. For alone He desireth to find thee, alone without thoughts – alone without desires – alone without thy own will. Seek not for crosses indiscreetly, without the

---

36. De Sales, *Letters to Persons in the World*, 324.

37. Alacoque, *Spiritual Letters*, letter 84, Kindle edition.

38. Croiset, *Devotion to the Sacred Heart of Jesus*, 68.

39. Alacoque, *Spiritual Letters*, letter 132, Kindle edition.

counsel of thy ghostly father, but dispose thyself rather to suffer, for love of Him, whatsoever He may please, and how it shall please Him. Do not thy will, but let God's Will be done in thee.[40]

I said earlier that we sometimes have the reaction to be too hard on ourselves, and sometimes to be too easy on ourselves. It plays out here in fashioning for ourselves crosses that are too heavy or too light. The value of a cross can be detected in its weight, but how the same cross weighs on one person is different from how it weighs on another. Grou thinks we have numerous ways to deceive ourselves.

> Do you claim that they should at lest be crosses of your own choice? For you often say: If it were any other cross I should bear it willingly. This is a delusion. The cross you are carrying is always the one you find heavy and particularly unpleasant. You would say the same of any other if it were laid on your shoulders, and perhaps you would find it heavier ... If crosses were left to your choice you would choose none, or else you would choose badly and repent of it afterwards. God knows better than you what is suitable for you; He loves you more than you love yourself ... If He strikes you on a sensitive spot it is because the malady is there and He is applying the remedy.[41]

Camus remembers de Sales saying that "the crosses fashioned by us for ourselves are always of the lightest and slenderest, and that he valued an ounce of resignation to suffering above pounds' weight of painful toil, good though it may be in itself, undertaken of one's own accord."[42] Some sorts of Christians shallowly say it is necessary to be crucified in order to belong to the divine Master, but deep down, Libermann finds them saying "'I do indeed desire to suffer, but I wish God would be pleased to give me some other cross than the one I have.' And they always find plausible reasons for this. This

---

40. Bovilla, *The Quiet of the Soul*, 16-17.

41. Grou, *The School of Jesus Christ*, 182.

42. Camus, *The Spirit of St. Francis de Sales*, 152.

attitude is wrong. We should take the cross Jesus gives us and carry it wholeheartedly the way He hands it to us, never wearying."[43] Resignation teaches us not to "set limits to the crosses you are willing to bear. Accept all that, as so many precious stones and be afraid to let any escape from your grasp. What are you afraid of? Haven't you the Heart of Jesus on which to rest where you will find the strength and love necessary to bear them?"[44]

After being told how necessary it is to desire crosses, we are now forewarned not to desire the wrong ones. A few saints have been given the privilege of seeking out a very heavy, very hard cross, but Grou thinks most of us should be content with the ones that come to us.

> You are not required to desire crosses, or seek them out, or ask God to send them to you ... Such feelings as these are experienced only by the very few, and are the result, either of a very high degree of acquired perfection, or of a special inspiration. What is required of you is to expect crosses without going out to meet them, and not to be surprised when they come to you, as though you were especially privileged to be free from them; to submit humbly to them when they cannot be avoided; to bear them patiently, with the help of the great motives that religion supplies; to appeal confidently to God for his support and hope steadfastly that He will not forsake you.[45]

The goal is not suffering; the goal is love; suffering is a means. That is why Fenelon says "the crosses which originate with ourselves, are not near as efficient in eradicating self-love, as those which come in the daily allotments of God."[46] The crosses should not

---

43. Libermann, *Letters to Clergy and Religious,* Spiritan Series 8, vol. 4, 116.

44. Libermann, *Letters to Religious Sisters and Aspirants,* Spiritan Series 5, vol. 1, 144.

45. Grou, *The School of Jesus Christ,* 181-82.

46. Fenelon, *Spiritual Progress,* 53.

come from our imagination, our pride, our choice, our piety, or our schemes. "Do not ask God for crosses but bear those sent you."[47] That is best, says Libermann.

One benefit to all of this is to not get ahead of ourselves. We boast that we are willing to accept big crosses instead of little ones, but that is because we suspect that we are less likely to receive the former than the latter! Some saints are given heroic crosses, true, and we admire them for it. But, as de Sales said, some actions "are more admirable than imitable."[48] "Do not desire crosses, unless you have borne those already laid upon you well – it is an abuse to long after martyrdom while unable to bear an insult patiently."[49] Bona supposes these great occasions and heroic acts of virtue "are very rare, but the lesser sort happen almost every moment. We ought therefore to mind little things ... No body is evil on a sudden, but as the wise man says, *He that despiseth small things, shall fall away by little and little.*"[50] Probably abnegation brings austerities to mind, and the latter most certainly have a role to play in mortification. But Gerbet concurs that "Great occasions of conquering self are rare, real persecutions, profound humiliations, excessive toil or privation come but rarely, and do not involve such entire subjugation of self-will as the never-ending daily duties of a Christian life."[51] Accordingly, he adds, we find people who have achieved hard things giving way under trifles; people who practice severe bodily austerities, but give undue license to their tongue; people who bear real persecution, but are keenly sensitive to a sharp word. The purpose of austerity has been not driven home yet. "Such persons may go bravely through severe temptations, and fall helplessly under some trifling assault; they will dream great things of all they would bear, even to death, for God's sake, thereby fostering vanity and self-conceit; and all the while they cannot put up with a disagreeable remark. No doubt it is easier to make one rare great effort than to keep up the ceaseless struggle against self, involved in what are called little things."[52] It

---

47. Libermann, *Letters to Religious Sisters and Aspirants*, Spiritan Series 5, vol. 1, 31.

48. De Sales, *Treatise on the Love of God*, 285.

49. De Sales, *Introduction to the Devout Life*, 171.

50. Bona, *The Principles of Christianity*, 85. Emphasis in original.

51. Gerbet, Self-Renunciation, 43

52. Gerbet, Self-Renunciation, 43

is probably the reason we daydream about one great effort of abnegation – because it is rare, and singular – and we can give up on the unending mundane abnegations that occur frequently and regularly. We are wrong when we call those occasions little. We are wrong when we think only some states of life are called to it, Croiset reiterates. "It is a great error to think that we cannot attain perfection without doing something extraordinary; we may be very eminent saints only by acquitting ourselves exactly the duties of our callings."[53]

We deceive ourselves (though not God) by boasting that we would be willing to undergo physical martyrdom, expecting in the meantime to be spared mundane crosses. Vianney thinks when we do this we have the wrong kind of martyrdom in mind, anyway. "The good God does not require of us the martyrdom of the body; He requires only the martyrdom of heart, and of the will ... Our Lord is our model; let us take up our cross, and follow Him."[54] The delusion we suffer is a symptom of pride, and vividly so. Grou says:

> A desire for great things is generally a delusion of self-love and presumption. Do you wish to practice great austerities in their heavy crosses in imitation of some saint of God? Beware of pride and self-esteem; the saints never conceived any such desires. You will probably grow slack as soon as the first excitement is passed, and in spite of all your ambition, you will very likely break down under some little cross which

53. Croiset, *A Spiritual Retreat for One Day in Every Month*, 52.

54. Vianney, *The Little Catechism of the Curé of Ars*, ch 18.

you had despised. It is better to wish for nothing, to choose nothing, to take things as God sends them.[55]

Therefore, rather than imagining oneself a companion of the apostle in the mission field, or the saint in the hermitage, or the monk in the desert, de Castaniza thinks "it is far better to take crosses, when, where, and how we find them, than to make them ourselves; for this is loss of time and nourishes self-love."[56] Be content with the present crosses, Fenelon advises, and "before you seek for others, bear these well."[57] Camus calls to mind another conversation with de Sales on this topic.

> Perhaps there is nothing of which men are more apt to complain than that of their own condition in life. This temptation to discontent and unhappiness is a favorite device of the enemy of souls. The holy Bishop [de Sales] used to say: "Away with such thoughts! Do not sow wishes in other people's gardens; do not desire to be what you are not, but rather try most earnestly to be the best of what you are. Try with all your might to perfect yourself in the state in which God has placed you, and bear manfully whatever crosses, heavy or light, may be laid upon your

---

55. Grou, *The Hidden Life of the Soul*, 218-19. He repeats the point in *Manual for Interior Souls:* "I should like to practice great austerities, like such and such a saint; I should like to bear great crosses: this is all pride, all vain-glory. The saints never formed such desires. Now, what happens to us when we do? We try of our own will to perform great austerities; then our fervour cools down, and we give them up; then some very ordinary crosses present themselves to us, and the soul, which thought it could bear such great things, finds it cannot bear the smallest. Let us desire nothing, let us choose nothing, let us take things just as God sends them to us, and just when He chooses to send them to us" (117).

56. De Castaniza, *The Spiritual Conflict and Conquest*, 436.

57. Fenelon, *An English Nun in Exile Translates the Spiritual Letters of Archbishop Fenelon to Madame Guyon*, 195.

shoulders. Believe me, this is the fundamental principle of the spiritual life."[58]

Here is a piece of good news, anyway, says de Caussade. God loves us so much, we will not have to go hunting for crosses, they will find us! "Blessed be God for all. He sows crosses everywhere!"[59]

The divine crosses (the ones given to us by God) work more powerfully and perfectly than human crosses (the ones we select for ourselves), if for no other reason than the fact that God knows the purpose he wants to accomplish with the affliction, and we do not. Bona urges us to trust providence. "*God has given to every man his proper cross, adapted to his strength, and equal to the glory which he has graciously prepared for each. As marble therefore, if it were capable of reasoning, would bear the strokes of the carver patiently, and give him hearty thanks; so it behooves us to rejoice, that God is pleased to finish and polish us with various tribulations, that we may be placed in a higher part of his house.*"[60] The human pairing to divine providence is discretion, and Collins says "discretion is needed in the embracing of crosses. Some people take it as a maxim that whatever is disagreeable is the best, spiritually speaking. This is a delusion."[61] He gives the example of Mary and Martha to make his point. Mary would have found it disagreeable to leave the Lord and help her sister in the household work – would it have been a cross because she found it disagreeable? Certainly not. "Only those crosses sanctify which our Lord lays upon us. To take up crosses at random, or through self-will, is not the road to perfection. Discretion tells us when, where, and how to handle a cross; which crosses to leave and which to take up.[62]

---

58. Camus, *The Spirit of St. Francis de Sales*, 340-41.

59. De Caussade, *Abandonment to Divine Providence*, 176.

60. Bona, *The Principles of Christianity*, 124.

61. Henry Collins, *Heaven Opened; Or, Our Home in Heaven and the Way Thither. A Manual of Guidance for Devout Souls* (London: Thomas Richardson and Son, 1880) 201.

62. Collins, *Heaven Opened*, 201.

When is an affliction liturgical? When it serves God's glory and our salvation (the twin purposes of liturgy). There are other reasons one might suffer, but suffering is liturgical when it serves the glorification of God and the sanctification of man, so it is best to bear the cross of God gives, and to do so simply. Fenelon thinks the means God uses will "accomplish his design much more rapidly and effectually than all the efforts of the creature; for they destroy self-love at its very root, where, with all our pains, we could scarce discover it. God knows all its windings, and attacks it in its strongest holds."[63] Look within. Slow down. Wait patiently. Expect crosses now. Expect crosses where you are. Abandon yourself, Libermann says, "to the guidance of the Master. Follow Him step-by-step, never wishing to rush ahead of Him or to anticipate things."[64] De Sales wrote the following words to a woman during an illness: "Behold a quantity of crosses and mortifications which you have neither chosen nor wished. God has given you them with his holy hand; receive them, kiss them, love them. My God! they are all perfumed with the dignity of the place whence they come."[65]

Bearing a cross is an exercise of obedience, and this begins with accepting the cross God chooses for us – how else could it be an act of obedience? The objective in bearing a crosses to do God's will; he is the master guide to abnegation, and Grou thinks accepting his choice of cross is the very first act of bearing that cross. We would avoid touching our weak point, which is why we

> generally prefer any other cross to that one which we actually have to bear. It wounds us and revolts against our nature. We cry aloud in our despair, or excess of agony renders us silent.

> It was, therefore, necessary to strike the blow there; for there nature was alive, self-love was sorrowful because of it; and if it could have been master

---

63. Fenelon, *Spiritual Progress*, 112.

64. Libermann, *Letters to Clergy and Religious,* Spiritan Series 9, vol. 5, 185.

65. De Sales, *Letters to Persons in the World,* 217.

of the occasion, it would have struck the blow anywhere else, where the
suffering would have been less deep.[66]

Selecting our own crosses will backfire and actually strengthen our self-will rather than
diminish it. How ironic, thinks Fenelon. "It is the fact of their being His selection which
disturbs and roots out self-will. Crosses which you picked out and thought well to bear,
so far from being crosses and means of death unto self, would be all that was wanted to
sustain and strengthen self-will."[67] Any crosses not given by divine grace will not pierce
as far as the spirit, which is what exactly where God intends them to reach. Baker then
finds them only working on the surface, and not piercing to the spirit. Though a surface
treatment may prevent some of the effects of self-love, it is "far from expelling that secret
self-love which lurks in the inmost centre of our souls; so that they may remain grievously
full of stains and infirmities, and the divine love feeble and easy to be extinguished,
notwithstanding the effects of such crosses."[68]

What makes God so expert in picking crosses? He knows his children, like a Father; he
knows our disease, like a Physician; he knows our vagrancy, like a Good Shepherd. That
is why Fenelon thinks

> God is ingenious in making us crosses. He makes them of iron and of lead,
> which are heavy in themselves. He makes them of straw which seems to
> weigh nothing, and which are less difficult to carry. He makes them of
> gold and of precious stones, which dazzle the spectators, which excite the
> envy of the public, but which crucify no less than the crosses which are
> most despised. He makes them of all the things which we like the best,
> and turns them to bitterness. Favour brings vexation and importunity. It
> gives what we do not want, and takes away what we should like.[69]

---

66. Grou, *Meditations upon the Love of God*, 173.

67. Fenelon, *Letters to Men*, 243.

68. Baker, *Holy Wisdom*, 214.

69. Fenelon, *Christian Perfection*, 16.

God knows how to select crosses, and how to distribute crosses, and how to work crosses, so what are you even thinking of when you want to take charge of this? "Where are your thoughts," in Camus' phrase, "when you do not only wish another cross, but even dare to demand it of God, as though you were wiser than that eternal wisdom, to discern what is most convenient for you? O what a presumption, how blind an inconsideration, what an immortification is this! What irresignation, what self-love! No, my Theopiste, no, not as thou wilt, but as God will: his will not your be done."[70]

The success of crosses depends upon the wisdom of God. Only God knows how to go far enough; we always stop short (Fenelon).

> It is the circumcision of the heart which makes us children and inheritors
> of Abraham's faith ... Our own hand always stops short in superficial
> prunings. Self-love stays the hand, and spares us; it will not cut down
> into the very quick for itself. Moreover, there is always a choice, and an
> exercise of self-love in that choice, which deadens the blow. But when
> God's Hand is lifted, it deals unexpected blows; it knows precisely where
> to hit the joints so as to sunder the soul from self; it searches all things.
> Then self-love becomes the patient, and we must let it cry out.[71]

Only God knows how deep to go; we always remain superficial (Grou). "It was, therefore, necessary to strike the blow there; for their nature was alive, self-love was sorrowful because of it; and if it could have been master of the occasion, it would have struck the blow anywhere else, where the suffering would have been less deep. This is the reason why God sends us ordinary crosses."[72] Only God knows how to reach the quick; we always remain shallow (Fenelon). "God always attacks us on our weak side; we do not aim to kill a person by striking a blow at his insensible parts, such as the hair or nails, but by endeavoring to reach at once the noble organs, the immediate seats of life. When God

---

70. Camus, *A Spiritual Combat*, 153-54

71. Fenelon, *Letters to Men*, 261-62.

72. Grou, *Meditations upon the Love of God*, 173.

would have us die to self, he always touches the tenderest spot, that which is fullest of life. It is thus that he distributes crosses. Suffer yourself to be humbled."[73]

What of us, then? What is required of us? Is there not something we must be doing? Yes, we must be willing. We must accept the divine crosses voluntarily. We must stay at Calvary. "Alas!" Faber warns: "the world is full of deserters from Calvary, so full that politic or disdainful grace seems to take no trouble to arrest them. For grace crucifies no one against his will."[74]

Liturgical abnegation does not suppose that we will accept crosses at the beginning with pleasure. There are trials, admittedly. Yet even so, even at the beginning stage, de Castaniza thinks we can say "You are welcome, Cross of my God; I embrace you with a resigned will; make me suffer until my self-love becomes crucified and dead."[75] The world cannot understand how the Christian passes a threshold from enduring crosses to welcoming them, because it has never experienced this transition. Boudon is certain that joy follows the esteem of crosses, but he does "not believe that we can imagine the joy of the soul which carries them as is necessary; only those who have the experience of it can indeed know it."[76] Yet the unimaginable is true. Faith precedes experience. Knowledge follows experience.

Then a most remarkable thing happens. A marvel unfolds when the cross kills corrupt nature. "When this stage has been reached, one desires no longer to be free from crosses"[77] (Libermann). A change of desire is one of the effects of love, and only love for God could change a desire to be free from crosses into a desire to welcome them. Boudon thinks "it is proper to love to transform," and therefore, "the soul which loves Jesus is more in Him than in itself; it lives no longer, it is Jesus Who lives in it. It only looks, then, at things as He sees them, it enjoys them as He enjoys them: so all his liking is for pains and crosses,

---

73. Fenelon, *Spiritual Progress*, 102.

74. Faber, Foot of the Cross, 333

75. De Caussade, *Abandonment to Divine Providence*, 215.

76. Boudon, *The Holy Slavery of the Admirable Mother of God*, 185.

77. Libermann, *Letters to Clergy and Religious,* Spiritan Series 8, vol. 4, 333.

all his joy in sorrows."[78] The soul's life, vision, and liking have been Christified. This operation of love is invisible to the world, just as the work of the cross is invisible to the world. Sometimes the world even salutes a person as having good fortune, when, actually, Fenelon understands that God is doing something completely different underneath. "The world does not see your cross ... Everything that dazzles the spectators disappears in the eyes of the person who possesses it, and God really crucifies him while all the world envies his good fortune."[79]

The sinner and the believer have different reactions, for good reason, Vianney finds. "Most men turn their backs on crosses, and fly before them. The more they run, the more the cross pursues them," but a believer goes in the opposite direction, toward the cross, because "He is pleased to meet them; he loves them; he carries them courageously. They unite him to Our Lord; they purify him; they detach him from this world; they remove all obstacles from his heart; they help him to pass through life, as a bridge helps us to pass over water."[80] This is a liturgical reaction to crosses: namely, a reception of crosses in order to liturgize Jesus' Father, as he did on his own cross. There is a glory in the secret of crosses, and if it sometimes confounds even the devout Christian, then certainly worldly men will never understand anything of it. Boudon explains in detail.

Whatever reading they do, whatever sermon they hear, their mind has no access to it. The proud and the self-sufficient will never understand it; it will always be a word hidden from human prudence: lovers of themselves will always be ignorant of it; and those who seek themselves will not find it: only the spirit of death and annihilation makes the soul disposed to the understanding of it which Our Lord gives. There are, then, those who do not savor the knowledge of it, because they are delicate people, who love their ease, who work to give some satisfaction to their mind and their body: people interested in honor and eager for glory, who place their joy in the applause of men, who desire their esteem, who love to be loved by

---

78. Boudon, *The Holy Slavery of the Admirable Mother of God*, 173.

79. Fenelon, *Christian Perfection*, 16.

80. Vianney, *The Little Catechism of the Curé of Ars,* ch 18.

them: people who are afraid of creatures, very timid in the contradictions which can happen to them, who have no courage to resist them, and to suffer rejections from them. All these people say that the word of the cross is very hard, and that there is no way to understand it; they are even afraid of crucified persons: they would not dare to frequent them, for fear of sharing in their crosses.[81]

Will one come to welcome crosses? The proper synonym for "welcome" is joy, and it is time to make that explicit.

Welcoming the cross means being joyful in the midst of tribulations. This is "not a joy of the senses," Fenelon admits. "It is a joy of pure will."[82] This joy of pure will is not an emotional fervor, which would easily evaporate. The joy of pure will belongs to the liturgist. Without this, Libermann admits a soul will quickly feel crushed by crosses. "But a soul that is wholly given to God, is animated by a spirit of sacrifice, and is firmly attached to Him, becomes accustomed to suffer joyfully the crosses that are sent to it. It ends by enjoying them, by finding in them great facility for union with God and a much greater and unshakable peace than that which is the result of an emotional (sensible) devotion."[83] The joy of the will is not partial and penultimate, it is full and ultimate, Boudon finds. "It is not enough to suffer without complaining, it is not enough to suffer in patience, it is not enough to suffer with joy; but crosses have to be the fullness of our joy."[84]

Only one thing could possibly account for this joy: it is the climax of the life of the soul. Tronson observes the soul as one that has reverence for spiritual things; she cares that the name of God is magnified; she maintains the splendor of God's house, the Church; she does devout participation in the holy sacraments; she is so jealous for the honor and glory of God that disobedience rendered by the world causes are intense grief, and in preparation for these insults she "is willing to suffer whatever crosses may be appointed

---

81. Boudon, *The Holy Slavery of the Admirable Mother of God*, 194.

82. Fenelon, *Christian Perfection*, 98.

83. Libermann, *The Rule by Nicolas*, 179.

84. Boudon, *The Holy Slavery of the Admirable Mother of God*, 187.

for her, and to endure them joyfully, if she may thereby contribute to the glory of God."[85] If the soul's suffering is liturgized – if the cross the soul receives contributes to mystical latria – then she will endure it joyfully. Joy in the face of the cross is accounted for by sanctifying union with Christ and the glorification of our Father. I call the joy liturgical; Libermann describes it as "a joy given us by the Spirit of Jesus who operates in the tried soul and is united to the soul. Joy and peace are always the fruits of the Spirit of Jesus, but since in this case He operates by means of crosses and afflictions in the afflicted soul, he does likewise in us. You see, then, how ideal it is to be empty of all existence in creatures and by creatures, in ourselves and by ourselves."[86] (We are back to annihilation.) It is joy that arises from the matrix of union with Christ, the Holy Spirit, nothingness, and love.

Especially love. The crosses appear as trials in the eyes of the world, but Christians are not of this world. Vianney has observed them abnegating this world in favor of their Father's house.

> Trials are not chastisements; they are graces to those whom God loves ...
> We must not consider the labor, but the recompense. A merchant does
> not consider the trouble he undergoes in his commerce, but the profit he
> gains by it ... What are twenty years, thirty years, compared to eternity?
> What, then, have we to suffer? A few humiliations, a few annoyances, a
> few sharp words; that will not kill us. It is glorious to be able to please
> God, so little as we are![87]

In fact, the sense of our littleness, and the growing sense of our unworthiness, are themselves signs of our increase of love. "It becomes a pain to us that we have so little to offer to God," moans Faber. "The more we know Him, and the more we approach to thoughts at least a little more worthy of His blessed Majesty, the more this feeling increases upon us, and, as I say, becomes a pain. It is this which drives the saints to yearn for suffering

---

85. Tronson, *Examination of Conscience*, 20.

86. Libermann, *Letters to Clergy and Religious*, Spiritan Series 8, vol. 4, 312.

87. Vianney, *The Little Catechism of the Curé of Ars,* Preface. Elipses in original.

and to pray for crosses."[88] Grou provides an example. A person's mind may be convinced, but he should pray that God will go on to touch his heart, and

> make it love what should be dear to it on so many grounds. Grant that I
> may fear crosses no more, nor rebel and murmur against them; but may
> bear them in silence, patience, resignation, and submission in union with
> Thy holy will; and may love and bless Thee, like Job and Tobias, through
> all the tests that Thou art pleased to send me. Amen.[89]

Reason tells us that crosses are inevitable; religion teaches us that without them we cannot expiate our sins to merit heaven; but Christianity goes furthest, and teaches that crosses are precious because they give a resemblance to Jesus Christ. The cross has been taken down from Calvary and its wood refashioned into a yoke, and de Montfort rejoices that we can be joined to Christ by it.

> But if you suffer as you should, your cross will be a sweet yoke (Matt.
> 11:30), for Christ will share it with you. Your soul will be borne on it as
> on a pair of wings to the portals of Heaven. It will be the mast on your
> ship guiding you happily and easily to the harbor of salvation.

> Carry your cross with patience: a cross patiently borne will be your light
> in spiritual darkness, for he knows naught who knows not how to suffer
> (Eccl. 34:9).

---

88. Frederick Faber, *All for Jesus*, 134-35.

89. Grou, *The School of Jesus Christ*, 185.

Carry your cross with joy and you will be inflamed with divine love, for only in suffering can we dwell in the pure love of Christ.[90]

---

90. Louis de Montfort, "Letters to Friends of the Cross," in *The Saint Louis de Montfort Collection* (London: Catholic Way Publishing, 2013) Kindle 499.

EUCHARIST UNDERSTOOD AS ABNEGATION

Where have we been led by everything in the preceding chapters? To what has abnegation, providence, justice, hope, mercy, nothingness, humility, the problems of self, and the cross itself led us? To the altar of sacrifice, the table of thanksgiving, the bread of heaven, the body and blood of the risen crucified. Chardon finds Christ's abnegation binding him to the Eucharistic altar:

> His love holds Him there, reduced to a state wherein He has neither being, nor life, nor presence except for us. It is a state unworthy of His greatness, but it is just what we need. He is deprived of His external glory so that He may be useful to us ... The Eucharistic Christ does not disdain either the cabins of the poor or the huts of the lepers. He does not prefer the dwellings of princes or the magnificent palaces of monarchs. Cancerous lips touch His mouth, as well as lips that rival the roses in their color and sweetness. Nothing can daunt His loving inclination to give Himself ... Whether He is honored or scorned, adored or cursed, praised or held in abomination, it touches Him not, so long as He can leave upon earth the device of a God who loves to the point of ecstasy, with a love whose property it is to be a separating love.[1]

---

1. Louis Chardon, *The Cross of Jesus*, vol. 1 (St. Louis, MO: B. Herder Book Co., 1957) 104.

One might think that because these theologians of liturgical abnegation give so much attention to the interior life they would pay little attention to the Blessed Sacrament. One would be wrong.

- Fenelon: "Do not regulate your Communions by your life, but your life by your frequent Communions."[2]

- De Caussade: "For Holy Communion these two points will suffice: before Communion let us act like Martha, and after like Mary."[3]

- Croiset: "A single good Communion is enough to make a Saint."[4]

- Faber: "Some saints have been made saints by one thing. One Communion is enough to make a saint."[5]

- De Sales: "Salvation depends sometimes upon one Communion. How do you know whether this Communion may not be the one you omit?"[6]

I am going to confine my attention in these two chapters to the relationship of Eucharist to abnegation, and abnegation to Eucharist. There will not be time to consider other facets presented by the theologians of liturgical abnegation, namely, the doctrine of real presence and transubstantiation, the frequency with which one should receive communion (which is discussed quite a lot), spiritual versus sacramental communion, remote and proximate preparation, the effects of deification, and teachings about the joy and delight of receiving communion. Maybe an occasion to do treat these topics will present itself later.

This chapter will consider Eucharist as cause for a life of abnegation, and de Liguori can set us on our way. The Eucharist returns us to nothingness. "When Jesus comes to

---

2. Fenelon, *Letters to Men*, 221.

3. De Caussade, *Abandonment to Divine Providence*, 99.

4. Croiset, *Devotion to the Sacred Heart of Jesus*, 152.

5. Frederick Faber, *Spiritual Conferences* (New York: Benziger Brothers, 1800) 225

6. De Sales & Crasset, *The Secret of Sanctity*, 73.

dwell in a soul in the Holy Communion, oh, how clearly does she see and know her own nothingness by the bright light which the king of heaven brings with him!"[7] It causes abnegation of self-will. "I desire to receive Thee within myself, that Thou mayest be the God of my heart and of my will ... O Love, O God of love, reign, triumph over my entire self; destroy and sacrifice all in me which is mine and not Thine."[8] It makes us forget self-love. "O my God, O Blessed Sacrament, since Thou wilt have me to be all Thine, make me what Thou wouldst have me. Make me forget everything that does not belong to Thy love."[9] Renunciation of the world is the result of feeding on Jesus. "O my beloved Jesus, since Thou wilt feed me this morning with Thine own blood in the Holy Communion, it is but reasonable that I should willingly renounce all the delights and pleasures which the world might give me."[10] Because after feeding upon the Logos himself, what attraction could creatures possibly still hold? "Yes, I do renounce all other love, and choose for myself Thy sweet love, my God, my all. Begone, ye creatures! what do you want with me? Go and enjoy the love of those who seek you. I wish only for my God; for God alone will I keep all my heart and all my affections."[11] At the altar table one can witnesses again the lengths to which God has gone to captivate our love, therefore we give preference to him above every self-satisfaction. "Make me hunger to be continually in Thy presence in the Blessed Sacrament, to receive Thee into myself, and to keep Thee company. I should be indeed ungrateful did I not accept so sweet and gracious an invitation. Ah, Lord, annihilate in me all affection for created things!"[12] In short, union with God results in detachment from the world. A Christian is called to be in the world, but not of it. Detachment from the world is neither a penalty nor a condition – it is a result.

---

7. de Liguori, *The Sacrifice of Jesus Christ* in *The Holy Eucharist*, vol. 6 of *The Ascetical Works* (New York: Benziger Brothers, 1887) 85.

8. de Liguori, *Visits to the Blessed Sacrament and to the Blessed Virgin*, in *The Holy Eucharist*, vol. 6 of *The Ascetical Works* (New York: Benziger Brothers, 1887) 157

10. de Liguori, *The Sacrifice of Jesus Christ*, 88

11. de Liguori, *The Sacrifice of Jesus Christ*, 90

12. de Liguori, *Visits to the Blessed Sacrament and to the Blessed Virgin*, 179

So ought every soul to say who is united with Jesus in the Blessed Sacrament: Creatures, depart from me; go out altogether from my heart. I loved you once, because I was blind; now I love you not, nor can I ever love you again. I have found another good, infinitely more delightful than you; I have found in myself my Jesus, who has enamoured me by his beauty; to this love I have given myself entirely. He has already accepted me, so that I am no longer my own. Creatures, farewell: I am not, nor shall I ever again be yours; but I am and shall be always Christ's.[13]

When God passes by, he stirs up abnegation. When God draws us to himself, he simultaneously draws us away from all that is not him. De Granada notices that if, at the level of nature, "earthly Things, and even the Images and Figures of them, do so possess our hearts as to make us forget Thee," then why not let a more salutary forgetfulness occur at the level of supernature, and ask "Why does not Thy true and real Presence so surprisingly seize me, as to make me forget the whole World for Thee!"[14] This is the divine favor we invoke, exemplified by Bona's prayer: "O Sweetness of my heart, O life of my soul, O essence of my being, and delightful rest of my spirit, draw me away from all created things that I may repose alone in Thee."[15] Courbon makes a very similar prayer: "Draw me, O Lord, by your love; let your powerful grace disengage my heart from all creatures, that with you I may now be elevated on the cross, in order to reign with you eternally hereafter."[16] Drawn by God, abnegation, on the cross, eternal life. We run after God,

---

13. de Liguori, *The Sacrifice of Jesus Christ*, 98

14. Louis de Granada, *Meditations on the Lord's Prayer*, subjoined to the life of Nicolas Herman in *The Great Advantages that Arise to a Christian by Preserving in his Mind a constant Sense of the Divine Presence*. Edinburgh: Printed for Mr. W. Monro and W. Drummond, 1741) 150

15. Bona, The *Easy Way to God*, 120-21.

16. Courbon (Curé de Saint Cyr), *Meditations on the Passion of Our Lord Jesus Christ, in the Way of Familiar Colloquies, for Every Day in the Month* (Dublin: Richard Grace and Son, 1833) 137.

because he draws us after himself after passing by, and as a result Bona recommends the soul make these aspirations at the lifting up of the host and chalice:

> I love and worship Thee with my whole heart's affection. Wash me in Thy Blood, and grant me to suffer something for the love of Thee.

> Thou art the King of glory, O Christ, Thou art the everlasting Son of the Father.

> Most loving Jesus, by Thy Blood-shedding make me die to the world and to live to Thee, losing myself altogether.[17]

By the shedding of his precious blood, Jesus makes us die to the world and enrolls us as citizens in what Faber calls "the empire of the Precious Blood."

> We must first see in what its royal rights are founded. The Precious Blood ministers to all the perfections of God. It is the one grand satisfaction of His justice. It is one of the most excellent inventions of His wisdom. It is the principal feeder of His glory. It is the repose of His purity. It is the delight of His mercy. It is the participation of His power. It is the display of His magnificence. It is the covenant of His patience. It is the reparation of His honour. It is the tranquility of His anger. It is the imitation of His fruitfulness. It is the adornment of His sanctity. It is the expression of His love. But, above all, it ministers to the dominion of God. It is a conqueror and conquers for Him. It invades the kingdom of darkness, and sweeps whole regions with its glorious light. It humbles the rebellious, and brings home the exiles, and reclaims the aliens. It pacifies; it builds up; it gives

---

17. Bona *An Easy Way to God,* 214.

laws; it restores old things; it inaugurates new things. It grants amnesties; grants pardons.[18]

We are led to abnegation by the new life experienced when Christ takes up residence in us. De Berniere-Louvigny lists the effects of communion as (i) begetting love of crosses, (ii) being transformed, (iii) perfect and consummate union, (iv) conferring of the highest love, and (v) strength and perseverance in serving God, because the Eucharist "ought to produce in us such inclinations as very much resemble those which the hypostatical union produced in the sacred humanity." [19] Confidence in the mercy of God, experienced in Communion, permits our authors to say what they say with such force. No wonder Teresa of Avila recognizes that the devil thinks that when he "has succeeded in driving away a soul from Holy Communion he has gained his ends, and Jesus weeps."[20] We should laugh the devil to scorn. Contempt is a sort of scorn; scorn is mockery or derision; derision is ridicule and laughter; and when the devil tells us that the world (soon ending) is the final abode for a soul (which will not end), tells us that the things of earth have the same ineffable sweetness as the things of heaven, tells us that the taste of a corruptible good is as gratifying as a taste of the Supreme Good, then it is all we can do to stifle our laughter.

We are not rewarded with mystical union upon accomplishing nothingness by our own efforts; to the contrary, the soul is brought face to face with her nothingness upon being filled with love. When the soul is inebriated with the glad drink of the Spirit, then Bona hears her singing the song of the bridal chamber, and "full of love, [she] melts away, losing herself, and being, as it were, brought to nothing, she falls fainting into the bottomless deep of eternal love. There, dead to herself, she lives in God. She knows nothing, she feels nothing but love. She loses herself in the divine darkness, but such

---

18. Frederick Faber, *The Precious Blood; or, The Price of Our Salvation* (London: Burnes & Oates, Ltd., 1860) 77-78.

19. De Berniere-Louvigny, *The Interior Christian*, 187-99.

20. Therese Lisieux, *Thoughts of the Servant of God Therese of the Child Jesus* (New York: P.J. Kenedy & Sons, 1915) 160.

losing is a true finding."[21] The fact that we accept this mystical death makes it possible to think of every Eucharist as a viaticum: food given to a dying person as a supply of provisions for a journey. The soul is on a journey. She is traveling through this world, and liturgical abnegation keeps her eyes fixed on the heavenly prize, lest she be sidetracked by worldliness. Vianney says we can take it as a tribute to the soul's excellence that nothing less than God himself can feed her.

> To sustain the soul in the pilgrimage of life, God looked over creation, and found nothing that was worthy of it. He then turned to Himself, and resolved to give Himself. O my soul, how great you are, since nothing less than God can satisfy you! The food of the soul is the Body and Blood of God! ... How happy are the pure souls that have the happiness of being united to Our Lord by Communion! They will shine like beautiful diamonds in Heaven, because God will be seen in them.[22]

The world is totally mistaken when it thinks Christian doctrine debases the human being. Lallemant says conceiving humility as something that debases us is a totally false idea "It does just the opposite: for since it gives us the true understanding of ourselves, and since it is the pure truth, it brings us closer to God; and consequently it brings us true grandeur, which we seek in vain outside God. Humiliation debases us only in men's esteem, which is nothing; but it raises us in God's esteem, and that is true glory."[23] Christian humility derives from a loftier anthropology than can be found in any other philosophy or religion. Humility is a condition for union with God; union with God is the cause for our elevation above all created things; and this union is uniquely celebrated in the sacrament of Divine Love, the Eucharist. Liturgical life is imitation of Christ, and the perfection our imitation of Christ is liturgical abnegation. By the power of the Spirit, we glorify the Father by using the very liturgy the God-Man did in his life. Grou makes a series of connections: "Jesus in the eucharist is a model of interior and exterior

---

21. Bona, The *Easy Way to God*, 26.

22. Vianney, *The Little Catechism of the Curé of Ars*, ch 12.

23. Lallemant, *The Spiritual Doctrine*, ed. Ranum, 63.

silence; he is absorbed in communion with his Father ... He is an example also of perfect self-renunciation, of entire self-immolation."[24]

Most of our chapters have presented Jesus as our exemplar, that is, the one worthy of imitation and an example for us to follow. In the case of the Eucharist, the connection with Jesus is even more intimate, even more powerful, because Jesus' intention, in the words of de Granada, "is to unite to him the soul of the communicant, and to make of two but one thing; which is indeed a spiritual alliance."[25] An alliance with God made man? Yes, says Crasset. "If you have received Communion, persuade yourself that this incarnation is renewed, that the Word is made flesh in you and desires to dwell in you."[26] The incarnation being renewed? Yes, says Grou. "The Eucharist is truly an extension of the Incarnation, imparting to our souls the effects of that adorable mystery, and as the humanity of Christ is divinized by its union with the Word, so we in a manner participate in the divine nature by being incorporated with him. His flesh is truly united to ours; he is not transformed into us, but he transforms us into himself."[27] The Incarnation being extended? Yes, says Camus. "What shall we then say of the mystery of the most holy Eucharist, which is, as it were, an extension of the Incarnation! In the holy Eucharist the Son of God, in His overflowing mercy, not content with having made Himself the Son of Man, a sharer in our humanity and our Brother, has invented a wondrous way of communicating Himself to each one of us in particular."[28] The Incarnation was the communication of God in the worthiest manner possible, but what he applied to human nature in general must be applied to each human being in particular.

This is taught by St. Thomas (himself a great theologian of liturgical abnegation, but outside our timeframe) and his influence on our authors is noticeable. On this particular point of the Eucharist being an extension of the incarnation, Saint-Jure refers to him three times across the body of his work. First, this fact explains the holy union a soul has with

---

24. Grou, *The Interior of Jesus and Mary*, vol. 2, 93.

25. De Granada, *A Memorial of a Christian Life*, 230.

26. De Sales & Crasset, *Secrete of Sanctity*, 53.

27. Grou, *The Interior of Jesus and Mary*, vol. 2, 15.

28. Camus, *The Spirit of St. Francis de Sales*, 390.

Christ. "The Angelic Doctor teaches that the mystery of the Eucharist is an extension of the incarnation; because, as in it the Divinity is united to a particular human nature, so in the holy Communion the Divinity is united to all who approached the holy table."[29] Second, it explains how the river of grace reaches us from God. "The Incarnate Word unites himself to all individual men who receive the Eucharist, and becomes incarnate in a certain manner in them. It likewise effectively represents the death of Christ, it transmits the grace of his death, and communicates its salutary effects ... It is the chief channel through which flow to us the merits of the cross and the gifts of God."[30] And third, it explains a parallel between the Eucharist and the Trinity.

> St. Thomas calls this Sacrament an extension of the Incarnation, and, as it is an extension of the infinite communication which the Father makes of Himself to the Son, and consequently the most sublime and divine communication which God could make outside Himself, so the Sacrament of the Eucharist is an extension of the Incarnation for every faithful soul that receives it, and by consequence, the most excellent imperfect participation that God can give of Himself in the order of grace, whereby He elevates and unites the soul to Himself, transforms, perfects and deifies it in Himself.[31]

Though Jesus Christ ascended, he did not separate himself from his Church. Indeed, the ascension makes possible a more intimate union, with a more multitudinous company, than he ever could have reached in the flesh. Now his divinity under the flesh is extended in his real presence under the eucharistic species, so Rodriguez makes three comparisons and contrasts of the incarnation with the Eucharist. (i) Where did Jesus hide himself? "In the incarnation he has hid his divinity under the veil of flesh, that we may see him; and in the blessed Sacrament, he has hid both his divinity and humanity, under

---

29. Saint-Jure, *The Spiritual Man*, 20.

30. Saint-Jure, *Union with Our Lord*, 344.

31. Saint-Jure, *A Treatise on the Knowledge and Love of Our Lord Jesus Christ*, vol. 1, 611..

the accidents of bread and wine, that we may eat him."[32] (ii) Where is man received? "In the former, God has received man into his bosom and bowels, by uniting human nature to the Divine Word; and in the latter, he wishes that you yourself receive him into your heart and bowels."[33] (iii) And how is the union of the Son to the Father realized in us?

> Man is united to God by the first; God and man unite themselves to you by the second: in the first the communication and union is made with one individual nature, which is the sacred humanity of Jesus Christ, personally united to the Divine Word; but in the second, an union is made with all those who receive his body and his blood. He becomes the same thing with them, not truly by an hypostatical and personal union, but at least, after that, by the most intimate and strict one that is possible.[34]

The Eucharist is a catholic extension of the Incarnation: I mean catholic as universal, in this case. It is an extension to all humanity, across the face of the earth. Christ comes in the Eucharist, says Saint-Jure, "to unite His Divinity to all men in particular. He extends to all men in this mystery of love what He extended only to one in the Incarnation, since He communicates Himself really and personally to all who receive him."[35] In other words (those of Libermann), the Eucharist is how the historical event becomes mystically present: "we receive all the graces contained in the Incarnation, the Nativity, the hidden life, the public life, the Cross, the Resurrection, the Ascension and in the eternal glorification of our adorable head. All these mysteries were realised in his sacred flesh. That is why he gives us this flesh that these fruits may flow as from their source into our

---

32. Rodriguez, *Christian Perfection*, vol. 2, 416. This is a unified quotation, but I have broken it into three elements for clarity.

33. Rodriguez, *Christian Perfection*, vol. 2, 416.

34. Rodriguez, *Christian Perfection*, vol. 2, 416.

35. Saint-Jure, *A Treatise on the Knowledge and Love of our Lord Jesus Christ*, vol. 1, 674.

36. Libermann, *Jesus Through Jewish Eyes*, vol. 2, 83.

souls."[36] The Eucharist is how the tendrils of the tree of life reach new places, new times, and new persons. Eudes contrasts there and here, then and now:

> There He sacrificed Himself on Calvary only; here He sacrifices Himself all over the world by means of the Blessed Eucharist. There He immolated Himself once only; here He sacrifices Himself thousands of times daily. It is true that the Sacrifice of the Cross was accomplished in a sea of sorrows and that it is accomplished here in an ocean of joy and felicity, but the Heart of our Redeemer is still, in our day, as flaming with love for us as it was then. Jesus is ready, if it were possible and necessary for our salvation, to undergo the same sufferings that He bore in His immolation on Calvary, as many times as He sacrifices Himself on the altars throughout the world because of His infinite love for us.[37]

The appropriate response to Jesus in the flesh was to follow him; the appropriate response to Jesus under the species is to hunger for him. And Blosius finds the soul dissolving in prayer. "Hail, sweet Jesus! praise, and honor, and glory be to Thee, who out of Thine Divine unspeakable love, didst institute the Sacrament of the Eucharist, and hast in it given Thyself to us with wondrous liberality, so that Thou mightest remain with us even bodily unto the end of the world. Give me, I beseech Thee, an earnest longing, and enkindle in my inmost soul, an intense hunger for this adorable sacrament."[38] The Eucharist is like the gathering of additional grains of wheat to be ground under the millstone of the cross and baked into the Bread of life. It is like a harvesting of additional faithful souls to be kneaded into the loaf of Christ.

If I may say this in a surprising way, for the sake of effect, Jesus was the first man to live the Christian life. What is the Christian life? Submission to God, love of the cross, union with God, obedience to the Father's will, and so forth, and so on. Who lived that Christian life first? Our Lord. We attach ourselves to his cross, and bear in ourselves his

---

36. Libermann, *Jesus Through Jewish Eyes*, vol. 2, 83.

37. Eudes, *The Sacred Heart of Jesus*, 33.

38. Blosius, *The Oratory of the Faithful Soul*, 28.

mortification, de Sales says, because "there is no other road to Heaven. Our Lord travelled it first."[39] De Berniere-Louvigny describes the law of Christianity as nothing more than loving abjection, and the cross, and humiliation, and abnegation – all to increase the glory of God. "It is the law of Christianity that we ought to love abjection, Jesus having loved it by his Father's order: and he is the grand example we must imitate."[40] And "the more a soul participates of the spirit and interior of the Son of God the more she esteems and loves the cross, and, consequently, does the more glorify God the Father. For, to suffer, is to make a continual sacrifice of our pleasures and interests; uniting ourselves to the design the Son of God had by suffering, viz.: – to repair the glory of his Father."[41] We only arrive at union with God by resembling the hypostatical union, and this is a gift of holy communion. "It ought to produce in us such inclinations as very much resemble those which the hypostatical union produced in the sacred humanity, that is to say, it should incline us to love the cross, poverty, humiliations, and all other manner of sufferings."[42] When Jesus comes into our souls – we may even say "becomes incarnate in us" – he reigns there as a Sovereign, yet Bourdaloue finds that "His greatness is not a hindrance which prevents Him from identifying Himself with us, and in some manner becoming incarnate in us; and we have not grasped the first idea of the mystery of His Body and Blood, if we be ignorant that He makes that infinite condescension minister to His greatness."[43] He confers the love of the cross as his most signal grace, and we follow the path he has taken to restore glory to his Father.

Eudes titles one of his sections as "*The Christian Life Must Be a Continuation of the Most Holy Life Which Jesus Lived on Earth.*" He goes on to explain:

---

39. Francis de Sales, *The Sermons of St. Francis de Sales for Advent and Christmas: vol. 4 in the Series* (Frederick, MD: Visitation Monastery, 1987) 38.

40. De Berniere-Louvigny, *The Interior Christian*, 35.

41. De Berniere-Louvigny, *The Interior Christian*, 47.

42. De Berniere-Louvigny, *The Interior Christian*, 188.

43. Louis Bourdaloue, *Eight Sermons for Holy Week and Easter* (London: Wells Gardner, Darton & Co., 1884) 21.

You are united with Him spiritually by faith and by the grace he gave you in Holy Baptism. You are united with Him corporally in the union of His Most Sacred Body with yours in the Blessed Eucharist. It necessarily follows that, just as the members are animated by the spirit of the head, and live the same life, so you must also be animated by the spirit of Jesus, live his life, walk in his ways, be clothed with His sentiments and inclinations, and perform all your actions in the dispositions and intentions that actuated His. In a word, you must carry on and perpetuate the life, religion and devotion which He exercised upon earth.[44]

Liturgical abnegation is our pursuit of Christ after he has lured us to himself. He is a fisher of men, baiting his hook with his own flesh. But alas, how often we eat, but do not live, grieves Saint-Jure. "Oh! incomparable effect of the Blessed Sacrament! He who receives it must lead a life of the Son of God, if the Son of God speaks truly. Where is that divine life I lead? Is my life always even a reasonable life? Is it not often a passionate life, and animal life? What then have so many Communions during so many years accomplished in me?"[45]

What objects did our Savior have in view when he instituted the holy Eucharist? Libermann sums them as three. First, to unite us with himself,

And do you know what kind of life our Lord Jesus wishes to lead in us? It is a life of separation from all creatures and of total surrender into the hands of His heavenly Father. He does not seek to be honored, loved and esteemed by creatures; He does not pursue the pleasures and enjoyments of the earth; He turns aside from them. He does not live for the sake of being quiet and content upon earth; He never seeks to gratify Himself, nor to do anything for His own satisfaction. On the contrary, He wishes

44. Eudes, *The Life and Kingdom of Jesus in Christian Souls*, 3.

45. Saint-Jure, *Union with our Lord Jesus Christ in his Principal Mysteries*, 392.

to lead in us a pure and holy life, wholly abandoned to His heavenly
Father. [46]

Second, to make a share for us in his union with his Father

It is His will that we seek nothing, desire, love and will nothing but His
heavenly Father. We may, therefore be assured that every movement of
our soul that does not tend directed toward God, is not coming from
Jesus living in us; consequently, such a movement is [spiritually] dead or
insignificant. [47]

And third, to make us live his own life.

If we wish to prepare for Holy Communion, we must be disposed to live
only the life of our Divine Savior. We should, therefore, purify our souls
from every earthly affection, and rid ourselves of every natural movement
and desire.[48]

In feeding us with his own death, Christ makes us deny self, deny vanity, deny the
corruptible, deny all selfish loves, so that we will love nothing but God with single-minded
intensity. Grou says it happens incrementally. "Little by little, we are transformed into
the image of Jesus Christ, and each good Communion adds some more perfect strokes to
this transformation."[49] Each Eucharist can contribute to this, he adds, because in each
Eucharist Christ offers us to his eternal Father, with himself, and "we have but to unite
in that twofold oblation, adopting at the same time intentions and dispositions similar

---

46. Libermann, *Letters to Clergy & Religious*, Spiritan Series 8, vol. 4, 88-89.

47. Libermann, *Letters to Clergy & Religious*, Spiritan Series 8, vol. 4, 89.

48. Libermann, *Letters to Clergy & Religious*, Spiritan Series 8, vol. 4, 89.

49. Grou, *Manual for Interior Souls*, 360.

to his."[50] De Berniere-Louvigny says each Eucharist displays the aim of abnegation. The soul "ought to aim at no other thing in all the actions of her life than to receive this bread of life, to the end she live the life of Jesus, and keep herself continually in such dispositions as she sees in him in the Blessed Sacrament."[51] This means more than dropping a model for us to imitate under our own power; it means delivering on the very prayer Jesus made to his Father when he instituted the Eucharist: "*Rogo, Pater, ut sint unum*; I ask of Thee, O Father! that they may be made partakers of the union that is between us. Wherefore the union he enjoys with God the Father is the model of that which he desires we should contract with him by means of this divine sacrament."[52]

Grou says we should find each Eucharist reproducing in our hearts the love of the cross that was in Christ's heart on the evening of its institution.

> Do you desire to communicate profitably, and in accordance with His Intentions? Come with a special desire that you may thereby grow in love for His Cross, that is for humiliation and suffering, self-renunciation, and self-oblation. Let this be the test of your Communions. Do not hold them to be good, because you have been kindled with warm glowing feelings, but rather if you have come away with fresh courage to conquer self, to fight against your own will, to bear whatever God may lay upon you; if, in short, you are more able to seek God for Himself, more willing to love His corrections as well as His favors.[53]

Do you wish to communicate profitably? It will have been a good communion if it leads you to better liturgical abnegation. Bruyere is on the lookout for an increased imitation of Christ. "Our Lord's Eucharistic life is one of total abnegation, silence,

---

50. Grou, *The Interior of Jesus and Mary*, vol. 2, 20.

51. De Berniere-Louvigny, *The Interior Christian*, 178.

52. De Berniere-Louvigny, *The Interior Christian*, 194.

53. Grou, *The Hidden Life of the Soul*, 109.

poverty, obedience, absolute isolation and tranquil self-surrender which seem to be the ideal of what the soul's life will be when it has become perfectly united with God."[54]

The grace received in the antecedent Eucharist must manifest in the dispositions then brought to the subsequent Eucharist. If the food the body takes in does not empower the body's movement, what good is it? The same is true of spiritual food, Grou suggests: it should empower the soul's movement.

> The Body of Christ is the food whereby our spiritual strength is sustained; it follows that that strength is the test how far our Communions are profitable. It is plain that such strength is to be used in overcoming self, our natural inclinations and dislikes, our sloth, our weakness, our inconsistency, the horror we have of all contradiction, restraint and humiliation; in short all that resists God's Grace within us. If this strength increases with each Communion, if we acquire self-control, if we are less self-indulgent, more devoted, more patient, more steadfast in our resolutions, more indifferent to the world's praise and blame, more docile to the leadings of grace, we may rest satisfied that our Communions are good.[55]

Our theologians regret what I will call "weak communions." Saint-Jure notices pious persons who communicate often "without advancing in virtue, and who, after fifty or a hundred communions, are as proud, as vain, as subject to anger, as deceitful, as full of themselves, and as void of God, as if they had never communicated."[56] This is a depressing thought (though we must not let it become a despairing one). "You have received him so many times, yet no such results have appeared! So many journeys that he has made from heaven to earth for you, so many miracles that he has worked in himself and in nature,

---

54. Bruyere, *Spiritual Life and Prayer*, 64.

55. Grou, *The Hidden Life of the Soul*, 110-11.

56. Saint-Jure, *A Treatise on the Knowledge and Love of Our Lord Jesus Christ*, vol. 1, 630.

have produced nothing in you!"[57] Croiset sees the clear reason why: "we prefer to give up Communion rather than our vices ... The love of Jesus Christ is inconvenient to us."[58] The body of Christ on which we feed should empower us to run the race, and instead, we seem to simply be running in place.

> For a year, for ten years perhaps, you have said Mass every day. You have received the Body and Blood of Jesus Christ more than three thousand times in your life; and yet, for a year, for ten years, you have been fighting against some imagination, some fancy, you say, which hinders you from belonging entirely to God ... If, then, unhappily we find that by communicating every week, or even oftener, or by celebrating Mass daily, we derive no profit from this adorable Sacrament, do not amend, misuse Holy Communion, do not love Jesus Christ more, always feel the same tepidity and weaknesses, are we therefore to leave off Communion? Must we give up saying Mass daily? No; but we must regulate our life and free ourselves from the vices and failings that hinder us from profiting by it.[59]

The synergy of divine, gratuitous grace with human, responsive abnegation is worked out before the altar of the Eucharist more precisely than anywhere else. The sacraments work *ex opere operato*, but the fruitfulness of the sacraments requires dispositions of us. Dalgairns recalls a helpful illustration.

> Devotion does not drop from the clouds, nor does grace makes its way into a soul which wilfully puts an obstacle to it. Let us never forget that we must do something on our part to obtain these dispositions, and moreover, that they are necessary ... the action of grace, *ex opere operato*, has been sometimes compared to that of fire burning wood; the dryness

---

57. Saint-Jure, *Union with our Lord Jesus Christ in his Principal Mysteries*, 379.

58. Croiset, *Devotion to the Sacred Heart of Jesus*, 212.

59. Croiset, *Devotion to the Sacred Heart of Jesus*, 94-95.

of the wood is in no way the cause of the application of the fire, yet it is a condition of its catching.[60]

Saint-Jure uses another image. The one who goes to the river with a thimble will bring back less water than the one who goes with a bucket. "Though all the sacraments operate grace of themselves, and in virtue of their institution, yet they do this in a manner proportioned to the dispositions of those who receive them; so that he who is but little disposed receives but little grace. The Sacrament of the Eucharist, then, gives very little when we receive it negligently."[61] Why don't we receive the grace the sacrament is supposed to bring? In a word, "it is for want of due preparation," which de Sales says consists of three elements: "the first preparation is purity of intention; the second is attention; the third is humility."[62] But, really, all these preparations can be united under the title of abnegation. They must join together for the chief result of "total abandonment of ourselves to the mercy of God, the submission of our will and all our affections, without reserve, to His dominion. I say without reserve, because such miserable creatures are weak, that we are always reserving something for ourselves."[63]

Love causes a desire to give up whatever hinders the growth of that love. So also, here, the Sacrament of Love enkindles a willingness to abnegate self, esteem, and worldly vanity so that the growth of our love for Sacramental Jesus is not hindered. Grou suggests this means there is work to be done both going from and coming to the altar. Our preparation for liturgy uses instruments from the toolchest of abnegation.

> You repeat a great number of prayers, but your mind is not attending to
> them and the prayers do not come from your heart. You are praying only

---

60. John Dalgairns, *The Holy Communion, Its Philosophy, Theology, and Practice*, 315-16

61. Saint-Jure, *A Treatise on the Knowledge and Love of Our Lord Jesus Christ*, vol. 1, 646-47.

62. De Sales, *The Spiritual Conferences*, 348.

63. De Sales, *The Spiritual Conferences*, 350.

with a view to your own interests, and you forget that nothing serves your interests better than loving God well. You ask Him for everything except love, which is the thing you should ask for most of all. You perform good works, but self-love plays a large part in them; you have worldly motives or you have a personal interest in the matter, and although the works are many there is hardly one that is done simply for God's sake.[64]

We should approach the altar from a recognition of our weakness, and not from a position of pretended strength. Here the forthright acknowledgment that we are sinners might persuade even those who have had a severe reaction against the grammar of nothingness. Blosius advises that when you are about to "receive the most Holy Eucharist, see that thou art not present unworthily at that tremendous and heavenly Table. Keep thyself low, hide thyself in the Valley of profound humiliation; confess – yea, confess thyself to be wholly a sinner. Pray to the Lord that He would deign to purify thy soul, and adorn it with His merits and virtues."[65] Abnegation is not a condition we must fulfill before God will approach us, but it is conditional disposition for receiving God, because everything works through the mediatorship of Jesus.

Essentially, the dispositions which will make the Eucharist fruitful in us are those we have been discussing throughout this work thus far. Libermann summarizes them as sacrifice, self-denial, and self-annihilation:

> First, Our Lord wanted us to share in His spirit of sacrifice, for the Most Holy Eucharist is a sacrifice ... This shows that our first preparation for Holy Communion should be a spirit of renunciation to every desire, to all affection and self-will. We must refuse ourselves every satisfaction, every joy; for the quality of a victim demands a complete annihilation. We must annihilate spiritually in ourselves every natural being, which must be sacrificed to God, so that we may live no other life than that of God.[66]

---

64. Grou, *The School of Jesus Christ*, 64.

65. Blosius, *The Manual of the Spiritual Life*, 60-61.

66. Libermann, *Letters to Clergy & Religious*, Spiritan Series 8, vol. 4, 50.

He elsewhere adds withdrawal from the deceits of the world, from self-pleasing vainglory, and from the temptation to feed an infinite hunger with corruptible goods:

> If a soul is not faithful, if, instead of withdrawing its affection from the joys it experiences, to attach oneself to God alone, who is the source of it, it always seeks to feast on pleasures, it will not the least progress in renouncing itself; she will always preserve her spiritual faculties curved towards creatures; she will not acquire this habit of directly attaching her faculties to God, and will never really be united to her ... what a frightful sacrilege to use God himself to procure pleasure. It is as if we were using the adorable bread of the Most Holy Eucharist to satisfy [our] bodily hunger.[67]

Croiset summarizes them as poverty, humility, and spiritual hunger:

> The general dispositions which we ought to bring to Communion are: profound humility and a sincere acknowledgment of our poverty; a certain spiritual hunger, which indicates, at the same time, the need we have of this food, and our good dispositions to profit by it; a great purity of heart, an ardent love of Jesus Christ, or at least an ardent desire of loving Him, and of accomplishing the design which He had in giving Himself to us in the Eucharist – namely, to unite us intimately to Him by a perfect conformity of heart and mind. Those who, at Communion, have no sentiment of devotion, no fervour, no tenderness, are certainly without some of these dispositions.[68]

And de Caussade summarizes them as abasement, humiliation, and annihilation.

> Let yourself be abased, humiliated, annihilated. Nothing is better calculated to purify your soul, and you could not approach Holy

---

68. Croiset, *Devotion to the Sacred Heart of Jesus*, 153.

Communion in a disposition more in keeping with the state of annihilation to which Jesus Christ has reduced Himself in this mystery.[69]

Christ's self-annihilation was denial of a glory that was rightfully his; our self-annihilation is a denial of vainglory that we wrongfully hold. Christ's Nativity and his Passion are both expressions of the economy of kenosis, by which he worked our redemption. Kenosis is God's *modus operandi* on this side of the eschaton: his way among us is one of self-emptying, humiliation, poverty, and abandonment. Grou will not be surprised, therefore, to find traces of kenotic descent in the hiddenness of the Eucharist. "Already to unite Thyself to human nature, Thou hast emptied Thyself, in the Incarnation, of the Majesty of Thy Divine Being; once more Thou dost will to annihilate Thyself in the Eucharist, that Thou mayest unite Thyself to me."[70] Eucharist is linked to abnegation because God hopes to find our hearts empty. De Sales says, "Our Lord, desiring to give Himself wholly to us, wishes that we, on our part, should give ourselves entirely to Him ... [He] finds our hearts all full of desires, affections, and petty wishes. This is not what He seeks, for He hopes to find them empty, that He may make Himself their Master and Ruler."[71] This desire on his part is not resentfulness, as if he is offended by some autonomy on our part. The objective is not to lessen us, but to elevate us.

Rigoleuc connects Eucharist and abnegation by supposing the shared trait of sacrifice. "Be assured of this, that excepting that of the Altar you cannot make a more glorious sacrifice to God, than by *divesting yourself entirely of yourself* for the love of Him, trampling underfoot those idols of self-love and self-esteem."[72] Apparently, daily abnegation can carry the Eucharistic sacrifice with us throughout the day.

---

69. De Caussade, *Abandonment to Divine Providence*, 185.

70. Grou, *The Practical Science of the Cross*, 107.

71. De Sales, *The Spiritual Conferences*, 350-51.

72. Rigoleuc, *Walking with God*, 258.

ABNEGATION UNDERSTOOD AS EUCHARISTIC

Abnegation is linked to the Eucharist because God hopes to find our hearts empty, so he can fill them with himself; he hopes to find us hungry, so he can feed us with himself; he hopes to find us humble, so he can exalt us to his side; he hopes to find us willing, so he can be our Lord and Master. Eymard connects this to the imagery of the wedding garment, without which one guest answered the king's invitation. This man "had not been asked to bring wedding presents, but only to be suitably attired. The others, who had on white garments, remained, poor and maimed though they were; their very misery gave them their right of admission to the banquet" (21). "Our Lord demands nothing of us but the will to come. He gives us our wedding garment in the Sacrament of Penance. He calls all of us, the poor, the halt, the crippled, vagabonds, and beggars" (132). "Then let us be pure; Jesus Christ wills it. Let us labor to make our heavenly garment ever whiter and whiter" (276). "Though we should have only a speck of dust on our wedding garment, we may not enter into heaven until we have cleansed it in the Blood of the Lamb" (281).[1] It is a banquet of grace – grace invites the guests, grace is on the menu – and grace inspires obedience to a labor of abnegation to make our garment whiter and whiter.

Abnegation is Eucharistic because the way he comes to us is how we should go to him. In the words of Saint-Jure:

> In order to come to us, He deigns to obey the voice of a man, to abase
> Himself, to make Himself little, to lead a hidden life in the general

---

1. Peter Eymard, *Holy Communion* (New York: The Sentinel Press, 1940). Page numbers listed in text.

mortifications of His senses ... so, to go to Him, we ought to practice heroic acts of obedience, humility, recollection and mortification; to separate things most closely united, that is, to separate ourselves from attachment to our honor, our convenience, our judgment, and all that is imperfect in us.[2]

And in the words of Eudes:

Our Lord Jesus Christ comes to you in the Blessed Eucharist, with the greatest humility, debasing Himself so far as to take the form and appearance of bread, to give Himself to you, and with the most ardent love that impels Him to give you, in this Sacrament, all the greatest, most dear, and most precious things He has. You also should receive Him in this same Sacrament with the deepest humility and the greatest love. These are the two principal dispositions you should have when you go to Holy Communion.[3]

And in the words of Vianney:

We ought always to devote at least a quarter of an hour to preparing ourselves to hear Mass well; we ought to annihilate ourselves before God, after the example of his profound annihilation in the Sacrament of the Eucharist."[4]

Our abnegation is modeled upon Christ's kenosis at the Incarnation, on the Cross, and upon the altar. Berulle says we must consider the perpetuity of these mysteries of Jesus,

---

2. Saint-Jure, *A Treatise on the Knowledge and Love of Our Lord Jesus Christ*, vol. 1, 671.

3. Eudes, *The Life and the Kingdom of Jesus in Christian Souls*, 132.

4. Vianney, *The Little Catechism of the Curé of Ars*, 33.

"for they are over in certain respects, [but] they remain present and continue forever in another way. They are over as to their execution, but they are present as to their power; and their power never ends, nor will the love in which they were accomplished ever end."[5] Saint-Jure thus describes Jesus in the Eucharist as a continued annihilation.

> At the simple word of a priest, He descends from heaven to earth; ...
> He hides His greatness and infinite Majesty under the species of bread
> and wine; He hides therein the noblest union the divine wisdom could
> form, the hypostatic union of the Divine Word with human nature; ...
> He annihilates Himself in some manner for love of us; ... He obeys, He
> humbles Himself, He exposes Himself to outrages and elevates Himself
> above nature for love of us. Urged by a reciprocal love, we will practice,
> especially today, obedience, humility, mortification, we will stifle within
> us all the movements of corrupt nature, and do all in our power to prepare
> worthily for His visit.[6]

Christ's arrival is gratuitous, and the slave will never make himself worthy of the King's visit. But the slaved can dispose himself for the visit by imitating the King's disposition. Jesus loves us with boundless liberality, therefore we give ourselves to him without any reserve. For God to be All, we embrace our nothingness.

Like molding clay being shaped around a solid form, our liturgical abnegation is shaped round Jesus' Eucharistic kenosis. He comes to us in greatest humility; we go to him with greatest abnegation. He comes to us in greatest poverty; we go to him without shame of our impoverishment. He comes to us in a kind of annihilation; we join him in it, and then, de Caussade says, we can approach "with confidence, with complete abandonment to the state of poverty and deprivation in which it has pleased God to place you. Remain in it as though sacrificed, annihilated and unseen like Jesus Christ in His Sacrament, because He is there in a kind of annihilation. Unite yours to His. Where there is nothing left that is

---

5. Berulle, *Discourses on the State and Grandeurs of Jesus*, 14.

6. Saint-Jure, *A Treatise on the Knowledge and Love of Our Lord Jesus Christ*, vol. 1, 677, 679.

created, or human, there is God."[7] In transubstantiation, Christ is made present under the sacramental species according to the state in which he is, which is one of resurrected and ascended glory, yet Grou says we can still dare approach him on the altar because "He wills to be in the Eucharist with still more simplicity than He lay in the manger, that He may receive with equal welcome poor and rich, shepherds and kings."[8] This is an boundless marvel, on par with Creation, Incarnation, and Resurrection. Boudon is amazed.

> O infinite wonder! ... Can He, I would ask, conceal Himself more perfectly? Assuredly it must be confessed that the love of this God-Man for the hidden life is most intense and most amazing. But in saying this, remember, O my soul, and never forget, that it is thy vainglory, by desire of being of importance and appearing of importance, and the same dispositions on the part of creatures like thyself, that caused these terrible annihilations of a God. After such a spectacle shall we grieve it being left unnoticed or disregarded?[9]

Now all the earlier language about loving the cross finally makes sense. Now all the earlier language connecting annihilation and liturgy finally makes sense. Gay describes adoration as the first movement in the soul of Christ at his conception, and "it was an act of complete annihilation of Itself, which precisely constitutes adoration."[10]

The language of Trent about bloody and unbloody sacrifice proves beneficial, which Grou works out in a number of his books. "The true Sacrifice was consummated on Calvary; all the others ceased. The Sacrifice of the Cross will perpetuate itself only

---

7. De Caussade, *Abandonment to Divine Providence*, 260.

8. Grou, *The Practical Science of the Cross*, 194.

9. Boudon, *The Hidden Life of Jesus*, 64-65.

10. Charles Gay, *The Christian Life and Virtues Considered in the Religious* State, vol. 2 (London: Burns & Oates, 1878) 314.

in the Eucharist, in another form, but always the same."[11] "By virtue of the Divine Consecration, Jesus Christ is after a mysterious manner in the Eucharist such as He was upon the Cross, in a state of immolation and death."[12] Christ made his bloody sacrifice on the historical cross; therefore, when that sacrifice is present in its unbloody form, it will return us to the cross, and create love for the cross in the hearts of all who love his sacrifice. "Since the effect of Holy Communion is to fasten us to the cross, and to help us die there, it follows that our dispositions in communicating, and the effects which it produces in us, are always relative and in proportion to the different states of death to ourselves in which we are found."[13] Liturgical abnegation plumbs the different states of death in which we are found, and this, in turn, reveals new depths in the Eucharist. "What is the Eucharist? A sacrament, and a sacrifice; the most excellent sacrament, and the only sacrifice. In the Eucharist, Jesus Christ renews and perpetuates to the end of time, the sacrifice of the cross."[14] Jesus's love fastened him to the cross; our love must fasten us to the place where he waits for us. "Thou dost fasten to my heart the same Body which Thy Love fastened to the Cross; Thou dost shed there the same Blood, Thou art therein again consumed; Thy Love makes Thee in some sort die therein again, and my soul becomes the sepulchre where my Savior buries Himself, and where He wills to bury me with Him."[15]

If we die, Jesus will bury himself in us; if he did not fear the stone sepulchre, he will not fear to be buried in our hearts; if he rose from the tomb, he will raise us up when he has sanctified us. So de Condren connects cross, resurrection and communion: "as it is by the sacrifice of the Cross that Jesus Christ has redeemed us, so it is by His Resurrection, and by the Eucharistic Sacrifice and communion which correspond to it, that He sanctifies us."[16]

We may imagine four altars: the wood altar of Calvary, the mystical stone altar of the Church, the spiritual altar of our hearts, and the celestial altar in heaven. Christ is at

---

11. Grou, *The Practical Science of the Cross*, 81.

12. Grou, *The Practical Science of the Cross*, 124.

13. Grou, *Manual for Interior Souls*, 369.

14. Grou, *The Interior of Jesus and Mary*, vol. 2, 14-15.

15. Grou, *The Practical Science of the Cross*, 105-06.

work upon them all; the cross is connected to them all; Jesus appears as one single victim on them all, even though one is bloody, one is sacramental, one is interior, and one is supernal. The reason for multiple altars is the restless outreach of charity. Jesus could just not let it rest! Huby writes,

> In order to content the immense desire he has of remaining with us, his love multiplies him and communicates him to every country of the world, to every church of the same town.

> Perhaps Jesus imparts himself to us for some years, for some ages only? No, again. The bonds of love which hold Jesus captive under the sacred species, will detain him on our altars as long as there shall be one single man on earth.[17]

Grou explains that lest the memory of a sacrifice in time be effaced from our minds, Jesus "willed to find in the contrivances of His Love effectual means to apply its merits to His members in every place and every age: He willed, so to speak, to found His Cross in the Eucharist, and to change it into an inexhaustible Fount."[18] The historical and bloody sacrifice could be offered only once, but the whole point of the ecclesial altar is its perpetuity. The Eucharist has "this advantage over the Cross, that It is not only the perpetual sacrifice of the Cross, but moreover an inexhaustible source of life."[19] "What else is the Eucharist," asks Bourdaloue, "but a perpetual representation of the Passion of the Saviour; and what was His intention in instituting it, if not that His Sacrifice on Calvary should be, not merely shadowed forth, but incessantly pleaded and offered on our altars?"[20]

---

17. Huby, *The Spiritual Retreat*, 135.

18. Grou, *The Practical Science of the Cross*, 79.

19. Grou, *The Practical Science of the Cross*, 95.

20. Bourdaloue, *Eight Sermons for Holy Week*, 95.

Leonard of Port Maurice recounts a story in which an ignorant poor woman put this truth terms that cannot be forgotten, and which also shed light on the real presence. During the transit of the Most Holy Viaticum to a sick person, all the faithful knelt and adored the Most Blessed Sacrament as it passed, except a Jew who was standing there and showed no sign of reverence. When the woman asked why not, the Jew's answer was "What true God? If the true God were there it would follow that there are many gods, as you say there is one on each of your altars during Mass."

> The woman immediately took a sieve and placing it between the Jew's eyes and the sun, told him to look at the rays which shone through the apertures. When he had done so, she said to him, "Tell me now, Jew, are there many suns or only one passing through the openings in this sieve?" The Jew answering said that there was but one sun. "Then," replied the woman, "why dost thou wonder if the God-Man, veiled in the Sacrament, though one, indivisible and unchanged, should, through excess of love for us, leave Himself really and truly present on different altars at the same time?"[21]

The spiritual altar of the heart receives the fruits of these sacrifices, but first this heart requires a harrowing. Its hard earth needs breaking up. Christ's expiation for sin was the prelude by which He prepares and disposes the heart for the reception of his benefits. De Condren knows "the expiation was made by His blood and His death, but the grace of Jesus Christ is communicated and His Spirit shed abroad in our hearts by Baptism and the other sacraments, especially the holy Eucharist, which contains the virtue and perfection of all the others; and this is the fruit of the Communion of the sacrifice of the Cross."[22] And all this is for the sake of bringing us home to the beatitude of everlasting liturgy.

A union can be forged between the sacramental altar and the altar of the heart, and thus it is, says Berniere-Louvigny that "sometimes, when communicating, I picture to myself that my heart is an altar, and that Jesus Christ comes to remain upon it in the

---

21. St. Leonard of Port Maurice, *The Hidden Treasure: or, the Value and Excellence of the Holy Sacrifice of the Mass* (Dublin: James Duffy And Co., `895) 12-13.

22. De Condren, *The Eternal Sacrifice*, 115.

same manner as on the altar where Holy Mass is celebrated. Wherefore my heart received him lovingly and simply; and united itself to all his divine operations relating both to his heavenly Father, and to creatures."[23] There should be a synergy between external devotion and the interior life, but, alas, too many Christians separate the two. Grou warns that in such a system "they daily devote allotted hours to prayer and pious reading; they hear Mass regularly; they assist at the offices of the Church; they frequent the sacraments of penance in the holy Eucharist; they are exact in availing of indulgences, and occasionally they perform an act of charity," and yet, while that occurs on the outside, they still cling to the world, and "interiorly revolt against the slightest mark of contempt, the most trivial humiliation, the least deficiency of deference and detentions; they are engrossed with the love of rank, dignity, merit, reputation, or, it may be, of perishable riches."[24] What a joy if Jesus would change places with us on the altar of our heart, exclaims de Sales in one of his most famous remarks. "Oh my God! how happy should I be, if one day, after Holy Communion, I should find my own wretched heart gone from my breast, and the Heart of my Saviour in its place."[25]

The problem is not solved by merely multiplying the number and frequency of reception, which Grou finds to be a common ill-use of the sacraments.

> Many persons think themselves saints, because they communicate weekly, or daily, who yet never dream of correcting their faults; and who perhaps do not even know them, because they are so blinded by self-love; they are impatient, harsh, censorious, full of self-esteem and contempt of their neighbour, proud of the multitude of their external observances, and destitute of the slightest idea of internal mortification. All the fruit they derive from their Communions and other pious exercises, consists in spiritual vanity, secret pride, and all the subtle vices engendered by devotion grafted on self-seeking.[26]

---

23. De Berniere-Louvigny, *The Interior Christian*, 181-82.

24. Grou, *The Interior of Jesus and Mary*, vol. 1, 356-57.

25. De Sales, quoted in de Chantal, *The Depositions of St. Jane Frances de Chantal*, 89.

26. Grou, *The Spiritual Maxims of Pere Grou*, 51.

To communicate fruitfully, we must fulfill the intentions of Jesus, and receive his body with the express desire that he will produce in us a love of the cross. In other words, a love of abnegation, "that is to say, the love of humiliations and sufferings, the desire of dying to ourselves, and of being sacrificed, as Jesus Christ was, to the good pleasure of God. Let us judge by our love of the cross of the fruit of our Communions."[27] This is the sacrament of love, after all. Not only does the love of God descend to us in the Eucharist, the depth of a soul trained in abnegation must reach out to meet him. Barbanson describes their rendezvous in the heart.

> When thy love as shown in the Holy Eucharist meets thy love in the depth of the soul, what words could express what divine secrets pass between the soul and her Beloved? For by the interior motion of the will the creature receives the Holy Spirit dwelling within her and ever communicating itself in a more and more perfect manner; while by the external sacrament duly received she is united in body and soul to the divine person of the Eternal Word made man for us, and receives an increase of the fundamental root of grace and charity. From the God-Man, Jesus Christ, as from her mystical head, she receives her spiritual operation and wholly godlike operations.[28]

The body and blood, soul and divinity of Christ operates on both a sacramental and spiritual plane so that we, his mystical body, can receive sanctification. Since we are both body and soul, his love operates on both planes.

When the Eucharist stirs up our interior self we find the sacrament reaching into our daily life and daily struggles. Even a visit to the Blessed Sacrament can produce effects, which, at the time, are neither immediate nor cognizable to the senses, nevertheless produce effects that Saint-Jure calls spiritual and may later cause a capacity for abnegation.

---

27. Grou, *Manual for Interior Souls*, 365.

28. Barbanson, *Secret Paths of Divine Love*, 210.

But when on that day and the following days you make an act of humility, obedience, patience or charity; when you quell a motion to anger, when you stifle sentiments of vanity, the grace for this, and which is given you, is the fruit of the visit you have made ... Our Lord, to produce these happy effects, asks not so much movement of the body as movement of the soul, that is to say, acts of faith, hope, charity, contrition, respect, etc., and that hence a person retired in his house can receive the sweet influence of the power of Jesus Christ in the Holy Eucharist, provided he produce the acts of which we speak.[29]

This is the power of grace working in the deepest abyss of the soul, working an annihilation of anything that opposes God, or ignores him. De Berniere-Louvigny thinks abnegation is integrated into this universe of grace. "To live in death – (as Jesus seems to do in the Blessed Sacrament) to change glory for contempt – to be most delighted when one is annihilated and even sacrificed – is the true character of the life of grace. It makes all things die to the exterior, and live only to the interior ... Then she annihilates herself in his presence, suspended with admiration of those divine grandeurs which she sees annihilated in the holy Eucharist."[30]

This admiration of divine grandeur will come to full fruition in eternal beatitude, but it can b experienced now in temporal liturgy. Abnegation is essentially interior sacrifice, done to liturgize God, and Grou says it is accomplished by being united to the sacrifice of the mass.

The perpetual Sacrifice which He exacts from His members must be wholly interior, as is His own in the Divine Eucharist; it must be still more the Sacrifice of their souls than of their bodies, the Sacrifice of their natural inclinations and of their earthly desires than of the goods of the earth, the Sacrifice of their will ever submissive to the Will of God; ever annihilated, as that of Jesus Christ in the Will of God. The characteristic

---

29. Saint-Jure, *A Treatise on the Knowledge and Love of Our Lord Jesus Christ*, vol. 2, 49-50.

30. De Berniere-Louvigny, *The Interior Christian*, 176-77.

of the perpetual Sacrifice of Jesus Christ is His perfect submission to this Divine Will.[31]

When this happens, the Eucharist is embedded in the heart and at work everywhere. There is no moment lived outside the liturgical circulation between God and ourselves.

The hidden work of divine love is "communicated to us through every creature under veils, like the Eucharistic species,"[32] de Caussade notices, and it is surprising that we do not see our Lord everywhere, in a sort of Eucharistic liturgy of the mundane.

> Do we not know that by all creatures, and by every event the divine love desires to unite us to Himself, that He has ordained, arranged, or permitted everything about us, everything that happens to us with a view to this union? This is the ultimate object of His designs to obtain which He makes use of the worst of His creatures as well as of the best, and of the most distressing events as well as of those which are pleasant and agreeable ... If this be true, every moment of our lives may be a kind of communion with the divine love, and this communion of every moment may produce as much fruit in our souls is that which we receive in the Communion of the Body and Blood of the Son of God.[33]

Our Shepherd has given his sheep a divine food capable of producing abnegation, deep love, daily latria, constant companionship, and spiritual reformation.

The grass is not good for the sheep because it is sweet, it is good if it nourishes the sheep's deification, and our theologians apply this principle of abnegation to the Eucharistic liturgy by warning us against being seduced by what Bona calls a sort of *spiritual gluttony*. "They sin by spiritual gluttony who, in spiritual exercises, hunt after delights of the soul and sensible consolations, rather than purity and true devotion ... When they communicate, [they] make every effort, not that they may worship God

---

31. Grou, *The Practical Science of the Cross*, 188.

32. De Caussade, *Abandonment to Divine Providence,* 26.

33. De Caussade, *Abandonment to Divine Providence,* 26.

present, but that they may elicit some sense of sweetness, which they also do in prayer and in every spiritual exercise. As a rule, these are lukewarm, addicted to their own will, and enemies of mortification and self-denial."[34] Communion should be done with pure intention, and de Sales says we can know the intention is pure if, "after Holy Communion you feel no consolation, you nevertheless can be at peace."[35]

Was it a good communion? That is not answered by whether we have enjoyed consolations upon its reception; it is answered by whether we come away filled with new courage to wage war against sin and self-love. A good communion is not judged according to any affectations it causes, it is judged according to its production of mortification.

Grou returns to this point repeatedly. In one place he says, "let us think our Communions are good and fruitful when we learn there to seek God no longer for our own consolation, but to seek Him and love Him purely for Himself alone."[36] In another place he says, "our state at Communion generally corresponds to our state in prayer; and the further we advance in mortification of self, the more we are weaned from all sweetnesses. If the heavenly food is then less delicious, it is more strengthening. The soul, in its trials, needs consolation less than strength, which latter is abundantly bestowed in those Communions in which nothing seems to be imparted.[37] In another place he urges us to go to the table of life with the same disposition Christ had when he went to the tree of life.

> Do you desire to communicate profitably, and in accordance with His
> Intentions? Come with a special desire that you may thereby grow in
> love for His Cross, that is for humiliation and suffering, self-renunciation,
> and self-oblation. Let this be the test of your Communions. Do not hold
> them to be good, because you have been kindled with warm glowing
> feelings, but rather if you have come away with fresh courage to conquer
> self, to fight against your own will, to bear whatever God may lay upon

---

34. Bona, *A Treatise of Spiritual Life*, 175-76.

35. De Sales, *The Spiritual Conferences*, 348.

36. Grou, *Manual for Interior Souls*, 366.

37. Grou, *The Spiritual Maxims of Pere Grou*, 62-63.

you; if, in short, you are more able to seek God for Himself, more willing to love His corrections as well as His favours.[38]

The effects of a good Communion are proven "if we acquire more mastery over ourselves, if we are less delicate and sensitive, more generous in undertaking, more patient in suffering, more faithful to our good resolutions, more indifferent to the esteem or contempt of men, more obedient to all the impulses of Divine grace, more ready for all the sacrifices God asks of us."[39] And in one final place, he gives a masterful summary.

If Holy Communion detaches me more and more from the good things of this world, if it makes them insipid to me, and wearisome, and insupportable – if in all matters of ordinary human life Holy Communion only teaches me what is my duty, and how I ought to practise all Christian virtues – if it teaches me to look upon myself only as traveler and a pilgrim whose true home is in Heaven, and who must only make use of the things he meets with on his way in such a manner that by them he may reach his home more quickly and surely – if Holy Communion inspires me with a taste for recollection, for prayer, for mortification, for the renunciation of myself and my own judgment – if it reforms my thoughts and my affections on the perfect model of the thoughts and affections of Jesus Christ, so that His doctrine becomes to me familiar, and, as it were, natural to my heart, and I take pleasure in practicing it on all occasions – if, like Jesus Christ, I begin to have a horror of the world and its false maxims – if I begin to despise what the world esteems, and to fly from what it most seeks after – if, on the contrary, and still like my Divine Lord and Master, I begin to seek after and embrace all that the world most shuns and abhors – then I have the greatest assurance, and at the same time the only true and solid assurance I can have in this

---

38. Grou, *The Hidden Life of the Soul*, 109.

39. Grou, *Manual for Interior Souls*, 367.

life, of the good effect of my Communions; then I may believe that Jesus
Christ dwells in me, and I in Him.[40]

Our reception of the Eucharist is right and just when it produces a liturgical power of
abnegation.

This might be a difficult lesson for persons of piety to accept. Like the Pharisee among
the Jews (Luke 18:11: "I thank you that I am not like other men ..."), the Pharisee among
the Christians will thank God his communion has "wrung forth a few tears," and his
soul can fancy herself "lifted altogether above this world, and gifted with eagles' wings for
the loftiest flights."[41] To cure us, God may withdraw his misused consolations and soon
send along occasions of humiliation. Afflictions arranged by providence are often given
precisely to combat spiritual pride. John of Avila says the fruit of Holy Communion is
the "greater strength to serve and love our Lord, to resist temptations, to bear our trials
with patience," it is not to "afford us sweetness or pleasant feelings, which are usually
signs of imperfection and may even be sent by the devil to deceive us."[42] Do not strive
for consolation if the Lord does not choose to send it; and if he does, then be doubly
cautious about the presumption of "despising your neighbour because he is without
them, for, very possibly, he is holier and more dear to God than you are."[43] The apostle
gave the Corinthians milk, and not meat, because they were not able to bear the latter,
and Libermann compares consolations to the former. "Don't seek so much spiritual joys
in Holy Communion; do not esteem them too highly. Such joys are but milk which Our
Lord gives to children who are still weak in faith."[44]

Advancement in perfection means moving from a faith buttressed by comforts, to
pure faith, true faith, often called naked faith. Naked faith is independent of sensible
devotion, yet walks undismayed in darkness. Eymard says God rouses temptations to

---

40. Grou, *Manual for Interior Souls*, 359.

41. Grou, *The Spiritual Maxims of Pere Grou*, 200.

42. John of Avila, *Letters*, 31.

43. John of Avila, *Letters*, 31.

44. Libermann, *Letters to People in the World*, Spiritan Series 6, vol. 2, 191.

discouragement "to show men's virtue in the highest degree of confidence, in naked faith grounded on His word alone,"[45] and counsels a friend that "you will only lay hold of our Lord by a continual detachment from yourself, by a spirit of naked faith – This is what God has been doing in you for a long time – The world is dead for you, now you must cross the desert of yourself."[46] Faber acknowledges that "never did any one so walk by faith, simple, naked faith, as Mary did that day [on Golgotha]. There was faith enough to save a whole world in her single heart."[47] John of St. Samson is happy for the soul that has been overwhelmed with the divine delights of paradise, "still there are some souls to whom this has never happened, and never will happen, unless it be at the moment of death. Meanwhile, they are fixed in this state and gaze steadily upon God in himself by means of a simple and naked faith."[48] And John Evangelist of Boisleduc lists it among four required mortifications of the soul:

> She obtains recollection in herself by abnegation of all external created
> things; by resignation she becomes simple and unified in herself; pure love
> converts her to God and opens to her a way above herself; and the naked
> faith fixes her therein. The knowledge which she has that God is within
> her quietens and quells all desires and longings, and in the centre of her
> soul her will is recollected in a high peace, where God is truly present.[49]

The aridity felt in the dark night of the soul can also be felt at the communion altar rail, and both for the same reasons: it is for our good. John of the Cross thinks true faith understands "that the least of the blessings of the Most Holy Sacrament is that which touches the senses, and that the invisible grace It confers is far greater; for God

---

45. Eymard, *The Eucharist and Christian Perfection* (New York: Fathers of the Blessed
   Sacrament, 1912) 97.

46. Eymard, *Life and Letters of Saint Peter Julian Eymard*, Vol. 1, 706.

47. Faber, *The Foot of the Cross*, 316

48. John of St. Samson, *Prayer, Aspiration and Contemplation*, 131

49. John Evangelist of Boisleduc, *The Kingdom of God in the Soul*, 53.

frequently withholds these sensible favours from men, that they may fix the eyes of faith upon Himself."[50] It is a mistake to think the hand of God is absent if we do not derive sensible sweetness from communion. After all, even if a sweetness was experienced, it will soon evaporate, while the effects of the Eucharist do not disappear. These effects should remain with us as spiritual abnegations, which Grou lists:

> You should return to your own homes on leaving the Holy Altar, with
> more love than you carried thither with you; and so with the desire
> and the determination to be more firmly and closely united to God,
> to be more attentive and more faithful to grace; more watchful over
> yourselves; more courageous to fight and to do violence to yourselves;
> more charitable towards your neighbour, more gentle and patient in
> bearing with him; more careful in fulfilling the duties of your station;
> more generous in giving to God; stronger in suffering all those crosses
> which may come into your way.[51]

Jesus said the kingdom of heaven suffers violence, and the violent bear it away (Matthew 11:12). To whom is this violence done? Segneri identifies two targets: "To God, by means of prayer; for although He gives thee Paradise most willingly, yet He chooses for thy good to act as though thy hand had to take it by violence ... [And] thou art to do violence to thyself by complete self-abnegation."[52] Horstius further describes the latter by saying "to offer violence to heaven is to lose thy own life, to overcome thy own self, and the evil impulses of thy own mind, and to crush the desires of the flesh. To one who loves surely this is no difficult thing; nay, it will become pleasant."[53] The sacramental liturgy

---

50. John of the Cross, *The Obscure Night of the Soul*, in *The Complete Works of Saint John of the Cross*, vol. 1, 342

51. Grou, *Meditations Upon the Love of God*, 120.

52. Segneri, *Manna of the Soul*, vol. 2, 378.

53. Horstius, *The Paradise of the Christian Soul*, 429.

should be connected to the great liturgy of life, and evidence of the power of the Eucharist will come in signs of liturgical abnegation.

Further investigation into the after-effects of the Eucharist is worthwhile. Here is a list from Crasset: "This beauty without stain, this perfection without blemish, this sanctity without spot, this grace, this perfect charity, are effects of the sacrament. It was to produce all these effects in our hearts by frequent reception of the Eucharist that it was instituted."[54] And one from Eudes: after Holy Communion "1. You should prostrate yourself in spirit at the feet of the Son of God abiding within you ... 2. You must thank Him for having given Himself to you ... 3. [Y]ou should give yourself all to Him, and beg Him to destroy in you everything that is contrary to Him and to establishing you forever the empire of His love and glory."[55] The sacramental graces and the gifts of the Holy Spirit should increase in a person each time he or she communicates in a good state, and yet, Lallemant admits, "we do not perceive their effects in our daily life. Whence comes this? From our unmortified passions, our attachments and disorderly and affections, and our habitual faults. We allow these vicious principles to have more dominion over us than sacramental graces and the gifts of the Holy Spirit."[56] If we do not perceive the effects of Communion, enter within to discover our interior state and correct its disorders. If we want the results of the Eucharist to take full effect in us, we should place ourselves in spirit with Mary on Calvary as we contemplate the Lamb of God mystically renewing that sacrifice. The eye is fixed on the altar, as Mary's eye was fixed on the cross, because love fixes the eye upon the beloved, and conceals all else.

The cross is being presented again, this time in our hearts and not outside the city walls, but Saint-Jure believes our interior communion with Christ will become joy-filled because the cross is healing our heart. "When you have communicated you are filled with Jesus Christ entire, because you possess his body, his soul, his divinity, and all that he is. Being thus filled with Jesus Christ, this divine plenitude should spread over your soul, your body, and your senses, to impress upon them a disposition of conformity to him, and

---

54. De Sales & Crasset, *Secret of Sanctity*, 71.

55. Eudes, *The Life and the Kingdom of Jesus in Christian Souls*, 135.

56. Lallemant, *The Spiritual Doctrine of Father Louis Lallemant*, ed. Faber 222.

to communicate to them his virtues."[57] There is a cost to this joy (the cost which has been the subject of this book), but Surin says "this joy, this perfect satisfaction, produced by the immediate presence of our Lord ... is only for those who, by complete self abnegation, and a general renunciation of all that is not God, and that does not tend to God, have perfectly emptied themselves of all creatures. It is to them that our Lord communicates himself, He honors them with His familiar converse."[58] When we discover our nothingness by having poured ourselves out entirely to God, when our humility positions our prayer, when we replace self-will with God's will, when the creation gives delight because it illuminates the Creator, when we are no longer tricked by the deceits of the world, then we receive this gift of joy, and de Sales commands us to "go to Holy Communion boldly; we shall gradually become accustomed to this heavenly food and learn to digest it to our profit."[59]

If Christ gives us all – namely, himself – then why would we keep back anything of ourselves? If Christ gives us all – namely, himself – then why would we seek anything more? Saint-Jure admits that the holy Eucharist has had extraordinary effects of odors and savors in some saints, but "considering only its common effects, we say that this divine Sacrament by the increase of charity it procures the soul and by the special assistance it gives, blunts the sting of sin which is within us, and thus hinders the disorderly movements of appetite, or moderates them when they appear, extinguishes the fire of concupiscence, and renders the flesh pure and submissive to the spirit."[60]

The Eucharist braces liturgical abnegation. The gift is not automatic (accomplished without wills), the gift is personal (between persons), and de Ravignan understands that we abnegate in response to this divine boon. "God gives, what has He not given? He gives His very Self, He identifies Himself with us by every means of union, especially in the Blessed Eucharist and in prayer ... And what else must I do? I must also give up everything – organs, memory, intelligence, affections, will, sufferings, in a word, everything appertaining to self I shall give myself up and sacrifice myself, and this oblation

---

57. Saint-Jure, *Union with our Lord Jesus Christ in his Principal Mysteries*, 368.

58. Surin, *The Foundations of Spiritual Life*, 108.

59. De Sales, *Maxims and Counsels of St. Francis de Sales*, 125.

60. Saint-Jure, *A Treatise on the Knowledge and Love of Our Lord Jesus Christ*, vol. 1, 618.

I shall make through obedience."[61] All is given; all is asked for – these are the twin blades of liturgical abnegation. Mortification is both preparatory and consequential because Olier calls it proportioned to the grace being communicated. "Our Lord communicates his grace to us in the Sacrament of the Eucharist, according to the whole extent of his divine charity, which is unbounded; but the graces which we receive by meditation and the sighs of our heart, are given us in proportion to the mortification of the old man, and the fidelity with which we renounce ourselves in the inclinations of nature."[62] Not all abnegation is liturgical; that which is, is identified by the "therefore" – because of Christ's graces, *therefore* we deny world, self, vanity. There is a hinge connecting grace and abnegation, which De Granada describes thus:

> Since thou hast already done me the favor to receive me into thy company, to place me at thy table, to give me share of thy banquet, to heap on me thy benefits, to bind me to thee with such strong and strait bonds of love, I from this time, O my Saviour, renounce all earthly things for love of thee. Let there be no longer any world for me, or any worldly vanity; begone from me ye deceitful goods, which I have so much loved; here is the only and sovereign good. It is not reasonable that, having tasted the bread of Angels, I should return to the food of beasts; it is not fit that, having received God into my house, I should let anything vain or unprofitable enter into it. Should a woman of mean condition be married to a king, she would soon leave that state of poverty which environed her, to appear in the equipage of a queen.[63]

A new love is created in the soul that has experienced a higher good.

How shall we define love? asks Bona. He answers: "Love is a certain Delight or Satisfaction we take in that which is Good: the first impression that affects the Appetite; proceeding from the Pleasure we take in a known Good ... All Good comes from the

---

61. De Ravignan, *Ravignan's Last Retreat*, 183-84.

62. Olier, *Catechism of an Interior Life*, 184-85.

63. De Granada, *A Memorial of a Christian Life*, 293.

sovereign Good, and thither it tends ... So great is the Power of Love, that it does in a manner, transform the Lover, into the thing belov'd."[64] God has infinite love for himself because God is the infinite Good. The Trinity dips low enough in the Eucharist to take us up into its energy, and our pleasure is increased by an expansive love for a higher good. Grou falls to his knees in prayer in recognition of it. "O Jesus, we have no virtue but that which Thou gavest us; our souls free not themselves from the clay of the body but in rising to Thee; they become disgusted with the vain conversation of the world only by talking with Thee. Our cold hearts are never warmed but when we approach the fire which Thy Love kindles in the Divine Eucharist."[65] Liturgical delight in God's supreme Goodness renders all lesser goods as nothing in our eyes – we do not look down with disdain, we look up with desire.

The heavenly food of the Eucharist fills the soul with delights proper to the spirit, so Scaramelli describes this sacrament as having "the special property of giving a delight which is felt by the souls of devout receivers; even as bodily food gives pleasure to the palate of him that partakes of it. Saint Cyprian adds, that the pleasure which the soul receives from this Bread of Angels is so intense as to alienate and detachment from all worldly gratifications."[66] Once the eye has a glint of heaven in it, the corruptible world no longer feeds the soul.

Those trained in liturgical abnegation discover that worldly gratifications have become like food that lacks the nourishment to feed a body. Christ bestows virtue (power) not to enable us to fulfill our own designs, which is a selfish use, but to deaden self-love so we will fulfill his own designs. The holy and virginal flesh we eat in the sacrifice of the altar has a different purpose, says Grou. "It has the virtue of deadening in our hearts the fire of cupidity, of extinguishing the order of our passions, of purifying our thoughts, of regulating our desires, of repressing the revolt of our senses, and of submitting the flesh to the spirit."[67] When this mystery takes hold, then we can come from communion with the words of Simeon on our lips (translated by de Berniere-Louvigny): "It is time, O

---

64. Bona, *Manductio ad Coelum: or, a Guide to Eternity*, 103-05.

65. Grou, *The Practical Science of the Cross*, 197.

66. Scaramelli, *Directorium Asceticum; Or, Guide to the Spiritual Life*, vol. 1, 614.

67. Grou, *The Practical Science of the Cross*, 171.

Lord; now permit my soul to depart in peace, and to quit this mortal life, because I receive within me the spring and source of immortality."[68] Only the Resurrection holds the key to liturgical abnegation, because the reason why Christ feeds us with his death is so we might rise with him to eternal life.

We like the idea of being conformed to a Savior who lived long ago, and will not disturb us now, but this all becomes more real and practical when he shows up in the Eucharist. He walks out of the pages of history to be enthroned on the altar before us, in order to assure us, says Saint-Jure, "that whoever eats Him will live by Him, as He lives by His Father, that is ... He will communicate Himself to him, imprint on him the traits of His perfections, enable him to lead a holy and divine life, and render him as a god on earth."[69]

Christ's virtues are a power to deify us: *Jesus ought to form Jesus in us.*

De Berniere-Louvigny picks up this thought by seeing that

> the principal effect of communion is to produce in us an intimate union with Jesus. This union is a perfect assimilation to his states and mysteries. And this assimilation is what they call a transformation into God, which renders a person wholly divine, and devoted to the interests of the Almighty. By this privileged grace we become divine – having no other inclinations than those of God – living by the life of God – and desiring nothing but the love and glory of God.[70]

However, as the cross led to Christ's resurrection, the cross comes before our deification. Abnegation is for the sake of theosis; theosis is the cause of abnegation.

> O my God, separate me by thy holy grace from every thing which hinders this divine transformation., Grant that I may cease to be what I am according to nature, and that I may become what thou art by the power

---

68. De Berniere-Louvigny, *The Interior Christian*, 193.

69. Saint-Jure, *A Treatise on the Knowledge and Love of Our Lord Jesus Christ*, vol. 1, 634.

70. De Berniere-Louvigny, *The Interior Christian*, 191.

of grace. When shall I be wholly united and transformed into thee? ...
The grace bestowed on us in the holy communion tends principally to
annihilate in us all inclinations of nature; and, in their place, introduce
others more conformable to those of Jesus Christ.[71]

The Apostle Paul has already warned us that exterior actions alone do not make an
acceptable sacrifice to God. Giving goods to the poor, the practice of fasting, even giving
up one's body to be burned, is as nothing if charity does not reign in us (1 Corinthians
13). God intends to penetrate more deeply than we might have expected of him when
we felt his first touch. Grou says it is more a matter of a sacrifice of the soul than of the
body. "The perpetual Sacrifice of which Jesus Christ gives the example, is not merely
exterior. It does not consist in the mere contempt of the vain grandeurs of the world,
nor in the mere forsaking of worldly goods," rather, on those who would be saved, He
imposed the obligations of keeping the commandments, "of sacrificing interiorly to God
the corrupt inclinations of their hearts, and of conforming their wills in all things to His.
The perpetual Sacrifice which He exacts from His members must be wholly interior, as is
His own in the Divine Eucharist."[72]

God is jealous for our souls and our hearts. Jealousy is not a vice when the objects are
God's possession in the first place. When he takes back his property (not a bad definition
of exorcism), then the soul in liberty has a taste of the Supreme Good, and from this union
Bona finds, flowing into the soul, "all good things, as rivulets of water from a welling
spring ... From this source also come that beaming brightness, and clear illumination,
those burnings of love, and ineffable sweetness. The contempt of all things of earth, and
the insatiable longings for heaven flow from this ... The soul is annihilated before God in
a mystical death."[73]

All morality, all philosophy, even all religions of the earth, are no more than a
preparation for the liturgy of heaven, and de Condren says Christians have a foretaste
of this liturgy in the Eucharist. "The Eucharistic Sacrifice and Communion, greatest and

---

71. De Berniere-Louvigny, *The Interior Christian*, 192.

72. Grou, *The Practical Science of the Cross*, 190.

73. Bona, The *Easy Way to God*, 27.

holiest of our mysteries, are but the means intended to fit us for offering the Holocaust of the Church of the saints."[74] The Christian liturgy does not come out of human ingenuity, or human resourcefulness, or even human desires; the Christian liturgy comes forth from the God-man, and if we are united with him eucharistically, then we love what he loves, and we have inclinations that resemble what the Word sought in his hypostatic union. This is why de Berniere-Louvigny thinks the

> most inward and the most perfect of all the unions that a creature can have with his God is the personal or hypostatical one, which produced in the humanity of Jesus a love of the cross, and of poverty. Insomuch, that the humanity was no sooner divinely assumed than it was inflamed with the love of suffering; and it esteemed nothing, next to the divinity, so worthy of love. Now it is evident we cannot arrive at any union with God so much resembling the hypostatical union as that which we obtain by the holy communion: whence it follows that it ought to produce in us such inclinations as very much resemble those which the hypostatical union produced in the sacred humanity, that is to say, it should incline us to love the cross, poverty, humiliations, and all other manner of sufferings.[75]

Christ becomes our interior Master in liturgical abnegation, thereby correcting our understanding and nerving our will.

The whole economy of salvation is designed for liturgizing God and deifying man, both of which climax in the Eucharist. Eudes identifies the cast of characters involved:

- the Eternal Father in eternity is continually occupied in producing His Son in Himself

- the Father outside Himself has formed his Son within the pure Virgin at the Incarnation

- the Son of God on earth formed himself within his holy Mother and in His

---

74. De Condren, *Eternal Sacrifice*, 199-200.

75. De Berniere-Louvigny, *The Interior Christian*, 188.

Eucharist

- the Holy Ghost formed Jesus within the womb of the virgin

- the Virgin never did anything more perfect than when she cooperated in this divine and wonderful formation of Jesus within her

- the Holy Church has no more important work than the production of Jesus in the Eucharist, and the formation of Jesus in the souls of all Christians.[76]

And us? Our task? "It should be your desire, your care and your chief occupation to form Jesus in you, to make Him live and reign in you together with His spirit, His devotion, His virtues, His sentiments, His inclinations and dispositions ... God places this task in your hands, for you to work at it without interruption."[77]

As we near the conclusion, we find everything tangling up together. Surin says, "what mystics call 'perfect annihilation,' 'transformation,' 'deiformity,' is no other thing than this entire application of the soul to God, by which we die to all things and to ourselves, and live for God alone ... In asking all, He excludes nothing; and in consequence, if we give to God all that He ought to have, nothing will remain to us, neither for ourselves nor for creatures, unless in so far as we and they have relation to God."[78] Abnegation is concerned with virtue, but not for virtue's sake. At least, not for horizontal virtue's sake. Abnegation is concerned with eternal powers. Lacordaire says the virtues that God communicates to us give "truth to our intelligence, justice to our will, goodness to our heart," which is basically "the same mode of thought, will, and feeling as God himself, who is by His essence truth, justice, and goodness ... There lies the point by which [our

---

76. Eudes, *Life and Kingdom of Jesus in Christian Souls*, 78.

77. Eudes, *Life and Kingdom of Jesus in Christian Souls*, 79.

78. Jean-Joseph Surin, *Spiritual Letters of Father Surin, S.J.* (London: Art and Book Company, 1892) 69-70.

nature] is susceptible of that enlargement and transformation which theology does not fear to call deifical."[79]

Give to God all he ought to have (liturgy) and nothing will remain to us (abnegation). Desire nothing (abnegation) but what may contribute to his service and glory (liturgy). When the soul becomes deiform, then it has no other life than that of God, which is why, Chardon says,

> nothing is capable of exerting an effect on the soul, of attracting the faculties, of exciting the desires, or of giving rest to the heart which is elevated, suspended, and transformed in this separation, solitude, and purity ... It is at this point that one realizes the nothingness of all things. To speak exactly, it is not so much a knowledge of this nothingness as a complete disregard for the existence of all created things ... In this light, then, the soul learns, in the emptiness of all that is sensible and of all that might reach its reason, that God is all and, consequently, that all else is nothing.[80]

Receiving the form of Jesus requires a complete annihilation of self-love, self-opinion, self-pride, self-vanity, because we cannot fit him into a heart already full of ourselves. Then we may be turned outward to the Father through Christ in the Holy Spirit. We liturgize in union with the Christ established in our hearts, so we can give the Father and Himself the love and glory they deserve. The Eucharist concerns holiness, transformation, and the implanting of Christ's life in us, Grou observes. "In uniting Himself to us in the Eucharist, He lives, He acts Himself within us in an ineffable manner: He communicates to us His Divine Life, He renders us partakers of His Holiness, He changes us, He transforms us into Himself, He engraves upon our hearts the living image of His Cross with the same Blood with which it was dyed on Calvary."[81] Our love for Christ is a love for a crucified

---

79. Jean-Baptiste Henri Lacordaire, *Life: Conferences Delivered at Toulouse* (New York: P. O'Shea Publisher, 1875) 149.

80. Chardon, *The Cross of Jesus*, vol. 2, 112-13.

81. Grou, *The Practical Science of the Cross*, 63.

one, therefore to unite with him, we add our mortification. This is why liturgy is the foundation for abnegation.

If one believes – truly believes – that deification is a human being's telos and omega, target and summation, end and purpose, then everything is changed. "Despise this present world," says de Estella, "and thou shalt come unto thy desired: this only end may suffice to persuade thee for to despise the vanity of the world, to know that thou wast created for heaven."[82] We speak of sin and pride as imperfections only because they prevent man's perfection, so Ullathorne suggests a number of broader definitions. "That which is the living image of another can only be perfect in so far as it has the life of that other."[83] Pride is an inordinate appetite for one's own greatness, in *substitution* for the greatness man will receive from God. "What is not made for itself but to receive something better is a very imperfect creature until it has received the nobler existence for which it is made."[84] A garden is imperfect if it grows weeds instead of receiving flowers and fruits; a house is imperfect if it is empty instead of having someone living in it; a body is corrupt if has not the soul for which it was made a habitation. "A soul, then, without the Spirit of God, is an existence without its object, a mere failure from the reason of its existence; like a house that is never inhabited, or a body that is never animated."[85]

Liturgical abnegation is striving for Christian perfection. It is not the disparagement of our human existence, it is the striving for the Supreme Good for which our souls are made, a good that the Father shows us in Jesus, and a good that Jesus gives us by his Spirit. Abnegation is not loss, it is gain. Abnegation is in service to the Christian's perfection. The soul is constituted in her nature as an image of God, and that soul can only be perfected in so far as she possesses the life of God, which she is fed sacramentally at the Eucharist, and with which she is infused mystically for the life of the virtues.

This life is a time of probation (trial, testing, growth), and that changes one's perception of the afflictions one might undergo temporarily. The pangs of birth are different from the pangs of death. The humiliations, adversities, afflictions, and sufferings

---

82. De Estella, *The Contempt of the World and the Vanities Thereof* 508.

83. Ullathorne, *The Groundwork of Christian Virtues*, 265.

84. Ullathorne, *The Groundwork of Christian Virtues*, 265.

85. Ullathorne, *The Groundwork of Christian Virtues*, 265.

all change in meaning, because, although painful, they are steps on a pathway leading to love – the very love that gives the name "Sacrament of Love" to the Eucharist. As a result, we can make a trustful surrender to providence, as de la Colombiere writes.

> If you would be convinced that in all He allows and in all that happens to you God has no other end in view but your real advantage and your eternal happiness, reflect a moment on all He has done for you; you are now suffering, but remember that the author of this suffering is He who chose to spend His life suffering to save you from everlasting suffering, whose angel is always at your side guarding your body and soul by His order, who sacrifices Himself daily on the altar to expiate your sins and appease His Father's anger, who comes lovingly to you in the Holy Eucharist and whose greatest pleasure is to be united to you. We must be very ungrateful to mistrust Him after He has shown such proofs of His love and to imagine that He can intend us harm.[86]

The crucified Lord in the Eucharist causes liturgical abnegation in us, and liturgical abnegation causes us to rejoice. And such rejoicing is a liturgy we carry around with us, everywhere, every day, because the love encountered is repeated. The act of Eucharist becomes a state of Eucharist, as Gay describes:

> To make acts of love is a thing as easy as it is sweet. A hundred times, a thousand times a day, look back into your hearts, enter into yourselves, into that centre of your soul, where the Infinite has His Throne, and there, kneeling in spirit, say to this Sacred Host, I love Thee, I love Thee; Thou knowest, Master, that I love Thee (St. John 21:16). Tell Him so on the occasion of all that happened to you, of the lights you have discerned, of the graces you have received, of the disappointments that have occurred, of the trials you have undergone, even of the faults you

---

86. Saint-Jure & de la Colombiere, *Trustful Surrender to Divine Providence*. 100-101.

have committed. Tell Him so, for no particular purpose whatever, but simply from the natural exuberance of love. [87]

---

87. Charles Gay, *The Christian Life and Virtues*, vol. 3, 29.

BIBLIOGRAPHY OF WORKS CONSULTED

Acarie, Barbe. https://www.madame-acarie.org/en/home-english/

_____. *A Gracious Life. Being the Life of Barbara Acarie*, by Emily Bowles. London: Burns and Oates, 1879.

_____. *Barbe Acarie: Wife an Mystic*, by Lancelot Sheppard. London: Burns and Oates, 1953.

Alacoque, Margaret Mary. *The Autobiography of Saint Margaret Mary*. Charlotte, NC: TAN Books, 2012. Kindle edition.

_____. *The Letters of St. Margaret Mary Alacoque*. Charlotte, NC: TAN Books, 2012. Kindle edition.

Anonymous. *The Redeemer's Call to Consecrated Souls.* Tarpon Springs, FL: Logos Institute Press, 2012.

Baker, Augustine. *Holy Wisdom, Or Directions for the Prayer of Contemplation Extracted out of more than Forty Treatises*, ed. R. F. Serenus Cressy. New York: Burns & Oates, 1911.

_____. *Confessions of Venerable Augustine Baker*. London: Burns Oates & Washbourne, Ltd., 1922.

_____. *The Fall and Restitution of Man*. Salzburg: Analecta Cartusiana, 2013.

_____. *The Inner Life of Dame Gertrude More*, vol 1. London: R. & T. Washbourne, Ltd., 1911.

_____. *The Inner Life and the Writings of Dame Gertrude More*, vol 2. R. & T. Washbourne, Ltd., 1911.

Barbanson, Constantine. *The Secret Paths of Divine Love*. London: Burns Oates & Washbourne, Ltd., 1928.

Bellarmine, Robert. *The Soul's Ascension to God by the Steps of Creation.* London: for Robert Gibson, 1703.

_____. *The Autobiography of St. Robert Bellarmine.* The Woodstock Letters, Vol. 84, Issue 1, 3-30

_____. *A Short Catechism, or Christian Doctrine.* 1677.

Bellecius, Aloysius. *Solid Virtue, or A Treatise on the Obstacles to Solid Virtue, the Means of Acquiring, and Motives for Practicing It.* London: R & T Washbourne, Ltd., 1914.

Berthier. Jean-Baptiste. *States of the Christian Life and Vocation, According to the Doctors and Theologians of the Church.* New York: P. O'Shea, 1879.

Binet, Etienne. *Divine Favors Granted to Saint Joseph.* Rockford, IL: TAN Books, 1983.

_____. *Purgatory Surveyed.* London: Burns and Oates, 1874.

Blosius (Louis of Blois). *A Book of Spiritual Instruction: Institutio Spiritualis.* St. Louis: B. Herder, 1800.

_____. *Comfort for the Fainthearted.* Westminster: Art and Book Company, 1908.

_____. *A Mirror for Monks.* London: C. J. Stewart, 1872.

_____. *Oratory of the Faithful Soul.* London: Richardson and Son, 1848.

_____. *Spiritual Works of Louis of Blois.* London: R. & T. Washbourne, 1903.

_____. *Seven Exercises or Meditations by which a Man May be, in Short Time, Established in the Fear of God, and in a Good and Holy Life.* London: M. Turner at the Lamb, 1686.

_____. *Spiritual Works of Louis of Blois.* London: R & T Washbourne, 1903.

Bona, Giovanni. *An Easy Way to God.* London: Burns Oates & Washbourne, Ltd., 1876.

_____. *Guidance to Heaven.* Rockford, IL: TAN Books and Publishers, Inc., 1995.

_____. *Manductio ad Coelum: or, a Guide to Eternity.* London: Printed for Henry Brome, 1680.

_____. *Moral Essay on Friendship.* London: Printed for John Harsley, 1702.

_____. *Precepts and Practical Rules for a Truly Christian Life.* London: Printed by M. Clark, 1678.

_____. *The Principles of Christianity.* London: Printed for C. Dilly, 1783.

_____. *A Treatise of Spiritual Life.* Poplar Bluff, MO: The author, 1893.

Borgia, Francis. *Spiritual Works of St. Francis Borgia.* London: Thomas Richardson and Sons, 1875.

_____. *Spiritual Works of St. Francis Borgia.* London: Thomas Richardson and Sons, 1875.

Bossuet, Jacques-Benigne. *A Catholic's Manual: Exposition of Controverted Doctrines of the Catholic Church.* New York: John McSweeny, 1836.

_____. *Devotion to the Blessed Virgin Mary.* London: Longmans, Green, and Co., 1899.

_____. *Great French Sermons from Bossuet, Bourdaloue, and Massillon.* London: Sands and Co., 1917.

_____. *Letters of Spiritual Direction.* London: A. R. Mowbray & Co., 1958

_____. *Selections from Meditations on the Gospels,* vol. 1. Chicago: Henry Regnery Co., 1962.

_____. *Selections from Meditations on the Gospels,* vol. 2. Chicago: Henry Regnery Co., 1962.

_____. *Select Sermons.* London: W. Clarke, 1800.

_____. *A Treatise of Communion Under Both Species.* Paris: Sebastian Marks Cramoisy, 1685.

Boudon, Henri-Marie. *The Book of Perpetual Adoration; or The Love of Jesus in the Most Holy Sacrament.* London: R. Washbourne, 1873.

_____. *Devotion to the Nine Choirs of Holy Angels.* London: Burns, Oates, & Co., 1869.

_____. *God is Everywhere Present.* London, JP Coghlan

_____. *The Hidden Life of Jesus.* London: Burns, Oates, & Co., 1869.

_____. *The Holy Slavery of the Admirable Mother of God.* CreateSpace Independent Publishing Platform, 2013.

_____. *The Holy Ways of the Cross.* London: Burnes, Oates, & Co., 1875.

Bourdaloue, Louis. *Eight Sermons for Holy Week and Easter.* London: Wells Gardner, Darton & Co., 1844.

_____. *Sermons, and Moral Discourses, on the Important Duties of Christianity,* vol 1. Dublin: James Duffy, 1843.

_____. *Sermons, and Moral Discourses, on the Important Duties of Christianity,* vol 2. Dublin: James Duffy, 1843,

_____. *Bourdalou* [sic] *at Versailles, 1670.* New York: Brentano's, 1919.

_____. *Spiritual Exercises: Readings for a Retreat of Seven Days. Translated and Abridged from the French of Bourdaloue*. London: Joseph Masters, 1868.

Boutauld, Michel. *The Counsels of Wisdom: Or a Collection of such Maxims of Solomon as are most Necessary for the Prudent Conduct of Life*. Oxford: At the Theatre, 1736.

_____. *A Method of Conversing with God*. Liege: H. Dessain, 1789.

Bremond, Henri. *A Literary History of Religious Thought in France, vol 1: Devout Humanism*. New York: Macmillan Company, 1928.

_____. *A Literary History of Religious Thought in France, vol 2: The Coming of Mysticism*. New York: Macmillan Company, 1930.

_____. *A Literary History of Religious Thought in France, vol 3: The Triumph of Mysticism*. New York: Macmillan Company, 1935.

Brother Lawrence. *The Practice of the Presence of God*. London: H. R. Allenson, 1906.

_____. *Maxims*

Bruyere, Abbess Cecile J. *Spiritual Life and Prayer According to Holy Scripture and Monastic Tradition*. New York: Benziger Brothers, 1905.

Burke, Christy. *No Longer Slaves: The Mission of Francis Libermann (1802-1852)*. Dublin: Columba Press, 2010.

Butler, Charles. *The Life of Fenelon, Archbishop of Cambray*. London: Longman, Hurst, Rees, and Orme, 1810.

_____. *The Life of Fenelon, To Which are Added the Lives of St Vincent of Paul and Henri-Marie de Boudon*. London: John Murray, 1819.

Camus, Jean Pierre. *The Beauties of St Francis de Sales*. London: Longman, Rees, Orme, Brown, and Green, 1829.

_____. *A Draught of Eternitie. English Recusant Literature 1558-1640, vol. 111*. London: Scolar Press, 1972.

_____. *The Spirit of St. Francis de Sales*. London: Burns, Oates & Washbourne, Ltd., 1925.

_____. *A Spiritual Combat*. London: The Scolar Press, 1974.

_____. *The Spiritual Director, Disinteressed. English Recusant Literature 1558-1640, Vol. 181*. London: The Scolar Press, 1974.

Canfield, Benedict. *A Bright Starre, Leading to & Centering in, Christ our Perfection. The Third part of the Rule of Perfection*. London: Henry Overton, 1646.

_____. *The Holy Will of God: A Short Rule of Perfection*. London: Thomas Richardson and Sons, 1878.

_____. *The Rule of Perfection: Contayning a Breif* [sic] *and Perspicuous Abridgement of All the Whole Spiritual Life,* parts 1-2. Rouan, France: Cardin Hamilton, 1609.

Catholick Sermons, A Selection Collection of, Vol. 1. London: 1841.

Catholick Sermons, A Selection Collection of, Vol. 2. London: 1841.

Cepari, Virgilio. *The Life of St. Mary Magdalene of Pazzi.* London: Thomas Richardson and Son, 1849.

Clerissac, Humbert. *The Mystery of the Church.* Cluny Media Edition, 2016.

Challoner, Richard. *Think Well On't: Reflections on the Great Truths of the Christian Religion for Every Day in the Month.* Manchester: T. Haydock, 1801.

Chardon, Louis. *The Cross of Jesus,* vol 1. St. Louis, Mo: B Herder Book Co., 1957.

_____. *The Cross of Jesus,* vol 2. St. Louis, Mo: B Herder Book Co., 1959.

Codrington, Thomas. *A Sermon Preached before their Majesties, in Saint James's, on Advent-Sunday.* London: Nathaniel Thompson, 1687.

Collins, Henry. *Heaven Opened; or, Our Home in Heaven, and the Way Thither.* London: Thomas Richardson and Son, 1880.

_____. *The Spirit and Mission of the Cistercian Order.* London: Simpkin Marhsall & Co., 1866.

_____. *Spiritual Conferences on the Mysteries of Faith and the Interior Life.* London: R. Washbourne, 1875.

Courbon, Abbe (Curé de Saint Cyr). *Familiar Instructions on Mental Prayer, vol 1 & 2.* London: Joseph Masters, 1856.

_____. *Meditations on the Passion of our Lord Jesus Christ.* Dublin: Richard Grace and Son, 1833

Cross, Nicholas. *The Cynosura, or a Saving Star that Leads to Eternity.* London: I. Redmayne for Thomas Books, 1679.

_____. *Pious Reflections, and Devout Prayers, on Several Points of Faith and Morality, from Man's Creation to His Consummation.* Doway: M. Mairesse, 1695.

Crasset, John. *Meditations for Every Day in the Year from the Christian Considerations of Father John Crasset, S. J.* London: R. Washbourne, 1888.

_____. *Christian Considerations; or, Devout Meditations for Every Day in the Year.* New York: P. O'Shea, 1864.

_____. *The Devotion of Calvary; or Meditations on the Passion of Our Lord and Saviour Jesus Christ.* Liverpool: Booker & Co., 1844.

Croiset, John. *Devotion to the Sacred Heart of Jesus*. London: Burns & Lambert, 1863.

_____. *A Spiritual Retreat for One Day in Every Month*. London: Printed by Thomas Hales, 1704

Dalgairns, John Bernard. *The Devotion to the Heart of Jesus*. London: Thomas Richardson and Sons, 1853.

_____. *The Holy Communion, Its Philosophy, Theology, and Practice*. New York: The Catholic Publication House, 1868.

De Alacantra, Peter. *A Golden Treatise of Mental Prayer, With Divers Spiritual Rules and Directions*. Philadelphia: M. Fithian, 1844.

De Bausset, M. L. F. *The Life of Fenelon, Archbishop of Cambrai*, 2 vols. London: Sherwood, Neely, and Jones, 1810.

De Bergamo, Gaetano Maria. *The Humility of Heart*. Mandeville, LA: Founding Father Films Publishing, 2015.

_____. *Thoughts and Affections on the Passion of Jesus Christ For Every Day of the Year, Taken from Holy Scripture and the Writings of the Fathers of the Church*. New York: Benziger Brothers, 1905

Berniere-Louvigny, Jean. *The Interior Christian in Eight Books*. New York: The Catholic Publication Society, 1843.

De Berulle, Pierre. *Discourses on the State and Grandeurs of Jesus: The Ineffable Union of the Deity with Humanity*. Washington, DC: Catholic University of America Press, 2023.

_____. *Berulle and the French School: Selected Writings*. New York: Paulist Press, 1989.

De Blois, Georges. *A Benedictine of the Sixteenth Century (Blosius)*. London: Burns and Oates, 1878,

De Bonilla, John. *Pax Animae: A Short Treatise*. (Attributed to Peter Alcantara). London: Burns & Oates.

_____. *The Quiet of the Soul*. London: Thomas Richardson and Sons, 1876.

De Castaniza, Juan. *The Spiritual Conflict and Conquest*. London: Burns and Oates, 1874.

De Caussade, Jean Pierre. *Abandonment to Divine Providence*. St. Louis: B. Herder Book Company, 1921.

_____. *On Prayer: Spiritual instructions on the Various States of Prayer According to the Doctrine of Bossuet, Bishop of Meaux*. New York: Brenziger Brothers, 1931.

_____. *The Sacrament of the Present Moment.* San Francisco: HarperSanFrancisco Reissue edition, 2009.

De Chantal, Jane. *Meditations for Retreats taken from Writings of St. Francis de Sales.* New York: Benziger Brothers, 1900.

_____. *The Depositions of St. Jane Frances de Chantal in the Cause of the Canonisation of St. Francis de Sales* in *Library of St. Francis de Sales.* London: Burnes & Oates, Ltd., 1908.

De Condren, Charles. *The Eternal Sacrifice.* London: Thomas Baker, 1906.

De Estella, Diego. *Meditations on the Love of God.* London: Burns & Oates, 1898.

_____. *Contempt for the World and he Vanities Thereof.* S. Omers: for John Heigham, 1622.

De Granada, Louis. *An Excellent Treatise of Consideration and Prayer.* London: John Harison, 1601.

_____. *Considerations on the Mysteries of the Faith.* London: Joseph Masters, 1862.

_____. *Counsels on Holiness of Life: Being the First Part of The Sinner's Guide.* London: Rivingtons, 1869.

_____. *An Exhortation to Alms-Deeds.* London: J. P. Coghlan, 1775.

_____. *Fr. Granada's Meditations Containing Fourteen Devout Exercises for the Seven Days of the Week.* London: Joseph Browne, 1623.

_____. *Life of Dom Bartholomew of the Martyrs.* London: Thomas Baker, 1890.

_____. *A Memorial of a Christian Life.* New York: The Catholic Publication Society, 1870.

_____. *Meditations on the Lord's Prayer*, subjoined to the life of Nicolas Herman in *The Great Advantages that Arise to a Christian by Preserving in his Mind a constant Sense of the Divine Presence.* Edinburgh: Printed for Mr. W. Monro and W. Drummond, 1741.

_____. *The Sinner's Guide in Two Books.* Philadelphia: Henry McGrath, 1845.

De la Bedoyere, Michael. *The Archbishop and the Lady.* New York: Patheon, 1956.

De la Colombiere, Claude. *Faithful Servant: Spiritual Retreats and Letters of La Colombiere.* St. Louis, MO: B. Herder Book Co., 1960.

_____, *Sermons: vol 1, Christian Conduct.* DeKalb, IL: NIU Press, 2014.

_____, *The Spiritual Direction of Saint Claude de la Colombiere.* San Francisco: Ignatius Press, 1998.

De Laredo, Bernardino. *The Ascent of Mount Sion.* Ed. E. Allison Peers, New York: Harper & Brothers, 1950.

De Liguori, Alphonsus. *Saint Alphonsus de Liguori: 20 Books.* Aeterna Press, Kindle book, 2016.

———. *Alphonsus de Liguori: Selected Writings.* New York: Paulist Press, 1999.

———. *Preparation for Death.* Philadelphia: J. B. Lippincott & Co., 1869.

———. *The Great Means of Salvation and of Perfection.* New York: Benziger Brothers, 1886.

———. *The Glories of Mary.* New York: P.J. Kenedy & Sons, 1888.

———. *The Holy Mass,* vol. 13 of *The Complete Works of Saint Alphonsus de Liguori, The Ascetical Works.* New York: Benziger Brothers, 1889.

———. *The Holy Eucharist,* vol. 6 of *The Complete Works of Saint Alphonsus de Liguori, The Ascetical Works.* New York: Benziger Brothers, 1887.

———. *The Passion and the Death of Jesus Christ.* New York: Benziger Brothers, 1887.

———. *The True Spouse of Jesus Christ, or, The Nun Sanctified by the Virtue of Her State.* New York: Benziger Brothers, 1899.

———. *Uniformity with God's Will.* Christian Classics Ethereal Library, https://www.ccel.org/ccel/alphonsus/uniformity.html

———. *The Way of Salvation and Perfection,* vol. 2 of *The Complete Works of Saint Alphonsus de Liguori.* New York: Benziger Brothers, 1886.

De Lombez, Ambrose. *A Treatise on Interior Peace.* New York: Alba House, 1996.

———. *A Treatise on the Joy of the Christian Soul.* London: S. Anselm's Society, 1894.

De Montfort, Louis. *God Alone: The Collected Writings of St. Louis Mary de Montfort.* Bay Shore, NY: Montfort Publications, 1988.

———. *The Love of Eternal Wisdom.* Bay Shore, NY: Montfort Publications, 1960.

———. *The Secret of Sanctity Revealed to Mary.* Boston: Thomas B. Noonan & Co., 1887.

———. *The Secret of the Rosary.* Bay Shore, NY: Montfort Publications, 2004.

———. *True Devotion to Mary.* Bay Shore, NY: Montfort Publications, 1954.

De Osuna, Francisco. *The Third Spiritual Alphabet.* New York: Benziger Brothers, 1931.

De Ponte, Louis. *Meditations on the Mysteries of Our Holy Faith*, vol 1. London: Richardson and Son, 1852.

_____. *Meditations on the Mysteries of Our Holy Faith*, vol 2. London: Richardson and Son, 1852.

_____. *Meditations on the Mysteries of Our Holy Faith*, vol 3. London: Richardson and Son, 1852.

_____. *Meditations on the Mysteries of Our Holy Faith*, vol 4. London: Richardson and Son, 1853.

_____. *Meditations on the Mysteries of Our Holy Faith*, vol 5. London: Richardson and Son, 1854.

_____. *Meditations on the Mysteries of Our Holy Faith*, vol 6. London: Richardson and Son, 1854.

_____. *A Treatise on Mental Prayer*. London: Burns Oates & Washbourne, Ltd., 1929.

De Ponlevoy, *The Life of Father de Ravignan of the Society of Jesus*. Dublin: William Kelly, 1869.

De Ravignan, Gustave Francois Xavier. *Conferences on the Spiritual Life*. London: R. Washbourne, 1873.

_____. *On The Life and Institute of the Jesuits*. Philadelphia: W. J. Cunningham, 1845.

_____. *Ravignan's Last Retreat*. London: Burns and Oates, 1859.

De Sales, Francis. *Finding God's Will for You*. Manchester, NH: Sophia Institute Press, 1998.

_____. *Introduction to the Devout Life*. New York: Vintage Spiritual Classics, 2002.

_____. *Library of St. Francis de Sales: vol 1, Letters to Persons in the World*. London: Burns & Oates, Ltd., 1894.

_____. *Library of St. Francis de Sales: vol 3, The Catholic Controversy*. London: Burns & Oates, Ltd, 1909.

_____. *Library of St. Francis de Sales: vol 4, Letters to Persons in Religion*. London: Burns & Oates, Ltd., 1909.

_____. *Library of St. Francis de Sales: vol. 5, The Spiritual Conferences*. London: Burns & Oates, Ltd., 1909.

_____. *Library of St. Francis de Sales: vol. 6, I. The Mystical Explanation of the Canticle of Canticles: By St. Francis de Sales; II. The Depositions of St. Jane Frances de*

Chantal in the Cause of the Canonisation of St. Francis de Sales. London: Burns & Oates, Ltd., 1908.

_____. *Maxims and Counsels of St Francis de Sales for Every Day of the Year*. Dublin: M. H. Gill & Son, 1884.

_____. *Mystical Exposition of the Canticle of Canticles*. DeSales University: Salesian Center for Faith & Culture, 2008.

_____. *The Mystical Flora: The Christian Life Under the Emblem of Plants*. Dublin: M. H. Gill & Son, 1877.

_____. *The Sermons of St. Francis de Sales for Advent and Christmas: vol 4 in the Series*. Frederick, MD: Visitation Monastery, 1987.

_____. *The Sermons of St. Francis de Sales on Our Lady: vol 2 in the Series*. Frederick, MD: Visitation Monastery, 1985.

_____. *The Spiritual Conferences*. London: Burns & Oates, Ltd., 1909.

_____. *Treatise on the Love of God*. Blacksburg, VA: Wilder Publications, 2011.

_____. *The Spiritual Director of Devout and Religious Souls*. Dublin: printed by James Mehain, 1777.

_____. Francis de Sales, Jane de Chantal. *Letters of Spiritual Direction*. New York: Paulist Press, 1988.

_____. *Sermons On Prayer*. https://www.theworkofgod.org/Library/Sermons/F_Sales.htm

De Sales, Francis, and Crasset, Jean. *The Secret of Sanctity According to St. Francis de Sales and Father Crasset, S. J.* New York: Benziger Brothers, 1892.

Duguet, Jacques Joseph. *The Characters and Properties of True Charity Displayed*. London: C. Davis, 1737.

_____. *The Principles of the Christian Faith*, vol 1. Edinburgh: G. Hamilton, 1755.

_____. *The Principles of the Christian Faith*, vol 2. Edinburgh: G. Hamilton, 1755.

Elizabeth of the Trinity. *I Have Found God: Complete Works*, vol 1. Washington, D.C.: ICS Publications, 2014.

_____. *The Complete Works: Letters from Carmel*, vol 2. Washington, D.C.: ICS Publications, 2014.

_____. *Sister Elizabeth of the Trinity: Spiritual Writings. Letters, Retreats, and Unpublished Notes*, ed. M.M. Philipon. New York: P. J. Kenedy & Sons, 1962.

_____. *The Praise of Glory: Reminiscences of Sr. Elizabeth of the Trinity*. London: R. & T. Washbourne, Ltd., 1914.

Eudes, John. *The Admirable Heart of Mary*. New York: P. J. Kenedy & Sons, 1948.

_____. *Letters and Shorter Works*. New York: P. J. Kenedy & Sons, 1948.

_____. *Life and Kingdom of Jesus in Christian Souls*. CreateSpace Independent Publishing Platform, 2013.

_____. *Man's Contract with God in Baptism*. Philadelphia: Peter F. Cunningham, 1859.

_____. *Meditations on Various Subjects*. New York: P. J. Kenedy & Sons, 1947.

_____. *Sacred Heart of Jesus*. New York: P. J. Kenedy & Sons, 1946.

_____. *St. John Eudes: Selections from his Writings*. London: Burnes Oates & Washbourne, Ltd., 1925.

_____. *The Priest: His Dignity and Obligations*. New York: P. J. Kenedy & Sons, 1947.

Eymard, Peter. *The Divine Eucharist, First Series: The Real Presence*. New York: Fathers of the Blessed Sacrament, 1907.

_____. *The Divine Eucharist, Second Series: Holy Communion*. New York: The Sentinel Press, 1927.

_____. *The Divine Eucharist, Third Series: Retreats at the Feet of Jesus Eucharistic*. New York: Fathers of the Blessed Sacrament, 1909.

_____. *The Divine Eucharist, Fourth Series: The Eucharist and Christian Perfection*. New York: Fathers of the Blessed Sacrament, 1912

_____. *In the Light of the Monstrance*. New York: Blessed Sacrament Fathers, 1947.

_____. *Month of Saint Joseph*. New York: Sentinel Press, 1948.

_____. *Month of Our Lady of the Blessed Sacrament*. New York: Sentinel Press, 1903.

_____. *How to Get More out of Communion*. Manchester, NH: Sophia Institute Press, 2000.

_____. *Rule of Life*. Congregation of the Blessed Sacrament, 1973.

_____. *Eucharistic Handbook for Members of the People's Eucharistic League*. New York: The Sentinel Press, 1948.

_____. *Life and Letters of Saint Peter Julian Eymard*, Vol 1. Electronic version by Curia Generalizia, Congregation of the Blessed Sacrament, Rome, 2010

_____. *Life and Letters of Saint Peter Julian Eymard*, Vol 2. Electronic version by Curia Generalizia, Congregation of the Blessed Sacrament, Rome, 2010

Faber, Frederick. *All for Jesus: or, The Easy Ways of Divine Love*. Baltimore: John Murphy & Co., 1855.

_____. *Bethlehem*. London: Thomas Richardson and Son, 1860.

_____. *The Blessed Sacrament: or, The Works and Ways of God*. London: Burns Oats & Washbourne, Ltd., 1861.

_____. *The Creator and the Creature, or, The Wonders of Divine* Love. London: Thomas Richardson and Son, 1858.

_____. *The Foot of the Cross: or, The Sorrows of Mary*. London: Thomas Richardson and Son, 1858.

_____. *Ethel's Book; or, Tales of the Angels*. London: Thomas Richardson and Son, 1858.

_____. *Growth in Holiness; or, The Progress of the Spiritual Life*. Baltimore: John Murphy & Co., 1855.

_____. *Notes on Doctrinal and Spiritual Subjects: Mysteries and Festivals*, vol. 1. London: Thomas Richardson and Son, 1866.

_____. *Notes on Doctrinal and Spiritual Subjects: The Faith and the Spiritual Life* vol. 2. London: Thomas Richardson and Son, 1866.

_____. *Spiritual Conferences*. New York: Benziger Brothers, 1800.

_____. *The Precious Blood; or, The Price of Our Salvation*. London: Burnes & Oates, Ltd., 1860.

_____. *Tracts on the Church and Her Offices*. London: J.G.F. & J. Rivington, 1840.

Fagerberg, David. *Consecrating the World: On Mundane Liturgical Theology*. Brooklyn, NY: Angelico Press, 2016.

_____. *Liturgical Mysticism*. Steubenville, OH: Emmaus Academic Press, 2020.

_____. *On Liturgical Asceticism*. Washington, DC: Catholic University of America Press, 2013.

_____. *Desiring to Desire God*. Brooklyn, NY: Angelico Press, 2024.

Fenelon, Francois. *The Archbishop of Cambray's Pastoral Letter Concerning the Love of God*. London: Robert Nelson, 1715.

_____. *Christian Perfection*. New York: Harper & Brothers, 1947.

_____. *The Complete Fenelon*. Brewster, MA: Paraclete Press, 2008.

_____. *A Demonstration of the Existence of God*. London: John Murray, 1769.

_____. *An English Nun in Exile Translates the Spiritual Letters of Archbishop Fenelon to Madame Guyon*. http://www.umilta.net/cambray2.html

_____. *Dialogues of the Dead*. London: D. Browne, 1760.

_____. *Directions for a Holy Life, and the Attaining Christian Perfection*. London: Darton & Harvey, 1795.

_____. *Dissertation on Pure Love*. London: sold by G. Thomson, 1750.

_____. *Extracts from the Writings of Francis Fenelon, with some Memoirs of His Life*, ed. John Kendall. Philadelphia: Kimber, Conrad & Co., 1804.

_____. *Fenelon: Selected Writings*. New York: Paulist Press, 2006.

_____. *Letters & Reflections*, ed. Thomas Kepler. New York: The World Publishing Co., 1955.

_____. *Fenelon: Letters of Love and Counsel*, ed. John McEwen. New York: Harcourt, Brace & World, Inc., 1964.

_____. *Letters to the Duke of Burgundy*. Dublin: W. Watson, 1758.

_____. *Maxims of the Saints*, www.ccel.org/ccel/fenelon/maxims/maxims.htm

_____. *On the Use of the Bible*. London: Booker, New Bond Street, 1837

_____. *Pious Thoughts Concerning the Knowledge and Love of God*. London: W. and J. Innys, 1720.

_____. *Sixteen Short Sermons*. Boston: New-England Tract Society, 1815.

_____. *Spiritual Letters of Archbishop Fenelon. Letters to Men*. London: Rivingtons, 1877.

_____. *Spiritual Letters of Archbishop Fenelon. Letters to Women*. London: Longmans, Green, and Co., 1900.

_____. *Spiritual Letters of Francois De Salignac De La Mothe-Fenelon* [to Countess Gramont]. Cornwall-on-Hudson, NY: Idlewild Press, 1945.

_____. *Spiritual Progress*. New York: M. W. Dodd, 1853.

_____. *The Seeking Heart*. Jacksonville, FL: SeedSowers Publishing, 1992.

_____. *Telemachus, son of Ulysses*. New York: Cambridge University Press, 1994.

_____. *Three Dialogues on Pulpit Eloquence*. Philadelphia: John McVey, 1897.

_____. *Thoughts on Spiritual Subjects*. Boston: Samuel G. Simpkins, 1843.

Foley, H. *The Life of Blessed Alphonsus Rodriguez* [Alonso]. London: Burns and Oates, 1873.

Froget, Barthelemy. *The Indwelling of Holy Spirit in Souls of the Just*. New York: Paulist Press, 1921.

Gabriel of Mary Magdalen. *Divine Intimacy: Meditations on the Interior Life for Every Day of the Liturgical Year*. Rockford, IL: TAN Books and Publishers, Inc., 1996.

Gay, Charles. *The Christian Life and Virtues Considered in the Religious State*, vol. 1. London: Burnes & Oates, 1878.

_____. *The Christian Life and Virtues Considered in the Religious State*, vol. 2. London: Burnes & Oates, 1878.

_____. *The Christian Life and Virtues Considered in the Religious State*, vol. 3. London: Burnes & Oates, 1879.

_____. *The Religious Life and the Vows*. London: Burnes & Oates, 1989.

Gerbet, Olympe Philippe. *The Lily of Israel: The Life of the Blessed Virgin*. Dublin: M. H. Gill and Son.

_____. *Considerations on the Eucharist viewed as the Generative Dogma of Catholic Piety*. London: C. Dolman, 1840.

Gilbert, Alphonse. *A Gentle Way to God: The Spiritual Teaching of Francis Libermann CSSp*. London: Paraclete Press, 1990.

_____. *You Have Laid Your Hand on Me: a Message of Ven. Francis Libermann for Our Time*. Pittsburgh: Duquesne, University, 2021.

Goepfert, Prosper. *The Life of the Venerable Francis Mary Paul Libermann*. Dublin: M. H. Gill & Son, 1881.

Goldie, Francis. *The Life of St. Alonso Rodriguez*. London: Burns and Oates, 1889.

Gorday, Peter J. *Francois Fenelon: A Biography – The Apostle of Pure Love*. Brewster, MA: Paraclete Press, 2012.

Grou, Jean Nicolas. *The Characteristics of True Devotion*. New York: Benziger Brothers, 1895.

_____. *The Christian Sanctified by the Lord's Prayer*. New York: Thomas Whitaker, 1885.

_____. *The Hidden Life of the Soul*, selections by Henrietta Lear. London: Rivingtons, 1871.

_____. *How to Pray*. London: Thomas Baker, 1901.

_____. *Manual for Interior Souls: A Collection of Unpublished Writings*. London: S. Anselm's Society, 1890.

_____. *The Interior of Jesus and Mary*, vol. 1. New York: Benziger Brothers, 1893.

_____. *The Interior of Jesus and Mary*, vol. 2. Dublin: James Duffy, 1847.

_____. *Meditations Upon the Love of God*. London: T. Baker, 1905.

_____. *Morality, Extracted from the Confessions of Saint Austin*, vol 1. London: J. P. Coghlan, 1791.

_____. *Morality, Extracted from the Confessions of Saint Austin*, vol 2. London: J. P. Coghlan, 1791.

_____. *Practical Science of the Cross*. London: Joseph Masters, 1871.

_____. *Self-Consecration, or the Gift of One's Self to God*. New York: E. & J. B. Young & Co., 1887.

_____. *The School of Jesus Christ*. London: Burns Oates & Washbourne, Ltd., 1932.

_____. *The Spiritual Maxims of Pere Grou*. London: J. T. Hayes, 1874.

Guillore, Francois. *Self-Renunciation*. London: Rivingtons, 1871.

_____. *Spiritual Guidance*. London: Rivingtons, 1873.

Grunewald, Charles. *The Venerable Francis Mary Paul Libermann*. Detroit: Fathers of the Holy Ghost, 1902.

Guyon, Jeanne. *A Short and Easy Method of Prayer*. https://www.ccel.org/ccel/g/guyon/prayer/cache/prayer.pdf

_____. *Justifications*, 3 vols. Linden, MI: Peter-John Parisis, 2004.

_____. *On the Way to God: State of Union*. https://hendersonvilletinting.com/StudyingGodsWord/Guyon/JeanneGuyonOnTheWayToGod.pdf

_____. *The Prison Narratives*. New York: Oxford University Press, 2012.

_____. *The Song of Songs of Solomon*. New York: A. W. Dennett, 1879.

_____. *The Unabridged Collected Works of Jeanne Guyon*. Kahley House Publishing, 2006.

Harpain, Eustelle. *The Writings of Marie-Eustelle Harpain*, Stephen Russell, yet to be published.

Horstius. *The Paradise of the Soul of a True Christian*. London: Burns & Lambert, 1850.

Huby, Vincent. *The Spiritual Retreat of the Reverend Father Vincent Huby*. Philadelphia: Printed for Mathew Carey, 1795

_____. *Spiritual Works*. London: Burns Oates & Washbourne Ltd. 1930.

Huguet, Jean-Joseph. *The Consoling Thoughts of St. Francis de Sales*. Dublin: M. H. Gill & Son, 1877.

Ignatius of Loyola. *The Autobiography of St. Ignatius*. New York: Benziger Brothers, 1900.

_____ *Letters and Instructions of St. Ignatius Loyola*, vol. 1. St. Louis: B. Herder, 1914.

_____. *The Letters of St. Ignatius of Loyola*. Chicago: Loyola University Press, 1959.

_____. *The Spiritual Exercises of St. Ignatius*, transl. Louis Puhl. Westminster, MD: The Newman Press, 1951.

Janet, Paul. *Life and Works of Fenelon*. London: Sir Isaac Pitman & Sons, Ltd., 1914.

Jenks, Sylvester. *The Blind Obedience of an Humble Penitent: The Best Cure for Scruples*. London: Burns Oates and Washbourne, 1926.

_____. *A Contrite and Humble Heart*. Dublin: P. Wogan, 1799.

_____. *An Essay Upon the Art of Love*. London. 1702.

_____. *Practical Discourses Upon the Morality of the Gospel, vol 1*. London, 1699.

_____. *Practical Discourses Upon the Morality of the Gospel, vol 2*. London, 1700.

John Evangelist of Boisleduc (Balduke). *The Kingdom of God in the Soul*. London: Sheed & Ward, 1930.

John of Avila. *Audi, Filia – Listen, O Daughter*. New York: Paulist Press, 2006.

_____. *The Holy Ghost*. London: Scepter Limited, 1959.

_____. *Letters of Blessed John of Avila*. London: Burns & Oates Ltd., 1904.

John of St. Samson. *Prayer, Aspiration and Contemplation*. New York: Alba House, 1975.

John of the Cross. *The Complete Works of Saint John of the Cross*, vol. 1. London: Longman, Green, Longman, Roberts & Green, 1864.

_____. *The Complete Works of Saint John of the Cross*, vol. 2. London: Longman, Green, Longman, Roberts & Green, 1864.

Kelly, Bernard. *Life Began at Forty: The Second Conversion of Francis Libermann*. Dublin: Paraclete Press, 2005.

Koren, Henry J. *The Spiritans: A History of the Congregation of the Holy Ghost*. Spiritan Series 1. Pittsburgh: Duquesne University Press, 1958.

Lacordaire, Henri-Dominique. *Jesus Christ, God, God and Man. Conferences Delivered at Notre Dame in Paris*. London: Chapman and Hall, 1884.

_____. *Letters to Young Men*. London: Art and Book Company, 1903.

_____. *Life: Conferences Delivered at Toulouse*. New York: P. O'Shea, 1875.

_____. *Life of Saint Dominic*. London: Burns and Oates, 1883.

_____. *Saint Mary Magdalene*. London: Thomas Richardson and Sons, 1860.

_____. *An Historical Sketch of the Order of St Dominic; or, a Memorial to the French People*. New York: P. O'Shea, 1869.

Lallemant, Louis. *The Spiritual Doctrine of Father Louis Lallemant*, ed. Frederick Faber. London: Burns & Lambert, 1855.

_____. *The Spiritual Doctrine of Louis Lallemant*, ed. Patrcia Ranum. Boston: Boston College Institute of Jesuit Sources, 2016.

Languet de Gergy, Jean-Joseph. *Confidence in the Mercy of God*. London: R. Washbourne, 1876.

Lawrence, Brother. *The Practice of the Presence of God: the Best Rule of a Holy Life*. New York: Fleming H. Revell Co., 1895.

_____. *The Spiritual Maxims*. Philadelphia: The Griffith and Rowland Press, 1907.

_____. *The Spiritual Maxims Together with The Character and Gathered Thoughts*. London: H.R. Allenson, 1907.

Lear, H.L. Sidney. *Bossuet and His Companions*. London: Rivingtons, 1874.

_____. *Fenelon, Archbishop of Cambrai: a Biographical Sketch*. London: Rivingtons, 1877.

_____. *St. Francis de Sales: Bishop and Prince of Geneva*. London: Rivingtons, 1876.

_____. *Henry Dominique Lacordaire: A Biographical Sketch*. London: Rivingtons, 1887.

_____. *The Revival of Priestly Life in the Seventeenth Century in France*. London: Rivingtons, 1873.

_____. *A Selection from The Spiritual Letters of S. Francis de Sales*, ed. Lear. New York: E. P. Dutton and Company, 1876.

Leonard of Port Maurice. *The Hidden Treasure; or, the Value of Excellence of the Holy Sacrifice of the Mass*. Dublin: James Duffy and Co., 1890.

Lebrun, Charles. *The Spiritual Teaching of St. John Eudes*. London: Sands & Co., 1934.

Lee, G. *The Life of Venerable Francis Libermann: Original Texts*. Fort Colins, CO: R. A. McCaffrey, 1999.

Leen, Edward. *Our Blessed Mother: Talks on Our Lady*. New York: P. J. Kenedy & Sons, 1946.

_____. *The Church Before Pilate*. Silver Spring, MD: The Preservation Press, 1939.

_____. *The Holy Ghost and His Work in Souls*. London: Sheed & Ward, 1940.

_____. *The Likeness of Christ*. New York: Sheed and Ward, 1936.

_____. *Progress Through Mental Prayer*. New York: Sheed and Ward, 1935.

_____. *The True Vine and Its Branches*. New York: P. J. Kenedy & Sons, 1939.

_____. *The Voice of a Priest*. New York: Sheed and Ward, 1946.

_____. *What is Education?* New York: Sheed and Ward, 1944.

_____. *Why the Cross?* New York: Sheed and Ward, 1938.

Leloir, Leon. *Libermann*. Washington, DC: Holy Ghost Fathers, 1943.

Libermann, Francis, and Poullart, Claude-Francois, *A Spiritan Anthology*,
ed. Christian de Mare. Rome: Congregazione dello Spirito Santo.
https://dsc.duq.edu/anthologie-spiritaine-english/

_____. *Instructions for Missionaries*.
https://dsc.duq.edu/cgi/viewcontent.cgi?article=1021&context=spiritan-rc

_____. *Jesus Through Jewish Eyes,* vol 1. Dublin: Paraclete Press, 1995.

_____. *Jesus Through Jewish Eyes,* vol 2. Dublin: Paraclete Press, 1999.

_____. *Jesus Through Jewish Eyes*, vol 3. Dublin: Paraclete Press, 2005.

_____. *Letters to Women Religious*, Spiritan Series 5, vol. 1. Pittsburgh: Duquesne
University Press, 1962.

_____. *Letters to People in the World*, Spiritan Series 6, vol. 2. Pittsburgh: Duquesne
University Press, 1963.

_____. *Letters to Clergy & Religious*, Spiritan Series 7, vol. 3. Pittsburgh: Duquesne
University Press, 1963.

_____. *Letters to Clergy & Religious*, Spiritan Series 8, vol. 4. Pittsburgh: Duquesne
University Press, 1964.

_____. *Letters to Clergy & Religious*, Spiritan Series 9, vol. 5. Pittsburgh: Duquesne
University Press, 1966.

_____. *Living with God: Instructions for Priests and Religious*. New York: Catholic
Book Publishing Co., 1949.

_____. *The Birth of Missionary Spirituality: Provisional Rule of the Missionaries of
Libermann*. Pittsburgh: Center for Spiritual Studies, 2015.

_____. *The Provisional Rule of the Missionaries of the Holy Heart of Mary: Text and
Libermann's Commentary*. Pittsburgh: Duquesne University, 1967.

Malaval, Francois. *A Simple Method of Raising the Soul to Contemplation: In the Form
of a Dialogue*. London: J. M. Dent and Sons, 1931.

Massillon, John-Baptist. *Sermons by John-Baptist Massillon*. London: Thomas Tegg,
1839.

Malinkowski, F.X. *The Holy Spirit in Francis Libermann*. Spiritan Horizons Journal,
Issue 10, Fall 2015. 7-18.

_____. *Meeting the Holy Spirit in the Writings of Francis Libermann: Original Texts.*
https://www.duq.edu/assets/Documents/spiritans/Holy%20Spirit%20Resources/Libermann%20and%20the%20Holy%20Spirit/Meeting%20the%20Holy%20Spirit%20in%20the%20Writings%20of%20Father%20Francis%20Libermann,%20C.S.Sp..pdf

Maria Magdalena de' Pazzi. *Selected Writings.* New York: Paulist Press, 2000.

Monnin, Alfred. *Life of Saint John-Baptist Vianney, Cure d'Ars.* London: Burns Oates & Washbourne, 1862.

_____. *The Spirit of the Cure of Ars.* London: Burns, Lambert, and Oates, 1865,

More, Gertrude. *The Holy Practices of a Divine Lover, or The Saintly Ideot's [sic] Devotions.* London: Sands & Co., 1909.

_____. *The Writings of Gertrude More.* London: R. & T. Washbourne, Ltd., 1910.

Mudge, James. *Fenelon: The Mystic.* New York: Eaton and Mains, 1906.

Nepveu, Francois. *The Hidden Life.* London: J. Masters, 1871.

_____. *Meditations for Every Day in the Month.* New York: Benziger Brothers, 1911.

_____. *The Method of Mental Prayer, Rendered Practical and Easie for all sorts of Persons.* London: Thomas Hales, 1694.

_____. *Of the Love of our Lord Jesus Christ, and the Means of Acquiring It.* London: Burns, Oates, & Co., 1869.

_____. *The Spirit of Christianity, or the Conformity of the Christian with Christ.* New York: Edward Dunigan & Brother, 1859.

Neumayr, Francis. *The Science of the Spiritual Life.* London: Burns and Oates, 1876.

Oddi, Longaro Degli. *Life of the Blessed Master John of Avila.* London: Burns and Oates, Ltd., 1898.

Olier, Jean-Jacques. *Catechism of an Interior Life.* Baltimore: Murphy & Co., 1852.

Philip, Sr. Mary. *A Jesuit at the English Court: The Life of Venerable Claude de la Colombiere.* London: Burns Oates & Washbourne, Ltd., 1922.

Philipon, M.M. *The Sacraments in the Christian Life.* Westminster, MD: The Newman Press, 1954.

_____. *The Spiritual Doctrine of Sister Elizabeth of the Trinity.* Westminster, MD: The Newman Press, 1948.

Premord, Charles Leonore. *The Rules of a Christian Life.* Taunton: J. W. Marriott, 1834.

_____. *Reflections on Communities of Women and Monastic Institutes*. Taunton: J. Poole, 1815.

Pollien, Francois, ed. Joseph Tissot. *The Interior Life Simplified and Reduced to Fundamental Principle*. London: Burns Oates & Washbourne, Ltd., 1927.

Pourrat, Pierre. *Christian Spirituality, vol 3. Later Developments, Part 1: From the Renaissance to Jansenism*. Westminster, MD: The Newman Press, 1953.

_____. *Christian Spirituality, vol 4. Later Developments, Part 2: From Jansenism to Modern Times*. Westminster, MD: The Newman Press, 1955.

Quadrupani, R. P. *Light and Peace: Instructions for Devout Souls to Dispel their Doubts and Allay Their Fears*. St. Louis, MO: B. Herder Book Co., 1918.

Quarre, John. *A Spiritual Treasure: Containing our Obligations to God, and the Vertues Necessary to a Perfect Christian*. London: for Thomas Dring, 1664.

_____. *Devout Entertainments of a Christian Soule*. Paris, 1648.

Ramsay, Andrew Michael. *The Life of Francois Fenelon, Archbishop and Duke of Cambray*. London: printed for Paul Vaillant, 1723.

Rigoleuc, Jean. *Walking with God: Or, Dwellers in the Recreation House of the Lord*. London: Thomas Richardson and Son, 1859.

Rodriguez, Alonso. *St. Alphonsus Rodriguez: Autobiography*. London: Geoffrey Chapman: London, 1964.

Rodriguez, Alphonsus. *The Practice of Christian and Religious Perfection*, vol 1. London: James Duffy, 1861.

_____. *The Practice of Christian and Religious Perfection*, vol 2. London: James Duffy, 1861.

_____. *The Practice of Christian and Religious Perfection*, vol 3. London: James Duffy, 1861.

Saint-Jure, Jean Baptiste and de la Colombiere, Claude. *Trustful Surrender to Divine Providence*. Rockford, IL: TAN Books and Publishers, 1983.

Saint-Jure, Jean Baptiste. *Christ our Teacher* (Baltimore: McCauley & Kilner , 1891).

_____. *The Holy Life of Monsieur de Renty, a Late Nobleman of France*. London: printed for Benj. Tooke, 1684.

_____. *The Religious: A Treatise on the Vows and Virtues of the Religious State*, vol. 1. New York: P. O'Shea, 1882.

_____. *The Religious: A Treatise on the Vows and Virtues of the Religious State*, vol. 2. New York: P. O'Shea, 1882.

_____. *The Spiritual Man; or, The Spiritual Life Reduced to its First Principles.* London: Burns and Oates, 1878.

_____. *A Treatise on the Knowledge and Love of Our Lord Jesus Christ*, vol 1. New York: P. O'Shea, 1870.

_____. *A Treatise on the Knowledge and Love of Our Lord Jesus Christ*, vol 2. New York: P. O'Shea, 1875.

_____. *A Treatise on the Knowledge and Love of Our Lord Jesus Christ*, vol 3. New York: P. O'Shea, 1875.

_____. *Union with Our Lord Jesus Christ in His Principal Mysteries for All Seasons of the Year.* New York: D. & J. Sadlier & Co., 1876.

Sanders, E. K. *Fenelon: His Friends and His Enemies 1651-1715.* London: Longmans, Green, and Co., 1901.

Scaramelli, John Baptist. *Directorium Asceticum or, Guide to the Spiritual Life*, vol 1. New York: Benziger Bros, 1902.

_____. *Directorium Asceticum or, Guide to the Spiritual Life*, vol 2. New York: Benziger Bros, 1902.

_____. *Directorium Asceticum or, Guide to the Spiritual Life*, vol 3. New York: Benziger Bros, 1902.

_____. *Directorium Asceticum or, Guide to the Spiritual Life*, vol 4. New York: Benziger Bros, 1902.

Scupoli, Lorenzo. *The Spiritual Combat, with The Path of Paradise.* London: James Burns, 1845.

Segneri, Paul. *Devout Client of Mary.* London: Burns & Lambert, 1857.

_____. *The Knowledge of Ourselves; With Practical Thoughts of Humility Divided into Meditations for Every Day in the Week.* York: C. Croshaw, 1834.

_____. *Lenten Sermons*, vol 1. New York: Christian Publication House, 1872.

_____. *Lenten Sermons*, vol 2. New York: Christian Press Association, 1874.

_____. *The Manna of the Soul: Meditations for Every Day of the Year*, vol 1. New York: Benziger Brothers, 1892.

_____. *The Manna of the Soul: Meditations for Every Day of the Year*, vol 2. New York: Benziger Brothers, 1892.

_____. *The Messenger of the Sacred Heart of Jesus, Organ of the Apostleship of Prayer*, vol 2, July to December. Dublin: M. H. Gill and Son, 1884.

_____. *The Panegyrics of Father Segneri, of the Society of Jesus*. London: R. Washbourne, 1877.

_____. *The Quaresimale of P. Paolo Segneri*, London: Joseph Masters, 1869.

_____. *Sentimenti; or, Lights in Prayer*. London: Burns & Oates, 1876.

_____. *The Penitent Instructed*. London: 1703.

_____. *True Wisdom: Or Considerations for Every Day of the Week*. 1716

Surin, John-Joseph. *Into the Dark Night and Back: The Mystical Writings of Surin*. Boston: Brill Publishing, 2019.

_____. *The Foundations of The Spiritual Life: Drawn from the Book of the Imitation of Jesus Christ*. London: James Burns, 1844.

_____. *The Spiritual Letters of Father Surin*. London: Art & Book Co., 1892.

Swetchine, Madame. *The Writings of Madam Swetchine*, ed. De Falloux. Boston: Roberts Brothers, 1869.

_____. *Life and Letters of Madame Swetchine*, by de Falloux. New York: The Catholic Publication House, 1869.

Teresa of Avila. *Collection*. Aeterna Press, Kindle, 2016.

_____. *The Interior Castle; or, the Mansions*. London: T. Jones, 1852.

_____. *Life of Saint Teresa Written by Herself*. New York: P. J. Kenedy & Sons, 1870.

_____. *Saint Teresa of Avila Collected Works*. Washington, D.C.: ICS Publications, 1987.

_____. *The Life and Letters of St,. Teresa*, vol 1. London: Burns and Oates, Ltd., 1893.

_____. *The Life and Letters of St,. Teresa*, vol 2. London: Burns and Oates, Ltd., 1895.

_____. *The Way of Perfection*. New York: A Doubleday Image Book, 1964.

Therese of Lisieux. *The Autobiography of Saint Therese of Lisieux: the story of a Soul*. New York: Image Books, 1989.

_____. *Thoughts of the Servant of God: Therese of the Child Jesus*. New York: P.J. Kenedy & Sons, 1915.

Tesniere, Albert. *Blessed Peter Julian Eymard: the Priest of the Eucharist*. New York: Fathers of the Blessed Sacrament, 1936.

Thompson, William M., ed. *Berulle and the French School: Selected Writings*. New York: Paulist Press, 1989.

Thompson, Edward Healy. *The Life of Jean-Jacques Olier*. London: Burns and Oates, 1885.

_____. *The Life of St. Aloysius Gonzaga*. London: Burns & Oates, 1867..

_____. *The Life of the Baron de Renty; or, Perfection in the World Exemplified*. London: Burns & Oates, 1873.

_____. *The Life of Henri-Marie Boudon, Archdeacon of Evreux*. London: Burns and Oates, 1880.

-------. *Library of Religious Biography. Vol 2, Marie-Estelle Harpain*. London: Burns, Oates & Co., 1868.

_____. *The Glories of St. Joseph*. London: Burns & Oates, 1891.

Trochu, Francis. *The Curé d'Ars: A Shorter Biography*. Westminster, MD: The Newman Press, 1955.

_____. *The Curé d'Ars: St. Jean-Marie-Baptiste Vianney According to the Acts of the Process of Canonization and Numerous Hitherto Unpublished Documents*.

Tronson, Louis. *Examination of Conscience Upon Special Subjects*. Oxford: Rivingtons, 1870.

Ullathorne, William. *The Autobiography of Archbishop Ullathorne, With Selections from His Letters*. London: Burns & Oates, 1892.

_____. *Christian Patience: The Strength and Discipline of the Soul*. London: Burns & Oates, 1886.

_____. *The Endowments of Man Considered in their Relations with His Final End*. London: Burns & Oates, 1880.

_____. *The Groundwork of the Christian Virtues*. London: Burns & Oates, 1890.

_____. *The Immaculate Conception of the Mother of God. An Exposition*. London: Richardson and Son, 1855.

Van Kaam, Adrian. *A Light to the Gentiles*. Eugene, OR: Wipf & Stock, 2009.

Van der Kley, Francesca. *Marian Mystic: A short Life of St Mary Magdalen de' Pazzi*. Chicago, Carmelite Third Order Press, 1957

Vercruysse, Bruno. *Practical Meditations for Every Day in the Year on the Life of Our Lord Jesus Christ: Composed Chiefly for the Use of Religious by a Father of the Society of Jesus,* vol 1. London: Burns Oates & Washbourne, 1868

_____. *Practical Meditations for Every Day in the Year on the Life of Our Lord Jesus Christ: Composed Chiefly for the Use of Religious by a Father of the Society of Jesus,* vol 2. London: Burns Oates & Washbourne, 1868

Vianney, John. *Sermons of the Curé of Ars*. Chicago: H. Regnery, 1960.

_____. *The Little Catechism of the Curé of Ars*. Rockford, IL: TAN books, 1951.

_____. *Thoughts of the Curé of Ars*, transl. Pauline Stump. Boston: Flynn & Mahony, 1896.

_____. *Thoughts of the Curé d'Ars,* compiled W.M.B. Rockford, IL: TAN Books, 1967.

_____. *Sermons for the Sundays and Feasts of the Year*. Long Prairie, MN: The Neumann Press, 1995.

Von Cochem, Martin. *The Four Last Things: Death, Judgment, Hell, Heaven.* New York: Benziger Brothers, 1899.

DATES OF THE LIVES OF AUTHORS

Alacoque, Margaret Mary. 1647-1690. French Visitation Nun.

Baker, Augustine. 1575-1641. English Benedictine Congregation

Barbanson, Constantine. 1581-1631. Belgian Capuchin.

Bellecius, Aloysius. 1704-1757. German Jesuit.

Berthier, Jean-Baptiste. 1840-1908. French founder of the Missionaries of the Holy Family.

Binet, Etienne. 1569-1639. French Jesuit.

Blosius (Louis of Blois). 1506-1566. Flemish Benedictine.

Bona, Giovanni. 1609-1674. Italian Cistercian, cardinal.

Borgia, Francis. 1510-1572. Spanish Jesuit.

Bossuct, Jacques Benigne. 1627-1704. French bishop.

Boudon, Henri-Marie.1624-1702. French abbot.

Bourdaloue, Louis. 1632-1704. French Jesuit preacher.

Boutauld, Michel. 1625-1688. French Jesuit.

Bruyere, Cecile. 1845-1909. French Benedictine.

Camus, Jean Pierre. 1584-1652. French bishop.

Canfield, Benedict. 1562-1610. English Capuchin Friar.

Challoner, Richard. 1691-1781. English bishop.

Chardon, Louis. 1595-1651. Dominican theologian.

Collins, Henry. 1827-1919. English Catholic priest.

Courbon, Abbe. d. 1710. Curé of Saint-Cyr.

Cross, Nicolas (also Nicolas of the holy Cross). English Franciscan 1616-1698.

Crasset, John. 1618-1692. French Jesuit.

Croiset, John. 1656-1738. French Jesuit.

Dalgairns, John. 1818-1876. English Catholic priest.

De Alacantara, Peter. 1499-1562. Spanish Franciscan.

De Bergamo, Gaetano Maria. 1672-1753. Italian Capuchin.

De Bernieres-Louvigny, Jean. 1602-1659. French contemplative.

De Berulle, Pierre. 1575-1629. French Cardinal, founder French Oratory.

De Bovilla, John. 16th c. Franciscan.

De Castaniza, Juan. 1555-1599. Spanish Benedictine.

De Caussade, Jean Pierre. 1675-1751. French Jesuit.

De Chantal, Jane Francis. 1572-1641. French Order of the Visitation of Holy Mary.

De Condren, Charles. 1588-1641. French Oratory.

De Estella, Diego. 1524-1578. Spanish Franciscan.

De Granada, Louis. 1504-1588. Spanish Dominican.

De la Colombiere, Claude. 1641-1682. French Jesuit.

De Laredo, Bernardino. 1482-1540. Spanish Franciscan.

De Liguori, Alphonsus. 1696-1787. Italian Redemptorist.

De Lombez, Ambrose. 1708-1778. French Capuchin.

De Montfort, Louis-Marie Grignion. 1673-1716. French priest.

De Osuna, Francisco. 1492-1540. Spanish Franciscan.

De Ponte, Louis (Luis de la Puente). 1554-1624. Spanish Jesuit.

De Ravignan, Gustave Francois Xavier. 1795-1858. French Jesuit.

De Sales, Francis. 1567-1622. French Bishop of Geneva.

Elizabeth of the Trinity. 1880-1906. French Discalced Carmelite.

Eudes, John. 1601-1680. French founder of The Eudists.

Eymard, Peter. 1811-1868. French Priest

Faber, Frederick. 1814-1863. English Oratorian.

Fénelon, François. 1651-1715. French Archbishop of Cambrai.

Gerbet, Olympe Philippe. 1798-1864. French bishop.

Grou, Jean. 1731-1803, French Jesuit.

Guillore, Francois. 1615-1684. French Jesuit.

Harpain, Marie-Eustelle. 1814-1842. Lay woman "angel of the Eucharist"

Horstius, Jacob Merlo. 1597-1644. Catholic priest.

Huby, Vincent. 1608-1693. French Jesuit.

Huguet, Jean-Joseph. 1812-1884. French Priest.

Ignatius of Loyola. 1491-1556. Spanish founder of Jesuits.

John Evangelist of Bois-le-duc (Balduke). d. 1637. Dutch Capuchin.

John of Avila. 1499-1569. Spanish priest.

John of St. Samson. 1571-1636. French Carmelite.

John of the Cross. 1542-1591. Spanish Carmelite.

Lacordaire, Jean-Baptiste. 1802-1861. French Dominican.

Lallemant, Louis. 1588-1635. French Jesuit.

Languet de Gergy, Jean-Joseph. 1677-1753. French archbishop.

Lawrence, Brother. 1614-1691. Lay Carmelite brother.

Leen, Edward. 1885-1944. Irish, Congregation of the Holy Ghost.

Libermann, Francis. 1802-1852. French Spiritan.

Malaval, Francois. 1627-1719. Blind Dominican, theology and canon law.

Maria Magdalena de'Pazzi. 1566-1607. Italian Carmelite.

Massillon, Jean Baptiste. 1663-1742. French Oratory, Bishop of Clermont.

More, Gertrude. 1606-1633. English Benedictine Nun.

Nepveu, Francois. 1639-1708. French Jesuit.

Neumayr, Franz (Francis). 1697-1765. German Jesuit.

Olier, Jean-Jacques. 1608-1657. French founder of the Sulpicians.

Pollien, Francois. 1853-1936. French Carthusian.

Premord, Charles. 1760-1837. French priest.

Quadrupani, Carlo Giuseppe 1740-1806. Italian Barnabite.

Quarre, John (Jean-Hugues). 1580-1656.

Rigoleuc, Jean. 1596-1658. French Jesuit.

Rodriguez, Alphonsus (Alonso). 1532-1617. Spanish Jesuit brother.

Rodriguez, Alphonsus(Alfonso). 1538-1616. Spanish Jesuit priest.

Saint-Jure, Jean Baptiste. 1588-1657. French Jesuit.

Scaramelli, John Baptist. 1687-1752. Italian Jesuit.

Scupoli, Lorenzo. 1530-1610. Italian priest.

Segneri, Paul. 1624-1694. Italian Jesuit.

Surin, John-Joseph. 1600-1665. French Jesuit.

Teresa of Avila. 1515-1582. Spanish Discalced Carmelite.

Therese of Lisieux. 1873-1897. French Carmelite.

Tronson, Louis. 1622-1700. French Sulpician.

Ullathorne, William Bernard. 1806-1889. Bishop of Birmingham.

Vercruysse, Bruno. 1797-1880. Jesuit priest.

Vianney, Jean Baptiste. 1786-1859. French parish priest.